Alexander Roberts, James Donaldson

The Writings of Quintus Tertullianus

Volume 1

Alexander Roberts, James Donaldson

The Writings of Quintus Tertullianus
Volume 1

ISBN/EAN: 9783742856876

Manufactured in Europe, USA, Canada, Australia, Japa

Cover: Foto ©ninafisch / pixelio.de

Manufactured and distributed by brebook publishing software (www.brebook.com)

Alexander Roberts, James Donaldson

The Writings of Quintus Tertullianus

Works Published by T. and T. Clark, Edinburgh.

Books for the Library of Clergymen and Educated Laymen.

CLARK'S FOREIGN THEOLOGICAL LIBRARY.

Annual Subscription, One Guinea (payable in advance) for Four Volumes, Demy 8vo.

When not paid in advance, the Retail Bookseller is entitled to charge 24s.

N.B.—A single Year's Books (except in the case of the current Year) cannot be supplied separately. Non-subscribers, price 10s. 6d. each volume, with exceptions marked.

1866.
KEIL'S COMMENTARY ON SAMUEL. One Volume.
DELITZSCH'S COMMENTARY ON JOB. Two Volumes.
MARTENSEN'S SYSTEM OF CHRISTIAN DOCTRINE. One Volume.

1867.
DELITZSCH'S SYSTEM OF BIBLICAL PSYCHOLOGY. (12s.)
DELITZSCH'S COMMENTARY ON ISAIAH. Two Volumes.
AUBERLEN ON THE DIVINE REVELATION. One Volume.

1868.
KEIL'S COMMENTARY ON THE MINOR PROPHETS. Two Volumes.
DELITZSCH'S COMMENTARY ON EPISTLE TO THE HEBREWS. Volume first.
HARLESS' SYSTEM OF CHRISTIAN ETHICS. One Volume.

1869.
STIER ON THE WORDS OF THE APOSTLES. One Volume. } First Issue.
HENGSTENBERG'S COMMENTARY ON EZEKIEL. One Volume. }

MESSRS. CLARK have resolved to allow a SELECTION of TWENTY VOLUMES (*or more at the same ratio*) from the various Series previous to the above,

At the Subscription Price of Five Guineas.

They trust that this will still more largely extend the usefulness of the FOREIGN THEOLOGICAL LIBRARY, which has so long been recognised as holding an important place in modern Theological literature.

The following are the works from which a Selection may be made (non-subscription prices within brackets):—

Shedd's History of Christian Doctrine. 2 Volumes. (£1, 1s.)
Gieseler's Compendium of Ecclesiastical History. 5 Volumes. (£2, 12s. 6d.)
Neander's General Church History. 9 Volumes. (£2, 11s. 6d.)
Olshausen on the Gospels and Acts. 4 Volumes. (£2, 2s.)
Olshausen on the Romans. (10s. 6d.)
Olshausen on the Corinthians. (9s.)
Olshausen on the Galatians, Ephesians, Colossians, and Thessalonians. (10s. 6d.)
Olshausen on Philippians, Titus, and Timothy. (10s. 6d.)
Olshausen and Ebrard on the Hebrews. (10s. 6d.)

Works Published by T. and T. Clark, Edinburgh.

CLARK'S FOREIGN THEOLOGICAL LIBRARY.

LIST OF WORKS FOR SELECTION—continued.

Havernick's General Introduction to the Old Testament. (10s. 6d.)
Macdonald's Introduction to the Pentateuch. 2 Volumes. (£1, 1s.)
Hengstenberg's Commentary on the Psalms. 3 Volumes. (£1, 13s.)
Hengstenberg's Egypt and the Books of Moses. 1 Volume. (7s. 6d.)
Hengstenberg's Christology of the Old Testament. 4 Volumes. (£2, 2s.)
Hengstenberg's Commentary on the Gospel of St. John. 2 Volumes. (£1, 1s.)
Hengstenberg's Commentary on Ecclesiastes. 1 Volume. (9s.)
Ackermann on the Christian Element in Plato. 1 Volume. (7s. 6d.)
Robinson's Greek Lexicon of the New Testament. 1 Volume. (9s.)
Stier on the Words of the Lord Jesus. 8 Volumes. (£4, 4s.)
Stier on the Words of the Risen Saviour, and Commentary on St. James. 1 Vol. (10s. 6d.)
Ullmann's Reformers before the Reformation. 2 Volumes. (£1, 1s.)
Gerlach's Commentary on the Pentateuch. 1 Volume. (10s. 6d.)
Baumgarten's Apostolic History. 3 Volumes. (£1, 7s.)
Müller on the Doctrine of Sin. 2 Volumes. (£1, 1s.)
Kurtz's History of the Old Covenant. 3 Volumes. (£1, 11s. 6d.)
Kurtz's Sacrificial Worship of the Old Testament. 1 Volume. (10s. 6d.)
Tholuck on the Gospel of St. John. 1 Volume. (9s.)
Tholuck on Christ's Sermon on the Mount. 1 Volume. (10s. 6d.)
Ebrard on Epistles of John. 1 Volume. (10s. 6d.)
Ebrard's Gospel History. 1 Volume. (10s. 6d.)
Dorner on the Person of Christ. 5 Volumes. (£2, 12s. 6d.)
Lange on St. Matthew and St. Mark. 3 Volumes. (£1, 11s. 6d.)
Lange's Commentary on the Acts of the Apostles. 2 Volumes. (£1, 1s.)
Oosterzee and Lange on St. Luke's Gospel. 2 Volumes. (18s.)
Keil and Delitzsch's Commentary on the Pentateuch. 3 Volumes. (£1, 11s. 6d.)
Keil and Delitzsch on Joshua, Judges, and Ruth. (10s. 6d.)

The above, in 94 Volumes (including 1868), price £24, 14s., form an *apparatus* without which it may be truly said *no Theological Library can be complete;* and the Publishers take the liberty of suggesting that no more appropriate gift could be presented to a Clergyman than the Series, in whole or in part.

⁂ *In reference to the above, it must be noted that* NO DUPLICATES *can be included in the Selection of Twenty Volumes; and it will save trouble and correspondence if it be distinctly understood that* NO LESS *number than twenty can be supplied, unless at non-subscription price.*

Subscribers' Names received by all Retail Booksellers.

CHEQUES on COUNTRY BANKS for sums under £2, 2s. must have 6d. added for Bank charge.

EDINBURGH: T. & T. CLARK.
LONDON: (*For Works at Non-subscription price only*) HAMILTON, ADAMS, & Co.

Works Published by T. & T. Clark, Edinburgh.

MESSRS CLARK *beg to offer a Selection of Eight Volumes from the following List of Works (chiefly forming the* BIBLICAL CABINET, *the first series of translations published by them),*

For ONE GUINEA, remitted with order.

The price affixed is that at which they can be had separately, which is also much reduced.

ERNESTI'S PRINCIPLES OF BIBLICAL INTERPRETATION OF NEW TESTAMENT. Translated by Bishop Terrot. 2 vols., 8s.

PHILOLOGICAL TRACTS. 3 vols., 4s. each.

Vol. I.—Rossi and Pfannkuche on the Language of Palestine in the Age of Christ; Planck on the Nature and Genius of the Diction of New Testament; Tholuck on the Importance of the Study of Old Testament; Beckhaus on the Interpretation of the Tropical Language of New Testament. Vol. II.—Storr on the Meaning of 'The Kingdom of Heaven;' Storr on the Parables; Storr on the word 'ΠΛΗΡΩΜΑ;' Hengstenberg on Isaiah liii. Vol. III.—Ullmann on Christ's Sinlessness; Rückert on the Resurrection of the Dead; Lange on the Resurrection of the Body; M. Stuart on Future Punishment.

THOLUCK'S COMMENTARY ON THE EPISTLE TO THE ROMANS. 2 vols., 8s.
PAREAU O; THE INTERPRETATION OF OLD TESTAMENT. 2 vols., 8s.
STUART'S SYNTAX OF THE NEW TESTAMENT. 4s.
UMBREIT'S EXPOSITION OF THE BOOK OF JOB. 2 vols., 8s.
STEIGER'S COMMENTARY ON FIRST PETER. 2 vols., 8s.
BILLROTH'S COMMENTARY ON THE CORINTHIANS. 2 vols., 8s.
KRUMMACHER'S CORNELIUS THE CENTURION. 3s.
WITSIUS' EXPOSITION OF THE LORD'S PRAYER. 4s.
ROSENMULLER'S BIBLICAL GEOGRAPHY OF CENTRAL ASIA. 2 vols., 8s.
ROSENMULLER'S BIBLICAL GEOGRAPHY OF ASIA MINOR, PHŒNICIA, & ARABIA. 4s.
ROSENMULLER'S BIBLICAL MINERALOGY AND BOTANY. 4s.
WEMYSS' CLAVIS SYMBOLICA; or, Key to Symbolical Language of Scripture. 4s.
CALVIN ON THE EPISTLES TO GALATIANS AND EPHESIANS. 4s.
GESS ON THE REVELATION OF GOD IN HIS WORD. 3s.
ROSENMULLER ON THE MESSIANIC PSALMS. 4s.
COVARD'S LIFE OF CHRISTIANS DURING FIRST THREE CENTURIES. 4s.
THOLUCK'S COMMENTARY ON THE EPISTLE TO THE HEBREWS, with Dissertations on Citations from Old Testament in New Testament, and on the Idea of Sacrifice and Priest in Old and New Testaments. 2 vols., 8s.
CALVIN AND STORR ON THE PHILIPPIANS AND COLOSSIANS. 4s.
SEMISCH'S LIFE, WRITINGS, AND OPINIONS OF JUSTIN MARTYR. 2 vols., 8s.
ROHR'S HISTORICO-GEOGRAPHICAL ACCOUNT OF PALESTINE IN THE TIME OF CHRIST. 4s.
TITTMANN'S EXEGETICAL, CRITICAL, AND DOCTRINAL COMMENTARY ON ST JOHN'S GOSPEL. 2 vols., 8s.
BARBACOVIS' LITERARY HISTORY OF MODERN ITALY. 2s. 6d.
MY OLD HOUSE; or, The Doctrine of Changes. 4s.
NEGRIS' EDITION OF HERODOTUS, with English Notes. 4s. 6d.
„   „   PINDAR,   „   „   4s. 6d.
„   „   XENOPHON,   „   „   2s.
WELSH'S ELEMENTS OF CHURCH HISTORY. 5s.
NEANDER ON THE EPISTLE TO THE PHILIPPIANS AND ON THE EPISTLE OF ST JAMES. 8s.
EDERSHEIM'S HISTORY OF THE JEWISH NATION AFTER THE DESTRUCTION OF JERUSALEM UNDER TITUS. 6s.

Works Published by T. & T. Clark, Edinburgh.

Works from the BIBLICAL CABINET, etc., continued.

HOFFMANN'S CHRISTIANITY IN THE FIRST CENTURY. 4s. 6d.
KAHNIS' INTERNAL HISTORY OF GERMAN PROTESTANTISM. 4s. 6d.
ULRICH VON HUTTEN, HIS LIFE AND TIMES. 4s.
NETTLETON AND HIS LABOURS. Edited by Rev. A. Bonar. 4s. 6d.
PATTERSON'S ILLUSTRATIONS, EXPOSITORY AND PRACTICAL, OF THE FAREWELL DISCOURSE OF OUR LORD. 6s.
WILSON'S KINGDOM OF OUR LORD JESUS CHRIST. 7s. 6d.
THORNLEY'S SKELETON THEMES. 3s.
THORNLEY'S TRUE END OF EDUCATION, AND THE MEANS ADAPTED TO IT. 3s. 6d.
ANDERSON'S CHRONICLES OF THE KIRK. 3s. 6d.

The following Tracts, issued in the STUDENT'S CABINET LIBRARY OF USEFUL TRACTS, *are also offered as under:—*

LOWMAN'S ARGUMENT à priori FOR THE BEING OF A GOD. 6d.
JOUFFROY ON THE METHOD OF PHILOSOPHICAL STUDY. 1s.
JOUFFROY'S ESSAYS ON HISTORY OF PHILOSOPHY; PHILOSOPHY OF HISTORY; INFLUENCE OF GREECE ON THE DEVELOPMENT OF HUMANITY; AND PRESENT STATE OF HUMANITY. 9d.
JOUFFROY ON SCEPTICISM OF PRESENT AGE; FACULTIES OF HUMAN SOUL; GOOD AND EVIL; ECLECTICISM IN MORALS; AND ON PHILOSOPHY AND COMMON SENSE. 1s.
COUSIN ON THE DESTINY OF MODERN PHILOSOPHY. 6d.
COUSIN'S EXPOSITION OF ECLECTICISM. 1s. 6d.
MURDOCK'S SKETCHES OF MODERN PHILOSOPHY, especially among the Germans. 1s.
EDWARDS' STATE OF SLAVERY IN ANCIENT GREECE. 4d.
EDWARDS' STATE OF SLAVERY IN THE EARLY AND MIDDLE AGES OF THE CHRISTIAN ERA. 6d.
HITCHCOCK ON THE CONNECTION BETWEEN GEOLOGY AND NATURAL RELIGION. 4d.
HITCHCOCK'S HISTORICAL AND GEOLOGICAL DELUGES COMPARED. 2 Parts, 9d. each.
EICHHORN'S LIFE AND WRITINGS OF MICHAELIS. 6d.
STÄUDLIN'S HISTORY OF THEOLOGICAL KNOWLEDGE AND LITERATURE. 4d.
VERPLANCK ON THE RIGHT MORAL INFLUENCE & USE OF LIBERAL STUDIES. 4d.
WARE ON THE CHARACTER AND DUTIES OF A PHYSICIAN. 4d.
STORY ON THE PROGRESS OF LITERATURE, SCIENCE, AND GOVERNMENT. 2 Parts, 4d. and 9d.
LIFE OF NIEBUHR. By his Son. 6d.

LIFE OF MADAME DE STAEL. 9d.
SAWYER'S POPULAR TREATISE ON BIBLICAL INTERPRETATION. 6d.
STUART'S PHILOLOGICAL VIEW OF MODERN DOCTRINES OF GEOLOGY. 6d.
LIFE OF LADY RUSSELL. 9d.
CHANNING ON SLAVERY. 6d.
WARE ON EXTEMPORANEOUS PREACHING. 9d.
CHANNING ON FENELON. 4d.
CHANNING ON NAPOLEON BONAPARTE. 6d.
EVERETT ON THE IMPORTANCE OF SCIENTIFIC KNOWLEDGE. 9d.
SIR JOSHUA REYNOLDS' DISCOURSES TO THE STUDENTS OF ROYAL ACADEMY. 1s. 6d.
CHANNING ON SELF-CULTURE. 6d.
CHANNING ON THE IMPORTANCE OF A NATIONAL LITERATURE. 4d.
NEGRIS' LITERARY HISTORY OF MODERN GREECE. 4d.
REYNOLDS ON THE NECESSITY OF PHYSICAL CULTURE TO LITERARY MEN. 4d.
HITCHCOCK ON THE CONNECTION BETWEEN GEOLOGY AND THE MOSAIC ACCOUNT OF CREATION. 1s.
STORY'S HISTORY OF THE LAW. 9d.
LORD STOWELL'S JUDGMENT IN CASE OF DALRYMPLE v. DALRYMPLE. 1s. 6d.
LORD STOWELL'S JUDGMENT IN CASES OF THE 'MARIA' AND 'GRATITUDINE.' 1s. 6d.
LORD LIVERPOOL ON THE CONDUCT OF GREAT BRITAIN IN RESPECT OF NEUTRAL NATIONS. 1s. 6d.
CONTROVERSY RELATIVE TO PRUSSIA'S ATTACHMENT OF BRITISH FUNDS IN REPRISAL FOR CAPTURES. 1s. 6d.
BURKE'S LETTER TO A NOBLE LORD. 6d.
WARNKÖNIG'S ANALYSIS OF SAVIGNY ON THE LAW OF POSSESSION. 6d.

STORIES FOR CHILDREN.

THE FLOWER BASKET. By Schmid. 1s. 6d.
EASTER EGGS, AND ROBIN REDBREAST. By Schmid. 6d.
THE LITTLE LAMB. By Schmid. 6d.

THE LITTLE DOVE. By Krummacher. 4d.
THE MINISTER OF ANDOUSE. By Mowes. 1s. 6d.

NOTICE TO SUBSCRIBERS.

MESSRS. CLARK have the pleasure of forwarding to their Subscribers the 11th and 12th Volumes of the ANTE-NICENE LIBRARY, viz. :

>TERTULLIAN, Volume I., and
>CLEMENT OF ALEXANDRIA, Volume II.

The whole of the remaining works to be comprised in the Series are in active preparation. May the Publishers request an early remittance of the Subscription for fourth year (Vols. 13–16).

It will be observed that the Volume of TERTULLIAN now issued is numbered Volume I. The Subscribers are aware that the *Treatise against Marcion* has been already published; and as the works of TERTULLIAN will likely extend to FOUR Volumes, the Publishers propose that it shall be considered the *fourth*, and a Title-page accordingly will be supplied in due time.

They again sincerely thank their Subscribers for the continued support they receive.

₊ *The Binders will please notice that part of this Volume has been signatured* VOL. II. *instead of* VOL. I.

EDINBURGH, *May* 1869.

ANTE-NICENE

CHRISTIAN LIBRARY:

TRANSLATIONS OF
THE WRITINGS OF THE FATHERS
DOWN TO A.D. 325.

EDITED BY THE
REV. ALEXANDER ROBERTS, D.D.,
AND
JAMES DONALDSON, LL.D.

VOL. XI.
THE WRITINGS OF TERTULLIAN.
VOL. I.

EDINBURGH:
T. & T. CLARK, 38, GEORGE STREET.
MDCCCLXIX.

MURRAY AND GIBB, EDINBURGH,
PRINTERS TO HER MAJESTY'S STATIONERY OFFICE.

THE WRITINGS

OF

QUINTUS SEPT. FLOR. TERTULLIANUS.

VOLUME I.

EDINBURGH:
T. & T. CLARK, 38, GEORGE STREET.
LONDON: HAMILTON & CO.   DUBLIN: JOHN ROBERTSON & CO.
MDCCCLXIX.

THE Treatises in this volume, beginning with page 141 and ending with page 332, are translated by Rev. S. THELWALL, late Scholar of Christ's College, Cambridge; and the "Ad Nationes" by Rev. Dr. HOLMES, the Translator of Tertullian's Treatise against Marcion, already published in this Series.

CONTENTS.

	PAGE
I. TO THE MARTYRS,	1
II. ON THE SPECTACLES,	8
III. ON THE TESTIMONY OF THE SOUL,	36
IV. TO SCAPULA,	46
V. APOLOGY,	53
VI. ON IDOLATRY,	141
VII. ON PRAYER,	178
VIII. OF PATIENCE,	205
IX. ON BAPTISM,	231
X. ON REPENTANCE,	257
XI. TO HIS WIFE,	279
XII. ON FEMALE DRESS,	304
XIII. ON THE SOLDIER'S CHAPLET,	333
XIV. ON FLIGHT IN PERSECUTION,	356
XV. THE ANTIDOTE TO THE SCORPION'S BITE,	379
XVI. TO THE NATIONS,	416

I.

AD MARTYRAS.

1. BLESSED Martyrs Designate,—Along with the provision which our lady mother the church from her bountiful breasts, and each brother out of his private means, makes for your bodily wants in the prison, accept also from me some contribution to your spiritual sustenance. For it is not good that the flesh be feasted and the spirit starve: nay, if that which is weak is carefully looked to, it is but right that that which is still weaker should not be neglected. Not that I am specially entitled to exhort you; yet not only the trainers and overseers, but even the unskilled, nay, all who choose, without the slightest need for it, are wont to animate from afar by their cries the most accomplished gladiators, and from the mere throng of onlookers useful suggestions have sometimes come. First, then, O blessed, grieve not the Holy Spirit,[1] who has entered the prison with you. For if He had not gone with you there, you would not have been there this day. And do you give all endeavour therefore to retain Him; so let Him lead you thence to your Lord. The prison, indeed, is the devil's house as well, wherein he keeps his family. But you have come within its walls for the very purpose of trampling the wicked one under foot in his chosen abode. You had already in pitched battle outside utterly overcome him; let him have no reason, then, to say to himself, "They are now in my domain; with vile hatreds I shall tempt them, with defections or dissensions among themselves." Let him fly from your presence, and skulk away into his own abysses, shrunken and torpid, as though he were an outcharmed or

[1] Eph. iv. 30.

outsmoked snake. Give him not the success in his own
kingdom of setting you at variance with each other, but let
him find you armed and fortified with concord; for peace
among you is battle with him. You know that some, not
able to find this peace in the church, have been used to seek
it from the imprisoned martyrs. And so you ought to have
it dwelling with you, and to cherish it, and to guard it, that
you may be able perhaps to bestow it upon others.

2. Other things, hindrances equally of the soul, may have
accompanied you as far as the prison gate, to which also your
relatives may have attended you. There and thenceforth
you were severed from the world; how much more from the
ordinary course of worldly life and all its affairs! Nor let
this separation from the world alarm you. For if we reflect
that the world is more really the prison, we shall see that you
have gone out of a prison rather than into one. The world
has the greater darkness, blinding men's hearts. The world
imposes the more grievous fetters, binding men's very souls.
The world breathes out the worst impurities—human lusts.
The world contains the larger number of criminals, even the
whole human race. Then, last of all, it awaits the judgment,
not of the proconsul, but of God. Wherefore, O blessed,
you may regard yourselves as having been translated from a
prison to, we may say, a place of safety. It is full of darkness, but ye yourselves are light; it has bonds, but God has
made you free. Unpleasant exhalations are there, but ye
are an odour of sweetness. The judge is daily looked for,
but ye shall judge the judges themselves. Sadness may be
there for him who sighs for the world's enjoyments. The
Christian outside the prison has renounced the world, but in
the prison he has renounced a prison too. It is of no consequence where you are in the world—you who are not of it.
And if you have lost some of life's sweets, it is the way of
business to suffer present loss, that after gains may be the
larger. Thus far I say nothing of the rewards to which
God invites the martyrs. Meanwhile let us compare the life
of the world and of the prison, and see if the spirit does not
gain more in the prison than the flesh loses. Nay, by the

care of the church and the love of the brethren, even the flesh does not lose there what is for its good, while the spirit obtains besides important advantages. You have no occasion to look on strange gods, you do not run against their images; you have no part in heathen holidays, even by mere bodily mingling in them; you are not annoyed by the foul fumes of idolatrous solemnities; you are not pained by the noise of the public shows, nor by the atrocity or madness or immodesty of their celebrants; your eyes do not fall on stews and brothels; you are free from causes of offence, from temptations, from unholy reminiscences; you are free now from persecution too. The prison does the same service for the Christian which the desert did for the prophet. Our Lord Himself spent much of His time in seclusion, that He might have greater liberty to pray, that He might be quit of the world. It was in a mountain solitude, too, He showed His glory to the disciples. Let us drop the name of prison; let us call it a place of retirement. Though the body is shut in, though the flesh is confined, all things are open to the spirit. In spirit, then, roam abroad; in spirit walk about, not setting before you shady paths or long colonnades, but the way which leads to God. As often as in spirit your footsteps are there, so often you will not be in bonds. The leg does not feel the chain when the mind is in the heavens. The mind compasses the whole man about, and whither it wills it carries him. But where thy heart shall be, there shall be thy treasure.[1] Be there our heart, then, where we would have our treasure.

3. Grant now, O blessed, that even to Christians the prison is unpleasant. But we were called to the warfare of the living God in our very response to the sacramental words. Well, no soldier comes out to the campaign laden with luxuries, nor does he go to action from his comfortable chamber, but from the light and narrow tent, where every kind of hardness and roughness and disagreeableness must be put up with. Even in peace soldiers inure themselves to war by toils and inconveniences—marching in arms, running

[1] Matt. vi. 21.

over the plain, working at the ditch, making the *testudo*, engaging in many arduous labours. The sweat of the brow is in everything, that bodies and minds may not shrink at having to pass from shade to sunshine, from sunshine to icy cold, from the robe of peace to the coat of mail, from silence to clamour, from quiet to tumult. In like manner, O blessed, count whatever is hard in this lot of yours as a discipline of your powers of mind and body. You are about to pass through a noble struggle, in which the living God acts the part of superintendent, in which the Holy Ghost is your trainer, in which the prize is an eternal crown of angelic essence, citizenship in the heavens, glory everlasting. Therefore your Master, Jesus Christ, who has anointed you with His Spirit, and led you forth to the arena, has seen it good, before the day of conflict, to take you from a condition more pleasant in itself, and imposed on you a harder treatment, that your strength might be the greater. For the athletes, too, are set apart to a more stringent discipline, that they may have their physical powers built up. They are kept from luxury, from daintier meats, from more pleasant drinks; they are pressed, racked, worn out; the harder their labours in the preparatory training, the stronger is the hope of victory. "And they," says the apostle, "that they may obtain a corruptible crown."[1] We, with the crown eternal in our eye, look upon the prison as our training-ground, that at the goal of final judgment we may be brought forth well disciplined by many a trial; since virtue is built up by hardships, as by voluptuous indulgence it is overthrown.

4. From the saying of our Lord we know that the flesh is weak, the spirit willing.[2] Let us not, withal, take delusive comfort from the Lord's acknowledgment of the weakness of the flesh. For precisely on this account He first declared the spirit willing, that He might show which of the two ought to be subject to the other—that the flesh might yield obedience to the spirit—the weaker to the stronger; the former thus from the latter getting strength. Let the spirit

---

[1] 1 Cor. ix. 25.   [2] Matt. xxvi. 41.

hold converse with the flesh about the common salvation, thinking no longer of the troubles of the prison, but of the wrestle and conflict for which they are the preparation. The flesh, perhaps, will dread the merciless sword, and the lofty cross, and the rage of the wild beasts, and that punishment of the flames, of all most terrible, and all the skill of the executioner in torture. But, on the other side, let the spirit set clearly before both itself and the flesh, how these things, though exceeding painful, have yet been calmly endured by many,—nay, have even been eagerly desired for the sake of fame and glory; and this not only in the case of men, but of women too, that you, O holy women, may be worthy of your sex. It would take me too long to enumerate one by one the men who at their own self-impulse have put an end to themselves. As to women, there is a famous case at hand: the violated Lucretia, in the presence of her kinsfolk, plunged the knife into herself, that she might have glory for her chastity. Mucius burned his right hand on an altar, that this deed of his might dwell in fame. The philosophers have been outstripped,—for instance Heraclitus, who, smeared with cow-dung, burned himself; and Empedocles, who leapt down into the fires of Ætna; and Peregrinus, who not long ago threw himself on the funeral pile. For women even have despised the flames. Dido did so, lest, after the death of a husband very dear to her, she should be compelled to marry again; and so did the wife of Hasdrubal, who, Carthage now on fire, that she might not behold her husband suppliant at Scipio's feet, rushed with her children into the conflagration, in which her native city was destroyed. Regulus, a Roman general, who had been taken prisoner by the Carthaginians, declined to be exchanged for a large number of Carthaginian captives, choosing rather to be given back to the enemy. He was crammed into a sort of chest; and everywhere pierced by nails driven from the outside, he endured so many crucifixions. Woman has voluntarily sought the wild beasts, and even asps, those serpents worse than bear or bull, which Cleopatra applied to herself, that she might not fall into the hands of her enemy. But the fear of death is not so great as the fear of torture. And so the Athenian courtezan succumbed to the executioner, when, subjected to torture by the tyrant for having taken part in a conspiracy, still making no betrayal of her confederates, she at last bit off her tongue and spat it in the tyrant's face, that he might be convinced of the uselessness of his torments, however long they should be continued. Everybody knows what to this day is the great Lacedæmonian solemnity—the διαμαστίγωσις, or scourging; in which sacred rite the Spartan youths are beaten with scourges before the altar, their parents and kinsmen standing by and exhorting them to stand it bravely out. For it will be always counted more honourable and glorious, that the soul rather than the body has given itself to stripes. But if so high a value is put on the earthly glory, won by mental and bodily vigour, that men, for the praise of their fellows, I may say, despise the sword, the fire, the cross, the wild beasts, the torture; these surely are but trifling sufferings to obtain a celestial glory and a divine reward. If the bit of glass is so precious, what must the true pearl be worth? Are we not called on, then, most joyfully to lay out as much for the true as others do for the false?

5. I leave out of account now the motive of glory. All these same cruel and painful conflicts, a mere vanity you find among men—in fact, a sort of mental disease—has trampled under foot. How many ease-lovers does the conceit of arms give to the sword? They actually go down to meet the very wild beasts in vain ambition; and they fancy themselves more winsome from the bites and scars of the contest. Some have sold themselves to fires, to run a certain distance in a burning tunic. Others, with most enduring shoulders, have walked about under the hunters' whips. The Lord has given these things a place in the world, O blessed, not without some reason: for what reason, but *now* to animate us, and on that day to confound us if we have feared to suffer for the truth, that we might be saved, what others out of vanity have eagerly sought for to their ruin?

6. Passing, too, from examples of enduring constancy having such an origin as this, let us turn to a simple con-

templation of man's estate in its ordinary conditions, that mayhap from things which happen to us whether we will or no, and which we must set our minds to bear, we may get instruction. How often, then, have fires consumed the living! How often have wild beasts torn men in pieces, it may be in their own forests, or it may be in the heart of cities, when they have chanced to escape from their dens! How many have fallen by the robber's sword! How many have suffered at the hands of enemies the death of the cross, after having been tortured first, yes, and treated with every sort of contumely! One may even suffer in the cause of a man what he hesitates to suffer in the cause of God. In reference to this indeed, let the present times bear testimony, when so many persons of rank have met with death in a mere human being's cause, and that though from their birth and dignities and bodily condition and age such a fate seemed most unlikely; either suffering at his hands if they have taken part against him, or from his enemies if they have been his partisans.

II.

DE SPECTACULIS.

1. YE servants of God, about to draw near to God, that you may make solemn consecration of yourselves to Him, seek well to understand the condition of faith, the reasons of the truth, the laws of Christian discipline, which forbid, among other sins of the world, the pleasures of the public shows; ye who have testified and confessed that you have already done so, review the subject, that there may be no sinning, whether through real or wilful ignorance. For such is the power of earthly pleasures, that, to retain the opportunity of still partaking of them, it contrives to prolong a willing ignorance, and bribes knowledge into playing a dishonest part. To both things, perhaps, some among you are allured by the views of the heathens, who in this matter are wont to press us with such arguments as these: That the exquisite enjoyments of ear and eye we have in external things are not in the least opposed to religion in the mind and conscience; and that surely no offence is offered to God in any human enjoyment, at any of our pleasures which, with all due reverence and honour secured to Him, it is not sinful to partake of in its own time and place. But this is precisely what we are ready to prove—that these things are not consistent with true religion, and true obedience to the true God. There are some who imagine that Christians, a sort of people ever ready to die, are trained into the abstinence they practise, with no other object than that of making it less difficult to despise life—the fastenings to it being, as it were, severed,—of quenching all desire for what they have emptied, so far as they are concerned, of all that is desirable; so it is thought to be rather

a thing of human planning and foresight, than clearly laid down by divine command. It were a grievous thing, forsooth, for Christians, while continuing in the enjoyment of pleasures so great, to die for God! It is not as they say; though, if it were, even Christian obstinacy might well give all submission to a plan so suitable, to a rule so excellent.

2. Then, again, every one is ready with the argument that all things, as we teach, were created by God, and given to man for his use, and that they must all be good as coming all from so good a source, but that among them are found the various constituent elements of the public shows, such as the horse, the lion, bodily strength, and musical voice. It cannot, then, be thought that what exists by God's own creative will is either foreign or hostile to Him; and if it is not opposed to Him, it cannot be regarded as injurious to His worshippers, as certainly it is not foreign to them. Beyond all doubt, too, the very buildings connected with the places of public amusement, composed as they are of rocks, stones, marbles, pillars, are things of God, who has given these various things for the earth's embellishment; nay, the very scenes are enacted under God's own heaven. How skilful a pleader seems human wisdom to herself, especially if she has the fear of losing any of her delights—any of the sweet enjoyments of worldly existence! In fact, you will find not a few whom the imperilling of their pleasures rather than their life holds back from us. For even the weakling has no strong dread of death *as a debt* he knows is due by him; while the wise man does not look with contempt on pleasure, regarding it as a precious gift—in fact, the one blessedness of life, whether to philosopher or fool. Now nobody denies what nobody is ignorant of—for Nature herself is teacher of it—that God is the Maker of the universe, and that it is good, and that it is man's by free gift of its Maker. But having no intimate acquaintance with the Highest, knowing Him only by natural revelation, and not as His "friends"—afar off, and not as those who have been brought nigh to Him—men cannot but be in ignorance alike of what He enjoins and what He forbids in regard to the administration of His world. They must

be ignorant, too, of the hostile power which works against Him, and perverts to wrong uses the things His hand has formed; for you cannot know either the will or the adversary of a God you do not know. We must not, then, consider merely by whom all things were made, but by whom they have been perverted. We shall find out for what use they were made at first, when we find for what they were not. There is a vast difference between the corrupted state and that of primal purity, just because there is a vast difference between the Creator and the corrupter. Why, all sorts of evils, which as indubitably evils even the heathens prohibit, and against which they guard themselves, come from the works of God. Take, for instance, murder, whether committed by iron, by poison, or by magical enchantments. Iron and herbs and demons are all equally creatures of God. Has the Creator, withal, provided these things for man's destruction? Nay, He puts His interdict on every sort of man-killing by that one summary precept, "Thou shalt not kill." Moreover, who but God, the Maker of the world, put in it gold, brass, silver, ivory, wood, and all the other materials used in the manufacture of idols? Yet has He done this that men may set up a worship in opposition to Himself? On the contrary, idolatry in His eyes is the crowning sin. What is there offensive to God which is not God's? But in offending Him, it ceases to be His; and in ceasing to be His, it is in His eyes an offending thing. Man himself, guilty as he is of every iniquity, is not only a work of God—he is His image, and yet both in soul and body he has severed himself from his Maker. For we did not get eyes to minister to lust, and the tongue for speaking evil with, and ears to be the receptacle of evil speech, and the throat to serve the vice of gluttony, and the belly to be gluttony's ally, and the genitals for unchaste excesses, and hands for deeds of violence, and the feet for an erring life; or was the soul placed in the body that it might become a thought-manufactory of snares, and frauds, and injustices? I think not; for if God, as the righteous exactor of innocence, hates everything like malignity, if He hates utterly such plotting of evil, it is clear

beyond a doubt, that, of all things that have come from His
hand, He has made none to lead to works which He condemns,
even though these same works may be carried on by things
of His making; for, in fact, it is the one ground of condemnation that the creature misuses the creation. We,
therefore, who in our knowledge of the Lord have obtained
some knowledge also of His foe, who in our discovery of the
Creator have at the same time laid hands upon the great
corrupter, ought neither to wonder nor to doubt that, as the
prowess of the corrupting and God-opposing angel overthrew
in the beginning the virtue of man, the work and image of God,
the possessor of the world, he has entirely changed man's nature
—created, like his own, for perfect sinlessness—into his own
state of wicked enmity against his Maker, that in the very thing
whose gift to man, but not to him, had grieved him, he might
make man guilty in God's eyes, and set up his own supremacy.

3. Fortified by this knowledge against heathen views, let
us rather turn to the unworthy reasonings of our own people.
For the faith of some, either too simple or too scrupulous,
demands direct authority from Scripture for giving up the
shows, and holds out that the matter is a doubtful one, because such abstinence is not clearly and in words imposed
upon God's servants. Well, we never find it expressed with
the same precision, "Thou shalt not enter circus or theatre,
thou shalt not look on combat or show;" as it is plainly laid
down, "Thou shalt not kill; thou shalt not worship an idol;
thou shalt not commit adultery or fraud."[1] But we find that
that first word of David bears on this very sort of thing:
"Blessed," he says, "is the man who has not gone into the
assembly of the impious, nor stood in the way of sinners, nor
sat in the seat of scorners."[2] For though he seems to have
predicted beforehand of that just man, that he took no part
in the meetings and deliberations of the Jews, taking counsel
about the slaying of our Lord, yet divine Scripture has ever
far-reaching applications: after the immediate sense has been
exhausted, in all directions it fortifies the practice of the religious life, so that here also you have an utterance which is

[1] Ex. xx. 14. [2] Ps. i. 1.

not far from a plain interdicting of the shows. For if he called those few Jews an assembly of the wicked, how much more will he so designate so vast a gathering of heathens! Are the heathens less impious, less sinners, less enemies of Christ, than the Jews were then? And see, too, how other things agree. For at the shows they also stand in the way. For they call the spaces between the seats going round the amphitheatre, and the passages which separate the people running down, ways. The place in the curve where matrons sit is called a chair. Therefore on the contrary it holds, unblessed is he who has entered any council of wicked men, and has stood in any way of sinners, and has sat in any chair of scorners. We may understand a thing as spoken generally, even when it requires a certain special interpretation to be given to it. For some things spoken with a special reference contain in them general truth. When God admonishes the Israelites of their duty, or sharply reproves them, He has surely a reference to all men; when He threatens destruction to Egypt and Ethiopia, He surely pre-condemns every sinning nation whatever. If, reasoning from *species* to *genus*, every nation that sins against them is an Egypt and Ethiopia; so also, reasoning from genus to species, with reference to the origin of shows, every show is an assembly of the wicked.

4. Lest any one think that we are dealing in mere argumentative subtleties, I shall turn to that highest authority of our "seal" itself. When entering the water, we make profession of the Christian faith in the words of its rule; we bear public testimony that we have renounced the devil, his pomp, and his angels. Well, is it not in connection with idolatry, above all, that you have the devil with his pomp and his angels? from which, to speak briefly—for I do not wish to dilate—you have every unclean and wicked spirit. If, therefore, it shall be made plain that the entire apparatus of the shows is based upon idolatry, beyond all doubt that will carry with it the conclusion that our renunciatory testimony in the laver of baptism has reference to the shows, which through their idolatry have been given over to the devil, and his pomp, and his angels. We shall set forth, then, their

several origins, in what nursing-places they have grown to manhood; next the titles of some of them, by what names they are called; then their apparatus, with what superstitions they are observed; then their places, to what patrons they are dedicated; then the arts which minister to them, to what authors they are traced. If any of these shall be found to have had no connection with an idol-god, it will be held as free at once from the taint of idolatry, and as not coming within the range of our baptismal abjuration.

5. In the matter of their origins, as these are somewhat obscure and but little known to many among us, our investigations must go back to a remote antiquity, and our authorities be none other than books of heathen literature. Various authors are extant who have published works on the subject. The origin of the games as given by them is this. Timæus tells us that immigrants from Asia, under the leadership of Tyrrhenus, who, in a contest about his native kingdom, had succumbed to his brother, settled down in Etruria. Well, among other superstitious observances under the name of religion, they set up in their new home public shows. The Romans, at their own request, obtain from them skilled performers—the proper seasons—the name too, for it is said they are called *Ludi*, from *Lydi*. And though Varro derives the name of *Ludi* from *Ludus*, that is, from play, as they called the Luperci also *Ludii*, because they ran about making sport; still that sporting of young men belongs, in his view, to festal days and temples, and objects of religious veneration. However, it is of little consequence the origin of the name, when it is certain that the thing springs from idolatry. For the Liberalia, under the general designation of Ludi, clearly declared the glory of Father Bacchus; for to Bacchus these festivities were first consecrated by grateful peasants, in return for the boon he conferred on them, as they say, making known the pleasures of wine. Then the Consualia were called *Ludi*, and at first were in honour of Neptune, for Neptune has the name of Consus also. Thereafter Romulus dedicated the Equiria to Mars, though they claim the Consualia too for Romulus, on the ground that he con-

secrated them to Consus, the god, as they will have it, of counsel; of the counsel, forsooth, in which he planned the rape of the Sabine virgins for wives to his soldiers. An excellent counsel truly; and still I suppose reckoned just and righteous by the Romans themselves, I may not say by God. For this goes also to taint the origin: you cannot surely hold that to be good which has sprung from sin, from shamelessness, from violence, from hatred, from a fratricidal founder, from a son of Mars. Even now, at the first turning-post in the circus, there is a subterranean altar to this same Consus, with an inscription to this effect: "Consus great in counsel, Mars in battle, mighty tutelar deities." The priests of the state sacrifice at it on the nones of July; the priest of Romulus and the Vestals on the twelfth before the Kalends of September. In addition to this, Romulus instituted games in honour of Jupiter Feretrius on the Tarpeian Hill, according to the statement Piso has handed down to us, called both Tarpeian and Capitoline. After him Numa Pompilius instituted games to Mars and Robigo (for they have also invented a goddess of rust); then Tullus Hostilius; then Ancus Martius; and various others in succession did the like. As to the idols in whose honour these games were established, ample information is to be found in the pages of Suetonius Tranquillus. But we need say no more to prove the accusation of idolatrous origin.

6. To the testimony of antiquity is added that of later games instituted in their turn, and betraying their origin from the titles which they bear even at the present day, in which it is imprinted as on their very face for what idol and for what religious object games, whether of the one kind or the other, were designed. You have festivals bearing the name of the great Mother and Apollo, of Ceres too, and Neptune, and Jupiter Latiaris, and Flora, all celebrated for a common end; the others have their religious origin in the birthdays and solemnities of kings, in public successes, in municipal holidays. There are also testamentary exhibitions, in which funeral honours are rendered to the memories of private persons; and this according to an institution of ancient

times. For from the first the "Ludi" were regarded as of two sorts, sacred and funereal, that is, in honour of the heathen deities and of the dead. But in the matter of idolatry, it makes no difference with us under what name or title it is practised, while it has to do with the wicked spirits whom we abjure. If it is lawful to offer homage to the dead, it will be just as lawful to offer it to their gods: you have the same origin in both cases; there is the same idolatry; there is on our part the same solemn renunciation against all idolatry.

7. The two kinds of public games, then, have one origin; and they have common names, as owning the same parentage. So, too, as they are equally tainted with the sin of idolatry, their foundress, they must needs be like each other in their pomp. But the more ambitious preliminary display of the circus games, to which the name procession specially belongs, is in itself the proof to whom the whole thing appertains, in the many images, the long line of statues, the chariots of all sorts, the thrones, the crowns, the dresses. What high religious rites besides, what sacrifices precede, come between, and follow, how many guilds, how many priesthoods, how many offices are set astir, is known to the inhabitants of the great city in which the demon convention has its headquarters. If these things are done in humbler style in the provinces, in accordance with their inferior means, still all circus games must be counted as belonging to that from which they are derived; the fountain from which they spring defiles them. For the tiny streamlet from its very spring-head, the little twig from its very budding, contains in it the essential nature of its origin. It may be grand or mean, no matter, any circus procession whatever is offensive to God. Though there be few images to grace it, there is idolatry in one; though there be no more than a single sacred car, it is a chariot of Jupiter: anything of idolatry whatever, whether meanly arrayed or modestly rich and gorgeous, taints it in its origin.

8. To follow out my plan in regard to places: the circus is chiefly consecrated to the Sun, whose temple stands in the middle of it, and whose image shines forth from its temple summit; for they have not thought it proper to pay sacred

honours underneath a roof to an object they have itself in open
space. Those who assert that the first spectacle was exhibited
by Circe, and in honour of the Sun her father, as they will
have it, maintain also the name of circus was derived from her.
Plainly, then, the enchantress did this in the name of the
parties whose priestess she was—I mean the demons and
spirits of evil. What an aggregation of idolatries you see,
accordingly, in the decoration of the place! Every ornament
of the circus is a temple by itself. The eggs are regarded
as sacred to the Castors, by men who are not ashamed to
profess faith in their production from the egg of a swan,
which was no other than Jupiter himself. The Dolphins
vomit forth in honour of Neptune. Images of Sessia, so
called as the goddess of sowing; of Messia, so called as the
goddess of reaping; of Tutulina, so called as the fruit-pro-
tecting deity—load the pillars. In front of these you have
three altars to these three gods—Great, Mighty, Victorious.
They reckon these of Samo-Thrace. The huge Obelisk, as
Hermeteles affirms, is set up in public to the Sun; its inscription, as its origin, belongs to Egyptian superstition. Cheerless
were the demon-gathering without their *Mater Magna;* and
so she presides there over the Euripus. Consus, as we have
mentioned, lies hidden under ground at the Murcian Goals.
These two sprang from an idol. For they will have it that
Murcia is the goddess of love; and to her, at that spot, they
have consecrated a temple. See, Christian, how many impure names have taken possession of the circus! You have
nothing to do with a sacred place which is tenanted by such
multitudes of diabolic spirits. And speaking of places, this
is the suitable occasion for some remarks in anticipation of
a point that some will raise. What, then, you say; shall I
be in danger of pollution if I go to the circus when the
games are not being celebrated? There is no law forbidding the mere places to us. For not only the places for
show-gatherings, but even the temples, may be entered without any peril of his religion by the servant of God, if he has
only some honest reason for it, unconnected with their proper
business and official duties. Why, even the streets, and the

market-place, and the baths, and the taverns, and our very dwelling-places, are not altogether free from idols. Satan and his angels have filled the whole world. It is not by merely being in the world, however, that we lapse from God, but by touching and tainting ourselves with the world's sins. I shall break with my Maker, that is, by going to the Capitol or the temple of Serapis to sacrifice or adore, as I shall also do by going as a spectator to the circus and the theatre. The places in themselves do not contaminate, but what is done in them, from which even the places themselves, we maintain, become defiled. The polluted things pollute us. It is on this account that we set before you to whom places of the kind are dedicated, that we may prove the things which are done in them to belong to the idol-patrons to whom the very places are sacred.

9. Now as to the kind of performances peculiar to the circus exhibitions. In former days equestrianism was practised in a simple way on horseback, and certainly its ordinary use had nothing sinful in it; but when it was dragged into the games, it passed from the service of God into the employment of demons. Accordingly this kind of circus performances is regarded as sacred to Castor and Pollux, to whom, Stesichorus tells us, horses were given by Mercury. And Neptune, too, is an equestrian deity, by the Greeks called Hippius. In regard to the team, they have consecrated the chariot and four to the sun; the chariot and pair to the moon. But, as the poet has it, "Erichthonius first dared to yoke four horses to the chariot, and to ride upon its wheels with victorious swiftness." Erichthonius, the son of Vulcan and Minerva, fruit of unworthy passion upon earth, is a demon-monster, nay, the devil himself, and no mere snake. But if Trochilus the Argive is maker of the first chariot, he dedicated that work of his to Juno. If Romulus first exhibited the four-horse chariot at Rome, he too, I think, has a place given him among idols, at least if he and Quirinus are the same. But as chariots had such inventors, the charioteers were naturally dressed, too, in the colours of idolatry: for at first these were only two, namely

white and red,—the former sacred to the winter with its glistening snows, the latter sacred to the summer with its ruddy sun; but afterwards, in the progress of luxury as well as of superstition, red was dedicated by some to Mars, and white by others to the Zephyrs, while green was given to Mother Earth, or spring, and azure to the sky and sea, or autumn. But as idolatry of every kind is condemned by God, that form of it surely shares the condemnation which is offered to the elements of nature.

10. Let us pass on now to theatrical exhibitions, which we have already shown have a common origin with the circus, and bear like idolatrous designations—even as from the first they have borne the name of "Ludi," and equally minister to idols. They resemble each other also in their pomp, having the same procession to the scene of their display from temples and altars and that mournful profusion of incense and blood, with music of pipes and trumpets, all under the direction of the soothsayer and the undertaker, those two foul masters of funeral rites and sacrifices. So as we went on from the origin of the "Ludi" to the circus games, we shall now direct our course thence to those of the theatre, beginning with the place of exhibition. At first the theatre was properly a temple of Venus; and, to speak briefly, it was owing to this that stage performances were allowed to escape censure, and got a footing in the world. For ofttimes the censors, in the interests of morality, put down above all the rising theatres, foreseeing as they did that there was great danger of their leading to a general profligacy; so that already, from this accordance of their own people with us, there is a witness to the heathen, and in the anticipatory judgment of human knowledge even a confirmation of our views. Accordingly Pompey the Great, less only than his theatre, when he had erected that citadel of all impurities, fearing some time or other censorian condemnation of his memory, superposed on it a temple of Venus; and summoning by public proclamation the people to its consecration, he called it not a theatre, but a temple, "under which," said he, "we have placed tiers of seats for viewing the

shows." So he threw a veil over a structure on which condemnation had been often passed, and which is ever to be held in reprobation, by pretending that it was a sacred place; and by means of superstition he blinded the eyes of a virtuous discipline. But Venus and Bacchus are close allies. These two evil spirits are in sworn confederacy with each other, as the patrons of drunkenness and lust. So the theatre of Venus is as well the house of Bacchus: for they properly gave the name of Liberalia also to other theatrical amusements—which besides being consecrated to Bacchus (as were the Dionysia of the Greeks), were instituted by him; and, without doubt, the performances of the theatre have the common patronage of these two deities. That immodesty of gesture and attire which so specially and peculiarly characterizes the stage are consecrated to them—the one deity wanton by her sex, the other by his drapery; while its services of voice, and song, and lute, and pipe, belong to Apollos, and Muses, and Minervas, and Mercuries. You will hate, O Christian, the things whose authors must be the objects of your utter detestation. So we would now make a remark about the arts of the theatre, about the things also whose authors in the names we execrate. We know that the names of the dead are nothing, as are their images; but we know well enough, too, who, when images are set up, under these names carry on their wicked work, and exult in the homage rendered to them, and pretend to be divine —none other than spirits accursed, than devils. We see, therefore, that the arts also are consecrated to the service of the beings who dwell in the names of their founders; and that things cannot be held free from the taint of idolatry whose inventors have got a place among the gods for their discoveries. Nay, as regards the arts, we ought to have gone further back, and barred all further argument by the position that the demons, predetermining in their own interests from the first, among other evils of idolatry, the pollutions of the public shows, with the object of drawing man away from his Lord and binding him to their own service, carried out their purpose by bestowing on him the artistic gifts which the shows require. For none but themselves would have made provision and preparation for the objects they had in view; nor would they have given the arts to the world by any but those in whose names, and images, and histories they set up for their own ends the artifice of consecration.

11. In fulfilment of our plan, let us now go on to consider the combats. Their origin is akin to that of the games (*ludi*). Hence they are kept as either sacred or funereal, as they have been instituted in honour of the idol-gods of the nations or of the dead. Thus, too, they are called Olympian in honour of Jupiter, known at Rome as the Capitoline; Nemean, in honour of Hercules; Isthmian, in honour of Neptune; the rest "*mortuarii*," as belonging to the dead. What wonder, then, if idolatry pollutes the combat-parade with profane crowns, with sacerdotal chiefs, with attendants belonging to the various colleges, last of all with the blood of its sacrifices? To add a completing word about the "place"—in the common place for the college of the arts sacred to the Muses, and Apollo, and Minerva, and also for that of the arts dedicated to Mars, they with contest and sound of trumpet emulate the circus in the arena, which is a real temple—I mean of the god whose festivals it celebrates. The gymnastic arts also originated with their Castors, and Herculeses, and Mercuries.

12. It remains for us to examine the "spectacle" most noted of all, and in highest favour. It is called a dutiful service (*munus*), from its being an office, for it bears the name of "*officium*" as well as "*munus*." The ancients thought that in this solemnity they rendered offices to the dead; at a later period, with a cruelty more refined, they somewhat modified its character. For formerly, in the belief that the souls of the departed were appeased by human blood, they were in the habit of buying captives or slaves of wicked disposition, and immolating them in their funeral obsequies. Afterwards they thought good to throw the veil of pleasure over their iniquity. Those therefore whom they had provided for the combat, and then trained in arms as best they could, only that they might learn to die, they on the funeral

day killed at the places of sepulture. They alleviated death by murders. Such is the origin of the "Munus." But by degrees their refinement came up to their cruelty; for these human wild beasts could not find pleasure exquisite enough, save in the spectacle of men torn to pieces by wild beasts. Offerings to propitiate the dead then were regarded as belonging to the class of funeral sacrifices; and these are idolatry: for idolatry, in fact, is a sort of homage to the departed; the one as well as the other is a service to dead men. Moreover, demons have abode in the images of the dead. To refer also to the matter of names, though this sort of exhibition has passed from honours of the dead to honours of the living, I mean, to quæstorships and magistracies—to priestly offices of different kinds, yet since idolatry still cleaves to the dignity's name, whatever is done in its name partakes of its impurity. The same remark will apply to the procession of the "Munus" as we look at that in the pomp which is connected with these honours themselves; for the purple robes, the fasces, the fillets, the crowns, the proclamations too, and edicts, the sacred feasts of the day before, are not without the pomp of the devil, without invitation of demons. What need, then, of dwelling on the place of horrors, which is too much even for the tongue of the perjurer? For the amphitheatre is consecrated to names more numerous and more dire than is the Capitol itself, temple of all demons as it is. There are as many unclean spirits there as it holds men. To conclude with a single remark about the arts which have a place in it, we know that its two sorts of amusement have for their patrons Mars and Diana.

13. We have, I think, faithfully carried out our plan of showing in how many different ways the sin of idolatry clings to the shows, in respect of their origins, their titles, their equipments, their places of celebration, their arts; and we may hold it as a thing beyond all doubt, that for us who have twice renounced all idols, they are utterly unsuitable. "Not that an idol is anything,"[1] as the apostle says, but that the homage they render is to demons, who are the real

[1] 1 Cor. viii. 4.

occupants of these consecrated images, whether of dead men or (as they think) of gods. On this account, therefore, because they have a common source—for their dead and their deities are one—we abstain from both idolatries. Nor do we dislike the temples less than the monuments: we have nothing to do with either altar, we adore neither image, we do not offer sacrifices to the gods, and we make no funeral oblations to the departed; nay, we do not partake of what is offered either in the one case or the other, for we cannot partake of God's feast and the feast of devils.[1] If, then, we keep throat and belly free from such defilements, how much more do we withhold our nobler parts, our ears and eyes, from the idolatrous and funereal enjoyments, which are not passed through the body, but are digested in the very spirit and soul, whose purity much more than that of our bodily organs God has a right to claim from us.

14. Having sufficiently established the charge of idolatry, which alone ought to be reason enough for our giving up the shows, let us now *ex abundanti* look at the subject in another way, for the sake of those especially who keep themselves comfortable in the thought that the abstinence we urge is not in so many words enjoined, as if in the condemnation of the lusts of the world there was not involved a sufficient declaration against all these amusements. For as there is a lust of money, or rank, or eating, or impure enjoyment, or glory, so there is also a lust of pleasure. But the show is just a sort of pleasure. I think, then, that under the general designation of lusts, pleasures are included; in like manner, under the general idea of pleasures, you have as a specific class the "shows." But we have spoken already of how it is with the places of exhibition, that they are not polluting in themselves, but owing to the things that are done in them from which they imbibe impurity, and then spirt it again on others.

15. Having done enough, then, as we have said, in regard to that principal argument, that there is in them all the taint of idolatry, having sufficiently dealt with that, let us now

[1] 1 Cor. x. 21.

contrast the other characteristics of the things of the show with the things of God. God has enjoined us to deal calmly, and gently, and quietly, and peacefully with the Holy Spirit, because these things are alone in keeping with the goodness of His nature, with His tenderness and sensitiveness, not to vex Him with rage, or ill-nature, or anger, or grief. Well, how shall this be made to accord with the shows? For the show always leads to spiritual agitation. For where there is pleasure, there is keenness of feeling giving pleasure its zest; and where there is keenness of feeling, there is rivalry giving in turn its zest to that. Then, too, where you have rivalry, you have rage, and bitterness, and wrath, and grief, and all bad things which flow from them—the whole entirely out of keeping with the religion of Christ. For even suppose one should enjoy the shows in a moderate way, as befits his rank or age or nature, still he is not undisturbed in mind, without some unuttered movings of the inner man. No one partakes of pleasures such as these without their strong excitements; no one comes under their excitements without their natural lapses. These lapses, again, create passionate desire. But if there is no desire, there is no pleasure, and he is chargeable with trifling who goes where nothing is gotten. But in my view, even that is foreign to us. And, moreover, a man pronounces his own condemnation in the very act of taking his place among those with whom, by his disinclination to be like them, he confesses he has no sympathy! It is not enough that we do no such things ourselves, unless we break all connection also with those who do. "If thou sawest a thief," says the Scripture, "thou consentedst with him."[1] Would that we did not even inhabit the same world with these wicked men! But though that wish cannot be realized, yet even now we are separate from them in what is of the world; for the world is God's, but the worldly is the devil's.

16. Since, then, all passionate excitement is forbidden us, we are debarred from every kind of spectacle, and especially from the circus, where such excitement presides as in its proper element. See the people coming to it already under

[1] Ps. xlix. 18.

strong emotion, already tumultuous, already passion-blind, already agitated about their bets. The prætor is too slow for them: their eyes are ever rolling as though along with the lots in his urn; then they hang all eager on the signal; there is the united shout of a common madness. Observe how "out of themselves" they are by their foolish speeches. "He has thrown it!" they exclaim; and they announce each one to his neighbour what all have seen. I have clearest evidence of their blindness; they do not see what is really thrown. They think it a "signal cloth," but it is the likeness of the devil cast headlong from on high. And the result accordingly is, that they fly into rages, and passions, and discords, and all that they who are consecrated to peace ought never to indulge in. Then there are curses and reproaches, with no cause of hatred; there are cries of applause, with nothing to merit them. What are the partakers in all this—not their own masters—to obtain of it for themselves? unless, it may be, that which makes them not their own: they are saddened by another's sorrow, they are gladdened by another's joy. Whatever they desire on the one hand, or detest on the other, is entirely foreign to themselves. So love with them is a useless thing, and hatred is unjust. Or is a causeless love perhaps more legitimate than a causeless hatred? God certainly forbids us to hate even with a reason for our hating; for He commands us to love our enemies. God forbids us to curse, though there be some ground for doing so, in commanding that those who curse us we are to bless. But what is more merciless than the circus, where people do not spare even their rulers and fellow-citizens? If any of its madnesses are becoming elsewhere in the saints of God, they will be seemly in the circus too; but if they are nowhere right, so neither are they there.

17. Are we not, in like manner, enjoined to put away from us all immodesty? On this ground, again, we are excluded from the theatre, which is immodesty's own peculiar abode, where nothing is in repute but what elsewhere is disreputable. So the best path to the highest favour of its god is the vileness which the Atellan gesticulates, which the

buffoon in woman's clothes exhibits, destroying all natural modesty, so that they blush more readily at home than at the play, which finally is done from his childhood on the person of the pantomime, that he may become an actor. The very harlots, too, victims of the public lust, are brought upon the stage, their misery increased as being there in the presence of their own sex, from whom alone they are wont to hide themselves: they are paraded publicly before every age and every rank—their abode, their gains, their praises, are set forth, and that even in the hearing of those who should not hear such things. I say nothing about other matters, which it were good to hide away in their own darkness and their own gloomy caves, lest they should stain the light of day. Let the Senate, let all ranks, blush for very shame! Why, even these miserable women, who by their own gestures destroy their modesty, dreading the light of day, and the people's gaze, know something of shame at least once a year. But if we ought to abominate all that is immodest, on what ground is it right to hear what we must not speak? For all licentiousness of speech, nay, every idle word, is condemned by God. Why, in the same way, is it right to look on what it is disgraceful to do? How is it that the things which defile a man in going out of his mouth, are not regarded as doing so when they go in at his eyes and ears?—when eyes and ears are the immediate attendants on the spirit; and that can never be pure whose servants-in-waiting are impure. You have the theatre forbidden, then, in the forbidding of immodesty. If, again, we despise the teaching of secular literature as being foolishness in God's eyes, our duty is plain enough in regard to those spectacles, which from this source derive the tragic or comic play. If tragedies and comedies are the bloody and wanton, the impious and licentious inventors of crimes and lusts, it is not good even that there should be any calling to remembrance the atrocious or the vile. What you reject in deed, you are not to bid welcome to in word.

18. But if you argue that the racecourse is mentioned in Scripture, I grant it at once. But you will not refuse to

admit that the things which are done there are not for you to look upon: the blows, and kicks, and cuffs, and all the recklessness of hand, and everything like that disfiguration of the human countenance, which is nothing less than the disfiguration of God's own image. You will never give your approval to those foolish racing and throwing feats, and yet more foolish leapings; you will never find pleasure in injurious or useless exhibitions of strength; certainly you will not regard with approval those efforts after an artificial body which aim at surpassing the Creator's work; and you will have the very opposite of complacency in the athletes Greece, in the inactivity of peace, feeds up. And the wrestler's art is a devil's thing. The devil wrestled with, and crushed to death, the first human beings. Its very attitude has power in it of the serpent kind, firm to hold—tortuous to clasp—slippery to glide away. You have no need of crowns; why do you strive to get pleasure from crowns?

19. We shall now see how the Scriptures condemn the amphitheatre. If we can maintain that it is right to indulge in the cruel, and the impious, and the fierce, let us go there. If we are what we are said to be, let us regale ourselves there with human blood! It is good, no doubt, to have the guilty punished. Who but the criminal himself will deny that? And yet the innocent can find no pleasure in another's sufferings: he rather mourns that a brother has sinned so heinously as to need a punishment so dreadful. But who is my guarantee that it is always the guilty who are adjudged to the wild beasts, or to some other doom, and that the guiltless never suffer from the revenge of the judge, or the weakness of the defence, or the pressure of the rack? How much better, then, is it for me to remain ignorant of the punishment inflicted on the wicked, lest I am obliged to know also of the good coming to untimely ends—if I may speak of goodness in the case at all! At any rate, gladiators not chargeable with crime are offered in sale for the games, that they may become the victims of the public pleasure. Even in the case of those who are judicially condemned to the amphitheatre, what a monstrous thing it is, that, in

undergoing their punishment, they, from some less serious delinquency, advance to the criminality of manslayers! But I mean these remarks for heathens. As to Christians, I shall not insult them by adding another word as to the aversion with which they should regard this sort of exhibition; though no one is more able than myself to set forth fully the whole subject, unless it be one who is still in the habit of going to the shows. I would rather withal be incomplete than set memory a-working.

20. How vain, then—nay, how desperate—is the reasoning of persons, who, just because they decline to lose a pleasure, hold out that we cannot point to the specific words or the very place where this abstinence is mentioned, and where the servants of God are directly forbidden to have anything to do with such assemblies! I heard lately a novel defence of himself by a certain play-lover. "The sun," said he, "nay, God Himself, looks down from heaven on the show, and no pollution is contracted." Yes, and the sun, too, pours down his rays into the common sewer without being defiled. As for God, would that all crimes were hid from His eye, that we might all escape judgment! But He looks on robberies too; He looks on falsehoods, and adulteries, and frauds, and idolatries, and these same shows; and precisely on that account *we* will not look on them, lest the All-seeing see us. You are putting on the same level, O man, the criminal and the judge; the criminal who is a criminal because he is seen, and the Judge who is a Judge because He sees. Are we set, then, on playing the madman outside the circus boundaries? Outside the gates of the theatre are we bent on lewdness, and outside the course on arrogance, and outside the amphitheatre on cruelty, because outside the porticoes and the tiers and the curtains, too, God has eyes? Never and nowhere is that free from blame which God ever condemns; never and nowhere is it right to do what you may not do at all times and in all places. It is the freedom of the truth from change of opinion and varying judgments which constitutes its perfection, and gives it its claims to full mastery, and unchanging reverence, and faithful obedience. That which

is really good or really evil cannot be ought else. But in all things the truth of God is immutable.

21. The heathens, who have not a full revelation of the truth, for they are not taught of God, hold a thing evil and good as it suits self-will and passion, making that which is good in one place evil in another, and that which is evil in one place in another good. So it strangely happens, that the same man who can scarcely in public lift up his tunic, even when necessity of nature presses him, takes it off in the circus, as if bent on exposing himself before everybody; that the father who carefully protects and guards his virgin daughter's ears from every polluting word, takes her to the theatre himself, exposing her to all its vile words and attitudes; he, again, who in the streets lays hands on or covers with reproaches the brawling pugilist, in the arena gives all encouragement to combats of a much more serious kind; and he who looks with horror on the corpse of one who has died under the common law of nature, in the amphitheatre gazes down with most patient eyes on bodies all mangled and torn and smeared with their own blood; nay, the very man who comes to the show, because he thinks murderers ought to suffer for their crime, drives the unwilling gladiator to the murderous deed with rods and scourges; and one who demands the lion for every manslayer of deeper dye, will have the staff for the savage swordsman, and rewards him with the cap of liberty: yes, and he must have the poor victim back again, that he may get a sight of his face—with zest inspecting near at hand the man whom he wished torn in pieces at safe distance from him: so much the more cruel he if that was not his wish.

22. What wonder is there in it? Such inconsistencies as these are just such as we might expect from men, who confuse and change the nature of good and evil in their inconstancy of feeling and fickleness in judgment. Why, the authors and managers of the spectacles, in that very respect with reference to which they highly laud the charioteers, and actors, and wrestlers, and those most loving gladiators, to whom men prostitute their souls, women too their bodies, slight and trample on them, though for their sakes they are guilty of

the deeds they reprobate; nay, they doom them to ignominy and the loss of their rights as citizens, excluding them from the Curia, from the rostra, from senatorial and equestrian rank, and from all other honours as well as certain distinctions. What perversity! They have pleasure in those whom yet they punish; they put all slights on those to whom, at the same time, they award their approbation; they magnify the art and brand the artist. What an outrageous thing it is, to blacken a man on account of the very things which make him meritorious in their eyes! Nay, what a confession that the things are evil, when their authors, even when in highest favour, are not without a mark of disgrace upon them!

23. Seeing, then, man's own reflections, even in spite of the sweetness of pleasure, lead him to think that people such as these should be condemned to a hapless lot of infamy, losing all the advantages connected with the possession of the dignities of life, how much more does the divine righteousness inflict punishment on those who give themselves to these arts! Will God have any pleasure in the charioteer who disquiets so many souls, who rouses up so many furious passions, and creates so many various moods, either crowned like a priest or wearing the colours of a pimp,—decked out by the devil that he may be whirled away in his chariot, as though with the object of taking off Elijah? Will He be pleased with him who applies the razor to himself, and completely changes his features; who, with no respect for his face, is not content with making it as like as possible to Saturn and Isis and Bacchus, but gives it quietly over to contumelious blows, as if in mockery of our Lord? The devil, forsooth, makes it part, too, of his teaching, that the cheek is to be meekly offered to the smiter! In the same way, with their high shoes, he has made the tragic actors taller, because "none can add a cubit to his stature."[1] His desire is to make Christ a liar. And in regard to the wearing of masks, I ask is that according to the mind of God, who forbids the making of every likeness, and especially then the likeness of man who is His own image? The Author of truth hates all the false;

[1] Matt. vi. 27.

He regards as adultery all that is unreal. Condemning, therefore, as He does hypocrisy in every form, He never will approve any putting on of voice, or sex, or age; He never will approve pretended loves, and wraths, and groans, and tears. Then, too, as in His law it is declared that the man is cursed who attires himself in female garments,[1] what must be His judgment of the pantomime, who is even brought up to play the woman! And will the boxer go unpunished? I suppose he received these cæstus-scars, and the thick skin of his fists, and these growths upon his ears, at his creation! God, too, gave him eyes for no other end than that they might be knocked out in fighting! I say nothing of him who, to save himself, thrusts another in the lion's way, that he may not be too little of a murderer when he puts to death that very same man on the arena.

24. In how many other ways shall we yet further show that nothing which is peculiar to the shows has God's approval, or without that approval is becoming in God's servants? If we have succeeded in making it plain that they were instituted entirely for the devil's sake, and have been got up entirely with the devil's things (for all that is not God's, or is not pleasing in His eyes, belongs to His wicked rival), this simply means that in them you have that pomp of the devil which in the "seal" of our faith we abjure. But we should have no connection with the things which we abjure, whether in deed or word, whether by looking on them or looking forward to them. But do we not abjure and rescind that baptismal pledge, when we cease to bear its testimony? Does it then remain for us to apply to the heathens themselves? Let them tell us, then, whether it is right in Christians to frequent the show. Why, the rejection of these amusements is the chief sign to them that a man has adopted the Christian faith. If any one, then, puts away the faith's distinctive badge, he is plainly guilty of denying it. What hope can you possibly retain in regard to a man who does that? When you go over to the enemy's camp, you throw down your arms, desert the standards and the oath of allegi-

---

[1] Deut. xxii. 5.

ance to your chief: you cast in your lot for life or death with your new friends.

25. Seated where there is nothing of God, will one be thinking of his Maker? Will there be peace in his soul when there is eager strife there for a charioteer? Wrought up into a frenzied excitement, will he learn to be modest? Nay, in the whole thing he will meet with no greater temptation than that gay attiring of the men and women. The very intermingling of emotions, the very agreements and disagreements with each other in the bestowment of their favours, where you have such close communion, blow up the sparks of passion. And then there is scarce any other object in going to the show, but to see and to be seen. When a tragic actor is declaiming, will one be giving thought to prophetic appeals? Amid the measures of the effeminate player, will he call up to himself a psalm? And when the athletes are hard at struggle, will he be ready to proclaim that there must be no striking again? And with his eye fixed on the bites of bears, and the sponge-nets of the net-fighters, can he be moved by compassion? May God avert from His people any such passionate eagerness after a cruel enjoyment! For how monstrous it is to go from God's church to the devil's—from the sky to the stye, as they say; to raise your hands to God, and then to weary them in the applause of an actor; out of the mouth, from which you uttered Amen over the Holy Thing, to give witness in a gladiator's favour; to cry "for ever" to any one else but God and Christ!

26. Why may not those who go into the temptations of the show become accessible also to evil spirits? We have the case of the woman—the Lord Himself is witness—who went to the theatre, and came back possessed. In the outcasting, accordingly, when the unclean creature was upbraided with having dared to attack a believer, he firmly replied, "And in truth I did it most righteously, for I found her in my domain." Another case, too, is well known, in which a woman had been hearing a tragedian, and on the very night she saw in her sleep a linen cloth—the actor's name being mentioned at the same time with strong disapproval—and

five days after that woman was no more. How many other undoubted proofs we have had in the case of persons who, by keeping company with the devil in the shows, have fallen from the Lord! For no one can serve two masters.[1] What fellowship has light with darkness, life with death?[2]

27. We ought to detest these heathen meetings and assemblies, if on no other account than that there God's name is blasphemed—that there the cry " To the lions!" is daily raised against us—that from thence persecuting decrees are wont to emanate, and temptations are sent forth. What will you do if you are caught in that heaving tide of impious judgments? Not that there any harm is likely to come to you from men: nobody knows that you are a Christian; but think how it fares with you in heaven. For at the very time the devil is working havoc in the church, do you doubt that the angels are looking down from above, and marking every man, who speaks and who listens to the blaspheming word, who lends his tongue and who lends his ears to the service of Satan against God? Shall you not then shun those tiers where the enemies of Christ assemble, that seat of all that is pestilential, and the very superincumbent atmosphere all impure with wicked cries? Grant that you have there things that are pleasant, things both agreeable and innocent in themselves; even some things that are excellent. Nobody dilutes poison with gall and hellebore: the accursed thing is put into condiments well seasoned and of sweetest taste. So, too, the devil puts into the deadly draught which he prepares, things of God most pleasant and most acceptable. Everything there, then, that is either brave, or noble, or loud-sounding, or melodious, or exquisite in taste, hold it but as the honey drop of a poisoned cake; nor make so much of your taste for its pleasures, as of the danger you run from its attractions.

28. With such dainties as these let the devil's guests be feasted. The places and the times, the inviter too, are theirs. Our banquets, our nuptial joys, are yet to come. We cannot sit down in fellowship with them, as neither can they with us. Things in this matter go by their turns. Now they have

[1] Matt. vi. 24.   [2] 2 Cor. vi. 14.

gladness and we are troubled. "The world," says Jesus, "shall rejoice; ye shall be sorrowful."[1] Let us mourn, then, while the heathen are merry, that in the day of their sorrow we may rejoice; lest, sharing now in their gladness, we share then also in their grief. Thou art too dainty, Christian, if thou wouldst have pleasure in this life as well as in the next; nay, a fool thou art, if thou thinkest this life's pleasures to be really pleasures. The philosophers, for instance, give the name of pleasure to quietness and repose; in that they have their bliss; in that they find entertainment: they even glory in it. You long for the goal, and the stage, and the dust, and the place of combat! I would have you answer me this question: Can we not live without pleasure, who cannot but with pleasure die? For what is our wish but the apostle's, to leave the world, and be taken up into the fellowship of our Lord?[2] You have your joys where you have your longings.

29. Even as things are, if your thought is to spend this period of existence in enjoyments, how are you so ungrateful as to reckon insufficient, as not thankfully to recognise the many and exquisite pleasures God has bestowed upon you? For what more delightful than to have God the Father and our Lord at peace with us, than revelation of the truth, than confession of our errors, than pardon of the sins so numerous of our past life? What greater pleasure than distaste of pleasure itself, than contempt of all that the world can give, than true liberty, than a pure conscience, a contented life, and freedom from all fear of death? What nobler than to tread under foot the gods of the nations—to exorcise evil spirits—to perform cures—to seek divine revealings—to live to God? These are the pleasures, these the spectacles that befit Christian men—holy, everlasting, free. Count of these as your circus games, fix your eyes on the courses of the world, the gliding seasons, reckon up the periods of time, long for the goal of the final consummation, defend the societies of the churches, be startled at God's signal, be roused up at the angel's trump, glory in the palms of martyrdom.

[1] John xvi. 20.   [2] Phil. i. 23.

If the literature of the stage delight you, we have literature in abundance of our own—plenty of verses, sentences, songs, proverbs; and these not fabulous, but true; not tricks of art, but plain realities. Would you have also fightings and wrestlings? Well, of these there is no lacking, and they are not of slight account. Behold unchastity overcome by chastity, perfidy slain by faithfulness, cruelty stricken by compassion, impudence thrown into the shade by modesty: these are the contests we have among us, and in these *we* win our crowns. But would you have something of blood too? You have Christ's.

30. But what a spectacle is that fast-approaching advent of our Lord, now owned by all, now highly exalted, now a triumphant One! What that exultation of the angelic hosts! what the glory of the rising saints! what the kingdom of the just thereafter! what the city New Jerusalem! Yes, and there are other sights: that last day of judgment, with its everlasting issues; that day unlooked for by the nations, the theme of their derision, when the world, hoary with age, and all its many products, shall be consumed in one great flame! How vast a spectacle then bursts upon the eye! What there excites my admiration? what my derision? Which sight gives me joy? which rouses me to exultation?— as I see so many illustrious monarchs, whose reception into the heavens was publicly announced, groaning now in the lowest darkness with great Jove himself, and those, too, who bore witness of their exaltation; governors of provinces, too, who persecuted the Christian name, in fires more fierce than those with which in the days of their pride they raged against the followers of Christ! What world's wise men besides, the very philosophers, in fact, who taught their followers that God had no concern in ought that is sublunary, and were wont to assure them that either they had no souls, or that they would never return to the bodies which at death they had left, now covered with shame before the poor deluded ones, as one fire consumes them! Poets also, trembling not before the judgment-seat of Rhadamanthus or Minos, but of the unexpected Christ! I shall have a better oppor-

tunity then of hearing the tragedians, louder-voiced in their own calamity; of viewing the play-actors, much more "dissolute" in the dissolving flame; of looking upon the charioteer, all glowing in his chariot of fire; of witnessing the wrestlers, not in their gymnasia, but tossing in the fiery billows; unless even then I shall not care to attend to such ministers of sin, in my eager wish rather to fix a gaze insatiable on those whose fury vented itself against the Lord. "This," I shall say, "this is that carpenter's or harlot's son, that Sabbathbreaker, that Samaritan and devil-possessed! This is He whom you purchased from Judas! This is He whom you struck with reed and fist, whom you contemptuously spat upon, to whom you gave gall and vinegar to drink! This is He whom His disciples secretly stole away, that it might be said He had risen again, or the gardener abstracted, that his lettuces might come to no harm from the crowds of visitants!" What quæstor or priest in his munificence will bestow on you the favour of seeing and exulting in such things as these? And yet even now we in a measure have them by faith in the picturings of imagination. But what are the things which eye has not seen, and ear has not heard, and which have not so much as dimly dawned upon the human heart? Whatever they are, they are nobler, I believe, than circus, and both theatres,[1] and every racecourse.

[1] Viz. the theatre and amphitheatre.

III.

DE TESTIMONIO ANIMÆ.

1. IF, with the object of convicting the rivals and persecutors of Christian truth, from their own authorities, of the crime of at once being untrue to themselves and doing injustice to us, one is bent on gathering testimonies in its favour from the writings of the philosophers, or the poets, or other masters of this world's learning and wisdom, he has need of a most inquisitive spirit, and a still greater memory, to carry out the research. Indeed, some of our people, who still continued their inquisitive labours in ancient literature, and still occupied memory with it, have published works we have in our hands of this very sort; works in which they relate and attest the nature and origin of their traditions, and the grounds on which opinions rest, and from which it may be seen at once that we have embraced nothing new or monstrous—nothing for which we cannot claim the support of ordinary and well-known writings, whether in ejecting error from our creed, or admitting truth into it. But the unbelieving hardness of the human heart leads them to slight even their own teachers, otherwise approved and in high renown, whenever they touch upon arguments which are used in defence of Christianity. Then the poets are fools, when they describe the gods with human passions and stories; then the philosophers are without reason, when they knock at the gates of truth. He will thus far be reckoned a wise and sagacious man who has gone the length of uttering sentiments that are almost Christian; while if, in a mere affectation of judgment and wisdom, he sets himself to reject their ceremonies, or to convicting the world of its sin, he is sure to be branded as a

Christian. We will have nothing, then, to do with the literature and the teaching, perverted in its best results, which is believed in its errors rather than its truth. We shall lay no stress on it, if some of their authors have declared that there is one God, and one God only. Nay, let it be granted that there is nothing in heathen writers which a Christian approves, that it may be put out of his power to utter a single word of reproach. For all are not familiar with their teachings; and those who are, have no assurance in regard to their truth. Far less do men assent to our writings, to which no one comes for guidance unless he is already a Christian. I call in a new testimony, yea, one which is better known than all literature, more discussed than all doctrine, more public than all publications, greater than the whole man —I mean all which is man's. Stand forth, O soul, whether thou art a divine and eternal substance, as most philosophers believe—if it is so, thou wilt be the less likely to lie,—or whether thou art the very opposite of divine, because indeed a mortal thing, as Epicurus alone thinks—in that case there will be the less temptation for thee to speak falsely in this case: whether thou art received from heaven, or sprung from earth; whether thou art formed of numbers, or of atoms; whether thine existence begins with that of the body, or thou art put into it at a later stage; from whatever source, and in whatever way, thou makest man a rational being, in the highest degree capable of thought and knowledge,—stand forth and give thy witness. But I call thee not as when, fashioned in schools, trained in libraries, fed up in Attic academies and porticoes, thou belchest forth thy wisdom. I address thee, simple and rude, and uncultured and untaught, such as they have thee who have thee only, that very thing pure and entire, of the road, the street, the workshop. I want thine inexperience, since in thy small experience no one feels any confidence. I demand of thee the things thou bringest with thee into man, which thou knowest either from thyself, or from thine author, whoever he may be. Thou art not, as I well know, Christian; for a man becomes a Christian, he is not born one. Yet Christians earnestly press thee for a testimony; they press thee, though an alien, to bear witness against thy friends, that they may be put to shame before thee, for hating and mocking us on account of things which convict thee as an accessory.

2. We give offence by proclaiming that there is one God, to whom the name of God alone belongs, from whom all things come, and who is Lord of the whole universe. Bear thy testimony, if thou knowest this to be the truth; for openly and with a perfect liberty, such as we do not possess, we hear thee both in private and in public exclaim, "Which may God grant," and, "If God so will." By expressions such as these thou declarest that there is one who is distinctively God, and thou confessest that all power belongs to Him to whose will as Sovereign thou dost look. At the same time, too, thou deniest any others to be truly gods, in calling them by their own names of Saturn, Jupiter, Mars, Minerva; for thou affirmest Him to be God alone to whom thou givest no other name than God; and though thou sometimes callest these others gods, thou plainly usest the designation as one which does not really belong to them, but is, so to speak, a borrowed one. Nor is the nature of the God we declare unknown to thee: "God is good, God does good," thou art wont to say; plainly suggesting further, "But man is evil." In asserting an antithetic proposition, thou in a sort of indirect and figurative way reproachest man with his wickedness in departing from a God so good. So, again, as among us, as belonging to the God of benignity and goodness, "Blessing" is a most sacred thing in our religion and our life, thou too sayest as readily as a Christian needs, "God bless thee;" and when thou turnest the blessing of God into a curse, in like manner thy very words confess with us that His power over us is absolute and entire. There are some who, though they do not deny the existence of God, hold withal that He is neither Searcher, nor Ruler, nor Judge; treating with especial disdain those of us who go over to Christ out of fear of a coming judgment, as they think, honouring God in freeing Him from the cares of keeping watch, and the trouble of taking note,—not even

regarding Him as capable of anger. For if God, they say, gets angry, then He is susceptible of corruption and passion; but that of which passion and corruption can be affirmed may also perish, which God cannot do. But these very persons elsewhere, confessing that the soul is divine, and bestowed on us by God, stumble against a testimony of the soul itself, which affords an answer to these views: for if either divine or God-given, it doubtless knows its giver; and if it knows Him, it undoubtedly fears Him too, and especially as having been by Him endowed so amply. Has it no fear of Him whose favour it is so desirous to possess, and whose anger it is so anxious to avoid? Whence, then, the soul's natural fear of God, if God cannot be angry? How is there any dread of Him whom nothing offends? What is feared but anger? Whence comes anger, but from observing what is done? What leads to watchful oversight, but judgment in prospect? Whence is judgment, but from power? To whom does supreme authority and power belong, but to God alone? So thou art always ready, O soul, from thine own knowledge, nobody casting scorn upon thee, and no one preventing, to exclaim, "God sees all," and "I commend thee to God," and "May God repay," and "God shall judge between us." How happens this, since thou art not Christian? How is it that, even with the garland of Ceres on the brow, wrapped in the purple cloak of Saturn, wearing the white robe of the goddess Isis, thou invokest God as judge? Standing under the statue of Æsculapius, adorning the brazen image of Juno, arraying the helmet of Minerva with dusky figures, thou never thinkest of appealing to any of these deities. In thine own forum thou appealest to a God who is elsewhere; thou permittest honour to be rendered in thy temples to a foreign god. Oh, striking testimony to truth, which in the very midst of demons obtains a witness for us Christians!

3. But when we say that there are demons—as though, in the simple fact that we alone expel them from the men's bodies, we did not also prove their existence—some disciple of Chrysippus begins to curl the lip. Yet thy curses sufficiently

attest that there are such beings, and that they are objects of thy strong dislike. As what comes to thee as a fit expression of thy strong hatred of him, thou callest the man a devil who annoys thee with his filthiness, or malice, or insolence, or any other vice which we ascribe to evil spirits. In expressing vexation, or contempt, or abhorrence, thou hast Satan constantly upon thy lips; the very same we hold to be the angel of evil, the source of error, the corrupter of the whole world, by whom in the beginning man was entrapped into breaking the commandment of God, and being given over to death on account of his sin, the entire human race, tainted in their descent from him, were made a channel for transmitting his condemnation. Thou seest, then, who your destroyer is; and though he is fully known only to Christians, or to any other sect that confesses the one true God, yet, as thy hatred of him proves, thou hast had some acquaintance with him as well as others.

4. Even now, as the matter refers to thy opinion on a point the more closely belonging to thee, in so far as it bears on thy personal well-being, we maintain that after life has passed away thou still remainest in existence, and lookest forward to a day of judgment, and according to thy deserts art assigned to misery or bliss, in either way of it for ever; that, to be capable of this, thy former substance must needs return to thee, the matter and the memory of the very same human being: for neither good nor evil couldst thou feel if thou wert not endowed again with that sensitive bodily organization, and there would be no grounds for judgment without the presentation of the very person to whom the sufferings of judgment were due. That Christian view, though much nobler than the Pythagorean, as it does not transfer thee into beasts; though more complete than the Platonic, since it endows thee again with a body; though more worthy of honour than the Epicurean, as it preserves thee from annihilation,—yet, because of the name connected with it, it is held to be nothing but vanity and folly, and, as it is called, a mere presumption. But we are not ashamed of ourselves if our presumption is found to have thy support. Well, in

the first place, when thou speakest of one who is dead, thou sayest of him, "Poor man"—poor, surely, not because he has been taken from the good of life, but because he has been given over to punishment and condemnation. But at another time thou speakest of the dead as free from trouble; thou professest to think life a burden, and death a blessing. Thou art wont, too, to speak of the dead as in repose, when, returning to their graves beyond the city gates with food and dainties, thou art wont to present offerings to thyself rather than to them; or when, coming from the graves again, thou art staggering under the effects of wine. But I want thy sober opinion. Thou callest the dead poor when thou speakest thine own thoughts, when thou art at a distance from them. For at their feast, where in a sense they are present and recline along with thee, it would never do to cast reproach upon their lot. Thou canst not but adulate those for whose sake thou art feasting it so sumptuously. Dost thou then speak of him as "poor" who feels not? How happens it that thou cursest, as one capable of suffering from thy curse, the man whose memory comes back on thee with the sting in it of some old injury? It is thine imprecation that the earth may lie heavy on him, and that there may be trouble to his ashes in the realm of the dead. In like manner, in thy kindly feeling to him to whom thou art indebted for favours, thou entreatest repose to his bones and ashes, and thy desire is that among the dead he may have pleasant rest. If thou hast no power of suffering after death, if no feeling remains,—if, in a word, severance from the body is the annihilation of thee, what makes thee lie against thyself, as if thou couldst suffer in another state? Nay, why dost thou fear death at all? There is nothing after death to be feared, if there is nothing to be felt. For though it may be said that death is dreadful not for anything it threatens afterwards, but because it deprives us of the good of life; yet, on the other hand, as it puts an end to life's discomforts, which are far more numerous, death's terrors are mitigated by a gain that more than outweighs the loss. And there is no occasion to be troubled about a loss of good things, which is amply made up for by so great a blessing as relief from every trouble. There is nothing dreadful in that which delivers from all that is to be dreaded. If thou shrinkest from giving up life because thy experience of it has been sweet, at any rate there is no need to be in any alarm about death if thou hast no knowledge that it is evil. Thy dread of it is the proof that thou art aware of its evil. Thou wouldst never think it evil—thou wouldst have no fear of it at all—if thou wert not sure that after it there is something to make it evil, and so a thing of terror. Let us leave unnoticed at this time that natural way of fearing death. It is a poor thing for any one to fear what is inevitable. I take up the other side, and argue on the ground of a joyful hope beyond our term of earthly life; for desire of posthumous fame is with almost every class an inborn thing. I have not time to speak of the Curtii, and the Reguli, or the brave men of Greece, who afford us innumerable instances of death despised for after-death renown. Who at this day is without the desire that he may be often remembered when he is dead? Who does not give all endeavour to preserve his name by works of literature, or by the simple glory of his virtues, or by the splendour even of his tomb? How is it the nature of the soul to have these posthumous ambitions, and to prepare with such amazing effort things it can only use after its decease? It would care nothing about the future, if the future were quite unknown to it. But perhaps thou thinkest thyself surer of continuing still to feel after thy exit from the body than of any future resurrection, which is a doctrine laid at our door as one of our presumptuous suppositions. But it is also the doctrine of the soul; for if any one inquires about a person lately dead as though he were alive, it occurs at once to say, "He has gone." He is expected to return, then.

5. These testimonies of the soul are simple as true, commonplace as simple, universal as commonplace, natural as universal, divine as natural. I don't think they can appear frivolous or feeble to any one, if he reflect on the majesty of nature, from which the soul derives its authority. If

you acknowledge the authority of the mistress, you will own it also in the disciple. Well, nature is the mistress here, and her disciple is the soul. But everything the one has taught or the other learned, has come from God—the Teacher of the teacher. And what the soul may know from the teachings of its chief instructor, thou canst judge from that which is within thee. Think of that which enables thee to think; reflect on that which in forebodings is the prophet, the augur in omens, the foreseer of coming events. Is it a wonderful thing, if, being the gift of God to man, it knows how to divine? Is it anything very strange, if it knows the God by whom it was bestowed? Even fallen as it is, the victim of the great adversary's machinations, it does not forget its Creator, His goodness and law, and the final end both of itself and of its foe. Is it singular then, if, divine in its origin, its revelations agree with the knowledge God has given to His own people? But he who does not regard those outbursts of the soul as the teaching of a congenital nature and the secret deposit of an inborn knowledge, will say that the habit and, so to say, the vice of speaking in this way has been acquired and confirmed from the opinions of published books widely spread among men. Unquestionably the soul existed before letters, and speech before books, and ideas before the writing of them, and man himself before the poet and philosopher. Is it then to be believed, that before literature and its publication no utterances of the sort we have pointed out came from the lips of men? Did nobody speak of God and His goodness, nobody of death, nobody of the dead? Speech went a-begging, I suppose; nay, it could not exist at all (the subjects being still awanting, without which it cannot even exist at this day, when it is so much more copious, and rich, and wise), if the things which are now so easily suggested, that cling to us so constantly, that are so very near to us, that are somehow born on our very lips, had no existence in ancient times, before letters had any existence in the world —before there was a Mercury, I think, at all. And whence was it, I pray, that letters themselves came to know, and to disseminate for the use of speech, what no mind had ever conceived, or tongue put forth, or ear taken in? But, clearly, since the Scriptures of God, whether belonging to Christians or Jews—into whose olive tree we have been grafted—are much more ancient than any secular literature, or, let us only say, are of a somewhat earlier date, as we have shown in its proper place when proving their trustworthiness; if the soul have taken these utterances from writings at all, we must believe it has taken them from ours, and not from yours, its instruction coming more naturally from the earlier than the later works, which latter indeed waited for their own instruction from the former; and though we grant that light has come from you, still it has flowed from the first fountainhead originally; and we claim as entirely ours, all you may have taken from us and handed down. Since it is thus, it matters little whether the soul's knowledge was put into it by God or by His book. Why, then, O man, wilt thou maintain a view so groundless, as that those testimonies of the soul have gone forth from the mere human speculations of your literature, and got hardening of common use?

6. Believe, then, your own books, and as to our Scriptures so much the more believe writings which are divine, but in the witness of the soul itself give like confidence to nature. Choose the one of these you observe to be the most faithful friend of truth. If your own writings are distrusted, neither God nor nature lie. And if you would have faith in God and nature, have faith in the soul; thus you will believe yourself. Certainly you value the soul as giving you your true greatness,—that to which you belong, which is all things to you, without which you can neither live nor die, on whose account you even put God away from you. Since, then, you fear to become a Christian, call the soul before you, and put her to the question. Why does she worship another? why name the name of God? Why does she speak of demons, when she means to denote spirits to be held accursed? Why does she make her protestations towards the heavens, and pronounce her ordinary execrations earthwards? Why does she render service in one place, in another invoke the Avenger? Why does she pass judgments

on the dead ? What Christian phrases are those she has got, though Christians she neither desires to see nor hear ? Why has she either bestowed them on us, or received them from us ? Why has she either taught us them, or learned them as our scholar ? Regard with suspicion this accordance in words, while there is such difference in practice. It is utter folly—denying a universal nature—to ascribe this exclusively to our language and the Greek, which are regarded among us as so near akin. The soul is not a boon from heaven to Latins and Greeks alone. Man is the one name belonging to every nation upon earth : there is one soul and many tongues, one spirit and various sounds; every country has its own speech, but the subjects of speech are common to all. God is everywhere, and the goodness of God is everywhere ; demons are everywhere, and the cursing of them is everywhere; the invocation of divine judgment is everywhere, death is everywhere, and the sense of death is everywhere, and all the world over is the witness of the soul. There is not a soul of man that does not, from the light that is in itself, proclaim the very things we are not permitted to speak above our breath. Most justly, then, every soul is a culprit as well as a witness : in the measure that it testifies for truth, the guilt of error lies on it; and on the day of judgment it will stand before the courts of God, without a word to say. Thou proclaimedst God, O soul, but thou didst not seek to know Him ; evil spirits were detested by thee, and yet they were the objects of thy adoration ; the punishments of hell were foreseen by thee, but no care was taken to avoid them ; thou hadst a savour of Christianity, and withal wert the persecutor of Christians.

IV.

AD SCAPULAM.

1. WE are not in any great perturbation or alarm about the persecutions we suffer from the ignorance of men; for we have attached ourselves to this sect, fully accepting the terms of its covenant, so that, as men whose very lives are not their own, we engage in these conflicts, our desire being to obtain God's promised rewards, and our dread lest the woes with which He threatens an unchristian life should overtake us. So we shrink not from the grapple with your utmost rage, coming even forth of our own accord to the contest; and condemnation gives us more pleasure than acquittal. We have sent therefore this tract to you in no alarm about ourselves, but in much concern for you and for all our enemies, to say nothing of our friends. For our religion commands us to love even our enemies, and to pray for those who persecute us, aiming at a perfection all its own, and seeking in its disciples something of a higher type than the commonplace goodness of the world. For all love those who love them; it is peculiar to Christians alone to love those that hate them. Therefore, mourning over your ignorance, and compassionating human error, and looking on to that future of which every day shows threatening signs, necessity is laid on us to come forth in this way also, that we may set before you the truths you will not listen to openly and publicly.

2. We are worshippers of one God, of whose existence and character nature teaches all men; at whose lightnings and thunders you tremble, whose benefits minister to your happiness. You think that others, too, are gods, the same we know to be devils. However, it is a fundamental human right, a

privilege of nature, that every man should worship according to his own convictions: one man's religion neither harms nor helps another man. It is assuredly no part of religion to compel religion—to which free-will and not force should lead us—the sacrificial victims even being required of a willing mind. You will render no real service to your gods by compelling us to sacrifice. For they can have no desire of offerings from the unwilling, unless they are animated by a spirit of contention, which is a thing altogether undivine. Accordingly the true God bestows His blessings alike on wicked men and on His own elect; upon which account He has appointed an eternal judgment, when both thankful and unthankful will have to stand before His bar. Yet you have never detected us—sacrilegious wretches though you reckon us to be—in any theft, far less in any sacrilege. But the robbers of your temples, all of them swear by your gods, and worship them; they are not Christians, and yet it is they who are found guilty of sacrilegious deeds. We have not time to unfold in how many other ways your gods are mocked and despised by their own votaries. So, too, treason is falsely laid to our charge, though no one has ever been able to find followers of Albinus, or Niger, or Cassius, among Christians; while the very men who had sworn by the genii of the emperors, who had offered and vowed sacrifices for their safety, who had often pronounced condemnation on Christ's disciples, are till this day found traitors to the imperial throne. A Christian is enemy to none, least of all to the Emperor of Rome, whom he knows to be appointed by His God, and so cannot but love and honour, and whose wellbeing, moreover, he must needs desire, with that of the empire over which he reigns so long as the world shall stand —for so long as that shall Rome continue. To the emperor, therefore, we render such reverential homage as is lawful for us and good for him; regarding him as the human being next to God, who from God has received all his power, and is less than God alone. And this will be according to his own desires. For thus—as less only than the true God—he is greater than all besides. Thus he is greater than the very gods themselves, even they, too, being subject to him. We therefore sacrifice for the emperor's safety, but to our God and his, but after the manner God has enjoined, in simple prayer. For God, Creator of the universe, has no need of odours or of blood. These things are the food of devils. But we not only reject those wicked spirits: we overcome them; we hold them daily up to contempt; we exorcise them from their victims, as multitudes can testify. So all the more we pray for the imperial well-being, as those who seek it at the hands of Him who is able to bestow it. And one would think it must be abundantly clear to you that the religious system under whose rules we act is one inculcating a divine patience; since, though our numbers are so great—constituting all but the majority in every city—we conduct ourselves so quietly and modestly; I might perhaps say, known rather as individuals than as organized communities, and remarkable only for the reformation of our former vices. For far be it from us to take it ill that we have laid on us the very things we wish, or in any way plot the vengeance at our own hands, which we expect to come from God.

3. However, as we have already remarked, it cannot but distress us that no state shall bear unpunished the guilt of shedding Christian blood; as you see, indeed, in what took place during the presidency of Hilarian, for when there had been some agitation about places of sepulture for our dead, and the cry arose, "No *areæ*—no burial-grounds for the Christians," it came about that their own *areæ*, their threshing-floors, were awanting, for they gathered in no harvests. As to the rains of the bygone year, it is abundantly plain of what they were intended to remind men—of the deluge, no doubt, which in ancient times overtook human unbelief and wickedness; and as to the fires which lately hung all night over the walls of Carthage, they who saw them know what they threatened; and what the preceding thunders pealed, *they* who were hardened by them can tell. All these things are signs of God's impending wrath, which we must needs publish and proclaim in every possible way; and in the meanwhile we must pray it may be only local. Sure are

they to experience it one day in its universal and final form, who interpret otherwise these samples of it. That sun, too, in the metropolis of Utica, with light all but extinguished, was a portent which could not have occurred from an ordinary eclipse, situated as the lord of day was in his height and house. You have the astrologers, consult them about it. We can point you also to the deaths of some provincial rulers, who in their last hours had painful memories of their sin in persecuting the followers of Christ. Vigellius Saturninus, who first here used the sword against us, lost his eyesight. Claudius Lucius Herminianus in Cappadocia, enraged that his wife had become a Christian, had treated the Christians with great cruelty : well, left alone in his palace, suffering under a contagious malady, he boiled out in living worms, and was heard exclaiming, "Let nobody know of it, lest the Christians rejoice, and Christian wives take encouragement." Afterwards he came to see his error in having tempted so many from their stedfastness by the tortures he inflicted, and died almost a Christian himself. In that doom which overtook Byzantium, Cæcilius Capella could not help crying out, "Christians, rejoice!" Yes, and the persecutors who seem to themselves to have acted with impunity shall not escape the day of judgment. For you we sincerely wish it may prove to have been a warning only, that, immediately after you had condemned Mavilus of Adrumetum to the wild beasts, you were overtaken by those troubles, and that even now for the same reason you are being called to a bloodreckoning. But do not forget the future.

4. We who are without fear ourselves are not seeking to frighten you, but we would save all men if possible by warning them not to fight with God. You may perform the duties of your charge, and yet remember the claims of humanity; if on no other ground than that you are liable to punishment yourself, [you ought to do so]. For is not your commission simply to condemn those who confess their guilt, and to give over to the torture those who deny? You see, then, how you trespass yourself against your instructions to wring from the confessing a denial. It is, in fact, an acknowledgment of

our innocence that you refuse to condemn us at once when we confess. In doing your utmost to extirpate us, if that is your object, it is innocence you assail. But how many rulers, men more resolute and more cruel than you are, have contrived to get quit of such causes altogether,—as Cincius Severus, who himself suggested the remedy at Thysdris, pointing out how the Christians should answer that they might secure an acquittal; as Vespronius Candidus, who dismissed from his bar a Christian, on the ground that to satisfy his fellow-citizens would break the peace of the community; as Asper, who, in the case of a man who gave up his faith under slight infliction of the torture, did not compel the offering of sacrifice, having owned before, among the advocates and assessors of court, that he was annoyed at having had to meddle with such a case. Pudens, too, at once dismissed a Christian who was brought before him, perceiving from the indictment that it was a case of vexatious accusation; tearing the document in pieces, he refused so much as to hear him without the presence of his accuser, as not being consistent with the imperial commands. All this might be officially brought under your notice, and by the very advocates, who are themselves also under obligations to us, although in court they give their voice as it suits them. For the clerk of one of them who was liable to be thrown upon the ground by an evil spirit, was set free from his affliction; as was also the relative of another, and the little boy of a third. And how many men of rank (to say nothing of common people) have been delivered from devils, and healed of diseases! Even Severus himself, the father of Antonine, was graciously mindful of the Christians. For he sought out the Christian Proculus, surnamed Torpacion, the steward of Euhodias, and in gratitude for his having once cured him by anointing, he kept him in his palace till the day of his death. Antonine, too, brought up as he was on Christian milk, was intimately acquainted with this man. Both women and men of highest rank, whom Severus knew well to be Christians, were not merely permitted by him to remain uninjured; but he even bore distinguished testimony in their favour, and gave them publicly back to us from the hands of a raging populace. Marcus Aurelius also, in his expedition to Germany, by the prayers his Christian soldiers offered to God, got rain in that well-known thirst. When, indeed, have not droughts been put away by our kneelings and our fastings? At times like these, moreover, the people crying to "the God of gods, the alone Omnipotent," under the name of Jupiter, have borne witness to our God. Then we never deny the deposit placed in our hands; we never pollute the marriage bed; we deal faithfully with our wards; we give aid to the needy; we render to none evil for evil. As for those who falsely pretend to belong to us, and whom we, too, repudiate, let them answer for themselves. In a word, who has complaint to make against us on other grounds? To what else does the Christian devote himself, save the affairs of his own community, which during all the long period of its existence no one has ever proved guilty of the incest or the cruelty charged against it? It is for freedom from crime so singular, for a probity so great, for righteousness, for purity, for faithfulness, for truth, for the living God, that we are consigned to the flames; for this is a punishment you are not wont to inflict either on the sacrilegious, or on undoubted public enemies, or on the treason-tainted, of whom you have so many. Nay, even now our people are enduring persecution from the governors of Legio and Mauritania; but it is only with the sword, as from the first it was ordained that we should suffer. But the greater our conflicts, the greater our rewards.

5. Your cruelty is our glory. Only see you to it, that in having such things as these to endure, we do not feel ourselves constrained to rush forth to the combat, if only to prove that we have no dread of them, but on the contrary, even invite their infliction. When Arrius Antoninus was driving things hard in Asia, the whole Christians of the province, in one united band, presented themselves before his judgment-seat; on which, ordering a few to be led forth to execution, he said to the rest, "O miserable men, if you wish to die, you have precipices or halters." If we should

take it into our heads to do the same thing here, what will you make of so many thousands, of such a multitude of men and women, persons of every sex and every age and every rank, when they present themselves before you? How many fires, how many swords will be required? What will be the anguish of Carthage itself, which you will have to decimate, as each one recognises there his relatives and companions, as he sees there it may be men of your own order, and noble ladies, and all the leading persons of the city, and either kinsmen or friends of those of your own circle? Spare thyself, if not us poor Christians! Spare Carthage, if not thyself! Spare the province, which the indication of your purpose has subjected to the threats and extortions at once of the soldiers and of private enemies.

We have no master but God. *He is before* you, and cannot be hidden from you, but to Him you can do no injury. But those whom you regard as masters are only men, and one day they themselves must die. Yet still this community will be undying, for be assured that just in the time of its seeming overthrow it is built up into greater power. For all who witness the noble patience of its martyrs, as struck with misgivings, are inflamed with desire to examine into the matter in question; and as soon as they come to know the truth, they straightway enrol themselves its disciples.

V.

APOLOGETICUS.

1. RULERS of the Roman Empire, if, seated for the administration of justice on your lofty tribunal, under the gaze of every eye, and occupying there all but the highest position in the state, you may not openly inquire into and sift before the world the real truth in regard to the charges made against the Christians; if in this case alone you are afraid or ashamed to exercise your authority in making public inquiry with the carefulness which becomes justice; if, finally, the extreme severities inflicted on our people in recently private judgments, stand in the way of our being permitted to defend ourselves before you, you cannot surely forbid the Truth to reach your ears by the secret pathway of a noiseless book. She has no appeals to make to you in regard of her condition, for that does not excite her wonder. She knows that she is but a sojourner on the earth, and that among strangers she naturally finds foes; and more than that, that her origin, her dwelling-place, her hope, her recompense, her honours, are above. One thing, meanwhile, she anxiously desires of earthly rulers—not to be condemned unknown. What harm can it do to the laws, supreme in their domain, to give her a hearing? Nay, for that part of it, will not their absolute supremacy be more conspicuous in their condemning her, even after she has made her plea? But if unheard sentence is pronounced against her, besides the odium of an unjust deed, they will incur the merited suspicion of doing it with some idea that it is unjust, as not wishing to hear what they may not be able to hear and condemn. We lay this before you as the first ground on which we urge that your hatred to the

name of Christian is unjust. And the very reason which seems to excuse this injustice (I mean ignorance) at once aggravates and convicts it. For what is there more unfair than to hate a thing of which you know nothing, even though it deserve to be hated? Hatred is only merited when it is *known* to be merited. But without that knowledge, whence is its justice to be vindicated? for that is to be proved, not from the mere fact that an aversion exists, but from acquaintance with the subject. When men, then, give way to a dislike simply because they are entirely ignorant of the nature of the thing disliked, why may it not be precisely the very sort of thing they should not dislike? So we maintain that they are both ignorant while they hate us, and hate us unrighteously while they continue in ignorance, the one thing being the result of the other either way of it. The proof of their ignorance, at once condemning and excusing their injustice, is this, that those who once hated Christianity because they knew nothing about it, no sooner come to know it than they all lay down at once their enmity. From being its haters they become its disciples. By simply getting acquainted with it, they begin now to hate what they had formerly been, and to profess what they had formerly hated; and their numbers are as great as are laid to our charge. The outcry is that the State is filled with Christians—that they are in the fields, in the citadels, in the islands: they make lamentation as for some calamity, that both sexes, every age and condition, even high rank, are passing over to the profession of the Christian faith; and yet for all, their minds are not awakened to the thought of some good they have failed to notice in it. They must not allow any truer suspicions to cross their minds; they have no desire to make closer trial. Here alone the curiosity of human nature slumbers. They like to be ignorant, though to others the knowledge has been bliss. Anacharsis reproved the rude venturing to criticise the cultured; how much more this judging of those who know, by men who are entirely ignorant, might he have denounced! Because they already dislike, they want to know no more. But thus they prejudge that of which they are ignorant to be such, that, if they came to know it, it could no longer be the object of their aversion; since, if inquiry finds nothing worthy of dislike, it is certainly proper to cease from an unjust dislike,—while if its bad character comes plainly out, instead of the detestation entertained for it being thus diminished, a stronger reason for perseverance in that detestation is obtained, even under the authority of justice itself. But, says one, a thing is not good merely because multitudes go over to it; for how many have the bent of their nature towards whatever is bad! how many go astray into ways of error! It is undoubted. Yet a thing that is thoroughly evil, not even those whom it carries away venture to defend as good. Nature throws a veil either of fear or shame over all evil. For instance, you find that criminals are eager to conceal themselves, avoid appearing in public, are in trepidation when they are caught, deny their guilt when they are accused; even when they are put to the rack, they do not easily or always confess; when there is no doubt about their condemnation, they grieve for what they have done. In their self-communings they admit their being impelled by sinful dispositions, but they lay the blame either on fate or on the stars. They are unwilling to acknowledge that the thing is theirs, because they own that it is wicked. But what is there like this in the Christian's case? The only shame or regret he feels, is at not having been a Christian earlier. If he is pointed out, he glories in it; if he is accused, he offers no defence; interrogated, he makes voluntary confession; condemned, he renders thanks. What sort of evil thing is this, which wants all the ordinary peculiarities of evil—fear, shame, subterfuge, penitence, lamenting? What! is that a crime in which the criminal rejoices? to be accused of which is his ardent wish, to be punished for which is his felicity? You cannot call it madness, you who stand convicted of knowing nothing of the matter.

2. If, again, it is certain that we are the most wicked of men, why do you treat us so differently from our fellows, that is, from other criminals, it being only fair that the same crime should get the same treatment? When the charges

made against us are made against others, they are permitted to make use both of their own lips and of hired pleaders to show their innocence. They have full opportunity of answer and debate; in fact, it is against the law to condemn anybody undefended and unheard. Christians alone are forbidden to say anything in exculpation of themselves, in defence of the truth, to help the judge to a righteous decision, all that is cared about is having what the public hatred demands—the confession of the name, not examination of the charge; while in'your ordinary judicial investigations, on a man's confession of the crime of murder, or sacrilege, or incest, or treason, to take the points of which we are accused, you are not content to proceed at once to sentence,—you do not take that step till you thoroughly examine the circumstances of the confession—what is the real character of the deed, how often, where, in what way, when he has done it, who were privy to it, and who actually took part with him in it. Nothing like this is done in our case, though the falsehoods disseminated about us ought to have the same sifting, that it might be found how many murdered children each of us had tasted; how many incests each of us had shrouded in darkness; what cooks, what dogs had been witness of our deeds. Oh, how great the glory of the ruler who should bring to light some Christian who had devoured a hundred infants! But, instead of that, we find that even inquiry in regard to our case is forbidden. For the younger Pliny, when he was ruler of a province, having condemned some Christians to death, and driven some from their stedfastness, being still annoyed by their great numbers, at last sought the advice of Trajan, the reigning emperor, as to what he was to do with the rest, explaining to his master that, except an obstinate disinclination to offer sacrifices, he found in their religious services nothing but meetings at early morning for singing hymns to Christ and[1] God, and sealing home their way of life by a united pledge to be faithful to their religion, forbidding murder, adultery, dishonesty, and other crimes. Upon which Trajan wrote back that Christians were by no means to be sought

---

[1] Another reading is " ut Deo," *as God.*

after; but if they were brought before him, they should be punished. O miserable deliverance,—under the necessities of the case, a self-contradiction! It forbids them to be sought after as innocent, and it commands them to be punished as guilty. It is at once merciful and cruel; it passes by, and it punishes. Why dost thou play a game of evasion upon thyself, O Judgment? If thou condemnest, why dost thou not also inquire? If thou dost not inquire, why dost thou not also absolve? Military stations are distributed through all the provinces for tracking robbers. Against traitors and public foes every man is a soldier; search is made even for their confederates and accessaries. The Christian alone must not be sought, though he may be brought and accused before the judge; as if a search had any other end than that in view! And so you condemn the man for whom nobody wished a search to be made when he is presented to you, and who even now does not deserve punishment, I suppose, because of his guilt, but because, though forbidden to be sought, he was found. And then, too, you do not in that case deal with us in the ordinary way of judicial proceedings against offenders; for, in the case of others denying, you apply the torture to make them confess— Christians alone you torture, to make them deny; whereas, if we were guilty of any crime, we should be sure to deny it, and you with your tortures would force us to confession. Nor indeed should you hold that our crimes require no such investigation merely on the ground that you are convinced by our confession of the name that the deeds were done,— *you* who are daily wont, though you know well enough what murder is, none the less to extract from the confessed murderer a full account of how the crime was perpetrated. So that with all the greater perversity you act, when, holding our crimes proved by our confession of the name of Christ, you drive us by torture to fall from our confession, that, repudiating the name, we may in like manner repudiate also the crimes with which, from that same confession, you had assumed that we were chargeable. I suppose, though you believe us to be the worst of mankind, you do not wish us to perish. For thus, no doubt, you are in the habit of bidding the murderer deny, and of ordering the man guilty of sacrilege to the rack if he persevere in his acknowledgment! Is that the way of it? But if thus you do not deal with us as criminals, you declare us thereby innocent, when as innocent you are anxious that we do not persevere in a confession which you know will bring on us a condemnation of necessity, not of justice, at your hands. "I am a Christian," the man cries out. He tells you what he is; you wish to hear from him what he is not. Occupying your place of authority to extort the truth, you do your utmost to get lies from us. "I am," he says, "that which you ask me if I am. Why do you torture me to sin? I confess, and you put me to the rack. What would you do if I denied?" Certainly you give no ready credence to others when they deny. When we deny, you believe at once. Let this perversity of yours lead you to suspect that there is some hidden power in the case under whose influence you act against the forms, against the nature of public justice, even against the very laws themselves. For, unless I am greatly mistaken, the laws enjoin offenders to be searched out, and not to be hidden away. They lay it down that persons who own a crime are to be condemned, not acquitted. The decrees of the senate, the commands of your chiefs, lay this clearly down. The power of which you are servants is a civil, not a tyrannical domination. Among tyrants, indeed, torments used to be inflicted even as punishments: with you they are mitigated to a means of questioning alone. Keep to your law in these as necessary till confession is obtained; and if the torture is anticipated by confession, there will be no occasion for it: sentence should be passed; the criminal should be given over to the penalty which is his due, not released. Accordingly, no one is eager for the acquittal of the guilty; it is not right to desire that, and so no one is ever compelled to deny. Well, you think the Christian a man of every crime, an enemy of the gods, of the emperor, of the laws, of good morals, of all nature; yet you compel him to deny, that you may acquit him, which without his denial you could not do. You play fast and loose with the laws. You wish him to deny his guilt, that you may, even against his will, bring him out blameless and free from all guilt in reference to the past! Whence is this strange perversity on your part? How is it you do not reflect that a spontaneous confession is greatly more worthy of credit than a compelled denial; or consider whether, when compelled to deny, a man's denial may not be in good faith, and whether acquitted, he may not, then and there, as soon as the trial is over, laugh at your hostility, a Christian as much as ever? Seeing, then, that in everything you deal differently with us than with other criminals, bent upon the one object of taking from us our name (indeed, it is ours no more if we do what Christians never do), it is made perfectly clear that there is no crime of any kind in the case, but merely a name which a certain system, ever working against the truth, pursues with its enmity, doing this chiefly with the object of securing that men may have no desire to know for certain what they know for certain they are entirely ignorant of. Hence, too, it is that they believe about us things of which they have no proof, and they are disinclined to have them looked into, lest the charges, they would rather take on trust, are all proved to have no foundation, that the name so hostile to that rival power—its crimes presumed, not proved—may be condemned simply on its own confession. So we are put to the torture if we confess, and we are punished if we persevere, and if we deny we are acquitted, because all the contention is about a name. Finally, why do you read out of your tablet-lists that such a man is a Christian? why not also that he is a murderer? And if a Christian is a murderer, why not guilty, too, of incest, or any other vile thing you believe of us? In our case alone you are either ashamed or unwilling to mention the very names of our crimes. If [to be called] a "Christian" does not imply any crime, the name is surely very hateful, when that of itself is made a crime.

3. What are we to think of it, that most people so blindly knock their heads against the hatred of the Christian name; that when they bear favourable testimony to any one, they mingle with it abuse of the name he bears? "A good man,"

says one, "is Gaius Seius, only that he is a Christian." So another, "I am astonished that a wise man like Lucius should have suddenly become a Christian." Nobody thinks it needful to consider whether Gaius is not good and Lucius wise, on this very account that he is a Christian; or a Christian, for the reason that he is wise and good. They praise what they know, they abuse what they are ignorant of, and they inspire their knowledge with their ignorance; though in fairness you should rather judge of what is unknown from what is known, than what is known from what is unknown. Others, in the case of persons whom, before they took the name of Christian, they had known as loose, and vile, and wicked, put on them a brand from the very thing which they praise. In the blindness of their hatred, they fall foul of their own approving judgment! "What a woman she was! how wanton! how gay! What a youth he was! how profligate! how libidinous!—they have become Christians!" So the hated name is given to a reformation of character. Some even barter away their comforts for that hatred, content to bear injury, if they are kept free at home from the object of their bitter enmity. The wife, now chaste, the husband, now no longer jealous, casts out of his house; the son, now obedient, the father, who used to be so patient, disinherits; the servant, now faithful, the master, once so mild, commands away from his presence: it is a high offence for any one to be reformed by the detested name. Goodness is of less value than hatred of Christians. Well now, if there is this dislike of the name, what blame can you attach to names? What accusation can you bring against mere designations, save that something in the word sounds either barbarous, or unlucky, or scurrilous, or unchaste? But Christian, so far as the meaning of the word is concerned, is derived from anointing. Yes, and even when it is wrongly pronounced by you "Chrestianus" (for you do not even know accurately the name you hate), it comes from sweetness and benignity. You hate, therefore, in the guiltless, even a guiltless name. But the special ground of dislike to the sect is, that it bears the name of its Founder. Is there anything new in a religious sect getting for its followers a designation from its master? Are not the philosophers called from the founders of *their* systems—Platonists, Epicureans, Pythagoreans? Are not the Stoics and Academics so called also from the places in which they assembled and stationed themselves? and are not physicians named from Erasistratus, grammarians from Aristarchus, cooks even from Apicius? And yet the bearing of the name, transmitted from the original institutor with whatever he has instituted, offends no one. No doubt, if it is proved that the sect is a bad one, and so its founder bad as well, that will prove that the name is bad and deserves our aversion, in respect of the character both of the sect and its author. Before, therefore, taking up a dislike to the name, it behoved you to consider the sect in the author, or the author in the sect. But now, without any sifting and knowledge of either, the mere name is made matter of accusation, the mere name is assailed, and a sound alone brings condemnation on a sect and its author both, while of both you are ignorant, because they have such and such a designation, not because they are convicted of anything wrong.

4. And so, having made these remarks as it were by way of preface, that I might show in its true colours the injustice of the public hatred against us, I shall now take my stand on the plea of our blamelessness; and I shall not only refute the things which are objected to us, but I shall also retort them on the objectors, that in this way all may know that Christians are free from the very crimes they are so well aware prevail among themselves, that they may at the same time be put to the blush for their accusations against us,—accusations I shall not say of the worst of men against the best, but now, as they will have it, against those who are only their fellows in sin. We shall reply to the accusation of all the various crimes we are said to be guilty of in secret, such as we find them committing in the light of day, and as being guilty of which we are held to be wicked, senseless, worthy of punishment, deserving of ridicule. But since, when our truth meets you successfully at all points, the authority of the laws as a last resort is set up against it, so that it is

either said that their determinations are absolutely conclusive, or the necessity of obedience is, however unwillingly, preferred to the truth, I shall first, in this matter of the laws, grapple with you as with their chosen protectors. Now first, when you sternly lay it down in your sentences, "It is not lawful for you to exist," and with unhesitating rigour you enjoin this to be carried out, you exhibit the violence and unjust domination of mere tyranny, if you deny the thing to be lawful, simply on the ground that you wish it to be unlawful, not because it ought. But if you would have it unlawful because it *ought* not to be lawful, without doubt that should have no permission of law which does harm; and on this ground, in fact, it is already determined that whatever is beneficial is legitimate. Well, if I have found what your law prohibits to be good, as one who has arrived at such a previous opinion, has it not lost its power to debar me from it, though that very thing, if it were evil, it would justly forbid to me? If your law has gone wrong, it is of human origin, I think; it has not fallen from heaven. Is it wonderful that man should err in making a law, or come to his senses in rejecting it? Did not the Lacedæmonians amend the laws of Lycurgus himself, thereby inflicting such pain on their author that he shut himself up, and doomed himself to death by starvation? Are you not yourselves every day, in your efforts to illumine the darkness of antiquity, cutting and hewing with the new axes of imperial rescripts and edicts, that whole ancient and rugged forest of your laws? Has not Severus, that most resolute of rulers, but yesterday repealed the ridiculous Papian laws which compelled people to have children before the Julian laws allow matrimony to be contracted, and that though they have the authority of age upon their side? There were laws, too, in old times, that parties against whom a decision had been given might be cut in pieces by their creditors; however, by common consent that cruelty was afterwards erased from the statutes, and the capital penalty turned into a brand of shame. By adopting the plan of confiscating a debtor's goods, it was sought rather to pour the blood in blushes over his face than to pour it out. How many laws lie hidden out of sight which still require to be reformed! For it is neither the number of their years nor the dignity of their maker that commends them, but simply that they are just; and therefore, when their injustice is recognised, they are deservedly condemned, even though they condemn. Why speak we of them as unjust? nay, if they punish mere names, we may well call them irrational. But if they punish acts, why in our case do they punish acts solely on the ground of a name, while in others they must have them proved not from the name, but from the wrong done? I am a practiser of incest (so they say); why do they not inquire into it? I am an infant-killer; why do they not apply the torture to get from me the truth? I am guilty of crimes against the gods, against the Cæsars; why am I, who am able to clear myself, not allowed to be heard on my own behalf? No law forbids the sifting of the crime which it prohibits, for a judge never inflicts a righteous vengeance if he is not well assured that a crime has been committed; nor does a citizen render a true subjection to the law, if he does not know the nature of the thing on which the punishment is inflicted. It is not enough that a law is just, nor that the judge should be convinced of its justice; those from whom obedience is expected should have that conviction too. Nay, a law lies under strong suspicions which does not care to have itself tried and approved: it is a positively wicked law, if, unproved, it tyrannizes over men.

5. To say a word about the origin of laws of the kind to which we now refer, there was an old decree that no god should be consecrated by the emperor till first approved by the senate. Marcus Æmilius had experience of this in reference to his god Alburnus. And this, too, makes for our case, that among you divinity is allotted at the judgment of human beings. Unless gods give satisfaction to men, there will be no deification for them: the god will have to propitiate the man. Tiberius accordingly, in whose days the Christian name made its entry into the world, having himself received intelligence from Palestine of events which had clearly shown the truth of Christ's divinity, brought the

matter before the senate, with his own decision in favour of Christ. The senate, because it had not given the approval itself, rejected his proposal. Cæsar held to his opinion, threatening wrath against all accusers of the Christians. Consult your histories; you will there find that Nero was the first who assailed with the imperial sword the Christian sect, making progress then especially at Rome. But we glory in having our condemnation hallowed by the hostility of such a wretch. For any one who knows him, can understand that not except as being of singular excellence did anything bring on it Nero's condemnation. Domitian, too, a man of Nero's type in cruelty, tried his hand at persecution; but as he had something of the human in him, he soon put an end to what he had begun, even restoring again those whom he had banished. Such as these have always been our persecutors, — men unjust, impious, base, of whom even you yourselves have no good to say, the sufferers under whose sentences you have been wont to restore. But among so many princes from that time to the present day, with anything of divine and human wisdom in them, point out a single persecutor of the Christian name. So far from that, we, on the contrary, bring before you one who was their protector, as you will see by examining the letters of Marcus Aurelius, that most grave of emperors, in which he bears his testimony that that Germanic drought was removed by the rains obtained through the prayers of the Christians who chanced to be fighting under him. And as he did not by public law remove from Christians their legal disabilities, yet in another way he put them openly aside, even adding a sentence of condemnation, and that of greater severity, against their accusers. What sort of laws are these which the impious alone execute against us—and the unjust, the vile, the bloody, the senseless, the insane?—which Trajan to some extent made naught by forbidding Christians to be sought after; which neither a Hadrian, though fond of searching into all things strange and new, nor a Vespasian, though the subjugator of the Jews, nor a Pius, nor a Verus, ever enforced? It should surely be judged something more natural for bad men to be eradicated by good princes as being their natural enemies, than by those of a spirit kindred with their own.

6. I would now have these most religious protectors and vindicators of the laws and institutions of their fathers, tell me, in regard to their own fidelity, and the honour and submission themselves show to ancestral institutions, if they have departed from nothing—if they have in nothing gone out of the old paths—if they have not put aside whatsoever is most useful and necessary as rules of a virtuous life. What has become of the laws' repressing expensive and ostentatious ways of living? which forbade more than a hundred *asses* to be expended on a supper, and more than one fowl to be set on the table at a time, and that not a fatted one; which expelled a patrician from the senate on the serious ground, as it was counted, of aspiring to be too great, because he had acquired ten pounds of silver; which put down the theatres as quickly as they arose to debauch the manners of the people; which did not permit the insignia of official dignities or of noble birth to be rashly or with impunity usurped? For I see the Centenarian suppers must now bear the name, not from the hundred asses, but from the hundred sestertia[1] expended on them; and that mines of silver are made into dishes (it were little if this applied only to senators, and not to freedmen or even mere whip-spoilers[2]). I see, too, that neither is a single theatre enough, nor are theatres unsheltered: no doubt it was that immodest pleasure might not be torpid in the winter-time, the Lacedæmonians invented their woollen cloaks for the plays. I see now no difference between the dress of matrons and prostitutes. In regard to women, indeed, those laws of your fathers, which used to be such an encouragement to modesty and sobriety, have also fallen into desuetude, when a woman had yet known no gold upon her save on the finger, which with the bridal ring her husband had sacredly pledged to himself; when the abstinence of women from wine was carried so far, that a matron, for

[1] As = 2½ farthings. Sestertium = £7, 16s. 3d.
[2] Slaves still bearing the marks of the scourge.

opening the compartments of a wine cellar, was starved to death by her friends,—while in the times of Romulus, for merely tasting wine, Mecenius killed his wife, and suffered nothing for the deed. With reference to this also, it was the custom of women to kiss their relatives, that they might be detected by their breath. Where is that happiness of married life, ever so desirable, which distinguished our earlier manners, and as the result of which for about 600 years there was not among us a single divorce? Now, women have every member of the body heavy laden with gold; wine-bibbing is so common among them, that the kiss is never offered with their will; and as for divorce, they long for it as though it were the natural consequence of marriage. The laws, too, your fathers in their wisdom had enacted concerning the very gods themselves, you their most loyal children have rescinded. The consuls, by the authority of the senate, banished Father Bacchus and his mysteries not merely from the city, but from the whole of Italy. The consuls Piso and Gabinius, no Christians surely, forbade Serapis, and Isis, and Arpocrates, with their dogheaded friend,[1] admission into the Capitol—in the act casting them out from the assembly of the gods—overthrew their altars, and expelled them from the country: they were anxious to prevent the vices of their base and lascivious religion from spreading. But you have restored them, and conferred highest honours on them. What has come of your religion—of the veneration due by you to your ancestors? In your dress, in your food, in your style of life, in your opinions, and last of all in your very speech, you have renounced your progenitors. You are always praising antiquity, and yet every day you have novelties in your way of living. From your having failed to maintain what you should, you make it clear, that while you abandon the good ways of your fathers, you retain and guard the things you ought not. Yet the very tradition of your fathers, which you still seem so faithfully to defend, and in which you find your principal matter of accusation against the Christians—I mean zeal in the worship of the gods, the point

---

[1] Anubis.

in which antiquity has mainly erred—although you have rebuilt the altars of Serapis, now a Roman deity; although to Bacchus, now become a god of Italy, you offer up your orgies,—I shall in its proper place show you despise and neglect, and overthrow, throwing entirely aside the authority of the men of old. I go on meantime to reply to that infamous charge of secret crimes, clearing my way to things of open day.

7. Monsters of wickedness, we are accused of observing a holy rite in which we kill a little child and then eat it, in which after the feast we practise incest, the dogs—our pimps, forsooth, overturning the lights and getting us the shamelessness of darkness for our impious lusts. This is what is constantly laid to our charge, and yet you take no pains to elicit the truth of what we have been so long accused. Either bring, then, the matter to the light of day if you believe it, or give it no credit as having never inquired into it. On the ground of your double dealing, we are entitled to lay it down to you that there is no reality in the thing which you dare not expiscate. You impose on the executioner, in the case of Christians, a duty the very opposite of expiscation: he is not to make them confess what they do, but to make them deny what they are. We date the origin of our religion, as we have mentioned before, from the reign of Tiberius. Truth and the hatred of truth come into our world together. As soon as truth appears, it is regarded as an enemy. It has as many foes as there are strangers to it: the Jews, as was to be looked for, from a spirit of rivalry; the soldiers, out of a desire to extort money; our very domestics, by their nature. We are daily beset by foes, we are daily betrayed; we are oftentimes surprised in our meetings and congregations. Whoever happened withal upon an infant wailing, according to the common story? Whoever kept for the judge, just as he had found them, the gory mouths of Cyclops and Sirens? Whoever found any traces of uncleanness in their wives? Where is the man who, when he had discovered such atrocities, concealed them; or, in the act of dragging the culprits before the judge, was bribed into silence? If we always keep

our secrets, when were our proceedings made known to the world? Nay, by whom could they be made known? Not, surely, by the guilty parties themselves; even from the very idea of the thing, the fealty of silence being ever due to mysteries. The Samothracian and Eleusinian make no disclosures—how much more will silence be kept in regard to such as are sure in their unveiling to call forth punishment from man at once, while wrath divine is kept in store for the future? If, then, Christians are not themselves the publishers of their crime, it follows of course it must be strangers. And whence have they their knowledge, when it is also a universal custom in religious initiations to keep the profane aloof, and to beware of witnesses, unless it be that those who are so wicked have less fear than their neighbours? Every one knows what sort of thing rumour is. It is one of your own sayings, that "among all evils, none flies so fast as rumour." Why is rumour such an evil thing? Is it because it is fleet? Is it because it carries information? Or is it because it is in the highest degree mendacious? a thing not even when it brings some truth to us without a taint of falsehood, either detracting, or adding, or changing from the simple fact? Nay more, it is the very law of its being to continue only while it lies, and to live but so long as there is no proof; for when the proof is given, it ceases to exist, and, as having done its work of merely spreading a report, it delivers up a fact, and is henceforth held to be a fact, and called a fact. And then no one says, for instance, "They say that it took place at Rome," or, "There is a rumour that he has obtained a province," but, "He has got a province," and, "It took place at Rome." Rumour, the very designation of uncertainty, has no place when a thing is certain. Does any but a fool put his trust in it? For a wise man never believes the dubious. Everybody knows, however zealously it is spread abroad, on whatever strength of asseveration it rests, that some time or other from some one fountain it has its origin. Thence it must creep into propagating tongues and ears; and a small seminal blemish so darkens all the rest of the story, that no one can determine whether the lips, from which it first came forth, planted the seed of falsehood, as often happens, from a spirit of opposition, or from a suspicious judgment, or from a confirmed, nay, in the case of some, an inborn, delight in lying. It is well that time brings all to light, as your proverbs and sayings testify, by a provision of nature, which has so appointed things that nothing long is hidden, even though rumour has not disseminated it. It is just then as it should be, that fame for so long a period has been alone aware of the crimes of Christians. This is the witness you bring against us—one that has never been able to prove the accusation it some time or other sent abroad, and at last by mere continuance made into a settled opinion in the world; so that I confidently appeal to nature herself, ever true, against those who groundlessly hold that such things are to be credited.

8. See now, we set before you the reward of these enormities. They give promise of eternal life. Hold it meanwhile as your own belief. I ask you, then, whether, so believing, you think it worth attaining with a conscience such as you will have. Come, plunge your knife into the babe, enemy of none, accused of none, child of all; or if that is another's work, simply take your place beside a human being dying before he has really lived, await the departure of the lately given soul, receive the fresh young blood, saturate your bread with it, freely partake. The while as you recline at table, take note of the places which your mother and your sister occupy; mark them well, so that when the dog-made darkness has fallen on you, you may make no mistake, for you will be guilty of a crime—unless you perpetrate a deed of incest. Initiated and sealed into things like these, you have life everlasting. Tell me, I pray you, is eternity worth it? If it is not, then these things are not to be credited. Even although you had the belief, I deny the will; and even if you had the will, I deny the possibility. Why then can others do it, if you cannot? why cannot you, if others can? I suppose we are of a different nature—are we Cynopæ or Sciapodes?[1] You are a man yourself as well as the Chris-

[1] Fabulous monsters.

tian: if you cannot do it, you ought not to believe it of others. For a Christian is a man as well as you. But the ignorant, forsooth, are deceived and imposed on. They were quite unaware of anything of the kind being imputed to Christians, or they would certainly have looked into it for themselves, and searched the matter out. Instead of that, it is the custom for persons wishing initiation into sacred rites, I think, to go first of all to the master of them, that he may explain what preparations are to be made. Then, in this case, no doubt he would say, "You must have a child still of tender age, that knows not what it is to die, and can smile under thy knife; bread, too, to collect the gushing blood; in addition to these, candlesticks, and lamps, and dogs—with tit-bits to draw them on to the extinguishing of the lights: above all things, you will require to bring your mother and your sister with you." But what if mother and sister are unwilling? or if there be neither the one nor the other? What if there are Christians with no Christian relatives? He will not be counted, I suppose, a true follower of Christ, who has not a brother or a son. And what now, if these things are all in store for them without their knowledge? At least afterwards they come to know them; and they bear with them, and pardon them. They fear, it may be said, lest they have to pay for it if they let the secret out: nay, but they will rather in that case have every claim to protection; they will even prefer, one might think, dying by their own hand, to living under the burden of such a dreadful knowledge. Admit that they have this fear; yet why do they still persevere? For it is plain enough that you will have no desire to continue what you would never have been, if you had had previous knowledge of it.

9. That I may refute more thoroughly these charges, I will show that in part openly, in part secretly, practices prevail among you which have led you perhaps to credit similar things about us. Children were openly sacrificed in Africa to Saturn as lately as the proconsulship of Tiberius, who exposed to public gaze the priests suspended on the sacred trees overshadowing their temple, so many crosses on

which the punishment which justice craved overtook their crimes, as the soldiers of our country still can testify who did that very work for that proconsul. And even now that sacred crime still continues to be done in secret. It is not only Christians, you see, who despise you; for all that you do there is neither any crime thoroughly and abidingly eradicated, nor does any of your gods reform his ways. When Saturn did not spare his own children, he was not likely to spare the children of others; whom indeed the very parents themselves were in the habit of offering, gladly responding to the call which was made on them, and keeping the little ones pleased on the occasion, that they might not die in tears. At the same time, there is a vast difference between homicide and parricide. A more advanced age was sacrificed to Mercury in Gaul. I hand over the Tauric fables to their own theatres. Why, even in that most religious city of the pious descendants of Æneas, there is a certain Jupiter whom in their games they lave with human blood. It is the blood of a beast-fighter, you say. Is it less, because of that, the blood of a man? Or is it viler blood because it is from the veins of a wicked man? At any rate it is shed in murder. O Jove, thyself a Christian, and in truth only son of thy father in his cruelty! But in regard to child-murder, as it does not matter whether it is committed for a sacred object, or merely at one's own self-impulse—although there is a great difference, as we have said, between parricide and homicide—I shall turn to the people generally. How many, think you, of those crowding around and gaping for Christian blood,—how many even of your rulers, notable for their justice to you and for their severe measures against us, may I charge in their own consciences with the sin of putting their offspring to death? As to any difference in the kind of murder, it is certainly the more cruel way to kill by drowning, or by exposure to cold and hunger and dogs. A maturer age has always preferred death by the sword. In our case, murder being once for all forbidden, we may not destroy even the fœtus in the womb, while as yet the human being derives blood from other parts of the body for its sustenance. To hinder a birth is merely a speedier man-killing; nor does it matter whether you take away a life that is born, or destroy one that is coming to the birth. That is a man which is going to be one; you have the fruit already in its seed. As to meals of blood and such tragic dishes, read—I am not sure where it is told (it is in Herodotus, I think)—how blood taken from the arms, and tasted by both parties, has been the treaty bond among some nations. I am not sure what it was that was tasted in the time of Catiline. They say, too, that among some Scythian tribes the dead are eaten by their friends. But I am going far from home. At this day, among ourselves, blood consecrated to Bellona, blood drawn from a punctured thigh and then partaken of, seals initiation into the rites of that goddess. Those, too, who at the gladiator shows, for the cure of epilepsy, quaff with greedy thirst the blood of criminals slain in the arena, as it flows fresh from the wound, and then rush off—to whom do they belong? those, also, who make meals on the flesh of wild beasts at the place of combat—who have keen appetites for bear and stag? That bear in the struggle was bedewed with the blood of the man whom it lacerated: that stag rolled itself in the gladiator's gore. The entrails of the very bears, loaded with as yet undigested human viscera, are in great request. And you have men rifting up man-fed flesh? If you partake of food like this, how do your repasts differ from those you accuse us Christians of? And do those, who, with savage lust, seize on human bodies, do less because they devour the living? Have they less the pollution of human blood on them because they only lick up what is to turn into blood? They make meals, it is plain, not so much of infants, as of grown-up men. Blush for your vile ways before the Christians, who have not even the blood of animals at their meals of simple and natural food; who abstain from things strangled and that die a natural death, for no other reason than that they may not contract pollution, so much as from blood secreted in the viscera. To clench the matter with a single example, you tempt Christians with sausages of blood, just because you are perfectly aware that the thing by which you thus try to get them to transgress they hold unlawful. And how unreasonable it is to believe that those, of whom you are convinced that they regard with horror the idea of tasting the blood of oxen, are eager after blood of men; unless, mayhap, you have tried it, and found it sweeter to the taste! Nay, in fact, there is here a test you should apply to discover Christians, as well as the fire-pan and the censer. They should be proved by their appetite for human blood, as well as by their refusal to offer sacrifice, just as otherwise they should be affirmed to be free of Christianity by their refusal to taste of blood, as by their sacrificing; and there would be no want of blood of men, amply supplied as that would be in the trial and condemnation of prisoners. Then who are more given to the crime of incest than those who have enjoyed the instruction of Jupiter himself? Ctesias tells us that the Persians have illicit intercourse with their mothers. The Macedonians, too, are suspected on this point; for on first hearing the tragedy of Œdipus they made mirth of the incest-doer's grief, exclaiming, ἤλαυνε εἰς τὴν μητέρα. Even now reflect what opportunity there is for mistakes leading to incestuous comminglings—your promiscuous looseness supplying the materials. You first of all expose your children, that they may be taken up by any compassionate passer-by, to whom they are quite unknown; or you give them away, to be adopted by those who will do better to them the part of parents. Well, some time or other, all memory of the alienated progeny must be lost; and when once a mistake has been made, the transmission of incest thence will still go on—the race and the crime creeping on together. Then, further, wherever you are—at home, abroad, over the seas—your lust is an attendant, whose general indulgence, or even its indulgence in the most limited scale, may easily and unwittingly anywhere beget children, so that in this way a progeny scattered about in the commerce of life may have intercourse with those who are their own kin, and have no notion that there is any incest in the case. A persevering and stedfast chastity has protected us from anything like this: keeping as we do from adulteries and all post-matrimonial unfaithfulness, we are not exposed to incestuous mishaps. Some of us, making matters still more secure, beat away from them entirely the power of sensual sin, by a virgin continence, still boys in this respect when they are old. If you would but take notice that such sins as I have mentioned prevail among you, that would lead you to see that they have no existence among Christians. The same eyes would tell you of both facts. But the two blindnesses are apt to go together; so that those who do not see what is, think they see what is not. I shall show it to be so in everything. But now let me speak of matters which are more clear.

10. "You do not worship the gods," you say; "and you do not offer sacrifices for the emperors." Well, we do not offer sacrifice for others, for the same reason that we do not for ourselves,—namely, that your gods are not at all the objects of our worship. So we are accused of sacrilege and treason. This is the chief ground of charge against us— nay, it is the sum-total of our offending; and it is worthy then of being inquired into, if neither prejudice nor injustice be the judge, the one of which has no idea of discovering the truth, and the other simply and at once rejects it. We do not worship your gods, because we know that there are no such beings. This, therefore, is what you should do: you should call on us to demonstrate their non-existence, and thereby prove that they have no claim to adoration; for only if your gods were truly so, would there be any obligation to render divine homage to them. And punishment even were due to Christians, if it were made plain that those to whom they refused all worship were indeed divine. But you say, They are gods. We protest and appeal from yourselves to your knowledge; let that judge us; let that condemn us, if it can deny that all these gods of yours were but men. If even it venture to deny that, it will be confuted by its own books of antiquities, from which it has got its information about them, bearing witness to this day, as they plainly do, both of the cities in which they were born, and the countries in which they have left traces of their exploits, as well as where also they are proved to have been buried.

Shall I now, therefore, go over them one by one, so numerous and so various, new and old, barbarian, Grecian, Roman, foreign, captive and adopted, private and common, male and female, rural and urban, naval and military? It were useless even to hunt out all their names: so I may content myself with a compend; and this not for your information, but that you may have what you know brought to your recollection. For undoubtedly you act as if you had forgotten all about them. No one of your gods is earlier than Saturn: from him you trace all your deities, even those of higher rank and better known. What, then, can be proved of the first, will apply to those that follow. So far, then, as books give us information, neither the Greek Diodorus or Thallus, neither Cassius Severus or Cornelius Nepos, nor any writer upon sacred antiquities, have ventured to say that Saturn was any but a man: so far as the question depends on facts, I find none more trustworthy than those—that in Italy itself we have the country in which, after many expeditions, and after having partaken of Attic hospitalities, Saturn settled, obtaining cordial welcome from Janus, or, as the Salii will have it, Janis. The mountain on which he dwelt was called Saturnius; the city he founded is called Saturnia to this day; last of all, the whole of Italy, after having borne the name of Oenotria, was called Saturnia from him. He first gave you the art of writing, and a stamped coinage, and thence it is he presides over the public treasury. But if Saturn were a man, he had undoubtedly a human origin; and having a human origin, he was not the offspring of heaven and earth. As his parents were unknown, it was not unnatural that he should be spoken of as the son of those elements from which we might all seem to spring. For who does not speak of heaven and earth as father and mother, in a sort of way of veneration and honour? or from the custom which prevails among us of saying that persons of whom we have no knowledge, or who make a sudden appearance, have fallen from the skies? In this way it came about that Saturn, everywhere a sudden and unlooked-for guest, got everywhere the name of the Heaven-born. For even the common folk call persons whose stock is unknown, sons of earth. I say nothing of how men in these rude times were wont to act, when they were impressed by the look of any stranger happening to appear among them, as though it were divine, since even at this day men of culture make gods of those whom, a day or two before, they acknowledged to be dead men by their public mourning for them. Let these notices of Saturn, brief as they are, suffice. It will thus also be proved that Jupiter is as certainly a man as from a man he sprung; and that one after another the whole swarm is mortal like the primal stock.

11. And since, as you dare not deny that these deities of yours once were men, you have taken it on you to assert that they were made gods after their decease, let us consider what necessity there was for this. In the first place, you must concede the existence of one higher God—a certain wholesale dealer in divinity, who has made gods of men. For they could neither have assumed a divinity which was not theirs, nor could any but one himself possessing it have conferred it on them. If there was no one to make gods, it is vain to dream of gods being made when thus you have no god-maker. Most certainly, if they could have deified themselves, with a higher state at their command, they never would have been men. If, then, there be one who is able to make gods, I turn back to an examination of any reason there may be for making gods at all; and I find no other reason than this, that the great God has need of their ministrations and aids in performing the offices of Deity. But first it is an unworthy idea that He should need the help of a man, and in fact a dead man, when, if He was to be in want of this assistance from the dead, He might more fittingly have created some one a god at the beginning. Nor do I see any place for his action. For this entire world-mass—whether self-existent and uncreated, as Pythagoras maintains, or brought into being by a creator's hands, as Plato holds—was manifestly, once for all, in its original construction disposed, and furnished, and ordered, and supplied with a government of perfect wisdom. That cannot be imperfect

which has made all perfect. There was nothing waiting on for Saturn and his race to do. Men will make fools of themselves if they refuse to believe that from the very first rain poured down from the sky, and stars gleamed, and light shone, and thunders roared, and Jove himself dreaded the lightnings you put in his hands; that in like manner before Bacchus, and Ceres, and Minerva, nay, before the first man, whoever that was, every kind of fruit burst forth plentifully from the bosom of the earth, for nothing provided for the support and sustenance of man could be introduced after his entrance on the stage of being. Accordingly, these necessaries of life are said to have been discovered, not created. But the thing you discover existed before; and that which had a pre-existence must be regarded as belonging not to him who discovered it, but to him who made it. For of course it had a being before it could be found. But if, on account of his being the discoverer of the vine, Bacchus is raised to godship, Lucullus, who first introduced the cherry from Pontus into Italy, has not been fairly dealt with; for as the discoverer of a new fruit, he has not, as though he were its creator, been awarded divine honours. Wherefore, if the universe existed from the beginning, thoroughly furnished, with its system working under certain laws for the performance of its functions, there is in this respect an entire absence of all reason for electing humanity to divinity; for the positions and powers which you have assigned to your deities have been from the beginning precisely what they would have been, although you had never deified them. But you turn to another reason, telling us that the conferring of deity was a way of rewarding worth. And hence you grant, I conclude, that the god-making God is of transcendent righteousness,—one who will neither rashly, nor improperly, nor needlessly bestow a reward so great. I would have you then consider whether the merits of your deities are of a kind to have raised them to the heavens, and not rather to have sunk them down into the lowest depths of Tartarus,—the place which you regard, with many, as the prison-house of infernal punishments. For into this dread place are wont to be cast all who offend against filial piety, and such as are guilty of incest with sisters, and seducers of wives, and ravishers of virgins, and boy-polluters, and men of furious tempers, and murderers, and thieves, and deceivers; all, in short, who tread in the footsteps of your gods, not one of whom you can prove free from crime or vice, save by denying that they had ever a human existence. But as you cannot deny that, you have those foul blots also as an added reason for not believing that they were made gods afterwards. For if you rule for the very purpose of punishing such deeds; if every virtuous man among you rejects all correspondence, and converse, and intimacy with the wicked and the base, while, on the other hand, the high God has taken up their mates to a share of His majesty, on what ground is it that you thus condemn those whose fellow-actors you adore? Your goodness is an affront in the heavens. Deify your vilest criminals, if you would please your gods. You honour them by giving divine honours to their fellows. But to say no more about a way of acting so unworthy, there have been men virtuous, and pure, and good. Yet how many of these nobler men you have left in the regions of doom! as Socrates, so renowned for his wisdom, Aristides for his justice, Themistocles for his warlike genius, Alexander for his sublimity of soul, Polycrates for his good fortune, Crœsus for his wealth, Demosthenes for his eloquence. Which of these gods of yours is more remarkable for gravity and wisdom than Cato, more just and warlike than Scipio? which of them more magnanimous than Pompey, more prosperous than Sylla, of greater wealth than Crassus, more eloquent than Tally? How much better it would have been for the God Supreme to wait, that He might have taken such men as these to be His heavenly associates, prescient as He must have surely been of their worthier character! He was in a hurry, I suppose, and straightway shut heaven's gates; and now He must surely feel ashamed at these worthies murmuring over their lot in the regions below.

12. But I pass from these remarks, for I know and I am going to show what your gods are not, by showing what they are. In reference, then, to these, I see only names of dead

men of ancient times; I hear fabulous stories; I recognise sacred rites founded on mere myths. As to the actual images, I regard them as simply pieces of matter akin to the vessels and utensils in common use among us, or even undergoing in their consecration a hapless change from these useful articles at the hands of reckless art, which in the transforming process treats them with utter contempt, nay, in the very act commits sacrilege; so that it might be no slight solace to us in all our punishments, suffering as we do because of these same gods, that in their making they suffer as we do themselves. You put Christians on crosses and stakes: what image is not formed from the clay in the first instance, set on cross and stake? The body of your god is first consecrated on the gibbet. You tear the sides of Christians with your claws; but in the case of your own gods, axes, and planes, and rasps are put to work more vigorously on every member of the body. We lay our heads upon the block; before the lead, and the glue, and the nails are put in requisition, your deities are headless. We are cast to the wild beasts, while you attach them to Bacchus, and Cybele, and Cælestis. We are burned in the flames; so, too, are they in their original lump. We are condemned to the mines; from these your gods originate. We are banished to islands; in islands it is a common thing for your gods to have their birth or die. If it is in this way a deity is made, it will follow that as many as are punished are deified, and tortures will have to be declared divinities. But plain it is these objects of your worship have no sense of the injuries and disgraces of their consecrating, as they are equally unconscious of the honours paid to them. O impious words! O blasphemous reproaches! Gnash your teeth upon us—foam with maddened rage against us—ye are the persons, no doubt, who censured a certain Seneca speaking of your superstition at much greater length, and far more sharply! In a word, if we refuse our homage to statues and frigid images, the very counterpart of their dead originals, with which hawks, and mice, and spiders are so well acquainted, does it not merit praise instead of penalty, that we have rejected what we have come to see is error? We cannot surely be made out to injure those who we are certain are nonentities. What does not exist, is in its non-existence secure from suffering.

13. "But they are gods to us," you say. And how is it, then, that in utter inconsistency with this, you are convicted of impious, and sacrilegious, and irreligious conduct to them, neglecting those you imagine to exist, destroying those who are the objects of your fear, making mock of those whose honour you avenge? See now if I go beyond the truth. First, indeed, seeing you worship, some one god, and some another, of course you give offence to those you do not worship. You cannot continue to give preference to one without slighting another, for selection implies rejection. You despise, therefore, those whom you thus reject; for in your rejection of them, it is plain you have no dread of giving them offence. For, as we have already shown, every god depended on the decision of the senate for his godhead. No god was he whom man in his own counsels did not wish to be so, and thereby condemned. The family deities you call Lares, you exercise a domestic authority over, pledging them, selling them, changing them—making sometimes a cooking-pot of a Saturn, a firepan of a Minerva, as one or other happens to be worn done, or broken in its long sacred use, or as the family head feels the pressure of some more sacred home necessity. In like manner, by public law you disgrace your state gods, putting them in the auction-catalogue, and making them a source of revenue. Men seek to get the Capitol, as they seek to get the herb market, under the voice of the crier, under the auction spear, under the registration of the quæstor. Deity is struck off and farmed out to the highest bidder. But indeed lands burdened with tribute are of less value; men under the assessment of a poll-tax are less noble; for these things are the marks of servitude. In the case of the gods, on the other hand, the sacredness is great in proportion to the tribute which they yield; nay, the more sacred is a god, the larger is the tax he pays. Majesty is made a source of gain. Religion goes about the taverns begging. You demand a price for the privilege of standing on temple ground,

for access to the sacred services; there is no gratis knowledge of your divinities permitted—you must buy their favours with a price. What honours in any way do you render to them that you do not render to the dead? You have temples in the one case just as in the other; you have altars in the one case as in the other. Their statues have the same dress, the same insignia. As the dead man had his age, his art, his occupation, so is it with the deity. In what respect does the funeral feast differ from the feast of Jupiter? or the bowl of the gods from the ladle of the manes? or the undertaker from the soothsayer, as in fact this latter personage also attends upon the dead? With perfect propriety you give divine honours to your departed emperors, as you worship them in life. The gods will count themselves indebted to you; nay, it will be matter of high rejoicing among them that their masters are made their equals. But when you adore Larentina, a public prostitute—I could have wished that it might at least have been Lais or Phryne—among your Junos, and Cereses, and Dianas; when you instal in your Pantheon Simon Magus, giving him a statue and the title of Holy God; when you make an infamous court page a god of the sacred synod, although your ancient deities are in reality no better, they will still think themselves affronted by you, that the privilege antiquity conferred on them alone, has been allowed to others.

14. I wish now to review your sacred rites; and I pass no censure on your sacrificing, when you offer the worn-out, the scabbed, the corrupting; when you cut off from the fat and the sound the useless parts, such as the head and the hoofs, which in your house you would have assigned to the slaves or the dogs; when of the tithe of Hercules you do not lay a third upon his altar (I am disposed rather to praise your wisdom in rescuing something from being lost); but turning to your books, from which you get your training in wisdom and the nobler duties of life, what utterly ridiculous things I find!—that for Trojans and Greeks the gods fought among themselves like pairs of gladiators; that Venus was wounded by a man, because she would rescue her son Æneas when he

was in peril of his life from the same Diomede; that Mars was almost wasted away by a thirteen months' imprisonment; that Jupiter was saved by a monster's aid from suffering the same violence at the hands of the other gods; that he now laments the fate of Sarpedon, now foully makes love to his own sister, recounting [to her] former mistresses, now for a long time past not so dear as she. After this, what poet is not found copying the example of his chief, to be a disgracer of the gods? One gives Apollo to king Admetus to tend his sheep; another hires out the building labours of Neptune to Laomedon. A well-known lyric poet, too—Pindar, I mean—sings of Æsculapius deservedly stricken with lightning for his greed in practising wrongfully his art. A wicked deed it was of Jupiter—if he hurled the bolt—unnatural to his grandson, and exhibiting envious feeling to the Physician. Things like these should not be made public if they are true; and if false, they should not be fabricated among people professing a great respect for religion. Nor indeed do either tragic or comic writers shrink from setting forth the gods as the origin of all family calamities and sins. I do not dwell on the philosophers, contenting myself with a reference to Socrates, who, in contempt of the gods, was in the habit of swearing by an oak, and a goat, and a dog. In fact, for this very thing Socrates was condemned to death, that he overthrew the worship of the gods. Plainly, at one time as well as another, that is, always truth disliked. However, when rueing their judgment, the Athenians inflicted punishment on his accusers, and set up a golden image of him in a temple, the condemnation was in the very act rescinded, and his witness was restored to its former value. Diogenes, too, makes utter mock of Hercules; and the Roman cynic Varro brings forward three hundred Joves, or Jupiters they should be called, all headless.

15. Others of your writers, in their wantonness, even minister to your pleasures by vilifying the gods. Examine those charming farces of your Lentuli and Hostilii, whether in the jokes and tricks it is the buffoons or the deities which afford you merriment; such farces I mean as Anubis the

Adulterer, and Luna of the masculine gender, and Diana under the lash, and the reading the will of Jupiter deceased, and the three famishing Herculeses held up to ridicule. Your dramatic literature, too, depicts all the vileness of your gods. The Sun mourns his offspring[1] cast down from heaven, and you are full of glee; Cybele sighs after the scornful swain,[2] and you do not blush; you brook the stage recital of Jupiter's misdeeds, and the shepherd[3] judging Juno, Venus, and Minerva. Then, again, when the likeness of a god is put on the head of an ignominious and infamous wretch, when one impure and trained up for the art in all effeminacy, represents a Minerva or a Hercules, is not the majesty of your gods insulted, and their deity dishonoured? Yet you not merely look on, but applaud. You are, I suppose, more devout in the arena, where after the same fashion your deities dance on human blood, on the pollutions caused by inflicted punishments, as they act their themes and stories, doing their turn for the wretched criminals, except that these, too, often put on divinity and actually play the very gods. We have seen in our day a representation of the mutilation of Attis, that famous god of Pessinus, and a man burnt alive as Hercules. We have made merry amid the ludicrous cruelties of the noon-day exhibition, at Mercury examining the bodies of the dead with his hot iron; we have witnessed Jove's brother,[4] mallet in hand, dragging out the corpses of the gladiators. But who can go into everything of this sort? If by such things as these the honour of deity is assailed, if they go to blot out every trace of its majesty, we must explain them by the contempt in which the gods are held, alike by those who actually do them, and by those for whose enjoyment they are done. This it will be said, however, is all in sport. But if I add—it is what all know and will admit as readily to be the fact—that in the temples adulteries are arranged, that at the altars pimping is practised, that often in the houses of the temple-keepers and priests, under the sacrificial fillets, and the sacred hats, and the purple robes, amid the fumes of incense, deeds of licentiousness are done, I am not sure but your gods have more

[1] Phaethon. [2] Atys or Attis. [3] Paris. [4] Pluto.

reason to complain of you than of Christians. It is certainly among the votaries of your religion that the perpetrators of sacrilege are always found. For Christians do not enter your temples even in the day-time. Perhaps they too would be spoilers of them, if they worshipped in them. What then do they worship, since their objects of worship are different from yours? Already indeed it is implied as the corollary from their rejection of the lie, that they render homage to the truth; nor continue longer in an error which they have given up in the very fact of recognising it to be an error. Take this in first of all, and when we have offered a preliminary refutation of some false opinions, go on to derive from it our entire religious system.

16. For, like some others, you are under the delusion that our god is an ass's head. Cornelius Tacitus first put this notion into people's minds. In the fifth book of his histories, beginning the [narrative of the] Jewish war with an account of the origin of the nation; and theorizing at his pleasure about the origin, as well as the name and the religion of the Jews, he states that having been delivered, or rather, in his opinion, expelled from Egypt, in crossing the vast plains of Arabia, where water is so scanty, they were in extremity from thirst; but taking the guidance of the wild asses, which it was thought might be seeking water after feeding, they discovered a fountain, and thereupon in their gratitude they consecrated a head of this species of animal. And as Christianity is nearly allied to Judaism, from this, I suppose, it was taken for granted that we too are devoted to the worship of the same image. But the said Cornelius Tacitus (the very opposite of *tacit* in telling lies) informs us in the work already mentioned, that when Cneius Pompeius captured Jerusalem, he entered the temple to see the arcana of the Jewish religion, but found no image there. Yet surely if worship was rendered to any visible object, the very place for its exhibition would be the shrine; and that all the more that the worship, however unreasonable, had no need there to fear outside beholders. For entrance to the holy place was permitted to the priests alone, while all vision was forbidden to

others by an outspread curtain. You will not, however, deny that all beasts of burden, and not parts of them, but the animals entire, are with their goddess Epona objects of worship with you. It is this perhaps which displeases you in us, that while your worship here is universal, we do homage only to the ass. Then, if any of you think we render superstitious adoration to the cross, in that adoration he is sharer with us. If you offer homage to a piece of wood at all, it matters little what it is like when the substance is the same: it is of no consequence the form, if you have the very body of the god. And yet how far does the Athenian Pallas differ from the stock of the cross, or the Pharian Ceres as she is put up uncarved to sale, a mere rough stake and piece of shapeless wood! Every stake fixed in an upright position is a portion of the cross; we render our adoration, if you will have it so, to a god entire and complete. We have shown before that your deities are derived from shapes modelled from the cross. But you also worship victories, for in your trophies the cross is the heart of the trophy. The camp religion of the Romans is all through a worship of the standards, a setting the standards above all gods. Well, all those images decking out the standards are ornaments of crosses. All those hangings of your standards and banners are robes of crosses. I praise your zeal: you would not consecrate crosses unclothed and unadorned. Others, again, certainly with more information and greater verisimilitude, believe that the sun is our god. We shall be counted Persians perhaps, though we do not worship the orb of day painted on a piece of linen cloth, having himself everywhere in his own disk. The idea no doubt has originated from our being known to turn to the east in prayer. But you, many of you, also, under pretence sometimes of worshipping the heavenly bodies, move your lips in the direction of the sunrise. In the same way, if we devote Sun-day to rejoicing, from a far different reason than Sun-worship, we have some resemblance to those of you who devote the day of Saturn to ease and luxury, though they too go far away from Jewish ways, of which indeed they are ignorant. But lately a new edition of our god has been given to the world in that great city: it originated with a certain vile man who was wont to hire himself out to cheat the wild beasts, and who exhibited a picture with this inscription: The God of the Christians, born of an ass.[1] He had the ears of an ass, was hoofed in one foot, carried a book,[2] and wore a toga. Both the name and the figure gave us amusement. But our opponents ought straightway to have done homage to this biformed divinity, for they have acknowledged gods dog-headed and lion-headed, with horn of buck and ram, with goat-like loins, with serpent legs, with wings sprouting from back or foot. These things we have discussed *ex abundanti*, that we might not seem willingly to pass by any rumour against us unrefuted. Having thoroughly cleared ourselves, we turn now to an exhibition of what our religion really is.

17. The object of our worship is the One God, He who by His commanding word, His arranging wisdom, His mighty power, brought forth from nothing this entire mass of our world, with all its array of elements, bodies, spirits, for the glory of His majesty; whence also the Greeks have bestowed on it the name of Κοσμος. The eye cannot see Him, though He is (spiritually) visible. He is incomprehensible, though in grace He is manifested. He is beyond our utmost thought, though our human faculties conceive of Him. He is therefore equally real and great. But that which, in the ordinary sense, can be seen and handled and conceived, is inferior to the eyes by which it is taken in, and the hands by which it is tainted, and the faculties by which it is discovered; but that which is infinite is known only to itself. This it is which gives some notion of God, while yet beyond all our conceptions — our very incapacity of fully grasping Him affords us the idea of what He really is. He is presented to our minds in His transcendent greatness, as at once known and unknown. And this is the crowning guilt of men, that they will not recognise One, of whom they cannot possibly be

---

[1] Onocoites. If with Oehler, Onochoietes, the meaning is "asinarius sacerdos" (Oehler).

[2] Referring evidently to the Scriptures; and showing what the Bible was to the early Christians.

ignorant. Would you have the proof from the works of His hands, so numerous and so great, which both contain you and sustain you, which minister at once to your enjoyment, and strike you with awe; or would you rather have it from the testimony of the soul itself? Though under the oppressive bondage of the body, though led astray by depraving customs, though enervated by lusts and passions, though in slavery to false gods; yet, whenever the soul comes to itself, as out of a surfeit, or a sleep, or a sickness, and attains something of its natural soundness, it speaks of God; using no other word, because this is the peculiar name of the true God. " God is great and good "—" Which may God give," are the words on every lip. It bears witness, too, that God is judge, exclaiming, " God sees," and, " I commend myself to God," and, " God will repay me." O noble testimony of the soul by nature Christian! Then, too, in using such words as these, it looks not to the Capitol, but to the heavens. It knows that there is the throne of the living God, as from Him and from thence itself came down.

18. But, that we might attain an ampler and more authoritative knowledge at once of Himself, and of His counsels and will, God has added a written revelation for the behoof of every one whose heart is set on seeking Him, that seeking he may find, and finding believe, and believing obey. For from the first He sent messengers into the world,—men whose stainless righteousness made them worthy to know the Most High, and to reveal Him,—men abundantly endowed with the Holy Spirit, that they might proclaim that there is one God only who made all things, who formed man from the dust of the ground (for He is the true Prometheus who gave order to the world by arranging the seasons and their course),—who have further set before us the proofs He has given of His majesty in His judgments by floods and fires, the rules appointed by Him for securing His favour, as well as the retribution in store for the ignoring and forsaking and keeping them, as being about at the end of all to adjudge His worshippers to everlasting life, and the wicked to the doom of fire at once without ending and without break, raising up

again all the dead from the beginning, reforming and renewing them with the object of awarding either recompense. Once these things were with us, too, the theme of ridicule. We are of your stock and nature: men are made, not born, Christians. The preachers of whom we have spoken are called prophets, from the office which belongs to them of predicting the future. Their words, as well as the miracles which they performed, that men might have faith in their divine authority, we have still in the literary treasures they have left, and which are open to all. Ptolemy, surnamed Philadelphus, the most learned of his race, a man of vast acquaintance with all literature, emulating, I imagine, the book enthusiasm of Pisistratus, among other remains of the past which either their antiquity or something of peculiar interest made famous, at the suggestion of Demetrius Phalereus, who was renowned above all grammarians of his time, and to whom he had committed the management of these things, applied to the Jews for their writings—I mean the writings peculiar to them and in their tongue, which they alone possessed. For from themselves, as a people dear to God for their fathers' sake, their prophets had ever sprung, and to them they had ever spoken. Now in ancient times the people we call Jews bare the name of Hebrews, and so both their writings and their speech were Hebrew. But that the understanding of their books might not be wanting, this also the Jews supplied to Ptolemy; for they gave him seventy-two interpreters—men whom the philosopher Menedemus, the well-known asserter of a Providence, regarded with respect as sharing in his views. The same account is given by Aristæus. So the king left these works unlocked to all, in the Greek language. To this day, at the temple of Serapis, the libraries of Ptolemy are to be seen, with the identical Hebrew originals in them. The Jews, too, read them publicly. Under a tribute-liberty, they are in the habit of going to hear them every Sabbath. Whoever gives ear will find God in them; whoever takes pains to understand, will be compelled to believe.

19. Their high antiquity, first of all, claims authority for these writings. With you, too, it is a kind of religion to

demand belief on this very ground. Well, all the substances, all the materials, the origins, classes, contents of your most ancient writings, even most nations and cities illustrious in the records of the past and noted for their antiquity in books of annals,—the very forms of your letters, those revealers and custodiers of events, nay (I think I speak still within the mark), your very gods themselves, your very temples and oracles, and sacred rites, are less ancient than the work of a single prophet, in whom you have the *thesaurus* of the entire Jewish religion, and therefore too of ours. If you happen to have heard of a certain Moses, I speak first of him: he is as far back as the Argive Inachus; by nearly four hundred years —only seven less—he precedes Danaus, your most ancient name, while he antedates by a millennium the death of Priam. I might affirm, too, that he is five hundred years earlier than Homer, and have supporters of that view. The other prophets also, though of later date, are even the most recent of them as far back as the first of your philosophers, and legislators, and historians. It is not so much the difficulty of the subject, as its vastness, that stands in the way of a statement of the grounds on which these statements rest; the matter is not so arduous as it would be tedious. It would require the anxious study of many books, and the fingers' busy reckoning. The histories of the most ancient nations, such as the Egyptians, the Chaldeans, the Phœnicians, would need to be ransacked; the men of these various nations who have information to give, would have to be called in as witnesses. Manetho the Egyptian, and Berosus the Chaldean, and Iromus the Phœnician king of Tyre; their successors too, Ptolemy the Mendesian, and Demetrius Phalereus, and King Juba, and Apion, and Thallus, and their critic the Jew Josephus, the native vindicator of the ancient history of his people, who either authenticates or refutes the others. Also the Greek censors' lists must be compared, and the dates of events ascertained, that the chronological connections may be opened up, and thus the reckonings of the various annals be made to give forth light. We must go abroad into the histories and literature of all nations. And, in fact, we have already brought the proof in part before you, in giving those hints as to how it is to be effected. But it seems better to delay the full discussion of this, lest in our haste we do not sufficiently carry it out, or lest in its thorough handling we make too lengthened a digression.

20. To make up for our delay in this, we bring under your notice something of even greater importance; we point to the majesty of our Scriptures, if not to their antiquity. If you doubt that they are as ancient as we say, we offer proof that they are divine. And you may convince yourselves of this at once, and without going very far. Your instructors, the world, and the age, and the event, are all before you. All that is taking place around you was fore-announced; all that you now see with your eye was previously heard by the ear. The swallowing up of cities by the earth; the theft of islands by the sea; wars, bringing external and internal convulsions; the collision of kingdoms with kingdoms; famines and pestilences, and local massacres, and widespread desolating mortalities; the exaltation of the lowly, and the humbling of the proud; the decay of righteousness, the growth of sin, the slackening interest in all good ways; the very seasons and elements going out of their ordinary course, monsters and portents taking the place of nature's forms—it was all foreseen and predicted before it came to pass. While we suffer the calamities, we read of them in the Scriptures; as we examine, they are proved. Well, the truth of a prophecy, I think, is the demonstration of its being from above. Hence there is among us an assured faith in regard to coming events as things already proved to us, for they were predicted along with what we have day by day fulfilled. They are uttered by the same voices, they are written in the same books—the same Spirit inspires them. All time is one to prophecy foretelling the future. Among men, it may be, a distinction of times is made while the fulfilment is going on: from being future we think of it as present, and then from being present we count it as belonging to the past. How are we to blame, I pray you, that we believe in things to come as though they already were, with the grounds we have for our faith in these two steps?

21. But having asserted that our religion is supported by the writings of the Jews, the oldest which exist, though it is generally known, and we fully admit that it dates from a comparatively recent period—no further back indeed than the reign of Tiberius—a question may perhaps be raised on this ground about its standing, as if it were hiding something of its presumption under shadow of an illustrious religion, one which has at any rate undoubted allowance of the law, or because, apart from the question of age, we neither accord with the Jews in their peculiarities in regard to food, nor in their sacred days, nor even in their well-known bodily sign, nor in the possession of a common name, which surely behoved to be the case if we did homage to the same God as they. Then, too, the common people have now some knowledge of Christ, and think of Him as but a man, one indeed such as the Jews condemned, so that some may naturally enough have taken up the idea that we are worshippers of a mere human being. But we are neither ashamed of Christ —for we rejoice to be counted His disciples, and in His name to suffer—nor do we differ from the Jews concerning God. We must make, therefore, a remark or two as to Christ's divinity. In former times the Jews enjoyed much of God's favour, when the fathers of their race were noted for their righteousness and faith. So it was that as a people they flourished greatly, and their kingdom attained to a lofty eminence; and so highly blessed were they, that for their instruction God spake to them in special revelations, pointing out to them beforehand how they should merit His favour and avoid His displeasure. But how deeply they have sinned, puffed up to their fall with a false trust in their noble ancestors, turning from God's way into a way of sheer impiety, though they themselves should refuse to admit it, their present national ruin would afford sufficient proof. Scattered abroad, a race of wanderers, exiles from their own land and clime, they roam over the whole world without either a human or a heavenly king, not possessing even the stranger's right to set so much as a simple footstep in their native country. The sacred writers withal, in giving previous warning of these

things, all with equal clearness ever declared that, in the last days of the world, God would, out of every nation, and people, and country, choose for Himself more faithful worshippers, upon whom He would bestow His grace, and that indeed in ampler measure, in keeping with the enlarged capacities of a nobler dispensation. Accordingly, He appeared among us, whose coming to renovate and illuminate man's nature was pre-announced by God—I mean Christ, that Son of God. And so the supreme Head and Master of this grace and discipline, the Enlightener and Trainer of the human race, God's own Son, was announced among us, born—but not so born as to make Him ashamed of the name of Son or of His paternal origin. It was not His lot to have as His father, by incest with a sister, or by violation of a daughter or another's wife, a god in the shape of serpent, or ox, or bird, or lover, for his vile ends transmuting himself into the gold of Danaus. They are your divinities upon whom these base deeds of Jupiter were done. But the Son of God has no mother in any sense which involves impurity; she whom men suppose to be His mother in the ordinary way, had never entered into the marriage bond. But, first, I shall discuss His essential nature, and so the nature of His birth will be understood. We have already asserted that God made the world, and all which it contains, by His Word, and Reason, and Power. It is abundantly plain that your philosophers, too, regard the Logos—that is, the Word and Reason—as the Creator of the universe. For Zeno lays it down that he is the creator, having made all things according to a determinate plan; that his name is Fate, and God, and the soul of Jupiter, and the necessity of all things. Cleanthes ascribes all this to spirit, which he maintains pervades the universe. And we, in like manner, hold that the Word, and Reason, and Power, by which we have said God made all, have spirit as their proper and essential substratum, in which the Word has in-being to give forth utterances, and reason abides to dispose and arrange, and power is over all to execute. We have been taught that He proceeds forth from God, and in that procession He is generated; so that He is the Son of God, and is called God from unity of substance with God. For God, too, is a Spirit. Even when the ray is shot from the sun, it is still part of the parent mass; the sun will still be in the ray, because it is a ray of the sun—there is no division of substance, but merely an extension. Thus Christ is Spirit of Spirit, and God of God, as light of light is kindled. The material matrix remains entire and unimpaired, though you derive from it any number of shoots possessed of its qualities; so, too, that which has come forth out of God is at once God and the Son of God, and the two are one. In this way also, as He is Spirit of Spirit and God of God, He is made a second in manner of existence—in position, not in nature; and He did not withdraw from the original source, but went forth. This ray of God, then, as it was always foretold in ancient times, descending into a certain virgin, and made flesh in her womb, is in His birth God and man united. The flesh formed by the Spirit is nourished, grows up to manhood, speaks, teaches, works, and is the Christ. Receive meanwhile this fable, if you choose to call it so—it is like some of your own—while we go on to show how Christ's claims are proved, and who the parties are with you by whom such fables have been set agoing to overthrow the truth, which they resemble. The Jews, too, were well aware that Christ was coming, as those to whom the prophets spake. Nay, even now His advent is expected by them; nor is there any other contention between them and us, than that they believe the advent has not yet occurred. For two comings of Christ having been revealed to us: a first, which has been fulfilled in the lowliness of a human lot; a second, which impends over the world, now near its close, in all the majesty of Deity unveiled; and, by misunderstanding the first, they have concluded that the second—which, as matter of more manifest prediction, they set their hopes on—is the only one. It was the merited punishment of their sin not to understand the Lord's first advent: for if they had, they would have believed; and if they had believed, they would have obtained salvation. They themselves read how it is written of them that they are deprived of wisdom and understanding—of the use of eyes and ears.[1] As, then, under the force of their pre-judgment, they had convinced themselves from His lowly guise that Christ was no more than man, it followed from that, as a necessary consequence, that they should hold Him a magician from the powers which He displayed,—expelling devils from men by a word, restoring vision to the blind, cleansing the leprous, reinvigorating the paralytic, summoning the dead to life again, making the very elements of nature obey Him, stilling the storms and walking on the sea; proving that He was the Logos of God, that primordial first-begotten Word, accompanied by power and reason, and based on Spirit,—that He who was now doing all things by His word, and He who had done that of old, were one and the same. But the Jews were so exasperated by His teaching, by which their rulers and chiefs were convicted of the truth, chiefly because so many turned aside to Him, that at last they brought Him before Pontius Pilate, at the time Roman governor of Syria, and, by the violence of their outcries against Him, extorted a sentence giving Him up to them to be crucified. He Himself had predicted this; which, however, would have mattered little had not the prophets of old done it as well. And yet, nailed upon the cross, He exhibited many notable signs, by which His death was distinguished from all others. At His own free-will, He with a word dismissed from Him His spirit, anticipating the executioner's work. In the same hour, too, the light of day was withdrawn, when the sun at the very time was in his meridian blaze. Those who were not aware that this had been predicted about Christ, no doubt thought it an eclipse. You yourselves have the account of the world-portent still in your archives. Then, when His body was taken down from the cross and placed in a sepulchre, the Jews in their eager watchfulness surrounded it with a large military guard, lest, as He had predicted His resurrection from the dead on the third day, His disciples might remove by stealth His body, and deceive even the incredulous. But, lo, on the third day there was a sudden shock of earthquake, and the stone which

---

[1] Isa. vi. 10.

sealed the sepulchre was rolled away, and the guard fled off in terror: without a single disciple near, the grave was found empty of all but the clothes of the buried One. But nevertheless, the leaders of the Jews, whom it nearly concerned both to spread abroad a lie, and keep back a people tributary and submissive to them from the faith, gave it out that the body of Christ had been stolen by His followers. For the Lord, you see, did not go forth into the public gaze, lest the wicked should be delivered from their error; that faith also, destined to a great reward, might hold its ground in difficulty. But He spent forty days with some of His disciples down in Galilee, a region of Judea, instructing them in the doctrines they were to teach to others. Thereafter, having given them commission to preach the gospel through the world, He was encompassed with a cloud and taken up to heaven,—a fact more certain far than the assertions of your Proculi concerning Romulus.[1] All these things Pilate did to Christ; and now in fact a Christian in his own convictions, he sent word of Him to the reigning Cæsar, who was at the time Tiberius. Yes, and the Cæsars too would have believed on Christ, if either the Cæsars had not been necessary for the world, or if Christians could have been Cæsars. His disciples also spreading over the world, did as their Divine Master bade them; and after suffering greatly themselves from the persecutions of the Jews, and with no unwilling heart, as having faith undoubting in the truth, at last by Nero's cruel sword sowed the seed of Christian blood at Rome. Yes, and we shall prove that even your own gods are effective witnesses for Christ. It is a great matter if, to give you faith in Christians, I can bring forward the authority of the very beings on account of whom you refuse them credit. Thus far we have carried out the plan we laid down. We have set forth this origin of our sect and name, with this account of the Founder of Christianity. Let no one henceforth charge us with infamous wickedness; let no one think that it is otherwise than we have represented, for none may give

[1] Proculus was a Roman senator, who affirmed that Romulus had appeared to him after his death.

a false account of his religion. For in the very fact that he says he worships another god than he really does, he is guilty of denying the object of his worship, and transferring his worship and homage to another; and in the transference he ceases to worship the god he has repudiated. We say, and before all men we say, and torn and bleeding under your tortures, we cry out, " We worship God through Christ." Count Christ a man, if you please; by Him and in Him God would be known and be adored. If the Jews object, we answer that Moses, who was but a man, taught them their religion; against the Greeks we urge that Orpheus at Pieria, Musæus at Athens, Melampus at Argos, Trophonius in Bœotia, imposed religious rites; turning to yourselves, who exercise sway over the nations, it was the man Numa Pompilius who laid on the Romans a heavy load of costly superstitions. Surely Christ, then, had a right to reveal Deity, which was in fact His own essential possession, not with the object of bringing boors and savages by the dread of multitudinous gods, whose favour must be won, into some civilisation, as was the case with Numa; but as one who aimed to enlighten men already civilised, and under illusions from their very culture, that they might come to the knowledge of the truth. Search, then, and see if that divinity of Christ be true. If it be of such a nature that the acceptance of it transforms a man, and makes him truly good, there is implied in that the duty of renouncing what is opposed to it as false; especially on every ground that which, hiding itself under the names and images of the dead, labours to convince men of its divinity by certain signs, and miracles, and oracles.

22. And we affirm indeed the existence of certain spiritual essences. Nor is their name unfamiliar. The philosophers acknowledge there are demons; Socrates himself waiting on a demon's will. Why not? since it is said an evil spirit attached itself specially to him even from his childhood— turning his mind no doubt from what was good. The poets are all acquainted with demons too; even the ignorant common people make frequent use of them in cursing. In fact, they call upon Satan the demon-chief in their execrations, as

though from some instinctive soul-knowledge of him. Plato also admits the existence of angels. The dealers in magic, no less, come forward as witnesses to the existence of both kinds of spirits. We are instructed, moreover, by our sacred books how from certain angels, who fell of their own free-will, there sprang a more wicked demon-brood, condemned of God along with the authors of their race, and that chief we have referred to. It will for the present be enough, however, that some account is given of their work. Their great business is the ruin of mankind. So, from the very first, spiritual wickedness sought our destruction. They inflict, accordingly, upon our bodies diseases and other grievous calamities, while by violent assaults they hurry the soul into sudden and extraordinary excesses. Their marvellous subtleness and tenuity give them access to both parts of our nature. As spiritual, they can do great harm; for, invisible and intangible, we are not cognizant of their action save by its effects, when some inexplicable, unseen poison in the breeze blights the apples and the grain while in the flower, or kills them in the bud, or destroys them when they have reached maturity; as though by the tainted atmosphere in some unknown way spreading abroad its pestilential exhalations. So, too, by an influence equally obscure, demons and angels breathe into the soul and rouse up its corruptions with furious passions and vile excesses, or with cruel lusts accompanied by various errors, of which the worst is that by which these deities are commended to the favour of deceived and deluded human beings, that they may get their proper food of flesh-fumes and blood when that is offered up to idol-images. And what is daintier food to the spirit of evil, than turning men's minds away from the true God by the illusions of a false divination? And here I shall explain how these illusions are managed. Every spirit is possessed of wings. This is a common property of both angels and demons. So they are everywhere in a single moment; the whole world is as one place to them; all that is done over the whole extent of it, it is as easy for them to know as to report. Their swiftness of motion is taken for divinity, because their nature is unknown. Thus they would have themselves thought sometimes the authors of the things which they announce; and sometimes, no doubt, the bad things are their doing, never the good. The purposes of God, too, they took up of old from the lips of the prophets, even as they spoke them; and they gather them still from their works, when they hear them read aloud. Thus getting, too, from this source some intimations of the future, they set themselves up as rivals of the true God, while they steal His divinations. But the skill with which their responses are shaped to meet events, your Crœsi and Pyrrhi know too well. On the other hand, it was in that way we have explained, the Pythian was able to declare that a tortoise was being cooked with the flesh of a lamb; in a moment he had been to Lydia. From dwelling in the air, and their nearness to the stars, and their commerce with the clouds, they have means of knowing the preparatory processes going on in these upper regions, and thus can give promise of the rains which they already feel. Very kind too, no doubt, they are in regard to the healing of diseases. For, first of all, they make you ill; then, to get a miracle out of it, they command the application of remedies either altogether new, or contrary to those in use, and straightway withdrawing hurtful influence, they are supposed to have wrought a cure. What need, then, to speak of their other artifices, or yet further of the deceptive power which they have as spirits? —of these Castor apparitions, and water carried by a sieve, and a ship drawn along by a girdle, and a beard reddened by a touch,—all done with the one object of showing that men should believe in the deity of stones, and not seek after the only true God?

23. Moreover, if sorcerers call forth ghosts, and even make what seem the souls of the dead to appear; if they put boys to death, in order to get a response from the oracle; if, with their juggling illusions, they make a pretence of doing various miracles; if they put dreams into people's minds by the power of the angels and demons whose aid they have invited, by whose influence, too, goats and tables are made to divine,— how much more likely is this power of evil to be zealous in

doing with all its might, of its own inclination, and for its own objects, what it does to serve the ends of others! Or if both angels and demons do just what your gods do, where in that case is the pre-eminence of deity, which we must surely think to be above all in might? Will it not then be more reasonable to hold that these spirits make themselves gods, giving as they do the very proofs which raise your gods to godhead, than that the gods are the equals of angels and demons? You make a distinction of places, I suppose, regarding as gods in their temple those whose divinity you do not recognise elsewhere; counting the madness which leads one man to leap from the sacred houses, to be something different from that which leads another to leap from an adjoining house; looking on one who cuts his arms and secret parts as under a different furor from another who cuts his throat. The result of the frenzy is the same [in both cases], and the manner of instigation is one. But thus far we have been dealing only in words: we now proceed to a proof of facts, in which we shall show that under different names you have real identity. Let a person be brought before your tribunals, who is plainly under demoniacal possession. The wicked spirit, bidden speak by a follower of Christ, will as readily make the truthful confession that he is a demon, as elsewhere he has falsely asserted that he is a god. Or, if you will, let there be produced one of the god-possessed, as they are supposed, who, inhaling at the altar, conceive divinity from the fumes, who are delivered of it by retching, who vent it forth in agonies of gasping. Let that same Virgin Cælestis herself the rain-promiser, let Æsculapius discoverer of medicines, ready to prolong the life of Socordius, and Tenatius, and Asclepiodotus, now in the last extremity, if they would not confess, in their fear of lying to a Christian, that they were demons, then and there shed the blood of that most impudent follower of Christ. What clearer than a work like that? what more trustworthy than such a proof? The simplicity of truth is thus set forth; its own worth sustains it; no ground remains for the least suspicion. Do you say that it is done by magic, or some trick of that sort?

You will not say anything of the sort, if you have been allowed the use of your ears and eyes. For what argument can you bring against a thing that is exhibited to the eye in its naked reality? If, on the one hand, they are really gods, why do they pretend to be demons? Is it from fear of us? In that case your divinity is put in subjection to Christians; and you surely can never ascribe deity to that which is under authority of man, nay (if it adds aught to the disgrace) of its very enemies. If, on the other hand, they are demons or angels, why, inconsistently with this, do they presume to set themselves forth as acting the part of gods? For as beings who put themselves out as gods would never willingly call themselves demons, if they were gods indeed, that they might not thereby in fact abdicate their dignity; so those whom you know to be no more than demons, would not dare to act as gods, if those whose names they take and use were really divine. For they would not dare to treat with disrespect the higher majesty of beings, whose displeasure they would feel was to be dreaded. So this divinity of yours is no divinity; for if it were, it would not be pretended to by demons, and it would not be denied by gods. But since on both sides there is a concurrent acknowledgment that they are not gods, gather from this that there is but a single race—I mean the race of demons, the real race in both cases. Let your search, then, now be after gods; for those whom you had imagined to be so you find to be spirits of evil. The truth is, as we have thus not only shown from your own gods that neither themselves nor any others have claims to deity, you may see at once who is really God, and whether that is He and He alone whom we Christians own; as also whether you are to believe in Him, and worship Him, after the manner of our Christian faith and discipline. But at once they will say, Who is this Christ with his fables? is he an ordinary man? is he a sorcerer? was his body stolen by his disciples from its tomb? is he now in the realms below? or is he not rather up in the heavens, thence about to come again, making the whole world shake, filling the earth with dread alarms, making all but Christians wail—as the Power of God, and the Spirit of God, and the Word, and the Reason, and the Wisdom, and the Son of God? Mock as you like, but get the demons if you can to join you in your mocking; let *them* deny that Christ is coming to judge every human soul which has existed from the world's beginning, clothing it again with the body it laid aside at death; let *them* declare it, say, before your tribunal, that this work has been allotted to Minos and Rhadamanthus, as Plato and the poets agree; let them put away from them at least the mark of ignominy and condemnation. They disclaim being unclean spirits, which yet we must hold as indubitably proved by their relish for the blood and fumes and foetid carcases of sacrificial animals, and even by the vile language of their ministers. Let them deny that, for their wickedness condemned already, they are kept for that very judgment-day, with all their worshippers and their works. Why, all the authority and power we have over them is from our naming the name of Christ, and recalling to their memory the woes with which God threatens them at the hands of Christ as Judge, and which they expect one day to overtake them. Fearing Christ in God, and God in Christ, they become subject to the servants of God and Christ. So at our touch and breathing, overwhelmed by the thought and realization of those judgment fires, they leave at our command the bodies they have entered, unwilling, and distressed, and before your very eyes put to an open shame. You believe them when they lie; give credit to them, then, when they speak the truth about themselves. No one plays the liar to bring disgrace upon his own head, but for the sake of honour rather. You give a readier confidence to people making confessions against themselves, than denials in their own behalf. It has not been an unusual thing, accordingly, for those testimonies of your deities to convert men to Christianity; for in giving full belief to them, we are led to believe in Christ. Yes, your very gods kindle up faith in our Scriptures, they build up the confidence of our hope. You do homage, as I know, to them also with the blood of Christians. On no account, then, would they lose those who are so useful and dutiful to them, anxious even to hold you fast, lest some day or other as Christians you might put them to the rout,—if under the power of a follower of Christ, who desires to prove to you the Truth, it were at all possible for them to lie.

24. This whole confession of these beings, in which they declare that they are not gods, and in which they tell you that there is no God but one, the God whom we adore, is quite sufficient to clear us from the crime of treason, chiefly against the Roman religion. For if it is certain the gods have no existence, there is no religion in the case. If there is no religion, because there are no gods, we are assuredly not guilty of any offence against religion. Instead of that, the charge recoils on your own head: worshipping a lie, you are really guilty of the crime you charge on us, not merely by refusing the true religion of the true God, but by going the further length of persecuting it. But now, granting that these objects of your worship are really gods, is it not generally held that there is one higher and more potent, as it were the world's chief ruler, endowed with absolute power and majesty? For the common way is to apportion deity, giving an imperial and supreme domination to one, while its offices are put into the hands of many, as Plato describes great Jupiter in the heavens, surrounded by an array at once of deities and demons. It behoves us, therefore, to show equal respect to the procurators, prefects, and governors of the divine empire. And yet how great a crime does he commit, who, with the object of gaining higher favour with the Cæsar, transfers his endeavours and his hopes to another, and does not confess that the appellation of God as of Emperor belongs only to the Supreme Head, when it is held a capital offence among us to call, or hear called, by the highest title any other than Cæsar himself! Let one man worship God, another Jupiter; let one lift suppliant hands to the heavens, another to the altar of Fides; let one—if you choose to take this view of it —count in prayer the clouds, and another the ceiling pannels; let one consecrate his own life to his God, and another that of a goat. For see that you do not give a further ground for the charge of irreligion, by taking away religious liberty, and forbidding free choice of deity, so that I may no

longer worship according to my inclination, but am compelled to worship against it. Not even a human being would care to have unwilling homage rendered to him; and so the very Egyptians have been permitted the legal use of their ridiculous superstition, liberty to make gods of birds and beasts, nay, to condemn to death any one who kills a god of their sort. Every province even, and every city, has its god. Syria has Astarte, Arabia has Dusares, the Norici have Belenus, Africa has its Cælestis, Mauritania has its own princes. I have spoken, I think, of Roman provinces, and yet I have not said their gods are Roman; for they are not worshipped at Rome any more than others who are ranked as deities over Italy itself by municipal consecration, such as Delventinus of Casinum, Visidianus of Narnia, Ancharia of Asculum, Nortia of Volsinii, Valentia of Ocriculum, Hostia of Satrium, Father Curis of Falisci, in honour of whom, too, Juno got her surname. In fact, we alone are prevented having a religion of our own. We give offence to the Romans, we are excluded from the rights and privileges of Romans, because we do not worship the gods of Rome. It is well that there is a God of all, whose we all are, whether we will or no. But with you liberty is given to worship any god but the true God, as though He were not rather the God all should worship, to whom all belong.

25. I think I have offered sufficient proof upon the question of false and true divinity, having shown that the proof rests not merely on debate and argument, but on the witness of the very beings whom you believe are gods, so that the point needs no further handling. However, having been led thus naturally to speak of the Romans, I shall not avoid the controversy which is invited by the groundless assertion of those who maintain that, as a reward of their singular homage to religion, the Romans have been raised to such heights of power as to have become masters of the world; and that so certainly divine are the beings they worship, that those prosper beyond all others, who beyond all others honour them. This, forsooth, is the wages the gods have paid the Romans for their devotion. The progress of the empire is to be ascribed

to Sterculus, and Mutunus, and Larentina! For I can hardly think that foreign gods would have been disposed to show more favour to an alien race than to their own, and given their own fatherland, in which they had their birth, grew up to manhood, became illustrious, and at last were buried, over to invaders from another shore! As for Cybele, if she set her affections on the city of Rome as sprung of the Trojan stock saved from the arms of Greece, she herself forsooth being of the same race, —if she foresaw her transference[1] to the avenging people by whom Greece the conqueror of Phrygia was to be subdued, let her look to it (in regard of her native country's conquest by Greece). Why, too, even in these days the *Mater Magna* has given a notable proof of her greatness which she has conferred as a boon upon the city, when, after the loss to the State of Marcus Aurelius at Sirmium, on the sixteenth before the Kalends of April, that most sacred high priest of hers was offering, a week after, impure libations of blood drawn from his own arms, and issuing his commands that the ordinary prayers should be made for the safety of the emperor already dead. O tardy messengers, O sleepy despatches, through whose fault Cybele had not an earlier knowledge of the imperial decease, that the Christians might have no occasion to ridicule a goddess so unworthy. Jupiter, again, would surely never have permitted his own Crete to fall at once before the Roman Fasces, forgetful of that Idean cave and the Corybantian cymbals, and the sweet odour of her who nursed him there. Would he not have exalted his own tomb above the entire Capitol, that the land which covered the ashes of Jove might rather be the mistress of the world? Would Juno have desired the destruction of the Punic city, beloved even to the neglect of Samos, and that by a nation of Æneadæ? As to that I know, "Here were her arms, here was her chariot, this kingdom, if the Fates permit, the goddess tends and cherishes to be mistress of the nations." Jove's hapless wife and sister had no power to prevail against the Fates! "Jupiter himself is sustained by fate." And yet the Romans have never done such homage to the Fates,

[1] Her image was taken from Pessinus to Rome.

which gave them Carthage against the purpose and the will of Juno, as to the abandoned harlot Larentina. It is undoubted that not a few of your gods have reigned on earth as kings. If, then, they now possess the power of bestowing empire, when they were kings themselves, from whence had they received their kingly honours? Whom did Jupiter and Saturn worship? A Sterculus, I suppose. But did the Romans, along with the native-born inhabitants, afterwards adore also some who were never kings? In that case, however, they were under the reign of others, who did not yet bow down to them, as not yet raised to godhead. It belongs to others, then, to make gift of kingdoms, since there were kings before these gods had their names on the roll of divinities. But how utterly foolish it is to attribute the greatness of the Roman name to religious merits, since it was after Rome became an empire, or call it still a kingdom, that the religion she professes made its chief progress! Is it the case now? Has its religion been the source of the prosperity of Rome? For though Numa set agoing an eagerness after superstitious observances, yet religion among the Romans was not yet a matter of images or temples. It was frugal in its ways, and its rites were simple, and there were no capitols struggling to the heavens; but the altars were offhand ones of turf, and the sacred vessels were yet of Samian earthenware, and from these the odours rose, and no likeness of God was to be seen. For at that time the skill of the Greeks and Tuscans in image-making had not yet overrun the city with the products of their art. The Romans, therefore, were not distinguished for their devotion to the gods before they attained to greatness; and so their greatness was not the result of their religion. Indeed, how could religion make a people great who have owed their greatness to their irreligion? For, if I am not mistaken, kingdoms and empires are acquired by wars, and are extended by victories. More than that, you cannot have wars and victories without the taking, and often the destruction, of cities. That is a thing in which the gods have their share of calamity. Houses and temples suffer alike; there is indiscriminate slaughter of priests and citizens; the hand of rapine is laid equally upon sacred and on common treasure. Thus the sacrileges of the Romans are as numerous as their trophies. They boast as many triumphs over the gods as over the nations; as many spoils of battle they have still, as there remain images of captive deities. And the poor gods submit to be adored by their enemies, and they ordain illimitable empire to those whose injuries rather than their simulated homage should have had retribution at their hands. But divinities unconscious are with impunity dishonoured, just as in vain they are adored. You certainly never can believe that devotion to religion has evidently advanced to greatness a people who, as we have put it, have either grown by injuring religion, or have injured religion by their growth. Those, too, whose kingdoms have become part of the one great whole of the Roman empire, were not without religion when their kingdoms were taken from them.

26. Examine then, and see if *He* be not the dispenser of kingdoms, who is Lord at once of the world which is ruled, and of man himself who rules; if He have not ordained the changes of dynasties, with their appointed seasons, who was before all time, and made the world a body of times; if the rise and the fall of states are not the work of Him, under whose sovereignty the human race once existed without states at all. How do you allow yourselves to fall into such error? Why, the Rome of rural simplicity is older than some of her gods; she reigned before her proud, vast Capitol was built. The Babylonians exercised dominion, too, before the days of the Pontiffs; and the Medes before the Quindecemvirs; and the Egyptians before the Salii; and the Assyrians before the Luperci; and the Amazons before the Vestal Virgins. And to add another point: if the religions of Rome give empire, ancient Judea would never have been a kingdom, despising as it did one and all these idol deities; Judea, whose God you Romans once honoured with victims, and its temple with gifts, and its people with treaties; and which would never have been beneath your sceptre but for that last and crowning offence against God, in rejecting and crucifying Christ.

27. Enough has been said in these remarks to confute the

charge of treason against your religion; for we cannot be held to do harm to that which has no existence. When we are called therefore to sacrifice, we resolutely refuse, relying on the knowledge we possess, by which we are well assured of the real objects to whom these services are offered, under profaning of images and the deification of human names. Some, indeed, think it a piece of insanity that, when it is in our power to offer sacrifice at once, and go away unharmed, holding as ever our convictions, we prefer an obstinate persistence in our confession to our safety. You advise us, forsooth, to take unjust advantage of you; but we know whence such suggestions come, who is at the bottom of it all, and how every effort is made, now by cunning suasion, and now by merciless persecution, to overthrow our constancy. No other than that spirit, half devil and half angel, who, hating us because of his own separation from God, and stirred with envy for the favour God has shown us, turns your minds against us by an occult influence, moulding and instigating them to all that perversity in judgment, and that unrighteous cruelty, which we have mentioned at the beginning of our work, when entering on this discussion. For, though the whole power of demons and kindred spirits is subject to us, yet still, as ill-disposed slaves sometimes conjoin contumacy with fear, and delight to injure those of whom they at the same time stand in awe, so is it here. For fear also inspires hatred. Besides, in their desperate condition, as already under condemnation, it gives them some comfort, while punishment delays, to have the usufruct of their malignant dispositions. And yet, when hands are laid on them, they are subdued at once, and submit to their lot; and those whom at a distance they oppose, in close quarters they supplicate for mercy. So when, like insurrectionary workhouses, or prisons, or mines, or any such penal slaveries, they break forth against us their masters, they know all the while that they are not a match for us, and just on that account, indeed, rush the more recklessly to destruction. We resist them unwillingly, as though they were equals, and contend against them by persevering in that which they assail; and our triumph over them is never more complete than when we are condemned for resolute adherence to our faith.

28. But as it was easily seen to be unjust to compel freemen against their will to offer sacrifice (for even in other acts of religious service a willing mind is required), it should be counted quite absurd for one man to compel another to do honour to the gods, when he ought ever voluntarily, and in the sense of his own need, to seek their favour, lest in the liberty which is his right he should be ready to say, "I want none of Jupiter's favours; pray who art thou? Let Janus meet me with angry looks, with whichever of his faces he likes; what have you to do with me?" You have been led, no doubt, by these same evil spirits to compel us to offer sacrifice for the well-being of the emperor; and you are under a necessity of using force, just as we are under an obligation to face the dangers of it. This brings us, then, to the second ground of accusation, that we are guilty of treason against a majesty more august; for you do homage with a greater dread and an intenser reverence to Cæsar, than Olympian Jove himself. And if you knew it, upon sufficient grounds. For is not any living man better than a dead one, whoever he be? But this is not done by you on any other ground than regard to a power whose presence you vividly realize; so that also in this you are convicted of impiety to your gods, inasmuch as you show a greater reverence to a human sovereignty than you do to them. Then, too, among you, people far more readily swear a false oath in the name of all the gods, than in the name of the single genius of Cæsar.

29. Let it be made clear, then, first of all, if those to whom sacrifice is offered are really able to protect either emperor or anybody else, and so adjudge us guilty of treason, if angels and demons, spirits of most wicked nature, do any good, if the lost save, if the condemned give liberty, if the dead (I refer to what you know well enough) defend the living. For surely the first thing they would look to would be the protection of their statues, and images, and temples, which rather owe their safety, I think, to the watch

kept by Cæsar's guards. Nay, I think the very materials of which these are made come from Cæsar's mines, and there is not a temple but depends on Cæsar's will. Yes, and many gods have felt the displeasure of the Cæsar. It makes for my argument if they are also partakers of his favour, when he bestows on them some gift or privilege. How shall they who are thus in Cæsar's power, who belong entirely to him, have Cæsar's protection in their hands, so that you can imagine them able to give to Cæsar what they more readily get from him? This, then, is the ground on which we are charged with treason against the imperial majesty, to wit, that we do not put the emperors under their own possessions; that we do not offer a mere mock service on their behalf, as not believing their safety rests in leaden hands. But you are impious in a high degree who look for it where it is not, who seek it from those who have it not to give, passing by Him who has it entirely in His power. Besides this, you persecute those who know where to seek for it, and who, knowing where to seek for it, are able as well to secure it.

30. For we offer prayer for the safety of our princes to the eternal, the true, the living God, whose favour, beyond all others, they must themselves desire. They know from whom they have obtained their power; they know, as they are men, from whom they have received life itself; they are convinced that He is God alone, on whose power alone they are entirely dependent, to whom they are second, after whom they occupy the highest places, before and above all the gods. Why not, since they are above all living men, and the living, as living, are superior to the dead? They reflect upon the extent of their power, and so they come to understand the highest; they acknowledge that they have all their might from Him against whom their might is nought. Let the emperor make war on heaven; let him lead heaven captive in his triumph; let him put guards on heaven; let him impose taxes on heaven! He cannot. Just because he is less than heaven, he is great. For he himself is His to whom heaven and every creature appertains. He gets his sceptre where he first got his humanity; his power where he got the

breath of life. Thither we lift our eyes, with hands outstretched, because free from sin; with head uncovered, for we have nothing whereof to be ashamed; finally, without a monitor, because it is from the heart we supplicate. And, without ceasing, for all our emperors we offer prayer. We pray for life prolonged; for security to the empire; for protection to the imperial house; for brave armies, a faithful senate, a virtuous people, the world at rest,—whatever, as man or Cæsar, an emperor would wish. These things I cannot ask from any but the God from whom I know I shall obtain them, both because He alone bestows them and because I have claims upon Him for their gift, as being a servant of His, rendering homage to Him alone, persecuted for His doctrine, offering to Him, at His own requirement, that costly and noble sacrifice of prayer[1] despatched from a chaste body, an unstained soul, a sanctified spirit,—not the few grains of incense a farthing buys—tears of an Arabian tree,—not a few drops of wine,—not the blood of some worthless ox to whom death is a relief, and, in addition to other offensive things, a polluted conscience, so that one wonders, when your victims are examined by these vile priests, why the examination is not rather of the sacrificers than the sacrifices. With our hands thus stretched out and up to God, rend us with your iron claws, hang us up on crosses, wrap us in flames, take our heads from us with the sword, let loose the wild beasts on us,—the very attitude of a Christian praying is one of preparation for all punishment. Let this, good rulers, be your work: wring from us the soul, beseeching God on the emperor's behalf. Upon the truth of God, and devotion to His name, put the brand of crime.

31. But we merely, you say, flatter the emperor, and feign these prayers of ours to escape persecution. Thank you for your mistake. For you give us the opportunity of proving our allegations. Do you, then, who think that we care nothing for the welfare of Cæsar, look into God's revelations, examine our sacred books, which we do not keep in hiding, and which many accidents put into the hands of

[1] Heb. x. 22.

those who are not of us. Learn from them. that a large benevolence is enjoined upon us, even so far as to supplicate God for our enemies, and to beseech blessings on our persecutors.[1] Who, then, are greater enemies and persecutors of Christians, than the very parties with treason against whom we are charged? Nay, even in terms, and most clearly, the Scripture says, "Pray for kings, and rulers, and powers, that all may be peace with you."[2] For when there is disturbance in the empire, if the commotion is felt by its other members, surely we too, though we are not thought to be given to disorder, are to be found in some place or other which the calamity affects.

32. There is also another and a greater necessity for our offering prayer in behalf of the emperors, nay, for the complete stability of the empire, and for Roman interests in general. For we know that a mighty shock impending over the whole earth—in fact, the very end of all things threatening dreadful woes—is only retarded by the continued existence of the Roman empire. We have no desire, then, to be overtaken by these dire events; and in praying that their coming may be delayed, we are lending our aid to Rome's duration. More than this, though we decline to swear by the genii of the Cæsars, we swear by their safety, which is worth far more than all your genii. Are you ignorant that these genii are called "Dæmones," and thence the diminutive name "Dæmonia" is applied to them? We respect in the emperors the ordinance of God, who has set them over the nations. We know that there is that in them which God has willed; and to what God has willed we desire all safety, and we count an oath by it a great oath. But as for dæmons, that is, your genii, we have been in the habit of exorcising them, not of swearing by them, and thereby conferring on them divine honour.

33. But why dwell longer on the reverence and sacred respect of Christians to the emperor, whom we cannot but look up to as called by our Lord to his office? so that on valid grounds I might say Cæsar is more ours than yours,

[1] Matt. v. 44.   [2] 1 Tim. ii. 2.

for our God has appointed him. Therefore, as having this
propriety in him, I do more than you for his welfare, not
merely because I ask it of Him who can give it, or because
I ask it as one who deserves to get it, but also because, in
keeping the majesty of Cæsar within due limits, and putting
it under the Most High, and making it less than divine, I
commend him the more to the favour of Deity, to whom I
make him alone inferior. But I place him in subjection to
one I regard as more glorious than himself. Never will I call
the emperor God, and that either because it is not in me to
be guilty of falsehood; or that I dare not turn him into ridicule; or that not even himself will desire to have that high
name applied to him. If he is but a man, it is his interest
as man to give God His higher place. Let him think it
enough to bear the name of emperor. That, too, is a great
name of God's giving. To call him God, is to rob him of
his title. If he is not a man, emperor he cannot be. Even
when, amid the honours of a triumph, he sits on that lofty
chariot, he is reminded that he is only human. A voice at
his back keeps whispering in his ear, "Look behind thee;
remember thou art but a man." And it only adds to his
exultation, that he shines with a glory so surpassing as to
require an admonitory reference to his condition. It adds
to his greatness that he needs such a reminiscence, lest he
should think himself divine.

34. Augustus, the founder of the empire, would not even
have the title Lord; for that, too, is a name of Deity. For
my part, I am willing to give the emperor this designation,
but in the common acceptation of the word, and when I am
not forced to call him Lord as in God's place. But my relation to him is one of freedom; for I have but one true Lord,
God omnipotent and eternal, who is Lord of the emperor as
well. How can he, who is truly father of his country, be its
lord? The name of piety is more grateful than the name of
power; so the heads of families are called fathers rather than
lords. Far less should the emperor have the name of God.
We can only profess our belief that he is that by the most
unworthy, nay, a fatal flattery; it is just as if, having an

emperor, you call another by the name, in which case will you not give great and unappeasable offence to him who actually reigns?—an offence he, too, needs to fear on whom you have bestowed the title. Give all reverence to God, if you wish Him to be propitious to the emperor. Give up all worship of, and belief in, any other being as divine. Cease also to give the sacred name to him who has need of God himself. If such adulation is not ashamed of its lie, in addressing a man as divine, let it have some dread at least of the evil omen which it bears. It is the invocation of a curse, to give Cæsar the name of god before his apotheosis.

35. This is the reason, then, why Christians are counted public enemies: that they pay no vain, nor false, nor foolish honours to the emperor; that, as men believing in the true religion, they prefer to celebrate their festal days with a good conscience, instead of with the common wantonness. It is, forsooth, a notable homage to bring fires and couches out into the public, to have feasting from street to street, to turn the city into one great tavern, to make mud with wine, to run in troops to acts of violence, to deeds of shamelessness, to lust allurements! What! is public joy manifested by public disgrace? Do things unseemly at other times beseem the festal days of princes? Do they who observe the rules of virtue out of reverence for Cæsar, for his sake turn aside from them? And shall piety be a licence to immoral deeds, and shall religion be regarded as affording the occasion for all riotous extravagance? Poor we, worthy of all condemnation! For why do we keep the votive days and high rejoicings in honour of the Cæsars with chastity, sobriety, and virtue? Why, on the day of gladness, do we neither cover our door-posts with laurels, nor intrude upon the day with lamps? It is a proper thing, at the call of a public festivity, to dress your house up like some new brothel! However, in the matter of this homage to a lesser majesty, in reference to which we are accused of a lower sacrilege, because we do not celebrate along with you the holidays of the Cæsars in a manner forbidden alike by modesty, decency, and purity,—in truth they have been established rather as

affording opportunities for licentiousness than from any worthy motive,—in this matter I am anxious to point out how faithful and true *you* are, lest perchance here also those who will not have us counted Romans, but enemies of Rome's chief rulers, be found themselves worse than we wicked Christians! I appeal to the inhabitants of Rome themselves, to the native population of the seven hills: does that Roman vernacular of theirs ever spare a Cæsar? The Tiber and the wild beasts' schools bear witness. Say now if nature had covered our hearts with a transparent substance through which the light could pass, whose hearts, all graven over, would not betray the scene of another and another Cæsar presiding at the distribution of a largess? And this at the very time they are shouting, "May Jupiter take years from us, and with them lengthen life to you,"—words as foreign to the lips of a Christian as it is out of keeping with his character to desire a change of emperor. But this is the rabble, you say; yet as the rabble they still are Romans, and none more frequently than they demand the death of Christians. Of course, then, the other classes, as befits their higher rank, are religiously faithful. No breath of treason is there ever in the senate, in the equestrian order, in the camp, in the palace. Whence, then, came a Cassius, a Niger, an Albinus? Whence they who beset the Cæsar[1] between the two laurel groves? whence they who practised wrestling, that they might acquire skill to strangle him? Whence they who in full armour broke into the palace,[2] more audacious than all your Tigerii and Parthenii?[3] If I mistake not, they were Romans; that is, they were not Christians. Yet all of them, on the very eve of their traitorous outbreak, offered sacrifices for the safety of the emperor, and swore by his genius, one thing in profession, and another in the heart; and no doubt they were in the habit of calling Christians enemies of the state. Yes, and persons who are now daily brought to light as confederates or approvers of these crimes and treasons, the still remanent gleanings after a vintage of

---

[1] Commodus.   [2] To murder Pertinax
[3] Tigerius and Parthenius were among the murderers of Commodus.

traitors, with what verdant and branching laurels they clad their door-posts, with what lofty and brilliant lamps they smoked their porches, with what most exquisite and gaudy couches they divided the Forum among themselves, not that they might celebrate public rejoicings, but that they might get a foretaste of their own votive seasons in partaking of the festivities of another, and inaugurate the model and image of their hope, changing in their minds the emperor's name. The same homage is paid, dutifully too, by those who consult astrologers, and soothsayers, and augurs, and magicians, about the life of the Cæsars,—arts which, as made known by the angels who sinned and forbidden by God, Christians do not even make use of in their own affairs. But who has any occasion to inquire about the life of the emperor, if he have not some wish or thought against it, or some hopes and expectations after it? For consultations of this sort have not the same motive in the case of friends as in the case of sovereigns. The anxiety of a kinsman is something very different from that of a subject.

36. If it is the fact that men bearing the name of Romans are found to be enemies of Rome, why are we, on the ground that we are regarded as enemies, denied the name of Romans? We may be at once Romans and foes of Rome, when men passing for Romans are discovered to be enemies of their country. So the affection, and fealty, and reverence, due to the emperors do not consist in such tokens of homage as these, which even hostility may be zealous in performing, chiefly as a cloak to its purposes; but in those ways which Deity as certainly enjoins on us, as they are held to be necessary in the case of all men as well as emperors. Deeds of true heart-goodness are not due by us to emperors alone. We never do good with respect of persons; for in our own interest we conduct ourselves as those who take no payment either of praise or premium from man, but from God, who both requires and remunerates an impartial benevolence. We are the same to emperors as to our ordinary neighbours. For we are equally forbidden to wish ill, to do ill, to speak ill, to think ill of all men. The thing we must not do to

an emperor, we must not do to any one else: what we should not do to anybody, *à fortiori*, perhaps we should not do to him whom God has been pleased so highly to exalt.

37. If we are enjoined, then, to love our enemies, as I have remarked above, whom have we to hate? If injured, we are forbidden to retaliate, lest we become as bad ourselves: who can suffer injury at our hands? In regard to this, recall your own experiences. How often you inflict gross cruelties on Christians, partly because it is your own inclination, and partly in obedience to the laws! How often, too, the hostile mob, paying no regard to you, takes the law into its own hand, and assails us with stones and flames! With the very frenzy of the Bacchanals, they do not even spare the Christian dead, but tear them, now sadly changed, no longer entire, from the rest of the tomb, from the asylum we might say of death, cut them in pieces, rend them asunder. Yet, banded together as we are, ever so ready to sacrifice our lives, what single case of revenge for injury are you able to point to, though, if it were held right among us to repay evil by evil, a single night with a torch or two could achieve an ample vengeance? But away with the idea of a sect divine avenging itself by human fires, or shrinking from the sufferings in which it is tried. If we desired, indeed, to act the part of open enemies, not merely of secret avengers, would there be any lacking in strength, whether of numbers or resources? The Moors, the Marcomanni, the Parthians themselves, or any single people, however great, inhabiting a distinct territory, and confined within its own boundaries, surpasses, forsooth, in numbers, one spread over all the world! We are but of yesterday, and we have filled every place among you—cities, islands, fortresses, towns, market-places, the very camp, tribes, companies, palace, senate, forum,—we have left nothing to you but the temples of your gods. For what wars should we not be fit, not eager, even with unequal forces, we who so willingly yield ourselves to the sword, if in our religion it were not counted better to be slain than to slay? Without arms even, and raising no insurrectionary banner, but simply in enmity to you, we could carry on the contest with you by

an ill-willed severance alone. For if such multitudes of men were to break away from you, and betake themselves to some remote corner of the world, why, the very loss of so many citizens, whatever sort they were, would cover the empire with shame; nay, in the very forsaking, vengeance would be inflicted. Why, you would be horror-struck at the solitude in which you would find yourselves, at such an all-prevailing silence, and that stupor as of a dead world. You would have to seek subjects to govern. You would have more enemies than citizens remaining. For now it is the immense number of Christians which makes your enemies so few, —almost all the inhabitants of your various cities being followers of Christ. Yet you choose to call us enemies of the human race, rather than of human error. Nay, who would deliver you from those secret foes, ever busy both destroying your souls and ruining your health? Who would save you, I mean, from the attacks of those spirits of evil, which without reward or hire we exorcise? This alone would be revenge enough for us, that you were henceforth left free to the possession of unclean spirits. But instead of taking into account what is due to us for the important protection we afford you, and though we are not merely no trouble to you, but in fact necessary to your well-being, you prefer to hold us enemies, as indeed we are, yet not of man, but rather of his error.

38. Ought not Christians, therefore, to receive not merely a somewhat milder treatment, but to have a place among the law-tolerated societies, seeing they are not chargeable with any such crimes as are commonly dreaded from societies of the illicit class? For, unless I mistake the matter, the prevention of such associations is based on a prudential regard to public order, that the state may not be divided into parties, which would naturally lead to disturbance in the electoral assemblies, the councils, the curiæ, the special conventions, even in the public shows by the hostile collisions of rival parties, especially when now, in pursuit of gain, men have begun to consider their violence an article to be bought and sold. But as those in whom all ardour in the pursuit of glory and

honour is dead, we have no pressing inducement to take part in your public meetings; nor is there aught more entirely foreign to us than affairs of state. We acknowledge one all-embracing commonwealth—the world. We renounce all your spectacles, as strongly as we renounce the matters originating them, which we know were conceived of superstition; when we give up the very things which are the basis of their representations. Among us nothing is ever said, or seen, or heard, which has anything in common with the madness of the circus, the immodesty of the theatre, the atrocities of the arena, the useless exercises of the wrestling-ground. Why do you take offence at us because we differ from you in regard to your pleasures? If we will not partake of your enjoyments, the loss is ours, if there be loss in the case, not yours. We reject what pleases you. You, on the other hand, have no taste for what is our delight. The Epicureans were allowed by you to decide for themselves one true source of pleasure —I mean equanimity; the Christian, on his part, has many such enjoyments—what harm in that?

39. I shall at once go on, then, to exhibit the peculiarities of the Christian society, that, as I have refuted the evil charged against it, I may point out its positive good. We are a body knit together as such by a common religious profession, by unity of discipline, and by the bond of a common hope. We meet together as an assembly and congregation, that, offering up prayer to God as with united force, we may wrestle with Him in our supplications. This violence God delights in. We pray, too, for the emperors, for their ministers and for all in authority, for the welfare of the world, for the prevalence of peace, for the delay of the final consummation. We assemble to read our sacred writings, if any peculiarity of the times makes either fore-warning or reminiscence needful. However it be in that respect with the sacred words, we nourish our faith, we animate our hope, we make our confidence more stedfast; and no less by inculcations of God's precepts we confirm good habits. In the same place also exhortations are made, rebukes and sacred censures are administered. For with a great gravity is the

work of judging carried on among us, as befits those who feel assured that they are in the sight of God; and you have the most notable example of judgment to come when any one has sinned so grievously as to require his severance from us in prayer, and the meeting, and all sacred intercourse. The tried men of our elders preside over us, obtaining that honour not by purchase, but by established character. There is no buying and selling of any sort in the things of God. Though we have our treasure-chest, it is not made up of purchase-money, as of a religion that has its price. On the monthly collection day, if he likes, each puts in a small donation; but only if it be his pleasure, and only if he be able: for there is no compulsion; all is voluntary. These gifts are, as it were, piety's deposit fund. For they are not taken thence and spent on feasts, and drinking-bouts, and eating-houses, but to support and bury poor people, to supply the wants of boys and girls destitute of means and parents, and of old persons confined now to the house; such, too, as have suffered shipwreck; and if there happen to be any in the mines, or banished to the islands, or shut up in the prisons, for nothing but their fidelity to the cause of God's church, they become the nurslings of their confession. But it is mainly the deeds of a love so noble that lead many to put a brand upon us. See, they say, how they love one another, for themselves are animated by mutual hatred; how they are ready even to die for one another, for they themselves will sooner put to death. And they are wroth with us, too, because we call each other brethren; for no other reason, as I think, than because among themselves names of consanguinity are assumed in mere pretence of affection. But we are your brethren as well, by the law of our common mother nature, though you are hardly men, because brothers so unkind. At the same time, how much more fittingly they are called and counted brothers who have been led to the knowledge of God as their common Father, who have drunk in one spirit of holiness, who from the same womb of a common ignorance have agonized into the same light of truth! But on this very account, perhaps, we are regarded as having less claim to be held true brothers, that no tragedy makes a noise about our brotherhood, or that the family possessions, which generally destroy brotherhood among you, create fraternal bonds among us. One in mind and soul, we do not hesitate to share our earthly goods with one another. All things are common among us but our wives. We give up our community where it is practised alone by others, who not only take possession of the wives of their friends, but most tolerantly also accommodate their friends with theirs, following the example, I believe, of those wise men of ancient times, the Greek Socrates and the Roman Cato, who shared with their friends the wives whom they had married, it seems for the sake of progeny both to themselves and to others; whether in this acting against their partners' wishes, I am not able to say. Why should they have any care over their chastity, when their husbands so readily bestowed it away? O noble example of Attic wisdom, of Roman gravity!—the philosopher and the censor playing pimps! What wonder if that great love of Christians towards one another is desecrated by you! For you abuse also our humble feasts, on the ground that they are extravagant as well as infamously wicked. To us, it seems, applies the saying of Diogenes: "The people of Megara feast as though they were going to die on the morrow; they build as though they were never to die!" But one sees more readily the mote in another's eye than the beam in his own. Why, the very air is soured with the eructations of so many tribes, and curiæ, and decuriae; the Salii cannot have their feast without going into debt; you must get the accountants to tell you what the tenths of Hercules and the sacrificial banquets cost; the choicest cook is appointed for the Apaturia, the Dionysia, the Attic mysteries; the smoke from the banquet of Serapis will call out the firemen. Yet about the modest supper-room of the Christians alone a great ado is made. Our feast explains itself by its name. The Greeks call it love. Whatever it costs, our outlay in the name of piety is gain, since with the good things of the feast we benefit the needy; not as it is with you, do parasites aspire to the glory of satisfying their licentious propensities, selling themselves for a belly-feast to all disgraceful treatment,—but as it is with God Himself, a peculiar respect is shown to the lowly. If the object of our feast be good, in the light of that consider its further regulations. As it is an act of religious service, it permits no vileness or immodesty. The participants, before reclining, taste first of prayer to God. As much is eaten as satisfies the cravings of hunger; as much is drunk as befits the chaste. They say it is enough, as those who remember that even during the night they have to worship God; they talk as those who know that the Lord is one of their auditors. After manual ablution, and the bringing in of lights, each is asked to stand forth and sing, as he can, a hymn to God, either one from the holy Scriptures or one of his own composing,—a proof of the measure of our drinking. As the feast commenced with prayer, so with prayer it is closed. We go from it, not like troops of mischief-doers, nor bands of roamers, nor to break out into licentious acts, but to have as much care of our modesty and chastity as if we had been at a school of virtue rather than a banquet. Give the meeting of the Christians its due, and hold it unlawful, if it is like assemblies of the illicit sort: by all means let it be condemned, if any complaint can be validly laid against it, such as lies against secret factions. But who has ever suffered harm from our assemblies? We are in our meetings just what we are when separated from each other; we are as a community what we are as individuals; we injure nobody, we trouble nobody. When the upright, when the virtuous meet together, when the pious, when the pure assemble in congregation, you ought not to call that a faction, but a *curia*—a sacred meeting.

40. On the contrary, *they* deserve the name of faction who conspire to bring odium on good men and virtuous, who cry out against innocent blood, offering as the justification of their enmity the baseless plea, that they think the Christians the cause of every public disaster, of every affliction with which the people are visited. If the Tiber rises as high as the city walls, if the Nile does not send its waters up over

the fields, if the heavens give no rain, if there is an earthquake, if there is famine or pestilence, straightway the cry is, "Away with the Christians to the lion!" What! shall you give such multitudes to a single beast? Pray, tell me how many calamities befell the world and particular cities before Tiberius reigned—before the coming, that is, of Christ? We read of the islands of Hiera, and Anaphe, and Delos, and Rhodes, and Cos, with many thousands of human beings, having been swallowed up. Plato informs us that a region larger than Asia or Africa was seized by the Atlantic Ocean. An earthquake, too, drank up the Corinthian sea; and the force of the waves cut off a part of Lucania, whence it obtained the name of Sicily. These things surely could not have taken place without the inhabitants suffering by them. But where—I do not say were Christians, those despisers of your gods—but where were your gods themselves in those days, when the flood poured its destroying waters over all the world, or, as Plato thought, merely the level portion of it? For that they are of later date than that calamity, the very cities in which they were born and died, nay, which they founded, bear ample testimony; for the cities could have no existence at this day unless as belonging to postdiluvian times. Palestine had not yet received from Egypt its Jewish swarm [of emigrants], nor had the race from which Christians sprung yet settled down there, when its neighbours Sodom and Gomorrha were consumed by fire from heaven. The country yet smells of that conflagration; and if there are apples there upon the trees, it is only a promise to the eye they give—you but touch them, and they turn to ashes. Nor had Tuscia and Campania to complain of Christians in the days when fire from heaven overwhelmed Vulsinii, and Pompeii was destroyed by fire from its own mountain. No one yet worshipped the true God at Rome, when Hannibal at Cannæ counted the Roman slain by the pecks of Roman rings. Your gods were all objects of adoration, universally acknowledged, when the Senones closely besieged the very Capitol. And it is in keeping with all this, that if adversity has at any time befallen cities, the temples and the walls have equally shared in the disaster, so that it is clear to demonstration the thing was not the doing of the gods, seeing it also overtook themselves. The truth is, the human race has always deserved ill at God's hand. First of all, as undutiful to Him, because when it knew Him in part, it not only did not seek after Him, but even invented other gods of its own to worship; and further, because, as the result of their willing ignorance of the Teacher of righteousness, the Judge and Avenger of sin, all vices and crimes grew and flourished. But had men sought, they would have come to know the glorious object of their seeking; and knowledge would have produced obedience, and obedience would have found a gracious instead of an angry God. They ought then to see that the very same God is angry with them now as in ancient times, before Christians were so much as spoken of. It was *His* blessings they enjoyed—created before they made any of their deities: and why can they not take it in, that their evils come from the Being whose goodness they have failed to recognise? They suffer at the hands of Him to whom they have been ungrateful. And, for all that is said, if we compare the calamities of former times, they fall on us more lightly now, since God gave Christians to the world. For from that time virtue put some restraint on the world's wickedness, and men began to pray for the averting of God's wrath. In a word, when the summer clouds give no rain, and the season is matter of anxiety, you indeed—full of feasting day by day, and ever eager for the banquet, baths and taverns and brothels always busy—offer up to Jupiter your rain-sacrifices, you enjoin on the people barefoot processions, you seek heaven at the Capitol, you look up to the temple-ceilings for the longed-for clouds—God and heaven not in all your thoughts: we, dried up with fastings, and our passions bound tightly up, holding back as long as possible from all the ordinary enjoyments of life, rolling in sackcloth and ashes, assail heaven with our importunities—touch God's heart—and when we have extorted divine compassion, why, Jupiter gets all the honour!

41. You, therefore, are the sources of trouble in human

affairs; on you lies the blame of public adversities, since you
are ever attracting them—you by whom God is despised and
images are worshipped. It should surely seem the more
natural thing to believe that it is the neglected One who
is angry, and not they to whom all homage is paid; or
most unjustly they act, if, on account of the Christians,
they send trouble on their own devotees, whom they are
bound to keep clear of the punishments of Christians. But
this, you say, hits your God as well, since He permits His
worshippers to suffer on account of those who dishonour
Him. But admit first of all His providential arrangings,
and you will not make this retort. For He who once for all
appointed an eternal judgment at the world's close, does not
precipitate the separation, which is essential to judgment,
before the end. Meanwhile He deals with all sorts of men
alike, so that all together share His favours and reproofs.
His will is, that outcasts and elect should have adversities
and prosperities in common, that we should have all the same
experience of His goodness and severity. Having learned
these things from His own lips, we love His goodness, we
fear His wrath, while both by you are treated with contempt;
and hence the sufferings of life, so far as it is our lot to be
overtaken by them, are in our case gracious admonitions,
while in yours they are divine punishments. We indeed are
not the least put about: for, first, only one thing in this life
greatly concerns us, and that is, to get quickly out of it; and
next, if any adversity befalls us, it is laid to the door of your
transgressions. Nay, though we are likewise involved in
troubles because of our close connection with you, we are
rather glad of it, because we recognise in it divine foretell-
ings, which, in fact, go to confirm the confidence and faith
of our hope. But if all the evils you endure are inflicted on
you by the gods you worship out of spite to us, why do you
continue to pay homage to beings so ungrateful, so unjust,
who, instead of being angry with you, should rather have
been aiding and abetting you by persecuting Christians—
keeping *you* clear of their sufferings?

42. But we are called to account as harm-doers on another

ground, and are accused of being useless in the affairs of life. How in all the world can that be the case with people who are living among you, eating the same food, wearing the same attire, having the same habits, under the same necessities of existence? We are not Indian Brahmins or Gymnosophists, who dwell in woods and exile themselves from ordinary human life. We do not forget the debt of gratitude we owe to God our Lord and Creator; we reject no creature of His hands, though certainly we exercise restraint upon ourselves, lest of any gift of His we make an immoderate or sinful use. So we sojourn with you in the world, abjuring neither forum, nor shambles, nor bath, nor booth, nor workshop, nor inn, nor weekly market, nor any other places of commerce. We sail with you, and fight with you, and till the ground with you; and in like manner we unite with you in your traffickings—even in the various arts we make public property of our works for your benefit. How it is we seem useless in your ordinary business, living with you and by you as we do, I am not able to understand. But if I do not frequent your religious ceremonies, I am still on the sacred day a man. I do not at the Saturnalia bathe myself at dawn, that I may not lose both day and night; yet I bathe at a decent and healthful hour, which preserves me both in heat and blood. I can be rigid and pallid like you after ablution when I am dead. I do not recline in public at the feast of Bacchus, after the manner of the beast-fighters at their final banquet. Yet of your resources I partake, *wherever* I may chance to eat. I do not buy a crown for my head. What matters it to you how I use them, if nevertheless the flowers are purchased? I think it more agreeable to have them free and loose, waving all about. Even if they are woven into a crown, we smell the crown with our nostrils: let those look to it who scent the perfume with their hair. We do not go to your spectacles; yet the articles that are sold there, if I need them, I will obtain more readily at their proper places. We certainly buy no frankincense. If the Arabias complain of this, let the Sabæans be well assured that their more precious and costly merchandise is expended as largely in the burying of Christians as in the fumigating of the gods. At any rate, you say, the temple revenues are every day falling off: how few now throw in a contribution! In truth, we are not able to give alms both to your human and your heavenly mendicants; nor do we think that we are required to give any but to those who ask for it. Let Jupiter then hold out his hand and get, for our compassion spends more in the streets than yours does in the temples. But your other taxes will acknowledge a debt of gratitude to Christians; for in the faithfulness which keeps us from fraud upon a brother, we make conscience of paying all their dues: so that, by ascertaining how much is lost by fraud and falsehood in the census declarations—the calculation may easily be made—it would be seen that the ground of complaint in one department of revenue is compensated by the advantages which others derive.

43. I will confess, however, without hesitation, that there are some who in a sense may complain of Christians that they are a sterile race: as, for instance, pimps, and panders, and bath-suppliers; assassins, and poisoners, and sorcerers; soothsayers, too, diviners, and astrologers. But it is a noble fruit of Christians, that they have no fruits for such as these. And yet, whatever loss your interests suffer from the religion we profess, the protection you have from us makes amply up for it. What value do you set on persons, I do not here urge who deliver you from demons, I do not urge who for your sakes present prayers before the throne of the true God, for perhaps you have no belief in that—but from whom you can have nothing to fear?

44. Yes, and no one considers what the loss is to the common weal,—a loss as great as it is real, no one estimates the injury entailed upon the state, when, men of virtue as we are, we are put to death in such numbers, when so many of the truly good suffer the last penalty. And here we call your own acts to witness, you who are daily presiding at the trials of prisoners, and passing sentence upon crimes. Well, in your long lists of those accused of many and various atrocities, has any assassin, any cutpurse, any

man guilty of sacrilege, or seduction, or stealing bathers' clothes, his name entered as being a Christian too? Or when Christians are brought before you on the mere ground of their name, is there ever found among them an ill-doer of the sort? It is always with your folk the prison is steaming, the mines are sighing, the wild beasts are fed: it is from you the exhibitors of gladiatorial shows always get their herds of criminals to feed up for the occasion. You find no Christian there, except simply as being such; or if one is there as something else, a Christian he is no longer.

45. We, then, alone are without crime. Is there ought wonderful in that, if it be a very necessity with us? For a necessity indeed it is. Taught of God Himself what goodness is, we have both a perfect knowledge of it as revealed to us by a perfect Master; and faithfully we do His will, as enjoined on us by a Judge we dare not despise. But your ideas of virtue you have got from mere human opinion; on human authority, too, its obligation rests: hence your system of practical morality is deficient, both in the fulness and authority requisite to produce a life of real virtue. Man's wisdom to point out what is good, is no greater than his authority to exact the keeping of it; the one is as easily deceived as the other is despised. And so, which is the ampler rule, to say, "Thou shalt not kill," or to teach, "Be not even angry?" Which is more perfect, to forbid adultery, or to restrain from even a single lustful look? Which indicates the higher intelligence, interdicting evil-doing, or evil-speaking? Which is more thorough, not allowing an injury, or not even suffering an injury done to you to be repaid? Though withal you know that these very laws also of yours, which seem to lead to virtue, have been borrowed from the law of God as the ancient model. Of the age of Moses we have already spoken. But what is the real authority of human laws, when it is in man's power both to evade them, by generally managing to hide himself out of sight in his crimes, and to despise them sometimes, if inclination or necessity leads him to offend? Think of these things, too, in the light of the brevity of any

punishment you can inflict—never to last longer than till death. On this ground Epicurus makes light of all suffering and pain, maintaining that if it is small, it is contemptible; and if it is great, it is not long-continued. No doubt about it, we, who receive our awards under the judgment of an all-seeing God, and who look forward to eternal punishment from Him for sin,—we alone make real effort to attain a blameless life, under the influence of our ampler knowledge, and the impossibility of concealment, and the greatness of the threatened torment, not merely long-enduring, but everlasting, fearing Him, whom he too should fear who the fearing judges,—fearing God, I mean, and not the proconsul.

46. We have sufficiently met, as I think, the accusation of the various crimes on the ground of which these fierce demands are made for Christian blood. We have made a full exhibition of our case; and we have shown you how we are able to prove that our statement is correct, from the trustworthiness, I mean, and antiquity of our sacred writings, from the confession likewise of the powers of spiritual wickedness themselves. Who will venture to undertake our refutation, not with skill of words, but, as we have managed our demonstration, on the basis of reality? But while the truth we hold is made clear to all, unbelief meanwhile, at the very time it is convinced of the worth of Christianity, which has now become well known for its benefits as well as from the intercourse of life, takes up the notion that it is not really a thing divine, but rather a kind of philosophy. These are the very things, it says, the philosophers counsel and profess—innocence, justice, patience, sobriety, chastity. Why, then, are we not permitted an equal liberty and impunity for our doctrines as they have, with whom, in respect of what we teach, we are compared? or why are not they, as so like us, not pressed to the same offices for declining which our lives are imperilled? For who compels a philosopher to sacrifice or take an oath, or put out useless lamps at midday? Nay, they openly overthrow your gods, and in their writings they attack your superstitions; and you applaud them for it. Many of them even, with your countenance,

bark out against your rulers, and they are rewarded with statues and salaries, instead of being given to the wild beasts. And very right it should be so. For they are called philosophers, not Christians. This name of philosopher has no power to put demons to the rout. Why are they not able to do that too? since philosophers count demons inferior to gods. Socrates used to say, "If the demon grant permission." Yet he, too, though in denying the existence of your divinities he had a glimpse of the truth, at his dying ordered a cock to be sacrificed to Æsculapius, I believe in honour of his father, for Apollo pronounced Socrates the wisest of men. Thoughtless Apollo! testifying to the wisdom of the man who denied the existence of his race. In proportion to the enmity the truth awakens, you give offence by faithfully standing by it; but the man who corrupts and makes a mere pretence of it, precisely on this ground gains favour with its persecutors. The truth which philosophers, these mockers and corrupters of it, with hostile ends merely affect to hold, and in doing so deprave, caring for nought but glory, Christians both intensely and intimately long for and maintain in its integrity, as those who have a real concern about their salvation. So that we are like each other neither in our knowledge nor our ways, as you imagine. For what certain information did Thales, the first of natural philosophers, give in reply to the inquiry of Crœsus regarding Deity, the delay for further thought so often proving in vain? There is not a Christian workman but finds out God, and manifests Him, and hence assigns to Him all those attributes which go to constitute a divine being, though Plato affirms that it is far from easy to discover the Maker of the universe; and when He is found, it is difficult to make Him known to all. But if we challenge you to comparison in the virtue of chastity, I turn to a part of the sentence passed by the Athenians against Socrates, who was pronounced a corrupter of youth. The Christian confines himself to the female sex. I have read also how the harlot Phryne kindled in Diogenes the fires of lust, and how a certain Speusippus, of Plato's school, perished in the adulterous act. The Christian husband has nothing to do with any but his own wife. Democritus, in putting out his eyes, because he could not look on women without lusting after them, and was pained if his passion was not satisfied, owns plainly, by the punishment he inflicts, his incontinence. But a Christian with grace-healed eyes is sightless in this matter; he is mentally blind against the assaults of passion. If I maintain our superior modesty of behaviour, there at once occurs to me Diogenes with filth-covered feet trampling on the proud couches of Plato, under the influence of another pride: the Christian does not even play the proud man to the pauper. If sobriety of spirit be the virtue in debate, why, there are Pythagoras at Thurii, and Zeno at Priene, ambitious of the supreme power: the Christian does not aspire to the ædileship. If equanimity be the contention, you have Lycurgus choosing death by self-starvation, because the Lacons had made some emendation of his laws: the Christian, even when he is condemned, gives thanks. If the comparison be made in regard to trustworthiness, Anaxagoras denied the deposit of his enemies: the Christian is noted for his fidelity even among those who are not of his religion. If the matter of sincerity is to be brought to trial, Aristotle basely thrust his friend Hermias from his place: the Christian does no harm even to his foe. With equal baseness does Aristotle play the sycophant to Alexander, instead of exercising his influence to keep him in the right way, and Plato allows himself to be bought by Dionysius for his belly's sake. Aristippus in the purple, with all his great show of gravity, gives way to extravagance; and Hippias is put to death laying plots against the state: no Christian ever attempted such a thing in behalf of his brethren, even when persecution was scattering them abroad with every atrocity. But it will be said that some of us, too, depart from the rules of our discipline. In that case, however, we count them no longer Christians; but the philosophers who do such things retain still the name and the honour of wisdom. So, then, where is there any likeness between the Christian and the philosopher? between the disciple of Greece and of heaven?

between the man whose object is fame, and whose object is life? between the talker and the doer? between the man who builds up and the man who pulls down? between the friend and the foe of error? between one who corrupts the truth, and one who restores and teaches it? between its thief and its custodier?

47. Unless I am utterly mistaken, there is nothing so old as the truth; and the already proved antiquity of the divine writings is so far of use to me, that it leads men more easily to take it in that they are the treasure-source whence all later wisdom has been taken. And were it not necessary to keep my work to a moderate size, I might launch forth also into the proof of this. What poet or sophist has not drunk at the fountain of the prophets? Thence, accordingly, the philosophers watered their arid minds, so that it is the things they have from us which bring us into comparison with them. For this reason, I imagine, philosophy was banished by certain states—I mean by the Thebans, by the Spartans also, and the Argives—its disciples sought to imitate our doctrines; and ambitious, as I have said, of glory and eloquence alone, if they fell upon anything in the collection of sacred Scriptures which displeased them, in their own peculiar style of research, they perverted it to serve their purposes: for they had no adequate faith in their divinity to keep them from changing them, nor had they any sufficient understanding of them either, as being still at the time under veil—even obscure to the Jews themselves, whose peculiar possession they seemed to be. For so, too, if the truth was distinguished by its simplicity, the more on that account the fastidiousness of man, too proud to believe, set to altering it; so that even what they found certain they made uncertain by their admixtures. Finding a simple revelation of God, they proceeded to dispute about Him, not as He had been revealed to them, but turned aside to debate about His properties, His nature, His abode. Some assert Him to be incorporeal; others maintain He has a body,—the Platonists teaching the one doctrine, and the Stoics the other. Some think that He is composed of atoms,

others of numbers: such are the different views of Epicurus and Pythagoras. One thinks He is made of fire; so it appeared to Heraclitus. The Platonists, again, hold that He administers the affairs of the world; the Epicureans, on the contrary, that He is idle and inactive, and, so to speak, a nobody in human things. Then the Stoics represent Him as placed outside the world, and whirling round this huge mass from without like a potter; while the Platonists place Him within the world, as a pilot is in the ship he steers. So, in like manner, they differ in their views about the world itself, whether it is created or uncreated, whether it is destined to pass away or to remain for ever. So again it is debated concerning the nature of the soul, which some contend is divine and eternal, while others hold that it is dissoluble. According to each one's fancy, He has either introduced something new, or refashioned the old. Nor need we wonder if the speculations of philosophers have perverted the older Scriptures. Some of their brood, with their opinions, have even adulterated our new-given Christian revelation, and corrupted it into a system of philosophic doctrines, and from the one path have struck off many and inexplicable by-roads. And I have alluded to this, lest any one becoming acquainted with the variety of parties among us, this might seem to him to put us on a level with the philosophers, and he might condemn the truth from the different ways in which it is defended. But we at once put in a plea in bar against these tainters of our purity, asserting that that is the rule of truth which comes down from Christ by transmission through His companions, to whom we shall prove that those devisers of different doctrines are all posterior. Everything opposed to the truth has been got up from the truth itself, the spirits of error carrying on this system of opposition. By them all corruptions of wholesome discipline have been secretly instigated; by them, too, certain fables have been introduced, that, by their resemblance to the truth, they might impair its credibility, or vindicate their own higher claims to faith; so that people might think Christians unworthy of credit because the poets or philosophers are so, or might regard the poets and philosophers as worthier of confidence from their not being followers of Christ. Accordingly, we get ourselves laughed at for proclaiming that God will one day judge the world. For, like us, the poets and philosophers set up a judgment-seat in the realms below. And if we threaten Gehenna, which is a reservoir of secret fire under the earth for purposes of punishment, we have in the same way derision heaped on us. For so, too, they have their Pyriphlegethon, a river of flame in the regions of the dead. And if we speak of Paradise, the place of heavenly bliss appointed to receive the spirits of the saints, severed from the knowledge of this world by that fiery zone as by a sort of enclosure, the Elysian plains have taken possession of their faith. Whence is it, I pray you, that you have all this, so like us, in the poets and philosophers? The reason simply is, that they have been taken from our religion. But if they are taken from our sacred things, as being of earlier date, then ours are the truer, and have higher claims upon belief, since even their imitations find faith among you. If they maintain their sacred mysteries to have sprung from their own minds, in that case ours will be reflections of what are later than themselves, which by the nature of things is impossible. For never does the shadow precede the body which casts it, or the image the reality.

48. Come now, if some philosopher affirms, as Laberius holds, following an opinion of Pythagoras, that a man may have his origin from a mule, a serpent from a woman, and with skill of speech twists every argument to prove his view, will he not gain acceptance for it, and work in some the conviction that, on account of this, they should even abstain from eating animal food? May any one have the persuasion that he should so abstain, lest by chance in his beef he eats of some ancestor of his? But if a Christian promises the return of a man from a man, and the very actual Gaius from Gaius, the cry of the people will be to have him stoned; they will not even so much as grant him a hearing. If there is any ground for the moving to and fro of human souls into dif-

ferent bodies, why may they not return into the very substance they have left, seeing this is to be restored, to be that which had been? They are no longer the very things they had been; for they could not be what they were not, without first ceasing to be what they had been. If we were inclined to give all rein upon this point, discussing into what various beasts one and another might probably be changed, we would need at our leisure to take up many points. But this we would do chiefly in our own defence, as setting forth what is greatly worthier of belief, that a man will come back from a man, any given person from any given person, still retaining his humanity; so that the soul, with its qualities unchanged, may be restored to the same condition, though not to the same outward framework. Assuredly, as the reason why restoration takes place at all is the appointed judgment, every man must needs come forth the very same who had once existed, that he may receive at God's hands a judgment, whether of good desert or the opposite. And therefore the body too will appear; for the soul is not capable of suffering without the solid substance, that is, the flesh; and for this reason also, that it is not right that souls should have all the wrath of God to bear: they did not sin without the body, within which all was done by them. But how, you say, can a substance which has been dissolved be made to reappear again? Consider thyself, O man, and thou wilt believe in it! Reflect on what you were before you came into existence. Nothing. For if you had been anything, you would have remembered it. You, then, who were nothing before you existed, reduced to nothing also when you cease to be, why may you not come into being again out of nothing, at the will of the same Creator whose will created you out of nothing at the first? Will it be anything new in your case? You who were not, *were* made; when you cease to be again, you *shall* be made. Explain, if you can, your original creation, and then demand to know how you shall be re-created. Indeed, it will be still easier surely to make you what you were once, when the very same creative power made you without difficulty what you never were before. There will be doubts, perhaps, as to the power of God, of Him who hung in its place this huge body of our world, made out of what had never existed, as from a death of emptiness and inanity, animated by the Spirit who quickens all living things, its very self the unmistakeable type of the resurrection, that it might be to you a witness—nay, the exact image of the resurrection. Light, every day extinguished, shines out again; and, with like alternation, darkness succeeds light's outgoing. The defunct stars re-live; the seasons, as soon as they are finished, renew their course; the fruits are brought to maturity, and then are reproduced. The seeds do not spring up with abundant produce, save as they rot and dissolve away;—all things are preserved by perishing, all things are refashioned out of death. Thou, man, of nature so exalted, if thou understandest thyself, taught even by the Pythian[1] words, lord of all these things that die and rise,—shalt thou die to perish evermore? Wherever your dissolution shall have taken place, whatever material agent has destroyed you, or swallowed you up, or swept you away, or reduced you to nothingness, it shall again restore you. Even nothingness is His who is Lord of *all*. You ask, Shall we then be always dying, and rising up from death? If so the Lord of all things had appointed, you would have to submit, though unwillingly, to the law of your creation. But, in fact, He has no other purpose than that of which He has informed us. The reason which made the universe out of diverse elements, so that all things might be composed of opposite substances in unity—of void and solid, of animate and inanimate, of comprehensible and incomprehensible, of light and darkness, of life itself and death—has also disposed time into order, by fixing and distinguishing its mode, according to which this first portion of it, which we inhabit from the beginning of the world, flows down by a temporal course to a close; but the portion which succeeds, and to which we look forward, continues for ever. When, there-

[1] "Know thyself."

fore, the boundary and limit, that millennial interspace, has been passed, when even the outward fashion of the world itself—which has been spread like a veil over the eternal economy, equally a thing of time—passes away, then the whole human race shall be raised again, to have its dues meted out according as it has merited in the period of good or evil, and thereafter to have these paid out through the immeasurable ages of eternity. And therefore after this there is neither death nor repeated resurrections, but we shall be the same that we are now, and still unchanged—the servants of God, ever with God, clothed upon with the proper substance of eternity; but the profane, and all who are not true worshippers of God, in like manner consigned to the punishment of everlasting fire—that fire which, from its very nature indeed, directly ministers to their incorruptibility. The philosophers are familiar as well as we with the distinction between a common and a secret fire. Thus that which is in common use is far different from that which we see in divine judgments, whether striking as thunderbolts from heaven, or bursting up out of the earth through mountain-tops; for it does not consume what it scorches, but while it burns it repairs. So the mountains continue ever burning; and a person struck by lightning is even now kept safe from any destroying flame. A notable proof this of the fire eternal! a notable example of the endless judgment which still supplies punishment with fuel! The mountains burn, and last. How will it be with the wicked and the enemies of God?

49. These are what are called presumptuous speculations in our case alone; in the philosophers and poets they are regarded as sublime speculations and illustrious discoveries. They are men of wisdom, we are fools. They are worthy of all honour, we are folk to have the finger pointed at; nay, besides that, we are even to have punishments inflicted on us. But let things which are the defence of virtue, if you will, have no foundation, and give them duly the name of fancies, yet still they are necessary; let them be absurd if you will,

yet they are of use: they make all who believe them better men and women, under the fear of never-ending punishment and the hope of never-ending bliss. It is not, then, wise to brand as false, nor to regard as absurd, things the truth of which it is expedient to presume. On no ground is it right positively to condemn as bad what beyond all doubt is profitable. Thus, in fact, you are guilty of the very presumption of which you accuse us, in condemning what is useful. It is equally out of the question to regard them as nonsensical; at any rate, if they are false and foolish, they hurt nobody. For they are just (in that case) like many other things on which you inflict no penalties—foolish and fabulous things, I mean, which, as quite innocuous, are never charged as crimes or punished. But in a thing of the kind, if this be so indeed, we should be adjudged to ridicule, not to swords, and flames, and crosses, and wild beasts, in which iniquitous cruelty not only the blinded populace exults and insults over us, but in which some of you too glory, not scrupling to gain the popular favour by your injustice. As though all you can do to us, did not depend upon our pleasure. It is assuredly a matter of my own inclination being a Christian. Your condemnation, then, will only reach me in that case, if I wish to be condemned; but when all you can do to me, you can do only at my will, all you can do is dependent on my will, and is not in your power. The joy of the people in our trouble is therefore utterly reasonless. For it is our joy they appropriate to themselves, since we would far rather be condemned than apostatize from God; on the contrary, our haters should be sorry rather than rejoice, as we have obtained the very thing of our own choice.

50. In that case, you say, why do you complain of our persecutions? You ought rather to be grateful to us for giving you the sufferings you want. Well, it is quite true that it is our desire to suffer, but it is in the way that the soldier longs for war. No one indeed suffers willingly, since suffering necessarily implies fear and danger. Yet the man who objected to the conflict, both fights with all his strength, and

when victorious, he rejoices in the battle, because he reaps from it glory and spoil. It is our battle to be summoned to your tribunals, that there, under fear of execution, we may battle for the truth. But the day is won when the object of the struggle is gained. This victory of ours gives us the glory of pleasing God, and the spoil of life eternal. But we are overcome. Yes, when we have obtained our wishes. Therefore we conquer in dying; we go forth victorious at the very time we are subdued. Call us, if you like, *Sarmenticii* and *Semaxii*, because, bound to a half-axle stake, we are burned in a circle-heap of fagots. This is the attitude in which we conquer, it is our victory-robe, it is for us a sort of triumphal car. Naturally enough, therefore, we do not please the vanquished; on account of this, indeed, we are counted a desperate, reckless race. But the very desperation and recklessness you object to in us, among yourselves lift high the standard of virtue in the cause of glory and of fame. Mucius of his own will left his right hand on the altar: what sublimity of mind! Empedocles gave his whole body at Catana to the fires of Ætna: what mental resolution! A certain foundress of Carthage gave herself away in second marriage to the funeral pile: what a noble witness of her chastity! Regulus, not wishing that his one life should count for the lives of many enemies, endured these crosses over all his frame: how brave a man—even in captivity a conqueror! Anaxarchus, when he was being beaten to death by a barley-pounder, cried out, "Beat on, beat on at the case of Anaxarchus; no stroke falls on Anaxarchus himself." O magnanimity of the philosopher, who even in such an end had jokes upon his lips! I omit all reference to those who with their own sword, or with any other milder form of death, have bargained for glory. Nay, see how even torture contests are crowned by you. The Athenian courtezan, having wearied out the executioner, at last bit off her tongue and spat it in the face of the raging tyrant, that she might at the same time spit away her power of speech, nor be longer able to confess her fellow-conspirators, if even overcome, that might be her inclination. Zeno the Eleatic, when he was asked by Dionysius what good philosophy did, on answering that it gave contempt of death, was, all unquailing, given over to the tyrant's scourge, and sealed his opinion even to the death. We all know how the Spartan lash, applied with the utmost cruelty under the very eyes of friends encouraging, confers on those who bear it honour proportionate to the blood which the young men shed. O glory legitimate, because it is human, for whose sake it is counted neither reckless foolhardiness, nor desperate obstinacy, to despise death itself and all sorts of savage treatment, for whose sake you may for your native place, for the empire, for friendship, endure all you are forbidden to do for God! And you cast statues in honour of persons such as these, and you put inscriptions upon images, and cut out epitaphs on tombs, that their names may never perish. In so far as you can by your monuments, you yourselves afford a sort of resurrection to the dead. Yet he who expects the true resurrection from God, is insane if for God he suffers! But go zealously on, good presidents, you will stand higher with the people if you sacrifice the Christians at their wish, kill us, torture us, condemn us, grind us to dust; your injustice is the proof that we are innocent. Therefore it is of God's permitting, [not of your mere will,] that we thus suffer. For but very lately, in condemning a Christian woman to the pimp rather than to the lion, you made confession that a taint on our purity is considered among us something more terrible than any punishment and any death. Nor does your cruelty, however exquisite, avail you; it is rather a temptation to us. The oftener we are mown down by you, the more in number we grow; the blood of Christians is seed. Many of your writers exhort to the courageous bearing of pain and death, as Cicero in the *Tusculans*, as Seneca in his *Chances*, as Diogenes, Pyrrhus, Callinicus. And yet their words do not find so many disciples as Christians do, teachers not by words, but by their deeds. That very obstinacy you rail against is the preceptress. For who that contemplates it, is not excited to inquire what is at the bottom of it? who, after inquiry, does not embrace our doctrines? and when he has embraced them, desires not to suffer that he may become partaker of the fulness of God's grace, that he may obtain from God complete forgiveness, by giving in exchange his blood? For that secures the remission of all offences. On this account it is that we return thanks on the very spot for your sentences. As the divine and human are ever opposed to each other, when we are condemned by you, we are acquitted by the Highest.

VI.

ON IDOLATRY.

CHAP. I.—*Wide scope of the word "Idolatry."*

THE principal crime of the human race, the highest guilt charged upon the world, the whole procuring cause of judgment, is idolatry. For, although each single fault retains its own proper feature, although it is destined to judgment under its own proper name also, yet it is marked off under the [general] count of idolatry. Set aside names, examine works, the idolater is likewise a murderer. Do you inquire whom he has slain? If it contributes ought to the aggravation of the indictment, no stranger nor personal enemy, but his own self. By what snares? Those of his error. By what weapon? The offence done to God. By how many blows? As many as are his idolatries. He who affirms that the idolater *perishes not*,[1] will affirm that the idolater has not committed murder. Further, you may recognise in the same crime[2] *adultery* and *fornication;* for he who serves false gods is doubtless an *adulterer*[3] of truth, because all falsehood is adultery. So, too, he is sunk in fornication. For who that is a fellow-worker with unclean spirits, does not stalk in general pollution

---

[1] Lit., "has not perished," as if the perishing were already complete; as, of course, it is *judicially*, as soon as the guilt is incurred, though not *actually*.

[2] *i.e.* in idolatry.

[3] A play on the word: we should say, "an *adulterator*."

and fornication? And thus it is that the Holy Scriptures[1] use the designation of fornication in their upbraiding of idolatry. The essence of *fraud*, I take it, is, that any should seize what is another's, or refuse to another his due; and, of course, fraud done toward *man* is a name of greatest crime. Well, but idolatry does fraud to God, by refusing to Him, and conferring on others, His honours; so that to fraud it also conjoins *contumely*. But if fraud, just as much as fornication and adultery, entails death, then, in these cases, equally with the former, idolatry stands unacquitted of the impeachment of murder. After such crimes, so pernicious, so devouring of salvation, all other crimes also, after some manner, and separately disposed in order, find their own essence represented in idolatry. In it also are the *concupiscences* of the world. For what solemnity of idolatry is without the circumstance of dress and ornament? In it are *lasciviousnesses* and *drunkennesses*; since it is, for the most part, for the sake of food, and stomach, and appetite, that these solemnities are frequented. In it is *unrighteousness*. For what more unrighteous than it, which knows not the Father of righteousness? In it also is *vanity*, since its whole system is vain. In it is *mendacity*, for its whole substance is false. Thus it comes to pass, that in idolatry all crimes are detected, and in all crimes idolatry. But even otherwise, since all faults savour of opposition to God, but there is nothing which savours of opposition to God which is not assigned to demons and unclean spirits, whose property idols are; doubtless, whoever commits a fault is chargeable with idolatry, for he does that which pertains to the proprietors of idols.

CHAP. II.—*Idolatry considered in its more limited sense. Its copiousness.*

But let the universal names of crimes withdraw to the specialities of their own works; let idolatry remain in that which it is itself. Sufficient to itself is a name so inimical to God, a substance of crime so copious, which reaches forth

[1] Oehler refers to Ezek. xxiii.; but many other references might be given—in the Pentateuch and Psalms, for instance.

so many branches, diffuses so many veins, that from this [name], for the greatest part, is drawn the material of all the modes in which the expansiveness of idolatry has to be foreguarded against by us, since in manifold wise it subverts the servants of God; and this not only when unperceived, but also when cloaked over. Most men simply regard idolatry as to be interpreted in these senses alone, viz.: if one burn incense, or immolate [a victim], or give a sacrificial banquet, or be bound to some sacred functions or priesthoods; just as if one were to regard adultery as to be accounted in kisses, and in embraces, and in actual fleshly contact; or murder as to be reckoned only in the shedding forth of blood, and in the actual taking away of life. But how far wider an extent the Lord assigns to those crimes we are sure: when He defines adultery [to consist] even in concupiscence,[1] "if one shall have cast an eye lustfully on [a woman]," and stirred his soul with immodest commotion; when He judges murder[2] [to consist] even in a word of curse or of reproach, and in every impulse of anger, and in the neglect of charity toward a brother: just as John teaches,[3] that he who hates his brother is a murderer. Else, both the devil's ingenuity in malice, and God the Lord's in the Discipline by which He fortifies us against the devil's depths,[4] would have but limited scope, if we were judged only in such faults as even the heathen nations have decreed punishable. How will our "righteousness abound above that of the Scribes and Pharisees," as the Lord has prescribed,[5] unless we shall have seen through the abundance of that adversary quality, that is, of *un*righteousness? But if the head of unrighteousness is idolatry, the first point is, that we be fore-fortified against the abundance of idolatry, while we recognise it not only in its palpable manifestations.

CHAP. III.—*Idolatry: origin and meaning of the name.*

Idol in ancient times there was none. Before the artificers of this monstrosity had bubbled into being,[6] temples stood

[1] Matt. v. 28.   [2] Matt. v. 22.   [3] 1 John iii. 15.   [4] Rev. ii. 24.
[5] Matt. v. 20.   [6] "Boiled out," "bubbled out."

solitary and shrines empty, just as to the present day in some places traces of the ancient practice remain permanently. Yet idolatry used to be practised, not under that name, but in that function; for even at this day it can be practised outside a temple, and without an idol. But when the devil introduced into the world artificers of statues and of images, and of every kind of likenesses, that former rude business of human disaster attained from idols both a name and a development. Thenceforward every art which in any way produces an idol instantly became a fount of idolatry. For it makes no difference whether a moulder cast, or a carver grave, or an embroiderer weave [the idol]; because neither is it a question of material, whether an idol be formed of gypsum, or of colours, or of stone, or of bronze,[1] or of silver, or of thread. For since even without an idol idolatry is committed, when the idol is there it makes no difference of what kind it be, of what material, of what shape; lest any should think *that* only to be held an idol which is consecrated in human shape. To establish this point, the interpretation of the word is requisite. " Eidŏs," in Greek, signifies " form ;" " eidōlŏn," derived diminutively from that, by an equivalent process in our language, makes " formling."[2] Every " form" or " formling," therefore, claims to be called an "idol." Hence "idolatry" is "all attendance and service about every idol." Hence also, every artificer of an idol is guilty of one and the same crime,[3] unless the People which consecrated for itself the likeness of a calf, and not of a man, fell short of incurring the guilt of idolatry.[4]

CHAP. IV.—*Idols not to be made, much less worshipped. Idols and idol-makers in the same category.*

God prohibits an idol as much to be *made* as to be *worshipped*. In so far as the *making* what may be worshipped is the prior act, so far is the prohibition to *make* (if the worship is unlawful) the prior prohibition. For this cause—the eradi-

---

[1] Or, "brass."   [2] *i.e.* "a little form."   [3] Idolatry, namely.
[4] See Ex. xxxii.; and compare 1 Cor. x. 7, where the latter part of Ex. xxxii. 6 is quoted.

cating, namely, of the material of idolatry—the divine law proclaims, "Thou shalt make no idol;"[1] and by conjoining, "Nor a similitude of the things which are in the heaven, and which are in the earth, and which are in the sea," has interdicted the servants of God from acts of that kind all the universe over. Enoch had preceded, predicting that "the demons, and the spirits of the angelic apostates,[2] would turn into idolatry all the elements, all the garniture of the universe, all things contained in the heaven, in the sea, in the earth, that they might be consecrated as God, in opposition to God." All things, therefore, does human error worship, except the Founder of all Himself. The images of those things are idols; the consecration of the images is idolatry. Whatever guilt idolatry incurs, must necessarily be imputed to every artificer of every idol. In short, the same Enoch fore-condemns in general menace both idol-worshippers and [idol-]makers together. And again: "I swear to you, sinners, that against the day of perdition of blood[3] repentance is being prepared. Ye who serve stones, and ye who make images of gold, and silver, and wood, and stones and clay, and serve phantoms, and demons, and spirits in fanes,[4] and all errors not according to knowledge, shall find no help from them." But Isaiah[5] says, "Ye are witnesses whether there is a God except Me." "And they who mould and carve out at that time were not: all vain! who do that which liketh them,

[1] Lev. xxvi. 1; Ex. xx. 4; Deut. v. 8. It must of course be borne in mind that Tertullian has defined the meaning of the word "idol" in the former chapter, and speaks with reference to that definition.

[2] Compare de Oratione, c. 23, and de Virg. Vel. c. 7.

[3] "Sanguinis perditionis:" such is the reading of Oehler and others. If it be correct, probably the phrase "perdition of blood" must be taken as equivalent to "bloody perdition," after the Hebrew fashion. Compare, for similar instances, 2 Sam. xvi. 7, Ps. v. 6, xxvi. 9, lv. 23, Ezek. xxii. 2, with the marginal readings. But Fr. Junius would read, "Of blood *and* of perdition"—sanguinis et perditionis. Oehler's own interpretation of the reading he gives—"blood-shedding"—appears unsatisfactory.

[4] "In fanis." This is Oehler's reading on conjecture. Other readings are—infamis, infamibus, insanis, infernis.

[5] Isa. xliv. 8 et seqq.

which shall not profit them!" And that whole ensuing discourse sets a ban as well on the artificers as the worshippers: the close of which is, "Learn that their heart is ashes and earth, and that none can free his own soul." In which sentence David equally includes the makers too. "Such," says he, "let them become who make them."[1] And why should I, a man of limited memory, suggest anything further? Why recall anything more from the Scriptures? As if either the voice of the Holy Spirit were not sufficient; or else any further deliberation were needful, whether the Lord cursed and condemned by priority the *artificers* of those things, of which He curses and condemns the *worshippers!*

CHAP. V.[2]—*The plea, "I have no other livelihood," answered; and sundry objections or excuses dealt with.*

We will certainly take more pains in answering the excuses of artificers of this kind, who ought never to be admitted into the house of God, if any have a knowledge of that Discipline.[3] To begin with, that speech, wont to be cast in our teeth, "I have nothing else whereby to live," may be more severely retorted, "You have, then, whereby to live? If by your own laws, what have you to do with God?"[4] Then, as to the argument they have the hardihood to bring even from the Scriptures, "that the apostle has said, 'As each has been found, so let him persevere.'"[5] We may all,

[1] Ps. cxv. 8. In our version, "They that make them are like unto them." Tertullian again agrees with the LXX.

[2] Cf. chaps. viii. and xii.

[3] *i.e.* the Discipline of the house of God, the Church. Oehler reads, "*eam* disciplinam," and takes the meaning to be, that no artificer of this class should be admitted into the Church, if he applies for admittance, with a knowledge of the law of God referred to in the former chapters, yet persisting in his unlawful craft. Fr. Junius would read, "*ejus* disciplinam."

[4] *i.e.*, If laws of your own, and not the will and law of God, are the source and means of your life, you owe no thanks and no obedience to God, and therefore need not to seek admittance into His house (Oehler).

[5] 1 Cor. vii. 20. In Eng. ver., "Let every man abide in the same calling wherein he was called."

therefore, persevere in *sins*, as the result of *that* interpretation! for there is not any one of us who has not been found as a *sinner*, since no other cause was the source of Christ's descent than that of setting *sinners* free. Again, they say the same apostle has left a precept, according to his own example, "That each one work with his own hands for a living."[1] If this precept is maintained in respect to *all* hands, I believe even the bath-thieves[2] live by their hands, and robbers themselves gain the means to live by their hands; forgers, again, execute their evil handwritings, not of course with their feet, but hands; actors, however, achieve a livelihood not with hands alone, but with their entire limbs. Let the Church, therefore, stand open to *all* who are supported by their hands and by their own work; if there is no exception of arts which the Discipline of God receives not. But some one says, in opposition to our proposition of "similitude being interdicted," "Why, then, did Moses in the desert make a likeness of a serpent out of bronze?" The figures, which used to be laid as a groundwork for some secret future dispensation, not with a view to the repeal of the law, but as a type of their own final cause, stand in a class by themselves. Otherwise, if we should interpret these things as the adversaries of the law do, do we, too, as the Marcionites do, ascribe inconsistency to the Almighty, whom *they*[3] in this manner destroy as being mutable, while in one place He forbids, in another commands? But if any feigns ignorance of the fact that that effigy of the serpent of bronze, after the manner of one uphung, denoted the shape of the Lord's cross, which was to free us from serpents—that is, from the devil's angels—while, through itself, it hanged up the devil slain—or whatever other exposition of that figure has been revealed to worthier men, no matter, provided we remember the apostle affirms that all things happened at that time to

[1] 1 Thess. iv. 11; 2 Thess. iii. 6-12.
[2] *i.e.* thieves who frequented the public baths, which were a favourite resort at Rome.
[3] The Marcionites.

the People[1] *figuratively;*[2] it is enough that the same God, as by law He forbade the making of similitude, did, by the extraordinary precept in the case of the serpent, interdict similitude.[3] If you reverence the same God, you have His law, "Thou shalt make no similitude."[4] If you look back, too, to the precept enjoining the subsequently made similitude, do you, too, imitate Moses: make not any likeness in opposition to the law, unless to *you*, too, God have bidden it.

CHAP. VI.—*Idolatry condemned by Baptism. To* MAKE *an idol is, in fact, to* WORSHIP *it.*

If no law of God had prohibited idols to be made by us; if no voice of the Holy Spirit uttered general menace no less against the makers than the worshippers of idols; from our sacrament itself we would draw our interpretation that arts of that kind are opposed to the faith. For how have we *renounced* the devil and his angels, if we *make* them? What divorce have we declared from them, I say not *with* whom, but *dependent on* whom, we live? What discord have we entered into with those to whom we are under obligation for the sake of our maintenance? Can you have denied with the tongue what with the hand you confess? unmake by word what by deed you make? preach one God, you who make so many? preach the true God, you who make false ones? "I *make*," says one, "but I *worship* not;" as if there were some cause for which he dare not *worship*, besides that for which he ought not also to *make*,— the offence done to God, namely, in either case. Nay, you who *make*, that they may be able to be worshipped, *do*

---

[1] *i.e.* the *Jewish* people, who are generally meant by the expression "the People" in the singular number in Scripture. We shall endeavour to mark that distinction by writing the word, as here, with a capital.

[2] See 1 Cor. x. 6, 11.

[3] On the principle that the exception proves the rule. As Oehler explains it: "By the fact of the extraordinary precept in that particular case, God gave an indication that likeness-making had before been forbidden and interdicted by Him."

[4] Ex. xx. 4, etc.

worship; and you worship, not with the spirit of some worthless perfume, but with your own; nor at the expense of a beast's soul, but of your own. To them you immolate your ingenuity; to them you make your sweat a libation; to them you kindle the torch of your forethought. More are you to them than a priest, since it is by *your* means they *have* a priest; *your* diligence is *their* divinity.[1] Do you affirm that you *worship* not what you *make*? Ah! but *they* affirm not so, to whom you slay this fatter, more precious and greater victim, your salvation!

CHAP. VII.—*Grief of the faithful at the admission of idol-makers into the church; nay, even into the ministry.*

A whole day the zeal of faith will direct its pleadings to this quarter: bewailing that a Christian should come from idols into the Church; should come from an adversary workshop into the house of God; should raise to God the Father hands which are the mothers of idols; should pray to God with the hands which, out of doors, are prayed to in opposition to God; should apply to the Lord's body those hands which confer bodies on demons. Nor is this sufficient. Grant that it be a small matter, if from other hands they receive what they contaminate; but even those very hands deliver to others what they have contaminated. Idol-artificers are chosen even into the ecclesiastical order. Oh wickedness! Once did the Jews lay hands on Christ; these mangle His body daily. Oh hands to be cut off! Now let the saying, "If thy hand make thee do evil, amputate it,"[2] see to it whether it were uttered by way of similitude [merely]. What hands more to be amputated than those in which scandal is done to the Lord's body?

[1] *i.e.*, Unless you *made* them, they would not *exist*, and therefore would not be regarded as *divinities*; therefore your diligence gives them their divinity.

[2] Matt. xviii. 8.

CHAP. VIII.—*Other arts made subservient to idolatry. Means of gaining a livelihood abundant, without having recourse to unlawful ones.*

There are also other species of very many arts which, although they extend not to the *making* of idols, yet, with the same criminality, *furnish the adjuncts* without which idols have no power. For it matters not whether you erect or equip: if you have embellished his temple, or altar, or niche, if you have pressed out gold-leaf, or have wrought his insignia, or even his house: work of that kind, which confers not *shape*, but *authority*, is more important. If the necessity of maintenance[1] is urged so much, the arts have other species withal to afford means of livelihood, without outstepping the path of discipline, that is, without the confiction of an idol. The plasterer knows both how to mend roofs, and lay on stuccoes, and polish a cistern, and trace ogees, and draw in relief on party-walls many other ornaments beside likenesses. The painter, too, and the marble-mason, and the bronze-worker, and every graver whatever, knows expansions[2] of his own art, of course much easier of execution. For how much more easily does he who delineates a statue overlay a sideboard![3] How much sooner does he who carves a Mars out of a lime-tree, fasten together a chest! No art but is either mother or kinswoman of some neighbour[4] art: nothing is independent of its neighbour. The veins of the arts are many as are the concupiscences of men. "But there is difference in wages and the rewards of handicraft;" therefore there is difference, too, in the labour required. Smaller wages are compensated by more frequent earning. How many are the party-walls which require statues? How many the temples and shrines which are built for idols? But

---

[1] See chaps. v. and xii.
[2] See chap. ii., "The *expansiveness* of idolatry."
[3] Abacum. The word has various meanings; but this, perhaps, is its most general use: as, for instance, in Horace and Juvenal.
[4] Alterius = ἑτέρου, which in the New Testament is = to "neighbour" in Rom. xiii. 8, etc.

houses, and official residences, and baths, and tenements, how many are they? Shoe- and slipper-gilding is daily work; not so the gilding of Mercury and Serapis. Let that suffice for the gain[1] of handicrafts. Luxury and ostentation have more votaries than all superstition. Ostentation will require dishes and cups more easily than superstition. Luxury deals in wreaths, also, more than ceremony. When, therefore, we urge men generally to such kinds of handicrafts as do not come in contact with an idol indeed, and with the things which are appropriate to an idol; since, moreover, the things which are common to idols are often common to men too; of this also we ought to beware, that nothing be, with our knowledge, demanded by any person from our hands for idols' service. For if we shall have made that concession, and shall not have had recourse to the remedies so often used, I think we are not free of the contagion of idolatry, we whose (not unwitting) hands[2] are found busied in the tendence, or in the honour and service, of demons.

CHAP. IX.—PROFESSIONS *of some kinds allied to idolatry. Of astrology in particular.*

We observe among the arts[3] also some professions liable to the charge of idolatry. Of astrologers there should be no speaking even; [4] but since one in these days has challenged us, defending on his own behalf perseverance in that profession, I will use a few words. I allege not that he honours idols, whose names he has inscribed on the heaven,[5] to whom he has attributed all God's power; because men, presuming that we are disposed of by the immutable arbitrament of the stars, think on that account that God is not

[1] Quæstum. Another reading is "questum," which would require us to translate "plaint."
[2] "Quorum manus non ignorantium," *i.e.* "the hands of whom not unwitting;" which may be rendered as above, because in English, as in the Latin, the adjective "unwitting" belongs to the "whose," not to the "hands."
[3] "Ars" in Latin is very generally used to mean "a *scientific* art."
[4] See Eph. v. 11, 12, and similar passages.
[5] *i.e.* by naming the stars after them.

to be sought after. One proposition I lay down: that those angels, the deserters from God, the lovers of women,[1] were likewise the discoverers of this curious art, on that account also condemned by God. Oh divine sentence, reaching even unto earth in its vigour, whereto even the unwitting render testimony! The astrologers are being expelled just like their angels! The city and Italy are being interdicted to the astrologers, just as heaven to their angels![2] There is the same penalty of exclusion for disciples and masters! "But Magi and astrologers came from the east."[3] We know the mutual alliance of magic and astrology. The interpreters of the stars, then, were the first to announce Christ's birth, the first to present Him "gifts." By this bond, I imagine, they put Christ under obligation to themselves! What then? Shall therefore the religion of those Magi act as patron now also to astrologers? Astrology now-a-days, forsooth, treats of Christ—is the science of the stars of Christ; not of Saturn, or Mars, and whomsoever else out of the same class of the dead[4] it pays observance to and preaches! But however, that science has been allowed until the Gospel, in order that after Christ's birth no one should thenceforward interpret any one's nativity by the heaven. For they therefore offered to the then infant Lord that frankincense and myrrh and gold, to be, as it were, the close of worldly[5] sacrifice and glory, which Christ was about to do away. What, then, the dream—sent, doubtless, of the will of God—suggested to the same Magi (namely, that they should go home, but by another way, not that by which they came) is this: that they should not walk in their ancient path,[6] not that Herod should not pursue them, who in fact did not pursue them; unwitting even that they had departed *by another*

---

[1] Comp. chap. iv., and the references there given. The idea seems founded on an ancient reading (found in the Codex Alexandrinus of the LXX.) in Gen. vi. 2, "angels of God," for "sons of God."

[2] See Tac. *Ann.* ii. 31, etc. (Oehler.)   [3] See Matt. ii.

[4] Because the names of the heathen divinities, which used to be given to the stars, were in many cases only names of dead men deified.

[5] Or, heathenish.   [6] Or, sect.

way, since he was withal unwitting by what way they *came*. Just so we ought to understand by it the right Way and Discipline. And so the precept was rather, that thenceforward they should *walk otherwise*. So, too, that other species of magic which operates by miracles, emulous even in opposition to Moses,[1] tried God's patience until the Gospel. For thenceforward both Simon Magus, just turned believer, was—since he was still thinking somewhat of his juggling sect; to wit, that among the miracles of his profession he might buy even the gift of the Holy Spirit through imposition of hands—cursed by the apostles, and ejected from the faith:[2] and that other magician, who was with Sergius Paulus, was—since he began opposing himself to the same apostles—mulcted with loss of eyes.[3] The same fate, I believe, would astrologers, too, have met, if any had fallen in the way of the apostles. But yet, when magic is being punished, of which astrology is a species, of course the species is condemned in the genus. After the Gospel, you will nowhere find either sophists, or Chaldeans, or enchanters, or diviners, or magicians, except as clearly punished. "Where is the wise, where the grammarian, where the disputer of this age? Hath not God made foolish the wisdom of this age?"[4] You know nothing, astrologer, if you knew not that you would be a Christian. If you did know it, you ought to have known this also, that you would have nothing more to do with that profession of yours. Itself, which fore-chants the climacterics of others, would instruct you of its own danger. There is no part nor lot for you in that system of yours.[5] He cannot hope for the kingdom of the heavens, whose finger or wand abuses[6] the heaven.

---

[1] See Ex. vii. viii., and comp. 2 Tim. iii. 8.
[2] See Acts viii. 9–24. [3] See Acts xiii. 6–11.
[4] 1 Cor. i. 20. [5] See Acts viii. 21.
[6] See 1 Cor. vii. 31, "They that use this world as not abusing it." The astrologer "abuses" the heaven, by putting the heavenly bodies to a sinful use.

CHAP. X.—*Of schoolmasters and their difficulties.*

Moreover, we must inquire likewise touching schoolmasters; nor only them, but also all other professors of literature. Nay, on the contrary, we must not doubt that they are in affinity with manifold idolatry: first, in that it is necessary for them to preach the gods of the nations, to express their names, genealogies, honourable distinctions, all and singular; further, to observe the solemnities and festivals of the same, as of them by whose means they compute their revenues. What schoolmaster, without a table of the seven idols,[1] will yet frequent the Quinquatria? The very first payment of every pupil he consecrates both to the honour and to the name of Minerva; so that, even though he be not said "to eat of that which is sacrificed to idols"[2] *nominally* (not being dedicated to any particular idol), he is shunned as an idolater. What less of defilement does he incur on that ground,[3] than a business which, both nominally and virtually, is publicly consecrated to an idol, brings? The Minervalia are as much Minerva's, as the Saturnalia Saturn's; Saturn's, which must necessarily be celebrated even by little slaves at the time of the Saturnalia. New-year's gifts likewise must be caught at, and the Septimontium kept; and all the presents of Midwinter and the feast of Dear Kinsmanship must be exacted; the schools must be wreathed with flowers; the flamens' wives and the ædiles sacrifice; the school is honoured on the appointed holy-days. The same thing takes place on an idol's birthday; every pomp of the devil is frequented. Who will think that these things are befitting to a Christian master, except him who shall think them suitable likewise to one who is not a master? We know it may be said, "If teaching literature is not lawful to God's servants, neither will learning be likewise;" and, "How would one be trained unto ordinary human intelligence, or unto any sense or action whatever, since literature is the means of training for all life? How do we repudiate secular studies, without which divine studies can-

---

[1] *i.e.* the seven planets. [2] See 1 Cor. viii. 10.
[3] *i.e.* because "he does not *nominally* eat," etc.

not be pursued?" Let us see, then, the necessity of literary erudition; let us reflect that partly it cannot be admitted, partly cannot be avoided. Learning literature is allowable for believers, rather than teaching; for the principle of learning and of teaching is different. If a believer teach literature, while he is teaching doubtless he commends, while he delivers he affirms, while he recalls he bears testimony to, the praises of idols interspersed therein. He seals the gods themselves with this name;[1] whereas the law, as we have said, prohibits "the names of gods to be pronounced,"[2] and this name[3] to be conferred on vanity.[4] Hence the devil gets men's early faith built up from the beginnings of their erudition. Inquire whether he who catechizes about idols commit idolatry. But when a believer *learns* these things, if he is already capable of understanding what idolatry is, he neither receives nor allows them; much more if he is not yet capable. Or, when he *begins* to understand, it behoves him first to understand what he has first learnt, that is, touching God and the faith. Therefore he will reject those things, and will not receive them; and will be as safe as one who knowingly *accepts* poison from one who knows it not, but does not *drink* it. To *him* necessity is attributed as an excuse, because he has no other way to learn. Moreover, the not *teaching* literature is as much easier than the not *learning*, as it is easier, too, for the pupil not to attend, than for the master not to frequent, the rest of the defilements incident to the schools from public and scholastic solemnities.

CHAP. XI.—*Connection between covetousness and idolatry. Certain trades, however gainful, to be consequently avoided.*

If we think over the rest of faults, tracing them from their generations,—beginning with covetousness, "a root of all evils,"[5] wherewith, indeed, some having been ensnared,

---

[1] *i.e.* the name of *gods.*
[2] Ex. xxiii. 13; Josh. xxiii. 7; Ps. xvi. 4; Hos. ii. 17; Zech. xiii. 2.
[3] *i.e.* the name of *God.*
[4] *i.e.* on an *idol*, which, as Isaiah says, is "vanity."
[5] 1 Tim. vi. 10.

"have suffered shipwreck about faith,"[1] (albeit covetousness is by the same apostle called *idolatry:*[2]) in the next place [proceeding to] mendacity, the minister of covetousness: of false swearing I am silent, since even swearing is not lawful:[3] —is *trade* adapted for a servant of God? But, covetousness apart, what is the motive for acquiring? When the motive for acquiring ceases, there will be no necessity for trading. Grant now that there be some righteousness in business, secure from the duty of watchfulness against covetousness and mendacity; I take it that that trade which pertains to the very soul and spirit of idols, which pampers every demon, falls under the charge of idolatry. Rather, is not that the *principal* idolatry? If the self-same merchandises—frankincense, I mean, and all other foreign productions—used as sacrifice to idols, are of use likewise to men for medicinal ointments, to us [Christians] also, over and above, for solaces of sepulture, let them see to it; at all events, while the pomps, while the priesthoods, while the sacrifices of idols, are being furnished by dangers, by losses, by inconveniences, by cogitations, by runnings to and fro, or trades, what else are you demonstrated to be but an idols' agent? Let none contend that, in this way, exception may be taken to *all* trades. All graver faults extend the sphere for diligence in watchfulness proportionably to the magnitude of the danger; in order that we may withdraw not only from the faults, but from the means through which they have being. For although the fault be done by others, it makes no difference if it be *by my means*. In no case ought I to be *necessary* to another, while he is doing what to me is unlawful. Hence I ought to understand that care must be taken by me, lest what I am forbidden to do be done *by my means*. In short, in another cause of no lighter guilt I observe that fore-judgment. For, in that I am interdicted from fornication, I furnish

---

[1] 1 Tim. i. 19.
[2] Col. iii. 5. It has been suggested that for "quamvis" we should read "quum bis;" *i.e.* "*seeing* covetousness *is twice* called," etc. The two places are Col. iii. 5 and Eph. v. 5.
[3] Matt. v. 34-37; Jas. v. 12.

nothing of help or connivance to others for that purpose; for, in that I have separated my own flesh itself from stews, I acknowledge that I cannot exercise the trade of pandering, or keep that kind of places for my neighbour's behoof. So, too, the interdiction of murder shows me that a trainer of gladiators also is excluded from the Church; nor will any one fail to be the means of doing what he subministers to another to do. Behold, here is a more kindred fore-judgment: if a purveyor of the public victims come over to the faith, will you permit him to remain permanently in that trade? or if one who is already a believer shall have undertaken that business, will you think that he is to be retained in the Church? No, I take it; unless any one will dissemble in the case of a frankincense-seller too. In sooth, the agency of *blood* pertains to some, that of *odours* to others. If, before idols were in the world, idolatry, hitherto shapeless, used to be transacted by these wares; if, even now, the work of idolatry is perpetrated, for the most part, without the idol, by burnings of odours; the frankincense-seller is an even more serviceable something, even toward demons: for idolatry is more easily carried on without the idol, than without the frankincense-seller's ware. Let us ask thoroughly the conscience of the faith itself. With what mouth will a Christian frankincense-seller, if he shall pass through temples, with what mouth will he spit down upon and blow out the smoking altars, for which himself has made provision? With what consistency will he exorcise his own foster-children,[1] to whom he affords his own house as store-room? Let not *him*, indeed, if he shall have ejected a demon,[2] congratulate himself on his faith, for he has not ejected an *enemy;* he ought to have easily had his prayer granted by one whom he is daily feeding.[3] No art, then, no profession, no trade, which administers either to equipping or forming idols, can be free from the title of idolatry; unless we interpret idolatry

---

[1] *i.e.* the demons, or idols, to whom incense is burnt.
[2] *i.e.* from one possessed.
[3] *i.e.* The demon, in gratitude for the incense which the man daily feeds him with, ought to depart out of the possessed at his request.

to be altogether something else than the service of idol-tendence.

CHAP. XII.—*Further answers to the plea, "How am I to live?"*

In vain do we flatter ourselves as to the necessities of human maintenance, if—after faith sealed[1]—we say, "I have no means to live?"[2] For here I will now answer more fully that abrupt proposition. It is advanced *too late.* For deliberation should have been made *before*, after the similitude of that most prudent builder,[3] who first computes the costs of the work, together with his own means; lest, when he has begun, he afterward blush to find himself spent. But even now you have the Lord's sayings, as examples taking away from you all excuse. For what is it you say? "I shall be in need." But the Lord calls the needy "happy."[4] "I shall have no food." But "think not," says He, "about food;"[5] and as an example of clothing we have the lilies.[6] "My work was my subsistence." Nay, but "all things are to be sold, and divided to the needy."[7] "But provision must be made for children and posterity." "None, putting his hand on the plough, and looking back, is fit" for work.[8] "But I was under contract." "None can serve two lords."[9] If you wish to be the Lord's disciple, it is necessary you "take your cross, and follow the Lord:"[10] [your cross;] that is, your own *straits* and *tortures*, or your *body* only, which is after the manner of a *cross*. Parents, wives, children, will have to be left behind, for God's sake.[11] Do you hesitate about arts and trades, and about professions likewise, for the sake of children and parents? Even there was it demonstrated to us, that both

---

[1] *i.e.* in baptism.   [2] See above, chap. v. and viii.
[3] See Luke xiv. 28–30.   [4] Luke vi. 20.
[5] Matt. vi. 25, 31, etc.; Luke xii. 22–24.
[6] Matt. vi. 28; Luke xii. 28.   [7] Matt. xix. 21; Luke xviii. 22.
[8] Luke ix. 62, where the words are, "is fit for the kingdom of God."
[9] Matt. vi. 24; Luke xvi. 13.
[10] Matt. xvi. 24; Mark viii. 34; Luke ix. 23, xiv. 27
[11] Luke xiv. 26; Mark x. 29, 30; Matt. xix. 27–30. Compare these texts with Tertullian's words, and see the testimony he thus gives to the deity of Christ.

"dear pledges,"[1] and handicrafts, and trades, are to be quite left behind for the Lord's sake; while James and John, called by the Lord, do leave quite behind both father and ship;[2] while Matthew is roused up from the toll-booth;[3] while even burying a father was too tardy a business for faith.[4] None of them whom the Lord chose to Him said, "I have no means to live." Faith fears not famine. It knows, likewise, that hunger is no less to be contemned by it for God's sake, than every kind of death. It has learnt not to respect *life;* how much more *food?* "How many have fulfilled these conditions?" But what with men is difficult, with God is easy.[5] Let us, however, comfort ourselves about the gentleness and clemency of God in such wise, as not to indulge our "necessities" up to the point of affinities with idolatry, but to avoid even from afar every breath of it, as of a pestilence; not merely in the cases forementioned, but in the universal series of human superstition; whether appropriated to its gods, or to the defunct, or to kings, as pertaining to the selfsame unclean spirits, sometimes through sacrifices and priesthoods, sometimes through spectacles and the like, sometimes through holy-days.

CHAP. XIII.—*Of the observance of holy-days connected with idolatry.*

But why speak of sacrifices and priesthoods? Of spectacles, moreover, and pleasures of that kind, we have already filled a volume of their own.[6] In this place must be handled the subject of holy-days and other extraordinary solemnities, which we accord sometimes to our wantonness, sometimes to our timidity, in opposition to the common faith and Discipline. The first point, indeed, on which I shall join issue is this: whether a servant of God ought to share with the very nations themselves in matters of this kind, either in

---

[1] *i.e.* any dear relations.
[2] Matt. iv. 21, 22; Mark i. 19, 20; Luke v. 10, 11.
[3] Matt. ix. 9; Mark ii. 14; Luke v. 29.   [4] Luke ix. 59, 60.
[5] Matt. xix. 26; Luke i. 37, xviii. 27.
[6] The treatise *De Spectaculis.*

dress, or in food, or in any other kind of their gladness. "To rejoice with the rejoicing, and grieve with the grieving,"[1] is said about *brethren* by the apostle when exhorting to unanimity. But, for *these* purposes, "There is nought of communion between light and darkness,"[2] between life and death; or else we rescind what is written, "The world shall rejoice, but ye shall grieve."[3] If we rejoice with the world, there is reason to fear that with the world we shall grieve too. But when the world rejoices, let us grieve; and when the world afterward grieves, we shall rejoice. Thus, too, Eleazar[4] in Hades,[5] attaining refreshment in Abraham's bosom; the rich man, on the other hand, set in the torment of fire; compensate, by an answerable retribution, their alternate vicissitudes of evil and good. There are certain gift-days, which with some adjust the claim of honour, with others the debt of wages. "Now, then," you say, "I shall receive back what is mine, or pay back what is another's." If men have consecrated for themselves this custom from superstition, why do you, estranged as you are from all their vanity, participate in solemnities consecrated to idols; as if for you also there were some prescript about a day, to prevent your paying or receiving what you owe a man, or what is owed you by a man, short of the observance of a particular day? Give me the form after which you wish to be dealt with. For why should you skulk withal, when you contaminate your own conscience by your neighbour's ignorance? If you are not unknown to be a Christian, you are tempted, and you act as if you were not a Christian against your neigh-

---

[1] Rom. xii. 15.

[2] See 2 Cor. vi. 14. In the *De Spect.* xxvi. Tertullian has the same quotation (Oehler). And there, too, he adds, as here, "between life and death."

[3] John xvi. 20. It is observable that Tertullian here translates κόσμος by "seculum."

[4] Luke xvi. 19–31.

[5] "Apud inferos," used clearly *here* by Tertullian of a place of happiness. Augustine says he never finds it so used in Scripture. See Usher's "Answer to a Jesuit" on the Article, "He descended into hell."

bour's conscience; if, however, you shall be disguised withal,[1] you are the slave of the temptation. At all events, whether in the latter or the former way, you are guilty of being "ashamed of God."[2] But "whosoever shall be ashamed of Me in the presence of men, of him will I too be ashamed," says He, "in the presence of my Father who is in the heavens."[3]

CHAP. XIV.—*Of blasphemy; and of St. Paul's saying, "I please all in all things."*

But, however, the majority [of Christians] have by this time induced the belief in their mind that it is pardonable if at any time they do what the heathen do, for fear "the Name be blasphemed." Now the blasphemy which must quite be shunned by us in every way is, I take it, this: If any of us lead a heathen into blasphemy with good cause, either by fraud, or by injury, or by contumely, or any other matter of worthy complaint, in which "the Name" is deservedly impugned, so that the Lord, too, be deservedly angry. Else, if of *all* blasphemy it has been said, "By your means My Name is blasphemed,"[4] we all perish at once; since the whole circus, with no desert of ours, assails "the Name" with wicked suffrages. Let us cease [to be Christians], and it will not be blasphemed. On the contrary, while we are, let it be blasphemed: in the observance, not the overstepping, of discipline; while we are being approved, not while we are being reprobated. Oh blasphemy, bordering on martyrdom, which now *attests* me to be a Christian, while for that very account it *detests* me! The cursing of well-maintained Discipline is a blessing of the Name. "If," says he, "I wished to please men, I should not be Christ's servant."[5] But the same apostle elsewhere bids us take care to please all: "As I," he says,

---

[1] *i.e.* if you *are* unknown to be a Christian: "dissimulaberis." This is Oehler's reading; but Latinius and Fr. Junius would read "dissimulaveris,"="if you dissemble the fact" of being a Christian, which perhaps is better.

[2] So Mr. Dodgson renders very well.

[3] Matt. x. 33; Mark viii. 38; Luke ix. 26; 2 Tim. ii. 12.

[4] Isa. lii. 5; Ezek. xxxvi. 20, 23. Cf. 2 Sam. xii. 14; Rom. ii. 24.

[5] St. Paul. Gal. i. 10.

"please all by all means."¹ No doubt he used to please them by celebrating the Saturnalia and New-year's day! or was it by moderation and patience? by gravity, by kindness, by integrity? In like manner, when he is saying, "I have become all things to all, that I may gain all,"² does he mean "to idolaters an idolater?" "to heathens a heathen?" "to the worldly worldly?" But albeit he does not prohibit us from having our conversation with idolaters and adulterers, and the other criminals, saying, "Otherwise ye would go out from the world,"³ of course he does not so slacken those reins of conversation that, since it is necessary for us both to *live* and to *mingle* with sinners, we may be able to *sin* with them too. Where there is the intercourse of life, which the apostle concedes, there is sinning, which no one permits. To live with heathens is lawful, to die with them⁴ is not. Let us live with all;⁵ let us be glad with them, out of community of nature, not of superstition. We are peers in soul, not in discipline; fellow-possessors of the world, not of error. But if we have no right of communion in matters of this kind with strangers, how far more wicked to celebrate them among brethren! Who can maintain or defend this? The Holy Spirit upbraids the Jews with their holy-days. "Your Sabbaths, and new moons, and ceremonies," says He, "My soul hateth."⁶ By us, to whom Sabbaths are strange, and the new moons and festivals formerly beloved by God, the Saturnalia and New-year's and Midwinter's festivals and Matronalia are frequented—presents come and go—New-year's gifts—games join their noise—banquets join their din! Oh better fidelity of the nations to their own sect, which claims no solemnity of the Christians for itself! Not the Lord's day, not Pentecost, even if they had known them, would they have shared with us; for they would fear lest they should seem to be Christians. *We* are not apprehensive lest we seem to

---

¹ 1 Cor. x. 32, 33. ² 1 Cor. ix. 22. ³ 1 Cor. v. 10.
⁴ *i.e.* by sinning; (Oehler:) for "the wages of sin is death."
⁵ There seems to be a play on the word "convivere" (whence "convivium," etc.), as in Cic. *de Sen.* xiii.
⁶ Isa. i. 14, etc.

be *heathens!* If any indulgence is to be granted to the flesh, you have it. I will not say your own days,[1] but more too; for to the *heathens* each festive day occurs but once annually: *you* have a festive day every eighth day. Call out the individual solemnities of the nations, and set them out into a row, they will not be able to make up a Pentecost.[2]

CHAP. XV.—*Concerning festivals in honour of emperors, victories, and the like. Examples of "the three children" and Daniel.*

But "let your works shine," saith He;[3] but now all our shops and gates shine! You will now-a-days find more doors of heathens without lamps and laurel-wreaths than of Christians. What does the case seem to be with regard to that species [of ceremony] also? If it is an idol's honour, without doubt an idol's honour is idolatry. If it is for a man's sake, let us again consider that all idolatry is for man's sake:[4] let us again consider that all idolatry is a worship done to men, since it is generally agreed even among their worshippers that aforetime the gods themselves of the nations were men; and so it makes no difference whether that superstitious homage be rendered to men of a former age or of this. Idolatry is condemned, not on account of the persons which are set up for worship, but on account of those its observances, which pertain to demons. "The things which are Cæsar's are to be rendered to Cæsar."[5] It is enough that He set in apposition thereto, "and to God the things which are God's." What things, then, are Cæsar's? Those, to wit, about which the consultation was then being held, whether the poll-tax were to be furnished to Cæsar or no. Therefore, too, the Lord demanded that the money should be shown Him, and inquired about the image, whose

---

[1] *i.e.* Perhaps your own birthdays. Oehler seems to think it means, "all other Christian festivals beside Sunday."

[2] *i.e.* a space of fifty days (see Deut. xvi. 10; and comp. Hooker, *Ecc. Pol.* iv. 13, 7, ed. Keble).

[3] Matt. v. 16.   [4] See chap. ix. p. 152, note 4.

[5] Matt. xxii. 21; Mark xii. 17; Luke xx. 25.

it were; and when He had heard it was Cæsar's, said, "Render what are Cæsar's to Cæsar, and what are God's to God;" that is, the image of Cæsar, which is on the coin, to Cæsar, and the image of God, which is on man,[1] to God; so as to render to Cæsar indeed money, to God yourself. Otherwise, what will be God's, if all things are Cæsar's? "Then," do you say, "the lamps before my doors, and the laurels on my posts, are an honour to God?" [They are there] of course, not because they are an honour to God, but to him who is honoured in God's stead by ceremonial observances of that kind, so far as is manifest, saving the religious performance, which is in secret appertaining to demons. For we ought to be sure if there are any whose notice it escapes through ignorance of this world's literature, that there are among the Romans even gods of entrances; Cardea (Hinge-goddess), called after hinges, and Forculus (Door-god) after doors, and Limentinus (Threshold-god) after the threshold, and Janus (Gate-god) himself after the gate: and of course we know that, though names be empty and feigned, yet, when they are being drawn down into superstition, demons and every unclean spirit seize them for themselves, through the bond of consecration. Otherwise demons have no name individually, but they there find a name where they find also a token. Among the Greeks likewise we read of Apollo Thyræus (*i.e.* of the door), and the Antelii (or Anthelii) demons, as presiders over entrances. These things, therefore, the Holy Spirit foreseeing from the beginning, fore-chanted, through the most ancient prophet Enoch, that even entrances would come into superstitious use. For we see too that other entrances[2] are adored in the baths. But if there are beings which are adored in *entrances*, it is to them that both the lamps and the laurels will pertain.

---

[1] See Gen. i. 26, 27, ix. 6; and comp. 1 Cor. xi. 7.

[2] The word is the same as that for "the mouth" of a river, etc. Hence Oehler supposes the "entrances" or "mouths" *here* referred to, to be the mouths of *fountains*, where *nymphs* were supposed to dwell. *Nympha* is supposed to be the same word as *Lympha*. See Hor. *Sat.* i. 5, 97; and Macleane's note.

To an idol you will have done whatever you shall have done to an *entrance*. In this place I call a witness on the authority also of God; because it is not safe to suppress whatever may have been shown to *one*, of course for the sake of *all*. I know that a brother was severely chastised, the same night, through a vision, because on the sudden announcement of public rejoicings his servants had wreathed his gates. And yet himself had not wreathed, or commanded them to be wreathed; for he had gone forth [from home] before, and on his return had reprehended the deed. So strictly are we appraised with God in matters of this kind, even with regard to the discipline of our family. Therefore, as to what relates to the honours due to kings or emperors, we have a prescript sufficient, that it behoves us to be in all obedience, according to the apostle's precept,[1] "subject to magistrates, and princes, and powers;"[2] but within the limits of discipline, so long as we keep ourselves separate from idolatry. For it is for this reason, too, that that example of the three brethren has forerun us, who, in other respects obedient toward king Nebuchodonosor, rejected with all constancy the honour to his image,[3] proving that whatever is extolled beyond the measure of human honour, unto the resemblance of divine sublimity, is idolatry. So too, Daniel, in all other points submissive to Darius, remained in his duty so long as it was free from danger to his religion;[4] for, to avoid undergoing *that* danger, *he* feared the royal lions no more than *they* the royal fires. Let, therefore, them who have no light, light their lamps daily; let them over whom [hell] fires are imminent, affix to their posts laurels doomed presently to burn: to them the testimonies of darkness and the omens of their penalties are suitable. *You* are a light of the world,[5] and a tree ever green.[6] If you have renounced temples, make not your own gate a temple. I have said too little. If you have renounced stews, clothe not your own house with the appearance of a new stew.

[1] Rom. xiii. 1, etc.; 1 Pet. ii. 13, 14.   [2] Tit. iii. 1.
[3] Dan. iii.   [4] Dan. vi.
[5] Matt. v. 14; Phil. ii. 15.   [6] Ps. i. 1-3, xcii. 12-15.

Chap. XVI.—*Concerning private festivals.*

Touching the ceremonies, however, of private and social solemnities — as those of the white toga, of espousals, of nuptials, of name-givings—I should think no danger need be guarded against from the breath of the idolatry which is mixed up with them. For the causes are to be considered to which the ceremony is due. Those above-named I take to be clean in themselves, because neither manly garb, nor the marital ring or union, descends from honours done to any idol. In short, I find no dress cursed by God, except a woman's dress on a man :[1] for " cursed," saith He, "is every man who clothes himself in woman's attire." The toga, however, is a dress of manly *name* as well as [of manly use].[2] Also, God no more prohibits nuptials to be celebrated than a name to be given. "But there are sacrifices appropriated to these occasions." Let me be invited, and let not the title of the ceremony be " assistance at a sacrifice," and the discharge of my good offices is at the service [of my friends]. Would that it were "at *their* service" indeed, and that we could escape *seeing* what is unlawful for us to *do*. But since the evil one has so surrounded the world with idolatry, it will be lawful for us to be present at some ceremonies which see us doing service to a *man*, not to an *idol*. Clearly, if invited unto priestly function and sacrifice, I will not go, for that is service peculiar to an idol; but neither will I furnish advice, or expense, or any other good office in a matter of *that* kind. If it is on account of the *sacrifice* that I be invited, and stand by, I shall be partaker of idolatry ; if any *other* cause conjoins me to the sacrificer, I shall be merely a spectator of the sacrifice.

[1] Tertullian should have added, "and a man's on a woman." See Deut. xxii. 5. Moreover, the word " cursed " is not used there, but " abomination " is.

[2] Because it was called *toga virilis*—" the *manly* toga."

CHAP. XVII.—*The cases of servants and other officials considered. What offices a Christian man may hold.*

But what shall believing servants or children[1] do? officials likewise, when attending on their lords, or patrons, or superiors, when sacrificing? Well, if any one shall have handed the wine to a sacrificer, nay, if by any single word necessary or belonging to a sacrifice he shall have aided him, he will be held to be a minister of idolatry. Mindful of this rule, we can render service even to "magistrates and powers," after the example of the patriarchs and the other forefathers,[2] who obeyed idolatrous kings up to the confine of idolatry. Hence arose, very lately, a dispute whether a servant of God should take the administration of any dignity or power, if he be able, whether by some special grace, or by adroitness, to keep himself intact from every species of idolatry; after the example that both Joseph and Daniel, clean from idolatry, administered both dignity and power in the livery and purple of the prefecture of entire Egypt or Babylonia. And so let us grant that it is possible for any one to succeed in moving, in whatsoever office, under the mere *name* of the office, neither sacrificing nor lending his authority to sacrifices; not farming out victims; not assigning to others the care of temples; not looking after their tributes; not giving spectacles at his own or the public charge, or presiding over the giving them; making proclamation or edict for no solemnity; not even taking oaths: moreover (what comes under the head of *power*), neither sitting in judgment on any one's life or character (for you might bear with his judging about *money*); neither condemning nor fore-condemning;[3] binding no one, imprisoning or torturing no one—if it is credible that all this is possible.

---

[1] This is Oehler's reading; Rigaltius and Fr. Junius read "liberti" = freedmen. I admit that in this instance I prefer their reading: among other reasons, it answers better to "patronis" = "patrons."

[2] Majores. Of course the word may be rendered simply "ancients;" but I have kept the common meaning "forefathers."

[3] "The judge condemns, the legislator fore-condemns."—RIGALTIUS. (Oehler.)

CHAP. XVIII.—*Concerning dress as connected with idolatry.*

But we must now treat of the garb only and apparatus of office. There is a dress proper to every one, as well for daily use as for office and dignity. That famous purple, therefore, and the gold as an ornament of the neck, were, among the Egyptians and Babylonians, ensigns of dignity, in the same way as bordered, or striped, or palm-embroidered togas, and the golden wreaths of provincial priests, are now; but not on the same terms. For they used only to be conferred, under the name of *honour*, on such as deserved the familiar friendship of kings (whence, too, such used to be styled the "purpled-men"[1] of kings, just as among us, some, from their white toga, are called "candidates"[2]); but *not* on the understanding that that garb should be tied to *priesthoods* also, or *to any idol-ceremonies*. For if *that* were the case, of course men of such holiness and constancy[3] would instantly have refused the defiled dresses; and it would instantly have appeared that Daniel had been no zealous slave to idols, nor worshipped Bel, nor the dragon, which long after *did* appear. That purple, therefore, was simple, and used not at that time to be a mark of *dignity*[4] among the barbarians, but of *nobility*.[5] For as both Joseph, who had been a slave, and Daniel, who through[6] captivity had changed his state, attained the freedom of the states of Babylon and Egypt through the dress of barbaric nobility;[7] so among us believers also, if need so be, the bordered toga will be able to be conceded to boys, and the stole to girls,[8] as ensigns of birth, not of power, of race, not of office, of rank, not of superstition. But the purple, or the other ensigns of dignities and powers, dedicated from the begin-

[1] Or, "purpurates." [2] Or, "white-men."
[3] Or, "consistency." [4] *i.e. Official* character.
[5] Or, "free" or "good" "birth." [6] Or, "during."
[7] *i.e.* the dress was the *sign* that they had obtained it.
[8] I have departed from Oehler's reading here, as I have not succeeded in finding that the "*stola*" was a *boy's* garment; and, for grammatical reasons, the reading of Gelenius and Pamelius (which I have taken) seems best.

ning to idolatry engrafted on the dignity and the powers, carry the spot of their own profanation; since, moreover, bordered and striped togas, and broad-barred ones, are put even on idols themselves; and fasces also, and rods, are borne before them; and deservedly, for demons are the magistrates of this world: they bear the fasces and the purples, the ensigns of one college. What end, then, will you advance if you use the garb indeed, but administer not the functions of it? In things unclean, none can appear clean. If you put on a tunic defiled in itself, it perhaps may not be defiled through you; but you, through it, will be unable to be clean. Now by this time, you who argue about "Joseph" and "Daniel," know that things old and new, rude and polished, begun and developed, slavish and free, are not always comparable. For they, even by their circumstances, were slaves; but you, the slave of none,[1] in so far as you are the slave of Christ alone,[2] who has freed you likewise from the captivity of the world, will incur the duty of acting after your Lord's pattern. That Lord walked in humility and obscurity, with no definite home: for "the Son of man," said He, "hath not where to lay His head;"[3] unadorned in dress, for else He had not said, "Behold, they who are clad in soft raiment are in kings' houses:"[4] in short, inglorious in countenance and aspect, just as Isaiah withal had fore-announced.[5] If, also, He exercised no right of power even over His own followers, to whom He discharged menial ministry;[6] if, in short, though conscious of His own kingdom,[7] He shrank back from being made a king,[8] He in the fullest manner gave His own an example for turning coldly from all the pride and garb, as well of dignity as of power. For [if they were to be used], who would rather have used them than the Son of God? What kind and what

---

[1] See 1 Cor. ix. 19.
[2] St. Paul in his epistles glories in the title, "Paul, a slave," or "bondman," "of Christ Jesus."
[3] Luke ix. 58; Matt. viii. 20.
[4] Matt. xi. 8; Luke vii. 25.
[5] Isa. liii. 2.
[6] See John xiii. 1–17.
[7] See John xviii. 36.
[8] John vi. 15.

number of fasces would escort Him? what kind of purple would bloom from His shoulders? what kind of gold would beam from His head, had He not judged the glory of the world to be alien both to Himself and to His? Therefore what He was unwilling to accept, He has rejected; what He rejected, He has condemned; what He condemned, He has counted as part of the devil's pomp. For He would not have condemned things, except such as were not His; but things which are not God's, can be no other's but the devil's. If you have forsworn "the devil's pomp,"[1] know that whatever there you touch is idolatry. Let even this fact help to remind you that all the powers and dignities of this world are not only alien to, but enemies of, God; that through them punishments have been determined against God's servants; through them, too, penalties prepared for the impious are ignored. But "both your birth and your substance are troublesome to you in resisting idolatry."[2] For avoiding it, remedies cannot be lacking; since, even if they be lacking, there remains that one by which you will be made a happier magistrate, not in the earth, but in the heavens.[3]

CHAP. XIX.—*Concerning military service.*

In that last section, decision may seem to have been given likewise concerning military service, which is between dignity and power. But now inquiry is made about this point, whether a believer may turn himself unto military service, and whether the military may be admitted unto the faith, even the rank and file, or each inferior grade, to whom there is no necessity for taking part in sacrifices or capital punishments. There is no agreement between the divine and the human sacrament,[4] the standard of Christ and the standard

---

[1] In baptism.

[2] *i.e.* From your birth and means, you will be expected to fill offices which are in some way connected with idolatry.

[3] *i.e.* Martyrdom (La Cerda, quoted by Oehler). For the idea of being "a magistrate in the heavens," compare such passages as Matt. xix. 28; Luke xxii. 28, 30; 1 Cor. vi. 2, 3; Rev. ii. 26, 27, iii. 21.

[4] "Sacramentum" in Latin is, among other meanings, "a military oath."

of the devil, the camp of light and the camp of darkness. One soul cannot be due to two [lords]—God and Cæsar. And yet Moses carried a rod,[1] and Aaron wore a buckle,[2] and John (Baptist) is girt with leather,[3] and Joshua the son of Nun leads a line of march; and the People warred: if it pleases you to sport with the subject. But how will [a Christian man] war, nay, how will he serve even in peace, without a sword, which the Lord has taken away?[4] For albeit soldiers had come unto John, and had received the formula of their rule;[5] albeit, likewise, a centurion had believed;[6] [still] the Lord afterward, in disarming Peter, unbelted every soldier. No dress is lawful among us, if assigned to any unlawful action.

CHAP. XX.—*Concerning idolatry in words.*

But, however, since the conduct according to the divine rule is imperilled, not merely by deeds, but likewise by words, (for, just as it is written, "Behold the man and his deeds;"[7] so, "Out of thy own mouth shalt thou be justified"[8]), we ought to remember that even in *words* also the inroad of idolatry must be foreguarded against, either from the defect of custom or of timidity. The law prohibits the gods of the nations from being named,[9] not of course that we are not to pronounce their names, the speaking of which common intercourse extorts from us: for this must very frequently be said, "You find him in the temple of Æsculapius;" and, "I live in Isis Street;" and, "He has been made priest of Jupiter;" and much else after this manner, since even on *men* names of

---

[1] "Virgam." The vine switch, or rod, in the Roman army was a mark of the centurion's (*i.e.* captain's) rank.

[2] To fasten the ephod; hence the buckle worn by soldiers here referred to would probably be the belt buckle. Buckles were sometimes given as military rewards (White and Riddle).

[3] As soldiers with belts.

[4] Matt. xxvi. 52; 2 Cor. x. 4; St. John xviii. 36.

[5] See Luke iii. 12, 13.   [6] Matt. viii. 5, etc.; Luke vii. 1, etc.

[7] Neither Oehler nor any editor seems to have discovered the passage here referred to.

[8] Matt. xii. 37.   [9] Ex. xxiii. 13

this kind are bestowed. For I do not honour Saturnus if I call a man so, [addressing him] by his own name. I honour him no more than I do Marcus, if I call a man Marcus. But it says, "Make not mention of the name of other gods, neither be it heard from thy mouth."[1] The precept it gives is this, that we do not call them *gods*. For in the first part of the law, too, "Thou shalt not," saith He, "use the name of the Lord thy God in a vain thing,"[2] that is, in an idol.[3] Whoever, therefore, honours an idol with the name of God, has fallen into idolatry. But if I must speak of them as gods, something must be added to make it appear that *I* do not call them gods. For even the Scripture names "gods," but adds "their," viz. "of the nations:" just as David does when he had named "gods," where he says, "But the gods of the nations are demons."[4] But this has been laid by me rather as a foundation for ensuing observations. However, it is a defect of custom to say, "By Hercules, "So help me the god of faith;"[5] while to the *custom* is added the *ignorance* of some, who are ignorant that it is an oath by Hercules. Further, what will an oath in the name of gods whom you have forsworn be, but a collusion of faith with idolatry? For who does not honour them in whose name he swears?

CHAP. XXI.—*Of silent acquiescence in heathen formularies.*

But it is a mark of timidity, when some other man binds you in the name of his gods, by the making of an oath, or by some other form of attestation, and you, for fear of dis-

---

[1] Ex. xxiii. 13.   [2] Ex. xx. 7.

[3] Because Scripture calls idols "vanities" and "vain things." See 2 Kings xvii. 15, Ps. xxiv. 4, Isa. lix. 4, Deut. xxxii. 21, etc.

[4] Ps. xcvi. 5. The LXX. (in whose version [ed. Tisch.] it is Ps. xcv.) read δαιμόνια, like Tertullian. Our version has "idols."

[5] Mehercule. Medius Fidius. I have given the rendering of the latter, which seems preferred by Paley (Ov. *Fast.* vi. 213, note), who considers it = *me dius* (*i.e. deus*) *fidius juvet*. Smith (*Lat. Dict. s.v.*) agrees with him, and explains it, *me deus fidius servet*. White and Riddle (*s.v.*) take the *me* (which appears to be *short*) as a "demonstrative" particle or prefix, and explain, "By the God of truth!" "As true as heaven," "Most certainly."

covery,[1] remain quiet. For you equally, by remaining quiet, affirm their majesty, by reason of which [majesty] you will seem to be bound. What matters it, whether you affirm the gods of the nations by calling them gods, or by hearing them so called? whether you swear by idols, or, when adjured by another, acquiesce? Why should we not recognise the subtleties of Satan, who makes it his aim, that, what he cannot effect by *our* mouth, he may effect by the mouth of his servants, introducing idolatry into us through our ears? At all events, whoever the adjurer is, he binds you to himself either in friendly or unfriendly conjunction. If in unfriendly, you are now being challenged unto battle, and know that you must fight. If in friendly, with how far greater security will you transfer your engagement unto the Lord, that you may dissolve the obligation of him through whose means the Evil One was seeking to annex you to the honour of idols, that is, to idolatry! All sufferance of that kind is idolatry. You honour those to whom, when imposed as authorities, you have rendered respect. I know that one (whom the Lord pardon!), when it had been said to him in public during a láw-suit, "Jupiter be wroth with you," answered, "On the contrary, with *you*." What else would a heathen have done who believed Jupiter to be a god? Even if he had not retorted the malediction in the name of the same Jupiter, or in the name of any like to Jupiter, he had affirmed Jupiter to be a god, at being cursed in whose name he, by returning the curse, had shown himself indignant. For what is there to be indignant at, [if cursed] in the name of one whom you know to be nothing? For if you rave, you immediately affirm his existence, and the profession of your fear will be an act of idolatry. How much more, while you are returning the malediction in the name of Jupiter himself, are you doing honour to Jupiter in the same way as he who provoked you! But a believer ought to laugh in such cases, not to rave; nay, according to the precept,[2] not to return a curse in the name of God even, but clearly to *bless* in the name

---

[1] *i.e.* for fear of being discovered to be a Christian (Oehler).
[2] See Matt. v. 44, 1 Pet. iii. 9, etc.

of God, that you may both demolish idols, and preach God, and fulfil discipline.

CHAP. XXII.—*Of accepting blessing in the name of idols.*

Equally, one who has been initiated into Christ will not endure to be blessed in the name of the gods of the nations, so as not always to reject the unclean benediction, and to cleanse it out for himself by converting it Godward. To be blessed in the name of the gods of the nations is to be cursed in the name of God. If I have given an alms, or shown any other kindness, and the recipient pray that his gods, or the Genius of the colony, may be propitious to me, my oblation or act will immediately be an honour to idols, in whose name he returns me the favour of blessing. But why should he not know that I have done it for God's sake; that God may rather be glorified, and demons may not be honoured in that which I have done for the sake of God? If God sees that I have done it for His sake, He equally sees that I have been unwilling to *show* that I did it for His sake, and have in a manner made His precept[1] a sacrifice to idols. Many say, "No one ought to divulge himself;" but I think neither ought he to *deny* himself. For whoever dissembles in any cause whatever, by being held as a heathen, does deny; and, of course, all denial is idolatry, just as all idolatry is denial, whether in deeds or in words.

CHAP. XXIII.—*Concerning written contracts in the name of idols, and tacit consent thereto.*

But there is a certain species of that class, doubly sharpened in deed and word, and mischievous on either side, although it flatter you, as if it were free of danger in each; while it does not seem to be a *deed*, because it is not laid hold of as a *word*. In borrowing money from heathens under pledged[2] securities, [Christians] give a guarantee under oath, and deny themselves [to have done so]. Of course, the time of the prosecution, and the place of the judgment-seat, and the

---

[1] *i.e.* the precept which enjoins me to "do good and lend."
[2] Or, "mortgaged."

person of the presiding judge, decide that they knew themselves [to have so done].[1] Christ prescribes that there is to be no swearing. "I wrote," says the debtor, "but I said nothing. It is the tongue, not the written letter, which kills." Here I call Nature and Conscience as my witnesses: Nature, because even if the *tongue* in dictating remains motionless and quiet, the hand can write nothing which the *soul* has not dictated; albeit even to the tongue itself the soul may have dictated either something conceived by itself, or else something delivered by another. Now, lest it be said, "Another dictated," I here appeal to Conscience [to witness] whether, what another dictated, the soul entertains,[2] and, whether with the concomitance or the inaction of the tongue, transmits unto the hand. And it is enough that the Lord has said that faults are committed in the mind and the conscience. If concupiscence or malice have ascended into a man's heart, He saith it is held as a deed.[3] You therefore have given a guarantee; which clearly has "ascended into your heart," which you can neither contend you were ignorant of nor unwilling; for when you gave the guarantee, you knew [that you did it]; when you knew, of course you

---

[1] This is perhaps the most obscure and difficult passage in the entire treatise. I have followed Oehler's reading, and given what appears to be his sense; but the readings are widely different, and it is doubtful whether any is correct. I can scarcely, however, help thinking that the "*se negant*" here, and the "*tamen non negavi*" below, are to be connected with the "*puto autem nec negare*" at the end of the former chapter; and that the true rendering is rather: "And [by so doing] deny themselves," *i.e.* deny their Christian name and faith. "Doubtless a time of persecution," such as the present time is—or "of prosecution," which would make very good sense—"and the place of the tribunal, and the person of the presiding judge, require them to *know* themselves," *i.e.* to have no shuffling or disguise. I submit this rendering with diffidence; but it does seem to me to suit the context better, and to harmonize better with the "Yet I have not denied," *i.e.* my name and faith, which follows, and with the "denying letters" which are mentioned at the end of the chapter.—Tr.

[2] Mr. Dodgson renders "conceiveth;" and the word is certainly capable of that meaning.

[3] See Matt. v. 28.

were willing: you did it as well in act as in thought; nor can you by the lighter charge exclude the heavier,[1] so as to say that it is clearly rendered false, by giving a guarantee for what you do not actually perform. " Yet I have not denied, because I have not sworn." [You have], since, even if you had done no such thing [as you have done], you would still even so be said to swear, if you have *consented* to have done it. Silence of voice is an unavailing plea in a case of *writing*, and muteness of sound in a case of *letters*. But, however, Zacharias, when punished with a temporary privation of *voice*, held colloquy with his *mind*, and, passing by his bootless tongue, with the help of his hands dictates from his heart, and without his mouth pronounces the name of his son:[2] in his pen there speaks, in his waxen tablet there is heard, a hand clearer than every sound, a letter more vocal than every mouth.[3] Inquire whether a man have *spoken* who is *understood* to have spoken. Pray we the Lord that no necessity for that kind of contract may ever encompass us; and if it *should* so fall out, may He give our brethren the means of helping us, or give us constancy to break off [the bonds of] all [such] necessity, lest those denying letters, the substitutes for our mouth, be brought forward against us in the day of judgment, sealed with the seals, not now of witnesses, but of angels!

Chap. XXIV.—*General conclusion.*

Amid these reefs and inlets, amid these shallows and straits of idolatry, Faith, her sails filled by the Spirit of God, navigates; safe if cautious, secure if intently watchful. But to such as are washed overboard is a deep whence is no out-swimming; to such as are run aground is inextricable shipwreck; to such

---

[1] Oehler understands "the lighter crime" or "charge" to be "swearing;" the "heavier," to be "denying the Lord Christ."

[2] See Luke i. 20, 22, 62, 63.

[3] This is how Mr. Dodgson renders, and the rendering agrees with Oehler's punctuation. But perhaps we may read thus: "He speaks in his pen; he is heard in his waxen tablet: the hand is clearer than every sound; the letter is more vocal than every mouth."

as are engulphed is a whirlpool, where there is no breathing—in idolatry. All waves thereof whatsoever suffocate; every eddy thereof sucks down unto Hades. Let no one say, "Who will so safely foreguard himself? We shall have to go out of the world!"[1] As if it were not as well worth while to go out, as to stand in the world as an idolater! Nothing can be easier than caution against idolatry, if the fear of it be our leading fear; any "necessity" whatever is too trifling compared to such a peril. The reason why the Holy Spirit did, when the apostles at that time were consulting, relax the bond and yoke for us,[2] was that we might be free to devote ourselves to the shunning of idolatry. This shall be our Law, the more fully to be administered the more ready it is to hand; [a Law] peculiar to Christians, by means whereof we are recognised and examined by heathens. This Law must be set before such as approach unto the Faith, and inculcated on such as are entering it; that in approaching they may deliberate, observing it may persevere, not observing it may renounce their name.[3] For we will see to it, if, after the type of the Ark, there shall be in the Church raven, and kite, and dog, and serpent. At all events, an idolater is not found in the type of the Ark: no animal has been fashioned to represent an idolater. Let not that be in the Church which was not in the Ark.

[1] 1 Cor. v. 10.   [2] Acts xv. 1–31.
[3] *i.e.* cease to be Christians (Rigalt. referred to by Oehler).

VII.

ON PRAYER.

CHAP. I.—*General introduction.*

THE Spirit of God, and the Word of God, and the Reason of God—Word of Reason, and Reason and Spirit of Word—Jesus Christ our Lord, namely, who is both the one and the other,[1]—has determined for us, the disciples of the New Testament, a new form of prayer; for in this particular also it was needful that new wine should be laid up in new skins, and a new breadth be sewn to a new garment.[2] Besides, whatever had been in bygone days, has either been quite changed, as circumcision; or else supplemented, as the rest of the Law; or else fulfilled, as Prophecy; or else perfected, as faith itself. For the new grace of God has renewed all things from carnal unto spiritual, by superinducing the Gospel, the obliterator of the whole ancient bygone system, in which [Gospel] our Lord Jesus Christ has been approved as the Spirit of God, and the Word of God, and the Reason of God: the Spirit, by which He was mighty; the Word, by which He taught; the Reason, by which He came.[3] So the prayer composed by Christ has been composed of three parts. In speech,[4] by which [prayer] is enunciated, in spirit, by

---

[1] Oehler's punctuation is followed here. The sentence is difficult, and has perplexed editors and commentators considerably.
[2] Matt. ix. 16, 17; Mark ii. 21, 22; Luke v. 36, 37.
[3] Routh suggests, "fortasse quâ sensit," referring to *T. adv. Praxeam*, c. 5.
[4] Sermone.

which alone it prevails, even John had taught his disciples to pray;[1] but all John's doings were laid as groundwork for Christ, until, when "He had increased"—just as the same John used to fore-announce "that it was needful" that "He should increase and himself decrease"[2]—the whole work of the forerunner passed over, together with his spirit itself, unto the Lord. Therefore, after what form of words John taught to pray is not extant, because earthly things have given place to heavenly. "He who is from the earth," says John, "speaketh earthly things; and He who is here from the heavens speaketh those things which He hath seen."[3] And what that is the Lord Christ's — as this method of praying is—is *not* heavenly? And so, blessed [brethren], let us consider His heavenly wisdom: first, touching the precept of praying secretly, whereby He exacted man's faith, that he should be confident that the sight and hearing of Almighty God are present beneath roofs, and extend even into the secret place; and required modesty in faith, that it should offer its religious homage to Him alone whom it believed to see and to hear everywhere. Further, since wisdom followed in the following precept, let it in like manner appertain unto faith, and the modesty of faith, that we think not that the Lord must be approached with a train of words, who, we are certain, takes unsolicited foresight for His own. And yet that very brevity—and let this make for the third grade of wisdom—is supported on the substance of a great and blessed interpretation, and is as diffuse in meaning as it is compressed in words. For it has embraced not only the special duties of prayer, be it veneration of God or petition for man, but almost every discourse of the Lord, every record of [His] Discipline; so

---

[1] This is Oehler's punctuation. The edition of Pamelius reads: "So the prayer composed by Christ was composed of three parts: of the speech, by which it is enunciated; of the spirit, by which alone it prevails; of the reason, by which it is taught." Rigaltius and subsequent editors read, "of the reason, by which it is conceived;" but this last clause is lacking in the MSS., and Oehler's reading appears, as he says, to "have healed the words."

[2] John iii. 30.   [3] John iii. 31, 32.

that, in fact, in the Prayer is comprised an epitome of the whole Gospel.

Chap. II.—*The first clause.*

The prayer begins with a testimony to God, and with the reward of faith, when we say, "Our Father who art in the heavens;" for [in so saying], we at once pray to God, and commend faith, whose reward this appellation is. It is written, "To them who believed on Him He gave power to be called sons of God."[1] However, our Lord very frequently proclaimed God as a Father to us; nay, even gave a precept "that we call no one on earth father, but the Father whom we have in the heavens:[2] and so, in thus praying, we are likewise obeying the precept. Happy they who recognise their Father! This is the reproach that is brought against Israel, to which the Spirit attests heaven and earth, saying, "I have begotten sons, and they have not recognised me."[3] Moreover, in saying "Father," we also call Him "God." That appellation is one both of filial duty and of power. Again, in the Father the Son is invoked; "for I," saith He, "and the Father are One."[4] Nor is even our mother the Church passed by, if, that is, in the Father and the Son is recognised the mother, from whom arises the name both of Father and of Son. In one general term, then, or word, we both honour God, together with His own,[5] and are mindful of the precept, and set a mark on such as have forgotten their Father.

Chap. III.—*The second clause.*

The name of "God the Father" had been published to none. Even Moses, who had interrogated Him on that very point, had heard a different name.[6] To us it has been revealed in the Son, for the Son is now the Father's new name. "I am come," saith He, "in the Father's name;"[7]

---

[1] John i. 12.   [2] Matt. xxiii. 9.   [3] Isa. i. 2.   [4] John x. 30.
[5] "*i.e.* together with the Son and the Holy Spirit" (Oehler); "His Son and His church" (Dodgson).
[6] Ex. iii. 13–16.   [7] John v. 43.

and again, "Father, glorify Thy name;"[1] and more openly, "I have manifested Thy name to men."[2] That [NAME], therefore, we pray may "be hallowed." Not that it is becoming for men to *wish* God *well*, as if there were any other[3] by whom He may be wished well, or as if He would suffer unless we do so wish. Plainly, it is universally becoming for God to be *blessed*[4] in every place and time, on account of the memory of His benefits ever due from every man. But this petition also serves the turn of a blessing. Otherwise, when is the name of God not "holy," and "hallowed" through Himself, seeing that of Himself He sanctifies all others—He to whom that surrounding circle of angels cease not to say, "Holy, holy, holy?"[5] In like wise, therefore, we too, candidates for angelhood, if we succeed in deserving it, begin even here on earth to learn by heart that strain hereafter to be raised unto God, and the function of future glory. So far for the glory of God. On the other hand, for our own petition, when we say, "Hallowed be Thy name," we pray this; that it may be hallowed *in us* who are in Him, as well as in all others for whom the grace of God is still waiting;[6] that we may obey this precept, too, in "praying for all,"[7] even for our personal enemies.[8] And therefore with suspended utterance, not saying, " Hallowed be it *in us*," we say, "[Hallowed be it] *in all*."

CHAP. IV.—*The third clause.*

According to this model,[9] we subjoin, "Thy will be done in the heavens and on the earth;"[10] not that there is some power withstanding[11] to prevent God's will being done, and we pray for Him the successful achievement of His will;

[1] John xii. 28.   [2] John xvii. 6.   [3] *i.e.* "any other *god.*"
[4] Ps. ciii. 22.   [5] Isa. vi. 3; Rev. iv. 8.
[6] Isa. xxx. 18.   [7] 1 Tim. ii. 1.   [8] Matt. v. 44.

[9] Mr. Dodgson renders, ":next to this clause;" but the "*forma*" referred to seems, by what Tertullian proceeds to add, to be what he had said above, "not that it becomes us to wish God well," etc.

[10] We learn from this and other places, that the comparative adverb was wanting in some ancient formulæ of the Lord's Prayer (Routh).

[11] See note 3.

but we pray for His will to be done *in all*. For, by figurative interpretation of *flesh* and *spirit, we* are "heaven" and "earth;" albeit, even if it is to be understood simply, still the sense of the petition is the same, that *in us* God's will be done on earth, to make it possible, namely, for it to be done also in the heavens. What, moreover, *does* God will, but that we should walk according to His Discipline? We petition, then, that He supply us with the substance of His will, and the capacity to do it, that we may be saved both in the heavens and on earth; because the sum of His will is the salvation of them whom He has adopted. There is, too, that will of God which the Lord accomplished in preaching, in working, in enduring: for if He Himself proclaimed that He did not His own, but the Father's, will, without doubt those things which He used to do *were* the Father's will;[1] unto which things, as unto exemplars, we are now provoked;[2] to preach, to work, to endure even unto death. And we *need* the will of God, that we may be able to fulfil these duties. Again, in saying, "Thy will be done," we are even wishing well to ourselves, in so far that there is nothing of *evil* in the will of God; even if, proportionably to each one's deserts, somewhat other [than we think *good*] is imposed on us. So by this expression we premonish our own selves unto patience. The Lord also, when He had wished to demonstrate to us, even in His own flesh, the flesh's infirmity, by [enduring] the reality of suffering, said, "Father, remove this Thy cup;" and remembering Himself, [added,] "save that not my will, but Thine be done."[3] Himself *was* the Will and the Power of the Father: and yet, for the demonstration of the patience which was due, He gave Himself up *to* the Father's Will.

CHAP. V.—*The fourth clause.*

"Thy kingdom come" has also reference to that whereto "Thy will be done" refers—*in us*, that is. For when does

---

[1] John vi. 38.
[2] For this use of the word "provoke," see Heb. x. 24, Eng. ver.
[3] Luke xxii. 42.

God not reign, in whose hand is the heart of all kings?[1] But whatever we wish for ourselves we augur for Him, and *to* Him we attribute what *from* Him we expect. And so, if the *manifestation* of the Lord's kingdom pertains unto the will of God and unto our anxious expectation, how do some pray for some protraction of the age,[2] when the kingdom of God, which we pray may arrive, tends unto the consummation of the age?[3] Our wish is, that our reign be hastened, not our servitude protracted. Even if it had not been prescribed in the Prayer that we should ask for the advent of the kingdom, we should, unbidden, have sent forth that cry, hastening toward the realization of our hope. The souls of the martyrs beneath the altar[4] cry in jealousy unto the Lord, "How long, Lord, dost Thou not avenge our blood on the inhabitants of the earth?"[5] for, of course, their avenging is regulated by[6] the end of the age. Nay, Lord, Thy kingdom come with all speed,—the prayer of Christians, the confusion of the nations, the exultation of angels, for the sake of which we suffer, nay, rather, for the sake of which we pray!

Chap. vi.—*The fifth clause.*

But how gracefully has the Divine Wisdom arranged the order of the prayer; so that *after* things heavenly—that is, after the "Name" of God, the "Will" of God, and the "Kingdom" of God—it should give earthly necessities also room for a petition! For the Lord had[7] withal issued His edict, "Seek ye first the kingdom, and then even these shall be added:"[8] albeit we may rather understand, "Give us this day our daily

---

[1] Prov. xxi. 1.   [2] Or, "world," *sæculo.*
[3] Or, "world," *sæculi.* See Matt. xxiv. 3, especially in the Greek. By "praying for some protraction in the age," Tertullian appears to refer to some who used to pray that the end might be deferred (Rigalt.).
[4] *altari.*   [5] Rev. vi. 10.
[6] So Dodgson aptly renders "*dirigitur a.*"
[7] This is a slight mistake of Tertullian. The words referred to, "Seek ye first," etc., do not occur till the *end* of the chapter in which the prayer is found, so that his pluperfect is out of place.
[8] Matt. vi. 33.

bread," *spiritually.* For *Christ* is our Bread; because Christ is Life, and bread is life. "I am," saith He, "the Bread of Life;"[1] and, a little above, "The Bread is the Word of the living God, who came down from the heavens."[2] Then [we find], too, that His body is reckoned [to be] in bread: "This is my body."[3] And so, in petitioning for "daily bread," we ask for perpetuity in Christ, and indivisibility from His body. But, because that word is admissible in a carnal sense too, it cannot be so used without the religious remembrance withal of spiritual Discipline; for [the Lord] commands that "*bread*" be prayed for, which is the only [food] necessary for believers; for "all other things the nations seek after."[4] The like lesson He both inculcates by examples, and repeatedly handles in parables, when He says, "Doth a father take away *bread* from his children, and hand it to dogs?"[5] and again, "Doth a father give his son a stone when he asks for *bread*?"[6] For He [thus] shows what it is that sons expect from their father. Nay, even that nocturnal knocker knocked for "*bread.*"[7] Moreover, He justly added, "Give us *this day*," seeing He had previously said, "Take no careful thought about the morrow, what ye are to eat."[8] To which subject He also adapted the parable of the man who pondered on an enlargement of his barns for his forthcoming fruits, and on seasons of prolonged security; but that very night he dies.[9]

Chap. VII.—*The sixth clause.*

It was suitable that, after contemplating the liberality of God,[10] we should likewise address His clemency. For what will aliments[11] profit us, if we are really *consigned* to them,

[1] John vi. 35.   [2] John vi. 33.
[3] Matt. xxvi. 26.   [4] Matt. vi. 32.
[5] Tertullian seems to refer to Matt. xv. 26, Mark vii. 27.
[6] Matt. vii. 9; Luke xi. 11.   [7] Luke xi. 5–9.
[8] Matt. vi. 34 and Luke xii. 29 seem to be referred to; but the same remark applies as in note 7 on the preceding page.
[9] Luke xii. 16–20.
[10] In the former petition, "Give us this day our daily bread."
[11] Such as "daily bread."

as it were a bull destined for a victim ?[1] The Lord knew Himself to be the only guiltless One; and so He teaches that we beg "to have our debts remitted us." A petition for pardon is a full confession; because he who begs for pardon fully admits his guilt. Thus, too, penitence is demonstrated acceptable to God, who desires it rather than the death of the sinner.[2] Moreover, *debt* is, in the Scriptures, a figure of *guilt;* because it is equally due to the sentence of judgment, and is exacted by it: nor does it evade the justice of exaction, unless the exaction be remitted, just as the lord remitted to that slave [in the parable] his debt;[3] for hither does the scope of the whole parable tend. For the fact withal, that the same servant, after being liberated by his lord, does not equally spare his own debtor; and, being on that account impeached before his lord, is made over to the tormentor to pay the uttermost farthing; (that is, every guilt, however small:) corresponds with our profession that "we also remit to our debtors;" indeed elsewhere, too, in conformity with this Form of Prayer, He saith, "Remit, and it shall be remitted you."[4] And when Peter had put the question whether remission were to be granted to a brother seven times, "Nay," saith He, "seventy-seven times;"[5] in order to remould the Law for the better; because in Genesis *vengeance* was assigned "seven times" in the case of Cain, but in that of Lamech " seventy-seven times."[6]

CHAP. VIII.—*The seventh or final clause.*

For the completeness of so brief a prayer He added—in order that we should supplicate not touching the remitting merely, but touching the entire averting, of acts of guilt—"Lead us not into temptation:" that is, suffer us not to be led into it, by him (of course) who tempts; but far be the

---

[1] That is, if we are just to be fed and fattened by them in *body*, as a bull which is destined for sacrifice is, and then, like him, *slain*—handed over to *death!*
[2] Ex. xviii. 23, 32, xxxiii. 11.
[4] Luke vi. 37.
[6] Gen. iv. 15, 24.
[3] Matt. xviii. 21-35.
[5] Matt. xviii. 21, 22.

thought that the Lord should seem to tempt,[1] as if He either were ignorant of the faith of any, or else were eager to overthrow it. Infirmity[2] and malice[3] are characteristics of the devil. For [God] had commanded even Abraham to make a sacrifice of his son, for the sake not of tempting, but proving, his faith; in order through him to make an example for that precept of His, whereby He was by and by to enjoin that he should hold no pledges of affection dearer than God.[4] He Himself, when tempted by the devil, demonstrated who it is that presides over and is the originator of temptation.[5] This passage He confirms by subsequent ones, saying, "Pray that ye be not tempted;"[6] yet they *were* tempted, [as they showed] by deserting their Lord, because they had given way rather to sleep than prayer.[7] The final clause, therefore, is consonant, and interprets the sense of "Lead us not into temptation;" for this [sense] is, "But convey us away from the Evil One."

Chap. ix.—*Recapitulation.*[8]

In summaries of so few words, how many utterances of the prophets, the Gospels, the apostles—how many discourses, examples, parables of the Lord, are touched on! How many duties are simultaneously discharged! The honour of God in the "Father;" the testimony of faith in the "Name;" the offering of obedience in the "Will;" the commemoration of hope in the "Kingdom;" the petition for life in the

[1] See Jas. i. 13.   [2] Implied in the one hypothesis—ignorance.
[3] Implied in the other—wishing to overthrow faith.
[4] *i.e.* no children even. The reference is apparently to Matt. x. 37 and Luke xiv. 26, with which may be compared Deut. xiii. 6–10 and xxxiii. 9. If Oehler's reading, which I have followed, be correct, the precept, which is not verbally given till ages after Abraham, is made to have a retrospective force on him.
[5] See Matt. iv. 10; Luke iv. 8.
[6] Luke xxii. 40; Matt. xxvi. 41; Mark xiv. 31.
[7] Routh refers us to *De Bapt.* c. 20, where Tertullian refers to the same event.
[8] Here begins the Codex Ambrosianus, with the title, "Here begins a treatise of Tertullian of divers necessary things;" and from it are taken the headings of the remaining chapters. (See Oehler and Routh.)

"Bread;" the full acknowledgment of debts in the prayer for their "Forgiveness;" the anxious dread of temptation in the request for "Protection." What wonder? God alone could teach how he wished Himself prayed to. The religious rite of prayer, therefore, ordained by Himself, and animated, even at the moment when it was issuing out of the Divine mouth, by His own Spirit, ascends, by its own prerogative, into heaven, commending to the Father what the Son has taught.

CHAP. X.—*We may superadd [prayers of our own to the Lord's prayer].*

Since, however, the Lord, the Foreseer of human necessities,[1] said separately, after delivering His Rule of Prayer, "Ask, and ye shall receive;"[2] and [since] there are petitions which are made according to the circumstances of each individual; our additional wants have the right—after beginning with the legitimate and customary prayers as a foundation, as it were—of rearing an outer superstructure of petitions, yet with remembrance of [the Master's] precepts.

CHAP. XI.—*When praying the Father, you are not to be angry with a brother.*

That we may not be as far from the ears of God as we are from His precepts,[3] the memory of His precepts paves for our prayers a way unto heaven; of which [precepts] the chief is, that we go not up unto God's altar[4] before we compose whatever of discord or offence we have contracted with our brethren.[5] For what sort of deed is it to approach the peace of God[6] without peace? the remission of debts[7] while

---

[1] See Matt. vi. 8. [2] Matt. vii. 7; Luke xi. 9.
[3] Oehler divides these two chapters as above. The generally adopted division unites this sentence to the preceding chapter, and begins the new chapter with, "The memory of His precepts;" and perhaps this is the preferable division.
[4] *altare.* [5] Matt v. 22, 23.
[6] Perhaps there may be an allusion to Phil. iv. 6, 7.
[7] See chap. vii. above, and compare Matt. vi. 14, 15.

you retain them? How will he appease his *Father* who is angry with his *brother*, when from the beginning "all anger" is forbidden us?[1] For even Joseph, when dismissing his brethren for the purpose of fetching their father, said, "And be not angry in the way."[2] He warned *us*, to be sure, at that time (for elsewhere our Discipline is called "the Way"[3]), that when, set in "the way" of prayer, we go not unto "the Father" with anger. After that, the Lord, "amplifying the Law,"[4] openly adds [the prohibition of] anger against a brother to [that of] murder.[5] Not even by an evil word does He permit it to be vented.[6] Even if we *must* be angry, our anger must not be maintained beyond sunset, as the apostle admonishes.[7] But how rash is it either to pass a day without prayer, while you refuse to make satisfaction to your brother; or else, by perseverance in anger, to lose your prayer?

CHAP. XII.—*We must be free likewise from* ALL *mental perturbation.*

Nor merely from anger, but altogether from *all* perturbation of mind, ought the exercise of prayer to be free, uttered from a spirit such as is the Spirit unto whom it is sent. For a defiled spirit cannot be acknowledged by a holy Spirit,[8] nor a sad by a joyful,[9] nor a fettered by a free.[10] No one grants reception to his adversary: no one grants admittance except to his compeer.

CHAP. XIII.—*Of washing the hands.*

But what reason is there in going to prayer with hands indeed washed, but the spirit foul?—inasmuch as to our

---

[1] "Ab initio" probably refers to the book of Genesis, the *initium*, or beginning of Scripture, to which he is about to refer. But see likewise Eph. iv. 31, Matt. v. 21, 22.

[2] Gen. xlv. 24; so the LXX.

[3] See Acts ix. 2, xix. 9, 23, in the Greek.

[4] See Matt. v. 17. [5] Matt. v. 21, 22.

[6] Matt. v. 21, 22; 1 Pet. iii. 9, etc. [7] Eph. iv. 26.

[8] Eph. iv. 30. [9] John xvii. 14; Rom. xiv. 17.

[10] Ps. li. 12.

hands themselves spiritual purities are necessary, that they may be "lifted up pure"[1] from falsehood, from murder, from cruelty, from poisonings,[2] from idolatry, and all the other blemishes which, conceived by the spirit, are effected by the operation of the hands. These are the true purities;[3] not those which most are superstitiously careful about, taking water at every prayer, even when they are coming from a bath of the whole body. When I was scrupulously making a thorough investigation of this practice, and searching into the reason of it, I ascertained it to be a commemorative act, bearing on the surrender[4] of our Lord. We, [however,] *pray* to the Lord: we do not *surrender* Him; nay, we ought even to set ourselves in opposition to the example of His surrenderer, and not, on that account, wash our hands. Unless any defilement contracted in human intercourse be a conscientious cause [for washing them], they are otherwise clean enough, which together with our whole body we once washed in Christ.[5]

CHAP. XIV.—*Apostrophe.*

Albeit Israel wash daily all his limbs over, yet is he never clean. His *hands*, at all events, are ever unclean, eternally dyed with the blood of the prophets, and of the Lord Himself; and on that account, as being hereditary culprits from their privity to their fathers' crimes,[6] they do not dare even to raise them unto the Lord,[7] for fear some Isaiah should cry out,[8] for fear Christ should utterly shudder. We, however, not only raise, but even expand them; and, taking our model from the Lord's passion,[9] even in prayer we confess[10] to Christ.

[1] 1 Tim. ii. 8.
[2] Or, "sorceries."
[3] See Matt. xv. 10, 11, 17-20, xxiii. 25, 26.
[4] By Pilate. See Matt. xxvii. 24.
[5] *i.e.* in baptism.
[6] See Matt. xxiii. 31; Luke xi. 48.
[7] I do not know Tertullian's authority for this statement. Certainly Solomon *did* raise *his* hands (1 Kings viii. 54), and David apparently his (see Ps. cxliii. 6, xxviii. 2, lxii. 4, etc.). Compare, too, Ex. xvii. 11, 12. But probably he is speaking only of the Israel of his own day.
[8] Isa. i. 15.
[9] *i.e.* from the expansion of the hands on the cross.
[10] Or, "give praise."

Chap. xv.—*Of putting off cloaks.*

But since we have touched on one special point of empty observance,[1] it will not be irksome to set our brand likewise on the other points against which the reproach of vanity may deservedly be laid; if, that is, they are observed without the authority of any precept either of the Lord, or else of the apostles. For matters of this kind belong not to religion, but to superstition, being studied, and forced, and of curious rather than rational ceremony;[2] deserving of restraint, at all events, even on this ground, that they put us on a level with Gentiles.[3] As, [for instance,] it is the custom of some to make prayer with cloaks doffed; for so do the nations approach their idols; which practice, of course, were its observance becoming, the apostles, who teach concerning the garb of prayer,[4] would have comprehended [in their instructions], unless any think that it was in prayer that Paul had left his cloak with Carpus![5] God, forsooth, would not hear cloaked suppliants, who plainly heard the three saints in the Babylonian king's furnace praying in their trousers and turbans.[6]

Chap. xvi.—*Of sitting after prayer.*

Again, for the custom which some have of sitting when prayer is ended, I perceive no reason, except that which children give.[7] For what if that Hermas, whose writing is generally inscribed with the title *The Shepherd*, had, after finishing his prayer, not sat down on his bed, but done some other thing: should we maintain that also as a matter for observance? Of course not. Why, even as it is, the sentence, "When I had prayed, and had sat down on my bed," is simply put with a view to the order of the narration, not as a model of discipline. Else we shall have to pray

---

[1] *i.e.* the hand-washing.
[2] Or, "reasonable service." See Rom. xii. 1.
[3] Or, "Gentile practices."   [4] See 1 Cor. xi. 3–16.
[5] 2 Tim. iv. 13.   [6] Dan. iii. 21, etc.
[7] *i.e.* that they have seen it done; for children imitate anything and everything (Oehler).

nowhere except where there is a bed! Nay, whoever sits in a *chair* or on a *bench,* will act contrary to that writing. Further: inasmuch as the nations do the like, in sitting down after adoring their petty images; even on this account the practice deserves to be censured in us, because it is observed in the worship of idols. To this is further added the charge of *irreverence,*—[a charge] intelligible even to the nations themselves, if they had any sense. If, on the one hand, it is irreverent to sit under the eye, and over against the eye, of him whom you most of all revere and venerate; how much more, on the other hand, is that deed *most* irreligious under the eye of the living God, while the angel of prayer is still *standing by,*[1] unless we are upbraiding God that prayer has wearied us!

CHAP. XVII.—*Of elevated hands.*

But we more commend our prayers to God when we pray with modesty and humility, with not even our hands too loftily elevated, but elevated temperately and becomingly; and not even our countenance over-boldly uplifted. For that publican who prayed with humility and dejection not merely in his supplication, but in his countenance too, went his way "more justified" than the shameless Pharisee.[2] The sounds of our voice, likewise, should be subdued; else, if we are to be heard for our noise, how large windpipes should we need! But God is the hearer not of the *voice,* but of the *heart,* just as He is its inspector. The demon of the Pythian oracle says:

"And I do understand the mute, and plainly hear the speechless one."[3]

Do the ears of God wait for sound? How, then, could Jonah's prayer find way out unto heaven from the depth of the whale's belly, through the entrails of so huge a beast; from the very abysses, through so huge a mass of sea?

---

[1] Routh and Oehler (after Rigaltius) refer us to Tob. xii. 12. They also, with Dodgson, refer to Luke i. 11. Perhaps there may be a reference to Rev. viii. 3, 4.

[2] Luke xviii. 9-14.   [3] Herod. i. 47.

What superior advantage will they who pray too loudly gain, except that they annoy their neighbours? Nay, by making their petitions audible, what less error do they commit than if they were to pray in public?[1]

Chap. XVIII.—*Of the kiss of peace.*

Another custom has now become prevalent. Such as are fasting withhold the kiss of peace, which is the seal of prayer, after prayer made with brethren. But when is peace more to be concluded with brethren than when, at the time of some religious observance,[2] our prayer ascends with more acceptability; that they may themselves participate in our observance, and thereby be mollified for transacting with their brother touching their own peace? What prayer is complete if divorced from the "holy kiss?"[3] Whom does peace impede when rendering service to his Lord? What kind of sacrifice is that from which men depart without peace? Whatever our prayer be, it will not be better than the observance of the precept by which we are bidden to conceal our fasts;[4] for *now*, by abstinence from the kiss we are known to be fasting. But even if there be some reason [for this practice], still, lest you offend against this precept, you may perhaps defer your "peace" *at home*, where it is not possible for your fast to be entirely kept secret; but wherever else you can conceal your observance, you ought to remember the precept: thus you may satisfy the requirements of Discipline abroad and of custom at home. So, too, on the day of the passover,[5] when the religious observance of a fast is general, and as it were public, we justly forego the kiss, caring nothing to conceal anything which we do in common with all.

---

[1] Which is forbidden, Matt. vi. 5, 6. [2] Such as fasting.
[3] See Rom. xvi. 16; 1 Cor. xvi. 20; 2 Cor. xiii. 12; 1 Thess. v. 26; 1 Pet. v. 14.
[4] Matt. vi. 16-18.
[5] *i.e.* "Good Friday," as it is now generally called.

Chap. XIX.—*Of Stations.*

Similarly, too, touching the days of Stations,[1] most think that they must not be present at the sacrificial prayers, on the ground that the Station must be dissolved by reception of the Lord's Body. Does, then, the Eucharist cancel a service devoted to God, or bind it more to God? Will not your *Station* be more solemn if you have withal *stood* at God's *altar*?[2] When the Lord's Body has been received and reserved,[3] each point is secured, both the participation of the sacrifice and the discharge of duty. If the "Station" has received its name from the example of military life—for we withal are God's military[4]—of course no gladness or sadness chancing to the camp abolishes the "stations" of the soldiers: for gladness will carry out discipline more willingly, sadness more carefully.

Chap. XX.—*Of women's dress.*

So far, however, as regards the dress of women, the variety of observance compels us—men, [as we are,] of no consideration whatever—to treat, presumptuously indeed, after the most holy apostle,[5] except in so far as it will not be presumptuously if we treat the subject in accordance with the apostle. Touching modesty of dress and ornamentation, indeed, the prescription of Peter[6] likewise is plain, checking as he does with the same mouth, because with the same Spirit, as Paul, the glory of garments, and the pride of gold, and the meretricious elaboration of the hair.

Chap. XXI.—*Of virgins.*

But that point which is promiscuously observed through-

---

[1] The word "*Statio*" seems to have been used in more than one sense in the ancient Church. A passage in the *Shepherd of Hermas*, referred to above (B. iii. Sim. 5), appears to make it = "fast."

[2] "Ara," not "altare."

[3] For eating at home apparently, when your "station" is over.

[4] See 2 Tim. ii. 1, etc.

[5] See 1 Cor. xi. 1–16; 1 Tim. ii. 9, 10.   [6] 1 Pet. iii. 1–6.

out the churches, whether virgins ought to be veiled or no, must be treated of. For they who allow to virgins immunity from head-covering, appear to rest on this; that the apostle has not defined "virgins" by name, but "women,"[1] as "to be veiled;" nor the sex generally, so as to say "females," but a *class* of the sex, by saying "women:" for if he had named the sex by saying "females," he would have made his limit absolute for *every* woman; but while he names one class of the sex, he separates another class by being silent: for, they say, he might either have named "virgins" specially; or generally, by a compendious term, "females."

CHAP. XXII.—*Answer to the foregoing arguments.*

They who make this concession[2] ought to reflect on the nature of the word itself—what is the meaning of "woman" from the very first records of the sacred writings. For they find it to be *the name of the sex,* not a *class of the sex*: if, that is, God gave to Eve, when she had not yet known a man, the surname "woman" and "female"[3]—["female," whereby the sex generally; "woman," whereby a class of the sex, is marked].[4] So, since at that time the as yet unwedded Eve was called by the word "woman," that word has been made common even to a virgin.[5] Nor is it wonderful that the apostle—guided, of course, by the same Spirit by whom, as all divine Scripture, so that book Genesis, was drawn up—has used the selfsame word in writing "women" which, by the example of Eve unwedded, is applicable too to a "virgin." In fact, all the other passages are in consonance herewith. For even by this very fact, that he has not *named*

---

[1] 1 Cor. xi. 5.

[2] As to the distinction between "women" and "virgins."

[3] Gen. ii. 23. In the LXX. and in the Eng. ver. there is but the one word "woman."

[4] These words are regarded by Dr. Routh as spurious, and not without reason. Mr. Dodgson likewise omits them, and refers to *de Virg. Vel.* cc. 4 and 5.

[5] In *de Virg. Vel.* 5, Tertullian speaks even more strongly: "And so you have the name, I say not now *common*, but *proper* to a virgin; a name which from the beginning a *virgin* received."

" virgins" (as he does in another place[1] where he is teaching
touching marrying), he sufficiently predicates that his remark
is made touching *every* woman, and touching *the whole* sex;
and that there is no distinction made between a "virgin"
[and any other], while he does not name her at all: for he
who elsewhere—namely, where the difference requires—remembers
to make the distinction, (moreover, he makes it by
designating each species by their appropriate names,) wishes,
where he makes *no* distinction (while he does not name
each), *no* difference to be understood. What of the fact
that in the Greek speech, in which the apostle wrote his
letters, it is usual to say " women " rather than " females ; "
that is, γυναῖκας (*gunaikas*) rather than θηλείας (*theleias*)?
Therefore if that word,[2] which by interpretation represents
what "female" (*femina*) represents,[3] is frequently used *instead*
of the name of the sex,[4] he has named the *sex* in saying
γυναῖκα; but in the *sex* even the *virgin* is embraced.
But, withal, the declaration is plain: "*Every* woman," saith
he, " praying and prophesying with head uncovered,[5] dishonoureth
her own head."[6] What is "*every* woman," but
[woman] of every age, of every rank, of every condition?
By saying "every" he excepts nought of womanhood, just
as he excepts nought of manhood either from *not* being
covered; for just so he says, "*Every* man."[7] As, then, in
the masculine sex, under the name of " man " even the
" youth " is *forbidden* to be veiled; so, too, in the feminine,
under the name of " woman," even the " virgin " is *bidden*
to be veiled. Equally in each sex let the younger age follow
the discipline of the elder; or else let the male " virgins,"[8]

---

[1] 1 Cor. vii. 34 et seq.   [2] γυνή.

[3] Mr. Dodgson appears to think that there is some transposition here;
and at first sight it may appear so. But when we look more closely,
perhaps there is no need to make any difficulty: the stress is rather
on the words " by *interpretation*," which, of course, is a different thing
from "*usage;*" and by *interpretation* γυνή appears to come *nearer* to
" femina " than to " mulier."

[4] θηλεία.   [5] Or, " unveiled."   [6] 1 Cor. xi. 5.

[7] 1 Cor. xi. 4.

[8] For a similar use of the word " virgin," see Rev. xiv. 4.

too, be *veiled*, if the female virgins withal are *not* veiled, because *they* are not mentioned by *name*. Let "man" and "youth" be different, if "woman" and "virgin" are different. For indeed it is "on account of the angels"[1] that he saith women must be veiled, because on account of "the daughters of men" angels revolted from God.[2] Who, then, would contend that "*women*" *alone*—that is,[3] such as were already wedded and had lost their virginity—were the objects of angelic concupiscence, unless "virgins" are incapable of excelling in beauty and finding lovers? Nay, let us see whether it were not "*virgins*" *alone* whom they lusted after; since Scripture saith "*the daughters* of men;"[4] inasmuch as it might have named "*wives* of men," or "females," indifferently.[5] Likewise, in that it saith, "And they took them to themselves for wives,"[6] it does so on this ground, that, of course, such [only] are "received *for wives*" as are devoid of that title. But it would have expressed itself differently concerning such as were *not* thus devoid. And so [they who are named] are devoid as much of *widowhood* as of *virginity*. So completely has [Paul], by naming the sex generally, mingled "daughters" and [all other] species together in the [common] genus. Again, while he says that "nature herself,"[7] which has assigned hair as a tegument and ornament to "women," "teaches that veiling is the duty of females," has not the same tegument and the same honour of the head been assigned also to "virgins?" If "it is shameful for 'a woman' to be shorn, it is similarly so to a virgin" too. From them, then, to whom is assigned one and the same *law* of the head,[8] one and the same *discipline*[9] of the head is

---

[1] 1 Cor. xi. 10.

[2] See Gen. vi. 2 in the LXX., with the *v. l.* ed. Tisch. 1860; and compare Tertullian, *de Idol.* c. 9, and the note there. Mr. Dodgson refers, too, to *de Virg. Vel.* c. 7, where this curious subject is more fully entered into.

[3] *i.e.* according to *their* definition, whom Tertullian is refuting.

[4] Gen. vi. 2.

[5] *i.e.* If *married women* had been meant, either word, "uxores" or "feminæ," could have been used indifferently.

[6] Gen. vi. 2. [7] 1 Cor. xi. 14. [8] *i.e.* long hair. [9] *i.e.* veiling.

exacted,—[a discipline which extends] even unto those virgins whom their childhood defends;[1] for from the first[2] [a "virgin"] was named "female." This custom,[3] in short, even Israel observes; but if [Israel] did *not* observe it, *our* Law,[4] amplified and supplemented, would vindicate the addition for itself; let it be excused for imposing the veil on virgins also. Under *our* dispensation, let that age [*only*] which is ignorant of its sex[5] retain the privilege of simplicity. For both Eve and Adam, when it befell them to be "wise,"[6] forthwith veiled what they had learnt to know.[7] At all events, with regard to those in whom girlhood has changed [into more advanced maturity], their age ought to remember its duties as to nature, so too to discipline; for they are being transferred to the rank of "women" both in their persons and in their functions. No one is a "virgin" from the time when she is capable of marriage; seeing that, in her, age has by that time been wedded to its own husband, that is, to time.[8] "But some particular [virgin] has devoted herself to God. From that very moment she both changes the fashion of her hair, and converts all her garb into that of a 'woman.'" Let her, then, maintain the character wholly, and perform the whole function of a "virgin:" what she conceals[9] for the sake of God, let her cover quite over.[10] It is our business to entrust to the knowledge of God alone that which the grace of God effects in us, lest we receive from man the reward we hope for from God.[11] Why do you denude before God[12] what you cover before men?[13] Will you be more modest in public than

---

[1] *i.e.* "exempts." [2] *i.e.* from her creation.
[3] Of the universal veiling of women.
[4] *i.e.*, as above, the Sermon on the Mount.
[5] *i.e.* mere infancy. [6] Gen. iii. 6.
[7] Gen. ii. 27 (or in the LXX. iii. 1), and iii. 7, 10, 11.
[8] Routh refers us to *de Virg. Vel.* c. 11.
[9] *i.e.* the redundance of her hair. [10] *i.e.* by a veil.
[11] *i.e.*, says Oehler, "lest we postpone the eternal favour of God, which we hope for, to the temporal veneration of men; a risk which those virgins seemed likely to run, who, when devoted to God, used to go veiled in public, but bareheaded in the church."
[12] *i.e.* in church. [13] *i.e.* in public; see note 11.

in the church? If [your self-devotion] is a grace of God,
and you have received it, "why do you boast," saith he, "as
if you have not received it?"[1] Why, by your ostentation
of yourself, do you judge other [virgins]? Is it that, by
your boasting, you invite others unto good? Nay, but even
you yourself run the risk of losing, if you boast; and you
drive others unto the same perils! What is assumed from
love of boasting is easily destroyed. Be veiled, virgin, if
virgin you are; for you ought to blush. If you are a virgin,
shrink from [the gaze of] many eyes. Let no one wonder
at your face; let no one perceive your falsehood.[2] You do
well in falsely assuming the married character, if you veil
your head; nay, you do not seem to assume it *falsely*, for
you *are* wedded to Christ: to Him you have surrendered
your flesh; act as becomes your Husband's discipline. If
He bids the brides of others to be veiled, His own, of course,
much more. "But each individual man[3] is not to think
that the institution of his predecessor is to be overturned."
Many yield up their own judgment, and its consistency, to
the custom of others. Granted that [virgins] be not *compelled* to be veiled, at all events such as *voluntarily are* so
should not be prohibited; who, likewise, cannot deny themselves to be virgins,[4] content, in the security of a good conscience before God, to damage their own fame.[5] Touching
such, however, as are betrothed, I can with constancy "above
my small measure"[6] pronounce and attest that they are to be
veiled from that day forth on which they shuddered at the

[1] 1 Cor. iv. 7.

[2] *i.e.* as Muratori, quoted by Oehler, says, your "pious" (?) fraud in pretending to be married when you are a virgin; because the "devoted" virgins used to dress and wear veils like married women, as being regarded as "wedded to Christ."

[3] *i.e.* each president of a church, or bishop.

[4] *i.e.* "are known to be such through the chastity of their manner and life" (Oehler).

[5] "By appearing in public as married women, while in heart they are virgins" (Oehler).

[6] Does Tertullian refer to 2 Cor. x. 13? or does "modulus" mean, as Oehler thinks, "my rule?"

first bodily touch of a man by kiss and hand. For in them everything has been forewedded: their age, through maturity; their flesh, through age; their spirit, through consciousness; their modesty, through the experience of the kiss; their hope, through expectation; their mind, through volition. And Rebecca is example enough for us, who, when her betrothed had been pointed out, veiled herself for marriage merely on recognition of him.[1]

CHAP. XXIII.—*Of kneeling.*

In the matter of *kneeling* also, prayer is subject to diversity of observance, through the act of some few who abstain from kneeling on the Sabbath; and since this dissension is particularly on its trial before the churches, the Lord will give His grace that the dissentients may either yield, or else indulge their opinion without offence to others. We, however (just as we have received), only on the day of the Lord's Resurrection ought to guard not only against kneeling, but every posture and office of solicitude; deferring even our businesses lest we give any place to the devil.[2] Similarly, too, in the period of Pentecost; which period we distinguish by the same solemnity of exultation.[3] But who would hesitate *every* day to prostrate himself before God, at least in the first prayer with which we enter on the daylight? At fasts, moreover, and Stations, no prayer should be made without kneeling, and the remaining customary marks of humility; for [then][4] we are not only *praying*, but *deprecating* [*wrath*], and making satisfaction to God our Lord.[5] Touching *times* of prayer nothing at all has been prescribed, except clearly "to pray at every time and every place."[6]

---

[1] Gen. xxiv. 64, 65.   [2] Eph. iv. 27.
[3] *i.e.* abstaining from kneeling: *kneeling* being more " a posture of solicitude" and of humility ; *standing*, of "exultation."
[4] *i.e.* at fasts and Stations.
[5] For the meaning of "satisfaction" as used by the Fathers, see Hooker, *Eccl. Pol.* vi. 5.
[6] Eph. vi. 18; 1 Thess. v. 17; 1 Tim. ii. 8.

Chap. XXIV.—*Of* place *for prayer*.

But how "in every place," since we are prohibited [from praying] in public? In every place, he means, which opportunity, or even necessity, may have rendered suitable: for that which was done by the apostles[1] (who, in gaol, in the audience of the prisoners, "began praying and singing to God") is not considered to have been done contrary to the precept;[2] nor yet that which was done by Paul,[3] who in the ship, in presence of all, "made thanksgiving to God."[4]

Chap. XXV.—*Of* time *for prayer*.

Touching the *time*, however, the extrinsic[5] observation of certain hours will not be unprofitable—those common hours, I mean, which mark the intervals of the day—the third, the sixth, the ninth—which we may find in the Scriptures to have been more solemn than the rest. The first infusion of the Holy Spirit into the congregated disciples took place at "the third hour."[6] Peter, on the day on which he experienced the vision of Universal Community,[7] [as exhibited] in that small vessel,[8] had ascended into the higher regions for prayer's sake "at the sixth hour."[9] The same [apostle] was going into the temple, with John, "at the ninth

---

[1] Paul and Silas (Acts xvi. 25).

[2] Matt. vi. 5, 6, which forbids praying in public.

[3] I have followed Muratori's reading here.

[4] Mr. Dodgson renders "celebrated the Eucharist;" but that rendering appears very doubtful. See Acts xxvii. 35.

[5] Mr. Dodgson supposes this word to mean "outward, as contrasted with the inward, 'praying always.'" Oehler interprets, "ex vita communi." But perhaps what Tertullian says lower down in the chapter, "albeit they stand *simply without any precept enjoining their observance*," may give us the true clue to his meaning; so that "extrinsecus" would = "extrinsic to any direct injunction of our Lord or His apostles."

[6] Acts ii. 1–4, 14, 15.

[7] Communitatis omnis (Oehler). Mr Dodgson renders, "of every sort of common thing." Perhaps, as Routh suggests, we should read "omnium."

[8] Vasculo. But in Acts it is, σκεῦός τι ὡς ὀθόνην μεγάλην.

[9] Acts x. 9.

[hour],"[1] when he restored the paralytic to his health. Albeit these [practices] stand simply without any *precept* for their observance, still it may be granted a good thing to establish some definite presumption, which may both add stringency to the admonition to pray, and may, as it were by a law, tear us out from our [ordinary] businesses unto such a duty; so that—what we read to have been observed by Daniel also,[2] in accordance (of course) with Israel's discipline—we pray at least not less than thrice in the day, debtors as we are to Three—Father, Son, and Holy Spirit; besides, of course, our regular prayers which are due, without any admonition, on the entrance of light and of night. But, withal, it becomes believers not to take food, and not to go to the bath, before interposing a prayer; for the refreshments and nourishments of the spirit are to be held prior to those of the flesh, and things heavenly prior to things earthly.

CHAP. XXVI.—*Of the parting of brethren.*

You will not dismiss a brother who has entered your house without prayer :—" Have you seen," says [Scripture], " a brother? you have seen your Lord;"[3]—especially " a stranger," lest perhaps he be " an angel." But again, when received yourself by brethren, you will not make[4] earthly refreshments prior to heavenly, for your faith will forthwith be judged. Or else how will you—according to the precept[5]—say, " Peace to this *house,*" unless you exchange mutual peace with them too who are *in* the house?

---

[1] Acts iii. 1; but the man is not said to have been "paralytic," but " lame from his mother's womb."

[2] Dan. vi. 10; comp. Ps. lv. 17 (in the LXX. it is liv. 18).

[3] I have ventured to turn the first part of the sentence into a question. What "scripture" this may be, no one knows. Perhaps, in addition to the passages in Gen. xviii. and Heb. xiii. 2, to which the editors naturally refer, Tertullian may allude to such passages as Mark ix. 37, Matt. xxv. 40, 45.

[4] I have followed Routh's conjecture, " feceris " for " fecerit," which Oehler does not even notice.

[5] Luke x. 5.

CHAP. XXVII.—*Of subjoining a psalm.*

The more diligent in prayer are wont to subjoin in their prayers the "Hallelujah,"[1] and such kind of psalms, in the closes of which the company respond. And, of course, every institution is excellent which, for the extolling and honouring of God, aims unitedly to bring Him enriched prayer as a choice victim.

CHAP. XXVIII.—*Of the spiritual victim, which prayer is.*

For this is the spiritual victim[2] which has abolished the pristine sacrifices. "To what purpose," saith He, "[bring ye] me the multitude of your sacrifices? I am full of holocausts of rams, and I desire not the fat of rams, and the blood of bulls and of goats. For who hath required these from your hands?"[3] What, then, God *has* required the Gospel teaches. "An hour will come," saith He, "when the true adorers shall adore the Father in spirit and truth. For God is a Spirit, and accordingly requires His adorers to be such."[4] We are the true adorers and the true priests,[5] who, praying in spirit,[6] sacrifice, in spirit, prayer,—a victim proper and acceptable to God, which assuredly He has required, which He has looked forward to[7] for Himself! This [victim], devoted from the whole heart, fed on faith, tended by truth, entire in innocence, pure in chastity, garlanded with love,[8] we ought to escort with the pomp[9] of good works, amid psalms and hymns, unto God's altar,[10] to obtain for us all things from God.

CHAP. XXIX.—*Of the power and effect of prayer.*

For what has God, who exacts it, [ever] denied[11] to prayer

---

[1] Perhaps "the great Hallelujah," *i.e.* the last five psalms.
[2] 1 Pet. ii. 5.   [3] Isa. i. 11. See the LXX.
[4] John iv. 23, 24.   [5] Sacerdotes; comp. *de Ex. Cast.* c. 7.
[6] 1 Cor. xiv. 15; Eph. vi. 18.   [7] Or, "provided."
[8] "Agape," perhaps "the love feast."
[9] Or, "procession."   [10] Altare.
[11] Routh would read, "What *will* God *deny?*"

coming from "spirit and truth?" How mighty specimens of its efficacy do we read, and hear, and believe! *Old-world* prayer, indeed, used to free [men] from fires,[1] and from beasts,[2] and from famine;[3] and yet it had not [then] received its form from Christ. But how far more amply operative is *Christian* prayer! It does not station the angel of dew in mid-fires,[4] nor muzzle lions, nor transfer to the hungry the rustics' bread;[5] it has no delegated grace to avert any sense of suffering;[6] but it supplies the suffering, and the feeling, and the grieving, with endurance: it amplifies grace by virtue, that faith may know what she obtains from the Lord, understanding what—for God's name's sake—she suffers. But in days gone by, withal, prayer used to call down[7] plagues, scatter the armies of foes, withhold the wholesome influences of the showers. Now, however, the prayer of righteousness averts all God's anger, keeps bivouac on behalf of personal enemies, makes supplication on behalf of persecutors. Is it wonder if [prayer] knows how to extort the *rains* of heaven[8] —[prayer] which was [of old] able to procure its *fires?*[9] Prayer is alone that which vanquishes God; but Christ has willed that it be operative for no evil: He has conferred on it all its virtue in the cause of good. And so it knows nothing save how to recall the souls of the departed from the very path of death, to transform the weak, to restore the sick, to purge the possessed, to open prison-bars, to loose the bonds of the innocent. Likewise it washes away faults, repels temptations, extinguishes persecutions, consoles the faint-spirited, cheers the high-spirited, escorts travellers, appeases waves, makes robbers stand aghast, nourishes the poor, governs the rich, upraises the fallen, arrests the falling, confirms the standing.

[1] Dan. iii.
[2] Dan. vi.
[3] 1 Kings xviii.; Jas. v. 17, 18.
[4] *i.e.* "the angel who preserved in the furnace the three youths besprinkled, as it were, with dewy shower" (Muratori, quoted by Oehler).
[5] 2 Kings iv. 42–44.
[6] *i.e.* in brief, its *miraculous* operations, as they are called, are suspended in these ways.
[7] Or, "inflict."
[8] See *Apolog.* c. 5 (Oehler).
[9] See 2 Kings i.

Prayer is the wall of faith: her arms and missiles [1] against the foe who keeps watch over us on all sides. And so, never walk we unarmed. By day, be we mindful of Station; by night, of vigil. Under the arms of prayer guard we the standard of our General; await we in prayer the angel's trump.[2] The angels, likewise, all pray; every creature prays; cattle and wild beasts pray and bend their knees; and when they issue from their layers and lairs,[3] they look up heavenward with no idle mouth, making their breath vibrate[4] after their own manner. Nay, the birds too, rising out of the nest, upraise themselves heavenward, and, instead of hands, expand the cross of their wings, and say somewhat to seem like prayer. What more, then, touching the office of prayer? Even the Lord Himself prayed; to whom be honour and virtue unto the ages of the ages!

[1] Or, "her armour defensive and offensive."
[2] 1 Cor. xv. 52: 1 Thess. iv. 16.   [3] Or, "pens and dens."
[4] As if in prayer.

VIII.

OF PATIENCE.

Chap. i.—*Of patience generally; and Tertullian's own unworthiness to treat of it.*

I FULLY confess unto the Lord God that it has been rash enough, if not even impudent, in *me* to have dared compose a treatise on Patience, for *practising* which I am all unfit, being a man of no goodness;[1] whereas it were becoming that such as have addressed themselves to the demonstration and commendation of some particular thing, should themselves first be conspicuous in the practice of that thing, and should regulate the constancy of their commonishing by the authority of their personal conduct, for fear their words blush at the deficiency of their deeds. And would that this "blushing" would bring a remedy, so that shame for *not* exhibiting that which we go to suggest to others should prove a tutorship into exhibiting it; except that the magnitude of some good things—just as of some ills too—is insupportable, so that only the grace of divine inspiration is effectual for attaining and practising them. For what is *most* good rests *most* with God; nor does any other than He who possesses it dispense it, as He deems meet to each. And so to discuss about that which it is not given one to enjoy, will be, as it were, a solace; after the manner of invalids, who, since they are without health, know not how to be silent about its blessings. So I, most miserable, ever sick with the heats of *impatience*, must of necessity sigh after, and invoke, and persistently plead for,

[1] "Nullius boni;" compare Rom. vii. 18.

that health of patience which I possess not; while I recall to mind, and, in the contemplation of my own weakness, digest, [the truth,] that the good health of faith, and the soundness of the Lord's discipline, accrue not easily to any unless patience sit by his side. So is patience set over the things of God, that one can obey no precept, fulfil no work well-pleasing to the Lord, if estranged from it. The good of it, even they who live outside it,[1] honour with the name of highest virtue. Philosophers indeed, who are accounted animals of some considerable wisdom, assign it so high a place, that, while they are mutually at discord with the various fancies of their sects and rivalries of their sentiments, yet, having a community of regard for patience alone, to this one of their pursuits they have joined in granting peace: for it they conspire; for it they league; it, in their affectation of [2] virtue, they unanimously pursue; concerning patience they exhibit all their ostentation of wisdom. Grand testimony this is to it, in that it incites even the vain schools of the world [3] unto praise and glory! Or is it rather an injury, in that a thing divine is bandied among worldly sciences? But let them look to that, who shall presently be ashamed of their wisdom, destroyed and disgraced together with the world [4] [it lives in].

CHAP. II.—*God Himself an example of patience.*

To *us* [5] no human affectation of canine [6] equanimity, modelled [7] by insensibility, furnishes the warrant for exercising patience; but the divine arrangement of a living and celestial discipline, holding up before us God Himself in the very first place as an example of patience; who scatters equally over just and unjust the bloom of this light; who suffers the

---

[1] *i.e.* who are strangers to it.
[2] Or, "striving after."
[3] Or, "heathendom"—sæculi.
[4] Sæculo.
[5] *i.e.* us Christians.
[6] *i.e.* cynical = κυνικός = dog-like. But Tertullian appears to use "caninæ" purposely, and I have therefore retained it rather than substitute (as Mr. Dodgson does) "cynical."
[7] *i.e.* the *affectation* is modelled by insensibility.

good offices of the seasons, the services of the elements, the tributes of entire nature, to accrue at once to worthy and unworthy; bearing with the most ungrateful nations, adoring [as they do] the toys of the arts and the works of their own hands, persecuting His Name together with His family; [bearing with] luxury, avarice, iniquity, malignity, waxing insolent daily:[1] so that by His own patience He disparages Himself; for the cause why many believe not in the Lord is that they are so long without knowing[2] that He is wroth with the world.[3]

CHAP. III.—*Jesus Christ in His incarnation and work a more imitable example thereof.*

And *this* species of the divine patience indeed being, as it were, at a distance, may perhaps be esteemed as among "things too high for us;"[4] but what is that which, in a certain way, has been grasped by hand[5] among men openly on the earth? God suffers Himself to be conceived in a mother's womb, and awaits [the time for birth]; and, when born, bears [the tedium] of growing up; and, when grown up, is not eager to be recognised, but is furthermore contumelious to Himself, and is baptized by His own servant; and repels with words alone the assaults of the tempter; while from being "Lord" He becomes "Master," teaching man to escape death, having been trained to the exercise of the absolute forbearance of offended patience.[6] He did not strive; He did not cry aloud; nor did any hear His voice in the streets. He did not break the bruised reed; the smoking flax He did not quench: for the prophet—nay, the attestation of God Himself, placing His own Spirit, together with patience in its entirety, in His Son—had not falsely spoken.

[1] See Ps. lxxiv. 23 in LXX. (it is Ps. lxxiii. in the LXX.)
[2] Because they see no visible proof of it.   [3] Sæculo.
[4] So Mr. Dodgson; and La Cerda, as quoted by Oehler. See Ps. cxxxi. 1 in LXX. (where it is Ps. cxxx.)
[5] 1 John i. 1.
[6] I have followed Oehler's reading of this very difficult and much disputed passage. For the expression, "having been trained," etc., compare Heb. v. 8.

There was none desirous of cleaving to Him whom He did not receive. No one's table or roof did He despise; indeed, Himself ministered to the washing of the disciples' feet; not sinners, not publicans, did He repel; not with that city even which had refused to receive Him was He wroth,[1] when even the disciples had wished that the celestial fires should be forthwith hurled on so contumelious a town. He cared for the ungrateful; He yielded to His ensnarers. This were a small matter, if He had not had in His company even His own betrayer, and stedfastly abstained from pointing him out. Moreover, while He is being betrayed, while He is being led up "as a sheep for a victim," (for "so He no more opens His mouth than a lamb under the power of the shearer,") He to whom, had He willed it, legions of angels would at one word have presented themselves from the heavens, approved not the avenging sword of even one disciple. The patience of the Lord was wounded in [the person of] Malchus. And so, too, He cursed for the time to come the works of the sword; and, by the restoration of health, made satisfaction to him whom Himself had not hurt, through Patience, the mother of Mercy. I pass by in silence [the fact] that He is crucified, for this was the end for which He had come; yet had the death which must be undergone had need of contumelies likewise?[2] [No]; but, when about to depart, He wished to be sated with the pleasure of patience. He is spitted on, scourged, derided, clad foully, more foully crowned. Wondrous is the faith of equanimity! He who had set before [Himself] the concealing of Himself in man's shape, imitated nought of man's impatience! Hence, even more than from any other trait, ought ye, Pharisees, to have recognised the Lord. Patience of this kind none of *men* would achieve. Such and so mighty evidences—the [very] magnitude of which proves to be among the nations indeed a cause for rejection of the faith, but among us its reason and rearing—proves manifestly enough (not by the sermons only, in enjoin-

---

[1] Luke ix. 51–56.

[2] Or, "yet had there been need of contumelies likewise for the undergoing of death?"

ing, but likewise by the sufferings of the Lord in enduring) to them to whom it is given to believe, that patience is God's nature, the effect and excellence of some inherent propriety [of His being].

CHAP. IV.—*Duty of imitating our Master taught us by slaves and beasts. But obedient imitation is founded on patience.*

Therefore, if we see all servants of probity and right feeling shaping their conduct suitably to the disposition of their lord; if, that is, the art of deserving favour is obedience,[1] while the rule of obedience is a compliant subjection; how much more does it behove *us* to be found with a character in accordance with our Lord,—servants as we are of the living God, whose judgment on His servants turns not on a fetter or a cap of freedom, but on an eternity either of penalty or of salvation; for the shunning of which severity or the courting of which liberality there needs a diligence in obedience[2] as great as are the comminations themselves which the severity utters, or the promises which the liberality freely makes.[3] And yet we exact obedience[4] not from *men* only, who have the bond of their slavery under their chin,[5] or in any other legal way are debtors to obedience,[6] but even from cattle,[7] even from brutes;[8] understanding that they have been provided and delivered for our uses by the Lord. Shall, then, [creatures] which God makes subject to us be better than we in the discipline of obedience?[9] Finally, [the

[1] "Obsequium," distinguished by Döderlein from "obedientia," as a more voluntary and spontaneous thing, founded less on authority than respect and love.

[2] Obsequii.   [3] "Pollicetur," not "promittit."   [4] Obedientiam.

[5] "Subnixis." Perhaps this may be the meaning, as in Virg. *Æn*. iv. 217. But Oehler notices "subnexis" as a conjecture of Jos. Scaliger, which is very plausible, and would mean nearly the same. Mr. Dodgson renders "supported by their slavery;" and Oehler makes "subnixis" = "præditis," "instructis."

[6] Obsequii.

[7] "Pecudibus," *i.e.* tame, domestic cattle.

[8] "Bestiis," irrational creatures, as opposed to "homines," here apparently *wild* beasts.

[9] Obsequii. For the sentiment, compare Isa. i. 3.

creatures] which obey, acknowledge [their masters]. Do we hesitate to listen diligently to Him to whom alone we are subjected—that is, the Lord? But how unjust is it, how ungrateful likewise, not to repay from yourself the same [service] which, through the indulgence of your neighbour, you obtain from others, to him through whom you obtain it! Nor needs there more words on [the subject of] the exhibition of obedience[1] due from us to the Lord God; for the acknowledgment[2] of God understands what is incumbent on it. Lest, however, we seem to have inserted [our remarks] on obedience[3] as something irrelevant, [let us remember] that obedience[3] itself is drawn from patience. Never does an *impatient* [man] render it, or a *patient* fail to find pleasure[4] in it. Who, then, could treat largely [enough] of the good of that [patience] which the Lord God, the Demonstrator and Acceptor of all good things, carried about in His own self?[5] To whom, again, would it be doubtful that every good thing ought, because it pertains[5] to God, to be earnestly pursued with the whole mind by such as [themselves] pertain to God? By means of which [considerations] both [our] commendation and [our] exhortation[6] on the subject of patience are briefly, and as it were in the compendium of a prescriptive rule, established.

CHAP. V.—*As God is the author of patience, so the devil is of impatience.*

Nevertheless, the proceeding[7] of a discussion on the necessaries of faith is not idle, because it is not unfruitful. In edification no loquacity is base, if it be base at any time.[8] And so, if the discourse be concerning some particular *good*, the

---

[1] Obsequii.

[2] See above, "the creatures ... *acknowledge* their masters."

[3] Obsequio.

[4] "Oblectatur" Oehler reads with the MSS. The editors, as he says, have emended "obluctatur," which Mr. Dodgson reads.

[5] See the previous chapter.   [6] See chap. i.

[7] "Procedere:" so Oehler, who, however, notices an ingenious conjecture of Jos. Scaliger—"procudere," the hammering out, or forging.

[8] As in *prayer*, Tertullian may perhaps wish to imply. See Matt. vi. 7.

subject requires us to review also the *contrary* of that good. For you will throw more light on what is to be pursued, if you first give a digest of what is to be avoided.

Let us therefore consider, concerning *Im*patience, whether, just as patience in God, so its adversary quality have been born and detected in our adversary, that from this consideration may appear how primarily adverse it is to faith. For that which has been conceived by God's rival, of course is not friendly to God's things. The discord of *things* is the same as the discord of their *authors*. Further, since God is best, the devil on the contrary worst, [of beings,] by their own very diversity they testify that neither works for[1] the other; so that anything of good can no more seem to be effected for us by the Evil One, than anything of evil by the Good. Therefore I detect the nativity of impatience in the devil himself, at that very time when he impatiently bore that the Lord God subjected the universal works which He had made to His own image, that is, to man.[2] For if he had endured [that], he would not have grieved; nor would he have envied man if he had not grieved. Accordingly he deceived him, because he had envied him; but he had envied because he had grieved: he had grieved because, of course, he had not patiently borne. What that angel of perdition[3] first was—malicious or impatient—I scorn to inquire: since manifest it is that either impatience took its rise *together with* malice, or else malice *from* impatience; that subsequently they conspired between themselves; and that they grew up indivisible in one paternal bosom. But, however; having been instructed, by his own experiment, what an aid unto sinning was that which he had been the first to feel, by means of which he had entered on his course of delinquency, he called the same to his assistance for the

---

[1] Facere. But Fulv. Ursinus (as Oehler tells us) has suggested a neat emendation—"favere," favours.

[2] See Ps. viii. 4–6.

[3] Compare the expression in *de Idol.* iv., "perdition of blood" = "bloody perdition," and the note there. So here "angel of perdition" may = "lost angel."

thrusting of man into crime. The woman,[1] immediately on being met by him—I may say so without rashness—was, through his very speech with her, breathed on by a spirit infected with impatience: so certain is it that she would never have sinned at all, if she had honoured the divine edict by maintaining her patience [under it] to the end. What [of the fact] that she endured not to have been met alone; but in the presence of Adam, not yet her husband, not yet bound to lend her his ears,[2] she is impatient of keeping silence, and makes him the transmitter of that which she had imbibed from the Evil One? Therefore another human being, too, perishes through the impatience of the one; presently, too, perishes of himself, through his own impatience committed in each respect, both in regard of God's premonition and in regard of the devil's cheatery; not enduring to observe the former nor to refute the latter. Hence, whence [arose the first origin] of delinquency, arose the first origin of judgment; hence, whence man was induced to offend, God began to be wroth. Whence [arose] the first indignation in God, thence [arose] His first patience; who, content at that time with malediction only, refrained in the devil's case from the instant infliction[3] of punishment. Else what crime, before this guilt of impatience, is imputed to man? Innocent he was, and in intimate friendship with God, and the husbandman[4] of paradise. But when once he succumbed to impatience, he quite ceased to be of sweet savour[5] to God; he quite ceased to be able to endure things celestial. Thenceforward, a creature[6] given to earth, and ejected from the sight of God, he begins to be easily turned by impatience unto every use offensive to God. For straightway that [impatience] conceived of the devil's seed, produced, in the fecundity of malice, anger as her son; and when brought forth, trained him in her own arts. For that very thing which had immersed Adam and Eve in death,

---

[1] Mulier. See *de Orat.* c. xxii.
[2] 1 Cor. vii. 8; compare also 1 Pet. iii. 7.
[3] Impetu.
[4] Colonus. Gen. ii. 15.
[5] Sapere. See *de Idol.* c. i. *sub fin.*
[6] Homo.

taught their son, too, to begin with murder. It would be idle for me to ascribe this to impatience, if Cain, that first homicide and first fratricide, had borne with equanimity and not impatiently the refusal by the Lord of his own oblations —if he is not wroth with his own brother—if, finally, he took away no one's life. Since, then, he could neither have killed unless he had been wroth, nor have been wroth unless he had been impatient, he demonstrates that what he did through wrath must be referred to that by which wrath was suggested during this cradle-time of impatience, then (in a certain sense) in her infancy. But how great presently were her augmentations! And no wonder. If she has been the first delinquent, it is a consequence that, because she *has* been the first, therefore she is the only, parent stem,[1] too, to *every* delinquency, pouring down from her own fount various veins of crimes.[2] Of *murder* we have spoken ; but, being from the very beginning the outcome of *anger*,[3] whatever [other] causes likewise it shortly found for itself it lays collectively to the account of impatience, as to its own origin. For whether from *private enmities*, or for the sake of *prey*, any one perpetrates that wickedness,[4] the earlier step is his becoming *impatient of*[5] either the hatred or the avarice. Whatever *compels* a man, without *impatience of itself* [on his part], it is not possible that it can be perfected [in deed]. Who [ever] committed *adultery* without impatience of *lust?* Moreover, if in females the sale of their modesty is forced [upon them] by [the hope of] the price, of course it is by impatience of contemning gain [6] that [this sale] is regulated.[7] These [I mention] as the principal delinquencies in the sight of the Lord;[8] for, to speak compendiously, *every* sin is ascrib-

[1] Matrix. Mr. Dodgson renders "womb," which is admissible ; but the other passages quoted by Oehler, where Tertullian uses this word, seem to suit better with the rendering given in the text.
[2] Compare a similar expression in *de Idol.* ii. *ad init.*
[3] Which Tertullian has just shown to be the result of *impatience.*
[4] *i.e.* murder.   [5] *i.e.* unable to restrain.
[6] *i.e.* want of power or patience to contemn gain.
[7] " Ordinatur ; " but " orditur " has been very plausibly conjectured.
[8] Mr. Dodgson refers to *ad Uxor.* i. 5, *q. v. sub fin.*

able to impatience. "Evil" is "impatience of good." None *immodest* is not *impatient* of *modesty*; *dishonest* of *honesty*; *impious* of *piety*;¹ *unquiet* of *quietness*. In order that each individual may become *evil*, he will be *unable to persevere*² in being *good*. How, therefore, can such a hydra of delinquencies fail to offend the Lord, the Disapprover of evils? Is it not manifest that it was through impatience that Israel himself also always failed in his duty toward God, from that time when,³ forgetful of the heavenly arm whereby he had been drawn out of his Egyptian affliction, he demands from Aaron "gods⁴ as his guides;" when he pours down for [the making of] an idol the contributions of his gold: for the so necessary delays of Moses, while he met with God, he had borne with impatience. After the edible rain of the manna, after the watery following⁵ of the rock, they despair of the Lord in not enduring a three-days' thirst;⁶ for this also is laid to their charge by the Lord as impatience. And—not to rove through individual cases—there was no instance in which it was not by failing in duty through impatience that they perished. How, moreover, did they [come to] lay hands on the prophets, except through impatience of hearing them? on the Lord moreover Himself, through impatience likewise of seeing Him? But had they entered [the path of] patience, they would have been set free.⁷

CHAP. VI.—*Patience both antecedent and subsequent to faith.*

Accordingly it is patience which is both subsequent and antecedent to faith. In short, Abraham believed God, and was accredited by Him with righteousness;⁸ but it was

¹ Or, "*unduteous* of *duteousness*."   ² *i.e. impatient*.
³ I have departed slightly here from Oehler's punctuation.
⁴ Ex. xxxii. 1; Acts vii. 39, 40.
⁵ *i.e.* the water which followed them, after being given forth by the smitten rock. See 1 Cor. x. 4.
⁶ See Num. xx. 1–6. But Tertullian has apparently confused this with Ex. xv. 22, which seems to be the only place where "a *three-days*' thirst" is mentioned.
⁷ Free, *i.e.* from the bondage of impatience and of sin.
⁸ See Gen. xv. 6; Rom. iv. 3, 9, 22; Gal. iii. 6; Jas. ii. 23.

patience which *proved* his faith, when he was bidden to immolate his son, with a view to (I would not say the temptation, but) the typical attestation of his faith. But God knew [the character of him] whom He had accredited with righteousness.[1] So heavy a precept, the perfect execution whereof was not even pleasing to the Lord, he patiently both heard, and (if God had willed) would have fulfilled. Deservedly then was he "blessed," because he was "faithful;" deservedly "faithful," because "patient." So faith, illumined by patience, when it was being propagated among the nations through "Abraham's seed, which is Christ,"[2] and was superinducing grace over the law,[3] made patience her pre-eminent coadjutrix for amplifying and fulfilling the law, because that alone had been lacking unto the doctrine of righteousness. For men were of old wont to require "eye for eye, and tooth for tooth,"[4] and to repay with usury "evil with evil;" for, as yet, patience was not on earth, because faith was not either. Of course, meantime, impatience used to enjoy the opportunities which the law gave [for its exercise]. That was easy, while the Lord and Master of patience was absent. But after He has supervened, and has united[5] the grace of faith with patience, *now* it is no longer lawful to assail even with *word*, nor to say "fool"[6] even, without "danger of the judgment." Anger has been prohibited, our spirits restrained, the petulance of the hand checked, the poison of the tongue[7] extracted. The law has found more than it has lost, while Christ says, "Love your personal enemies, and bless your cursers, and pray for your persecutors, that ye may be sons of your heavenly Father."[8] Do you see whom patience gains for us as a Father? In this principal precept

---

[1] *i.e.* The trial was necessary not to prove his faith to *God*, who knows all whom He accounts righteous, but "typically" to *us*.
[2] Gal. iii. 16.   [3] John i. 17 : Rom. vi. 14, 15.
[4] Matt. vi. 38, and the references there given.
[5] Composuit.
[6] See Matt. v. 22 ; and Wordsworth *in loco*, who thinks it probable that the meaning is "apostate."
[7] Ps. cxl. 3 ; Rom. iii. 13 ; Jas. iii. 8.
[8] Matt. v. 44, 45.

the universal discipline of patience is succinctly comprised, since evil-doing is not conceded even when it is deserved.

CHAP. VII.—*Causes of impatience, and their correspondent precepts.*

Now, however, while we run through the causes of impatience, all the other precepts also will answer in their own places. If our spirit is aroused by the loss of property, it is commonished by the Lord's Scriptures, in almost every place, to a contemning of the world;[1] nor is there any more powerful exhortation to contempt of money submitted[2] [to us], than [the fact] the Lord Himself is found amid no riches. He always justifies the poor, fore-condemns the rich. So He fore-ministered to patience "loss" [as her portion], and to opulence "contempt" [as her portion];[3] demonstrating, by means of [His own] *repudiation* of riches, that *hurts* done to them also are not to be much regarded. Of that, therefore, which we have not the smallest need to seek after (because the Lord did not seek after it either), we ought to endure without heart-sickness the cutting down or taking away. "Covetousness," the Spirit of the Lord has through the apostle pronounced "a root of all evils."[4] Let us not interpret that [covetousness] as consisting merely in the concupiscence of what is another's: for even what *seems* ours *is* another's; for nothing is ours, since all things are God's, whose are we also ourselves. And so, if, when suffering from a loss, we feel impatiently, grieving for what is lost from what is not our own, we shall be detected as bordering on covetousness: we *seek* what is another's when we ill brook *losing* what is another's. He who is greatly stirred with impatience of a loss, does, by giving things earthly the precedence over things heavenly, sin directly[5] against God;

---

[1] Sæculo. [2] Subjacet.
[3] This appears to be the sense of this very difficult passage as Oehler reads it; and of Fr. Junius' interpretation of it, which Oehler approves.
[4] 1 Tim. vi. 10. See *de Idol.* xi. *ad init.*
[5] De proximo. See above, c. v. *Deo de proximo amicus,* "a most intimate friend to God."

for the Spirit, which he has received from the Lord, he greatly shocks for the sake of a worldly matter. Willingly, therefore, let us lose things earthly, let us keep things heavenly. Perish the whole world,[1] so I may make patience my gain! In truth, I know not whether he who has not made up his mind to endure with constancy the loss of somewhat of his, either by theft, or else by force, or else even by carelessness, would himself readily or heartily lay hand on his own property in the cause of almsgiving: for who that endures not at all to be cut by another, himself draws the sword on his own body? Patience in losses is an exercise in bestowing and communicating. Who fears not to lose, finds it not irksome to give. Else how will one, when he has two coats, give the one of them to the naked,[2] unless he be a man likewise to offer to one who takes away his coat his cloak as well?[3] How shall we fashion to us friends from mammon,[4] if we love it so much as not to put up with its loss? We shall perish together with the lost [mammon]. Why do we *find* here, where it is our business to *lose*?[5] To exhibit impatience at all losses is the Gentiles' business, who give money the precedence perhaps over their soul; for so they do, when, in their cupidities of lucre, they encounter the gainful perils of commerce on the sea; when, for money's sake, even in the forum, there is nothing which damnation [itself] would fear which they hesitate to essay; when they hire themselves for sport and the camp; when, after the manner of wild beasts, they play the bandit along the highway. But us, according to the diversity by which we are distinguished from them, it becomes to lay down not our soul for money, but money for our soul, whether spontaneously in bestowing or patiently in losing.

---

[1] Sæculum.   [2] Luke iii. 11.
[3] Matt. v. 40; Luke vi. 29.   [4] Luke xvi. 9.
[5] "Alluding to Christ's words in Matt. x. 39" (Rigalt. quoted by Oehler).

CHAP. VIII.—*Of patience under personal violence and malediction.*

We who carry about our very soul, our very body, exposed in this world[1] to injury from all, and exhibit patience under that injury; shall we be hurt at the loss[2] of less important things?[3] Far from a servant of Christ be such a defilement as that the patience which has been prepared for greater temptations should forsake him in frivolous ones. If one attempt to provoke you by manual violence, the monition of the Lord is at hand: "To him," He saith, "who smiteth thee on the face, turn the other cheek likewise."[4] Let outrageousness[5] be wearied out by your patience. Whatever that blow may be, conjoined[6] with pain and contumely, it[7] shall receive a heavier one from the Lord. You wound that outrageous[8] one more by enduring: for he will be beaten by Him for whose sake you endure. If the tongue's bitterness break out in malediction or reproach, look back at the saying, "When they curse you, rejoice."[9] The Lord Himself was "cursed" in the eye of the law;[10] and yet is He the only Blessed One. Let us servants, therefore, follow our Lord closely; and be cursed patiently, that we may be able to be blessed. If I hear with too little equanimity some wanton or wicked word uttered against me, I must of necessity either myself retaliate the bitterness, or else I shall be racked with mute impatience. When, then, on being cursed, I smite [with my tongue], how shall I be found to have followed the doctrine of the Lord, in which it has been

---

[1] Sæculo.   [2] Delibatione.
[3] *i.e.* money and the like. Compare Matt. vi. 25; Luke xii. 23.
[4] Matt. v. 39.   [5] Improbitas.
[6] Constrictus. I have rendered after Oehler; but may not the meaning be " clenched," like the hand which deals the blow?
[7] As Oehler says "the blow" is said to "receive" that which, strictly, the dealer of it receives.
[8] Improbum.   [9] Matt. v. 11, 12; Luke vi. 22, 23.
[10] Deut. xxi. 23; Gal. iii. 13. Tertullian's quotations here are somewhat loose. He renders words which are distinct in the Greek by the same in his Latin.

delivered that "a man is defiled,[1] not by the defilements of vessels, but of the things which are sent forth out of his mouth." Again, [it is said] that "impeachment[2] awaits us for every vain and needless word."[3] It follows that, from whatever the Lord keeps us, the same He admonishes us to bear patiently from another. I will add [somewhat] touching the *pleasure* of patience. For every injury, whether inflicted by tongue or hand, when it has lighted upon patience, will be dismissed[4] with the same fate as some weapon launched against and blunted on a rock of most stedfast hardness. For it will wholly fall then and there with bootless and fruitless labour; and sometimes will recoil and spend its rage on him who sent it out, with retorted impetus. No doubt the reason why any one hurts you is that you may be pained; because the hurter's enjoyment consists in the pain of the hurt. When, then, you have upset his enjoyment by not being pained, *he* must needs be pained by the loss of his enjoyment. Then you not only go unhurt away, which even alone is enough for you; but gratified, into the bargain, by your adversary's disappointment, and revenged by his pain. This is the *utility* and the *pleasure* of patience.

CHAP. IX.—*Of patience under bereavement.*

Not even that species of impatience under the loss of our dear ones is excused, where some assertion of [the right of] grief acts the patron to it. For the consideration of the apostle's declaration must be set before us, who says, "Be not overwhelmed with sadness at the falling asleep of any one, just as the nations are who are without hope."[5] And justly; for, believing the resurrection of Christ, we believe also in our own, for whose sake He both died and rose again.

---

[1] Communicari—κοινοῦσθαι. See Mark vii. 15, "made common," *i.e.* profane, unclean. Compare Acts x. 14, 15 in the Greek.

[2] Reatum. See *de Idol.* i. *ad init.*, "the highest impeachment of the age."

[3] Matt. xii. 36. Tertullian has rendered ἀργόν by "vani et supervacui."

[4] Dispungetur: a word which, in the active, means technically "to balance accounts," hence "to discharge," etc.

[5] 1 Thess. iv. 13, not very strictly rendered.

Since, then, there is certainty as to the resurrection of the dead, grief for death is needless, and impatience of grief is needless. For why should you grieve, if you believe that [your loved one] is not perished? Why should you bear impatiently the temporary withdrawal of him who you believe will return? That which you think to be death is departure. He who goes before us is not to be lamented, but plainly [he is] to be longed for.[1] That longing also must be tempered with patience. For why should you bear without moderation [the fact that] one is gone away whom you will presently follow? Besides, impatience in matters of this kind bodes ill for our hope, and is a dealing insincerely with the faith. And we wound Christ when we accept not with equanimity the summoning out of this world of any by Him, as if they were to be pitied. "I desire," says the apostle, "to be now received, and to be with Christ."[2] How far better a desire does *he* exhibit! If, then, we grieve impatiently over such as *have* attained the desire of Christians, we show unwillingness ourselves to attain it.

Chap. x.—*Of revenge.*

There is, too, another chief spur of impatience, the lust of revenge, dealing with the business either of glory or else of malice. But "glory," on the one hand, is everywhere "vain;"[3] and malice, on the other, is always[4] odious to the Lord; in this case indeed most of all, when, being provoked by a neighbour's malice, it constitutes itself superior[5] in following out revenge, and by paying wickedness doubles [the evil] which has once been done. Revenge, in the estimation of error,[6] seems a solace of pain; in the estimation of truth, on the contrary, it is convicted of malignity. For what difference is there between provoker and provoked, except

---

[1] Desiderandus.
[2] Phil. i. 23, again loosely rendered: *e.g.* ἀναλῦσαι = "to weigh anchor," is rendered by Tertullian "recipi."
[3] See Gal. v. 26; Phil. ii. 3.   [4] Nunquam non.
[5] *i.e.* perhaps superior *in degree of malice.*
[6] *i.e.* of the world and its erroneous philosophies.

that the former is detected as prior in evil-doing, but the latter as posterior? Yet each stands impeached of hurting a man in the eye of the Lord, who both prohibits and condemns every wickedness. In evil-doing there is no account taken of *order*, nor does *place* separate what *similarity* conjoins. And the precept is absolute, that evil is not to be repaid with evil.[1] Like deed involves like merit. How shall we observe that principle, if in our loathing[2] we shall not loathe *revenge*? What honour, moreover, shall we be offering to the Lord God, if we arrogate to ourselves the arbitrament of vengeance? We are corrupt[3]—earthen vessels.[4] With our own servant-boys,[5] if they assume to themselves the right of vengeance on their fellow-servants, we are gravely offended; while such as make us the offering of their patience we not only approve as mindful of humility, of servitude, affectionately jealous of the right of their lord's honour; but we make them an ampler satisfaction than they would have pre-exacted[6] for themselves. Is there any risk of a different result in the case of a Lord so just in estimating, so potent in executing? Why, then, do we believe Him a Judge, if not an Avenger too? This He promises that He will be to us in return, saying, "[Leave] vengeance to me, and I will avenge;"[7] that is, [Offer] patience to me, and I will reward patience. For when He says, "Judge not, lest ye be judged,"[8] does He not require patience? For who will refrain from judging another, but he who shall be patient in not revenging himself? Who *judges* in order to *pardon*? And if he shall pardon, still he has taken care to indulge the impatience of a judger, and has taken away the honour of the one Judge, that is, God. How many mischances had impatience of this kind been wont to run into! How oft has

---

[1] Rom. xii. 17.
[2] Fastidientes, *i.e.* our loathing or abhorrence of *sin*. Perhaps the reference may be to Rom. xii. 9.
[3] Isa. lxiv. 6.   [4] Isa. lxiv. 8; 2 Cor. iv. 7.
[5] Servulis.   [6] Præsumpsissent.
[7] Deut. xxxii. 35; Ps. xciv. 1; Rom. xii. 19; Heb. x. 30.
[8] Matt. vii. 1; Luke vi. 37.

it repented of its revenge! How oft has its vehemence been found worse than the causes which led to it!—inasmuch as nothing undertaken with impatience can be effected without impetuosity: nothing done with impetuosity fails either to stumble, or else to fall altogether, or else to vanish headlong. Moreover, if you avenge yourself too slightly, you will be mad; if too amply, you will have to bear the burden.[1] What have I to do with vengeance, the measure of which, through impatience of pain, I am unable to regulate? Whereas, if I shall repose on patience, I shall not *feel* pain; if I shall not feel pain, I shall not *desire* to avenge myself.

CHAP. XI.—*Further reasons for practising patience. Its connection with " the Beatitudes."*

After these principal material causes of impatience, registered to the best of our ability, why should we wander out of our way among the rest,—what are found at home, what abroad? Wide and diffusive is the Evil One's operation, hurling manifold irritations of our spirit, and sometimes trifling ones, sometimes very great. But the trifling ones you may contemn from their very littleness; to the very great ones you may yield in regard of their overpoweringness. Where the injury is less, there is no necessity for impatience; but where the injury is greater, there more necessary is the remedy for the injury—patience. Let us strive, therefore, to endure the inflictions of the Evil One, that the counter-zeal of our equanimity may mock the zeal of the foe. If, however, we ourselves, either by imprudence or else voluntarily, draw upon ourselves anything, let us meet with equal patience what we have to blame ourselves for. Moreover, if we believe that some inflictions are sent on us by the Lord, to whom should we more exhibit patience than to the Lord? Nay, He teaches[2] us to give thanks and rejoice, over and above, at being thought worthy of divine chastisement.

[1] *i.e.* the penalty which the law will inflict.
[2] Docet. But a plausible conjecture, "decet," "it becomes us," has been made.

"Whom I love," saith He, "I chasten."[1] O blessed servant, on whose amendment the Lord is intent! with whom He deigns to be wroth! whom He does not deceive by dissembling His reproofs! On every side, therefore, we are bound to the duty of exercising patience, from whatever quarter, either by our own errors or else by the snares of the Evil One, we incur the Lord's reproofs. Of that duty great is the reward— happiness, namely. For whom but the patient has the Lord called happy, in saying, "Blessed are the poor in spirit, for theirs is the kingdom of the heavens?"[2] No one, assuredly, is "poor in spirit," except he be humble. Well, who is humble, except he be patient? For no one can abase himself without patience, in the first instance, to bear the act of abasement. "Blessed," saith He, "are the weepers and mourners."[3] Who, without patience, is tolerant of such unhappinesses? And so, to such, "consolation" and "laughter" are promised. "Blessed are the gentle:"[4] under this term, surely, the impatient cannot possibly be classed. Again, when He marks "the peacemakers"[5] with the same title of felicity, and names them "sons of God," pray have the impatient any affinity with "peace?" Even a fool may perceive that. When, however, He says, "Rejoice and exult, as often as they shall curse and persecute you; for very great is your reward in heaven,"[6] of course it is not to the *impatience* of exultation[7] that He makes that promise; because no one *will* "exult" in adversities unless he have first learnt to contemn them; no one will contemn them unless he have learnt to practise patience.

CHAP. XII.—*Certain other divine precepts, and the apostolic description of Charity, in their connection with patience.*

As regards the rule of peace, which [8] is so pleasing to God, who in the world that is prone to impatience[9] will even *once*

---

[1] Prov. iii. 11, 12; Heb. xii. 5, 6; Rev. iii. 19.
[2] Matt. v. 3.   [3] Matt. v. 4.   [4] Matt. v. 5.
[5] Matt. v. 9.   [6] Matt. v. 11, 12, inexactly quoted.
[7] Exultationis impatientiæ.   [8] *i.e.* peace.
[9] Impatientiæ natus: lit. "born for impatience." Comp. *de Pæn.* 12, *ad fin.:* "nec ulli rei nisi pænitentiæ natus."

forgive his brother, I will not say "seven times," or[1] "seventy-seven times?"[2] Who that is contemplating a suit against his adversary will compose the matter by agreement,[3] unless he first begin by lopping off [the shoots of] chagrin, hard-heartedness, and bitterness, which are in fact the poisonous outgrowths of impatience? How will you "remit, and remission shall be granted" you,[4] if the absence of patience makes you tenacious of [the memory of] a wrong? No one who is at variance with his brother in his mind, will finish offering his "duteous gift at the altar," unless he first, with intent to "re-conciliate his brother," return to patience.[5] If "the sun go down over our wrath," we are in jeopardy:[6] we are not allowed to remain one day without patience. But, however, since Patience takes the lead in[7] every species of salutary discipline, what wonder that she likewise ministers to Repentance, (accustomed as Repentance is to come to the rescue of such as have fallen,) when, on a disjunction of wedlock (for that cause, I mean, which makes it lawful, whether for husband or wife, to persist in the perpetual observance of widowhood[8]), she[9] waits for, she yearns for, she persuades by her entreaties, repentance in all who are one day to enter salvation? How great a blessing she confers on each! The one she prevents from becoming an adulterer; the other she amends. So, too, she is found in those holy examples touching patience in the Lord's parables. The shepherd's patience seeks and finds the straying ewe:[10] for *Im*patience would easily despise *one* ewe; but Patience undertakes the labour of the quest, and

---

[1] Oehler reads "sed," but the "vel" adopted in the text is a conjecture of Latinius, which Oehler mentions.

[2] Septuagies septies. The reference is to Matt. xviii. 21, 22. Compare *de Or*. vii. *ad fin*. and the note there.

[3] Matt. v. 25.   [4] Luke vi. 37.

[5] Matt. v. 23, 24.   [6] Eph. iv. 26. Compare *de Or*. xi.

[7] Gubernet.

[8] What that cause *is* is disputed. Opinions are divided as to whether Tertullian means by it "marriage with a heathen" (which, as Mr. Dodgson reminds us, Tertullian—*de Uxor*. ii. 3—calls "adultery"), or the case in which our Lord allowed divorce. See Matt. xix. 9.

[9] *i.e.* patience.   [10] Luke xv. 3–6.

the patient burden-bearer carries home on his shoulders the forsaken sinner.[1] That prodigal son also the father's patience receives, and clothes, and feeds, and makes excuses for, in the presence of the angry brother's *im*patience.[2] He, therefore, who "had perished" is saved, because he entered on [the path of] repentance. Repentance perishes not, because it finds Patience [ready to welcome it]. For by whose teachings but those of Patience is Charity[3]—the highest sacrament of the faith, the treasure-house of the Christian name, which the apostle commends with the whole strength of the Holy Spirit—trained? "Charity," he says, "is long-suffering;" thus she applies patience: "is beneficent;" Patience does no evil: "is not emulous;" that certainly is a peculiar mark of patience: "savours not of violence;"[4] she has drawn her self-restraint from patience: "is not puffed up; is not violent;"[5] for that pertains not unto patience: "nor does she seek her own;" [certainly not], if, [as she does,] she *offers* her own, provided she may benefit her neighbours: "nor is irritable;" if she were, what would she have left to *Im*patience [as her characteristic]? Accordingly he says, "Charity endures all things; tolerates all things;" of course because she is patient. Justly, then, "will she never fail;"[6] for all other things will be cancelled, will have their consummation. "Tongues, sciences, prophecies, become exhausted; faith, hope, charity, are permanent." Faith, which Christ's patience introduced; hope, which man's patience waits for; charity, which, with God as Master, patience accompanies.

CHAP. XIII.—*Of bodily patience.*

Thus far, finally, of patience simple and uniform, and as it

---

[1] Peccatricem, *i.e.* the ewe.   [2] Luke xv. 11-32.
[3] Dilectio = ἀγάπη. See Trench, *New Testament Syn. s. v.* ἀγάπη; and with the rest of this chapter compare carefully, in the Greek, 1 Cor. xiii.
[4] Protervum = Greek περπεριύεται.
[5] Proterit = Greek ἀσχημονεῖ.
[6] Excidet = Greek ἐκλείπει, suffers eclipse.

exists merely in the *mind:* though in many forms likewise I labour after it in *body,* for the purpose of "winning the Lord;"[1] inasmuch as it is [a quality] which has been exhibited by the Lord Himself in bodily virtue as well; if it is true that the ruling mind easily communicates the gifts[2] of the Spirit with its [corporeal] habitation. What, therefore, is the business of Patience *in the body?* In the first place, [her business is] the affliction[3] of the flesh—a victim[4] able to appease the Lord by means of the sacrifice of humiliation—in making a libation to the Lord of sordid[5] raiment, together with scantiness of food, content with simple diet and the pure drink of water; in conjoining fasts [to all this]; in inuring herself to sackcloth and ashes. This *bodily* patience adds a grace to our prayers for good, a strength to our prayers against evil; this opens the ears of Christ [our] God,[6] dissipates severity, elicits clemency. Thus that Babylonish king,[7] after being exiled from human form in his seven years' squalor and neglect, because he had offended the Lord; by the immolation of the patience of his body not only recovered his kingdom, but—what is more to be desired by a man—made satisfaction to God. Further, if we set down in order the higher and happier grades of bodily Patience, [we find that] it is she who is entrusted by holiness with the care of continence of the flesh: she keeps the widow [in widowhood],[8] and sets on the virgin the seal [of perpetual virginity],[9] and raises the self-made eunuch to the kingdoms of heaven.[10] That which springs from a virtue of the *mind* is perfected in the *flesh;* [and,] finally, by the patience of the flesh, does battle under persecution. If flight press [us] hard, the flesh wars with[11] the inconveniences of flight; if imprison-

---

[1] Phil. iii. 8.
[2] "Invecta," generally = moveables, household furniture.
[3] Or, mortification, "adflictatio."
[4] *i.e.* fleshly mortification is "a victim," etc.
[5] Or, "mourning." Comp. *de Pæn.* c. 9.   [6] Christi Dei.
[7] Dan. iv. 33-37. Comp. *de Pæn.* c. 12.
[8] 1 Tim. v. 3, 9, 10; 1 Cor. vii. 39, 40.
[9] 1 Cor. vii. 34, 35.   [10] Matt. xix. 12.
[11] Ad. It seems to mean the flesh has strength given it, by patience,

ment overtake [1] us, the flesh [endures] in bonds, the flesh in the gyve, the flesh in solitude,[2] and in that want of light, and in that patience of the world's misusage. When, however, it is led forth unto the final proof of happiness,[3] unto the occasion of the second baptism,[4] unto the act of ascending the divine seat, no patience is more needed *there* than *bodily* patience. If the "spirit is willing, but the flesh," *without* patience, " weak," [5] where [but *in* patience] is the safety of the spirit, and of the flesh itself? But when the Lord says this about the flesh, pronouncing it "weak," He shows what need there is of strengthening it,—by patience, namely,—to meet [6] every preparation for subverting or punishing faith; that it may bear with all constancy stripes, fire, cross, beasts, sword; all which prophets and apostles, by enduring, conquered!

CHAP. XIV.—*The power of this twofold (spiritual and bodily) patience, as exemplified in saints of old.*

[Armed] with this strength of patience, Esaias is cut [asunder], and ceases not to speak concerning the Lord; Stephen is stoned, and prays for pardon to his foes.[7] Oh, happy also he who met all the violence of the devil by the exertion of every species of patience![8]—whom neither the driving away of his cattle, nor those riches of his in sheep, nor the sweeping away of his children in one swoop of ruin, nor, finally, the agony of his own body in [one universal] wound, estranged from the patience and the faith which he had plighted to the Lord; whom the devil smote with all his might in vain. For by all his pains he was not drawn away from his reverence for God; but he has been set up as an example and testimony to us, for the thorough accomplishment of patience as well in spirit as in flesh, as well in mind

---

to meet the hardships of the flight. Compare the πρὸς πλησμονὴν τῆς σαρκός of St. Paul in Col. ii. 23.

[1] Præveniat; "prevent" us, before we have time to flee.
[2] Solo.   [3] *i.e.* martyrdom.   [4] Comp. Luke xii. 50.
[5] Matt. xxvi. 41.   [6] "Adversus," like the "ad" above.
[7] Acts vii. 59, 60.   [8] Job. See Job i. and ii.

as in body; in order that we succumb neither to damages of our worldly goods, nor to losses of them who are dearest, nor even to bodily afflictions. What a bier[1] for the devil did God erect in the person of that hero! What a banner did He rear over the enemy of His glory, when, at every bitter message, that man uttered nothing out of his mouth but thanks to God, while he denounced his wife, now quite wearied with ills, and urging him to resort to crooked remedies! How did God laugh,[2] how was the evil one cut asunder,[3] while Job with mighty equanimity kept scraping off[4] the unclean overflow of his own ulcer, while he sportively replaced the vermin that brake out thence, in the same caves and feeding-places of his pitted flesh [whence they had issued]! And so, when all the darts of temptations had blunted themselves against the corslet and shield of his patience, that instrument[5] of God's victory not only presently recovered from God the soundness of his body, but possessed in redoubled measure what he had lost. And if he had wished to have his children also restored, he might again have been called father; but he preferred to have them restored him "in that day."[6] Such joy as *that*—secure so entirely concerning the Lord—he deferred; meantime he endured a voluntary bereavement, that he might not live without *some* [exercise of] patience.

CHAP. XV.—*General summary of the virtues and effects of patience.*

So amply sufficient a Depositary of patience is God. If it be a wrong which you deposit in His care, He is an Avenger; if a loss, He is a Restorer; if pain, He is a Healer; if death, He is a Reviver. What honour is granted to Patience, to have God as her Debtor! And not without reason: for she

---

[1] "Feretrum"—for carrying trophies in a triumph, the bodies of the dead, and their effigies, etc.
[2] Compare Ps. ii. 4.   [3] *i.e.* with rage and disappointment.
[4] Job ii. 8.   [5] Operarius.
[6] See 2 Tim. iv. 8. There is no authority for this statement of Tertullian's in Scripture.

keeps all His decrees; she has to do with all His mandates. She fortifies faith; is the pilot of peace; assists charity; establishes humility; waits long for repentance; sets her seal on confession; rules the flesh; preserves the spirit; bridles the tongue; restrains the hand; tramples temptations under foot; drives away scandals; gives their crowning grace to martyrdoms; consoles the poor; teaches the rich moderation; overstrains not the weak; exhausts not the strong; is the delight of the believer; invites the Gentile; commends the servant to his lord, and his lord to God; adorns the woman; makes the man approved; is loved in childhood, praised in youth, looked up to in age; is beauteous in every sex, in every time of life. Come, now, [let us see] whether[1] we have a general idea of her mien and habit. Her countenance is tranquil and peaceful; her brow serene,[2] contracted by no wrinkle of sadness or of anger; her eyebrows evenly relaxed in gladsome wise, with eyes downcast in humility, not in unhappiness; her mouth sealed with the honourable mark of silence; her hue such as theirs who are without care and without guilt; the motion of her head frequent against the devil, and her laugh threatening;[3] her clothing, moreover, about her bosom white and well fitted to her person, as being neither inflated nor disturbed. For [Patience] sits on the throne of that calmest and gentlest Spirit, who is not found in the roll of the whirlwind, nor in the leaden hue of the cloud, but is [a Spirit] of soft serenity, open and simple, whom Elias saw at his third [vision].[4] For where God is, there too is His foster-child, namely Patience. When God's Spirit descends, then Patience accompanies Him indivisibly. If we do not give admission [to her] together

[1] Si. This is Oehler's reading, who takes "ai" to be = "an." But perhaps "sis" (= "si vis"), which is Fr. Junius' correction, is better: "Come, now, let us, if you please, give a general sketch of her mien and habit."

[2] Pura; perhaps "smooth."

[3] Compare with this singular feature, Isa. xxxvii. 22.

[4] *i.e.*, as Rigaltius (referred to by Oehler) explains, after the *two* visions of angels who appeared to him and said, "Arise and eat." See 1 Kings xix. 4–13.

with the Spirit, will [the Spirit] *always* tarry with us? Nay, I know not whether He would remain *any longer.* Without His companion and handmaid, He must of necessity be straitened in every place and at every time. Whatever blow His enemy may inflict He will be unable to endure alone, being without the instrumental means of enduring.

CHAP. XVI.—*The patience of the heathen very different from Christian patience. Theirs is doomed to perdition; ours destined to salvation.*

This is the rule, this the discipline, these the works of [that] patience [which is] heavenly and true ; that is, of Christian [patience], not like as is that patience [we spoke of] of the nations of the earth, false and disgraceful. For in order that in this also the devil might rival the Lord, he has as it were quite on a par (except that the very diversity of evil and good is exactly on a par with their magnitude [1]) taught *his* [disciples] also a patience of his own : that, I mean, which, making husbands venal for dowry, and teaching them to trade in panderings, makes them subject to the power of their wives ; which, with feigned affection, undergoes every toil of forced complaisance,[2] with a view to ensnaring the childless ;[3] which makes the slaves of the belly[4] submit to contumelious patronage, in the subjection of their liberty to their gullet. Such pursuits of patience the Gentiles are acquainted with ; and they eagerly seize a name of so great goodness to apply it to foul practices : patient they live of rivals, and of the rich, and of such as give them invitations ; impatient of God alone. But let their own and their leader's patience look to itself—[a patience] which the subterraneous fire awaits ! Let us, on the other hand, love the patience of God, the patience of Christ ; let us repay to Him the [patience] which He has paid down for us ! Let us offer [to Him] the patience of the spirit, the patience of the flesh, believing as we do in the resurrection of flesh and spirit.

[1] One is finite, the other infinite.   [2] Obsequii.
[3] And thus getting a place in their wills.
[4] *i.e.* professional " diners out." Comp. Phil. iii. 19.

IX.
ON BAPTISM.

CHAP. I.—*Introduction. Origin of the treatise.*

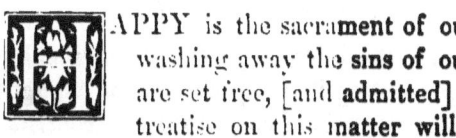APPY is the sacrament of our[1] water, in that, by washing away the sins of our early blindness, we are set free, [and admitted] into eternal life! A treatise on this matter will not be superfluous; instructing not only such as are just being formed [in the faith], but them who, content with having simply believed, without full examination of the grounds[2] of the traditions, carry [in their mind], through ignorance, an untried [and merely] probable faith. The consequence is, that a viper of the Cainite heresy, lately conversant in this quarter, has carried away a great number with her most venomous doctrine, making it her first aim to destroy baptism: [a course] which is quite in accordance with nature; for vipers and asps and basilisks themselves generally do affect arid and waterless places. But we, little fishes, after the example of our ΙΧΘΥΣ[3] Jesus Christ, are born in water, nor have we safety in any other way than by permanently abiding in

---

[1] *i.e.* Christian (Oehler).   [2] Rationibus.
[3] This curious allusion it is impossible, perhaps, to render in our language. The word ΙΧΘΥΣ (*ikhthus*) in Greek means "a fish;" and it was used as a name for our Lord Jesus, because the initials of the words Ἰησοῦς Χριστός Θεοῦ Υἱός Σωτήρ (*i.e.* Jesus Christ, the Son of God, the Saviour), make up that word.—(OEHLER, who gives abundant references on the point.)

[that] water. And so that most monstrous creature, who had no right to teach even sound doctrine,[1] knew full well how to kill the little fishes, by taking them away from the water!

CHAP. II.—*The very simplicity of God's means of working, a stumbling-block to the carnal mind.*

Well, but how great is the force of perversity for shaking the faith or entirely preventing its reception, that it impugns it on the very principles of which [the faith itself] consists! There is absolutely nothing which makes men's minds more obdurate than the simplicity of the divine works which are visible in the *act*, when compared with the grandeur which is promised thereto in the *effect;* so that from the very fact, that with so great simplicity, without pomp, without any considerable novelty of preparation, finally, without expense, a man is dipped in water, and, amid the utterance of some few words, is sprinkled, and then rises again, not much (or not at all) the cleaner, the consequent attainment of eternity[2] is esteemed the more incredible. I am a deceiver if, on the contrary, it is not from their circumstance, and preparation, and expense, that *idols'* solemnities or mysteries get their credit and authority built up. Oh, miserable incredulity, which quite deniest to God His own properties, simplicity and power! What then? Is it not wonderful, too, that death should be washed away by bathing? But it is the more to be believed if the wonderfulness be the reason why it is *not* believed. For what does it behove divine works to be in their quality, except that they be above all wonder?[3] We also ourselves wonder, but it is *because* we believe. Incredulity, on the other hand, wonders, but does *not* believe: for the simple [acts] it wonders at, as if they were vain; the grand [results], as if they were impossible. And grant that it be just as you think;[4] sufficient to meet each point is the divine declaration which has forerun: "The foolish things of

---

[1] As being a woman. See 1 Tim. ii. 11, 12.
[2] Consecutio æternitatis.   [3] Admirationem.
[4] *i.e.* that the simple be vain, and the grand impossible.

the world hath God elected to confound its wisdom;"[1] and, "The things very difficult with men are easy with God."[2] For if God is wise and powerful (which even they who pass Him by do not deny), it is with good reason that He lays the material causes of His own operation in the contraries of wisdom and of power, that is, in foolishness and impossibility; since every virtue receives its cause from those things by which it is called forth.

CHAP. III.—*Why should* WATER *be chosen as a vehicle of divine operation? Its prominence first of all in Creation.*

Mindful of this declaration as of a conclusive prescript, we nevertheless [proceed to] treat [the question], "How *foolish* and *impossible* it is to be formed anew by water. In what respect, pray, has this material substance merited an office of so high dignity?" The authority, I suppose, of the liquid element has to be examined.[3] This,[4] however, is found in abundance, and that from the very beginning. For [water] is one of those things which, before all the furnishing of the world, were quiescent with God in a yet unshapen[5] state. "In the first beginning," saith [Scripture], "God made the heaven and the earth. But the earth was invisible, and unorganized,[6] and darkness was over the abyss; and the Spirit of the Lord was hovering[7] over the waters."[8] The first thing, O man, which you have to venerate, is the *age* of the waters, in that their substance is ancient; the second, their *dignity*, in that they were the seat of the Divine Spirit, more pleasing [to Him], no doubt, than all the other then existing elements. For the darkness was total thus far, shapeless, without the ornament of stars; and the abyss gloomy; and the earth unfurnished; and the heaven unwrought: water[9] alone—always a perfect, gladsome, simple material substance, pure

---

[1] 1 Cor. i. 27, not quite exactly quoted.
[2] Luke xviii. 27, again inexact.
[3] Compare the Jews' question, Matt. xxi. 23.
[4] Its authority.
[5] Impolita.
[6] Incomposita.
[7] Ferebatur.
[8] Gen. i. 1, 2, and comp. the LXX.
[9] Liquor.

in itself—supplied a worthy vehicle to God. What [of the fact] that waters were in some way the regulating powers by which the disposition of the world thenceforward was constituted by God? For the suspension of the celestial firmament in the midst He caused by "dividing the waters;"[1] the suspension of "the dry land" He accomplished by "separating the waters." After the world had been hereupon set in order through [its] elements, when inhabitants were given it, "the waters" were the first to receive the precept "to bring forth living creatures."[2] Water was the first to produce that which had life, that it might be no wonder in baptism if waters know how to give life.[3] For was not the work of fashioning man himself also achieved with the aid of waters? Suitable material is found in the *earth*, yet not apt for the purpose unless it be moist and juicy; which [earth] "the waters," separated the fourth day before into their own place, temper with their remaining moisture to a clayey consistency. If, from that time onward, I go forward in recounting universally, or at more length [than I have already done], the evidences of the "authority" of this element which I can adduce to show how great is its power or its grace; how many ingenious devices, how many functions, how useful an instrumentality, it affords the world, I fear I may seem to have collected rather the praises of water than the reasons of baptism; although I should [thereby] teach all the more fully, that it is not to be doubted that God has made the material substance which He has disposed throughout all His products[4] and works, obey Him also in His own peculiar sacraments; that the [material substance] which governs terrestrial life acts as agent likewise in the celestial.

CHAP. IV.—*The primeval hovering of the Spirit of God over the waters typical of baptism. The universal element of water thus made a channel of sanctification. Resemblance between the outward sign and the inward grace.*

But it will suffice to have [thus] culled at the outset those points in which withal is recognised that primary principle

[1] Gen. i. 6, 7, 8.   [2] Animas.   [3] Animare.   [4] Rebus.

of baptism,—[a principle] which was even then fore-noted by the very attitude [which the Spirit assumed] for a type of baptism,—that the Spirit of God, who hovered over [the waters] from the beginning, would continue to linger over the waters of the baptized.[1] But a holy thing, of course, hovered over a holy; or else, from that which hovered over that which *was* hovered over borrowed a holiness, since it is necessary that in every case an underlying material substance should catch the quality of that which overhangs it, most of all a corporeal of a spiritual, adapted [as the spiritual is], through the subtleness of its substance, both for penetrating and insinuating. Thus the nature of the waters, sanctified by the Holy One, itself conceived withal the power of sanctifying. Let no one say, "Why then, are we, pray, baptized with the very waters which then existed in the first beginning?" Not with those very waters, of course, except in so far as the *genus* indeed is one, but the *species* very many. But what is an attribute to the *genus* reappears[2] likewise in the *species*. And accordingly it makes no difference whether a man be washed in a sea or a pool, a stream or a fount, a lake or a trough;[3] nor is there any distinction between those whom John baptized in the Jordan and those whom Peter baptized in the Tiber, unless withal [it be thought that] the eunuch whom Philip baptized in the midst of his journeys with chance water, derived [therefrom] more or less of salvation [than others].[4] All waters, therefore, in virtue of the pristine privilege of their origin, do, after invocation of God, attain the sacramental power of sanctification; for the Spirit immediately supervenes from the heavens, and rests over the waters, sanctifying them from Himself; and being thus sanctified, they imbibe at the same time the power of sanctifying. Albeit the similitude may be admitted to be suitable to the simple act; that, since we are defiled by sins, as it were by dirt, we should be washed from those stains in waters. But as sins do not show themselves in our *flesh* (inasmuch as no one carries on his skin the spot of idolatry, or fornication, or fraud), so persons of that kind are foul in

[1] Intinctorum. [2] Redundat. [3] Alveo. [4] Acts viii. 26-40.

the *spirit*, which is the author of the sin; for the spirit is lord, the flesh servant. Yet they each mutually share the guilt: the spirit, on the ground of command; the flesh, of subservience. Therefore, after the waters have been in a manner endued with medicinal virtue[1] through the intervention of the angel,[2] the spirit is corporeally washed in the waters, and the flesh is in the same spiritually cleansed.

CHAP. V.—*Use made of water by the heathen. Type of the angel at the pool of Bethsaida (Bethesda, Eng. ver.).*

"Well, but the nations, who are strangers to all understanding of spiritual powers, ascribe to their idols the imbuing of waters with the self-same efficacy." [So they do], but they cheat themselves with waters which are widowed.[3] For washing is the channel through which they are initiated into some sacred rites—[rites] of some notorious Isis or Mithras; [and] the gods themselves likewise they honour by washings. Moreover, by carrying water around, and sprinkling it, they everywhere expiate[4] country-seats, houses, temples, and whole cities: at all events, at the Apollinarian and Eleusinian games they are baptized; and they presume that the effect of their doing that is their regeneration, and the remission of the penalties due to their perjuries. Among the ancients, again, whoever had defiled himself with murder, was wont to go in quest of purifying waters. Therefore, if the mere nature of water, in that it is the appropriate material for washing away, leads men to flatter themselves with a belief in omens of purification, how much more truly will waters render that service through the authority of God, by whom all their nature has been constituted! If men think that water is endued with a medicinal virtue by religion, what religion is more effectual than that of the living God? Which fact being acknowledged, we recognise here also the zeal of the devil rivalling the things of God, while we find

---

[1] Medicatis. [2] See c. vi. *ad init.*, and c. v. *ad fin.*
[3] *i.e.*, as Oehler rightly explains, "lacking the Holy Spirit's presence and virtue."
[4] Or, "purify."

him, too, practising baptism in his [subjects]. What similarity is there? The unclean cleanses! the ruiner sets free! the damned absolves! He will, forsooth, destroy his own work, by washing away the sins which himself inspires! These [remarks] have been set down by way of testimony against such as reject the faith; if they put no trust in the things of God, the spurious imitations of which, in the case of God's rival, they do trust in. Are there not other cases too, in which, without any sacrament, unclean spirits brood on waters, in spurious imitation of that brooding[1] of the Divine Spirit in the very beginning? Witness all shady founts, and all unfrequented brooks, and the ponds in the baths, and the conduits[2] in [private] houses, or the cisterns and wells which are said to have the property of "spiriting away,"[3] through the power, that is, of a hurtful spirit. Men whom waters have drowned[4] or affected with madness or with fear, they call "nymph-caught,"[5] or "lymphatic," or "hydrophobic." Why have we adduced these instances? Lest any think it too hard [for belief] that a holy angel of God should grant his presence to waters, to temper them to man's salvation; while the evil angel holds frequent profane commerce with the selfsame element to man's ruin. If it seems a novelty for an angel to be present in waters, an example of what was to come to pass has forerun. An angel, by his intervention, was wont to stir the pool at Bethsaida.[6] They who were complaining of ill-health used to watch for him; for whoever had been the first to descend into them, ceased, after his washing, to complain [any more]. This figure of corporeal healing sang of a spiritual healing, according to the rule by which things carnal are always antecedent[7] as figurative of things spiritual. And thus, when the grace of God advanced to higher degrees among men,[8] an accession [of efficacy] was granted

[1] Gestationem. [2] Euripi. [3] Rapere. [4] Necaverunt.
[5] "Nympholeptos," restored by Oehler, = νυμφοληπτους.
[6] So Tertullian reads, and some copies, but not the best, of the New Testament in the place referred to (John v. 1-9).
[7] Compare 1 Cor. xv. 46. [8] John i. 16, 17.

to the waters and to the angel. They who[1] were wont to remedy bodily defects,[2] now heal the spirit; they who used to work temporal salvation,[3] now renew eternal; they who did set free but once in the year, now save peoples in a body[4] daily, death being done away through ablution of sins. The guilt being removed, of course the penalty is removed too. Thus man will be restored for God to His "likeness," who in days bygone had been [conformed] to "the image" of God; (the "image" is counted [to be] in his *form;* the "likeness" in his *eternity:*) for he receives again that Spirit of God which he had then first received from His afflatus, but had afterward lost through sin.

CHAP. VI.—*The angel the forerunner of the Holy Spirit. Meaning contained in the baptismal formula.*

Not that *in*[5] the waters we obtain the Holy Spirit; but in the water, under [the influence of] the angel, we are cleansed, and [thus] prepared *for* the Holy Spirit. In this case also a type has preceded; for thus was John beforehand the Lord's forerunner, "preparing His ways."[6] Thus, too, does the angel, the witness[7] of baptism, "make the paths straight"[8] for the Holy Spirit, who is about to come upon us, by the washing away of sins which faith, sealed in [the name of] the Father, and the Son, and the Holy Spirit, obtains. For if "in [the mouth of] three witnesses every word shall stand,"[9] how much more—while, through the benediction [uttered], we have the same [three] as witnesses of our faith whom we have as sureties[10] of our salvation too—does the number of the divine names suffice for the assurance of our hope likewise! Moreover, after the pledging both of the attestation of faith and the promise[11] of salvation under [the sanction of]

---

[1] "Qui," *i.e.* probably, "angeli qui."   [2] Vitia.
[3] Or, "health"—salutem.   [4] Conservant populos.
[5] Compare c. viii., where Tertullian appears to regard the Holy Spirit as given *after* the baptized had come up out of the waters and received the "unction."
[6] Luke i. 76.   [7] Arbiter.   [8] Isa. xl. 3; Matt. iii. 3.
[9] Deut. xix. 15; Matt. xviii. 16; 2 Cor. xiii. 1.
[10] Sponsores.   [11] Sponsio.

"three witnesses," there is added, of necessity, mention of the church;[1] inasmuch as, wherever there are three, (that is, the Father, the Son, and the Holy Spirit,) there is the church, which is a body of three.[2]

CHAP. VII.—*Of the unction.*

After this, when we have issued from the font,[3] we are thoroughly anointed with a blessed unction,—[a practice derived] from the old discipline, wherein, on entering the priesthood, [men] were wont to be anointed with oil from a horn, ever since Aaron was anointed by Moses;[4] whence Aaron is called "Christ,"[5] from the "chrism," which is "the unction;" which, when made spiritual, furnished an appropriate name to the Lord, because He was "anointed" with the Spirit by God the Father; as [we have it] in the Acts: "For truly they were gathered together in this city[6] against Thy Holy Son whom Thou hast anointed."[7] Thus, too, in *our* case, the unction runs [down our flesh] carnally, but profits spiritually, in the same way as the *act* of baptism itself too is carnal, in that we are plunged in water; the *effect* spiritual, in that we are freed from sins.

CHAP. VIII.—*Of the imposition of hands. Types of the deluge and the dove.*

In the next place the hand is laid on us, invoking and inviting the Holy Spirit through [the words of] benediction. Shall it be granted possible for human ingenuity to summon a spirit into water, and, by the application of hands from

---

[1] Compare *de Or.* c. ii. *sub fin.*
[2] Compare the *de Or.* quoted above, and *de Pa.* xxi.; and see Matt. xviii. 20.
[3] Lavacro.   [4] See Ex. xxix. 7; Lev. viii. 12; Ps. cxxxiii. 2.
[5] *i.e.* "Anointed." Aaron, or at least the priest, is actually so called in the LXX., in Lev. iv. 5, 16, ὁ ἱερεὺς ὁ Χριστός: as in the Hebrew it is the word whence "Messiah" is derived which is used.
[6] Civitate.
[7] Acts iv. 27. "In this city" (ἐν τῇ πόλει ταύτῃ) is omitted in the English version; and the name 'Ιησοῦν, "Jesus," is omitted by Tertullian. Compare Acts x. 38 and Lev. iv. 18 with Isa. lxi. 1 in the LXX.

above, to animate their union into one body¹ with another
spirit of so clear sound;² and shall it not be possible for God,
in the case of His own organ,³ to produce, by means of "holy
hands,"⁴ a sublime spiritual modulation? But this [practice]
as well as the former is derived from the old sacramental
rite in which Jacob blessed his grandsons, born of Joseph,
Ephrem⁵ and Manasses; with his hands laid on them and
interchanged, and indeed so transversely slanted one over the
other, that, by delineating Christ, they even portended the
future benediction into Christ.⁶ Then, over our cleansed
and blessed bodies willingly descends from the Father that
Holiest Spirit: over the waters of baptism, recognising as it
were His primeval seat,⁷ He reposes: [He who] glided down
on the Lord " in the shape of a dove," ⁸ in order that the
nature of the Holy Spirit might be declared by means of the
creature [which is the emblem] of simplicity and innocence,
because even in her bodily structure the dove is without
literal⁹ gall. And accordingly He says, "Be ye simple as
doves." ¹⁰ Even this is not without the supporting evidence ¹¹
of a preceding figure. For just as, after the waters of the
deluge, by which the old iniquity was purged—after the baptism, so to say, of the world—a *dove* was the herald which
announced to the earth the assuagement ¹² of celestial wrath,
when she had been sent her way out of the ark, and had
returned with the olive-branch (a sign which even among the
nations is the fore-token of *peace* ¹³); [so] by the self-same
law ¹⁴ of heavenly effect, to earth—that is, to our flesh ¹⁵—as

---

¹ Concorporationem.

² The reference is to certain hydraulic organs, which the editors tell
us are described by Vitruvius, ix. 9 and x. 13, and Pliny, *H. N.* vii. 37.

³ *i.e.* Man. There may be an allusion to Eph. ii. 10, "We are His
workmanship," and to Ps. cl. 4.

⁴ Compare 1 Tim. ii. 8.   ⁵ *i.e.* Ephraim.   ⁶ In Christum.

⁷ See c. iv.   ⁸ Matt. iii. 16; Luke iii. 22.

⁹ Ipso. The ancients held this.

¹⁰ Matt. x. 16. Tertullian has rendered ἀκέραιοι (" unmixed ") by
" simplices" (without fold).

¹¹ Argumento.   ¹² Pacem.   ¹³ Paci.

¹⁴ Dispositione.   ¹⁵ See *de Or.* iv. *ad init.*

it emerges from the font,[1] after its old sins, flies the *dove* of the Holy Spirit, bringing us the peace of God, sent out from the heavens, where is the church, the typified ark.[2] But the world returned unto sin; in which point baptism would ill be compared to the deluge. And so it is destined to fire; just as the man too is, who after baptism renews his sins: so that this also ought to be accepted as a sign for our admonition.

CHAP. IX.—*Types of the Red Sea, and the water from the rock.*

How many, therefore, are the pleas[3] of nature, how many the privileges of grace, how many the solemnities of discipline, the figures, the preparations, the prayers, which have ordained the sanctity of water? First, indeed, when the people, set unconditionally free,[4] escaped the violence of the Egyptian king by crossing over *through water*, it was *water* that extinguished[5] the king himself, with his entire forces.[6] What figure more manifestly fulfilled in the sacrament of baptism? The nations are set free from the world[7] by means of *water*, to wit: and the devil, their old tyrant, they leave quite behind, overwhelmed in the *water*. Again, *water* is restored from its defect of "bitterness" to its native grace of "sweetness" by the tree[8] of Moses. That tree was Christ,[9] restoring, to wit, of Himself, the *veins* of sometime envenomed and bitter nature into the all-salutary *waters* of baptism. This is the *water* which flowed continuously down for the people from the "accompanying rock;" for if Christ is "the Rock," without doubt we see baptism blest by the *water* in Christ. How mighty is the grace of *water*, in the sight of God and His Christ, for the confirmation of baptism!

[1] Lavacro. [2] Compare *de Idol.* xxiv. *ad fin.*
[3] Patrocinia—"*pleas in defence.*"
[4] "Libere expeditus," set free, and that without any conditions, such as Pharaoh had from time to time tried to impose. See Ex. viii. 25, 28, x. 10, 11, 24.
[5] "Extinxit," as it does *fire*. [6] Ex. xiv. 27–30.
[7] Sæculo. [8] See Ex. xv. 24, 25.
[9] "The Tree of Life," "the True Vine," etc.

Never is Christ without *water:* if, that is, [as is the case,] He is Himself baptized in *water;*[1] inaugurates in *water* the first rudimentary displays of His power, when invited to the nuptials;[2] invites the thirsty, when He makes a discourse, to His own sempiternal *water;*[3] approves, when teaching concerning love,[4] among works of charity,[5] the cup of *water* offered to a poor [child];[6] recruits His strength at a *well;*[7] walks over the *water;*[8] willingly crosses the *sea;*[9] ministers *water* to His disciples.[10] Onward even to the passion does the witness of baptism last: while He is being surrendered to the cross, *water* intervenes; witness Pilate's hands:[11] when He is wounded, forth from His side bursts *water;* witness the soldier's lance![12]

CHAP. X.—*Of John's baptism.*

We have spoken, so far as our moderate ability permitted, of the *generals* which form the groundwork of the sanctity[13] of baptism. I will now, equally to the best of my power, proceed to the rest of its character, touching certain minor questions.

The baptism announced by John formed the subject, even at that time, of a question, proposed by the Lord Himself indeed to the Pharisees, whether that baptism were heavenly, or truly earthly:[14] about which they were unable to give a consistent[15] answer, inasmuch as they understood not, because they believed not. But *we,* with but as poor a measure of understanding as of faith, *are* able to determine that that baptism was *divine* indeed, (yet in respect of the command [which authorized it], not in respect of efficacy[16] too, in that we read that John was *sent by the Lord* to perform this

---

[1] Matt. iii. 13-17. [2] John ii. 1-11.
[3] John vii. 37, 38. [4] Agape. See *de Or.* c. 28, *ad fin.*
[5] Dilectionis. See *de Pa.* c. xii. [6] Matt. x. 42.
[7] John iv. 6. [8] Matt. xiv. 25. [9] Mark iv. 36.
[10] John xiii. 1-12. [11] Matt. xxvii. 24. Comp. *de Or.* c. xiii.
[12] John xix. 34. See c. xviii. *sub fin.* [13] Religionem.
[14] Matt. xxi. 25; Mark xi. 30; Luke xx. 4.
[15] Constanter. [16] Potestate.

duty,)[1] but *human* in its nature: for it conveyed nothing celestial, but it fore-ministered to things celestial; being, to wit, appointed over [the work of] *repentance*, which is in man's power.[2] In fact, the doctors of the law and the Pharisees, who were unwilling to "believe," did not "repent" either.[3] But if repentance is a thing human, its baptism must necessarily be of the same nature: else, if it had been celestial, it would have given both the Holy Spirit and remission of sins. But none either pardons sins or freely grants the Spirit save God only.[4] Even the Lord Himself said that the Spirit would not descend on any other condition, but that He should first ascend to the Father.[5] What the Lord was not yet conferring, of course the servant could not furnish. Accordingly, in the Acts of the Apostles, we find that men who had "John's baptism" had not received the Holy Spirit, whom they knew not even by hearing.[6] That, then, was no celestial thing which furnished no celestial [endowments]: whereas the very thing which *was* celestial in John—the Spirit of prophecy—so completely failed, after the transfer of the whole Spirit to the Lord, that he presently sent to inquire whether He whom he had himself preached,[7] whom he had pointed out when coming to him, were "HE."[8] And so "the baptism of repentance"[9] was dealt with[10] as if it were a candidate for the remission and sanctification shortly about to follow in Christ: for in that John used to preach "baptism *for* the remission of sins,"[11] the declaration was made with reference to a *future* remission; if it be true, [as it is,] that repentance is antecedent, remission subsequent; and this is "preparing the way."[12] But he who "prepares" does not himself "perfect," but procures for another to perfect. John

[1] See John i. 33.
[2] It is difficult to see how this statement is to be reconciled with Acts v. 31.
[3] Matt. iii. 7-12, xxi. 23, 31, 32.
[4] Mark ii. 8; 1 Thess. iv. 8; 2 Cor. i. 21, 22, v. 5.
[5] John xvi. 6, 7.   [6] Acts xix. 1-7.
[7] Matt. iii. 11, 12; John i. 6-37.
[8] Matt. xi. 2-6; Luke vii. 18-23.   [9] Acts xix. 4.
[10] Agebatur.   [11] Mark i. 4.   [12] Luke i. 76.

himself professes that the celestial things are not his, but Christ's, by saying, "He who is from the earth speaketh concerning the earth; He who comes from the [realms] above is above all;"[1] and again, by saying that he "baptized in repentance only, but that One would shortly come who would baptize in the Spirit and fire;"[2]—of course because true and stable faith is baptized with *water*, unto salvation; pretended and weak faith is baptized with *fire*, unto judgment.

CHAP. XI.—*Answer to the objection that "the Lord did not baptize."*

"But behold," say some, "the Lord came, and baptized not; for we read, 'And yet He used not to baptize, but His disciples!'"[3] As if, in truth, John had preached that He would baptize with His own hands! Of course his words are not so to be understood, but as simply spoken after an ordinary manner; just as, for instance, we say, "The emperor set forth an edict," or, "The prefect cudgelled him." Pray does the emperor in person set forth, or the prefect in person cudgel? One whose ministers do a thing is always said to do it.[4] So "He will baptize you" will have to be understood as standing for, "Through Him," or "Into Him," "you will be baptized." But let not [the fact] that "He Himself baptized not" trouble any. For into whom should He baptize? Into repentance? Of what use, then, do you make His forerunner? Into remission of sins, which He used to give by a word? Into Himself, whom by humility He was concealing? Into the Holy Spirit, who had not yet descended from the Father? Into the church, which His apostles had not yet founded? And thus it was with the selfsame "baptism of John" that His disciples used to baptize, as ministers, with which John before had baptized as forerunner. Let none think it was with some other, because no other exists, except that of Christ subsequently; which at

---

[1] John iii. 30, 31, briefly quoted.
[2] Matt. iii. 11, not quite exactly given.   [3] John iv. 2.
[4] For instances of this, compare Matt. viii. 5 with Luke vii. 3, 7; and Mark x. 35 with Matt. xx. 20.

that time, of course, could not be given by His disciples, inasmuch as the glory of the Lord had not yet been fully attained,[1] nor the efficacy of the font[2] established through the passion and the resurrection; because neither can our death see dissolution except by the Lord's passion, nor our life be restored without His resurrection.

CHAP. XII.—*Of the necessity of baptism to salvation.*

When, however, the prescript is laid down that "without baptism, salvation is attainable by none" (chiefly on the ground of that declaration of the Lord, who says, "Unless one be born of water, he hath not life"[3]), there arise immediately scrupulous, nay rather audacious, doubts on the part of some, "how, in accordance with that prescript, salvation is attainable by the apostles, whom—Paul excepted—we do not find baptized in the Lord? Nay, since Paul is the only one of them who has put on [the garment of] Christ's baptism,[4] either the peril of all the others who lack the water of Christ is prejudged, that the prescript may be maintained, or else the prescript is rescinded if salvation has been ordained even for the unbaptized." I have heard—the Lord is my witness—doubts of that kind: that none may imagine me so abandoned as to excogitate, unprovoked, in the licence of my pen, ideas which would inspire others with scruple.

And now, as far as I shall be able, I will reply to them who affirm "that the apostles were unbaptized." For if they had undergone the human baptism of John, and were longing for that of the Lord, [then,] since the Lord Himself had defined baptism to be ONE;[5] (saying to Peter, who was desirous[6] of being thoroughly bathed, "He who hath once bathed hath no necessity [to wash] a second time;"[7] which, of course, He would not have said at all to one *not*

---

[1] Cf. 1 Pet. i. 11, *ad fin.*   [2] Lavacri.
[3] John iii. 5, not fully given.   [4] See Gal. iii. 27.
[5] See Eph. iv. 5.
[6] "Volenti," which Oehler notes as a suggestion of Fr. Junius, is adopted here in preference to Oehler's "nolenti."
[7] John xiii. 9, 10.

baptized;) even here we have a conspicuous[1] proof against those who, in order to destroy the sacrament of water, deprive the apostles even of John's baptism. Can it seem credible that "the way of the Lord," that is, the baptism of John, had not then been "prepared" in those persons who were being destined to *open* the way of the Lord throughout the whole world? The Lord Himself, though no "repentance" was due from *Him*, was baptized: was baptism not necessary for *sinners*? As for the fact, then, that "others were not baptized:" [true;] they, however, were not companions of Christ, but enemies of the faith, doctors of the law and Pharisees: from which fact is gathered an additional suggestion, that, since the *opposers* of the Lord *refused* to be baptized, they who *followed* the Lord *were* baptized, and were not like-minded with their own rivals: especially when, if there were any one to whom they clave, the Lord had exalted John above him by the testimony [He bare him], saying, "Among them who are born of women [there is] none greater than John the Baptist." [2]

Others make the suggestion—forced enough, clearly— "that the apostles then served the turn of baptism when, in their little ship, they were sprinkled and covered with the waves: that Peter himself also was immersed enough when he walked on the sea." [3] It is, however, as I think, one thing to be sprinkled or intercepted by the violence of the sea; another thing to be baptized in obedience to the discipline of religion. But that little ship did present a figure of the church, in that she is disquieted "in the sea," that is, in the world,[4] "by the waves," that is, by persecutions and temptations; the Lord, through patience, sleeping as it were, until, roused in their last extremities by the prayers of the saints, He checks the world,[5] and restores tranquillity to His own.

Now, whether they were baptized in any manner whatever, or whether they continued unbathed[6] to the end—so

---

[1] Exerta. Comp. c. xviii. *sub init.*; *ad Ux.* ii. c. i. *sub fin.*
[2] Matt. xi. 11 (ἐγήγερται omitted).   [3] Matt. viii. 24, xiv. 28, 29.
[4] Sæculo.   [5] Sæculum.   [6] Illoti.

that even that saying of the Lord touching the "one bath"[1] does, under the person of Peter, merely regard *us*—still, to determine concerning the salvation of the apostles is audacious enough, because on *them* the prerogative even of first choice,[2] and thereafter of undivided intimacy, might be able to confer the compendious grace of baptism, seeing they (I think) followed Him who was wont to promise salvation to every believer. "Thy faith," He would say, "hath saved thee;"[3] and, "Thy sins shall be remitted thee,"[4] on thy believing, of course, albeit thou be not [yet] baptized. If that[5] was wanting to the apostles, I know not in the faith of what things it was, that, roused by one word of the Lord, [one] left the toll-booth behind for ever;[6] [another] deserted father and ship, and the craft by which he gained his living;[7] [a third,] who disdained his father's obsequies,[8] fulfilled, before he heard it, that highest precept of the Lord, "He who prefers father or mother to me, is not worthy of me."[9]

CHAP. XIII.—*Another objection: "Abraham pleased God without being baptized." Answer thereto: Old things must give place to new; and baptism is now a law.*

Here, then, those miscreants[10] provoke questions. And so they say, "Baptism is not necessary for them to whom faith is sufficient; for withal, Abraham pleased God by a sacrament of no water, but of faith." [True;] but in all cases it is the *later* things which have a conclusive force, and the *subsequent* which prevail over the antecedent. Grant that, in days gone by, there was salvation by means of bare faith, before the passion and resurrection of the Lord. But now that faith has been enlarged, and is become a faith which

---

[1] Lavacrum.
[2] *i.e.* of being the first to be chosen.   [3] Luke xviii. 42 ; Mark x. 52.
[4] "Remittentur" is Oehler's reading; "remittuntur" others read: but the Greek is in the perfect tense. See Mark ii. 5.
[5] *i.e.* faith, or perhaps the "compendious grace of baptism."
[6] Matt. ix. 9.   [7] Matt. iv. 21, 22.
[8] Luke ix. 59, 60 ; but it is not said there that the man *did* it.
[9] Matt. x. 37.
[10] *i.e.* probably the Cainites. See c. i.

believes in His nativity, passion, and resurrection, there has been an amplification added to the sacrament,[1] [namely,] the sealing act of baptism; the clothing, in some sense, of the faith which before was bare, and which cannot exist now without its proper law. For the *law* of baptizing has been *imposed*, and the formula prescribed: " Go," saith [Christ], " teach the nations, baptizing them into the name of the Father, and of the Son, and of the Holy Spirit."[2] The comparison with this law of that definition, " Unless a man have been re-born of water and Spirit, he shall not enter into the kingdom of the heavens,"[3] has tied faith to the necessity of baptism. Accordingly, all [who] thereafter[4] [became] believers used to be baptized. *Then* it was, too,[5] that Paul, when he believed, was baptized; and this is the meaning of the precept which the Lord had given him when smitten with the plague of loss [of sight], saying, " Arise, and enter Damascus; there shall be demonstrated to thee what thou oughtest to do,"—be baptized, to wit, which was the only thing lacking to him: that point excepted, he had sufficiently *learnt and believed* " the Nazarene " to be " the Lord, the Son of God."[6]

CHAP. XIV.—*Of Paul's assertion, " that he had not been sent to baptize."*

But they roll back [upon us an objection] from [that] apostle himself, in that he said, " For Christ sent me not to baptize;"[7] as if by this argument baptism were done away! For [if so], why did he baptize Gaius, and Crispus, and the house of Stephanas?[8] However, even if Christ had not sent *him* to baptize, yet He had given *other* apostles the precept to baptize. But these words were written to the

---

[1] *i.e.* the sacrament, or obligation, of faith. See beginning of chapter.
[2] Matt. xxviii. 19: " all " omitted.
[3] John iii. 5: " shall not " for " cannot; " and " kingdom of the heavens"—an expression only occurring in Matthew—for " kingdom of God."
[4] *i.e.* from the time when the Lord gave the " law."
[5] *i.e.* not till *after* the " law " had been made.
[6] See Acts ix. 1–31.   [7] 1 Cor. i. 17.   [8] 1 Cor. i. 14, 16.

Corinthians in regard of the circumstances of that particular time; seeing that schisms and dissensions were being agitated among them, while one attributes [everything] to Paul, another to Apollos;[1] for which reason the "peacemaking"[2] apostle, for fear he should seem to claim all [gifts] for himself, says that he had been sent "not to baptize, but to preach." For preaching is the prior thing, baptizing the posterior. Therefore the preaching came *first:* but I think baptizing withal was *lawful* to him to whom preaching was.

CHAP. XV.—*Unity of baptism.* Remarks on HERETICAL and JEWISH *baptism.*

I know not whether any further point is mooted to bring baptism into controversy. Permit me to call to mind what I have omitted above, lest I seem to break off the train of impending thoughts in the middle. There is to us one, and but one, baptism; as well according to the Lord's gospel[3] as according to the apostle's letters,[4] inasmuch as [he says], "One God, and one baptism, and one church in the heavens."[5] But it must be admitted that the question, "What rules are to be observed with regard to heretics?" is worthy of being treated. For it is to *us*[6] that that assertion[7] refers. Heretics, however, have no fellowship in our discipline, whom the mere fact of their excommunication[8] testifies to be outsiders. I am not bound to recognise in *them* a thing which is enjoined on *me*, because they and we have not the same God, nor one—that is, *the same*—Christ: and therefore their baptism is not one [with ours] either, because it is not *the same;* [a baptism] which, since they have it not duly, doubtless they have *not [at all]*; nor is that capable of being *counted* which is not *had:*[9] thus they cannot *receive* it either, because they *have it*

---

[1] 1 Cor. i. 11, 12, iii. 3, 4.
[2] Matt. v. 9; referred to in *de Pa.* c. ii.
[3] Oehler refers us to c. xii. above, "He who hath once bathed."
[4] *i.e.* the Epistle to the Ephesians especially.
[5] Eph. iv. 4, 5, 6, but very inexactly quoted.
[6] *i.e.* us Christians; or "Catholics," as Oehler explains it.
[7] *i.e.* touching the "one baptism."
[8] Ademptio communicationis.   [9] Comp. Eccles. i. 15.

not. But this point has already received a fuller discussion from us in Greek. We enter, then, the font¹ *once: once* are sins washed away, because they ought never to be repeated. But the Jewish Israel bathes daily,² because he is daily being defiled: and, for fear that [daily defilement] should be practised among *us* also, therefore was the definition touching the one bathing³ made. Happy water, which *once* washes away; which does not mock sinners [with vain hopes]; which does not, by being infected with the repetition of impurities, again defile them whom it has washed!

CHAP. XVI.—*Of the second baptism—with blood.*

We *have* indeed, likewise, a *second* font,⁴ (itself withal *one* [with the former,]) of *blood*, to wit; concerning which the Lord said, "I have to be baptized with a baptism," ⁵ when He had been baptized already. For He had come "by means of water and blood," ⁶ just as John has written; that He might be baptized by the water, glorified by the blood; to make *us*, in like manner, *called* by *water, chosen*⁷ by *blood*. These two baptisms He sent out from the wound in His pierced side,⁸ in order that they who believed in His blood might be bathed with the water; they who had been bathed in the water might likewise drink the blood.⁹ This is the baptism which both stands in lieu of the fontal bathing¹⁰ when that has not been received, and restores it when lost.

CHAP. XVII.—*Of the power of conferring baptism.*

For concluding our brief subject,¹¹ it remains to put you in mind also of the due observance of giving and receiving baptism. Of giving it, the chief priest¹² (who is the bishop)

¹ Lavacrum.
² Compare *de Or.* c. xiv.
³ In John xiii. 10, and Eph. iv. 5.
⁴ Lavacrum.
⁵ Luke xii. 50, not given in full.
⁶ 1 John v. 6.
⁷ Matt. xx. 16; Rev. xvii. 14.
⁸ John xix. 34. See c. ix. *ad fin.*
⁹ See John vi. 53, etc.
¹⁰ Lavacrum.
¹¹ Materiolam.
¹² Summus sacerdos. Compare *de Or.* xxviii., "nos . . . veri sacerdotes," etc.; and *de Ex. Cast.* c. vii., "nonne et laici sacerdotes sumus?"

has the right: in the next place, the presbyters and deacons, yet not without the bishop's authority, on account of the honour of the church, which being preserved, peace is preserved. Beside these, even laymen have the right; for what is equally received can be equally given. Unless bishops, or priests, or deacons, be on the spot, [ordinary] disciples are called [to the work]. The word of the Lord ought not to be hidden by any: in like manner, too, baptism, which is equally God's property,[1] can be administered by all. But how much more is the rule[2] of reverence and modesty incumbent on laymen—seeing that these [powers[3]] belong [strictly] to their superiors — lest they assume to themselves the *specific*[4] function of the bishop! Emulation of the episcopal office is the mother of schisms. The most holy apostle has said, that "all things are *lawful*, but not all *expedient*."[5] Let it suffice assuredly, in cases of *necessity*, to avail yourself [of that rule[6]], if at any time circumstance either of place, or of time, or of person compels you [so to do]; for *then* the stedfast courage of the succourer, when the situation of the endangered one is urgent, is exceptionally admissible; inasmuch as he will be guilty of a human creature's loss if he shall refrain from bestowing what he had free liberty to bestow. But the woman of pertness,[7] who has usurped the power to teach, will of course not give birth for herself likewise to a right of baptizing, unless some new beast shall arise[8] like the former; so that, just as the one abolished baptism,[9] so some other should in her own right confer it! But if the writings which wrongly go under Paul's name, claim Thecla's example as a licence for

---

[1] Census. [2] Disciplina.
[3] *i.e.* the powers of administering baptism and "sowing the word."
[4] Dicatum.
[5] 1 Cor. x. 23, where μοι in the received text seems interpolated.
[6] Or, as Oehler explains it, of your power of baptizing, etc.
[7] Quintilla. See c. i.
[8] Evenerit. Perhaps Tertullian means literally—though that sense of the word is very rare—"shall issue out of her," alluding to his "pariet" above.
[9] See c. i. *ad fin.*

women's teaching and baptizing, let them know that, in Asia, the presbyter who composed that writing,[1] as if he were augmenting Paul's fame from his own store, after being convicted, and confessing that he had done it from love of Paul, was removed[2] from his office. For how credible would it seem, that he who has not permitted a *woman*[3] even to *learn* with over-boldness, should give a *female*[4] the power of *teaching* and of *baptizing!* "Let them be silent," he says, "and at home consult their own husbands."[5]

CHAP. XVIII.—*Of the persons to whom, and the time when, baptism is to be administered.*

But they whose office it is [to baptize], know that baptism is not rashly to be administered. "Give to every one who beggeth thee,"[6] has a reference of its own, appertaining especially to almsgiving. [With regard to baptism,] on the contrary, this [precept] is rather to be looked at carefully: "Give not the holy thing to the dogs, nor cast your pearls before swine;"[7] and, "Lay not hands easily on [any]; share not other men's sins."[8] If Philip so "easily" baptized the chamberlain, let us reflect that a manifest and conspicuous[9] evidence that the Lord deemed him worthy had been interposed.[10] The Spirit had enjoined Philip to proceed to that road: the eunuch himself, too, was not found idle, nor as one who was suddenly seized with an eager desire to be baptized; but, after going up to the temple for prayer's sake, being intently engaged on the divine Scripture, was thus suitably discovered—to whom God had, unasked, sent an apostle, which [apostle], again, the Spirit bade adjoin himself to the chamberlain's chariot: the Scripture [which he was reading][11] falls in opportunely with his faith; [Philip,]

[1] The allusion is to a spurious work entitled *Acta Pauli et Theclæ.*
[2] Decessisse.   [3] Mulieri.   [4] Fœminæ.
[5] 1 Cor. xiv. 34, 35.   [6] Luke vi. 30.   [7] Matt. vii. 6.
[8] 1 Tim. v. 22; μηδενὶ omitted, ταχίως rendered by "facile," and μηδὲ by "ne."
[9] "Exertam," as in c. xii.: "probatio exerta," "a conspicuous proof."
[10] Comp. Acts viii. 26–40.
[11] Acts viii. 28, 30, 32, 33, and Isa. liii. 7, 8, especially in LXX. The

being requested, is taken to sit beside him; the Lord is pointed out; faith lingers not; water needs no waiting for; the work is completed, and the apostle snatched away. "But Paul too was, in fact, 'speedily' baptized." [True;] for Simon,[1] his host, speedily recognised him to be " an appointed vessel of election." God's approbation sends sure premonitory tokens before it; every "petition"[2] [of man] may both deceive and be deceived. And so, according to the circumstances and disposition, and even age, of each individual, the delay of baptism is preferable; principally, however, in the case of little children. For why is it necessary—if [baptism itself] is not so [*indispensably*] necessary[3]—that the sponsors likewise should be thrust into danger; who both themselves, by reason of mortality, may fail to fulfil their promises, and may be disappointed by the development of an evil disposition [in the infant for whom they stood]? The Lord does indeed say, "Forbid them not to come unto me."[4] Let them "come," then, while they are growing up; let them "come" while they are learning, while they are being taught whither to come;[5] let them become Christians[6] when they have become able to know Christ. Why does the innocent period of life hasten to the "remission of sins?" More caution will be exercised in worldly[7] matters: so that one who is *not* trusted with earthly substance *is* trusted with divine! Let them know how to "ask" for salvation, that you may seem [at least] to have given "to him that asketh."[8] For no less cause must the unwedded also be deferred—in whom [the

quotation, as given in Acts, agrees nearly *verbatim* with the Cod. Alex. there.

[1] Tertullian seems to have confused the "Judas" with whom Saul stayed (Acts ix. 11) with the "Simon" with whom St. Peter stayed (Acts ix. 43); and it was Ananias, not Judas, to whom he was pointed out as "an appointed vessel," and by whom he was baptized.

[2] See the beginning of the chapter.

[3] Tertullian has already allowed (in c. xvi.) that baptism is not *indispensably* necessary to salvation.

[4] Matt. xix. 14; Mark x. 14; Luke xviii. 16.

[5] Or, "whither they are coming." [6] *i.e.* in baptism.

[7] Sæcularibus. [8] See beginning of chapter.

ground of] temptation is prepared, alike in such as *never were* wedded[1] by means of their maturity, and in the *widowed* by means of their freedom [from the nuptial yoke]—until they either marry, or else be more fully strengthened for [maintaining] continence. If any understand the weighty import of baptism, they will fear its reception more than its delay: sound faith is secure of salvation.

CHAP. XIX.—*Of the times most suitable for baptism.*

The Passover affords a more [than usually] solemn day for baptism; when, withal, the Lord's passion, in [the faith of] which we are baptized, was completed. Nor will it be incongruous to interpret figuratively [the fact] that, when the Lord was about to celebrate the last Passover, He said to the disciples who were sent to make preparation, "Ye will meet a man bearing water:"[2] He points out the place for celebrating the Passover by the sign of *water*. After that, [the space of] Pentecost is a most joyous space for conferring baptisms;[3] wherein, too, the resurrection of the Lord was repeatedly proved[4] among the disciples, and the hope of the advent of the Lord indirectly pointed to, in that, at that time, when He had been received back into the heavens, the angels[5] told the apostles that "He would so come, as He had withal ascended into the heavens;"[6] at Pentecost, of course. But, moreover, when Jeremiah says, "And I will gather them together from the extremities of the land in the feast-day," he signifies the day of the Passover and of Pentecost, which is properly a "feast-day."[7] However, *every* day is

---

[1] Virginibus; but he is speaking about men as well as women. Comp. *de Or.* c. xxii.

[2] Mark xiv. 13, Luke xxii. 10, "a small earthen pitcher of water."

[3] Lavacris.

[4] Frequentata, *i.e.* by His frequent appearance. See Acts i. 3, δι' ἡμερῶν τεσσαράκοντα ὀπτανόμενος αὐτοῖς.

[5] Comp. Acts i. 10 and Luke ix. 30: in each place St. Luke says, ἄνδρες δύο: as also in xxiv. 4 of his Gospel.

[6] Acts i. 10, 11; but it is οὐρανόν throughout in the Greek.

[7] Jer. xxxi. 8 (xxxviii. 8 in LXX., where ἐν ἑορτῇ φασίν is found, which is not in the English version).

the Lord's; every hour, every time, is apt for baptism: if there is a difference in the *solemnity*, in the *grace* distinction there is none.

CHAP. XX.—*Of preparation for, and conduct after, the reception of baptism.*

They who are about to enter baptism ought to pray with repeated prayers, fasts, and bendings of the knee, and vigils all the night through; and with the confession of all bygone sins, that they may express [the meaning] even of the baptism of John: " They were baptized," saith [the Scripture], " confessing their own sins."[1] To us it is matter for thankfulness if we do *now* publicly confess our iniquities or our turpitudes:[2] for we do at the same time both make satisfaction[3] for our former sins, by mortification of our flesh and spirit, and lay beforehand the foundation of defences against the temptations which will closely follow. " Watch and pray," saith [the Lord], " lest ye fall into temptation."[4] And the reason, I believe, why they *were* tempted was, that they fell asleep; so that they deserted the Lord when apprehended, and he who continued to stand by Him, and used the sword, even denied Him thrice: for withal the word had gone before, that "no one *un*tempted should attain the celestial kingdoms."[5] The Lord Himself forthwith after *baptism*[6] temptations surrounded, when in forty days He had kept fast. " Then," some one will say, " it becomes *us*, too, rather to fast *after* baptism."[7] Well, and who forbids you [so to do], unless it be the necessity for joy, and the thanksgiving for salvation? But so far as I, with my poor powers, understand, the Lord figuratively retorted upon Israel the reproach [which Israel

[1] Matt. iii. 6.
[2] Perhaps Tertullian is referring to Prov. xxviii. 13. If we confess *now*, we shall be forgiven, and not put to shame at the judgment-day.
[3] See *de Or.* c. xxiii. *ad fin.*, and the note there.
[4] Matt. xxvi. 41.
[5] What passage is referred to is doubtful. The editors point us to Luke xxii. 28, 29; but the reference is unsatisfactory.
[6] Lavacrum.
[7] Lavacro. Compare the beginning of the chapter.

had cast on the Lord].¹ For the people, after crossing the
sea, and being carried about in the desert during forty years,
although they were there nourished with divine supplies,
nevertheless were more mindful of their belly and their
gullet than of God. Thereupon the Lord, driven apart into
desert places after baptism,² showed, by maintaining a fast
of forty days, that the man of God lives "not by bread
alone," but "by the word of God;"³ and that temptations
incident to fulness or immoderation of appetite are shattered
by abstinence. Therefore, blessed [friends], whom the grace
of God awaits, when you ascend from that most sacred font⁴
of your new birth, and spread your hands⁵ for the first time
in the house of your mother,⁶ together with your brethren,
ask from the Father, ask from the Lord, that His own
specialties of grace [and] distributions of gifts⁷ may be
supplied you. "Ask," saith He, "and ye shall receive."⁸
Well, you *have* asked, and have received; you *have* knocked,
and it has been opened to you. Only, I pray that, when
you are asking, you be mindful likewise of Tertullian the
sinner.

¹ Viz. by their murmuring for bread (see Ex. xvi. 3, 7); and again—
nearly forty years after—in another place (see Num. xxi. 5).

² Aquam : just as St. Paul says the Israelites had been "*baptized*"
(or "*baptized themselves*") "into Moses in the cloud and in *the sea.*"
1 Cor. x. 2.

³ Matt. iv. 1–4.   ⁴ Lavacro.

⁵ In prayer : comp. *de Or.* c. xiv.

⁶ *i.e.* the church : comp. *de Or.* c. 2.   ⁷ 1 Cor. xii. 4–12.

⁸ Matt. vii. 7 ; Luke xi. 9 : αἰτεῖτε, καὶ δοθήσεται ὑμῖν, in both places.

X.

ON REPENTANCE.

Chap. I.—*Of heathen repentance.*

"REPENTANCE" that kind of men which even we ourselves were in days gone by—blind, without the Lord's light—understand, so far as nature is able, to be an emotion of the mind arising from disgust at some [previously cherished] worse sentiment.[1] From the *reason* of repentance, however, they are just as far as they are from the Author of reason Himself. *Reason*, in fact, is a thing of GOD, inasmuch as there is nothing which God the Maker of all has not provided, disposed, ordained *by reason*—nothing which He has not willed should be handled and understood *by reason*. All, therefore, who are ignorant of God, must necessarily be ignorant also of a thing which is His, because no treasure-house[2] at all is accessible to strangers. And thus, voyaging all the universal course of life without the rudder of reason, they know not how to shun the hurricane which is impending over the world.[3] Moreover, how irrationally they behave in the practice of repentance, it will be enough briefly to show just by this one fact, that they exercise it even in the case of their *good* deeds. They repent of good faith, of love, of simple-heartedness, of patience, of mercy, just in proportion as any deed [prompted by these feelings] has fallen on thankless soil. They execrate their own selves for having

---

[1] "Offensa sententiæ pejoris;" or possibly, "the *miscarriage* of some," etc.

[2] Thesaurus.   [3] Sæculo.

done good; and that species chiefly of repentance which is applied to the best works they fix in their heart, making it their care to remember never again to do a good turn. On repentance for *evil* deeds, on the contrary, they lay lighter stress. In short, they make this same [virtue] a means of *sinning* more readily than a means of *right-doing*.

CHAP. II.—*True repentance a thing divine, originated by God, and subject to His laws.*

But if they acted as men who had any part in God, and thereby in reason also, they would first weigh well the importance of repentance, and would never apply it in such a way as to make it a ground for [convicting themselves of] perverse self-amendment. In short, they would regulate the limit of their repentance, because they would reach [a limit] in sinning too—by fearing God, I mean. But where there is no fear, in like manner there is no amendment; where there is no amendment, repentance is of necessity vain, for it lacks the fruit for which God sowed it; that is, man's salvation. For God—after so many and so great sins of human temerity, begun by the first of the race, Adam, after the condemnation of man, together with the dowry of the world[1] [with which he had been endowed], after his ejection from paradise and subjection to death—when He had hasted back to His own mercy, did from that time onward inaugurate repentance in His own self, by rescinding the sentence of His first wrath, engaging to grant pardon to His own work and image.[2] And so He gathered together a people for Himself, and fostered them with many liberal distributions of His bounty, and, after so often finding them most ungrateful, ever exhorted them to repentance, and sent out the voices of the universal company of the prophets to prophesy. By and by, promising freely the grace which in the last times He was intending to pour as a flood of light on the universal world[3] through His Spirit, He bade the baptism of repentance lead the way, with the view of first preparing,[4] by means of the

---

[1] Sæculi dote. Comp. Gen. i. 28, Pa. viii. 4-8. [2] *i.e.* man.
[3] Orbi. [4] Componeret.

sign and seal of repentance, them whom He was calling, through grace, to [inherit] the promise surely made to Abraham. John holds not his peace, saying, "Enter upon repentance, for now shall salvation approach the nations"[1]—the Lord, that is, bringing salvation according to God's promise. To Him John, as His harbinger, directed the repentance [which he preached], whose province was the purging of men's minds, that whatever defilement inveterate error had imparted, whatever contamination in the heart of man ignorance had engendered, *that* repentance should sweep and scrape away, and cast out of doors, and thus prepare the home of the heart, by making it clean, for the Holy Spirit, who was about to supervene, that He might with pleasure introduce Himself thereinto, together with His celestial blessings. Of these blessings the title is [briefly] one—the salvation of man—the abolition of former sins being the preliminary step. This[2] is the [final] cause of repentance, this her work, in taking in hand the business of divine mercy. What is profitable to man does service to God. The *rule* of repentance, however, which we learn when we know the Lord, retains a definite form,—[namely,] that no violent hand, so to speak, be ever laid on *good* deeds or thoughts.[3] For God, never giving His sanction to the reprobation of good [deeds], inasmuch as they are His own (of which, being the author, He must necessarily be the defender too), is in like manner the acceptor of them, and if the acceptor, likewise the rewarder. Let, then, the ingratitude of men see to it,[4] if it attaches repentance even to good works; let their gratitude see to it too, if the desire of earning it be the incentive to well-doing: earthly and mortal are they each. For how small is your gain if you do good to a grateful man! or your loss if to an ungrateful! A *good* deed has GOD as its debtor, just as an *evil* has too; for a judge is a rewarder of every cause. Well, since God as Judge presides over the exacting and maintaining[5] of justice, which to Him is most

---

[1] Comp. Matt. iii. 1, 2; Mark i. 4; Luke iii. 4–6.
[2] *i.e.* man's salvation.   [3] See the latter part of c. i.
[4] Viderit.   [5] Or, "defending."

dear; and since it is with an eye to justice that He appoints all the sum of His discipline, is there room for doubting that, just as in all our acts universally, so also in the case of repentance, justice must be rendered to God?—which duty can indeed only be fulfilled on the condition that repentance be brought to bear *only* on *sins*. Further, no deed but an *evil* one deserves to be called *sin*, nor does any one err by well-doing. But if he does not err, why does he invade [the province of] repentance, the private ground of such as do err? Why does he impose on his goodness a duty proper to wickedness? Thus it comes to pass that, when a thing is called into play where it ought not, there, where it ought, it is neglected.

CHAP. III.—*Sins may be divided into corporeal and spiritual. Both equally subject, if not to human, yet to divine investigation and punishment.*

What things, then, they be for which repentance seems just and due—that is, what things are to be set down under the head of *sin*—the occasion indeed demands that I should note down; but [so to do] may seem to be unnecessary. For when the Lord is known, our spirit, having been "looked back upon"[1] by its own Author, emerges unbidden into the knowledge of the truth; and being admitted to [an acquaintance with] the divine precepts, is by them forthwith instructed that "that from which God bids us abstain is to be accounted *sin:*" inasmuch as, since it is generally agreed that God is some great [essence] of good, of course nothing but evil would be displeasing to good; in that, between things mutually contrary, friendship there is none. Still it will not be irksome briefly to touch upon the fact[2] that, of sins, some are carnal, that is, corporeal; some spiritual. For since man is composed of this combination of a two-fold substance, the sources of his sins are no other than the sources of his composition. But it is not the fact that body and spirit are two things that constitutes the sins mutually different—otherwise they are on this account rather *equal*,

[1] Luke xxii. 61. [2] Or, "briefly to lay down the rule."

because the *two* make up *one*—lest any make the distinction between their *sins* proportionate to the difference between their *substances,* so as to esteem the one lighter, or else heavier, than the other : if it be true, [as it is,] that both flesh and spirit are creatures of God ; one wrought by His hand, one consummated by His afflatus. Since, then, they equally pertain to the Lord, whichever of them *sins* equally *offends* the Lord. Is it for you to distinguish the acts of the flesh and the spirit, whose communion and conjunction in life, in death, and in resurrection, are so intimate, that " at that time "[1] they are equally raised up either for life or else for judgment ; because, to wit, they have equally either sinned or lived innocently ? This we would [once for all] premise, in order that we may understand that no less necessity for repentance is incumbent on *either* part of man, if in anything it have sinned, than on *both.* The *guilt* of both is common ; common, too, is the *Judge*—God, to wit ; common, therefore, is withal the healing medicine of repentance. The source whence sins are named " spiritual " and " corporeal " is the fact that every sin is matter either of *act* or else of *thought:* so that what is in *deed* is " corporeal," because a *deed,* like a *body,* is capable of being *seen* and *touched;* what is in the *mind* is " spiritual," because *spirit* is neither *seen* nor *handled:* by which consideration is shown that sins not of *deed* only, but of *will* too, are to be shunned, and by repentance purged. For if human finitude [2] judges only sins of *deed,* because it is not equal to [piercing] the lurking-places of the *will,* let us not on that account make light of crimes of the will in God's sight. God is all-sufficient. Nothing from whence any sin whatsoever proceeds is remote from His sight ; because He is neither ignorant, nor does He omit to decree it to judgment. He is no dissembler of, nor double-dealer with,[3] His own clearsightedness. What [shall we say of the fact] that *will* is the *origin* of *deed?* For if any sins are imputed to chance, or to necessity, or to ignorance, let them see to themselves : if

---

[1] *i.e.* in the judgment-day. Compare the phrase " that day and that hour " in Scripture.

[2] Mediocritas. [3] Prævaricatorem: comp. *ad Ux.* b. ii. c. ii. *ad init.*

these be excepted, there is no sinning save by *will*. Since, then, will is the origin of deed, is it not so much the rather amenable to penalty as it is first in guilt? Nor, if some difficulty interferes with its full accomplishment, is it even in that case exonerated; for it is itself imputed to itself: nor, having done the work which lay in its own power, will it be excusable by reason of that miscarriage of its accomplishment. In fact, how does the Lord demonstrate Himself as adding a superstructure to the Law, except by interdicting sins of the *will* as well [as other sins]; while He defines not only the man who had actually invaded another's wedlock to be an adulterer, but likewise him who had contaminated [a woman] by the concupiscence of his gaze?[1] Accordingly it is dangerous enough for the mind to set before itself what it is forbidden to perform, and rashly through the will to perfect its execution. And since the power of this will is such that, even without fully sating its self-gratification, it stands for a deed; as a deed, therefore, it shall be punished. It is utterly vain to say, "I *willed*, but yet I *did* not." Rather you *ought* to carry the thing through, *because* you will; or else not to will, because you do not carry it through. But, by the confession of your consciousness, you pronounce your own condemnation. For if you eagerly desired a *good* thing, you would have been anxious to carry it through; in like manner, as you do not carry an *evil* thing through, you ought not to have eagerly desired it. Wherever you take your stand, you are fast bound by guilt; because you have either *willed* evil, or else have not *fulfilled* good.

CHAP. IV.—*Repentance applicable to all the kinds of sin; and to be practised not only, nor chiefly, for the good it brings, but because God commands it.*

To all sins, then, committed whether by flesh or spirit, whether by deed or will, the same [God] who has destined penalty by means of judgment, has withal engaged to grant pardon by means of repentance, saying to the people, " Repent thee, and I will save thee;"[2] and again, " I live, saith the

[1] Matt. v. 27, 28 ; comp. *de Idol.* ii. [2] Comp. Ezek. xviii. 30, 32.

Lord, and I will [have] repentance rather than death."[1] Repentance, then, is "life," since it is preferred to "death." That repentance, O sinner, like myself (nay, rather, less than myself, for pre-eminence in sins I acknowledge to be mine[2]), do you so hasten to, so embrace, as a shipwrecked man the protection[3] of some plank. This will draw you forth when sunk in the waves of sins, and will bear you forward into the port of the divine clemency. Seize the opportunity of unexpected felicity: that you, who sometime were in God's sight nothing but "a drop of a bucket,"[4] and "dust of the threshing-floor,"[5] and "a potter's vessel,"[6] may thenceforward become that "tree which is sown beside[7] the waters, and is perennial in leaves, and bears fruit at its own time,"[8] which shall not see "fire,"[9] nor "axe."[10] Having found "the truth,"[11] repent of errors; repent of having loved what God loves not: for even we ourselves do not permit our slave-lads not to hate the things which are offensive to us; for the principle of voluntary obedience[12] consists in similarity of minds.

To reckon up the good of repentance, the subject-matter is copious, and therefore should be committed to great eloquence. Let us, however, in proportion to our narrow abilities, inculcate one point,—[namely,] that what God enjoins is good and best. I hold it audacity to dispute about the "good" of a divine precept; for, indeed, it is not the fact that it is good which binds us to obey, but the fact that God has enjoined it. To exact the rendering of obedience the majesty of divine power has the prior[13] right; the authority of Him who commands is prior to the utility of him who serves. "Is it good to repent, or no?" Why do you ponder? God enjoins; nay, He not merely enjoins, but likewise exhorts. He invites by [the hope of a] reward—

[1] The substance of this is found in Ezek. xxxiii. 11.
[2] Compare 1 Tim. i. 16.
[3] Fidem: comp. c. xii. sub fin.
[4] Isa. xl. 15.
[5] Dan. ii. 35; Matt. iii. 12.
[6] Ps. ii. 9; Rev. ii. 27.
[7] Penes.
[8] Ps. i. 3; Jer. xvii. 8. Compare Luke xxiii. 31.
[9] Jer. xvii. 8; Matt. iii. 10.
[10] Matt. iii. 10.
[11] John xiv. 6.
[12] Obsequii.
[13] Or, "paramount."

salvation, to wit; even by an oath, saying "I live,"[1] He desires that credence may be given Him. Oh blessed we, for whose sake God swears! Oh most miserable, if we believe not the Lord even when He swears! What, therefore, God so highly commends, what He even (after human fashion) attests on oath, we are bound of course to approach, and to guard with the utmost seriousness; that, abiding permanently in [the faith of] the solemn pledge[2] of divine grace, we may be able also to persevere in like manner in its fruit[3] and its benefit.

CHAP. V.—*Sin never to be returned to after repentance.*

For what I say is this, that the repentance which, being shown us and commanded us through God's grace, recalls us to grace[4] with the Lord, when once learned and undertaken by us ought never afterward to be cancelled by repetition of sin. No pretext of ignorance now remains to plead on your behalf; in that, after acknowledging the Lord, and accepting His precepts[5]—in short, after engaging in repentance of [past] sins—you again betake yourself to sins. Thus, in as far as you are removed from ignorance, in so far are you cemented[6] to contumacy. For if the ground on which you had repented of having sinned was that you had begun to fear the Lord, why have you preferred to rescind what you did for fear's sake, except because you have ceased to fear? For there is no other thing but contumacy which subverts fear. Since there is no exception which defends from liability to penalty even such as are ignorant of the Lord—because ignorance of God, openly as He is set before men, and comprehensible as He is even on the score of His heavenly benefits, is not possible[7]—how perilous is it for Him to be despised when known?

[1] See ref. 1 on the preceding page. The phrase is "As I live" in the English version.
[2] "Asseveratione:" apparently a play on the word, as compared with "perseverare," which follows.
[3] Or, "enjoyment."   [4] *i.e.* favour.
[5] Which is solemnly done in baptism.   [6] Adglutinaris.
[7] Acts xiv. 15–17: "licet" here may = "lawful," "permissible," "excusable."

Now, that man does despise Him, who, after attaining by His help to an understanding of things good and evil, offers an affront to his own understanding—that is, to God's gift—by resuming what he understands ought to be shunned, and what he has already shunned: he rejects the Giver in abandoning the gift; he denies the Benefactor in not honouring the benefit. How can he be pleasing to Him, whose gift is displeasing to himself? Thus he is shown to be not only contumacious toward the Lord, but likewise ungrateful. Besides, that man commits no light sin against the Lord, who, after he had by repentance renounced His rival the devil, and had under this appellation subjected him to the Lord, again upraises him by his own return [to him], and makes himself a ground of exultation to him; so that the Evil One, with his prey recovered, rejoices anew against the Lord. Does he not—[a thing] which is perilous even to say, but must be put forward with a view to edification—place the devil before the Lord? For he seems to have made the comparison who has known each; and to have judicially pronounced him to be the better whose [servant] he has preferred again to be. Thus he who, through repentance for sins, had begun to make satisfaction to the Lord, will, through another repentance of his repentance, make satisfaction to the devil, and will be the more hateful to God in proportion as he will be the more acceptable to His rival. But some say that "God is satisfied if He be looked up to with the heart and the mind, even if this be not done in [outward] act, and that thus they sin without damage to their fear and their faith:" that is, that they violate wedlock without damage to their chastity; they mingle poison for their parent without damage to their filial duty! Thus, then, they will themselves withal be thrust down into hell without damage to their pardon, while they sin without damage to their fear! Here is a primary example of perversity: they sin, because they fear![1] I suppose, if they feared not, they would not sin! Let him, therefore, who would not have God offended not revere Him at all, if

[1] "Timent," not "metuunt." "Metus" is the word Tertullian has been using above for religious, reverential fear.

fear[1] is the plea for offending! But these dispositions have [ever] been wont to sprout from the seed of hypocrites, whose friendship with the devil is indivisible, whose repentance never faithful.

CHAP. VI.—*Baptism not to be presumptuously received without preceding repentance, manifested by amendment of life.*

Whatever, then, our poor ability has attempted to suggest with reference to laying hold of repentance once for all, and perpetually retaining it, does indeed bear upon *all* who are given up to the Lord, as being all competitors for salvation in earning the favour of God; but is chiefly urgent in the case of those young novices who are only just beginning to bedew[2] their ears with divine discourses, and who, as whelps in yet early infancy, and with eyes not yet perfect, creep about uncertainly, and say indeed that they renounce their former deeds, and assume [the profession of] repentance, but neglect to complete it.[3] For the very end of desiring importunes them to desire somewhat of their former [deeds]; just as fruits, when they are already beginning to turn into the sourness or bitterness of age, do yet still in some part flatter[4] their own loveliness. Moreover, a presumptuous confidence in baptism introduces all kind of vicious delay and tergiversation with regard to repentance; for, feeling sure of undoubted pardon of their sins, [men] meanwhile steal the intervening time, and make it for themselves into a holiday-time[5] for sinning, rather than a time for learning not to sin. Further, how inconsistent is it to expect pardon of sins [to be granted] to a repentance which they have not fulfilled! This is to hold out your hand for merchandise, but not produce the price. For repentance is the price at which the Lord has determined to award pardon: He proposes the redemption[6] of release from penalty at this compensating exchange of repentance. If, then, sellers first examine the coin with which they make their bargains, to see

---

[1] Timor.   [2] Deut. xxxii. 2.   [3] *i.e.* by baptism.   [4] Adulantur.
[5] "Commeatus," a military word = "furlough," hence "holiday-time."
[6] *i.e.* repurchase.

whether it be cut, or scraped, or adulterated,[1] we believe likewise that the Lord, when about to make us the grant of so costly merchandise, even of eternal life, first institutes a probation of our repentance. "But meanwhile let us defer the reality of our repentance: it will then, I suppose, be clear that we are amended when we are absolved."[2] By no means; but [our emendation must be manifested] while, pardon being in abeyance, there is still a prospect of penalty; while [the penitent] does not yet merit—so far as merit we can—his liberation; while God is threatening, not while He is forgiving. For what slave, after his position has been changed by reception of freedom, charges himself with his [past] thefts and desertions? What soldier, after his discharge, makes satisfaction for his [former] brands? A sinner is bound to bemoan himself *before* receiving pardon, because the time of repentance is coincident with that of peril and of fear. Not that I deny that the divine benefit—the putting away of sins, I mean—is in every way sure to such as are on the point of entering the [baptismal] water; but what we have to labour for is, that it may be granted us to attain that blessing. For who will grant to you, a man of so faithless repentance, one single sprinkling of any water whatever? To approach it by stealth, indeed, and to get the minister appointed over this business misled by your asseverations, is easy; but God takes foresight for His own treasure, and suffers not the unworthy to steal a march upon it. What, in fact, does He say? "Nothing hid which shall not be revealed."[3] Draw whatever [veil of] darkness you please over your deeds, "God is light."[4] But some think as if God were under a *necessity* of bestowing, even on the unworthy, what He has engaged [to give]; and they turn His liberality into slavery. But if it is, [as in that case it is,] of *necessity* that God grants us the symbol of death,[5] then He does so *unwillingly*. But who permits a gift to be permanently retained which he has granted unwillingly? For do not many afterward fall out of [grace]? is not this gift taken

[1] Adulter; see *de Idol.* c. i. [2] *i.e.* in baptism. [3] Luke viii. 17. [4] 1 John i. 5.
[5] Symbolum mortis indulget. Comp. Rom. vi. 3, 4, 8; Col. ii. 12, 20.

away from many? These, no doubt, are they who do steal a
march upon [the treasure], who, after approaching to the faith
of repentance, set up on the sands a house doomed to ruin.
Let no one, then, flatter himself on the ground of being
assigned to the "recruit-classes" of learners, as if on that
account he have a licence even now to sin. As soon as you
"know the Lord,"[1] you should fear Him; as soon as you
have gazed on Him, you should reverence Him. But what
difference does *your* "knowing" Him make, while you rest
in the same practices as in days bygone, when you knew Him
not? What, moreover, is it which distinguishes you from
a perfected[2] servant of God? Is there one Christ for the
baptized, another for the learners? Have they some different
hope or reward? some different dread of judgment? some
different necessity for repentance? That [baptismal] washing is a sealing of faith, which faith is begun and is commended by the faith of repentance. We are not washed *in
order that* we *may* cease sinning, but *because* we *have* ceased,
since in *heart* we have *been* bathed[3] already. For the *first*
baptism of a learner is *this*, a perfect fear;[4] thenceforward,
in so far as you have understanding of the Lord, faith [is]
sound, the conscience having once for all embraced repentance. Otherwise, if it is [only] after the [baptismal] waters
that we cease sinning, it is of *necessity*, not of *free-will*, that
we put on innocence. Who, then, is pre-eminent in goodness?
he who is not *allowed*, or he whom *it displeases*, to be evil?
he who is *bidden*, or he whose *pleasure it is*, to be free from
crime? Let us, then, neither keep our hands from theft
unless the hardness of bars withstand us, nor refrain our
eyes from the concupiscence of fornication unless we be
withdrawn by guardians of our persons, if no one who has
surrendered himself to the Lord is to cease sinning unless he
be bound thereto by baptism. But if any entertain this
sentiment, I know not whether he, after baptism, do not feel
more sadness to think that he has *ceased* from sinning, than
gladness that he hath *escaped* from it. And so it is becoming

---

[1] Jer. xxxi. (LXX. xxxviii.) 34; Heb. viii. 11.   [2] *i.e.* in baptism.
[3] See John xiii. 10 and Matt. xxiii. 26.   [4] Metus integer.

that learners *desire* baptism, but do not hastily *receive* it: for he who desires it, honours it; he who hastily receives it, disdains it: in the one appears modesty, in the other arrogance; the former satisfies, the latter neglects it; the former covets to merit it, but the latter promises it to himself as a due return; the former takes, the latter usurps it. Whom would you judge worthier, except one who is more amended? whom more amended, except one who is more timid, and on that account has fulfilled the duty of true repentance? for he has feared to continue still in sin, lest he should not merit the reception [of baptism]. But the hasty receiver, inasmuch as he promised it himself [as his due], being forsooth secure [of obtaining it], *could* not fear: thus he fulfilled not repentance either, because he lacked the instrumental agent of repentance, that is, fear.[1] Hasty reception is the portion of irreverence; it inflates the seeker, it despises the Giver. And thus it sometimes deceives[2] [the hasty recipient himself:] for it promises to itself [the gift] before it be due; whereby He who is to furnish [the gift] is ever offended.

CHAP. VII.—*Of repentance, in the case of such as have lapsed after baptism.*

So long, Lord Christ, may the blessing of learning or hearing concerning the discipline of repentance be granted to Thy servants, as it likewise behoves them, while *learners*,[3] not to sin; in other words, may they thereafter know nothing of repentance, [and] require nothing of it. It is irksome to append mention of a *second*—nay, in that case, the *last*—hope; lest, by treating of a remedial repenting yet in reserve, we seem to be pointing to a yet further space for sinning. Far be it that any one so interpret our meaning, as if, because there is an opening for repenting, there were even now, on that account, an opening for sinning; and [as if] the redundance of celestial clemency constituted a licence for human temerity. Let no one be less, because God is more, good, by repeating his sin as often as he is forgiven. Otherwise he will find, be sure, an end of *escaping*, when he

[1] Metus.   [2] Or, "disappoints."   [3] *i.e. before* baptism.

shall not find one of *sinning*. We have escaped *once* : thus far [and no farther] let us commit ourselves to perils, even if we seem likely to escape a second time. Men in general, after escaping shipwreck, thenceforward declare divorce with ship and sea; and by [cherishing] the memory of the danger, honour the benefit conferred by God,—their deliverance, namely. I praise their fear, I love their reverence; they are unwilling a second time to be a burden to the divine mercy; they fear to seem to trample on [the benefit] which they have attained; they shun, with a solicitude which at all events is good, to make trial a second time of that which they have once learned to fear. Thus the limit of their temerity is the evidence of their fear. Moreover, man's fear[1] is an honour to God. But, however, that most stubborn foe [of ours] never gives his malice leisure; indeed, he is then most savage when he fully feels that a man is freed [from his clutches]; he then flames fiercest while he is fast being extinguished. Grieve and groan he must of necessity over the fact that, by the grant of pardon, so many works of death[2] in man have been overthrown, so many marks of the condemnation which formerly was his own erased. He grieves that that sinner, [now become] Christ's servant, is destined to judge him and his angels.[3] And so he observes, assaults, besieges him, in the hope that he may be able in some way either to strike his eyes with carnal concupiscence, or else to entangle his mind with worldly enticements, or else to subvert his faith by fear of earthly power, or else to wrest him from the sure way by perverse traditions: he is never deficient in stumbling-blocks nor in temptations. These poisons of his, therefore, God foreseeing, although the gate of forgiveness has been shut and fastened up with the bar of baptism, has permitted [it] still to stand somewhat open.[4] In the vestibule He has stationed repentance the second to open to such as knock: but now *once for all*, be-

---

[1] Timor.
[2] "Mortis opera," or "deadly works;" cf. *de Idol.* c. iv. (mid.), "perdition of blood," and the note there.
[3] 1 Cor. vi. 3. [4] Or, "has permitted somewhat still to stand open."

cause now for the second time; but never more, because the last time it had been in vain. For is not even this *once* enough? You have what you now deserved not, for you had lost what you had received. If the Lord's indulgence grants you the means of restoring what you had lost, be thankful for the benefit renewed, not to say amplified; for *restoring* is a greater thing than *giving*, inasmuch as *having lost* is more miserable than never having *received* at all. However, if any do incur the debt of a second repentance, his spirit is not to be forthwith cut down and undermined by despair. Let it by all means be irksome to *sin* again, but let not to *repent* again be irksome: irksome to imperil one's self again, but not to be again set free. Let none be ashamed. Repeated sickness must have repeated medicine. You will show your gratitude to the Lord by not refusing what the Lord offers you. You have offended, but can still be reconciled. You have One whom you may satisfy, and Him willing [to accept the satisfaction].

CHAP. VIII.—*Examples from Scripture to prove the Lord's willingness to pardon.*

This if you doubt, unravel[1] the meaning of "what the Spirit saith to the churches."[2] He imputes to the Ephesians "forsaken love;"[3] reproaches the Thyatirenes with "fornication," and "eating of things sacrificed to idols;"[4] accuses the Sardians of "works not full;"[5] censures the Pergamenes for teaching perverse things;[6] upbraids the Laodiceans for trusting to their riches;[7] and yet gives them all general monitions to repentance—under comminations, it is true; but He would not utter comminations to one *unrepentant* if He did not forgive the repentant. The matter were doubtful if He had not withal elsewhere demonstrated this profusion of His clemency. Saith He not,[8] "He who hath fallen

[1] Evolve: perhaps simply = "read."
[2] Rev. ii. 7, 11, 17, 29, iii. 6, 13, 21.   [3] Rev. ii. 4.
[4] Rev. ii. 20.   [5] Rev. iii. 2.   [6] Rev. ii. 14, 15.   [7] Rev. iii. 17.
[8] Jer. viii. 4 (in LXX.) appears to be the passage meant. The Eng. Ver. is very different.

shall rise again, and he who hath been *a*verted shall be *con*verted?" He it is, indeed, who "would have mercy rather than sacrifices."¹ The heavens, and the angels who are there, are glad at a man's repentance.² Ho! you sinner, be of good cheer! you see where it is that there is joy at your return. What meaning for us have those themes of the Lord's parables? Is not the fact that a woman has lost a drachma, and seeks it and finds it, and invites her female friends to share her joy, an example of a restored sinner?³ There strays, withal, one little ewe of the shepherd's; but the flock was not more dear than the one: that one is earnestly sought; the one is longed for instead of all; and at length she is found, and is borne back on the shoulders of the shepherd himself; for much had she toiled⁴ in straying.⁵ That most gentle father, likewise, I will not pass over in silence, who calls his prodigal son home, and willingly receives him repentant after his indigence, slays his best fatted calf, graces his joy with a banquet.⁶ Why not? He had found the son whom he had lost; he had felt *him* to be all the dearer of whom he had *made a gain*. Who is that father to be understood by us to be? God, surely: no one [is] so truly a Father;⁷ no one so rich in paternal love. He, then, will receive you, His own son,⁸ back, even if you have squandered what you had received from Him, even if you return naked—just because you *have* returned; and will joy more over your return than over the sobriety of the other;⁹ but [only] if you heartily repent—if you compare your own hunger with the plenty of your Father's "hired servants"—if you leave behind you the swine, that unclean herd—if you again seek your Father, offended though He be, saying, "I have sinned, nor am worthy any longer to be called Thine." Confession

---

¹ Hos. vi. 6; Matt. ix. 13. [The words in Hosea in the LXX. are, διότι ἵλεος θέλω ἢ θυσίαν (al. καὶ οὐ θυσίαν).]

² Luke xv. 7, 10.   ³ Luke xv. 8–10.   ⁴ Or, "suffered."

⁵ Luke xv. 3–7.   ⁶ Luke xv. 11–32.

⁷ Cf. Matt. xxiii. 9; and Eph. iii. 14, 15, in the Greek.

⁸ Publicly enrolled as such in baptism; for Tertullian here is speaking solely of the "second repentance."

⁹ See Luke xv. 29–32.

of sins lightens, as much as dissimulation aggravates them; for confession is counselled by [the desire of making] satisfaction, dissimulation by contumacy.

CHAP. IX.—*Concerning the outward manifestations by which this " second repentance" is to be accompanied.*

The narrower, then, the sphere of action of this second and only [remaining] repentance, the more laborious is its probation; in order that it may not be exhibited in the conscience alone, but may likewise be carried out in some [external] act. This act, which is more usually expressed and commonly spoken of under a Greek name, is ἐξομολό-γησις,[1] whereby we confess our sins to the Lord, not indeed as if He were ignorant of them, but inasmuch as by confession satisfaction is settled;[2] of confession repentance is born; by repentance God is appeased. And thus *exomologesis* is a discipline for man's prostration and humiliation, enjoining a demeanour calculated to move mercy. With regard also to the very dress and food, it commands [the penitent] to lie in sackcloth and ashes, to cover his body in mourning,[3] to lay his spirit low in sorrows, to exchange for severe treatment the sins which he has committed; moreover, to know no food and drink but such as is plain,—not for the stomach's sake, to wit, but the soul's; for the most part, however, to feed prayers on fastings, to groan, to weep and roar[4] unto the Lord your[5] God; to roll before the feet of the presbyters, and kneel to God's dear ones; to enjoin on all the brethren to be ambassadors to bear his[6] deprecatory supplication [before God]. All this *exomologesis* [does], that it may enhance repentance; may honour God by its fear of the [incurred] danger; may,

[1] Utter confession.
[2] For the meaning of "satisfaction," see Hooker, *Eccl. Pol.* vi. 5, where several references to the present treatise occur.
[3] Sordibus.
[4] Cf. Ps. xxii. 1 (in LXX. xxii. 3), xxxviii. 8 (in the LXX. xxxvii. 9). Cf. Heb. v. 7.
[5] Tertullian changes here to the second person, unless Oehler's "tuum" be a misprint for "suum."
[6] "Suæ," which looks as if the "tuum" above should be "suum."

by itself pronouncing against the sinner, stand in the stead of God's indignation, and by temporal mortification (I will not say frustrate, but) discharge eternal punishments. Therefore, while it abases the man, it raises him; while it covers him with squalor, it renders him more clean; while it *ac*cuses, it *ex*cuses; while it condemns, it absolves. The less quarter you give yourself, the more (believe me) will God give you.

CHAP. X.—*Of men's shrinking from this "second repentance" and "exomologesis," and of the unreasonableness of such shrinking.*

Yet [we see] most men either shun this work, as being a public exposure of themselves, or else defer it from day to day. I presume [they do so as being] more mindful of modesty than of salvation; just like men who, having contracted some malady in the more private parts of the body, avoid the privity of physicians, and so perish with their own bashfulness. It is intolerable, forsooth, to modesty to make satisfaction to the offended Lord! to be restored to its forfeited[1] salvation! Truly you are honourable in your modesty; bearing an open forehead for sinning, but an abashed one for deprecating! I give no place to bashfulness when I am a gainer by its loss; when itself in some sort exhorts the man, saying, "Respect not me; it is better that I perish through[2] you [than you through me]." At all events, the time when (if ever) its danger is serious, is when it is a butt for jeering speech in the presence of insulters, where one man raises himself on his neighbour's ruin, where there is upward clambering over the prostrate. But among brethren and fellow-servants, where there is common hope, fear,[3] joy, grief, suffering, because there is a common Spirit from a common Lord and Father, why do you think these [brethren and fellow-servants] to be anything other than your-

[1] Prodactæ.
[2] Per. But "per," according to Oehler, is used by Tertullian as = "propter"—on your account, for your sake.
[3] Metus.

self? Why flee from the partners of your own mischances, as from such as will derisively cheer them? The body cannot feel gladness at the trouble of any one member;[1] it must necessarily join with one consent in the grief, and in labouring for the remedy. In a company of two[2] is the church;[3] but the church is Christ.[4] When, then, you cast yourself at the brethren's knees, you are handling *Christ*, you are entreating *Christ*. In like manner, when they shed tears over you, it is *Christ* who suffers, *Christ* who prays the Father for mercy. What a son[5] asks is ever easily obtained. Grand indeed is the reward of modesty, which the concealment of our fault promises us! to wit, if we do hide somewhat from the knowledge of man, shall we equally conceal it from God? Are the judgment of men and the knowledge of God so put upon a par? Is it better to be damned in secret than absolved in public? "It is a miserable thing thus to come to *exomologesis*." [Miserable, I grant;] for evil does bring to misery; but where repentance is to be made, the misery ceases, because it is turned into something salutary. Miserable it is to be cut, and cauterized, and racked with the pungency of some [medicinal] powder: still, the things which heal by unpleasant means do, by the benefit of the cure, excuse their own offensiveness, and make present injury bearable for the sake[6] of the advantage to supervene.

CHAP. XI.—*Further strictures on the same subject.*

What if, besides the shame which they make the most account of, [men] dread likewise the bodily inconveniences [they must suffer]; in that, unwashen, sordidly attired, estranged from gladness, they must spend their time in the roughness of sackcloth, and the horridness of ashes, and the sunkenness of face caused by fasting? Is it then becoming for us to supplicate for our sins in scarlet and purple? Hasten hither with the pin for parting the hair, and the powder for polishing the teeth, and some forked implement of steel or brass

---

[1] 1 Cor. xii. 26.
[2] In uno et altero.
[3] See Matt. xviii. 20.
[4] *i.e.* as being His body.
[5] Or, "the Son." Comp. John xi. 41, 42.
[6] Or, "by the grace."

for cleaning the nails. Whatever of false brilliance, whatever of feigned redness, [is to be had,] let him diligently apply it to his lips or cheeks. Let him furthermore seek out baths of more genial temperature in some gardened or sea-side retreat; let him enlarge his expenses; let him carefully seek the rarest delicacy of fatted fowls; let him refine his old wine: and when any shall ask him, "On whom are you lavishing all this?" let him say, "I have sinned against God, and am in peril of eternally perishing: and so now I am drooping, and wasting and torturing myself, that I may reconcile God to myself, whom by sinning I have offended." Why, they who go about canvassing for the obtaining of civil office, feel it neither degrading nor irksome to struggle, in behalf of such their desires, with annoyances to soul and body; and not annoyances merely, but likewise contumelies of all kinds. What meannesses of dress do they not affect! what houses do they not beset with early and late visits! —bowing whenever they meet any high personage, frequenting no banquets, associating in no entertainments, but voluntarily exiled from the felicity of freedom and festivity: and all that for the sake of the fleeting joy of a single year! Do *we* hesitate, when eternity is at stake, to endure what the competitor for consulship or prætorship puts up with?[1] and shall we be tardy in offering to the offended Lord a self-chastisement in food and raiment, which[2] Gentiles lay upon themselves when they have offended no one at all? Such [hesitators] are they of whom Scripture makes mention: "Woe to them who bind their own sins as it were with a long rope."[3]

CHAP. XII.—*Final considerations to induce to exomologesis.*

If you shrink back from *exomologesis,* consider in your heart hell,[4] which *exomologesis* will extinguish for you; and imagine first the magnitude of the penalty, that you may not hesitate about the adoption of the remedy. What

---

[1] Quod securium virgarumque petitio sustinet.
[2] "Quae," neut. pl.   [3] Isa. v. 18 (comp. the LXX.).
[4] Gehennam. Comp. *ad Ux.* ii. c. vi. *ad fin.*

do we esteem that treasure-house of eternal fire to be, when small vent-holes[1] of it rouse such blasts of flames that neighbouring cities either are already no more, or are in daily expectation of the same fate? The haughtiest[2] mountains start asunder in the birth-throes of their inly-gendered fire; and—which proves to us the *perpetuity* of the judgment—though they start asunder, though they be devoured, yet come they never to an end. Who will not account these occasional punishments inflicted on the mountains as examples of the judgment which menaces [sinners]? Who will not agree that such sparks are but some few missiles and sportive darts of some inestimably vast centre of fire? Therefore, since you know that after the first bulwarks of the Lord's baptism[3] there still remains for you, in *exomologesis*, a second reserve of aid against hell, why do you desert your own salvation? Why are you tardy to approach what you know heals you? Even dumb irrational animals recognise in their time of need the medicines which have been divinely assigned them. The stag, transfixed by the arrow, knows that, to force out the steel, and its inextricable lingerings, he must heal himself with dittany. The swallow, if she blinds her young, knows how to give them eyes again by means of her own swallow-wort.[4] Shall the sinner, knowing that *exomologesis* has been instituted by the Lord for his restoration, pass that by which restored the Babylonian king[5] to his realms? Long time had he offered to the Lord his repentance, working out his *exomologesis* by a seven years' squalor, with his nails wildly growing after the eagle's fashion, and his unkempt hair wearing the shagginess of a lion. Hard handling! Him whom men were [all this while] shuddering at, God was receiving back [to Himself]. But, on the other

---

[1] Fumariola, *i.e.* the craters of volcanoes.

[2] Superbissimi: perhaps a play on the word, which is connected with "super" and "superus," as "haughty" with "high."

[3] For Tertullian's distinction between "the Lord's baptism" and "John's," see *de Bapt.* x.

[4] Or "celandine," which is perhaps only another form of "chelidonia" ("*Chelidonia major*," Linn.).

[5] Dan. iv. 25 sqq. See *de Pa.* xiii.

hand, the Egyptian emperor—who, after pursuing the once
afflicted people of God, long denied to their Lord, rushed
into the battle [1]—did, after so many warning plagues, perish
in the parted sea, (which was permitted to be passable to "the
people" alone,) by the backward roll of the waves: [2] for repentance and her handmaid [3] *exomologesis* he had cast away.

Why should I add more touching these two planks [4] (as it
were) of human salvation, caring more for the business of
the pen [5] than the duty of my conscience ? For, sinner as
I am of every dye,[6] and born for nothing save repentance, I
cannot easily be silent about that about which also the very
head and fount of the human race, and of human offence,
Adam, restored by *exomologesis* to his own paradise,[7] is not
silent.

[1] Proelium.   [2] Ex. xiv. 15-31.
[3] "Ministerium," the abstract for the concrete; so "servitia" = slaves.
[4] See c. iv.   [5] See *de Bapt.* xii. *sub init.*
[6] Lit. "of all *brands*." Comp. c. vi.: "Does the soldier . . . make satisfaction for his *brands*."
[7] Cf. Gen. iii. 24 with Luke xxiii. 43, 2 Cor. xii. 4, and Rev. ii. 7.

XI.

TO HIS WIFE.

BOOK I.

CHAP. I.—*Design of the treatise. Disavowal of personal motives in writing it.*

HAVE thought it meet, my best beloved fellow-servant in the Lord, even from this early period,[1] to provide for the course which you must pursue after my departure from the world,[2] if I shall be called before you; [and] to entrust to your honour[3] the observance of the provision. For in things worldly[4] we are active enough, and we wish the good of each of us to be consulted. If we draw up wills for *such* matters, why ought we not much more to take forethought for our posterity[5] in things divine and heavenly, and in a sense to bequeath a legacy to be received before the inheritance be divided,—[the legacy, I mean, of] admonition and demonstration touching those [bequests] which are allotted[6] out of [our] immortal goods, and from the heritage of the heavens? Only, that you may be able to receive in its entirety[7] this feoffment in trust[8] of my admonition, God grant; to whom be honour, glory, renown, dignity, and power, now and to the ages of the ages!

[1] Jam hinc.   [2] Sœculo.   [3] Fidei.   [4] Sæcularibus.
[5] Posteritati; or, with Mr. Dodgson, "our future."   [6] Deputantur.
[7] Solidum; alluding to certain laws respecting a widow's power of receiving " in its entirety " her deceased husband's property.
[8] Fidei commissum.

The precept, therefore, which I give you is, that, with all the constancy you may, you do, after our departure, renounce nuptials; not that you will on that score confer any benefit on me, except in that you will profit yourself. But to Christians, after their departure from the world,[1] no restoration of marriage is promised in the day of the resurrection, translated as they will be into the condition and sanctity of angels.[2] Therefore no solicitude arising from carnal jealousy will, in the day of the resurrection, even in the case of her whom they chose to represent as having been married to seven brothers successively, wound any one[3] of her so many husbands; nor is any [husband] awaiting her to put her to confusion.[4] The question raised by the Sadducees has yielded to the Lord's sentence. Think not that it is for the sake of preserving to the end for myself the entire devotion of your flesh, that I, suspicious of the pain of [anticipated] slight, am even at this early period[5] instilling into you the counsel of [perpetual] widowhood. There will at that day be no resumption of voluptuous disgrace between us. No such frivolities, no such impurities, does God promise to His [servants]. But whether to you, or to any other woman whatever who pertains to God, the advice which we are giving shall be profitable, we take leave to treat of at large.

CHAP. II.—*Marriage lawful, but not polygamy.*

We do not indeed forbid the union of man and woman, blest by God as the seminary of the human race, and devised for the replenishment of the earth[6] and the furnishing of the world,[7] and thereafter permitted, yet singly. For Adam was the one husband of Eve, and Eve his one wife, one woman, one rib.[8] We grant[9] that among our ancestors, and the patriarchs themselves, it was lawful[10] not only to marry,

---

[1] Sæculo.   [2] Luke xx. 36.   [3] Nulla ... neminem—two negatives.
[4] See Matt. xxii. 23-33; Mark xii. 18-27; Luke xx. 27-40.
[5] Jam hinc. See beginning of chapter.   [6] Orbi. Gen. i. 28.
[7] Sæculo.   [8] Gen. ii. 21, 22.   [9] Sane.
[10] "Fas," strictly *divine* law, opp. to "jus," *human* law; thus "lawful," as opp. to "legal."

but even to multiply wives.[1] There were concubines, too, [in those days.] But although the church did come in figuratively in the synagogue, yet (to interpret simply) it was necessary to institute [certain things] which should afterward deserve to be either lopped off or modified. For the Law was [in due time] to supervene. [Nor was that enough:] for it was meet that causes for making up the deficiencies of the Law should have forerun [Him who was to supply those deficiencies]. And so to the Law presently had to succeed the Word[2] of God introducing the spiritual circumcision.[3] Therefore, by means of the wide licence of those days, materials for subsequent emendations were furnished beforehand, of which materials the Lord by His Gospel, and then the apostle in the last days of the [Jewish] age,[4] either cut off the redundancies or regulated the disorders.

CHAP. III.—*Marriage good: celibacy preferable.*

But let it not be thought that my reason for premising thus much concerning the liberty granted to the old, and the restraint imposed on the later time, is that I may lay a foundation for teaching that Christ's advent was intended to dissolve wedlock, [and] to abolish marriage unions; as if from this period onward[5] I were prescribing an end to marrying. Let them see to that, who, among the rest of their perversities, teach the disjoining of the "one flesh in twain;"[6] denying Him who, after borrowing the female from the male, re-combined between themselves, in the matrimonial computation, the two bodies taken out of the consortship of the self-same material substance. In short, there is no

[1] Plurifariam matrimoniis uti. The neut. pl. "matrimonia" is sometimes used for "wives." Comp. c. v. *ad fin.* and *de Pæn.* c. xii. *ad fin.*
[2] Sermo, *i.e.* probably the personal Word. Comp. *de Or.* c. i. *ad init.*
[3] Rom. ii. 28, 29; Phil. iii. 3; Col. ii. 11.
[4] Sæculi. The meaning here seems clearly to be, as in the text, "the Jewish *age*" or *dispensation;* as in the passages referred to—1 Cor. x. 11, where it is τὰ τέλη τῶν αἰώνων; and Heb. ix. 26, where again it is τῶν αἰώνων, the Jewish and all preceding ages being intended.
[5] "Jam hinc," *i.e.* apparently from the time of Christ's advent.
[6] Matt. xix. 5, 6.

place at all where we read that nuptials are prohibited; of course on the ground that they are "a good thing." What, however, is *better* than this "good," we learn from the apostle, who *permits* marrying indeed, but *prefers* abstinence; the former on account of the insidiousnesses of temptations, the latter on account of the straits of the times.[1] Now, by looking into the reason thus given for each proposition, it is easily discerned that the ground on which the power of marrying is conceded is *necessity;* but whatever *necessity* grants, she by her very nature depreciates. In fact, in that it is written, "To marry is better than to burn," what, pray, is the nature of this "good" which is [only] commended by comparison with "evil," so that the reason why "marrying" is *more* good is [merely] that "burning" is *less?* Nay, but how far better is it neither to marry nor to burn? Why, even in persecutions it is *better* to take advantage of the permission granted, and "flee from town to town,"[2] than, when apprehended and racked, to deny [the faith].[3] And therefore more blessed are they who have strength to depart [this life] in blessed confession of their testimony.[4] I may say, What is *permitted* is not *good*. For how stands the case? I must of necessity die, [if I be apprehended and confess my faith.] If I think [that fate] deplorable, [then flight] is good; but if I have a fear of the thing which is permitted, [the permitted thing] has some suspicion attaching to the cause of its permission. But that which is "better" no one [ever] "permitted," as being undoubted, and manifest by its own inherent purity. There are some things which are not to be *desired* merely because they are not *forbidden*, albeit they *are* in a certain sense *forbidden* when other things are preferred to them; for the preference given to the higher things is a dissuasion from the lowest. A thing is not "good" merely because it is not "evil," nor is it "evil" merely because it is not "harmful."[5] Further: that which is fully "good" excels on this

---

[1] 1 Cor. vii.   [2] Matt. x. 23; perhaps confused with xxiii. 34.
[3] Comp. *de Idol.* c. xxiii., and the note there on "se negant."
[4] *i.e.* in martyrdom, on the ground of that open confession.
[5] Non obest.

ground, that it is not only not harmful, but profitable into the bargain. For you are bound to prefer what is profitable to what is [merely] not harmful. For the *first* place is what every struggle aims at; the *second* has consolation attaching to it, but not victory. But if we listen to the apostle, forgetting what is behind, let us both strain after what is before,[1] and be followers after the better rewards. Thus, albeit he does not "cast a snare[2] upon us," he points out what tends to utility when he says, "The unmarried woman thinks on the things of the Lord, that both in body and spirit she may be holy; but the married is solicitous how to please her husband."[3] But he nowhere permits marriage in such a way as not rather to wish us to do our utmost in imitation of his own example. Happy the man who shall prove like Paul!

CHAP. IV.—*Of the infirmity of the flesh, and similar pleas.*

But we read "that the flesh is weak;"[4] and hence we soothe[5] ourselves in some cases. Yet we read, too, that "the spirit is strong;"[6] for each clause occurs in one and the same sentence. Flesh is an earthly, spirit a heavenly, material. Why, then, do we, too prone to self-excuse, put forward [in our defence] the weak part of us, but not look at[7] the strong? Why should not the earthly yield to the heavenly? If the spirit is stronger than the flesh, because it is withal of nobler origin, it is our own fault if we follow the weaker. Now there are two phases[8] of human weakness which make marriages[9] necessary to such as are disjoined from matrimony.

---

[1] Phil. iii. 13, 14.

[2] Laqueum = βρόχος (1 Cor. vii. 35), "a noose," "lasso" ("snare," Eng. ver."). " Laqueo trahuntur inviti " (Bengel).

[3] See note 1. [4] Matt. xxvi. 41.

[5] Adulamur: "we fawn upon," or "caress," or "flatter." Comp. *de Pæn.* c. vi. *sub init.:* "flatter their own sweetness."

[6] "Firmum," opp. to "infirmam" above. In the passage there referred to (Matt. xxvi. 41) the word is πρόθυμον.

[7] Tuemur. Mr. Dodgson renders, "guard not." [8] Species.

[9] *i.e.* apparently *second* marriages: "disjunctis a matrimonio" can scarcely include such as were never "juncti;" and comp. the "præmissis maritis" below.

The first and most powerful is that which arises from *fleshly* concupiscence; the second, from *worldly* concupiscence. But by us, who are servants of God, who renounce both voluptuousness and ambition, each is to be repudiated. Fleshly concupiscence claims the functions of adult age, craves after beauty's harvest, rejoices in its own shame, pleads the necessity of a husband to the female sex, as a source of authority and of comfort, or to render it safe from evil rumours. To meet these its counsels, do you apply the examples of sisters of ours whose names are with the Lord,[1]—who, when their husbands have preceded them [to glory], give to no opportunity of beauty or of age the precedence over holiness. They prefer to be wedded to God. To God their beauty, to God their youth [is dedicated]. With Him they live; with Him they converse; Him they "handle"[2] by day and by night; *to* the Lord they assign their prayers as dowries; *from* Him, as oft as they desire it, they receive His approbation[3] as dotal gifts. Thus they have laid hold for themselves of an eternal gift of the Lord; and while on earth, by abstaining from marriage, are already counted as belonging to the angelic family. Training yourself to an emulation of [their] constancy by the examples of such women, you will by spiritual affection bury that fleshly concupiscence, in abolishing the temporal[4] and fleeting desires of beauty and youth by the compensating gain of immortal blessings.

On the other hand, this *worldly* concupiscence [to which I referred] has, as its causes, glory, cupidity, ambition, want of sufficiency; through which causes it trumps up the "necessity" for marrying,—promising itself, forsooth, heavenly things in return—to lord it, [namely,] in another's family; to roost[5] on another's wealth; to extort splendour from another's store; to lavish expenditure[6] which you do not feel! Far be all this from believers, who have no care about maintenance, unless it be that we distrust the promises of God, and [His] care and providence, who clothes

---

[1] Comp. Phil. iv. 3; 2 Tim. ii. 19; Mal. iii. 16; and similar passages.
[2] 1 John i. 1; Luke xxiv. 39; John xx. 17.   [3] Dignationem.
[4] Or, "temporary."   [5] Incubare.   [6] Cædere sumptum.

with such grace the lilies of the field;[1] who, without any labour on their part, feeds the fowls of the heaven;[2] who prohibits care to be taken about to-morrow's food and clothing,[3] promising that He knows what is needful for each of His servants—not indeed ponderous necklaces, not burdensome garments, not Gallic mules nor German bearers, which all add lustre to the glory of nuptials; but "sufficiency,"[4] which is suitable to moderation and modesty. Presume, I pray you, that you have need of nothing if you "attend upon the Lord;"[5] nay, that you have all things, if you have the Lord, whose are all things. Think often[6] on things heavenly, and you will despise things earthly. To widowhood signed and sealed before the Lord nought is necessary but perseverance.

CHAP. V.—*Of the love of offspring as a plea for marriage.*

Further reasons for marriage which men allege for themselves arise from anxiety for posterity, and the bitter bitter pleasure of children. To *us* this is idle. For why should we be eager to bear children, whom, when we have them, we desire to send before us [to glory][7] (in respect, I mean, of the distresses that are now imminent); desirous as we are ourselves, too, to be taken out of this most wicked world,[8] and received into the Lord's presence, which was the desire even of an apostle?[9] To the servant of God, forsooth, offspring is necessary! For of our own salvation we are secure enough, so that we have leisure for children! Burdens must be sought by us for ourselves which are avoided even by the majority of the Gentiles, who are compelled by laws,[10] who are decimated[11] by abortions;[12] burdens which, finally, are to *us* most of all unsuitable, as being perilous to faith. For why

---

[1] Matt. vi. 28–30. [2] Matt. vi. 26.
[3] Matt. vi. 31, 34. [4] Comp. Phil. iv. 19; 1 Tim. vi. 8.
[5] Comp. 1 Cor. vii. 35, esp. in Eng. ver. [6] Recogita.
[7] Comp. c. iv. above, "præmissis maritis;" "when their husbands have preceded them [to glory]."
[8] Sæculo. [9] Phil. i. 23; comp. *de Pa. c. ix. ad fin.*
[10] *i.e.* to get children. [11] Expugnantur.
[12] "Parricidiis." So Oehler seems to understand it.

did the Lord foretell a "woe to them that are with child, and them that give suck,"[1] except because He testifies that in that day of disencumbrance the encumbrances of children will be an inconvenience? It is to marriage, of course, that those encumbrances appertain; but that ["woe"] will not pertain to widows. [*They*] at the first trump of the angel will spring forth disencumbered — will freely bear to the end whatsoever pressure and persecution, with no burdensome fruit of marriage heaving in the womb, none in the bosom.

Therefore, whether it be for the sake of the flesh, or of the world,[2] or of posterity, that marriage is undertaken, nothing of all these "necessities" affects the servants of God, so as to prevent my deeming it enough to have once for all yielded to some one of them, and by one marriage appeased[3] all concupiscence of this kind. Let us marry daily, and in the midst of our marrying let us be overtaken, like Sodom and Gomorrha, by that day of fear![4] For *there* it was not only, of course, that they were dealing in marriage and merchandise; but when He says, "They were marrying and buying," He sets a brand[5] upon the very leading vices of the flesh and of the world,[6] which call men off the most from divine disciplines — the one through the pleasure of rioting, the other through the greed of acquiring. And yet that "blindness" *then* was felt long before "the ends of the world."[7] What, then, will the case be if God *now* keep us from the vices which *of old* were detestable before Him? "The time," says [the apostle], "is compressed.[8] It remaineth that they who have wives[9] act as if they had them not."

---

[1] Luke xxi. 23; Matt. xxiv. 19.   [2] Sæculi.

[3] "Expiasse" — a rare but Ciceronian use of the word.

[4] Luke xvii. 28, 29.   [5] Denotat.   [6] Sæculi.

[7] Sæculi. Comp. 1 Cor. x. 11; but the Greek there is, τὰ τέλη τῶν αἰώνων. By the "blindness," Tertullian may refer to Gen. xix. 11.

[8] Or, "short" (Eng. ver.); 1 Cor. vii. 29, ὁ καιρὸς συνεσταλμένος, "in collecto."

[9] "Matrimonia," neut. pl. again for the fem., the abstract for the concrete. See c. ii., "to multiply wives," and the note there. In the Greek (1 Cor. vii. 29) it is γυναῖκας; but the ensuing chapter shows that Tertullian refers the passage to women as well.

CHAP. VI.—*Examples of heathens urged as commendatory of widowhood and celibacy.*

But if they who *have* [wives] are [thus] bound to consign to oblivion what they have, how much more are they who have *not* prohibited from seeking a second time what they no longer have; so that she whose husband has departed from the world should thenceforward impose rest on her sex by abstinence from marriage—abstinence which numbers of Gentile women devote to the memory of beloved husbands! When anything seems difficult, let us survey others who cope with still greater difficulties. How many are there who from the moment of their baptism set the seal [of virginity] upon their flesh? How many, again, who by equal mutual consent cancel the debt of matrimony—voluntary eunuchs [1] for the sake of their desire after the celestial kingdom! But if, while the marriage-tie is still intact, abstinence is endured, how much more when it has been undone! For I believe it to be harder for what is intact to be quite forsaken, than for what has been lost not to be yearned after. A hard and arduous thing enough, surely, is the continence for God's sake of a holy woman after her husband's decease, when Gentiles,[2] in honour of their own Satan, endure sacerdotal offices which involve both virginity and widowhood![3] At Rome, for instance, they who have to do with the type of that "inextinguishable fire,"[4] keeping watch over the omens of their own [future] penalty, in company with the [old] dragon [5] himself, are appointed on the ground of *virginity*. To the Achæan Juno, at the town Ægium, a *virgin* is allotted; and the [priestesses] who rave at Delphi know not marriage. Moreover, we know that *widows* minister to the African Ceres; enticed away, indeed, from matrimony by a most stern oblivion: for not only do they withdraw from their still living husbands, but they even introduce other wives to them in their own room—the husbands, of course, smiling

---

[1] Comp. *de Pa.* xiii., and Matt. xix. 12. Comp. too, *de Ex. Cast.* c. i.
[2] *i.e.* Gentile *women*.   [3] Oehler marks this as a question.
[4] Matt. iii. 12.   [5] Comp. Rev. xii. 9, and *de Bapt.* i.

on it—all contact [with males], even as far as the kiss of
their sons, being forbidden them; and yet, with enduring
practice, they persevere in such a discipline of widowhood,
which excludes the solaces even of holy affection.[1] These
precepts has the devil given to his servants, and he is heard!
He challenges, forsooth, God's servants, by the continence
of his own, as if on equal terms! Continent are even the
priests of hell![2] For he has found a way to ruin men even
in good pursuits; and with him it makes no difference to slay
some by voluptuousness, some by continence.

CHAP. VII.—*The death of a husband is God's call to the
widow to continence. Further evidences from Scripture
and from heathenism.*

To us continence has been pointed out by the Lord of salvation as an instrument for attaining eternity[3]—as a testimony of [our] faith; as a commendation of this flesh of ours,
which is to be sustained for the "garment of immortality,"[4]
which is one day to supervene; for enduring, in fine, the will
of God. Besides, reflect, I advise you, that there is no one
who is taken out of the world[5] but by the will of God, if, [as
is the case,] not even a leaf falls from off a tree without the
will of God. The same who brings us into the world,[6] must
of necessity take us out of it too. Therefore when, through
the will of God, the husband is deceased, the marriage likewise by the will of God deceases. Why should *you* restore
what GOD has put an end to? Why do you, by repeating
the servitude of matrimony, spurn the liberty which is offered
you? "You have been bound to a wife," says the apostle;[7]
"seek not loosing. You have been loosed from a wife;" seek
not binding." For even if you do not "*sin*" in re-marrying,

---

[1] Pietatis.
[2] Gehennæ; comp. *de Pœn.* c. xii. *ad init.*
[3] *i.e.* eternal life; comp. "consecutio æternitatis," *de Bapt.* c. ii.
[4] 1 Cor. xv. 53; 2 Cor. v. 4.   [5] Sæculo.   [6] Mundo.
[7] "Matrimonio," or "by matrimony." Comp. 1 Cor. vii. 27: δέδεσαι
γυναικί; μὴ ζήτει λύσιν· λέλυσαι ἀπὸ γυναικός; μὴ ζήτει γυναῖκα.
Tertullian's rendering, it will be seen, is not *verbatim.*

still he says " pressure of the flesh ensues."[1] Wherefore, so far as we can, let us love the opportunity of continence; as soon as it offers itself, let us resolve to accept it, that what we have not had strength[2] [to follow] in matrimony we may follow in widowhood. The occasion must be embraced which puts an end to that which *necessity*[3] commanded. How detrimental to faith, how obstructive to holiness, second marriages are, the discipline of the church and the prescription of the apostle declare, when he suffers not men twice married to preside [over a church[4]], when he would not grant a widow admittance into the order unless she had been " the wife of one man;"[5] for it behoves God's altar[6] to be set forth pure. That whole halo[7] which encircles the church is represented [as consisting] of holiness. Priesthood is [a function] of widowhood and of celibacies among the nations. Of course [this is] in conformity with the devil's principle of rivalry. For the king of heathendom,[8] the chief pontiff,[9] to marry a second time is unlawful. How pleasing must holiness be to God, when even His enemy affects it!—not, of course, as having any affinity with anything good, but as contumeliously affecting what is pleasing to[10] God the Lord.

Chap. viii.—*Conclusion.*

For, concerning the honours which widowhood enjoys in the sight of God, there is a brief summary in one saying of His through the prophet: "Do thou[11] justly to the widow and to the orphan; and come ye,[11] let us reason, saith the Lord." These two names, left to the care of the divine mercy, in proportion as they are destitute of human aid, the

[1] 1 Cor. vii. 28.
[2] Or, "been able"—valuimus. But comp. c. vi.
[3] See c. iii., "quod autem *necessitas* præstat, depretiat *ipsa*," etc.
[4] 1 Tim. ii. 2; Tit. i. 6.   [5] 1 Tim. v. 9, 10.   [6] Aram.
[7] Comp. *de Cor.* c. i., " et de martyrii *candida* melius coronatus," and Oehler's note.
[8] Sæculi.   [9] Or, " Pontifex maximus."
[10] Or, " has been decreed by."
[11] So Oehler reads, with Rhenanus and the MSS. The other edd. have the plural in each case, as the LXX. in the passage referred to (Isa. i. 17, 18).

Father of all undertakes to defend. Look how the widow's benefactor is put on a level with the widow herself, whose champion shall "reason with the Lord!" Not to virgins, I take it, is so great a gift given. Although in *their* case perfect integrity and entire sanctity shall have the nearest vision of the face of God, yet the *widow* has a task more toilsome, because it is easy not to crave after that which you know not, and to turn away from what you have never had to regret.[1] More glorious is the continence which is aware of its own right, which knows what it has seen. The virgin may possibly be held the happier, but the widow the more hardly tasked; the former in that she has always kept "the good,"[2] the latter in that she has found "the good for herself." In the former it is grace, in the latter virtue, that is crowned. For some things there are which are of the divine liberality, some of our own working. The indulgences granted by the Lord are regulated by their own grace; the things which are objects of man's striving are attained by earnest pursuit. Pursue earnestly, therefore, the virtue of continence, which is modesty's agent; industry, which allows not women to be "wanderers;"[3] frugality, which scorns the world.[4] Follow companies and conversations worthy of God, mindful of that short verse, sanctified by the apostle's quotation of it, "Ill interviews good morals do corrupt."[5] Talkative, idle, winebibbing, curious tent-fellows,[6] do the very greatest hurt to the purpose of widowhood. Through talkativeness there creep in words unfriendly to modesty; through idleness they seduce one from strictness; through winebibbing they insinuate any and every evil; through curiosity they convey a spirit of rivalry in lust. Not one of such women knows how to speak of the good of single-husbandhood; for their "god," as the apostle says, "is their belly;"[7] and so, too, what is neighbour to the belly.

---

[1] Desideraveris. Oehler reads "desideres." [2] Comp. c. iii.
[3] 1 Tim. v. 13. [4] Sæculum.
[5] A verse said to be Menander's, quoted by St. Paul, 1 Cor. xv. 33; quoted again, but somewhat differently rendered, by Tertullian in B. i. c. iii.
[6] *i.e.* here "female companions." [7] Phil. iii. 19.

These considerations, dearest fellow-servant, I commend to you thus early,[1] handled throughout superfluously indeed, after the apostle, but likely to prove a solace to you, in that (if so it shall turn out[2]) you will cherish my memory in them.

BOOK II.

CHAP. I.—*Reasons which led to the writing of this second book.*

Very lately, best beloved fellow-servant in the Lord, I, as my ability permitted, entered for your benefit at some length into the question what course is to be followed by a holy woman when her marriage has (in whatever way) been brought to an end. Let us now turn our attention to the next best advice, in regard of human infirmity; admonished hereto by the examples of certain, who, when an opportunity for the practice of continence has been offered them, by divorce, or by the decease of the husband, have not only thrown away the opportunity of attaining so great a good, but not even in their re-marriage have chosen to be mindful of the rule that "above all[3] they marry in the Lord." And thus my mind has been thrown into confusion, in the fear that, having exhorted you myself to perseverance in single husbandhood and widowhood, I may now, by the mention of precipitate[4] marriages, put "an occasion of falling"[5] in your way. But if you are perfect in wisdom, you know, of course, that the course which is the more useful is the course which you must keep. But, inasmuch as that course is difficult, and not without its embarrassments,[6] and on this account is the highest aim of [widowed] life, I have paused somewhat [in my urging you

---

[1] Comp. c. i.   [2] *i.e.* if I be called before you; comp. c. i.
[3] Potissimum; Gr. "μόνον," 1 Cor. vii. 39.   [4] Proclivium.
[5] Ps. lxix. 23 (according to the "Great Bible" version, ed. 1539. This is the translation found in the "Book of Common Prayer"). Comp. Rom. xiv. 13.
[6] Necessitatibus.

to it]; nor would there have been any causes for my recurring
to that point also in addressing you, had I not by this time
taken up a still graver solicitude. For the nobler is the
continence of the flesh which ministers to widowhood, the
more pardonable a thing it seems if it be not persevered in.
For it is then when things are difficult that their pardon is
easy. But in as far as marrying "in the Lord" is permissible, as being within our power, so far more culpable is
it *not* to observe that which you *can* observe. Add to this
the fact that the apostle, with regard to widows and the unmarried, *advises* them to remain permanently in that state,
when he says, "But I desire all to persevere in [imitation of]
my example:"[1] but touching marrying "in the Lord," he
no longer *advises*, but plainly [2] *bids*.[3] Therefore in this case
especially, if we do not obey, we run a risk, because one may
with more impunity neglect an "advice" than an "order;"
in that the former springs from *counsel*, and is proposed to
the *will* [for acceptance or rejection]: the other descends
from *authority*, and is bound to *necessity*. In the former case,
to disregard appears *liberty*, in the latter, *contumacy*.

CHAP. II.—*Of the apostle's meaning in* 1 *Cor.* vii. 12-14.

Therefore, when in these days a certain woman removed
her marriage from the pale of the church, and united herself
to a Gentile, and when I remembered that this had in days
gone by been done by others: wondering at either their own
waywardness or else the double-dealing[4] of their advisers, in
that there is no scripture which holds forth a licence of this
deed,—"I wonder," said I, "whether they flatter themselves
on the ground of that passage of the first [Epistle] to the
Corinthians, where it is written: 'If any of the brethren has

---

[1] 1 Cor. vii. 6-8.

[2] Exerte. Comp. the use of "exertus" in *de Bapt.* cc. xii. and xviii.

[3] 1 Cor. vii. 39, where the μόνον ἐν Κυρίῳ is on the same footing as
γυνὴ δέδεται ἐφ' ὅσον χρόνον ζῇ ὁ ἀνὴρ αὐτῆς; comp. c. ix. and Rom. vii. 1
(in the Eng. ver. 2).

[4] Prævaricationem. Comp. *de Pæn.* c. iii.: "Dissimulator et præ-
varicator perspicaciæ suæ (Deus) non est."

an unbelieving wife, and she consents to the matrimony, let him not dismiss her; similarly, let not a believing woman, married to an unbeliever, if she finds her husband agreeable [to their continued union], dismiss him: for the unbelieving husband is sanctified by the believing wife, and the unbelieving wife by the believing husband; else were your children unclean.'"[1] It may be that, by understanding *generally* this monition regarding *married* believers, they think that licence is granted [thereby] to marry even *un*believers. God forbid that he who thus interprets [the passage] be *willingly* ensnaring himself! But it is manifest that this scripture points to those believers who may have been found by the grace of God in [the state of] Gentile matrimony; according to the words themselves: "If," it says, "any believer *has* an unbelieving wife;" it does not say, "*takes* an unbelieving wife." It shows that it is the duty of one who, already living in marriage with an unbelieving woman,[2] has presently been by the grace of God converted, to continue with his wife; for this reason, to be sure, in order that no one, after attaining to faith, should think that he must turn away from a woman[3] who is now in some sense an "alien" and "stranger."[4] Accordingly he subjoins withal a reason, that "we are called *in peace* unto the Lord God;" and that "the unbeliever may, through the use of matrimony, *be gained* by the believer."[5] The very closing sentence of the period confirms [the supposition] that this is thus to be understood. "As each," it says, "is called by the Lord, so let him persevere."[6] But it is *Gentiles* who "are called," I take it, not *believers*. But if he had been pronouncing *absolutely*, [in the words under discussion,] touching the marriage of believers merely, [then] had he [virtually] given to saints a permission to marry promiscuously. If, however, he had given such a permission, he would never have subjoined a declaration so diverse from

---

[1] 1 Cor. vii. 12-14, in sense, not *verbatim*.
[2] Mulieris. [3] Femina. [4] Comp. Eph. ii. 12, 19.
[5] Comp. 1 Cor. vii. 15, 16, and Phil. iii. 8, in Vulg., for the word "lucrifieri."
[6] 1 Cor. vii. 17, inexactly given, like the two preceding citations.

and contrary to his own permission, saying: "The woman, when her husband is dead, is free: let her marry whom she wishes, *only in the Lord*."[1] Here, at all events, there is no need for reconsidering; for what there *might* have been reconsideration about, the Spirit has oracularly declared. For fear we should make an ill use of what he says, "Let her marry whom she wishes," he has added, "only in the Lord," that is, in the name of the Lord, which is, undoubtedly, "to a Christian." That "Holy Spirit,"[2] therefore, who prefers that widows and unmarried women should persevere in their integrity, who exhorts us to a copy[3] of himself, prescribes no other manner of repeating marriage except "in the Lord:" to this condition alone does he concede the foregoing[4] of continence. "Only," he says, "in the Lord:" he has added to his law a weight—"*only*." Utter that word with what tone and manner you may, it is weighty: it both bids and advises; both enjoins and exhorts; both asks and threatens. It is a concise,[5] brief sentence; and by its own very brevity, eloquent. Thus is the divine voice wont [to speak], that you may instantly understand, instantly observe. For who but could understand that the apostle foresaw many dangers and wounds to faith in marriages of this kind, which he prohibits? and that he took precaution, in the first place, against the defilement of holy flesh in Gentile flesh? At this point some one says, "What, then, is the difference between him who is chosen by the Lord to Himself in [the state of] Gentile marriage, and him who was of old (that is, before marriage) a believer, that they should not be equally cautious for their flesh?—whereas the one is kept from marriage with an unbeliever, the other bidden to continue in it. Why, if we are defiled by a Gentile, is not the one disjoined, just as the other is not bound?" I will answer, if the Spirit give [me ability];

---

[1] 1 Cor. vii. 39, not *verbatim*.

[2] *i.e.* St. Paul, who, as inspired by the Holy Spirit, is regarded by Tertullian as merged, so to speak, in the Spirit.

[3] "Exemplum,"—a rarer use of the word, but found in Cic. The reference is to 1 Cor. vii. 7.

[4] Detrimenta.   [5] Districta (? = dis-stricta, "doubly strict").

alleging, before all [other arguments], that the Lord holds it more pleasing that matrimony should not be contracted, than than it should at all be dissolved: in short, divorce He prohibits, except for the cause of fornication; but continence He commends. Let the one, therefore, have the necessity of continuing; the other, further, even the power of not marrying. Secondly, if, according to the Scripture, they who shall be "apprehended"[1] by the faith in [the state of] Gentile marriage are not defiled [thereby] for this reason, that, together with themselves, others[2] also are sanctified: without doubt, they who have been sanctified *before* marriage, if they commingle themselves with "strange flesh,"[3] cannot sanctify that [flesh] in [union with] which they were not "apprehended." The grace of God, moreover, sanctifies that which it *finds*. Thus, what has not been able to be sanctified is unclean; what is unclean has no part with the holy, unless to defile and slay it by its own [nature].

CHAP. III.—*Remarks on some of the " dangers and wounds" referred to in the preceding chapter.*

If these things are so, it is certain that believers contracting marriages with Gentiles are guilty of fornication,[4] and are to be excluded from all communication with the brotherhood, in accordance with the letter of the apostle, who says that "with persons of that kind there is to be no taking of food even."[5] Or shall we "in that day"[6] produce [our] marriage certificates before the Lord's tribunal, and allege that a marriage such as He Himself has forbidden has been duly contracted? What is prohibited [in the passage just referred to] is not "adultery;" it is not "fornication." The admission of a strange man [to your couch] less violates

---

[1] Comp. Phil. iii. 12, and c. vii. *ad init.*   [2] See 1 Cor. vii. 14.
[3] Comp. Jude 7, and above, "an alien and stranger," with the reference there.
[4] Comp. *de Pa.* c. xii. (mid.), and the note there.
[5] Comp. 1 Cor. v. 11.
[6] The translator has ventured to read " *die* illo " here, instead of Oehler's " *de* illo."

"the temple of God,"[1] less commingles "the members of Christ" with the members of an adulteress.[2] So far as I know, "we are not our own, but bought with a price;"[3] and what kind of price? The blood of God.[4] In hurting this flesh of ours, therefore, we hurt Him directly.[5] What did that man mean who said that "to wed a 'stranger' was indeed a sin, but a very small one?" whereas in other cases (setting aside the injury done to the flesh which pertains to the Lord) *every* voluntary sin against the Lord is *great*. For, in as far as there was a power of avoiding it, in so far is it burdened with the charge of contumacy.

Let us now recount the other dangers or wounds (as I have said) to faith, foreseen by the apostle; most grievous not to the flesh merely, but likewise to the spirit too. For who would doubt that faith undergoes a daily process of obliteration by unbelieving intercourse? "Evil confabulations corrupt good morals;"[6] how much more fellowship of life, and indivisible intimacy! Any and every believing woman must of necessity obey God. And how can she serve two lords[7]—the Lord, and her husband—a Gentile to boot? For in obeying a Gentile she will carry out Gentile practices,—personal attractiveness, dressing of the head, worldly[8] elegancies, baser blandishments, the very secrets even of matrimony tainted: not as, among the saints, the duties of the sex are discharged with honour [shown] to the very necessity [which makes them incumbent], with modesty and temperance, as beneath the eyes of God.

CHAP. IV.—*Of the hindrances which an unbelieving husband puts in his wife's way.*

But let her see to [the question] how she discharges her

---

[1] 1 Cor. iii. 16, comp. vi. 19.   [2] 1 Cor. vi. 15.   [3] 1 Cor. vi. 19, 20.

[4] See the last reference, and Acts xx. 28, where the MSS. vary between Θεοῦ and Κυρίου.

[5] De proximo. Comp. *de. Pa.* cc. v. and vii. "Deo *de proximo* amicus;" "*de proximo* in Deum peccat."

[6] Comp. B. i. c. viii. *sub fin.*, where Tertullian quotes the same passage, but renders it somewhat differently.

[7] Comp. Matt. vi. 24; Luke xvi. 13.   [8] Sæculares.

duties to her husband. To the Lord, at all events, she is unable to give satisfaction according to the requirements of discipline; having at her side a servant of the devil, *his* lord's agent for hindering the pursuits and duties of believers: so that if a station[1] is to be kept, the husband at daybreak makes an appointment with his wife to meet him at the baths; if there are fasts to be observed, the husband that same day holds a convivial banquet; if a charitable expedition has to be made, never is family business more urgent. For who would suffer his wife, for the sake of visiting the brethren, to go round from street to street to other men's, and indeed to all the poorer, cottages? Who will willingly bear her being taken from his side by nocturnal convocations, if need so be? Who, finally, will without anxiety endure her absence all the night long at the paschal solemnities? Who will, without some suspicion of his own, dismiss her to attend that Lord's Supper which they defame? Who will suffer her to creep into prison to kiss a martyr's bonds? nay, truly, to meet any one of the brethren to exchange the kiss? to offer water for the saints' feet?[2] to snatch [somewhat for them] from her food, from her cup? to yearn [after them]? to have [them] in her mind? If a pilgrim brother arrive, what hospitality for him in an alien home? If bounty is to be distributed to any, the granaries, the storehouses, are foreclosed.

CHAP. V.—*Of sin and danger incurred even with a "tolerant" husband.*

"But some husband does endure our [practices], and not annoy us." *Here*, therefore, there is a sin; in that Gentiles *know* our [practices]; in that we are subject to the privity of the unjust; in that it is thanks to them that we do any [good] work. He who "endures" [a thing] cannot be ignorant of it; or else, if he is kept in ignorance because he does *not* endure [it], he is feared. But since Scripture commands each of two things—namely, that we work for the

---

[1] For the meaning of "statio," see *de Or.* c. xix.
[2] 1 Tim. v. 10.

Lord without the privity of any second person,[1] and without pressure upon ourselves, it matters not in which quarter you sin; whether in regard to your husband's privity, if he be tolerant, or else in regard of your own affliction in avoiding his intolerance. "Cast not," saith He, "your pearls to swine, lest they trample them to pieces, and turn round and overturn you also."[2] "Your pearls" are the distinctive marks[3] of even your daily conversation. The more care you take to conceal them, the more liable to suspicion you will make them, and the more exposed to the grasp of Gentile curiosity. Shall you escape notice when you sign your bed, [or] your body; when you blow away some impurity;[4] when even by night you rise to pray? And will you not be thought to be engaged in some work of magic? Will not your husband know what it is which you secretly taste before [taking] any food? and if he knows it to be bread, does he not believe it to be *that* [bread] which it is *said* to be? And will every [husband], ignorant of the reason of these things, simply endure them, without murmuring, without suspicion whether it be bread or poison? Some, [it is true,] *do* endure [them]; but it is that they may trample on, that they may make sport of, such women; whose secrets they keep in reserve against the danger which they believe in, in case they ever chance to be hurt: they do endure [wives], whose dowries, by casting in their teeth their [Christian] name, they make the wages of silence; while they threaten them, forsooth, with a suit before some spy[5] as arbitrator! which most women, not foreseeing, have been wont to discover either by the extortion of their property, or else by the loss of their faith.

CHAP. VI.—*Danger of having to take part in heathenish rites and revels.*

The handmaid of God[6] dwells amid alien labours; and

[1] Comp. Matt. vi. 1–4.   [2] Matt. vii. 6.
[3] Insignia.   [4] Comp. *de Idol.* c. xi. *sub fin.*
[5] " Speculatorem;" also = an executioner. Comp. Mark vi. 27.
[6] Comp. Luke i. 38, and *de Cult. Fem.* b. ii. c. i. *ad init.*

among these [labours], on all the memorial days [1] of demons, at all solemnities of kings, at the beginning of the year, at the beginning of the month, she will be agitated by the odour of incense. And she will have to go forth [from her house] by a gate wreathed with laurel, and hung with lanterns, as from some new consistory of public lusts; will have to sit with her husband ofttimes in club meetings, ofttimes in taverns; and, wont as she was formerly to minister to the "saints," will sometimes have to minister to the "unjust." [2] And will she not hence recognise a prejudgment of her own damnation, in that she *tends* them whom [formerly] she was expecting to *judge*? [3] whose hand will she yearn after? of whose cup will she partake? What will her husband sing [4] to her, or she to her husband? From the tavern, I suppose, she who sups upon God [5] will hear somewhat! From hell what mention of God [arises]? what invocation of Christ? Where are the fosterings of faith by the interspersion of the Scriptures [in conversation]? Where the Spirit? where refreshment? where the divine benediction? All things are strange, all inimical, all condemned; aimed by the Evil One for the attrition of salvation!

CHAP. VII.—*The case of a heathen whose wife is converted* AFTER *marriage with him very different, and much more hopeful.*

If these things may happen to those women also who, having attained the faith while in [the state of] Gentile matrimony, continue in that state, still they are excused, as

[1] Nominibus; al. honoribus.
[2] Sanctis—iniquis. Comp. St. Paul's antithesis of ἀδίκων and ἁγίων in 1 Cor. vi. 1.
[3] See 1 Cor. vi. 2, 3. [4] See Eph. v. 19.
[5] So Oehler understands (apparently) the meaning to be. The translator is inclined to think that, adopting Oehler's reading, we may perhaps take the "Dei" with "aliquid," and the "coenans" absolutely, and render, "From the tavern, no doubt, while supping, she will hear some [strain] of God," in allusion to the former sentence, and to such passages as Ps. cxxxvii. 4 (in the LXX. it is cxxxvi. 4).

having been "apprehended by God"[1] in these very circumstances; and they are *bidden* to persevere in their married state, and are sanctified, and have hope of "making a gain"[2] held out to them. "If, then, a marriage of this kind [contracted *before* conversion] stands ratified before God, why should not [one contracted *after* conversion] too go prosperously forward, so as not to be thus harassed by pressures, and straits, and hindrances, and defilements, having already [as it has] the partial sanction of divine grace?" Because, on the one hand, the wife[3] in the former case, called *from among* the Gentiles to the exercise of some eminent heavenly virtue, is, by the visible proofs of some marked [divine] regard, a terror to her Gentile husband, so as to make him less ready to annoy her, less active in laying snares for her, less diligent in playing the spy over her. He has felt "mighty works;"[4] he has seen experimental evidences; he knows her changed for the better: thus even he himself is, by his fear,[5] a candidate for God.[6] Thus men of this kind, with regard to whom the grace of God has established a familiar intimacy, are more easily "gained." But, on the other hand, to descend into forbidden ground unsolicited and spontaneously, is [quite] another thing. Things which are not pleasing to the Lord, of course offend the Lord, are of course introduced by the Evil One. A sign hereof is this fact, that it is *wooers* only who find the Christian name pleasing; and, accordingly, some heathen men are found not to shrink in horror from Christian women, just in order to exterminate them, to wrest them away, to exclude them from the faith. So long as marriage of this kind is procured by the Evil One, but condemned by God, you have a reason why you need not doubt that it can in no case be carried to a prosperous end.

---

[1] Comp. Phil. iii. 12, and c. ii. *sub fin.*

[2] Comp. 1 Cor. vii. 16 and 1 Pet. iii. 1.

[3] Tertullian here and in other places appears, as the best editors maintain, to use the masculine gender for the feminine.

[4] Magnalia. Comp. 2 Cor. xii. 12.   [5] Timore.

[6] Comp. *de Or.* c. iii. (*med.*), "angelorum candidati;" and *de Bapt.* c. x. *sub fin.*, "candidatus remissionis."

CHAP. VIII.—*Arguments drawn even from heathenish laws to discountenance marriage with unbelievers. The happiness of union between partners in the faith enlarged on in conclusion.*

Let us further inquire, as if we were in very deed inquisitors of divine sentences, whether they be lawfully [thus condemned]. Even among the nations, do not all the strictest lords and most tenacious of discipline interdict their own slaves from marrying out of their own house?—in order, of course, that they may not run into lascivious excess, desert their duties, purvey their lords' goods to strangers. Yet, further, have not [the nations] decided that such women as have, after their lords'[1] formal warning, persisted in intercourse with other men's slaves, may be claimed as slaves? Shall earthly disciplines be held more strict than heavenly prescripts; so that *Gentile* women, if united to strangers, lose their liberty; *ours* conjoin to themselves the devil's slaves, and continue in their [former] position? Forsooth, they will deny that any formal warning has been given them by the Lord through His own apostle![2]

What am I to fasten on as the cause of this madness, except the weakness of faith, ever prone to the concupiscences of worldly[3] joys?—which, indeed, is chiefly found among the wealthier; for the more any is rich, and inflated

[1] Oehler refers us to Tac. *Ann.* xii. 53, and the notes on that passage. (Consult especially Orelli's edition.)

[2] The translator inclines to think that Tertullian, desiring to keep up the parallelism of the last-mentioned case, in which (see note 1) the *slave's* master had to give the "warning," means by "domino" here, *not* "the Lord," who on his hypothesis is the *woman's* Master, not the *slave's*, but the "lord" of the "unbeliever," *i.e.* the devil: so that the meaning would be (with a bitter irony, especially if we compare the end of the last chapter, where "the Evil One" is said to "procure" these marriages, so far is he from "condemning" them): "Forsooth, they" (*i.e.* the Christian women) "will deny that a formal warning has been given them by the lord" (of the unbelievers, *i.e.* the Evil One) "through an apostle of his!" If the other interpretation be correct, the reference will be to c. ii. above.

[3] Sæcularium.

with the name of "matron," the more capacious house does she require for her burdens, as it were a field wherein ambition may run its course. To such the churches look paltry. A rich man is a difficult thing [to find] in the house of God;[1] and if such an one is [found there], difficult [is it to find such] unmarried. What, then, are they to do? Whence but from the devil are they to seek a husband apt for maintaining their sedan, and their mules, and their hair-curlers of outlandish stature? A Christian, even although rich, would perhaps not afford [all] these. Set before yourself, I beg of you, the examples of Gentiles. Most Gentile women, noble in extraction and wealthy in property, unite themselves indiscriminately with the ignoble and the mean, sought out for themselves for luxurious, or mutilated for licentious, purposes. Some take up with their own freedmen and slaves, despising public opinion, provided they may but have [husbands] from whom to fear no impediment to their own liberty. To a Christian believer it is irksome to wed a believer inferior to herself in estate, destined as she will be to have her wealth augmented in the person of a poor husband! For if it is "the poor," not the rich, "whose are the kingdoms of the heavens,"[2] the rich will find more in the poor [than she brings him, or than she would in the rich]. She will be dowered with an ampler dowry from the goods of him who is rich in God. Let her be on an equality with him on earth, who in the heavens will perhaps not be so. Is there need for doubt, and inquiry, and repeated deliberation, whether he whom God has entrusted with His own property[3] is fit for dotal endowments?[4] Whence are we to find [words] enough fully to tell the happiness of that marriage which the Church cements, and the oblation confirms, and the benediction signs and seals; [which] angels carry back

---

[1] Matt. xix. 23, 24; Mark x. 23, 24; Luke xviii. 24, 25; 1 Cor. i. 26, 27.

[2] Matt. v. 3; but Tertullian has omitted "spiritu," which he inserts in *de Pa.* c. xi., where he refers to the same passage. In Luke vi. 20 there is no τῷ πνεύματι.

[3] Censum.   [4] Invecta. Comp. *de Pa.* c. xiii. *ad init.*

the news of [to heaven], [which] the Father holds for ratified? For even on earth children[1] do not rightly and lawfully wed without their fathers' consent. What kind of yoke is that of two believers, [partakers] of one hope, one desire,[2] one discipline, one and the same service? Both [are] brethren, both fellow-servants, no difference of spirit or of flesh; nay, [they are] truly "two in one flesh."[3] Where the flesh is one, one is the spirit too. Together they pray, together prostrate themselves, together perform their fasts; mutually teaching, mutually exhorting,[4] mutually sustaining. Equally [are they] both [found] in the Church of God; equally at the banquet of God; equally in straits, in persecutions, in refreshments. Neither hides [ought] from the other; neither shuns the other; neither is troublesome to the other. The sick is visited, the indigent relieved, with freedom. Alms [are given] without [danger of ensuing] torment; sacrifices [attended] without scruple; daily diligence [discharged] without impediment: [there is] no stealthy signing, no trembling greeting, no mute benediction. Between the two echo psalms and hymns;[5] and they mutually challenge each other which shall better chant to their Lord. Such things when Christ sees and hears, He joys. To these He sends his own peace.[6] Where two [are], there withal [is] He Himself.[7] Where He [is], there the Evil One is not.

These are the things which that utterance of the apostle has, beneath its brevity, left to be understood by us. These things, if need shall be, suggest to your own mind. By these turn yourself away from the examples of some. To marry *otherwise* is, to believers, not "lawful;" is not "expedient."[8]

[1] Filii.
[2] Comp. *de Or.* c. v. *ad fin.*; *de Pa.* c. ix. *ad fin.*; *ad Ux.* i. c. v. *ad init.*
[3] Gen. ii. 24; Matt. xix. 5; Mark x. 8; Eph. v. 31.   [4] Col. iii. 16.
[5] Eph. v. 19; Col. iii. 16.   [6] Comp. John xiv. 27.
[7] Matt. xviii. 20.   [8] Comp. 1 Cor. x. 23.

XII.

ON FEMALE DRESS.

BOOK I.

Chap. i.—*Introduction. Modesty in apparel becoming to women, in memory of the introduction of sin into the world through a woman.*

IF there dwelt upon earth a faith as great as is the reward of faith which is expected in the heavens, no one of you at all, best beloved sisters, from the time that she had first "known the Lord," [1] and learned [the truth] concerning her own (that is, woman's) condition, would have desired too gladsome (not to say too ostentatious) a style of dress; so as not rather to go about in humble garb, and rather to affect meanness of appearance, walking about as Eve mourning and repentant, in order that by every garb of penitence [2] she might the more fully expiate that which she derives from Eve,—the ignominy, I mean, of the first sin, and the odium [attaching to her as the cause] of human perdition. "In pains and in anxieties dost thou bear [children], woman; and toward thine husband [is] thy inclination, and he lords it over thee." [3] And do you not know that you are [each] an Eve? The sentence of God on this sex of yours lives in this age: [4] the guilt must of necessity live too. *You are the devil's gateway: you are*

---

[1] Comp. Heb. viii. 11; Jer. xxxi. 34 (in the LXX. it is xxxviii. 34).
[2] Satisfactionis.   [3] Comp. Gen iii. 16, in Eng. ver. and in LXX.
[4] Sæculo.

the unsealer[1] of that [forbidden] tree : *you* are the first deserter of the divine law : *you* are she who persuaded[2] him whom the devil was not valiant enough to attack. *You* destroyed so easily God's image, man. On account of *your* desert—that is, death—even the Son of God had to die. And do you think about adorning yourself over and above your tunics of skins?[3] Come, now; if from the beginning of the world[4] the Milesians sheared sheep, and the Serians[5] spun trees, and the Tyrians dyed, and the Phrygians embroidered with the needle, and the Babylonians with the loom, and pearls gleamed, and onyx-stones flashed; if gold itself also had already issued, with the cupidity [which accompanies it], from the ground; if the mirror, too, already had licence to lie so largely, Eve, expelled from paradise, [Eve] already dead, would also have coveted *these* things, I imagine! No more, then, ought she *now* to crave, or be acquainted with (if she desires to live again), what, when she *was* living, she had neither had nor known. Accordingly these things are all the baggage of woman in her condemned and dead state, instituted as if to swell the pomp of her funeral.

CHAP. II.—*The origin of female ornamentation, traced back to the angels who had fallen.*[6]

For they, withal, who instituted them are assigned, under condemnation, to the penalty of death,—those angels, to wit, who rushed from heaven on the daughters of men; so that this ignominy also attaches to woman. For when to an age[7] much more ignorant [than ours] they had disclosed certain well-concealed material substances, and several not well-revealed scientific arts—if it is true that they had laid bare the operations of metallurgy, and had divulged the natural

---

[1] Resignatrix. Comp. the phrase " a *fountain sealed* " in Cant. iv. 12.
[2] " Suasisti " is the reading of the MSS. ; " persuasisti," a conjectural emendation adopted by Rig.
[3] See Gen. iii. 21.   [4] Rerum.   [5] *i.e.* Chinese.
[6] Comp. with this chapter, *de Idol.* c. ix. ; *de Or.* c. xxii. ; *de Cult. Fem.* l. ii. c. x. ; *de Virg. Vel.* c. vii.
[7] Sæculo.

properties of herbs, and had promulgated the powers of enchantments, and had traced out every curious art,[1] even to the interpretation of the stars—they conferred properly and as it were peculiarly upon women that instrumental mean of womanly ostentation, the radiances of jewels wherewith necklaces are variegated, and the circlets of gold wherewith the arms are compressed, and the medicaments of orchil with which wools are coloured, and that black powder itself wherewith the eyelids and eyelashes are made prominent.[2] What is the quality of these things may be declared meantime, even at this point,[3] from the quality and condition of their teachers; in that sinners could never have either shown or supplied anything conducive to integrity, unlawful lovers anything conducive to chastity, renegade spirits anything conducive to the fear of God. If [these things] are to be called *teachings*, ill masters must of necessity have taught ill; if as *wages of lust*, there is nothing base of which the wages are honourable. But why was it of so much importance to show these things as well as[4] to confer them? Was it that women, without material causes of splendour, and without ingenious contrivances of grace, could not please *men*, who, while still unadorned, and uncouth, and—so to say—crude and rude, had moved [the mind of] *angels?* or was it that the lovers[5] would appear sordid and—through gratuitous use—contumelious, if they had conferred no [compensating] gift on the women who had been enticed into connubial connection with them? But these questions admit of no calculation. Women who possessed angels [as husbands] could desire nothing more; they had, forsooth, made a grand match! Assuredly they who, of course, did sometimes think whence they had fallen,[6] and, after the heated impulses of their lusts, looked up toward heaven, thus requited that very excellence of women, natural beauty, as [having proved] a

---

[1] Curiositatem. Comp. *de Idol.* c. ix., and Acts xix. 19.
[2] Quo oculorum exordia producuntur. Comp. ii. 5.
[3] "Jam," *i.e.* without going any farther. Comp. c. iv. et seqq.
[4] Sicut. But Pam. and Rig. read "sive."
[5] *i.e.* the *angelic* lovers.   [6] Comp. Rev. ii. 5.

cause of evil, in order that their good fortune might profit them nothing; but that, being turned from simplicity and sincerity, they, together with [the angels] themselves, might become offensive to God. Sure they were that all ostentation, and ambition, and love of pleasing by carnal means, was *dis*pleasing to God. And these are the angels whom we are destined to judge :[1] these are the angels whom in baptism we renounce:[2] these, of course, are the reasons why they have deserved to be judged by man. What business, then, have their *things* with their *judges?* What commerce have they who are to condemn with them who are to be condemned? The same, I take it, as Christ has with Belial.[3] With what consistency do we mount that [future] judgment-seat to pronounce sentence against those whose gifts we [now] seek after? For you too, [women as you are,] have the self-same angelic nature promised[4] as your reward, the self-same sex as men : the self-same advancement to the dignity of judging, does [the Lord] promise you. Unless, then, we begin even here to *pre*judge, by pre-condemning their *things*, which we are hereafter to condemn in *themselves, they* will rather judge and condemn *us.*

CHAP. III.—*Concerning the genuineness of " the Prophecy of Enoch."*

I am aware that the Scripture of Enoch,[5] which has assigned this order [of action] to angels, is not received by some, because it is not admitted into the Jewish canon either. I suppose they did not think that, having been published before the deluge, it could have safely survived that world-wide calamity, the abolisher of all things. If that is the reason [for rejecting it], let them recall to their memory that Noah, the survivor of the deluge, was the great-grandson of Enoch himself ;[6] and he, of course, had heard and remembered, from

---

[1] See 1 Cor. vi. 3.   [2] Comp. *de Idol.* c. vi.
[3] Comp. 2 Cor. vi. 14–16.
[4] See Matt. xxii. 30; Mark xii. 25; Luke xx. 35, 36; and comp. Gal. iii. 28.
[5] Comp. *de Idol.* c. iv.   [6] See Gen. v. 21, 25, 28, 29.

domestic renown[1] and hereditary tradition, concerning his own great-grandfather's "grace in the sight of God,"[2] and concerning all his preachings;[3] since Enoch had given no other charge to Methuselah than that he should hand on the knowledge of them to his posterity. Noah therefore, no doubt, might have succeeded in the trusteeship of [his] preaching, or, had the case been otherwise, he would not have been silent alike concerning the disposition [of things] made by God, his Preserver, and concerning the particular glory of his own house.

If [Noah] had not had this [conservative power] by so short a route, there would [still] be this [consideration] to warrant[4] our assertion of [the genuineness of] this Scripture: he could equally have *renewed* it, under the Spirit's inspiration,[5] after it *had* been destroyed by the violence of the deluge, as, after the destruction of Jerusalem by the Babylonian storming of it, every document[6] of the Jewish literature is generally agreed to have been restored through Ezra.

But since Enoch in the same Scripture has preached likewise concerning the Lord, nothing at all must be rejected *by* us which pertains *to* us; and we read that "every Scripture suitable for edification is divinely inspired."[7] By the *Jews* it may now seem to have been rejected for that [very] reason, just like all the other [portions] nearly which tell of Christ. Nor, of course, is this fact wonderful, that they did not receive some Scriptures which spake of Him whom even in person, speaking in their presence, they were not to receive. To these considerations is added the fact that Enoch possesses a testimony in the Apostle Jude.[8]

CHAP. IV.—*Waiving the question of the* AUTHORS, *Tertullian proposes to consider the* THINGS *on their own merits.*

Grant now that no mark of pre-condemnation has been branded on womanly pomp by the [fact of the] fate[9] of its

---

[1] "Nomine;" perhaps = "account."
[2] Comp. Gen. vi. 8.
[3] Prædicatis.
[4] Tueretur.
[5] In spiritu.
[6] Instrumentum.
[7] See 2 Tim. iii. 16.
[8] See Jude 14, 15.
[9] Exitu.

authors; let nothing be imputed to those angels besides their repudiation of heaven and [their] carnal marriage :[1] let us examine the qualities of the things themselves, in order that we may detect the purposes also for which they are eagerly desired.

Female habit carries with it a twofold idea — dress and ornament. By "dress" we mean what they call "womanly gracing;"[2] by "ornament," what it is suitable should be called "womanly *disgracing*."[3] The former is accounted [to consist] in gold, and silver, and gems, and garments; the latter in care of the hair, and of the skin, and of those parts of the body which attract the eye. Against the one we lay the charge of ambition, against the other of prostitution; so that even from this early stage[4] [of our discussion] you may look forward and see what, out of [all] these, is suitable, handmaid of God, to *your* discipline, inasmuch as you are assessed on different principles [from other women],—those, namely, of humility and chastity.

CHAP. V.—*Gold and silver not superior in origin or in utility to other metals.*

Gold and silver, the principal material causes of worldly[5] splendour, must necessarily be identical [in nature] with that out of which they have their being: [they must be] earth, that is; [which earth itself is] plainly more glorious [than they], inasmuch as it is only after it has been tearfully wrought by penal labour in the deadly laboratories of accursed mines, and there left its name of "earth" in the fire behind it, that, as a fugitive from the mine, it passes from torments to ornaments, from punishments to embellishments, from ignominies to honours. But iron, and brass, and other the vilest material substances, enjoy a parity of condition [with silver and gold], both as to earthly origin and metallurgic operation; in order that, in the estimation of nature, the substance of gold and of silver may be judged not a whit more noble

[1] Matrimonium carnis. [2] Mundum muliebrem. Comp. Liv. xxxiv. 7.
[3] Immundum muliebrem.
[4] Jam hinc; comp. *ad. Ux.* i. 1 *ad init.* and *ad fin.*, and 8 *ad fin.*
[5] Sæcularis.

[than theirs]. But if it is from the quality of *utility* that gold and silver derive their glory, why, iron and brass excel them; whose usefulness is so disposed [by the Creator], that they not only discharge functions of their own more numerous and more necessary to human affairs, but do also none the less serve the turn of gold and silver, by dint of their own powers,[1] in the service of juster causes. For not only are rings made of iron, but the memory of antiquity still preserves [the fame of] certain vessels for eating and drinking made out of brass. Let the insane plenteousness of gold and silver look to it, if it serves to make utensils even for foul purposes. At all events, neither is the field tilled by means of gold, nor the ship fastened together by the strength of silver. No mattock plunges a golden edge into the ground; no nail drives a silver point into planks. I leave unnoticed the fact that the needs of our whole life are dependent upon iron and brass; whereas those rich materials themselves, requiring both to be dug up out of mines, and needing a forging process in every use [to which they are put], are helpless without the laborious vigour of iron and brass. Already, therefore, we must judge whence it is that so high dignity accrues to gold and silver, since they get precedence over material substances which are not only cousin-german to them in point of origin, but more powerful in point of usefulness.

Chap. vi.—*Of precious stones and pearls.*

But, in the next place, what am I to interpret those jewels to be which vie with gold in haughtiness, except little pebbles and stones and paltry particles of the self-same earth; but yet not necessary either for laying down foundations, or rearing party-walls, or supporting pediments, or giving density to roofs? The only edifice which they know how to rear is this silly pride of women: because they require slow rubbing that they may shine, and artful underlaying that they may show to advantage, and careful piercing that they may hang; and [because they] render to gold a mutual assistance in mere-

[1] De suo. Comp. *de Bapt.* c. xvii. *sub fin.*

tricious allurement. But whatever it is that ambition fishes up from the British or the Indian sea, it is a kind of conch not more pleasing in *savour* than—I do not say the oyster and the sea-snail, but—even the giant muscle.[1] For let me add that I know conchs [which are] sweet fruits of the sea. But if that [foreign] conch suffers from some internal pustule, that ought to be regarded rather as its defect than as its glory; and although it be called "pearl," still something else must be understood than some hard, round excrescence of the fish. Some say, too, that gems are culled from the foreheads of *dragons*, just as in the brains of fishes there is a certain stony substance. This also was wanting to the Christian woman, that she may add a grace to herself from the serpent! Is it thus that she will set her heel on the devil's head,[2] while she heaps ornaments [taken] from his head on her own neck, or on her very head?

CHAP. VII.—RARITY *the only cause which makes such things valuable.*

It is only from their rarity and outlandishness that all these things possess their grace; in short, within their own native limits they are not held of so high worth. Abundance is always contumelious toward itself. There are some barbarians with whom, because gold is indigenous and plentiful, it is customary to keep [the criminals] in their convict establishments chained with gold, and to lade the wicked with riches—the more guilty, the more wealthy. At last there has really been found a way to prevent even gold from being loved! We have also seen at Rome the nobility of gems blushing in the presence of our matrons at the contemptuous usage of the Parthians and Medes, and the rest of their own fellow-countrymen, only that [*their* gems] are not generally worn with a view to ostentation. Emeralds[3] lurk in their belts; and the sword [that hangs] below their bosom alone is witness to the cylindrical stones that decorate

---

[1] Peloris. Comp. Hor. S. ii. 4, 32, and Macleane's note there.
[2] See Gen. iii. 15.
[3] Smaragdi. Comp. Rev. iv. 3.

its hilt; and the massive single pearls on their boots are fain to get lifted out of the mud! In short, they carry nothing so richly gemmed as that which ought *not* to be gemmed if it is [either] not conspicuous, or else is conspicuous only that it may be shown to be also neglected.

CHAP. VIII.—*The same rule holds with regard to colours. God's creatures generally not to be used, except for the purposes to which He has appointed them.*

Similarly, too, do even the servants[1] of those barbarians cause the glory to fade from the colours of our garments [by wearing the like]; nay, even their party-walls use slightingly, to supply the place of painting, the Tyrian and the violet-coloured and the grand royal hangings, which you laboriously undo and metamorphose. Purple with them is more paltry than red ochre; [and justly,] for what legitimate honour can garments derive from adulteration with illegitimate colours? That which He Himself has not produced is not pleasing to God, unless He was *unable* to order sheep to be born with purple and sky-blue fleeces! If He was *able*, then plainly He was *unwilling:* what God willed not, of course ought not to be fashioned. Those things, then, are not the best by *nature* which are not from God, the *Author* of nature. Thus they are understood to be from *the devil*, from the *corrupter* of nature: for there is no other whose they *can* be, if they are not God's; because what are not God's must necessarily be His rival's.[2] But, beside the devil and his angels, other rival of God there is none. Again, if the *material substances* are of God, it does not immediately follow that such ways of *enjoying* them among men [are so too]. It is matter for inquiry not only whence come conchs,[3] but what sphere of embellishment is assigned them, and where it is that they exhibit their beauty. For all those profane pleasures of worldly[4] shows—as we have already published a volume of their own about them[5]—[ay, and] even idolatry itself, derive

[1] Or, "slaves."
[2] Comp. c. vi. above.
[3] Comp. *de Pæn.* c. v. *med.*
[4] Sæcularium.
[5] *i.e.* the treatise *de Spectaculis.*

their material causes from the creatures[1] of God. Yet a Christian ought not to attach himself[2] to the frenzies of the racecourse, or the atrocities of the arena, or the turpitudes of the stage, simply because God has given to man the horse, and the panther, and the power of speech: just as a Christian cannot commit idolatry with impunity either, because the incense, and the wine, and the fire which feeds[3] [thereon], and the animals which are made the victims, are God's workmanship;[4] since even the material thing which is adored is God's [creature]. Thus then, too, with regard to their active use, does the *origin* of the material substances, which descends from God, *excuse* [that use] as foreign to God, as guilty forsooth of worldly[5] glory!

CHAP. IX.—*God's distribution must regulate our desires, otherwise we become the prey of ambition and its attendant evils.*

For, as some particular things distributed by God over certain individual lands, and some one particular tract of sea, are mutually foreign one to the other, they are reciprocally either neglected or desired: [desired] among foreigners, as being rarities; neglected [rightly], if anywhere, among their own compatriots, because in *them* there is no such fervid longing for a glory which, among its own home-folk, is frigid. But, however, the rareness and outlandishness which arise out of that distribution of possessions which God has ordered as He willed, ever finding favour in the eyes of strangers, excites, from the simple fact of *not* having what God has made native to other places, the concupiscence of *having* it. Hence is educed another vice—that of *immoderate* having; because although, perhaps, *having* may be permissible, still a limit[6] is bound [to be observed]. This [second vice] will be ambition; and hence, too, its name is to be interpreted, in that from concupiscence *ambient* in the mind it is born, with

---

[1] Rebus.
[2] "Affici"—a rare use rather of "afficere," but found in Cic.
[3] Or perhaps "is fed" thereby; for the word is "vescitur."
[4] "Conditio"—a rare use again. [5] Sæcularis.
[6] Or, "moderation."

a view to the desire of glory,—a grand desire, forsooth, which (as we have said) is recommended neither by nature nor by truth, but by a vicious passion of the mind,—[namely,] concupiscence. And there are other vices connected with ambition and glory. Thus they have withal enhanced the *cost* of things, in order that [thereby] they might add fuel to themselves also; for concupiscence becomes proportionably greater as it has set a higher value upon the thing which it has eagerly desired. From the smallest caskets is produced an ample patrimony. On a single thread is suspended a million of sesterces. One delicate neck carries about it forests and islands.[1] The slender lobes of the ears exhaust a fortune; and the left hand, with its every finger, sports with a several money-bag. Such is the strength of ambition—[equal] to bearing on one small body, and that a woman's, the product of so copious wealth.

BOOK II.

CHAP. I.—*Introduction. Modesty to be observed not only in its essence, but in its accessories.*

Handmaids of the living God, my fellow-servants and sisters, the right which I enjoy with you—I, the most meanest[2] in that right of fellow-servantship and brotherhood—emboldens me to address to you a discourse, not, of course, of affection, but paving the way for affection in the cause of your salvation. That salvation—and not [the salvation] of women only, but likewise of men—consists in the exhibition principally of modesty. For since, by the introduction into and appropriation[3] [in] us of the Holy Spirit, we are all "the temple of God,"[4] Modesty is the sacristan and priestess of that temple, who is to suffer nothing unclean or profane

---

[1] "Saltus et insulæ," *i.e.* as much as would purchase them.
[2] Postremissimus. [3] Consecrato.
[4] See 1 Cor. iii. 16, 17, vi. 19, 20.

to be introduced [into it], for fear that the God who inhabits it should be offended, and quite forsake the polluted abode. But on the present occasion we [are to speak] not about modesty, for the enjoining and exacting of which the divine precepts which press [upon us] on every side are sufficient; but about the matters which pertain to it, that is, the manner in which it behoves you to walk. For most women (which very thing I trust God may permit me, with a view, of course, to my own personal censure, to censure in all), either from simple ignorance or else from dissimulation, have the hardihood so to walk as if modesty consisted only[1] in the [bare] integrity of the flesh, and in turning away from [actual] fornication; and there were no need for anything extrinsic to boot—in the matter (I mean) of the arrangement of dress and ornament,[2] the studied graces of form and brilliance:—wearing in their gait the self-same appearance as the women of the nations, from whom the sense of *true* modesty is absent, because in those who know not God, the Guardian and Master of truth, there is *nothing* true.[3] For if any modesty can be believed [to exist] in Gentiles, it is plain that it must be imperfect and undisciplined to such a degree that, although it be actively tenacious of itself in the *mind* up to a certain point, it yet allows itself to relax into licentious extravagances of attire; just in accordance with Gentile perversity, in craving after that of which it carefully shuns the effect.[4] How many a one, in short, is there who does not earnestly desire even to look pleasing to strangers? who does not on that very account take care to have herself painted out, and denies that she has [ever] been an object of [carnal] appetite? And yet, granting that even this is a practice familiar to Gentile modesty—[namely,] not actually to *commit* the sin, but still to be *willing* to do so; or even not to be *willing*, yet still not *quite* to refuse—what wonder? for all things which are not God's are perverse. Let those women therefore look to it, who, by not holding fast the

---

[1] Comp. *de Idol.* c. ii.
[2] Cultus et ornatus. For the distinction between them, see b. i. c. iv.
[3] Comp. *de Pæn.* c. i. [4] Or, "execution."

whole good, easily mingle with evil even what they do hold fast. Necessary it is that *you* turn aside from them, as in all other things, so also in your gait; since you ought to be "perfect, as [is] your Father who is in the heavens."[1]

CHAP. II.—*Perfect modesty will abstain from whatever* TENDS *to sin, as well as from sin itself. Difference between trust and presumption. If secure ourselves, we must not put temptation in the way of others. We must love our neighbour as ourself.*

You must know that in the eye of perfect, that is, Christian, modesty, [carnal] desire of one's self [on the part of others] is not only not to be desired, but even execrated, by you: first, because the study of making personal grace (which we know to be naturally the inviter of lust) a mean of pleasing does not spring from a sound conscience: why therefore excite toward yourself that evil [passion]? why invite [that] to which you profess yourself a stranger? secondly, because we ought not to open a way to temptations, which, by their instancy, sometimes achieve [a wickedness] which God expels from them who are His; [or,] at all events, put the spirit into a thorough tumult by [presenting] a stumbling-block [to it]. We ought indeed to walk so holily, and with so entire substantiality[2] of faith, as to be confident and secure in regard of our own conscience, *desiring* that that [gift] may abide in us to the end, yet not *presuming* [that it will]. For he who presumes feels less apprehension; he who feels less apprehension takes less precaution; he who takes less precaution runs more risk. Fear[3] is the foundation of salvation; presumption is an impediment to fear. More useful, then, is it to apprehend that we may possibly fail, than to presume that we cannot; for apprehending will lead us to fear, fearing to caution, and caution to salvation. On the other hand, if we presume, there will be

---

[1] See Matt. v. 48.
[2] Substantia. Comp. Heb. xi. 1, ἔστι δὲ πίστις ἐλπιζομένων ὑπόστασις.
[3] Timor.

neither fear nor caution to save us. He who acts securely, and not at the same time warily, possesses no safe and firm security; whereas he who is wary will be truly able to be secure. And for His own servants, may the Lord by His mercy take care that to *them* it may be lawful even to *presume* on His goodness! But why are we a [source of] danger to our neighbour? why do we import concupiscence into our neighbour? which concupiscence, if God, in "amplifying the law,"[1] do not[2] dissociate in [the way of] penalty from the actual commission of fornication,[3] I know not whether He allows impunity to him who[4] has been the cause of perdition to some other. For that other, as soon as he has felt concupiscence after your beauty, and has mentally already committed [the deed] which his concupiscence pointed to,[5] perishes; and you have been made[6] the sword which destroys him: so that, albeit you be free from the [actual] crime, you are not free from the odium [attaching to it]; as, when a robbery has been committed on some man's estate, the [actual] crime indeed will not be laid to the owner's charge, while yet the domain is branded with ignominy, [and] the owner himself aspersed with the infamy. Are we to paint ourselves out that our neighbours may perish? Where, then, is [the command], "Thou shalt love thy neighbour as thyself?"[7] "Care not merely about your own [things], but [about your] neighbour's?"[8] No enunciation of the Holy Spirit ought to be [confined] to the subject immediately in hand merely, and not applied and carried out with a view to *every* occasion to which its application is useful.[9] Since, therefore, both our own interest and that of others is implicated in the studious pursuit of most perilous [outward]

---

[1] Matt. v. 17. Comp. *de Or.* c. xxii. mid.; *de Pa.* c. vi. mid.; *de Pæn.* c. iii. *sub fin.*

[2] The second "non," or else the first, must apparently be omitted.

[3] Matt. v. 28. See *de Idol.* c. ii.; *de Pa.* c. vi.; *de Pæn.* c. iii.

[4] "Qui," Oehler; "quæ," Rig.

[5] Comp. *de Pæn.* c. iii. (latter half). [6] Tu *facta es.*

[7] Lev. xix. 18; Matt. xix. 19, xxii. 39; Mark xii. 31; Luke x. 27; Rom. xiii. 9; Gal. v. 14; Jas. ii. 8.

[8] Comp. 1 Cor. x. 24, xiii. 5; Phil. ii. 4.   [9] Comp. 2 Pet. i. 20.

comeliness, it is time for you to know[1] that not merely must the pageantry of fictitious and elaborate beauty be rejected by you; but that of even natural grace must be obliterated by concealment and negligence, as equally dangerous to the glances of [the beholder's] eyes. For, albeit comeliness is not to be *censured*,[2] as being a bodily happiness, as being an additional outlay of the divine plastic art, as being a kind of goodly garment[3] of the soul; yet it is to be *feared*, just on account of the injuriousness and violence of suitors:[4] which [injuriousness and violence] even the father of the faith,[5] Abraham,[6] greatly feared in regard of his own wife's grace; and Isaac,[7] by falsely representing Rebecca as his sister, purchased safety by insult![8]

CHAP. III.—*Grant that beauty be not to be feared: still it is to be shunned as unnecessary and vainglorious.*

Let it now be granted that excellence of form be not to be feared, as neither troublesome to its possessors, nor destructive to its desirers, nor perilous to its compartners;[9] let it be thought [to be] not exposed to temptations, not surrounded by stumbling-blocks: it is enough that to angels of God[10] it is not necessary. For, where modesty is, there beauty is idle; because properly the use and fruit of beauty is voluptuousness, unless any one thinks that there is some other harvest for bodily grace to reap.[11] Are women who think that, in furnishing to their *neighbour* that which is demanded of beauty, they are furnishing it to *themselves* also, to augment that [beauty] when [naturally] given them, and to strive after it when not [thus] given? Some one will say, "Why, then, if voluptuousness be shut out and chastity let

[1] Jam ... sciatis.
[2] Accusandus.
[3] Comp. Gen. xxvii. 15.
[4] Sectatorum.
[5] Comp. Rom. iv. 11, 16.
[6] Gen. xii. 10-20, and xx.
[7] Gen. xxvi. 6-11.
[8] "Salutem contumelia redemit;" the "insult" being the denial of her as his wife.
[9] Conjunctis.
[10] Angelis Dei. Comp. the opening sentence of the book.
[11] Comp. *ad Ux.* b. i. c. iv.

in, may [we] not enjoy the praise of beauty alone, and glory in a bodily good?" Let whoever finds pleasure in "glorying in the flesh"[1] see to that. To us, in the first place, there is no studious pursuit of "glory," because "glory" is the essence of *exaltation*. Now *exaltation* is incongruous for professors of *humility* according to God's precepts. Secondly, if *all* "glory" is "vain" and insensate,[2] how much more [glory] *in the flesh*, especially to *us?* For even if "glorying" is [allowable], we ought to wish our sphere of pleasing to lie in the graces[3] of the Spirit, not in the flesh; because we are "suitors"[4] of things spiritual. In those things wherein our sphere of labour lies, let our joy lie. From the sources whence we hope for salvation, let us cull our "glory." Plainly, a Christian *will* "glory" even in the *flesh;* but [it will be] when it has endured laceration for Christ's sake,[5] in order that the spirit may be crowned in it, not in order that it may draw the eyes and sighs of youths after it. Thus [a thing] which, from whatever point you look at it, is in *your* case superfluous, you may justly disdain if you have it not, and neglect if you have. Let a holy woman, if naturally beautiful, give none so great occasion [for carnal appetite]. Certainly, if even she be so, she ought not to set off, but even to obscure, [her beauty.][6]

CHAP. IV.—*Concerning the plea of "pleasing the husband."*

As if I were speaking to Gentiles, addressing you with a Gentile precept, and [one which is] common to all, [I would say,] "You are bound to please your husbands only."[7] But you will please *them* in proportion as you take no care to please *others*. Be ye without carefulness,[8] blessed [sisters]: no wife is "ugly" to her own husband. She "pleased" him enough when she was selected [by him as his wife]; whether commended by form or by character. Let

---

[1] See Gal. vi. 13 and 1 Cor. iii. 21, v. 6.
[2] Stuporata.
[3] Bonis.
[4] Sectatores.
[5] Comp. 2 Cor. xi. 18, xii. 10; Phil. iii. 3, 4.
[6] Non adjuvare, sed etiam impedire, debet.
[7] Comp. 1 Cor. vii. 34.
[8] Comp. 1 Cor. vii. 32.

none of you think that, if she abstain from the care of her person,[1] she will incur the hatred and aversion of husbands. Every husband is the exactor of *chastity;* but *beauty* a believing [husband] does not require, because we are not captivated by the same graces[2] which the Gentiles think [to be] graces:[3] an *un*believing, on the other hand, even regards with suspicion, just from that infamous opinion of us which the Gentiles have. . For whom, then, is it that you cherish your beauty? If for a believer, he does not exact it: if for an *un*believer, he does not believe in it unless it be artless.[4] Why are you eager to please either one who is suspicious, or else one who desires no [such pleasing]?

CHAP. V.—*Some refinements in dress and personal appearance lawful, some unlawful. Pigments come under the latter head.*

These suggestions are not made to you, of course, to be developed into an entire crudity and wildness of appearance; nor are we seeking to persuade you of the good of squalor and slovenliness; but of the limit and norm and just measure of cultivation of the person. There must be no overstepping of that line to which simple and sufficient refinements limit their desires—that line which is pleasing to God. For they who rub[5] their skin with medicaments, stain their cheeks with rouge, make their eyes prominent with antimony,[6] sin against HIM. To them, I suppose, the plastic skill[7] of God is displeasing! In their own persons, I suppose, they convict, they censure, the Artificer of all things! For censure they do when they amend, when they add to, [His work;] taking these their additions, of course, from the adversary artificer. That adversary artificer is the devil.[8] For who would show the way to change the *body*, but he who by wickedness transfigured man's *spirit?* He it is, undoubtedly, who adapted ingenious devices of this kind; that in your own persons it

[1] Compositione sui.   [2] Bonis.   [3] Bona.
[4] Simplicem.   [5] Urgent. Comp. *de Pæn.* c. xi.
[6] "Fuligine," lit. "soot." Comp. b. i. c. ii.
[7] See c. ii. *ad fin.*   [8] Comp. b. i. c. viii.

ON FEMALE DRESS.

may be apparent that you do, in a certain sense, do violence to God. Whatever is *born* is the work of God. Whatever, then, is *plastered on*[1] [that], is the devil's work. To superinduce on a divine work Satan's ingenuities, how criminal is it! Our servants borrow nothing from our personal enemies: soldiers eagerly desire nothing from the foes of their own general; for, to demand for [your own] use anything from the adversary of him in whose hand[2] you are, is a transgression. Shall a Christian be assisted in anything by that evil one? [If he do,] I know not whether this name [of "Christian"] will continue [to belong] to him; for he will be *his* in whose lore he eagerly desires to be instructed. But how alien from *your* schoolings[3] and professions are [these things], how unworthy the Christian name, to wear a fictitious face, [you,] on whom simplicity in every form is enjoined!—to lie in your appearance, [you,] to whom [lying] with the tongue is not lawful!—to seek after what is another's, [you,] to whom is delivered [the precept of] abstinence from what is another's!—to practise adultery in your mien,[4] [you,] who make modesty your study! Think,[5] blessed [sisters], how will you keep God's precepts if you shall not keep in your own persons His lineaments?

Chap. vi.—*Of dyeing the hair.*

I see some [women] turn [the colour of] their hair with saffron. They are ashamed even of their own nation, [ashamed] that their procreation did not assign them to Germany and to Gaul: thus, as it is, they transfer their *hair*[6] [thither]! Ill, ay, *most* ill, do they augur for themselves with their flame-coloured head,[7] and think that graceful which [in fact] they are polluting! Nay, moreover, the force of the cosmetics burns ruin into the hair; and the con-

---

[1] Infingitur.   [2] *i.e.* subject to whom.
[3] Disciplinis.   [4] Species.   [5] Credite.
[6] Jam capillos: so Oehler and Rig. But the others read *patriam capillo:* "they change their country by the instrumentality of their hair."
[7] Comp. *ad Ux.* b. i. c. vi.

stant application of even any *un*drugged moisture, lays up a store of harm for the head; while the sun's warmth, too, so desirable for imparting to the hair at once growth and dryness, is hurtful. What "grace" is compatible with "injury?" What "beauty" with "impurities?" Shall a Christian woman heap saffron on her head, as upon an altar?[1] For, whatever is wont to be burned to the honour of the unclean spirit, that—unless it is applied for honest, and necessary, and salutary uses, [to serve the end] for which God's creature was provided—may seem to be a sacrifice. But, however, God saith, "Which of you can make a white hair black, or out of a black a white?"[2] And so they refute the Lord! "Behold!" say they, "instead of white or black, we make it *yellow*,—more winning in grace."[3] And yet such as repent of having lived to old age do *attempt* to change it even from white to black! O temerity! The age which is the object of our wishes and prayers blushes [for itself]! a theft is effected! youth, wherein we have sinned,[4] is sighed after! the opportunity of sobriety is spoiled! Far from Wisdom's daughters be folly so great! The more old age tries to conceal itself, the more will it be detected. Here is a veritable eternity, in the [perennial] youth of your head! Here we have an "incorruptibility" to "put on,"[5] with a view to the new house of the Lord[6] which the divine monarchy promises! Well do you speed toward the Lord, well do you hasten to be quit of this most iniquitous world,[7] to whom to approach [your own] end is unsightly!

Chap. vii.—*Of elaborate dressing of the hair in other ways, and its bearing upon salvation.*

What service, again, does all the labour spent in *arranging* the hair render to [the cause of] salvation? Why is no rest allowed to your hair, which must now be bound, now loosed, now cultivated, now thinned out? Some are anxious to force their hair into curls, some to let it hang loose and

---

[1] Aram.   [2] See Matt. v. 36.   [3] Gratia faciliorem.
[4] Comp. Ps. xxv. 7 (in LXX. xxiv. 7).   [5] Comp. 1 Cor. xv. 53.
[6] Comp. 2 Cor. v. 1.   [7] Sæculo.

flying; not with good simplicity: beside which, you affix I know not what enormities of subtle and textile perukes; now, after the manner of a helmet of undressed hide, as it were a sheath for the head and a covering for the crown; now, a mass [drawn] backward toward the neck. The wonder is, that there is no [open] contending against the Lord's prescripts! It has been pronounced that no one can add to his own stature.[1] *You*, however, *do* add to your *weight* some kind of rolls, or shield-bosses, to be piled upon your necks! If you feel no shame at the enormity [of the gear], feel some at the pollution; for fear you may be fitting on a holy and Christian head the slough [2] of some one else's [3] head, unclean perchance, guilty perchance and destined to hell.[4] Nay, rather banish quite away from your "free"[5] head all this slavery of ornamentation. In vain do you labour to seem adorned, in vain do you call in the aid of all the most skilful manufacturers of false hair. God bids you "be veiled."[6] I believe [He does so] for fear the heads of some should be seen! And oh that in "that day"[7] of Christian exultation, I, most miserable [as I am], may elevate my head, even though below [the level of] your heels! I shall [then] see whether you will rise with [your] ceruse and rouge and saffron, and in all that parade of head-gear: [8] whether it will be women thus tricked out whom the angels carry up to meet Christ in the air![9] If these [decorations] are *now* good, and of God, they will *then* also present themselves to the rising bodies, and will recognise their several places. But nothing can rise except flesh and spirit sole and pure.[10] Whatever, therefore, does not rise in [the form of] [11] spirit and flesh is condemned, be-

---

[1] Mensuram. See Matt. vi. 27.   [2] Exuvias.
[3] "Alieni:" perhaps here = "alien," *i.e.* "heathen," as in other places.
[4] Gehennæ.   [5] Comp. Gal. iv. 31, v. 13.
[6] See 1 Cor. xi. 2–16; and comp. *de Or.* c. xxii., and the treatise *de Virg. Vel.*
[7] Comp. *ad Ux.* b. ii. c. iii.
[8] Ambitu [*habitu* is a conjectural emendation noticed by Oehler] capitis.
[9] See 1 Thess. iv. 13–17.   [10] Comp. 1 Cor. xv. 50 with 1 Thess. v. 23.
[11] Or, "within the limits of the flesh and the spirit."

cause it is not of God. From things which are condemned abstain, even at the present day. At the present day let God see you such as He will see you *then*.

CHAP. VIII.—MEN *not excluded from these remarks on personal adornment.*

Of course, now, I, a man, as being envious[1] of women, am banishing them quite from their own [domains]. Are there, in our case too, some things which, in respect of the sobriety[2] we are to maintain on account of the fear[3] due to God, are disallowed?[4] [There are,] if it is true, [as it is,] that in men, for the sake of women (just as in women for the sake of men), there is implanted, by a defect of nature, the will to please; and [if] this sex of ours acknowledges to itself deceptive trickeries of form peculiarly its own,—[such as] to cut the beard too sharply; to pluck it out here and there; to shave round about [the mouth]; to arrange the hair, and disguise its hoariness by dyes; to remove all the incipient down all over the body; to fix [each particular hair] in its place with [some] womanly pigment; to smooth all the rest of the body by the aid of some rough powder or other: then, further, to take every opportunity for consulting the mirror; to gaze anxiously into it:—while yet, when [once] the knowledge of God has put an end to all wish to please by means of voluptuous attraction, all these things are rejected as frivolous, as hostile to modesty. For where God is, there modesty is; there is sobriety,[5] her assistant and ally. How, then, shall we practise modesty without her instrumental mean,[6] that is, without sobriety?[7] How, moreover, shall we bring sobriety[8] to bear on the discharge of [the functions of] modesty, unless seriousness in appearance and in countenance, and in the general aspect[9] of the entire man, mark our carriage?

[1] Æmulus. [2] Gravitatis. [3] Metus.
[4] Detrahuntur. [5] Gravitas. [6] Comp. *de Pa.* c. xv. *ad fin.*
[7] Gravitate. [8] Gravitatem. [9] Contemplatione.

CHAP. IX.—*Excess in dress, as well as in personal culture, to be shunned. Arguments drawn from* 1 *Cor.* vii.

Wherefore, with regard to clothing also, and all the remaining lumber of your self-elaboration,[1] the like pruning off and retrenchment of too redundant splendour must be the object of your care. For what boots it to exhibit in your *face* temperance and unaffectedness, and a simplicity altogether worthy of the divine discipline, but to invest all the *other* parts of the body with the luxurious absurdities of pomps and delicacies? How intimate is the connection which these pomps have with the business of voluptuousness, and how they interfere with modesty, is easily discernible from the fact that it is by the allied aid of dress that they prostitute the grace of personal comeliness: so plain is it that if [the pomps] be wanting, they render [that grace] bootless and thankless, as if it were disarmed and wrecked. On the other hand, if natural beauty fails, the supporting aid of outward embellishment supplies a grace, as it were, from its own inherent power.[2] Those times of life, in fact, which are at last blest with quiet and withdrawn into the harbour of modesty, the splendour and dignity of dress lure away [from that rest and that harbour], and *dis*quiet seriousness by seductions of appetite, which compensate for the chill of age by the provocative charms of apparel. First, then, blessed [sisters], [take heed] that you admit not to your use meretricious and prostitutionary garbs and garments: and, in the next place, if there are any of you whom the exigences of riches, or birth, or past dignities, compel to appear in public so gorgeously arrayed as not to appear to have attained wisdom, take heed to temper an evil of this kind; lest, under the pretext of necessity, you give the rein without stint to the indulgence of licence. For how will you be able to fulfil [the requirements of] humility, which our [school]

[1] Impedimenta compositionis.
[2] De suo. Comp. *de Bapt.* c. xvii. (*sub fin.*), *de Cult. Fem.* b. i. c. v. (*med.*).

profess,[1] if you do not keep within bounds[2] the enjoyment of your riches and elegances, which tend so much to "glory?" Now it has ever been the wont of glory to *exalt*, not to *humble*. "Why, shall we not use what is our own?" Who prohibits your using it? Yet [it must be] in accordance with the apostle, who warns us "to use this world[3] as if we abuse it not; for the fashion[4] of this world[5] is passing away." And "they who buy are so to act as if they possessed not."[6] Why so? Because he had laid down the premiss, saying, "The time is wound up."[7] If, then, he shows plainly that even wives themselves are so to be had as if they be *not* had,[8] on account of the straits of the times, what would be his sentiments about these vain appliances of theirs? Why, are there not many, withal, who so *do*, and seal themselves up to eunuchhood for the sake of the kingdom of God,[9] spontaneously relinquishing a pleasure so honourable,[10] and (as we know) permitted? Are there not some who prohibit to themselves [the use of] the very "creature of God,"[11] abstaining from wine and animal food, the enjoyments of which border upon no peril or solicitude; but they sacrifice to God the humility of their soul even in the chastened use of food? Sufficiently, therefore, have you, too, used your riches and your delicacies, sufficiently have you cut down the fruits of your dowries, before [receiving] the knowledge of saving disciplines. We are they "upon whom the ends of the ages have met, having ended their course."[12] We have been predestined by God, before the world[13] was, [to arise] in the extreme end of the times.[14] And so we are trained by God for the purpose of chastising, and (so to say) emasculating, the world.[15] We are the circumcision[16]—spiritual and carnal—of all things; for

---

[1] See c. iii.   [2] Repastinantes.
[3] Mundo ; κόσμῳ. See 1 Cor. vii. 31.   [4] Habitus ; σχῆμα, *ib.*
[5] Κόσμου, *ib.*   [6] 1 Cor. vii. 30.   [7] 1 Cor. vii. 29.
[8] 1 Cor. vii. 29.   [9] Matt. xix. 12.   [10] Fortem.
[11] Comp. 1 Tim. iv. 4, 5.
[12] 1 Cor. x. 11, εἰς οὓς τὰ τέλη τῶν αἰώνων κατήντησεν.
[13] Mundum.
[14] In extimatione temporali. See Eph. i. 4 and 1 Pet. i. 20.
[15] Sæculo.   [16] Comp. Phil. iii. 3.

both in the spirit and in the flesh we circumcise worldly[1] [principles].

CHAP. X.—*Tertullian refers again to the question of the* ORIGIN *of all these ornaments and embellishments.*[2]

For it was God, no doubt, who showed the way to dye wools with the juices of herbs and the humours of conchs! It had escaped Him, when He was bidding the universe to come into being,[3] to issue a command for [the production of] purple and scarlet sheep! It was God, too, who devised by careful thought the manufactures of those very garments which, light and thin [in themselves], were to be heavy in price alone; God who produced such grand implements of gold for confining or parting the hair; God who introduced [the fashion of] finely-cut wounds for the ears, and set so high a value upon the tormenting of His own work and the tortures of innocent infancy, learning to suffer with its earliest breath, in order that from those scars of the body—born for the steel!—should hang I know not what [precious] grains, which, as we may plainly see, the Parthians insert, in place of studs, upon their very shoes! And yet even the gold itself, the "glory" of which carries you away, serves a certain race (so Gentile literature tells us) for chains! So true is it that it is not intrinsic worth,[4] but rarity, which constitutes the goodness [of these things]: the excessive labour, moreover, of working them with arts introduced by the means of the sinful angels, who were the revealers withal of the material substances themselves, joined with their rarity, excited their costliness, and hence a lust on the part of women to possess [that] costliness. But, if the selfsame angels who disclosed both the material substances of this kind and their charms—of gold, I mean, and lustrous[5] stones—and taught men how to work them, and by and by instructed them, among their other [instructions], in [the virtues of] eyelid-powder and the dyeings of fleeces, have been condemned by God, as Enoch tells us, how shall we please God while we joy in the

---

[1] Sæcularia. [2] Comp. i. cc. ii. iii. v. vii. viii.
[3] Universa nasci. [4] Veritate. [5] Illustrium.

things of those [angels] who, on these accounts, have provoked the *anger* and the *vengeance* of God?

Now, granting that God did foresee these things; that God permitted them; that Esaias finds fault with no garment of purple,[1] represses no coif,[2] reprobates no crescent-shaped neck ornaments;[3] still let *us* not, as the Gentiles do, flatter ourselves with thinking that God is merely a Creator, not likewise a Downlooker on His own creatures. For how far more usefully and cautiously shall we act, if we hazard the presumption that all these things were indeed provided[4] at the beginning and placed in the world[5] by God, in order that there should now be means of putting to the proof the discipline of His servants, in order that the licence of *using* should be the means whereby the experimental trials of *continence* should be conducted? Do not wise heads of families purposely offer and permit some things to their servants[6] in order to try whether and how they will use the things thus permitted; whether [they will do so] with honesty, whether with moderation? But how far more praiseworthy [the servant] who abstains entirely; who has a wholesome fear[7] even of his lord's indulgence! Thus, therefore, the apostle too: "All things," says he, "are lawful, but not all are expedient."[8] How much more easily will he fear[9] what is *un*lawful who has a reverent dread[10] of what is *lawful*?

CHAP. XI.—*Christian women, further, have not the same* CAUSES *for appearing in public, and hence for dressing in fine array, as Gentiles. On the contrary, their appearance should always* DISTINGUISH *them from such.*

Moreover, what causes have you for appearing in public in excessive grandeur, removed as you are from the occasions which call for such exhibitions? For you neither make the circuit of the temples, nor demand [to be present at] public shows, nor have any acquaintance with the holy days of the

---

[1] De conchylio.
[2] κοσύμβους. Isa. iii. 18 (in LXX.).
[3] Lunulas = μηνίσκους, *ib.*
[4] Or, "foreseen."
[5] Sæculo.
[6] Or, "slaves."
[7] Timuerit.
[8] 1 Cor. x. 23.
[9] Timebit.
[10] Verebitur.

Gentiles. Now it is for the sake of all these public gatherings, and of much seeing and being seen, that all pomps [of dress] are exhibited before the public eye; either for the purpose of transacting the trade of voluptuousness, or else of inflating "glory." *You*, however, have no cause of appearing in public, except such as is serious. Either some brother who is sick is visited, or else the sacrifice is offered, or else the word of God is dispensed. Whichever of these you like to name is a business of sobriety[1] and sanctity, requiring no extraordinary attire, with [studious] arrangement and [wanton] negligence.[2] And if the requirements of Gentile friendships and of kindly offices call you, why not go forth clad in your own armour; [and] all the more in that [you have to go] to such as are strangers to the faith? so that between the handmaids of God and of the devil there may be a difference; so that you may be an example to them; that they may be edified in you; so that (as the apostle says) "God may be magnified in your body."[3] But magnified He is in the *body* through modesty: of course, too, through attire suitable to modesty. Well, but it is urged by some, "Let not the Name be blasphemed in us,[4] if we make any derogatory change from our old style and dress." Let us, then, not abolish our old vices! let us maintain the same character, if we must maintain the same appearance [as before]; and then truly the nations will not blaspheme! A grand blasphemy is that by which it is said, "Ever since she became a Christian, she walks in poorer garb!" Will you fear to appear poorer, from the time that you have been made more wealthy; and *fouler*,[5] from the time when you have been made more clean? Is it according to the decree[6] of Gentiles, or according to the decree of God, that it becomes Christians to walk?

CHAP. XII.—*Such outward adornments meretricious, and therefore unsuitable to modest women.*

Let us only wish that we may be no cause for just blas-

[1] Gravitatis.   [2] Et composito et soluto.   [3] See Phil. i. 20.
[4] Comp. *de Idol.* c. xiv.   [5] Sordidior.
[6] Or, "pleasure:" placitum.

phemy! But how much more provocative of blasphemy is it that you, who are called modesty's priestesses, should appear in public decked and painted out after the manner of the *im*modest? Else, [if you so do,] what inferiority would the poor unhappy victims of the public lusts have [beneath you]? whom, albeit some laws were [formerly] wont to restrain them from [the use of] matrimonial and matronly decorations, now, at all events, the daily increasing depravity of the age[1] has raised so nearly to an equality with all the most honourable women, that the difficulty is to distinguish them. And yet, even the Scriptures suggest [to us the reflection], that meretricious attractivenesses of form are invariably conjoined with and appropriate[2] to bodily prostitution. That powerful state[3] which presides over[4] the seven mountains and very many waters, has merited from the Lord the appellation of a prostitute.[5] But what kind of garb is the instrumental mean of her comparison with that appellation? She sits, to be sure, "in purple, and scarlet, and gold, and precious stone." How accursed are the things without [the aid of] which an accursed prostitute could not have been described! It was the fact that Thamar "had painted out and adorned herself" that led Judah to regard her as a harlot,[6] and thus, because she was hidden beneath her "veil,"—the quality of her garb belying her as if she had been a harlot,—he judged [her to be one], and addressed and bargained with [her as such]. Whence we gather an additional confirmation of the lesson, that provision must be made in every way against all immodest associations[7] and suspicions. For why is the integrity of a chaste mind defiled by its neighbour's suspicion? Why is a thing from which I am averse hoped for in me? Why does not my garb pre-announce my character, to prevent my spirit from being wounded by shamelessness through [the channel of] my ears? Grant that it be lawful to assume the appearance of a modest woman:[8] to assume that of an *im*modest is, at all events, *not* lawful.

[1] Sæculi. [2] Debita. [3] Or, "city." [4] Or, "sits on high above."
[5] Comp. Rev. xvii. [6] Comp. Gen. xxxviii. 12–30.
[7] Congressus. [8] Videri pudicam.

CHAP. XIII.—*It is not enough that God know us to be chaste: we must seem so before men.* Especially in these times of persecution we must inure our bodies to the hardships which they may not improbably be called to suffer.

Perhaps some [woman] will say: " To me it is not necessary to be approved by men; for I do not require the testimony of men:[1] God is the inspector of the heart."[2] [That] we all know; provided, however, we remember what the same [God] has said through the apostle: " Let your probity appear before men."[3] For what purpose, except that malice may have no access at all to you, or that you may be an example and testimony to the evil? Else, what is [that]: " Let your works shine?"[4] Why, moreover, does the Lord call us the light of the world; why has He compared us to a city built upon a mountain;[5] if we do not shine in [the midst of] darkness, and stand eminent amid them who are sunk down? If you hide your lamp beneath a bushel,[6] you must necessarily be left quite in darkness, and be run against by many. The things which make us luminaries of the world are these—our good works. What is *good*, moreover, provided it be true and full, loves not darkness: it joys in being seen,[7] and exults over the very pointings which are made at it. To Christian modesty it is not enough to *be* so, but to *seem* so too. For so great ought its plenitude to be, that it may flow out from the mind to the garb, and burst out from the conscience to the outward appearance; so that even from the outside it may gaze, as it were, upon its own furniture,[8]—[a furniture] such as to be suited to retain faith as its inmate perpetually. For such delicacies as tend by their softness and effeminacy to unman the manliness[9] of faith are to be discarded. Otherwise, I know not whether

---

[1] Comp. John v. 34; 1 Cor. iv. 3.
[2] Comp. 1 Sam. xvi. 7; Jer. xxii. 10; Luke xvi. 15.
[3] See Phil. iv. 5, 8; Rom. xii. 17; 2 Cor. viii. 21.
[4] See Matt. v. 16; and comp. *de Idol.* c. xv. *ad init.*
[5] Matt. v. 14.   [6] Matt. v. 15; Mark iv. 21; Luke viii. 16, xi. 33.
[7] See John iii. 21.   [8] Supellectilem.   [9] Effeminari virtus.

the wrist that has been wont to be surrounded with the palm-leaf-like bracelet will endure till it grow into the numb hardness of its own chain! I know not whether the leg that has rejoiced in the anklet will suffer itself to be squeezed into the gyve! I fear the neck, beset with pearl and emerald nooses, will give no room to the broadsword! Wherefore, blessed [sisters], let us meditate on hardships, and we shall not feel them; let us abandon luxuries, and we shall not regret them. Let us stand ready to endure every violence, having nothing which we may fear to leave behind. It is these things which are the bonds which retard our hope. Let us cast away earthly ornaments if we desire heavenly. Love not gold; in which [one substance] are branded all the sins of the people of Israel. You ought to *hate* what ruined your fathers; what was adored by them who were forsaking God.[1] Even *then* [we find] gold is food for the fire.[2] But Christians always, and now more than ever, pass their times not in gold but in iron: the stoles of martyrdom are [now] preparing: the angels who are to carry us are [now] being awaited! Do you go forth [to meet them] already arrayed in the cosmetics and ornaments of prophets and apostles; drawing your whiteness from simplicity, your ruddy hue from modesty; painting your eyes with bashfulness, and your mouth with silence; implanting in your ears the words of God; fitting on your necks the yoke of Christ. Submit your head to your husbands, and you will be enough adorned. Busy your hands with spinning; keep your feet at home; and you will "please" better than [by arraying yourselves] in gold. Clothe yourselves with the silk of uprightness, the fine linen of holiness, the purple of modesty. Thus painted, you will have God as your Lover!

[1] Comp. Ex. xxxii.   [2] Ex. xxxii. 20.

XIII.

DE CORONA.

1. VERY lately it happened thus: The bounty of our most excellent emperors[1] was being dispensed in the camp; the soldiers, laurel-crowned, were approaching. One of them, more a soldier of God, more stedfast than the rest of his brethren, who had imagined that they could serve two masters, his head alone uncovered, the useless crown in his hand—already even by that peculiarity known to every one as a Christian—was nobly conspicuous. Accordingly, all began to mark him out, jeering him at a distance, gnashing on him near at hand. The murmur is wafted to the tribune, when the person had just left the ranks. The tribune at once puts the question to him, Why are you so different in your attire? He declared that he had no liberty to wear the crown with the rest. Being urgently asked for his reasons, he answered, I am a Christian. O soldier! boasting thyself in God. Then the case was considered and voted on; the matter was remitted to a higher tribunal; the offender was conducted to the prefects. At once he put away the heavy cloak, his disburdening commenced; he loosed from his foot the military shoe, beginning to stand upon holy ground; he gave up the sword, which was not necessary either for the protection of our Lord; from his hand likewise dropped the laurel crown; and now, purple-clad with the hope of his own blood [being shed], shod with the preparation of the gospel, girt with the

---

[1] "Emperors." The Emperor Severus associated his two sons with him in the possession of the imperial power; Caracalla in the year 198, Geta in 208.—TR.

sharper word of God, completely equipped in the apostles' armour, and crowned more worthily with the white crown of martyrdom, he awaits in prison the largess of Christ. Thereafter adverse judgments began to be passed upon his conduct—whether on the part of Christians I do not know, for those of the heathen are not different—as if he were headstrong and rash, and too eager to die, because, in being taken to task about a mere matter of dress, he brought trouble on the bearers of the [Christian] name,—he, forsooth, alone brave among so many soldier-brethren, he alone a Christian. It is plain that as they have rejected the prophecies of the Holy Spirit, they are also purposing the refusal of martyrdom. So they murmur that a peace so good and long is endangered for them. Nor do I doubt that some are already turning their back on the Scriptures, are making ready their luggage, are equipped for flight from city to city. For that is all of the gospel they care to remember. I know, too, their pastors are lions in peace, deer in the fight. As to the questions asked for extorting confessions from us, we shall teach elsewhere. But now, as they put forth also the objection: But where are we forbidden to be crowned? I shall take this point up, as more suitable to be treated of here,—being the essence, in fact, of the present contention: so that, on the one hand, the inquirers who are ignorant, but anxious, may be instructed; and on the other, those may be refuted who try to vindicate the sin, especially the laurel-crowned Christians themselves, to whom it is merely a question of debate, as if it might be regarded as either no trespass at all, or at least a doubtful one, because it may be made the subject of investigation. But that it is neither sinless nor doubtful, I shall now, however, show.

2. I affirm that not one of the faithful has ever a crown upon his head, except at a time of trial. That is the case with all, from catechumens to confessors and martyrs, or (as the case may be) deniers. Consider, then, whence the custom about which we are now chiefly inquiring got its authority. But when the question is raised why it is observed, it is meanwhile evident that it is observed. Therefore that can

neither be regarded as no offence, or an uncertain one, which is perpetrated against a practice which is capable of defence, on the ground even of its repute, and is sufficiently ratified by the support of general acceptance. It is undoubted, so that we ought to inquire into the reason of the thing, but without prejudice to the practice, not for the purpose of overthrowing it, but rather of building it up, that you may all the more carefully observe it, when you are also satisfied as to its reason. But what sort of procedure is it, for one to be bringing into debate a practice, when he has fallen from it, and to be seeking the explanation of his having ever had it, when he has left it off? Since, although he may wish to seem on this account desirous to investigate it, that he may show that he has not done wrong in giving it up, it is evident that he nevertheless transgressed previously in its presumptuous observance. For if he has done no wrong to-day in accepting the crown, he offended before in refusing it. And this treatise, therefore, will not be for those who are not in a proper condition for inquiry, but for those who, with the real desire of getting instruction, bring forward, not a question for debate, but a request for advice. For it is from this desire that a true inquiry always proceeds; and I praise the faith which has believed in the duty of complying with the rule, before it has learned the reason of it. And an easy thing it is at once to demand where it is written that we should not be crowned. But is it written that we should be crowned? Indeed, in urgently demanding the warrant of Scripture in a different side from their own, men prejudge that the support of Scripture ought no less to appear on their part. For if it shall be said that it is lawful to be crowned on this ground, that Scripture does not forbid it, it will as validly be retorted that just on this ground is the crown unlawful, because the Scripture does not enjoin it. What shall discipline do? Shall it accept both things, as if neither were forbidden? or shall it refuse both, as if neither were enjoined? But the thing which is not forbidden is freely permitted. I should rather say that is forbidden which has not been freely allowed.

3. And how long shall we draw the saw to and fro through this line, when we have an ancient practice, which by anticipation has made for us the state [of the question]? If no passage of Scripture has prescribed it, assuredly custom, which without doubt flowed from tradition, has confirmed it. For how can anything come into use, if it has not first been handed down? Even in pleading tradition, written authority, you say, must be demanded. Let us inquire, therefore, whether tradition, unless it be written, should not be admitted. Certainly we shall say that it ought not to be admitted, if no cases of other practices which, without any written instrument, we maintain on the ground of tradition alone, and the countenance thereafter of custom, affords us any precedent. To deal with this matter briefly, I shall begin with baptism. When we are going to enter the water, but a little before, in the presence of the congregation and under the hand of the president, we solemnly profess that we disown the devil, and his pomp, and his angels. Hereupon we are thrice immersed, making a somewhat ampler pledge than the Lord has appointed in the Gospel. Then, when we are taken up [as new-born children], we taste first of all a mixture of milk and honey, and from that day we refrain from the daily bath for a whole week. We take also, in meetings before daybreak, and from the hand of none but the presidents, the sacrament of the Eucharist, which the Lord both commanded to be eaten at meal-times, and enjoined to be taken by all [alike]. As often as the anniversary comes round, we make offerings for the dead as birthday honours. We count fasting or kneeling in worship on the Lord's day to be unlawful. We rejoice in the same privilege also from Easter to Whitsunday. We feel pained should any wine or bread, even though our own, be cast upon the ground. At every forward step and movement, at every going in and out, when we put on our clothes and shoes, when we bathe, when we sit at table, when we light the lamps, on couch, on seat, in all the ordinary actions of daily life, we trace upon the forehead the sign [of the cross].

4. If, for these and other such rules, you insist upon having positive Scripture injunction, you will find none. Tradition will be held forth to you as the originator of them, custom as their strengthener, and faith as their observer. That reason will support tradition, and custom, and faith, you will either yourself perceive, or learn from some one who has. Meanwhile you will believe that there is some reason to which submission is due. I add still one case more, as it will be proper to show you how it was among the ancients also. Among the Jews, so usual is it for their women to have the head veiled, that they may thereby be recognised. I ask in this instance for the law. I put the apostle aside. If Rebecca at once drew down her veil, when in the distance she saw her betrothed, this modesty of a mere private individual could not have made a law, or it will have made it only for those who have the reason which she had. Let virgins alone be veiled, and this when they are coming to be married, and not till they have recognised their destined husband. If Susanna also, who was subjected to unveiling on her trial,[1] furnishes an argument for the veiling of women, I can say here also, the veil was a voluntary thing. She had come accused, ashamed of the disgrace she had brought on herself, properly concealing her beauty, even because now she feared to please. But I should not suppose that, when it was her aim to please, she took walks with a veil on in her husband's avenue. Grant, now, that she was always veiled. In this particular case, too, I demand the dress-law, or, in fact, in that of any other. If I nowhere find a law, it follows that tradition has given custom the fashion in question at some future time to have the apostle's sanction, in his unfolding the true interpretation of its reason. These instances, therefore, will make it sufficiently plain that you can vindicate the keeping of even unwritten tradition when it has been established by custom, the proper witness for tradition whose truth has then been demonstrated by the long-continued observance of it. But even in civil matters custom is received instead of law, when positive legal enactment is wanting; and it is the same

---

[1] Vulgate, Dan. xiii. 32.

thing whether it depends on writing or on reason, since reason is, in fact, the basis of law. But, moreover, if reason is the ground of law, all will now have to be counted law, whoever brings it forward, which shall have reason as its ground. Or do you think that every believer is entitled to originate and establish a law, if only it be such as is agreeable to God, as is helpful to discipline, as promotes salvation, when the Lord says, "But why do you not even of your own selves judge what is right?"[1] And not merely in regard to a judicial sentence, but in regard to every decision in matters we are called on to consider, the apostle also says, "If of anything you are ignorant, God shall reveal it unto you;"[2] he himself, too, being accustomed to afford counsel though he had not the command of the Lord, and at his own hand to give deliverances, as possessing the Spirit of God who guides into all truth. Therefore his advice has, by the warrant of divine reason, become equivalent to nothing less than a divine command. Earnestly now inquire of this teacher, keeping intact your regard for tradition, 'from whomsoever it originally sprang; nor have regard to the author, but to the authority, and especially that of custom itself, which on this very account we should revere, that we may not want an interpreter; so that if reason too is God's gift, you may then learn, not whether custom has to be followed by you, but why.

5. The argument for Christian practices becomes all the stronger, when also nature, which is the first rule of all, supports them. Well, she is the first who lays it down that a crown does not become the head. But I think ours is the God of nature, who fashioned man, and, that he might desire, appreciate, become partaker of the pleasures afforded by His creatures, endowed him with certain senses [acting] through members which, so to speak, are their peculiar instruments. The sense of hearing he has planted in the ears; that of sight, lighted up in the eyes; that of taste, shut up in the mouth; that of smell, wafted into the nose; that of touch, fixed in the tips of the fingers. By means of these organs of the outer man doing duty to the inner man, the enjoyments of

[1] Luke xii. 27.   [2] Phil. iii. 15.

the divine gifts are conveyed by the senses to the soul. What, then, in flowers affords you enjoyment? For it is the flowers of the field which are the peculiar, at least the chief, material of crowns. Either smell, you say, or colour, or both together. What will be the senses of colour and smell? Those of seeing and smelling, I suppose. What members have had these senses allotted to them? The eyes and the nose, if I am not mistaken. With sight and smell, then, make use of flowers, for these are the senses by which they are meant to be enjoyed; use them by means of the eyes and nose, which are the members to which these senses belong. You have got the thing from God, the mode of it from the world; but an extraordinary mode does not prevent the use of the thing in the common way. Let flowers, then, both when fastened into each other and tied together in thread and rush, be what they are when free, when loose—things to be looked at and smelt. You count it a crown, let us say, when you have a bunch of them bound together in a series, that you may carry many at one time, that you may enjoy them all at once. Well, lay them in your bosom if they are so singularly pure, and strew them on your couch if they are so exquisitely soft, and consign them to your cup if they are so perfectly harmless. Have the pleasure of them in as many ways as they appeal to your senses. But what taste for a flower, what sense for anything belonging to a crown but its band, have you in the head, which is able neither to distinguish colour, nor to inhale sweet perfumes, nor to appreciate softness? It is as much against nature to long after a flower with the head, as it is to crave food with the ear, or sound with the nostril. But everything which is against nature deserves to be branded as monstrous among all men; but with us it is to be condemned also as sacrilege against God, the Lord and Creator of nature.

6. Demanding then a law of God, you have that common one prevailing all over the world, engraven on the natural tables to which the apostle too is wont to appeal, as when in respect of the woman's veil he says, "Does not even nature teach you?"[1]—as when [in the Epistle] to the Romans, affirm-

[1] 1 Cor. xi. 14.

ing that the heathen do by nature those things which the law requires,[1] he suggests both natural law and a law-revealing nature. Yes, and also in the first chapter of the epistle he authenticates nature, when he asserts that males and females changed among themselves the natural use of the creature into that which is unnatural,[2] by way of penal retribution for their error. We first of all indeed know God Himself by the teaching of nature, calling Him God of gods, taking for granted that He is good, and invoking Him as Judge. Is it a question with you whether, for the enjoyment of His creatures, nature should be our guide, that we may not be carried away in the direction in which the rival of God has corrupted, along with man himself, the entire creation which had been made over to our race for certain uses, whence the apostle says that it too unwillingly became subject to vanity, completely bereft of its original character, first by vain, then by base, and unrighteous, and ungodly uses? It is thus, accordingly, in the pleasures of the shows that the creature is dishonoured by those who by nature indeed perceive that all the materials of which shows are got up belong to God, but lack the knowledge to perceive as well that they have all been changed by the devil. But with this topic we have, for the sake of our own play-lovers, sufficiently dealt, and that, too, in a work in Greek.

7. Let these dealers in crowns then recognise in the meantime the authority of nature on the ground of a common sense as human beings, and the certifications of their peculiar religion, as, according to the last chapter, worshippers of the God of nature; and as it were thus over and above what is required, let them consider those other reasons too which forbid us wearing crowns, especially on the head, and indeed crowns of every sort. For we are obliged to turn from the rule of nature, which we share with mankind in general, that we may maintain the whole peculiarity of our Christian discipline, in relation also to other kinds of crowns which seem to have been provided for different uses, as being composed of different substances, lest, because they do

[1] Rom. ii. 14.   [2] Rom. i. 26.

not consist of flowers, the use of which nature has indicated
(as it does in the case of this military laurel one itself), they
may be thought not to come under the prohibition of our sect,
since they have escaped any objections of nature. I see,
then, that we must go into the matter both with more research, and more fully, from its beginnings on through its
successive stages of growth to its more erratic developments.
For this we need to turn to heathen literature. For things
belonging to the heathen must be proved from their own
documents. The little of this I have acquired, will, I believe,
be enough. If there really was a Pandora, whom Hesiod
mentions as the first of women, hers was the first head the
graces crowned, for she received gifts from all [the gods],
whence she got [her name] Pandora. But Moses, a prophet,
not a poet-shepherd, shows us the first woman Eve having
her loins more naturally girt about with leaves than her
temples with flowers. Pandora, then, is a myth. And so we
have to blush for the origin of the crown, even on the ground
of the falsehood connected with it; and, as will soon appear,
on the ground no less of its realities. For it is an undoubted
fact that certain persons either originated the thing, or shed
lustre on it. Pherecydes relates that Saturn was the first
who wore a crown; Diodorus, that Jupiter, after conquering
the Titans, was honoured with this gift by the rest of the
gods. To Priapus also the same author assigns fillets; and
to Ariadne a garland of gold and of Indian gems, the gift of
Vulcan, and afterwards of Bacchus, and subsequently turned
into a constellation. Callimachus has put a vine crown upon
Juno. So too at Argos, her statue, vine-wreathed, with a
lion's skin placed beneath her feet, exhibits the step-mother
exulting over the spoils of her two step-sons. Hercules displays upon his head sometimes poplar, sometimes wild-olive,
sometimes parsley. You have the tragedy of Cerberus, you
have Pindar, and besides Callimachus, who mentions that
Apollo, too, when he had killed the Delphic serpent, as a
suppliant put on a laurel garland; for among the ancients
suppliants were wont to be crowned. Harpocration argues
that Bacchus, the same as Osiris among the Egyptians, was

designedly crowned with ivy, because it is the nature of ivy to protect the brain against drowsiness. But that in another way also Bacchus was the originator of the laurel crown, [the crown] in which he celebrated his triumph over the Indians, even the rabble acknowledge, when they call the days dedicated to him the "great crown." If you open, again, the writings of the Egyptian Leo, you learn that Isis was the first who discovered and wore ears of corn upon her head—a thing more suited to the belly. Those who want additional information will find an ample exposition of the subject in Claudius Saturninus, a writer of distinguished talent who treats this question also. For he has a book on crowns, so explaining their beginnings as well as causes, and kinds, and rites, that you find all that is charming in the flower, all that is beautiful in the leafy branch, that every sod or vine-shoot has been dedicated to some head or other; making it abundantly clear how foreign to us we should judge the custom of the crowned head, introduced as it was by, and thereafter constantly managed for the honour of, those whom the world has believed to be gods. For if the devil, a liar from the beginning, is even in this matter working for his false system of godhead (idolatry), he had himself also without doubt provided for his god-lie being carried out. What sort of thing, then, must that be counted among the people of the true God, which was brought in by the nations in honour of the devil's candidates, and was set apart from the beginning to no other than these; and which even then received its consecration to idolatry by idols and in idols yet alive? Not as if an idol were anything, but seeing the things which *others* offer up to idols belong to demons. But if the things which others offer to them belong to demons, how much more what idols themselves offered to themselves, when they were in life! The demons themselves, doubtless, had made provision for themselves by means of those whom they had possessed, while in a state of desire and craving, before provision had been actually made.

8. Hold fast in the meantime this persuasion, while I examine a question which comes in our way. For I already

hear that it is said that many other things as well as crowns have been invented by those whom the world believes to be gods, and that they are notwithstanding to be met with both in our present usages and in those of early saints, and in the service of God, and in Christ Himself, who did His work as man by no other than these ordinary instrumentalities of human life. Well, let it be so; nor shall I inquire any further back into the origin of these things. Let Mercury have been the first who taught the knowledge of letters; I will own that they are requisite both for the business and commerce of life, and for performing our devotion to God. Nay, if he also first strung the chord to give forth melody, I will not deny, when listening to David, that this invention has been in use with the saints, and ministered to God. Let Æsculapius have been the first who sought and discovered cures: Esaias[1] mentions that he ordered Hezekiah medicine when he was sick. Paul, too, knows that a little wine does the stomach good.[2] Let Minerva have been the first who built a ship: I shall see Jonah and the apostles sailing. Nay, there is more than this: for even Christ, we shall find, has ordinary raiment; Paul, too, has his cloak.[3] If at once of every article of furniture and each household vessel you name some god of the world as the originator, well, I must recognise Christ, both as He reclines on a couch, and when He presents a basin for the feet of His disciples, and when He pours water into it from a ewer, and when He is girt about with a linen towel[4]—a garment specially sacred to Osiris. It is thus in general I reply upon the point, admitting indeed that we use along with others these articles, but challenging that this be judged in the light of the distinction between things agreeable and things opposed to reason, because the promiscuous employment of them is deceptive, concealing the corruption of the creature, by which it has been made subject to vanity. For we affirm that those things only are proper to be used, whether by ourselves or by those who lived before us, and alone befit the service of God and Christ Himself, which

[1] Isa. xxxviii. 21.
[2] 1 Tim. v. 23.
[3] 2 Tim. iv. 13.
[4] John xiii. 1-5.

to meet the necessities of human life supply what is simply useful and affords real assistance and honourable comfort, so that they may be well believed to have come from God's own inspiration, who first of all no doubt provided for, and taught and ministered to the enjoyment, I should suppose, of His own man; but as for the things which are out of this class, they are not fit to be used among us, especially those which on that account indeed are not to be found either with the world, or in the service of God, or in the ways of Christ.

9. In short, what patriarch, what prophet, what Levite, or priest, or ruler, or at a later period what apostle, or preacher of the gospel, or bishop, do you ever find the wearer of a crown? I think not even the temple of God itself was crowned; as neither was the ark of the testament, nor the tabernacle of witness, nor the altar, nor the candlestick crowned; though certainly, both on that first solemnity of the dedication, and in that second rejoicing for the restoration, crowning would have been most suitable if it were worthy of God. But if these things were figures of us (for we are temples of God, and altars, and lights, and sacred vessels), this too they in figure set forth, that the people of God ought not to be crowned. The reality must always correspond with the image. If, perhaps, you object that Christ Himself was crowned, to that you will get the brief reply: Be you too crowned, as He was; you have full permission. Yet even that crown of insolent ungodliness was not of any decree of the Jewish people. It was a device of the Roman soldiers, taken from the practice of the world,—a practice which the people of God never allowed either on the occasion of public rejoicing or to gratify innate luxury: so they returned from the Babylonish captivity with timbrels, and flutes, and psalteries, more suitably than with crowns; and after eating and drinking, uncrowned, they rose up to play. For neither would the account of the rejoicing nor the exposure of the luxury have been silent touching the honour or dishonour of the crown. Thus too Isaiah, as he says, "With timbrels, and psalteries, and flutes they drink wine,"[1] would have added

---

[1] Isa. v. 12.

"with crowns," if this practice had ever had place in the things of God.

10. So, when you allege that the ornaments of the heathen deities are found no less with God, with the object of claiming among these for general use the head-crown, you already lay it down for yourself, that we must not have among us, as a thing whose use we are to share with others, what is not to be found in the service of God. Well, what is so unworthy of God indeed as that which is worthy of an idol? But what is so worthy of an idol as that which is also worthy of a dead man? For it is the privilege of the dead also to be thus crowned, as they too straightway become idols, both by their dress and the service of deification, which [deification] is with us a second idolatry. Wanting, then, the sense, it will be theirs to use the thing for which the sense is wanting, just as if in full possession of the sense they wished to abuse it. When there ceases to be any reality in the use, there is no distinction between using and abusing. Who can abuse a thing, when the percipient nature with which he wishes to carry out his purpose is not his to use it? The apostle, moreover, forbids us to abuse, while he would more naturally have taught us not to use, unless on the ground that, where there is no sense for things, there is no wrong use of them. But the whole affair is meaningless, and is, in fact, a dead work so far as concerns the idols; though, without doubt, a living one as respects the demons to whom the religious rite belongs. "The idols of the heathen," says David, "are silver and gold." "They have eyes, and see not; a nose, and smell not; hands, and they will not handle."[1] By means of these organs, indeed, we are to enjoy flowers; but if he declares that those who make idols will be like them, they already are, so who use anything after the style of idol adornings. "To the pure all things are pure: so, likewise, all things to the impure are impure;"[2] but nothing is more impure than idols. But the substances are themselves as creatures of God without impurity, and in this their native state are free to the use of all. But the ministries to which in their

---

[1] Ps. cxv. 4-8.   [2] Tit. i. 15.

use they are devoted, makes all the difference; for I, too, kill a cock for myself, just as Socrates did for Æsculapius; and if the smell of some place or other offends me, I burn the Arabian product myself, but not with the same ceremony, nor in the same dress, nor with the same pomp with which it is done to idols. For if the creature is defiled by a mere word, as the apostle teaches, "But if any one say, This is offered in sacrifice to idols, you must not touch it,"[1] much more when it is polluted by the dress, and rites, and pomp of what is offered to the gods. Thus the crown also is made out to be an offering to idols; for with this ceremony, and dress, and pomp, it is presented in sacrifice to idols, its originators, to whom its use is specially given over, and chiefly on this account, that what has no place among the things of God may not be admitted into use with us as with others. Wherefore the apostle exclaims, "Flee idolatry:"[2] certainly idolatry whole and entire he means. Reflect on what a thicket it is, and how many thorns lie hid in it. Nothing must be given to an idol, and so nothing must be taken from one. If it is inconsistent with faith to recline in an idol temple, what is it to appear in an idol dress? What communion have Christ and Belial? And therefore flee from it; for he enjoins us to keep at a distance from idolatry— to have no close dealings with it of any kind. Even an earthly serpent sucks in men at some distance with its breath. Going still further, John says, "My little children, keep yourselves from idols,"[3]—not now from idolatry, as if from the service of it, but from idols—that is, from any resemblance to them; for it is an unworthy thing that you, the image of the living God, should become the likeness of an idol and a dead man. Thus far we assert, that this attire belongs to idols, both from the history of its origin, and from its use by false religion; on this ground, besides, that while it is not mentioned as connected with the worship of God, it is more and more given over to those in whose antiquities, as well as festivals and services, it is found. In a word, the very doors, the very victims and altars, the very

[1] 1 Cor. x. 28.   [2] 1 Cor. x. 14.   [3] 1 John v. 21.

servants and priests, are crowned. You have, in Claudius, the crowns of all the various colleges of priests. We have added also that distinction between things altogether different from each other—things, namely, agreeable, and things contrary to reason—in answer to those who, because there happens to be the use of some things in common, maintain the right of participation in all things. With reference to this part of the subject, therefore, it now remains that the special grounds for wearing crowns should be examined, that while we show these to be foreign, nay, even opposed to our Christian discipline, we may demonstrate that none of them has any plea of reason to support it, on the basis of which this article of dress might be vindicated as one in whose use we can participate, as even some others may whose instances are cast up to us.

11. To begin with the real ground of the military crown, I think we must first inquire whether warfare is proper at all for Christians. What sense is there in discussing the merely accidental, when that on which it rests is to be condemned? Do we believe it lawful for a human oath to be superadded to one divine, and for a man to come under promise to another master after Christ, and to abjure father and mother and all nearest kinsfolk, whom even the law has commanded us to honour and love next to God Himself, to whom the gospel, too, holding them only of less account than Christ, has in like manner rendered honour? Shall it be held lawful to make an occupation of the sword, when the Lord proclaims that he who uses the sword shall perish by the sword? And shall the son of peace take part in the battle when it does not become him even to sue at law? And shall he apply the chain, and the prison, and the torture, and the punishment, who is not the avenger even of his own wrongs? Shall he, forsooth, either keep watch-service for others more than for Christ, or shall he do it on the Lord's day, when he does not even do it for Christ Himself? And shall he keep guard before the temples which he has renounced? And shall he take a meal where the apostle has forbidden him?[1] And shall he diligently

[1] 1 Cor. viii. 10.

protect by night those whom in the day-time he has put to flight by his exorcisms, leaning and resting on the spear the while with which Christ's side was pierced? Shall he carry a flag, too, hostile to Christ? And shall *he* ask a watchword from the emperor who has already received one from God? Shall *he* be disturbed in death by the trumpet of the trumpeter, who expects to be aroused by the angel's trump? And shall the Christian be burned according to camp rule, when he was not permitted to burn incense to an idol, when to him Christ remitted the punishment of fire? Then how many other offences there are involved in the performance of camp offices, which we must hold to involve a transgression of God's law, you may see by a slight survey. The very carrying of the name over from the camp of light to the camp of darkness is a violation of it. Of course, if faith comes later, and finds any preoccupied with military service, their case is different, as in the instance of those whom John used to receive for baptism, and of those most faithful centurions, I mean the centurion whom Christ approves, and the centurion whom Peter instructs; yet, at the same time, when a man has become a believer, and faith has been sealed, there must be either an immediate abandonment of it, which has been the course with many; or all sorts of quibbling will have to be resorted to in order to avoid offending God, and that is not allowed even outside of military service;[1] or, last of all, for God the fate must be endured which a citizen-faith has been no less ready to accept. For neither does military service hold out escape from punishment of sins, or exemption from martyrdom.

---

[1] "Outside of the military service." By substituting *ex militia* for the corresponding words *extra militiam*, as has been proposed by Rigaltius, the sentence acquires a meaning such that desertion from the army is suggested as one of the methods by which a soldier who has become a Christian may continue faithful to Jesus. But the words *extra militiam* are a genuine part of the text. There is no good ground, therefore, for the statement of Gibbon: "Tertullian (*de Corona Militis*, c. xi.) suggests to them the expedient of deserting; a counsel which, if it had been generally known, was not very proper to conciliate the favour of the emperors towards the Christian sect."—Tr.

Nowhere does the Christian change his character. There is one gospel, and the same Jesus, who will one day deny every one who denies, and acknowledge every one who acknowledges God,—who will save, too, the life which has been lost for His sake; but, on the other hand, destroy that which for gain has been saved to His dishonour. With Him the faithful citizen is a soldier, just as the faithful soldier is a citizen.[1] A state of faith admits no plea of necessity; they are under no necessity to sin, whose one necessity is, that they do not sin. For if one is pressed to the offering of sacrifice and the sheer denial of Christ by the necessity of torture or of punishment, yet discipline does not connive even at that necessity; because there is a higher necessity to dread denying and to undergo martyrdom, than to escape from suffering, and to render the homage required. In fact, an excuse of this sort overturns the entire essence of our sacrament, removing even the obstacle to voluntary sins; for it will be possible also to maintain that inclination is a necessity, as involving in it, forsooth, a sort of compulsion. I have, in fact, disposed of this very allegation of necessity with reference to the pleas by which crowns connected with official position are vindicated, in support of which it is in common use, since for this very reason offices must be either refused, that we may not fall into acts of sin, or martyrdoms endured that we may get quit of offices. Touching this primary aspect of the question, as to the unlawfulness even of a military life itself, I shall not add more, that the secondary question may be restored to its place. Indeed, if, putting my strength to the question, I banish from us the military life, I should now to no purpose issue a challenge on the matter of the military crown. Suppose, then, that the military service is lawful, as far as the plea for the crown is concerned.

12. But I first say a word also about the crown itself. This laurel one is sacred to Apollo or Bacchus—to the former as the god of archery, to the latter as the god of triumphs.

---

[1] "The faithful," etc.; *i.e.* the kind of occupation which any one has cannot be pleaded by him as a reason for not doing all that Christ has enjoined upon His people.—Tr.

In like manner Claudius teaches, when he tells us that soldiers are wont too to be wreathed in myrtle. For the myrtle belongs to Venus, the mother of the Æneadæ, the mistress also of the god of war, who through Ilia and the Romuli is Roman. But I do not believe that Venus is Roman as well as Mars, because of the vexation the concubine [Ilia] gave her. When military service again is crowned with olive, the idolatry has respect to Minerva, who is equally the goddess of arms—but got a crown of the tree referred to, because of the peace she made with Neptune. In these respects, the superstition of the military garland will be everywhere defiled and all-defiling. And it is further defiled, I should think, also in the grounds of it. Lo! the yearly public pronouncing of vows, what does that bear on its face to be? It takes place first in the part of the camp where the general's tent is, and then in the temples. In addition to the places, observe the words also: "We vow that you, O Jupiter, will then have an ox with gold-decorated horns." What does the utterance mean? Without a doubt the denial [of Christ]. Albeit the Christian says nothing in these places with the mouth, he makes his response by having the crown on his head. The laurel is likewise commanded [to be used] at the distribution of the largess. So you see idolatry is not without its gain, selling, as it does, Christ for pieces of gold, as Judas did for pieces of silver. Will it be "Ye cannot serve God and mammon,"[1] to devote your energies to mammon, and to depart from God? Will it be "Render unto Cæsar the things which are Cæsar's, and unto God the things which are God's,"[2] not only not to render the human being to God, but even to take the denarius from Cæsar? Is the laurel of the triumph made of leaves, or of corpses? Is it adorned with ribbons, or with tombs? Is it bedewed with ointments, or with the tears of wives and mothers?—it may be of some Christians too; for Christ is also among the barbarians. Has not he who has carried [a crown for] this cause on his head, fought even against himself? Another sort of service belongs to the royal guards. And indeed

---

[1] Matt. vi. 24.   [2] Matt. xxii. 21.

crowns are called [Castrenses], as belonging to the camp; Munificæ likewise, from the duties they [the crowns] perform. But even then you are still the soldier and the servant of another; and if of two masters, of God and Cæsar: but assuredly then not of Cæsar, when you owe yourself to God, as having higher claims, I should think, even in matters in which both have an interest.

13. For state reasons, the various orders of the citizens also are crowned with laurel crowns; but the magistrates besides with golden ones, as at Athens, as at Rome. Even to those are preferred the Etruscan. This appellation is given to the crowns which, distinguished by their gems and oak leaves of gold, they put on with mantles, having an embroidery of palm branches, to conduct the chariots containing the images of the gods to the circus. There are also provincial crowns of gold, needing now the larger heads of images instead of those of men. But your orders, and your magistracies, and your very place of meeting, the church, are Christ's. You belong to Him, for you have been enrolled in the books of life.[1] There the blood of the Lord serves for your purple robe, and your broad stripe is His own cross; there the axe is already laid to the trunk of the tree;[2] there is the branch out of the root of Jesse.[3] Never mind the state. horses with their crown. Your Lord, when, according to the Scripture, He would enter Jerusalem in triumph, had not even an ass of His own. These [put their trust] in chariots, and these in horses; but we will seek our help in the name of the Lord our God.[4] From so much as a dwelling in that Babylon of John's Revelation[5] we are called away; much more then from its pomp. The rabble, too, are crowned, at one time because of some great rejoicing for the success of the emperors; at another, on account of some custom belonging to municipal festivals. For luxury strives to make her own every occasion of public gladness. But as for you, you are a foreigner in this world, a citizen of Jerusalem, the city above. Our citizenship, the apostle says, is in heaven.[6] You have your

[1] Phil. iv. 3.   [2] Matt. iii. 10.   [3] Isa. xi. 1.
[4] Ps. xx. 7.   [5] Rev. xviii. 4.   [6] Phil. iii. 20.

own registers, your own calendar; you have nothing to do with the joys of the world; nay, you are called to the very opposite. For "the world shall rejoice, but ye shall mourn."[1] And I think the Lord affirms, that those who mourn are happy, not those who are crowned. Marriage, too, decks the bridegroom with its crown; and therefore we will not have heathen brides, lest they seduce us even to the idolatry with which among them marriage is initiated. You have the law from the patriarchs indeed; you have the apostle enjoining people to marry in the Lord.[2] You have a crowning also on the making of a freeman. But *you* have been already ransomed by Christ, and that at a great price. How shall the world manumit the servant of another? Though it seems to be liberty, yet it will come to be found bondage. In the world everything is nominal, and nothing real. For even then, as ransomed by Christ, you were under no bondage to man; and now, though man has given you liberty, you are the servant of Christ. If you think the freedom of the world to be real, so that you even seal it with a crown, you have returned to the slavery of man, imagining it to be freedom; you have lost the freedom of Christ, fancying it is slavery. Will there be any dispute as to the cause of crown-wearing, which contests in the games in their turn supply, which, both as sacred to the gods and in honour of the dead, their own reason at once condemns? For it only remains, that the Olympian Jupiter, and the Nemean Hercules, and the wretched little Archemorus, and the hapless Antinous, should be crowned in a Christian, that he himself may become a spectacle disgusting to behold. We have recounted, as I think, all the various causes of the wearing of the crown, and there is not one which has any place with us: all are foreign to us, unholy, unlawful, having been abjured already once for all in the solemn declaration of the sacrament. For they were of the pomp of the devil and his angels, offices of the world, honours, festivals, popularity huntings, false vows, exhibitions of human servility, empty praises, base glories, and in them all idolatry, even in respect of the origin

---

[1] John xvi. 20.   [2] 1 Cor. vii. 39.

of the crowns alone, with which they are all wreathed. Claudius will tell us in his preface, indeed, that in the poems of Homer the heaven also is crowned with constellations, and that no doubt by God, no doubt for man; therefore man himself, too, should be crowned by God. But the world crowns brothels, and baths, and bakehouses, and prisons, and schools, and the very amphitheatres, and the chambers where the clothes are stripped from dead gladiators, and the very biers of the dead. How sacred and holy, how venerable and pure is this article of dress, determine not from the heaven of poetry alone, but from the traffickings of the whole world. But indeed a Christian will not even dishonour his own gate with laurel crowns, if so be he knows how many gods the devil has attached to doors; Janus so-called from gate, Limentinus from threshold, Forcus and Carna from leaves and hinges; among the Greeks, too, the Thyræan Apollo, and the evil spirits, the Antelii.

14. Much less may the Christian put the service of idolatry on his own head—nay, I might have said, upon Christ, since Christ is the Head of the Christian man—[for his head] is as free as even Christ is, under no obligation to wear a covering, not to say a band. But even the head which is bound to have the veil, I mean woman's, as already taken possession of by this very thing, is not open also to a band. She has the burden of her own inferiority to bear. If she ought not to appear with her head uncovered on account of the angels,[1] much more with a crown on it will she offend those [elders] who perhaps are then wearing crowns above.[2] For what is a crown on the head of a woman, but beauty made seductive, but mark of utter wantonness,—a notable casting away of modesty, a setting temptation on fire? Therefore a woman, taking counsel from the apostles' foresight,[3] will not too elaborately adorn herself, that she may not either be crowned with any exquisite arrangement of her hair. What sort of garland, however, I pray you, did He who is both the Head of the man and the glory of the woman, Christ Jesus, the

[1] 1 Cor. xi. 10.   [2] Rev. iv. 4.   [3] 1 Tim. ii. 9; 1 Pet. iii. 3.

Husband of the church, submit to in behalf of both sexes? Of thorns, I think, and thistles,—a figure of the sins which the soil of the flesh brought forth for us, but the power of the cross removed, blunting, in its endurance by the head of our Lord, death's every sting. Yes, and besides the figure, there is contumely with ready lip, and dishonour, and infamy, and the ferocity involved in the cruel things which then disfigured and lacerated the temples of the Lord, that you may now be crowned with laurel, and myrtle, and olive, and any famous branch, and which is of more use, with hundred-leaved roses too, culled from the garden of Midas, and with both kinds of lily, and with violets of all sorts, perhaps also with gems and gold, so as even to rival that crown of Christ which He afterwards obtained; for it was after the gall He tasted the honeycomb, and He was not greeted as King of Glory in heavenly places till He had been condemned to the cross as King of the Jews, having first been made by the Father for a time a little less than the angels, and so crowned with glory and honour. If for these things you owe your own head to Him, repay it if you can, such as He presented His for yours; or be not crowned with flowers at all, if you cannot be with thorns, because you may not be with flowers.

15. Keep for God His own property untainted; He will crown it if He choose. Nay, then, He does even choose. He calls us to it. To him who conquers He says, "I will give a crown of life."[1] Be *you*, too, faithful unto death, and fight *you*, too, the good fight, whose crown the apostle[2] feels so justly confident has been laid up for him. The angel[3] also, as he goes forth on a white horse, conquering and to conquer, receives a crown of victory; and another[4] is adorned with an encircling rainbow (as it were in its fair colours)—a celestial meadow. In like manner, the elders sit crowned around, crowned too with a crown of gold, and the Son of man Himself flashes out above the clouds. If such are the appearances in the vision of the seer, of what sort

---

[1] Rev. ii. 10; Jas. i. 12. [2] 2 Tim. iv. 8.
[3] Rev. vi. 2. [4] Rev. x. 1.

will be the realities in the actual manifestation? Look at those crowns. Inhale those odours. Why condemn you to a little chaplet, or a twisted headband, the brow which has been destined for a diadem? For Christ Jesus has made us even kings to God and His Father. What have you in common with the flower which is to die? You have a flower in the Branch of Jesse, upon which the grace of the Divine Spirit in all its fulness rested—a flower undefiled, unfading, everlasting, by choosing which the good soldier, too, has got promotion in the heavenly ranks. Blush, ye fellow-soldiers of his, henceforth not to be condemned even by him, but by some soldier of Mithras, who, at his initiation in the gloomy cavern, in the camp, it may well be said, of darkness, when at the sword's point a crown is presented to him, as though in mimicry of martyrdom, and thereupon put upon his head, is admonished to resist and cast it off, and, if you like, transfer it to his shoulder, saying that Mithras is his crown. And thenceforth he is never crowned; and he has that for a mark to show who he is, if anywhere he be subjected to trial in respect of his religion; and he is at once believed to be a soldier of Mithras if he throws the crown away—if he say that in his god he has his crown. Let us take note of the devices of the devil, who is wont to ape some of God's things with no other design than, by the faithfulness of his servants, to put us to shame, and to condemn us.

XIV.

DE FUGA IN PERSECUTIONE.

1. MY brother Fabius, you very lately asked, because some news or other were communicated, whether or not we ought to flee in persecution. For my part, having on the spot made some observations in the negative suited to the place and time, I also, owing to the rudeness of some persons, took away with me the subject but half treated, meaning to set it forth now more fully by my pen; for your inquiry had interested me in it, and the state of the times had already on its own account pressed it upon me. For as persecutions in increasing number threaten us, so the more are we called on to give earnest thought to the question of how faith ought to receive them. And the duty of carefully considering it concerns you no less, who no doubt, by not accepting the Comforter, the guide to all truth, have, as was natural, opposed us hitherto in regard to other questions also. We have therefore applied a methodical treatment, too, to your inquiry, as we see that we must first come to a decision as to how the matter stands in regard to persecution itself, whether it comes on us from God or from the devil, that with the less difficulty we may get on firm ground as to our duty to meet it; for of everything one's knowledge is clearer when it is known from whom it has its origin. It is enough indeed to lay it down, [in bar of all besides,] that nothing happens without the will of God. But lest we be diverted from the point before us, we shall not by this deliverance at once give occasion to the other discussions if one make answer—Therefore evil and sin are both from God; the devil henceforth, and even we ourselves, are entirely free. The question in hand is persecution. With respect to this, let me in the meantime

say, that nothing happens without God's will; on the ground that persecution is especially worthy of God, and, so to speak, requisite, for the approving, to wit, or if you will, the rejection of His professing servants. For what is the issue of persecution, what other result comes of it, but the approving and rejecting of faith, in regard to which the Lord will certainly sift His people? Persecution, by means of which one is declared either approved or rejected, is just the judgment of the Lord. But the judging properly belongs to God alone. This is that fan which even now cleanses the Lord's threshing-floor—the church, I mean—winnowing the mixed heap of believers, and separating the grain[1] of the martyrs from the chaff of the deniers; and this is also the ladder[2] of which Jacob dreams, on which are seen, some mounting up to higher places, and others going down to lower. So, too, persecution may be viewed as a contest. By whom is the conflict proclaimed, but by Him by whom the crown and the rewards are offered? You find in the Revelation its edict, setting forth the rewards by which He incites to victory—those, above all, whose is the distinction of conquering in persecution, in very deed contending in their victorious struggle not against flesh and blood, but against spirits of wickedness. So, too, you will see that the adjudging of the contest belongs to the same glorious One as umpire who calls us to the prize. The one great thing in persecution is the promotion of the glory of God, as He tries and casts away, lays on and takes off. But what concerns the glory of God will surely come to pass by His will. And when is trust in God more strong, than when there is a greater fear of Him, than when persecution breaks out? The church is awe-struck. Then is faith both more zealous in preparation, and better disciplined in fasts, and meetings, and prayers, and lowliness, in brotherly-kindness and love, in holiness and temperance. There is no room, in fact, for aught but fear and hope. So even by this very thing we have it clearly proved that persecution, improving as it does the servants of God, cannot be imputed to the devil.

2. If, because injustice is not from God, but from the

[1] Matt. iii. 12.   [2] Gen. xxviii. 12.

devil, and persecution consists of injustice (for what more unjust than that the bishops of the true God, that all the followers of the truth, should be dealt with after the manner of the vilest criminals?), persecution therefore seems to proceed from the devil, by whom the injustice which constitutes persecution is perpetrated, we ought to know, as you have neither persecution without the injustice of the devil, nor the trial of faith without persecution, that the injustice necessary for the trial of faith does not give a warrant for persecution, but supplies an agency; that in reality, in reference to the trial of faith, which is the reason of persecution, the will of God goes first, but that as the instrument of persecution, which is the way of trial, the injustice of the devil follows. For in other respects, too, injustice in proportion to the enmity it displays against righteousness affords occasion for attestations of that to which it is opposed as an enemy, that so righteousness may be perfected in injustice, as strength is perfected in weakness.[1] For the weak things of the world have been chosen by God to confound the strong, and the foolish things of the world to confound its wisdom.[2] Thus even injustice is employed, that righteousness may be approved in putting unrighteousness to shame. Therefore, since the service is not of free-will, but of subjection (for persecution is the appointment of the Lord for the trial of faith, but its ministry is the injustice of the devil, supplied that persecution may be got up), we believe that persecution comes to pass, no question, by the devil's agency, but not by the devil's origination. Satan will not be at liberty to do anything against the servants of the living God unless the Lord grant leave, either that He may overthrow Satan himself by the faith of the elect which proves victorious in the trial, or in the face of the world show that apostatizers to the devil's cause have been in reality His servants. You have the case of Job, whom the devil, unless he had received authority from God, could not have visited with trial, not even, in fact, in his property, unless the Lord had said, "Behold, all that he has I put at your disposal; but do not stretch out your

[1] 2 Cor. xii. 9.   [2] 1 Cor. i. 27, 28.

hand against himself."[1] In short, he would not even have stretched it out, unless afterwards, at his request, the Lord had granted him this permission also, saying, " Behold, I deliver him to you; only preserve his life." So he asked in the case of the apostles likewise an opportunity to tempt them, having it only by special allowance, since the Lord in the Gospel says to Peter, "Behold, Satan asked that he might sift you as grain; but I have prayed for you, that your faith fail not;"[2] that is, that the devil should not have power granted him sufficient to endanger his faith. Whence it is manifest that both things belong to God, the shaking of faith as well as the shielding of it, when both are sought from Him—the shaking by the devil, the shielding by the Son. And certainly, when the Son of God has faith's protection absolutely committed to Him, beseeching it of the Father, from whom He receives all power in heaven and on earth, how entirely out of the question is it that the devil should have the assailing of it in *his* own power! But in the prayer prescribed to us, when we say to our Father, "Lead us not into temptation"[3] (now what greater temptation is there than persecution?), we acknowledge that that comes to pass by His will whom we beseech to exempt us from it. For this is what follows, "But deliver us from the wicked one," that is, do not lead us into temptation by giving us up to the wicked one. For then are we delivered from the power of the devil, when we are not handed over to him to be tempted. Nor would the devil's legion have had power over the herd of swine[4] unless they had got it from God; so far are they from having power over the sheep of God. I may say that the bristles of the swine, too, were then counted by God, not to speak of the hairs of holy men. The devil, it must be owned, seems indeed to have power—in this case really his own—over those who do not belong to God, the nations being once for all counted by God as a drop of the bucket, and as the dust of the threshing-floor, and as the spittle of the mouth, and so thrown open to the devil as, in a sense, a free possession. But against those who belong to the household of God he may not do

[1] Job i. 12.   [2] Luke xxii. 31, 32.   [3] Matt. vi. 13.   [4] Mark v. 11.

ought as by any right of his own, because the cases marked out in Scripture show when—that is, for what reasons—he may touch them. For either, with a view to their being approved, the power of trial is granted to him, challenged or challenging, as in the instances already referred to, or, to secure an opposite result, the sinner is handed over to him, as though he were an executioner to whom belonged the inflicting of punishment, as in the case of Saul. "And the Spirit of the Lord," says Scripture, "departed from Saul, and an evil spirit from the Lord troubled and stifled him;"[1] or the design is to humble, as the apostle tells us, that there was given him a stake, the messenger of Satan, to buffet him;[2] and even this sort of thing is not permitted in the case of holy men, unless it be that at the same time strength of endurance may be perfected in weakness. For the apostle likewise delivered Phygellus and Hermogenes over to Satan, that by chastening they might be taught not to blaspheme.[3] You see, then, that the devil receives more suitably power even from the servants of God; so far is he from having it by any right of his own.

3. Seeing therefore, too, these cases occur in persecutions more than at other times, as there is then among us more of proving or rejecting, more of abasing or punishing, it must be that their general occurrence is permitted or commanded by Him at whose will they happen even partially; by Him, I mean, who says, "I am He who make peace and create evils,"[4]—that is, war, for that is the antithesis of peace. But what other war has our peace than persecution? If in its issues persecution emphatically brings either life or death, either wounds or healing, you have the author, too, of this. "I will smite and heal, I will make alive and put to death."[5] "I will burn them," He says, "as gold is burned; and I will try them," He says, "as silver is tried."[6] For when the flame of persecution is consuming us, then the stedfastness of our faith is proved. These will be the fiery darts of the devil, by which faith gets a ministry of burning and kindling; yet

---
[1] 1 Sam. xvi. 14.   [2] 2 Cor. xii. 7.   [3] 2 Tim. i. 15; 1 Tim. i. 20.
[4] Isa. xlv. 7.   [5] Deut. xxxii. 39.   [6] Zech. xiii. 9.

by the will of God. As to this I know not who can doubt, unless it be persons with frivolous and frigid faith, which seizes upon those who with trembling assemble together in the church. For you say, seeing we assemble without order, and assemble at the same time, and flock in large numbers to the church, the heathen are led to make inquiry about us, and we are alarmed lest we awaken their anxieties. Do ye not know that God is Lord of all? And if it is God's will, then you shall suffer persecution; but if it is not, the heathen will be still. Believe it most surely, if indeed you believe in that God without whose will not even the sparrow, a penny can buy, falls to the ground.[1] But we, I think, are better than many sparrows.

4. Well, then, if it is evident from whom persecution proceeds, we are able at once to satisfy your doubts, and to decide from these introductory remarks alone, that men should not flee in it. For if persecution proceeds from God, in no way will it be our duty to flee from what has God as its author; a twofold reason opposing: for what proceeds from God ought not on the one hand to be avoided, and it cannot be evaded on the other. It ought not to be avoided, because it is good; for everything must be good on which God has cast His eye. And with this idea has perhaps this statement been made in Genesis, "And God saw because it is good;" not that He would have been ignorant of its goodness unless He had seen it, but to indicate by this expression that it was good because it was viewed by God. There are many events indeed happening by the will of God, and happening to somebody's harm. Yet for all that, a thing is therefore good because it is of God, as divine, as reasonable. For what is divine, and not reasonable, not good? What is good, yet not divine? But if to the universal apprehension of mankind this seems to be the case, in judging, man's faculty of apprehension does not predetermine the nature of things, but the nature of things his power of apprehension. For every several nature is a certain definite reality, and it lays it on the perceptive power to perceive it

[1] Matt. x. 29.

just as it exists. Now, if that which comes from God is good indeed in its natural state (for there is nothing from God which is not good, because it is divine, because it is reasonable), but seems evil to the human faculty, all will be right in regard to the former; with the latter the fault will lie. In its real nature a very good thing is chastity, and so is truth, and so is righteousness; and yet they are distasteful to many. Is perhaps the real nature on this account sacrificed to the sense of perception? Thus persecution in its own nature too is good, because it is a divine and reasonable appointment; but those to whom it comes as a punishment do not feel it to be pleasant. You see that as proceeding from Him, even that evil has a reasonable ground, when one in persecution is cast out of a state of salvation, just as you see that you have a reasonable ground for the good also, when one by persecution has his salvation made more secure. Unless, as it depends on the Lord, one either perishes irrationally, or is irrationally saved, he will not be able to speak of persecution as an evil, which, while it is under the direction of reason, is, even in respect of its evil, good. So, if persecution is in every way a good, because it has a natural basis, we on valid grounds lay it down, that what is good ought not to be shunned by us, because it is a sin to refuse what is good, besides that what has been looked upon by God can no longer indeed be avoided, proceeding as it does from God, from whose will escape will not be possible. Therefore those who think that they should flee, either reproach God with doing what is evil, if they flee from persecution as an evil (for no one avoids what is good); or they count themselves stronger than God: so they think, who imagine it possible to escape when it is God's pleasure that such events should occur.

5. But, says some one, I flee, the thing it belongs to me to do, that I may not perish, if I deny; it is for Him on His part, if He chooses, to bring me, when I flee, back before the tribunal. First answer me this: Are you sure you will deny if you do not flee, or are you not sure? For if you are sure, you have denied already, because by presupposing that you will deny, you have given yourself up to that about which

you have made such a presupposition; and now it is vain for you to think of flight, that you may avoid denying, when in intention you have denied already. But if you are doubtful on that point, why do you not, in the incertitude of your fear wavering between the two different issues, presume that you are able rather to act a confessor's part and so add to your safety, that you may not flee, just as you presuppose denial to send you off a fugitive? The matter stands thus—we have either both things in our own power, or they wholly lie with God. If it is ours to confess or to deny, why do we not anticipate the nobler thing, that is, that we shall confess? If you are not willing to confess, you are not willing to suffer; and to be unwilling to confess is to deny. But if the matter is wholly in God's hand, why do we not leave it to His will, recognising His might and power in that, just as He can bring us back to trial when we flee, so is He able to screen us when we do not flee; yes, and even living in the very heart of the people? Strange conduct, is it not, to honour God in the matter of flight from persecution, because He can bring you back from your flight to stand before the judgment-seat; but in regard of witness-bearing, to do Him high dishonour by despairing of power at His hands to shield you from danger? Why do you not rather on this, the side of constancy and trust in God, say, I do my part; I depart not; God, if He choose, will Himself be my protector? It beseems us better to retain our position in submission to the will of God, than to flee at our own will. Rutilius, a saintly martyr, after having ofttimes fled from persecution from place to place, nay, having bought security from danger, as he thought, by money, was, notwithstanding the complete security he had, as he thought, provided for himself, at last unexpectedly seized, and being brought before the magistrate, was put to the torture and cruelly mangled,—a punishment, I believe, for his fleeing,—and thereafter he was consigned to the flames, and thus paid to the mercy of God the suffering which he had shunned. What else did the Lord mean to show us by this example, but that we ought not to flee from persecution because it avails us nothing if God disapproves?

6. Nay, says some one, he fulfilled the command, when he fled from city to city. For so a certain individual, but a fugitive likewise, has chosen to maintain, and others have done the same who are unwilling to understand the meaning of that declaration of the Lord, that they may use it as a cloak for their cowardice, although it has had its persons as well as its times and reasons to which it specially applies. "When they begin," He says, "to persecute you, flee from city to city."[1] We maintain that this belongs specially to the persons of the apostles, and to their times and circumstances, as the following sentences will show, which are suitable only to the apostles: "Do not go into the way of the Gentiles, and into a city of the Samaritans do not enter: but go rather to the lost sheep of the house of Israel."[2] But to us the way of the Gentiles is also open, as in it we in fact were found, and to the very last we walk; and no city has been excepted. So we preach throughout all the world; nay, no special care even for Israel has been laid upon us, save as also we are bound to preach to all nations. Yes, and if we are apprehended, we shall not be brought into Jewish councils, nor scourged in Jewish synagogues, but we shall certainly be sisted before Roman magistrates and judgment-seats.[3] So, then, the circumstances of the apostles even required the injunction to flee, their mission being to preach first to the lost sheep of the house of Israel. That therefore this preaching might be fully accomplished in the case of those among whom this behoved first of all to be carried out—that the sons might receive bread before the dogs, for that reason He commanded them to flee then for a time—not with the object of eluding danger, under the plea strictly speaking which persecution urges (rather He was in the habit of proclaiming that they would suffer persecutions, and of teaching that these must be endured), but in order to further the proclamation of the gospel message, lest by their being at once put down, the diffusion of the gospel too might be prevented. For neither were they to flee to any city as if by stealth, but as if everywhere about to proclaim their message, and for this every-

[1] Matt. x. 23.   [2] Matt. x. 5.   [3] Matt. x. 17.

where about to undergo persecutions, until they should fulfil their teaching. Accordingly the Saviour says, "Ye will not go over all the cities of Israel."[1] So the command to flee was restricted to the limits of Judea. But no command that shows Judea to be specially the sphere for preaching applies to us, now that the Holy Spirit has been poured out upon all flesh. Therefore Paul and the apostles themselves, mindful of the precept of the Lord, bear this solemn testimony before Israel, which they had now filled with their doctrine—saying, "It was necessary that the word of God should have been first delivered to you; but seeing ye have rejected it, and have not thought yourselves worthy of eternal life, lo, we turn to the Gentiles."[2] And from that time they turned their steps away, as those who went before them had laid it down, and departed into the way of the Gentiles, and entered into the cities of the Samaritans; so that, in very deed, their sound went forth into all the earth, and their words to the end of the world.[3] If, therefore, the prohibition against setting foot in the way of the Gentiles, and entering into the cities of the Samaritans, has come to an end, why should not the command to flee, which was issued at the same time, have come also to an end? Accordingly, from the time when, Israel having had its full measure, the apostles went over to the Gentiles, they neither fled from city to city, nor hesitated to suffer. Nay, Paul too, who had submitted to deliverance from persecution by being let down from the wall, as to do so was at this time a matter of command, refused in like manner now at the close of his ministry, and after the injunction had come to an end, to give in to the anxieties of the disciples, eagerly entreating him that he would not risk himself at Jerusalem, because of the sufferings in store for him which Agabus had foretold; but doing the very opposite, it is thus he speaks, "What do ye, weeping and disquieting my heart? For I could wish not only to suffer bonds, but also to die at Jerusalem, for the name of my Lord Jesus Christ."[4] And so they all said, "Let the will of the Lord be done." What was the will of the Lord? Certainly no longer to flee from persecution. Otherwise they

[1] Matt. x. 23. [2] Acts xiii. 36. [3] Ps. xix. 4. [4] Acts xxi. 13.

who had wished him rather to avoid persecution, might also have adduced that prior will of the Lord, in which He had commanded flight. Therefore, seeing even in the days of the apostles themselves, the command to flee was temporary, as were those also relating to the other things at the same time enjoined, that cannot continue with us which ceased with our teachers, even although it had not been issued specially for them; or if the Lord wished it to continue, the apostles did wrong who were not careful to keep fleeing to the last.

7. Let us now see whether also the rest of our Lord's ordinances accord with a lasting command of flight. In the first place, indeed, if persecution is from God, what are we to think of our being ordered to take ourselves out of its way, by the very party who brings it on us? For if He wanted it to be evaded, He had better not have sent it, that there might not be the appearance of His will being thwarted by another will. For He wished us either to suffer persecution or to flee from it. If to flee, how to suffer? If to suffer, how to flee? In fact, what utter inconsistency in the decrees of One who commands to flee, and yet urges to suffer, which is the very opposite! "Him who will confess me, *I* also will confess before my Father."[1] How will he confess, fleeing? How flee, confessing? "Of him who shall be ashamed of me, will I also be ashamed before my Father."[2] If I avoid suffering, I am ashamed to confess. "Happy they who suffer persecution for my name's sake."[3] Unhappy, therefore, they who, by running away, will not suffer according to the divine command. "He who shall endure to the end shall be saved."[4] How then, when you bid me flee, do you wish me to endure to the end? If views so opposed to each other do not comport with the divine dignity, they clearly prove that the command to flee had, at the time it was given, a reason of its own, which we have pointed out. But it is said, the Lord, providing for the weakness of some of His people, nevertheless, in His kindness, suggested also the haven of flight to them. For He was not able even without flight—a

[1] Matt. x. 32, 33.
[2] Mark viii. 38; Luke ix. 26.
[3] Matt. v. 11.
[4] Matt. x. 22.

protection so base, and unworthy, and servile—to preserve in persecution such as He knew to be weak! Whereas in fact He does not cherish, but ever rejects the weak, teaching first, not that we are to fly from our persecutors, but rather that we are not to fear them. "Fear not them who are able to kill the body, but are unable to do aught against the soul; but fear Him who can destroy both body and soul in hell."[1] And then what does He allot to the fearful? " He who will value his life more than me, is not worthy of me; and he who takes not up his cross and follows me, cannot be my disciple."[2] Last of all, in the Revelation, He does not propose flight to the " fearful,"[3] but a miserable portion among the rest of the outcast, in the lake of brimstone and fire, which is the second death.

8. He sometimes also fled from violence Himself, but for the same reason as had led Him to command the apostles to do so: that is, He wanted to fulfil His ministry of teaching; and when it was finished, I do not say He stood firm, but He had no desire even to get from His Father the aid of hosts of angels: finding fault, too, with Peter's sword. He likewise acknowledged, it is true, that His " soul was troubled, even unto death,"[4] and the flesh weak; with the design, [however,] first of all, that by having as His own trouble of soul and weakness of the flesh, He might show you that both the substances in Him were truly human, lest, as certain persons have now brought it in, you might be led to think either the flesh or the soul of Christ different from ours; and then, that, by an exhibition of their states, you might be convinced that they have no power at all of themselves without the spirit. And for this reason He puts first "the willing spirit,"[5] that, looking to the natures respectively of both the substances, you may see that you have in you the spirit's strength as well as the flesh's weakness, and even from this may learn what to do, and by what means to do it, and what to bring under what,—the weak, namely, under the strong, that you may not, as is now your fashion, make excuses on the ground of the

[1] Matt. x. 28.   [2] Matt. x. 37.   [3] Rev. xxi. 8.
[4] Matt. xxvi. 38.   [5] Matt. xxvi. 41.

weakness of the flesh, forsooth, but put out of sight the strength of the spirit. He also asked of His Father, that if it might be, the cup of suffering should pass from Him.[1] So ask you the like favour; but as He did, holding your position,—merely offering supplication, and adding, too, the other words: " but not what I will, but what Thou wilt." But when you run away, how will you make this request, taking, in that case, into your own hands the removal of the cup from you, and instead of doing what your Father wishes, doing what you wish yourself?

9. The teaching of the apostles was surely in everything according to the mind of God: they forgot and omitted nothing of the gospel. Where, then, do you show that they renewed the command to flee from city to city? In fact, it was utterly impossible that they should have laid down anything so utterly opposed to their own examples as a command to flee, while it was just from bonds, or the islands in which, for confessing, not fleeing from the Christian name, they were confined, they wrote their letters to the churches. Paul[2] bids us support the weak, but most certainly it is not when they flee. For how can the absent be supported by you? By bearing with them? Well, he says that people must be supported, if anywhere they have committed a fault through the weakness of their faith, just as [he enjoins] that we should comfort the fainthearted; he does not say, however, that they should be sent into exile. But when he urges us not to give place to evil,[3] he does not offer the suggestion that we should take to our heels, he only teaches that passion should be kept under restraint; and if he says that the time must be redeemed, because the days are evil,[4] he wishes us to gain a lengthening of life, not by flight, but by wisdom. Besides, he who bids us shine as sons of light,[5] does not bid us hide away out of sight as sons of darkness. He commands us to stand stedfast,[6] certainly not to act an opposite part by fleeing, and to be girt—to play the fugitive or oppose the gospel. He points out weapons, too, which persons who

[1] Matt. xxvi. 39.   [2] 1 Thess. v. 14.   [3] Eph. iv. 27.
[4] Eph. v. 16.   [5] 1 Thess. v. 5.   [6] 1 Cor. xv. 58.

intend to run away would not require. And among these he notes the shield[1] too, that ye may be able to quench the darts of the devil, when doubtless ye resist him, and sustain his assaults in their utmost force. Accordingly John also teaches that we must lay down our lives for the brethren;[2] much more, then, we must do it for the Lord. This cannot be fulfilled by those who flee. Finally, mindful of his own Revelation, in which he had heard the doom of the fearful, [and so] speaking from personal knowledge, he warns us that fear must be put away. "There is no fear," says he, "in love; but perfect love casteth out fear; because fear hath torment"—the fire of the lake, no doubt. "He that feareth is not perfect in love"[3]—to wit, the love of God. And yet who will flee from persecution, but he who fears? Who will fear, but he who has not loved? Yes; and if you ask counsel of the Spirit, what does He approve more than that utterance of the Spirit? For, indeed, it incites all almost to go and offer themselves in martyrdom, not to flee from it; so that we also make mention of it. If you are exposed to public infamy, says he, it is for your good; for he who is not exposed to dishonour among men is sure to be so before the Lord. Do not be ashamed; righteousness brings you forth into the public gaze. Why should you be ashamed of gaining glory? The opportunity is given you when you are before the eyes of men. So also elsewhere: seek not to die on bridal beds, nor in miscarriages, nor in soft fevers, but to die the martyr's death, that He may be glorified who has suffered for you.

10. But some, paying no attention to the exhortations of God, are readier to apply to themselves that Greek versicle of worldly wisdom, "He who fled will fight again;" perhaps also in the battle to flee again. And when will he who, as a fugitive, is a defeated man, be conqueror? A worthy soldier he furnishes to his commander Christ, who, so amply armed by the apostle, as soon as he hears persecution's trumpet, runs off from the day of persecution. I also will produce in answer a quotation taken from the world: "Is it a thing so very sad to die?"[4] He must die, in whatever way of it,

[1] Eph. vi. 16. [2] 1 John iii. 16. [3] 1 John iv. 18. [4] Æneid, xii. 646.

either as conquered or as conqueror. But although he has
succumbed in denying, he has yet faced and battled with the
torture. I had rather be one to be pitied than to be blushed
for. More glorious is the soldier pierced with a javelin in
battle, than he who has a safe skin as a fugitive. Do you
fear man, O Christian?—you who ought to be feared by the
angels, since you are to judge angels; who ought to be feared
by evil spirits, since you have received power also over evil
spirits; who ought to be feared by the whole world, since by
you, too, the world is judged. You are Christ-clothed, you
who flee before the devil, since into Christ you have been
baptized. Christ, who is in you, is treated as of small
account when you give yourself back to the devil, by becoming a fugitive before him. But, seeing it is from the Lord
you flee, you taunt all runaways with the futility of their purpose. A certain bold prophet also had fled from the Lord,
he had crossed over from Joppa in the direction of Tarsus,
as if he could as easily transport himself away from God;
but I find him, I do not say in the sea and on the land, but,
in fact, in the belly even of a beast, in which he was confined
for the space of three days, unable either to find death or
even thus escape from God. How much better the conduct
of the man who, though he fears the enemy of God, does not
flee from, but rather despises him, relying on the protection
of the Lord, or, if you will, having an awe of God all the
greater, the more that he has stood in His presence, says,
" It is the Lord, He is mighty. All things belong to Him;
wherever I am, I am in His hand: let Him do as He wills, I
go not away; and if it be His pleasure that I die, let Him
destroy me Himself, while I save myself for Him. I had
rather bring odium upon Him by dying by His will, than
by escaping through my own anger."

11. Thus ought every servant of God to feel and act,
even one in an inferior place, that he may come to have a
more important one, if he has made some upward step by his
endurance of persecution. But when persons in authority
themselves—I mean the very deacons, and presbyters, and
bishops—take to flight, how will a layman be able to see with

what view it was said, Flee from city to city? Thus, too, with the leaders turning their backs, who of the common rank will hope to persuade men to stand firm in the battle? Most assuredly a good shepherd lays down his life for the sheep, according to the word of Moses, when the Lord Christ had not as yet been revealed, but was already shadowed forth in himself: "If you destroy this people," he says, "destroy me also along with it."[1] But Christ, confirming these foreshadowings Himself, adds: "The bad shepherd is he who, on seeing the wolf, flees, and leaves the sheep to be torn in pieces."[2] Why, a shepherd like this will be turned off from the farm; the wages to have been given him at the time of his discharge will be kept from him as compensation; nay, even from his former savings a restoration of the master's loss will be required; for "to him who hath shall be given, but from him who hath not shall be taken away even that which he seemeth to have."[3] Thus Zechariah threatens: "Arise, O sword, against the shepherds, and pluck ye out the sheep; and I will turn my hand against the shepherds."[4] And against them both Ezekiel and Jeremiah declaim with kindred threatenings, for their not only wickedly eating of the sheep,—they feeding themselves rather than those committed to their charge,—but also scattering the flock, and, giving it over shepherdless, a prey to all the beasts of the field. And this never happens more than when in persecution the church is abandoned by the clergy. If any one recognises the Spirit also, he will hear him branding the runaways. But if it does not become the keepers of the flock to flee when the wolves invade it—nay, if that is absolutely unlawful (for He who has declared a shepherd of this sort a bad one has certainly condemned him; and whatever is condemned has, without doubt, become unlawful)—on this ground it will not be the duty of those who have been set over the church to flee in the time of persecution. But otherwise, if the flock should flee, the overseer of the flock would have no call to hold his ground, as his doing so in that

[1] Ex. xxxii. 32. [2] John x. 12.
[3] Luke viii. 18. [4] Zech. xiii. 7.

case would be, without good reason, to give to the flock protection, which it would not require in consequence of its liberty, forsooth, to flee.

12. So far, my brother, as the question proposed by you is concerned, you have our opinion in answer and encouragement. But he who inquires whether persecution ought to be shunned by us must now be prepared to consider the following question also: Whether, if we should not flee from it, we should at least buy ourselves off from it. Going further than you expected, therefore, I will also on this point give you my advice, distinctly affirming that persecution, from which it is evident we must not flee, must in like manner not even be bought off. The difference lies in the payment; but as flight is a buying off without money, so buying off is money-flight. Assuredly you have here too the counselling of fear. Because you fear, you buy yourself off; and so you flee. As regards your feet, you have stood; in respect of the money you have paid, you have run away. Why, in this very standing of yours there was a fleeing from persecution, in the release from persecution which you bought; but that you should ransom with money a man whom Christ has ransomed with His blood, how unworthy is it of God and His ways of acting, who spared not His own Son for you, that He might be made a curse for us, because cursed is he that hangeth on a tree,[1]—Him who was led as a sheep to be a sacrifice, and just as a lamb before its shearer, so opened not His mouth,[2] but gave His back to the scourges, nay, His cheeks to the hands of the smiter, and turned not away His face from spitting, and was numbered with the transgressors, and was delivered up to death, nay, the death of the cross. All this took place that He might redeem us from our sins. The sun ceded to us the day of our redemption; hell re-transferred the right it had in us, and our covenant is in heaven; the everlasting gates were lifted up, that the King of Glory, the Lord of might, might enter in,[3] after having redeemed man from earth, nay, from hell, that he might attain to heaven. What, now, are we to think of the man who strives against

[1] Rom. viii. 32; Gal. iii. 13.   [2] Isa. liii. 7.   [3] Ps. xxiv. 7.

that glorious One, nay, slights and defiles His goods, obtained at so great a ransom—no less, in truth, than His most precious blood? It appears, then, that it is better to flee than to fall in value, if a man will not lay out for himself as much as he cost Christ. And the Lord indeed ransomed him from the angelic powers which rule the world—from the spirits of wickedness, from the darkness of this life, from eternal judgment, from everlasting death. But *you* bargain for him with an informer, or a soldier, or some paltry thief of a ruler— under, as they say, the folds of the tunic—as if *he* were stolen goods whom Christ purchased in the face of the whole world, yes, and set at liberty. Will you value, then, this free man at any price, and possess him at any price, but the one, as we have said, it cost the Lord,—namely, His own blood? [And if not,] why then do you purchase Christ in the man in whom He dwells, as though He were some human property? No otherwise did Simon even try to do, when he offered the apostles money for the Spirit of Christ. Therefore this man also, who in buying himself has bought the Spirit of Christ, will hear that word, "Your money perish with you, since you have thought that the grace of God is to be had at a price!"[1] Yet who will despise him for being [what he is], a denier? For what says that extorter? Give me money: assuredly that he may not deliver him up, since he tries to sell you nothing else than that which he is going to give you for money. When you put that into his hands, it is certainly your wish *not* to be delivered up. But not delivered up, had you to be held up to public ridicule? While, then, in being unwilling to be delivered up, you are not willing to be thus exposed, by this unwillingness of yours you have denied that you are what you have been unwilling to have it made public that you are. Nay, you say, While I am unwilling to be held up to the public as being what I am, I have acknowledged that I am what I am unwilling to be so held up as being, that is, a Christian. Can Christ, therefore, claim that you, as a witness for Him, have stedfastly shown Him forth? He who buys himself off does

[1] Acts viii. 20.

nothing in that way. Before *one* it might, I doubt not, be said, You have confessed Him; so also, on the account of your unwillingness to confess Him before many you have denied Him. A man's very safety will pronounce that he has fallen while getting out of persecution's way. He has fallen, therefore, whose desire has been to escape. The refusal of martyrdom is denial. A Christian is preserved by his wealth, and for this end has his treasures, that he may not suffer, while he will be rich toward God. But it is the case that Christ was rich in blood for him. Blessed therefore are the poor, because, He says, the kingdom of heaven is theirs who have the soul only treasured up.[1] If we cannot serve God and mammon, can we be redeemed both by God and by mammon? For who will serve mammon more than the man whom mammon has ransomed? Finally, of what example do you avail yourself to warrant your averting by money the giving of you up? When did the apostles, dealing with the matter, in any time of persecution trouble, extricate themselves by money? And money they certainly had from the prices of lands which were laid down at their feet,[2] there being, without a doubt, many of the rich among those who believed—men, and also women, who were wont, too, to minister to their comfort. When did Onesimus, or Aquila, or Stephen,[3] give them aid of this kind when they were persecuted? Paul indeed, when Felix the governor hoped that he should receive money for him from the disciples,[4] about which matter he also dealt with the apostle in private, certainly neither paid it himself, nor did the disciples for him. Those disciples, at any rate, who wept because he was equally persistent in his determination to go to Jerusalem, and neglectful of all means to secure himself from the persecutions which had been foretold as about to occur there, at last say, "Let the will of the Lord be done." What was that will? No doubt that he should suffer for the name of the Lord, not that he should be bought off. For as Christ laid down His life for us, so, too, we

---

[1] Matt. v. 3.   [2] Acts iv. 34, 35.
[3] Stephanas is perhaps intended.—TR.   [4] Acts xxiv. 26.

should do for Him; and not only for the Lord Himself, nay, but likewise for our brethren on His account. This, too, is the teaching of John when he declares, not that we should pay for our brethren, but rather that we should die for them. It makes no difference whether the thing not to be done by you is to buy *off* a Christian, or to *buy* one. And so the will of God accords with this. Look at the condition—certainly of God's ordaining, in whose hand the king's heart is—of kingdoms and empires. For increasing the treasury there are daily provided so many appliances—registerings of property, taxes in kind, benevolences, taxes in money; but never up to this time has aught of the kind been provided by bringing Christians under some purchase-money for the person and the sect, although enormous gains could be reaped from numbers too great for any to be ignorant of them. Bought with blood, paid for with blood, we owe no money for our head, because Christ is our Head. It is not fit that Christ should cost us money. How could martyrdoms, too, take place to the glory of the Lord, if by tribute we should pay for the liberty of our sect? And so he who stipulates to have it at a price, opposes the divine appointment. Since, therefore, Cæsar has imposed nothing on us after this fashion of a tributary sect—in fact, such an imposition never can be made,—with Antichrist now close at hand, and gaping for the blood, not for the money of Christians—how can it be pointed out to me that there is the command, "Render to Cæsar the things which are Cæsar's?"[1] A soldier, be he an informer or an enemy, extorts money from me by threats, exacting nothing on Cæsar's behalf; nay, doing the very opposite, when for a bribe he lets me go—Christian as I am, and by the laws of man a criminal. Of another sort is the *denarius* which I owe to Cæsar, a thing belonging to him, about which the question then was started, it being a tribute coin due indeed by those subject to tribute, not by children. Or how shall I render to God the things which are God's,—certainly, therefore, His own likeness and money inscribed with His name, that is, a Christian man? But what do I owe God, as I do

[1] Matt. xxii. 21.

Cæsar the *denarius*, but the blood which His own Son shed for me? Now if I owe God, indeed, a human being and my own blood, but I am now in this juncture, that a demand is made upon me for the payment of that debt, I am undoubtedly guilty of cheating God if I do my best to withhold payment. I have well kept the commandment, if, rendering to Cæsar the things which are Cæsar's, I refuse to God the things which are God's.

13. But also to every one who asks me I will give on the plea of charity, not under any intimidation. Who asks?[1] He says. But he who uses intimidation does not ask. One who threatens if he does not receive, does not crave, but compel. It is not alms he looks for, who comes not to be pitied, but to be feared. I will give, therefore, because I pity, not because I fear, when the recipient honours God and returns me his blessing, not when rather he both believes that he has conferred a favour on me, and, beholding his plunder, says, "Guilt money." Shall I be angry even with an enemy? But enmities have also other grounds. Yet withal he did not say a betrayer, or persecutor, or one seeking to concuss you by his threats. For how much more shall I heap coals upon the head of a man of this sort, if I do not redeem myself by money? "In like manner," says Jesus, "to him who has taken away your coat, grant even your cloak also." But that refers to him who has sought to take away my property, not my faith. The cloak, too, I will grant, if I am not threatened with betrayal. If he threatens, I will demand even my coat back again. Even now, the declarations of the Lord have reasons and laws of their own. They are not of unlimited or universal application. And so He commands us to give to every one who asks, yet He Himself does not give to those who ask a sign. Otherwise, if you think that we should give indiscriminately to all who ask, that seems to me to mean that you would give, I say not wine to him who has a fever, but even poison or a sword to him who longs for death. But how we are to understand, "Make to yourselves friends of mammon,"[2] let

[1] Matt. v. 42.   [2] Luke xvi. 9.

the previous parable teach you. The saying was addressed to the Jewish people; inasmuch as, having managed ill the business of the Lord which had been entrusted to them, they ought to have provided for themselves out of the men of mammon, which we then were, friends rather than enemies, and to have delivered us from the dues of sins which kept us from God, if they bestowed the blessing upon us, for the reason given by the Lord, that when grace began to depart from them, they, betaking themselves to our faith, might be admitted into everlasting habitations. Hold now any other explanation of this parable and saying you like, if only you clearly see that there is no likelihood of our concussors, should we make them friends with mammon, then receiving us into everlasting abodes. But of what will not cowardice convince men? As if Scripture both allowed them to flee, and commanded them to buy off! Finally, it is not enough if one or another is so rescued. Whole churches have imposed tribute *en masse* on themselves. I know not whether it is matter for grief or shame when, among hucksters, and pickpockets, and bath-thieves, and gamesters, and pimps, Christians too are included as taxpayers in the lists of free soldiers and spies. Did the apostles, with so much foresight, make the office of overseer of this type, that the occupants might be able to enjoy their rule free from anxiety, under colour of providing [a like freedom for their flocks]? For such a peace, forsooth, Christ, returning to His Father, commanded to be bought from the soldiers by gifts like those you have in the Saturnalia!

14. But how shall we assemble together? say you; how shall we observe the ordinances of the Lord? To be sure, just as the apostles also did, who were protected by faith, not by money; which faith, if it can remove a mountain, can much more remove a soldier. Be your safeguard wisdom, not a bribe. For you will not have at once complete security from the people also, should you buy off the interference of the soldiers. Therefore all you need for your protection is to have both faith and wisdom: if you do not make use of these, you may lose even the deliverance which you

have purchased for yourself; while, if you do employ them, you can have no need of any ransoming. Lastly, if you cannot assemble by day, you have the night, the light of Christ luminous against its darkness. You cannot run about among them one after another. Be content with a church of threes. It is better that you sometimes should not see your crowds, than subject yourselves [to a tribute bondage]. Keep pure for Christ His betrothed virgin; let no one make gain of her. These things, my brother, seem to you perhaps harsh and not to be endured; but recall that God has said, "He who receives it, let him receive it,"[1] that is, let him who does not receive it go his way. He who fears to suffer, cannot belong to Him who suffered. But the man who does not fear to suffer, he will be perfect in love—in the love, it is meant, of God; "for perfect love casteth out fear."[2] "And therefore many are called, but few chosen."[3] It is not asked who is ready to follow the broad way, but who the narrow. And therefore the Comforter is requisite, who guides into all truth, and animates to all endurance. And they who have received Him will neither stoop to flee from persecution nor to buy it off, for they have the Lord Himself, One who will stand by us to aid us in suffering, as well as to be our mouth when we are put to the question.

[1] Matt. xix. 12.   [2] 1 John iv. 18.   [3] Matt. xxii. 14.

XV.

SCORPIACE.

ANTIDOTE FOR THE SCORPION'S STING.

1. THE earth brings forth, as if by suppuration, great evil from the diminutive scorpion. The poisons are as many as are the kinds of it, the disasters as many as are also the species of it, the pains as many as are also the colours of it. Nicander writes [on the subject of scorpions], and depicts them. And yet to smite with the tail—which tail will be whatever is prolonged from the hindmost part of the body, and scourges—is the one movement which they all use when making an assault. Wherefore that succession of knots in the scorpion, which in the inside is a thin poisoned veinlet, rising up with a bow-like bound, draws tight a barbed sting at the end, after the manner of an engine for shooting missiles. From which circumstance they also call after the scorpion, the warlike implement which, by its being drawn back, gives an impetus to the arrows. The point in their case is also a duct of extreme minuteness, to inflict the wound; and where it penetrates, it pours out poison. The usual time of danger is the summer season: fierceness hoists the sail when the wind is from the south and the south-west. Among cures, [certain] substances supplied by nature have very great efficacy; magic also puts on some bandage; the art of healing counteracts with lancet and cup. For some, making haste, take also beforehand a protecting draught; but sexual intercourse drains it off, and they are dry again. We have faith for a defence, if we are not smitten with distrust itself also, in immediately making the sign [of the cross over the wounded part],

and adjuring [that part in the name of Jesus], and besmearing the [poisoned] heel with [the gore of] the beast [when it has been crushed to death]. Finally, we often aid in this way even the heathen, seeing we have been endowed by God with that power which the apostle first used when he despised the viper's bite.[1] What, then, does this pen of yours offer, if faith is safe by what it has of its own? That it may be safe by what it has of its own also at other times, when it is subjected to scorpions of its own. These, too, have a troublesome littleness, and are of different sorts, and are armed in one manner, and are stirred up at a definite time, and that not another than one of burning heat. This among Christians is [a season of] persecution. When, therefore, faith is greatly agitated, and the church burning, as represented by the bush,[2] then the Gnostics break out, then the Valentinians creep forth, then all the opponents of martyrdoms bubble up, being themselves also hot, to strike, penetrate, kill. For, because they know that many are artless and also inexperienced, and weak moreover, that a very great number in truth are Christians who veer about with the wind and conform to its moods, they perceive that they are never to be approached more than when fear has opened the entrances to the soul, especially when some [display of] ferocity has already arrayed with a crown the faith of martyrs. Therefore, drawing along the tail hitherto, they first of all apply it to the feelings, or whip with it as if on empty space. Innocent persons undergo such suffering! So that you may suppose [the speaker] to be a brother or a heathen of the better sort. A sect troublesome to nobody so dealt with! Then they pierce. Men are perishing without a reason. For that they are perishing, and without a reason, is the first insertion. Then they now strike mortally. But the unsophisticated souls[3] know not what is written, and what meaning it bears, where and when and before whom we must confess, [or ought] save that this, to die for God, is, since He preserves me, not even artlessness, but folly, nay madness. If He kills me, how will

---

[1] Acts xxviii. 3.   [2] Ex. iii. 2.
[3] The opponents of martyrdoms are meant.—Tr.

it be His duty to preserve me? Once for all Christ died for us, once for all He was slain that we might not be slain. If He demands the like from me in return, does He also look for salvation from my death by violence? Or does God importune for the blood of men, especially if He refuses that of bulls and he-goats?[1] Assuredly He had rather have the repentance than the death of the sinner.[2] And how is He eager for the death of those who are not sinners? Whom will not these, and perhaps other subtle devices containing heretical poisons, pierce either for doubt if not for destruction, or for irritation if not for death? As for you, therefore, do you, if faith is on the alert, smite on the spot the scorpion with a curse, so far as you can, with your sandal, and leave it dying in its own stupefaction? But if it gluts the wound, it drives the poison inwards, and makes it hasten into the bowels; forthwith all the former senses become dull, the blood of the mind freezes, the flesh of the spirit pines away, loathing for the Christian name is accompanied by a sense of sourness. Already the understanding also seeks for itself a place where it may throw up; and thus, once for all, the weakness with which it has been smitten breathes out wounded faith either in heresy or in heathenism. And now the present state of matters is [such, that we are in] the midst of an intense heat, [under] the very dog-star of persecution, —a state originating doubtless with the dog-headed one himself.[3] Of some Christians the fire, of others the sword, of others the beasts, have made trial; others are hungering in prison for the martyrdoms of which they have had a taste in the meantime by being subjected to clubs and claws[4] besides. We ourselves, having been appointed for pursuit, are like hares being hemmed in from a distance; and heretics go about according to their wont. Therefore the state of the times has prompted me to prepare by my pen, in opposition to the little beasts which trouble our sect, our antidote against poison, that I may thereby effect cures. You who read will at the same time drink. Nor is the draught bitter. If the

[1] Ps. l. 13.   [2] Ezek. xxxiii. 11.   [3] i.e. the devil.—Tr.
[4] An instrument of torture, so called.—Tr.   [5] Ps. xix. 10.

utterances of the Lord are sweeter than honey and the honey-combs,[1] the juices are from that source. If the promise of God flows with milk and honey,[2] the ingredients which go to make that draught have the smack of this. "But woe to them who turn sweet into bitter, and light into darkness!"[3] For, in like manner, they also who oppose martyrdoms, representing salvation to be destruction, transmute sweet into bitter, as well as light into darkness; and thus, by preferring this very wretched life to that most blessed one, they put bitter for sweet, as well as darkness for light.

2. But not yet about the good to be got from martyrdom must we learn, without our having first about the duty of suffering it; nor must we about the usefulness of it, before we have about the necessity for it. The [question of the] divine warrant goes first—whether, [namely,] God has willed and also commanded ought of the kind, so that they who assert that it is not good are not plied with arguments for thinking it profitable save when they have been subdued [by those in favour of its having been divinely enjoined]. It is proper that heretics be driven[4] to duty, not enticed. Obstinacy must be conquered, not coaxed. And, certainly, that will be pronounced beforehand quite good enough, which will be shown to have been instituted and also enjoined by God. Let the Gospels wait a little while I set forth their root the Law, while I ascertain the will of God from those writings from which I recall to mind Himself also: "*I* am," says He, "God, thy God, who have brought thee out of the land of Egypt. Thou shalt have no other gods besides me. Thou shalt not make unto thee a likeness of those things which are in heaven, and which are in the earth beneath, and which are in the sea under the earth. Thou shalt not worship them, nor serve them. For I am the Lord thy God."[5] Likewise in the same [book of] Exodus: "Ye yourselves have seen that I have talked with you from heaven. Ye shall not make unto you gods of silver, neither shall ye

---

[1] Ps. xix. 10.
[2] Ex. iii. 17.
[3] Isa. v. 20.
[4] By argument, of course.—TR.
[5] Ex. xx. 2.

make unto you gods of gold."[1] To the following effect also, in Deuteronomy: "Hear, O Israel; The Lord thy God is one: and thou shalt love the Lord thy God with all thy heart and all thy might, and with all thy soul."[2] And again: "Neither do thou forget the Lord thy God, who brought thee forth from the land of Egypt, out of the house of bondage. Thou shalt fear the Lord thy God, and serve Him only, and cleave to Him, and swear by His name. Ye shall not go after strange gods, and the gods of the nations which are round about you, because the Lord thy God is also a jealous God among you, and lest His anger should be kindled against thee, and destroy thee from off the face of the earth."[3] But setting before them blessings and curses, He also says: "Blessings shall be yours, if ye obey the commandments of the Lord your God, whatsoever I command you this day, and do not wander from the way which I have commanded you, to go and serve other gods whom ye know not."[4] And as to rooting them out in every way: "Ye shall utterly destroy all the places wherein the nations, which ye shall possess by inheritance, served their gods, upon mountains and hills, and under shady trees. Ye shall overthrow all their altars, ye shall overturn and break in pieces their pillars, and cut down their groves, and burn with fire the graven images of the gods themselves, and destroy the names of them out of that place."[5] He further urges, [as to be kept in view by the Israelites] when they had entered the land of promise, and driven out its nations: "Take heed to thyself, that thou do not follow them after they be driven out from before thee, that thou do not inquire after their gods, saying, As the nations serve their gods, so let me do likewise."[6] But also says He: "If there arise among you a prophet himself, or a dreamer of dreams, and giveth thee a sign or a wonder, and it come to pass, and he say, Let us go and serve other gods, whom ye know not, do not hearken to the words of that prophet or dreamer, for the Lord your God proveth you, to know whether ye fear God with all your heart and with all your

[1] Ex. xx. 22, 23.   [2] Deut. vi. 4.   [3] Deut. vi. 12.
[4] Deut. xi. 27.   [5] Deut. xii. 2, 3.   [6] Deut. xii. 30.

soul. After the Lord your God ye shall go, and fear Him, and keep His commandments, and obey His voice, and serve Him, and cleave unto Him. But that prophet or dreamer shall die; for he has spoken to turn thee away from the Lord thy God."[1] But also in another section:[2] "If, however, thy brother, the son of thy father or of thy mother, or thy son, or thy daughter, or the wife of thy bosom, or thy friend who is as thine own soul, solicit thee, saying secretly, Let us go and serve other gods, which thou knowest not, nor did thy fathers, of the gods of the nations which are round about thee, very nigh unto thee or far off from thee, do not consent to go with him, and do not hearken to him. Thine eye shall not spare him, neither shalt thou pity, neither shalt thou preserve him; thou shalt certainly inform upon him. Thine hand shall be first upon him to kill him, and afterwards the hand of thy people; and ye shall stone him, and he shall die, seeing he has sought to turn thee away from the Lord thy God."[3] He adds likewise concerning cities, that if it appeared that one of these had, through the advice of unrighteous men, passed over to other gods, all its inhabitants should be slain, and everything belonging to it become accursed, and all the spoil of it be gathered together into all its places of egress, and be, even with all the people, burned with fire in all its streets in the sight of the Lord God; and, says He, "it shall not be for dwelling in for ever: it shall not be built again any more, and there shall cleave to thy hands nought of its accursed plunder, that the Lord may turn from the fierceness of His anger."[4] He has, from His abhorrence of idols, framed a series of curses too: "Cursed be the man who maketh a graven or a molten image, an abomination, the work of the hands of the craftsman, and putteth it in a secret place."[5] But in Leviticus He says: "Go not ye after idols, nor make to yourselves molten gods: I am the Lord your God."[6] And in other

---

[1] Deut. xiii. 1.

[2] Our division of the Scriptures by chapter and verse did not exist in the days of Tertullian.—Tr.

[3] Deut. xiii. 6.   [4] Deut. xiii. 16.   [5] Deut. xxvii. 15.   [6] Lev. xix. 4.

passages: "The children of Israel are my household servants; these are they whom I led forth from the land of Egypt:[1] I am the Lord your God. Ye shall not make you idols fashioned by the hand, neither rear you up a graven image. Nor shall ye set up a remarkable stone in your land [to worship it]: I am the Lord your God."[2] And these words indeed were first spoken by the Lord by the lips of Moses, being applicable certainly to whomsoever the Lord God of Israel may lead forth in like manner from the Egypt of a most superstitious world, and from the abode of human slavery. But from the mouth of every prophet in succession, sound forth also utterances of the same God, augmenting the same law of His by a renewal of the same commands, and in the first place announcing no other duty in so special a manner as the being on guard against all making and worshipping of idols; as when by the mouth of David He says: "The gods of the nations are silver and gold: they have eyes, and see not; they have ears, and hear not; they have a nose, and smell not; a mouth, and they speak not; hands, and they handle not; feet, and they walk not. Like to them shall be they who make them, and trust in them."[3]

3. Nor should I think it needful to discuss whether God pursues a worthy course in forbidding His own name and honour to be given over to a lie, or does so in not consenting that such as He has plucked from the maze of false religion should return again to Egypt, or does so in not suffering to depart from Him them whom He has chosen for Himself. Thus that, too, will not require to be treated by us, whether He has wished to be kept the rule which He has chosen to appoint, and whether He justly avenges the abandonment of the rule which He has wished to be kept; since He would have appointed it to no purpose if He had not wished it kept, and would have to no purpose wished it kept if He had been unwilling to uphold it. My next

---

[1] The words in the Septuagint are: ὅτι ἐμοὶ οἱ υἱοὶ Ἰσραὴλ οἰκέται εἰσίν, παῖδές μου οὗτοί εἰσιν οὓς ἐξήγαγον ἐκ γῆς Αἰγύπτου.
[2] Lev. xxv. 55, xxvi. 1.   [3] Ps. cxxxv. 15, cxv. 4.

step, indeed, is to put to the test these appointments of God
in opposition to false religions, the completely vanquished
as well as also the punished, since on these will depend the
entire argument for martyrdoms. Moses was apart with God
on the mountain, when the people, not brooking his absence,
which was so needful, seek to make gods for themselves, which,
for his own part, he will prefer to destroy.[1] Aaron is importuned, and commands that the earrings of their women be
brought together, that they may be thrown into the fire.
For the people were about to lose, as a judgment upon
themselves, the true ornaments for the ears, the words of
God. The wise fire makes for them the molten likeness of
a calf, reproaching them with having the heart where they
have their treasure also,—in Egypt, to wit, which clothed
with sacredness, among the other animals, a certain ox likewise. Therefore the slaughter of three thousand by their
nearest relatives, because they had displeased their so very
near relative God, solemnly marked both the commencement
and the deserts of the trespass. Israel having, as we are told
in Numbers,[2] turned aside [from their journey] at Sethim,
the people go to the daughters of Moab to gratify their lust:
they are allured to the idols, so that they committed whore-
dom with the spirit also: finally, they eat of their defiled
[sacrifices]; then they both worship the gods of the nation,
and are admitted to the rites of Beelphegor. For this lapse,
too, into idolatry, sister to adultery, it took the slaughter of
twenty-three thousand by the swords of their countrymen
to appease the divine anger. After the death of Joshua the
son of Nave they forsake the God of their fathers, and
serve idols, Baalim and Ashtaroth;[3] and the Lord in anger
delivered them up to the hands of spoilers, and they continued to be spoiled by them, and to be sold to their enemies,
and could not at all stand before their enemies. Whither-
soever they went forth, His hand was upon them for evil,
and they were greatly distressed. And after this God sets
judges (*critas*), the same as our censors, over them. But not
even these did they continue stedfastly to obey. So soon

[1] Ex. xxxii.   [2] Num. xxv. 1.   [3] Judg. ii. 8-13.

as one of the judges died, they proceeded to transgress more than their fathers had done by going after the gods of others, and serving and worshipping them. Therefore the Lord was angry. "Since, indeed," He says, "this nation have transgressed my covenant which I established with their fathers, and have not hearkened to my voice, I also will give no heed to remove from before them a man of the nations which Joshua left at his death."[1] And thus, throughout almost all the annals of the judges and of the kings who succeeded them, while the strength of the surrounding nations was preserved, He meted wrath out to Israel by war and captivity and a foreign yoke, as often as they turned aside from Him, especially to idolatry.

4. If, therefore, it is evident that from the beginning this kind of worship has both been forbidden—witness the commands so numerous and weighty—and that it has never been engaged in without punishment following, as examples so numerous and impressive show, and that no offence is counted by God so presumptuous as a trespass of this sort, we ought further to perceive the purport of both the divine threatenings and their fulfilments, which was even then commended not only by the not calling in question, but also by the enduring of martyrdoms, for which certainly He had given occasion by forbidding idolatry. For otherwise martyrdoms would not take place. And certainly He had supplied, as a warrant for these, His own authority, willing those events to come to pass for the occurrence of which He had given occasion. At present [it is important to bear that in mind], for we are getting severely stung concerning the will of God, and the scorpion repeats the prick, denying the existence of this will, finding fault with it, so that he either insinuates that there is another god, such that this is not his will, or none the less overthrows ours, seeing such is his will, or altogether denies [this] will of God, if he cannot deny Himself. But, for our part, contending elsewhere about [questions relating to] God, and about all the rest of the body of heretical teaching, we now draw before us definite

[1] Judg. ii. 20, 21.

lines[1] for one form of encounter, maintaining that this will, such as to have given occasion for martyrdoms, is that of not another god than the God of Israel, on the ground of the commandments relating to an always forbidden, as well as of the judgments upon a punished, idolatry. For if the keeping of a command involves the suffering of violence, this will be, so to speak, a command about keeping the command, requiring me to suffer that through which I shall be able to keep the command, violence namely, whatever of it threatens me when on my guard against idolatry. And certainly [in the case supposed] the Author of the command extorts compliance with it. He could not, therefore, have been unwilling that those events should come to pass by means of which the compliance will be manifest. The injunction is given me not to make mention of any other god, not even by speaking,—as little by the tongue as by the hand,—to fashion a god, and not to worship or in any way show reverence to another than Him only who thus commands me, whom I am both bid fear that I may not be forsaken by Him, and love with my whole being, that I may die for Him. Serving as a soldier under this oath, I am challenged by the enemy. If I surrender to them, I am as they are. In maintaining this oath, I fight furiously in battle, am wounded, hewn in pieces, slain. Who wished this fatal issue to his soldier, but he who sealed him by such an oath?

5. You have therefore the will of my God. We have cured this prick. Let us give good heed to another thrust touching the character of His will. It would be tedious to show that my God is good,—a truth with which the Marcionites have now been made acquainted by us. Meanwhile it is enough that He is called God for its being necessary that He should be believed to be good. For if any one make the supposition that God is evil, he will not be able to take his stand on both the constituents thereof: he will be bound either to affirm that he whom he has thought to be evil is not God, or that he whom he has proclaimed to be

---

[1] An allusion to what occurred in the games, there being lines to mark the space within which the contests were to be waged.—Tr.

God is good. Good, therefore, will be the will also of him who, unless he is good, will not be God. The goodness of the thing itself also which God has willed—of martyrdom, I mean—will show this, because only one who is good has willed what is good. I stoutly maintain that martyrdom is good, as required by the God by whom likewise idolatry is forbidden and punished. For martyrdom strives against and opposes idolatry. But to strive against and oppose evil cannot be ought but good. Not as if I denied that there is a rivalry in evil things with one another, as well as in good also; but this ground for it requires a different state of matters. For martyrdom contends with idolatry, not from some malice which they share, but from its own kindness; for it delivers from idolatry. Who will not proclaim that to be good which delivers from idolatry? What else is the opposition between idolatry and martyrdom, than that between life and death? Life will be counted to be martyrdom as much as idolatry to be death. He who will call life an evil, has death to speak of as a good. This frowardness also appertains to men,—to discard what is wholesome, to accept what is baleful, to avoid all dangerous cures, or, in short, to be eager to die rather than to be healed. For they are many who flee from the aid of physic also, many in folly, many from fear and false modesty. And the healing art has manifestly an apparent cruelty, by reason of the lancet, and of the burning iron, and of the great heat of the mustard; yet to be cut and burned, and pulled and bitten, is not on that account an evil, for it occasions helpful pains; nor will it be refused merely because it afflicts, but because it afflicts inevitably will it be applied. The good accruing is the apology for the frightfulness of the work. In short, that man who is howling and groaning and bellowing in the hands of a physician will presently load the same hands with a fee, and proclaim that they are the best operators, and no longer affirm that they are cruel. Thus martyrdoms also rage furiously, but for salvation. God also will be at liberty to heal for everlasting life by means of fires and swords, and all that is painful. But you will admire the physician at least even in that respect, that for the most part he employs like properties in the cures to counteract the properties of the diseases, when he aids, as it were, the wrong way, succouring by means of those things to which the affliction is owing. For he both checks heat by heat, by laying on a greater load; and subdues inflammation by leaving thirst unappeased, by tormenting rather; and contracts the superabundance of bile by every bitter little draught, and stops hemorrhage by opening a veinlet in addition. But you will think that God must be found fault with, and that for being jealous, if He has chosen to contend with a disease and to do good by imitating the malady, to destroy death by death, to dissipate killing by killing, to dispel tortures by tortures, to disperse[1] punishments by punishments, to bestow life by withdrawing it, to aid the flesh by injuring it, to preserve the soul by snatching it away. The wrongheadedness, as you deem it to be, is reasonableness; what you count cruelty is kindness. Thus, seeing God by brief [sufferings] effects cures for eternity, extol your God for your prosperity; you have fallen into His hands, but have happily fallen. He also fell into your sicknesses. Man always first provides employment for the physician; in short, he has brought upon himself the danger of death. He had received from his own Lord, as from a physician, the salutary enough rule to live according to the law, that he should eat of all indeed [that the garden produced], [and] should refrain from only one little tree which in the meantime the Physician Himself knew as a perilous one. He gave ear to him whom he preferred, and broke through self-restraint. He ate what was forbidden, and, surfeited by the trespass, suffered indigestion tending to death; he certainly richly deserving to lose his life altogether who wished to do so. But the inflamed tumour due to the trespass having been endured until in due time the medicine might be mixed, the Lord gradually prepared the means of healing—all the rules of faith, they also bearing a resemblance to [the causes of] the ailment, seeing they annul the word of death by the word of life, and diminish the trespass-

---

[1] Literally, "disperse in vapour."—Tr.

listening by a listening of allegiance. Thus, even when that Physician commands one to die, He drives out the lethargy of death. Why does man show reluctance to suffer now from a cure, what he was not reluctant then to suffer from a disorder? Does he dislike being killed for salvation, who did not dislike being killed for destruction? Will he feel squeamish with reference to the counter poison, who gaped for the poison?

6. But if, for the contest's sake, God had appointed martyrdoms for us, that thereby we might make trial with our opponent, in order that He may now keep bruising him by whom man chose to be bruised, here too generosity rather than harshness in God holds sway. For He wished to make man, now plucked from the devil's throat by faith, trample upon him likewise by courage, that he might not merely have escaped from, but also completely vanquished, his enemy. He who had called to salvation has been pleased to summon to glory also, that they who were rejoicing in consequence of their deliverance may be in transports when they are crowned likewise. With what good-will the world celebrates those games, the combative festivals and superstitious contests of the Greeks, involving forms both of worship and of pleasure, has now become clear in Africa also. As yet cities, by sending their congratulations severally, annoy Carthage, which was presented with the Pythian game after the racecourse had attained to an old age. Thus, by the world[1] it has been believed to be a most proper mode of testing proficiency in studies, to put in competition the forms of skill, to elicit the existing condition of bodies and of voices, the reward being the informer, the public exhibition the judge, and pleasure the decision. Where there are mere contests, there are some wounds: fists make reel, heels kick like butting rams, boxing-gloves mangle, whips leave gashes. Yet there will be no one reproaching the superintendent of the contest for exposing men to outrage. Suits for injuries lie outside the racecourse. But to the extent that those persons deal in discoloration, and gore, and swellings, he will design for them

[1] Literally, "age."—TR.

crowns, doubtless, and glory, and a present, political privileges, contributions by the citizens, images, statues, and—of such sort as the world can give—an eternity of fame, a resurrection by being kept in remembrance. The pugilist himself does not complain of feeling pain, for he wishes it; the crown closes the wounds, the palm hides the blood: he is excited more by victory than by injury. Will you count this man hurt whom you see happy? But not even the vanquished himself will reproach the superintendent of the contest for his misfortune. Shall it be unbecoming in God to bring forth kinds of skill and rules of His own into public view, into this open ground of the world, to be seen by men, and angels, and all powers?—to test flesh and spirit as to stedfastness and endurance?—to give to this one the palm, to this one distinction, to that one the privilege of citizenship, to that one pay?—to reject some also, and after punishing to remove them with disgrace? You dictate to God, forsooth, the times, or the ways, or the places in which to institute a trial concerning His own troop [of competitors], as if it were not proper for the Judge to pronounce the preliminary decision also. Well now, if He had put forth faith to suffer martyrdoms not for the contest's sake, but for its own benefit, ought it not to have had some store of hope, for the increase of which it might restrain desire of its own, and check its wish, in order that it might strive to mount up, seeing they also who discharge earthly functions are eager for promotion? Or how will there be many mansions in our Father's house, if not to accord with a diversity of deserts? How will one star also differ from another star in glory, unless in virtue of disparity in their rays?[1] But further, if, on that account, some increase of brightness also was appropriate to loftiness of faith, that gain ought to have been of some such sort as would cost great effort, poignant suffering, torture, death. But consider the requital, when flesh and life are paid away—than which in man there is nought more precious, the one from the hand of God, the other from His breath—that the very things are paid away in obtaining the

[1] 1 Cor. xv. 41.

benefit of which the benefit consists, that the very things are expended which may be acquired, that the same things are the price which are also the commodities. God had foreseen also other weaknesses incident to the condition of man,—the stratagems of the enemy, the deceptive aspects of the creatures, the snares of the world; that faith even after baptism would be endangered; that the most, after attaining unto salvation, would be lost again, through soiling the wedding-dress, through failing to provide oil for their torchlets—would be such as would have to be sought for over mountains and woodlands, and carried back upon the shoulders. He therefore appointed as second supplies of comfort, and the last means of succour, the fight of martyrdom and the baptism —thereafter free from danger—of blood. And concerning the happiness of the man who has partaken of these, David says: "Blessed are they whose iniquities are forgiven, and whose sins are covered. Blessed is the man to whom the Lord will not impute sin."[1] For, strictly speaking, there cannot any longer be reckoned ought against the martyrs, by whom in the baptism [of blood] life itself is laid down. Thus, "love covers the multitude of sins;"[2] and loving God, to wit, with all its strength (by which in the endurance of martyrdom it maintains the fight), with all its life[3] (which it lays down for God), it makes of a man a martyr. Shall you call these cures, counsels, methods of judging, spectacles, [illustrations of] even the barbarity of God? Does God covet man's blood? And yet I might venture to affirm that He does, if man also covets the kingdom of heaven, if man covets a sure salvation, if man also covets a second new birth. The exchange is displeasing to no one, which can plead, in justification of itself, that either benefit or injury is shared by the parties making it.

7. If the scorpion, swinging his tail in the air, still reproach us with having a murderer for our God, I shall shudder at the altogether foul breath of blasphemy which comes stinking from his heretical mouth; but I will embrace even such a God, with assurance derived from reason, by

[1] Ps. xxxii. 1; Rom. iv. 7, etc.   [2] 1 Pet. iv. 8.   [3] Matt. xxii. 37.

which reason even He Himself has, in the person of His own
Wisdom, by the lips of Solomon, proclaimed Himself to be
more than a murderer: Wisdom (Sophia), says He, has slain
her own children.[1] Sophia is Wisdom. She has certainly
slain them wisely if only into life, and reasonably if only
into glory. Of murder by a parent, oh the clever form!
Oh the dexterity of crime! Oh the proof of cruelty, which
has slain for this reason, that he whom it may have slain may
not die! And therefore what follows? Wisdom is praised
in hymns, in the places of egress; for the death of martyrs
also is praised in song. Wisdom behaves with firmness
in the streets, for with good results does she murder her
own sons.[2] Nay, on the top of the walls she speaks with
assurance, when indeed, according to Esaias, this one calls
out, "I am God's;" and this one shouts, "In the name of
Jacob;" and another writes, "In the name of Israel."[3] O good
mother! I myself also wish to be put among the number
of her sons, that I may be slain by her; I wish to be slain,
that I may become a son. But does she merely murder her
sons, or also torture them? For I hear God also, in another
passage, say, "I will burn them as gold is burned, and will
try them as silver is tried."[4] Certainly by the means of
torture which fires and punishments supply, by the testing
martyrdoms of faith. The apostle also knows what kind of
God he has ascribed to us, when he writes: "If God spared
not His own Son, but gave Him up for us, how did He not
with Him also give us all things?"[5] You see how divine
Wisdom has murdered even her own proper, first-born and
only Son, who is certainly about to live, nay, to bring back
the others also into life. I can say with the Wisdom of God:
It is Christ who gave Himself up for our offences.[6] Already
has Wisdom butchered herself also. The character of words

---

[1] Prov. ix. 2: "She hath killed her beasts." The corresponding words
in the Septuagint are, ἔσφαξε τὰ ἑαυτῆς θύματα. Augustine, in his *de
Civ. Dei*, xvii. 20, explains the victims (θύματα) to be *Martyrum victimas*.
—Tr.

[2] Prov. i. 20, 21; see the Septuagint version.   [3] Isa. xliv. 5.
[4] Zech. xiii. 9.   [5] Rom. viii. 32.   [6] Rom. iv. 25.

depends not on the sound only, but on the meaning also, and they must be heard not merely by ears, but also by minds. He who does not understand, believes God to be cruel; although for him also who does not understand, an announcement has been made to restrain his rashness in understanding otherwise [than aright]. "For who," says [the apostle], "has known the mind of the Lord? or who has been His counsellor, to teach Him? or who has pointed out to Him the way of understanding?"[1] But, indeed, the world has held it lawful for Diana of the Scythians, or Mercury of the Gauls, or Saturn of the Africans, to be appeased by human sacrifices; and in Latium to this day Jupiter has human blood given him to taste in the midst of the city; and no one makes it a matter of discussion, or imagines that it does not occur for some reason, or that it occurs by the will of his God, without having value. If our God, too, to have a sacrifice of His own, had required martyrdoms for Himself, who would have reproached Him for the deadly religion, and the mournful ceremonies, and the altar-pyre, and the undertaker-priest, and not rather have counted happy the man whom God should have devoured?

8. We keep therefore to the one position, and, in respect of this question only, summon to an encounter, whether martyrdoms have been commanded by God, that you may believe that they have been commanded by reason, if you know that they have been commanded by Him, because God will not command ought without reason. Since the death of His own saints is precious in His sight, as David sings,[2] it is not, I think, that one which falls to the lot of men generally, and is a debt due by all (rather is that one even disgraceful on account of the charge of trespass, and the desert of condemnation [to which it is to be traced]), but that [other] which is met in this very work—in bearing witness for religion, and maintaining the fight of confession in behalf of righteousness and the sacrament. As saith Esaias, "See how the righteous man perisheth, and no one layeth it to heart; and righteous men are taken away, and no one con-

[1] Rom. xi. 34.   [2] Ps. cxvi. 15.

sidereth it: for from before the face of unrighteousness the righteous man perisheth, and he shall have honour at his burial."[1] Here, too, you have both an announcement of martyrdoms, and [of] the recompense they bring. From the beginning, indeed, righteousness suffers violence. Forthwith, as soon as God has begun to be worshipped, religion has got ill-will for her portion. He who had pleased God is slain, and that by his brother. Beginning with kindred blood, in order that it might the more easily go in quest of that of strangers, ungodliness made the object of its pursuit, finally, that not only of righteous persons, but even of prophets also. David is persecuted; Elias put to flight; Jeremias stoned; Esaias cut asunder; Zacharias butchered between the altar and the temple, imparting to the hard stones lasting marks of his blood.[2] That person himself, at the close of the law and the prophets, and called not a prophet, but a messenger, is, suffering an ignominious death, beheaded to reward a dancing-girl. And certainly they who were wont to be led by the Spirit of God used to be guided by Himself to martyrdoms; so that they had even already to endure what they had also proclaimed as requiring to be borne. Wherefore the brotherhood of the three also, when the dedication of the royal image was the occasion of the citizens being pressed to offer worship, knew well what faith, which alone in them had not been taken captive, required,—namely, that they must resist idolatry to the death.[3] For they remembered also the words of Jeremias writing to those over whom that captivity was impending: "And now ye shall see borne upon [men's] shoulders the gods of the Babylonians, of gold and silver and wood, causing fear to the Gentiles. Beware, therefore, that *ye* also do not be altogether like the foreigners, and be seized with fear while ye behold crowds worshipping those gods before and behind, but say in your mind, Our duty is to worship Thee, O Lord."[4] Therefore, having got confidence from God, they said, when with strength of mind they set at defiance the king's threats against the disobedient: "There is no necessity for our making answer to this command of yours. For our

[1] Isa. lvii. 1. [2] Matt. xiv. 3. [3] Dan. iii. 12. [4] Baruch vi. 3.

God whom we worship is able to deliver us from the furnace of fire and from your hands; and then it will be made plain to you that we shall neither serve your idol, nor worship your golden image which you have set up."[1] O martyrdom even without suffering perfect! Enough did they suffer! enough were they burned, whom on this account God shielded, that it might not seem that they had given a false representation of His power. For forthwith, certainly, would the lions, with their pent-up and wonted savageness, have devoured Daniel also, a worshipper of none but God, and therefore accused and demanded by the Chaldeans, if it had been right that the worthy anticipation of Darius concerning God should have proved delusive. For the rest, every preacher of God, and every worshipper also, such as, having been summoned to the service of idolatry, had refused compliance, ought to have suffered, agreeably to the tenor of that argument too, by which the truth ought to have been recommended both to those who were then living and to those following in succession,—[namely,] that the suffering of its defenders themselves bespeak trust for it, because nobody would have been willing to be slain but one possessing the truth. Such commands as well as instances, remounting to earliest times, show that believers are under obligation to suffer martyrdom.

9. It remains for us, lest ancient times may perhaps have had the sacrament[2] [exclusively] their own, to review the modern Christian system, as though, being also from God, it might be different [from what preceded], and besides, therefore, opposed thereto in its code of rules likewise, so that its Wisdom knows not to murder her own sons! Evidently, in the case of Christ both the divine nature and the will and the sect are different [from any previously known]! He will have commanded either no martyrdoms at all, or those which must be understood in a sense different from the ordinary, being such a person as to urge no one to a risk of this kind, as to promise no reward to them who suffer for Him, because He does not wish them to suffer; and therefore does He

[1] Dan. iii. 16. [2] Tertullian means martyrdom.—Tr.

say, when setting forth His chief commands, "Blessed are they who are persecuted for righteousness' sake, for theirs is the kingdom of heaven."[1] The following statement, indeed, applies [in the first place] to all without restriction, then specially to the apostles themselves: " Blessed shall ye be when men shall revile you, and persecute you, and shall say all manner of evil against you, for my sake. Rejoice and be exceeding glad, since very great is your reward in heaven; for so used their fathers to do even to the prophets." So that He likewise foretold their having to be themselves also slain, after the example of the prophets. Though, even if He had appointed all this persecution in case He were obeyed for those only who were then apostles, assuredly through them, along with the entire sacrament, with the shoot of the name, with the layer of the Holy Spirit, the rule about enduring persecution also would have had respect to us too, as to disciples by inheritance, and, [as it were,] bushes from the apostolic seed. For even thus again does He address words of guidance to the apostles: "Behold, I send you forth as sheep in the midst of wolves;" and, "Beware of men, for they will deliver you up to the councils, and they will scourge you in their synagogues; and ye shall be brought before governors and kings for my sake, for a testimony against them and the Gentiles," etc.[2] Now when He adds, "But the brother will deliver up the brother to death, and the father the child; and the children shall rise up against their parents, and cause them to be put to death," He has clearly announced with reference to the others, [that they would be subjected to] this form of unrighteous conduct, which we do not find [exemplified] in the case of the apostles. For none of them had experience of a father or a brother as a betrayer, which very many of us have. Then He returns to the apostles: "And ye shall be hated of all men for my name's sake." How much more shall we, for whom there exists the necessity of being delivered up by parents too! Thus, by allotting this very betrayal, now to the apostles, now to all, He pours out the same destruction

[1] Matt. v. 10; Luke vi. 23.   [2] Matt. x. 16.

upon all the possessors of the name, on whom the name, along with the condition that it be an object of hatred, will rest. But he who will endure on to the end—this man will be saved. By enduring what but persecution, but betrayal, but death? For to endure to the end is nought else than to suffer the end. And therefore there immediately follows, "The disciple is not above his master, nor the servant above his own lord;" because, seeing the Master and Lord Himself was stedfast in suffering persecution and betrayal and death, much more will it be the duty of His servants and disciples to bear the same, that they may not seem as if superior to Him, to have got an immunity from the assaults of unrighteousness, since this itself should be glory enough for them, to be conformed to the sufferings of their Lord and Master; and, preparing them for the endurance of these, He reminds them that they must not fear such persons as kill the body only, but are not able to destroy the soul, but that they must dedicate fear to Him rather who has such power that He can kill both body and soul, and destroy them in hell. Who, pray, are these slayers of the body only, but the governors and kings aforesaid—men, I ween? Who is the ruler of the soul also, but God only? Who is this but the threatener of fires [hereafter], but He without whose will not even one of two sparrows falls to the ground, that is, not even one of the two substances of man, flesh or spirit, because the number of our hairs also has been recorded before Him? Fear ye not, therefore. When He adds, "Ye are of more value than many sparrows," He makes promise that we shall not in vain —that is, not without profit—fall to the ground if we choose to be killed by men rather than by God. "Whosoever therefore will confess in me before men, in him will I confess also before my Father who is in heaven;[1] and whosoever shall deny me before men, him will I deny also before my Father who is in heaven." Clear, as I think, are the terms used in announcing, and the way to explain, the confession

[1] The words in the Greek, though correctly rendered in our authorized version, are, when translated literally, what Tertullian represents them to be.—TR.

as well as the denial, although the mode of putting them is different. He who confesses himself a Christian, beareth witness that he is Christ's; he who is Christ's must be in Christ. If he is in Christ, he certainly confesses in Christ, when he confesses himself a Christian. For he cannot be this without being in Christ. Besides, by confessing in Christ he confesses Christ too; since, by virtue of being a Christian, he is in Christ, while [Christ] Himself also is in him. For if you have made mention of day, you have also held out to view the element of light which gives us day, although you may not have made mention of light. Thus, albeit He has not expressly said, "He who will confess me," [yet] the conduct involved in daily confession is not different from what is meant in our Lord's declaration. For he who confesses himself to be what he is, that is, a Christian, confesses that likewise by which he is it, that is, Christ. Therefore he who has denied that he is a Christian, has denied in Christ, by denying that he is in Christ while he denies that he is a Christian; and, on the other hand, by denying that Christ is in him, while He denies that he is in Christ, he will deny Christ too. Thus both he who will deny in Christ will deny Christ, and he who will confess in Christ will confess Christ. It would have been enough, therefore, though our Lord had made an announcement about confessing merely. For, from His mode of presenting confession, it might be decided beforehand with reference to its opposite too—denial, that is—that denial is repaid by the Lord with denial, just as confession is with confession. And therefore, since in the mould in which the confession has been cast the state of [the case with reference to] denial also may be perceived, it is evident that to another manner of denial belongs what the Lord has announced concerning it, in terms different from those in which He speaks of confession, when He says, "Who will deny me," not "Who will deny in me." For He had foreseen that this form of violence also would, for the most part, immediately follow when any one had been forced to renounce the Christian name,—that he who had denied that he was a Christian would be compelled to deny Christ Himself too by blaspheming Him. As not long ago, alas, we shuddered at the struggle waged in this way by some with their entire faith, which had had favourable omens. Therefore it will be to no purpose to say, "Though I shall deny that I am a Christian, I shall not be denied by Christ, for I have not denied Himself." For even so much will be inferred from that denial, by which, seeing he denies Christ in him by denying that he is a Christian, he has denied [Christ] Himself also. But there is more, because He threatens likewise shame with shame [in return]: "Whosoever shall be ashamed of me before men, of him will I also be ashamed before my Father who is in heaven." For He was aware that denial is produced even most of all by shame, that the state of the mind appears in the forehead, that the wound of shame precedes that in the body.

10. But as to those who think that not here, that is, not within this environment of earth, nor during this period of existence, nor before men possessing this nature shared by us all, has confession been appointed to be made, what a supposition is theirs, being at variance with the whole order of things of which we have experience in these lands, and in this life, and under human authorities! Doubtless, when the souls have departed from their bodies, and begun to be put upon trial in the several stories of the heavens, with reference to the engagement [under which they have come to Jesus], and to be questioned about those hidden mysteries of the heretics, they must then confess before the real powers and the real men,—the Teleti,[1] to wit, and the Abascanti,[2] and the Acineti[3] of Valentinus! For, say [the promulgators of such views], even the Demiurge himself did not uniformly approve of the men of our world, whom he counted as a drop of a bucket,[4] and the dust of the threshing-floor, and spittle and locusts, [and] put on a level even with brute beasts. Clearly, it is so written. Yet not therefore must we understand that there is, besides us, another kind of man, which—for it is evidently [thus in the case proposed]—has been able to assume without in-

[1] The perfect. [2] The spell-resisting. [3] The stedfast. [4] Isa. xl. 15.

validating a comparison [between the two kinds], both the characteristics of the race and a unique property. For even if the life was tainted, so that condemned to contempt it might be likened to objects held in contempt, the nature was not forthwith taken away, so that there might be supposed to be another under its name. Rather is the nature preserved, though the life blushes; nor does Christ know other men than those with reference to whom He says, "Whom do men say that I am?"[1] And, "As ye would that men should do to you, do ye likewise so to them."[2] Consider whether He may not have preserved a race such that He is looking for a testimony to Himself from them, as well as consisting of those on whom He enjoins the interchange of righteous dealing. But if I should urgently demand that those heavenly men be described to me, Aratus will sketch more easily Perseus, and Cepheus, and Erigone, and Ariadne, among the constellations. But who prevented the Lord from clearly prescribing that confession by men likewise has to be made where He plainly announced that His own would be; so that the statement might have run thus: "Whosoever shall confess in me before men in heaven, I also will confess in him before my Father who is in heaven?" He ought to have saved me from this mistake about confession on earth, which He would not have wished me to take part in, if He had commanded one in heaven; for I knew no other men but the inhabitants of the earth, man himself even not having up to that time been observed in heaven. Besides, what is the credibility of the things [alleged], that, being after death raised to heavenly places, I should be put to the test there, whither I would not be translated without being already tested, that I should there be tried in reference to a command where I could not come, but to find admittance? Heaven lies open to the Christian before the way to it does; because there is no way to heaven, but to him to whom heaven lies open; and he who reaches it will enter. What powers, keeping guard at the gate, do I hear you affirm to exist in accordance with Roman super-

[1] Matt. xvi. 18.   [2] Matt. vii. 12 and Luke vi. 31.

stition, with a certain Carnus, and a Forculus, and a Limentinus? What powers do you set in order at the railings? If you have ever read in David, "Lift up your gates, ye princes, and let the everlasting gates be lifted up; and the King of glory shall enter in;"[1] if you have also heard from Amos, "Who buildeth up to the heavens his way of ascent, and is such as to pour forth his abundance [of waters] over the earth;"[2] know that both that way of ascent was thereafter levelled with the ground, by the footsteps of the Lord, and an entrance thereafter opened up by the might of Christ, and that no delay or inquest will meet Christians on the threshold, since they have there to be not discriminated from one another, but owned, and not put to the question, but received in. For though you think heaven still shut, remember that the Lord left here to Peter, and through him to the church, the keys of it, which every one who has been here put to the question, and also made confession, will carry with him. But the devil stoutly affirms that we must confess there, to persuade us that we must deny here. I shall send before me fine documents, to be sure, [in support of my cause:] I shall carry with me excellent keys, the fear of them who kill the body only, but do nought against the soul: I shall be graced by the neglect of this command: I shall stand with credit in heavenly places, who could not stand in earthly: I shall hold out against the greater powers, who yielded to the lesser: I shall deserve to be at length let in, though now shut out. It readily occurs to one to remark further, "If it is in heaven that men must confess, it is here too that they must deny." For where the one is, there both are. For contraries always go together. There will need to be carried on in heaven persecution even, which is the occasion of confession or denial. Why, then, do you refrain, O most presumptuous heretic, from transporting to the world above the whole series of means proper to the intimidation of Christians, and especially to put there the very hatred for the name, where Christ rules at the right hand of the Father? Will you plant there both synagogues

[1] Ps. xxiv. 7. [2] Amos ix. 6.

of the Jews—fountains of persecution—before which the
apostles endured the scourge, and heathen assemblages with
their own circus, forsooth, where they readily join in the cry,
Death to the third race ?[1] But ye are bound to produce
in the same place both our brothers, and fathers, and children, and mothers-in-law, and daughters-in-law, and those of
our household, through whose agency the betrayal has been
appointed [to happen]; likewise kings, and governors, and
armed authorities, before whom the matter at issue must be
contested. Assuredly there will be in heaven a prison also,
destitute of the sun's rays or full of light unthankfully, and
fetters of the zones perhaps, and, for a rack-horse, the axis
itself which whirls [the heavens round]. Then, if a Christian
is to be stoned, hail-storms will be near; if burned, thunderbolts are at hand; if butchered, the armed Orion will exercise
his function; if put an end to by beasts, the north will send
forth the bears, the Zodiac the bulls and the lions. He who
will endure these assaults to the end, the same shall be saved.
Will there be then, in heaven, both an end, and suffering,
and killing, and the first confession? And where will be
the flesh requisite for all this? Where the body which
alone has to be killed by men? Unerring reason has commanded us to set forth these things in even a playful manner;
nor will any one thrust out the bar consisting in this objection [we have offered], so as not to be compelled to transfer
the whole array of means proper to persecution, all the
powerful instrumentality which has been provided for dealing with this matter, to the place where he has put the
court before which confession should be made. Since confession is elicited by persecution, and persecution ended in
confession, there cannot but be at the same time, in attendance upon these, the instrumentality which determines both
the entrance and the exit, that is, the beginning and the end.
But both hatred for the name will be here, and persecution
breaks out here, and betrayal brings men forth here, and

[1] More literally, "How long shall we suffer the third race!" The
Christians are meant; the first race being the heathen, and the second
the Jews.—Tr.

examination uses force here, and torture rages here, and confession or denial completes this whole course of procedure on the earth. Therefore, if the other things are here, confession also is not elsewhere; if confession is elsewhere, the other things also are not here. Certainly the other things are not elsewhere; therefore neither is confession in heaven. Or, if they will have it that the manner in which the heavenly examination and confession take place is different, it will certainly be also incumbent on them to devise a mode of procedure of their own of a very different kind, and opposed to that method which is indicated in the Scriptures. And we may be able to say, Let them consider [whether what they imagine to exist does so], if so be that this course of procedure, proper to examination and confession on earth— a course which has persecution as the source in which it originates, and which pleads dissension in the state—is preserved to its own faith, if so be that we must believe just as is also written, understand just as is spoken. Here I endure the entire course [in question], the Lord Himself not appointing a different quarter of the world [for my doing so]. For what does He add after finishing with confession and denial? "Think not that I am come to send peace on earth, but a sword,"—undoubtedly on the earth. "For I am come to set a man at variance against his father, and the daughter against her mother, and the mother-in-law against her daughter-in-law. And a man's foes shall be they of his own household."[1] For so is it brought to pass, that the brother delivers up the brother to death, and the father the son: and the children rise up against the parents, and cause them to die. And he who endureth to the end, let that man be saved.[2] So that this whole course of procedure characteristic of the Lord's sword, which has been sent not to heaven, but to earth, makes confession also to be there, which by enduring to the end is to issue in the suffering of death.

11. In the same manner, therefore, we maintain that the other announcements too refer to the condition of martyr-

[1] Matt. x. 34.   [2] Matt. x. 21.

dom. "He," says Jesus, "who will value his own life also more than me, is not worthy of me,"[1]—that is, he who will rather live by denying, than die by confessing, me; and " he who findeth his life shall lose it; but he who loseth it for my sake shall find it."[2] Therefore indeed he finds it, who in winning life denies; but he who thinks that he wins it by denying, will lose it in hell. On the other hand, he who, through confessing, is killed, will lose it for the present, but is also about to find it unto everlasting life. In fine, governors themselves, when they urge men to deny, say, Save your life; and, Do not lose your life. How would Christ speak, but in accordance with the treatment to which the Christian would be subjected? But when He forbids thinking about what answer to make at a judgment-seat,[3] He is preparing His own servants [for what awaited them], He gives the assurance that the Holy Spirit will answer [by them]; and when He wishes a brother to be visited in prison,[4] He is commanding that those about to confess be the objects of solicitude; and He is soothing their sufferings when He asserts that God will avenge His own elect.[5] In the parable also [which speaks] of the withering of the word-[corn][6] after the green blade had sprung up, He is drawing a picture with reference to the burning heat of persecutions. If these announcements are not understood as they are made, without doubt they signify something else than the sound indicates; and there will be one thing [expressed] in the words, another [contained] in their meanings, as is the case with allegories, with parables, with riddles. Whatever wind of reasoning, therefore, these scorpions may catch [in their sails], with whatever subtlety they may attack, there is now one line of defence:[7] an appeal will be made to the facts themselves, whether they occur as the Scriptures represent that they would; since another thing will then be meant in the Scriptures if that very one [which seems to be so] is not found in actual facts. For what is written, this will

[1] Luke xiv. 26. [2] Matt. x. 39. [3] Matt. x. 19.
[4] Matt. xxv. 36. [5] Luke xviii. 7. [6] Matt. xiii. 3.
[7] See note, a. 4.

needs come to pass. Besides, what is written will then come to pass, if something different does not. But, lo! we are both regarded as persons to be hated by all men for the sake of the name, as it is written; and are delivered up by our nearest of kin also, as it is written; and are brought before magistrates, and examined, and tortured, and make confession, and are ruthlessly killed, as it is written. So the Lord ordained. If He ordained these events otherwise, why do they not come to pass otherwise than He ordained them, that is, as He ordained them? And yet they do not come to pass otherwise than He ordained. Therefore, as they come to pass, so He ordained; and as He ordained, so they come to pass. For neither would they have been permitted to occur otherwise than He ordained, nor for His part would He have ordained otherwise than He would wish them to occur. Thus these passages of Scripture will not mean ought else than we recognise in actual facts; or if those events are not yet taking place which are announced, how are those taking place which have not been announced? For these events which are taking place have not been announced, if those which are announced are different, and not these which are taking place. Well now, seeing the very occurrences are met with in actual life which are believed to have been expressed with a different meaning in words, what would happen if they were found to have come to pass in a different manner [than had been revealed]? But this will be the waywardness of faith, not to believe what has been demonstrated, to assume the truth of what has not been demonstrated. And to this waywardness I will offer the following objection also, that if these events which occur as is written will not be the very ones which are announced, those too [which are meant] ought not to occur as is written, that they themselves also may not, after the example of these [others], be in danger of exclusion, since there is one thing in the words and another in the facts; and there remains that even the events which have been announced are not seen when they occur, if they are announced otherwise than they have to occur. And how will those be believed [to have come to pass], which will not have been announced as they come to pass? Thus heretics, by not believing what is announced as it has been shown to have taken place, believe what has not been even announced.

12. Who, now, should know better the marrow of the Scriptures than the school of Christ itself?—the persons whom the Lord both chose for Himself as scholars, certainly to be fully instructed in all points, and appointed to us for masters, certainly to instruct us in all points. To whom would He have rather made known the veiled import of His own language, than to him to whom He disclosed the likeness of His own glory—to Peter, to John, to James, and afterwards to Paul, to whom He granted participation in [the joys of] paradise too, prior to his martyrdom? Or do they also write differently from what they think—teachers using deceit, not truth? Addressing the Christians of Pontus, Peter, at all events, says, "How great indeed is the glory, if ye suffer patiently, without being punished as evil-doers! For this is a lovely feature, [and] even hereunto were ye called, since Christ also suffered for us, leaving you Himself as an example, that ye should follow His own steps."[1] And again: "Beloved, be not alarmed by the fiery trial which is taking place among you, as though some strange thing happened unto you. For, inasmuch as ye are partakers of Christ's sufferings, do ye rejoice; that, when His glory shall be revealed, ye may be glad also with exceeding joy. If ye are reproached for the name of Christ, happy are ye; because glory and the Spirit of God rest upon you: if only none of you suffer as a murderer, or as a thief, or as an evil-doer, or as a busybody in other men's matters; yet [if any man suffer] as a Christian, let him not be ashamed, but let him glorify God on this behalf."[2] John, in fact, exhorts us to lay down our lives even for our brethren,[3] affirming that there is no fear in love: "For perfect love casteth out fear, since fear has punishment; and he who fears is not perfect in love."[4] What fear would it be better to understand [as here meant], than that which gives rise to denial? What love does he assert to be perfect, but that which puts fear to

[1] 1 Pet. ii. 20. [2] 1 Pet. iv. 12. [3] 1 John iii. 16. [4] 1 John iv. 18.

flight, and gives courage to confess? What penalty will he appoint as the punishment of fear, but that which he who denies is about to pay, who has to be slain, body and soul, in hell? And if he teaches that we must die for the brethren, how much more for the Lord,—he being sufficiently prepared, by his own Revelation too, for giving such advice! For indeed the Spirit had sent the injunction to the angel of the church in Smyrna: "Behold, the devil shall cast some of you into prison, that ye may be tried ten days. Be thou faithful unto death, and I will give thee a crown of life."[1] Also to the angel of the church in Pergamus [mention was made] of Antipas,[2] the very faithful martyr, who was slain where Satan dwelleth. Also to the angel of the church in Philadelphia[3] [it was signified] that he who had not denied the name of the Lord was delivered from the last trial. Then to every conqueror the Spirit promises now the tree of life, and exemption from the second death; now the hidden manna, with the stone of glistening whiteness, and the name unknown [to every man save him that receiveth it]; now power to rule with a rod of iron, and the brightness of the morning star; now the being clothed in white raiment, and not having the name blotted out of the book of life, and being made in the temple of God a pillar with the inscription on it of the name of God and of the Lord, and of the heavenly Jerusalem; now a sitting with the Lord on His throne, —which once was persistently refused to the sons of Zebedee.[4] Who, pray, are these so blessed conquerors, but martyrs in the strict sense of the word? For indeed theirs are the victories whose also are the fights; theirs, however, are the fights whose also is the blood. But the souls of the martyrs both peacefully rest in the meantime under the altar,[5] and support their patience by the assured hope of revenge; and, clothed in their robes, wear the dazzling halo of brightness, until others also may fully share in their glory. For yet again a countless throng are revealed, clothed in white and distinguished by palms of victory, celebrating their triumph doubtless over

[1] Rev. ii. 10.   [2] Rev. ii. 13.   [3] Rev. iii. 10.
[4] Matt. xx. 20-28.   [5] Rev. vi. 9.

Antichrist, since one of the elders says, "These are they who come out of that great tribulation, and have washed their robes, and made them white in the blood of the Lamb."[1] For the flesh is the clothing of the soul. The uncleanness, indeed, is washed away by baptism, but the stains are changed into dazzling whiteness by martyrdom. For Esaias also promises, that out of red and scarlet there will come forth the whiteness of snow and wool.[2] When great Babylon likewise is represented as drunk with the blood of the saints,[3] doubtless the supplies needful for her drunkenness are furnished by the cups of martyrdoms; and what suffering the fear of martyrdoms will entail, is in like manner shown. For among all the castaways, nay, taking precedence of them all, are the fearful. "But the fearful," says John—and then come the others—"will have their part in the lake of fire and brimstone."[4] Thus fear, which, as stated in his epistle, love drives out, has punishment.

13. But how Paul, an apostle, from being a persecutor, who first of all shed the blood of the church, though afterwards he exchanged the sword for the pen, and turned the dagger into a plough[share], being [first] a ravening wolf of Benjamin, then himself supplying food as did Jacob,[5]— how he, [I say,] speaks in favour of martyrdoms, now to be chosen by himself also, when, rejoicing over the Thessalonians, he says, "So that we glory in you in the churches of God, for your patience and faith in all your persecutions and tribulations, in which ye endure a manifestation of the righteous judgment of God, that ye may be accounted worthy of His kingdom, for which ye also suffer!"[6] As also in his Epistle to the Romans: "And not only so, but we glory in tribulations also, being sure that tribulation worketh patience, and patience experience, and experience hope; and hope maketh not ashamed."[7] And again: "And if children, then heirs, heirs indeed of God, and joint-heirs with Christ: if so be that we suffer with Him, that we may be also glorified together. For I reckon that the sufferings of this time are

---

[1] Rev. vii. 14. [2] Isa. i. 18. [3] Rev. xvii. 6. [4] Rev. xxi. 8.
[5] Gen. xxv. 34, xxvii. 25. [6] 2 Thess. i. 4. [7] Rom. v. 3.

not worthy to be compared with the glory which shall be
revealed in us."[1] And therefore he afterward says: "Who
shall separate us from the love of God? Shall tribulation,
or distress, or famine, or nakedness, or peril, or sword? (As
it is written : For Thy sake we are killed all the day long;
we have been counted as sheep for the slaughter.) Nay, in
all these things we are more than conquerors, through Him
who loved us. For we are persuaded, that neither death,
nor life, nor power, nor height, nor depth, nor any other
creature, shall be able to separate us from the love of God,
which is in Christ Jesus our Lord."[2] But further, in recounting his own sufferings to the Corinthians, he certainly
decided that suffering must be borne: " In labours, [he
says,] more abundant, in prisons very frequent, in deaths
oft. Of the Jews five times received I forty stripes, save
one; thrice was I beaten with rods; once was I stoned,"[3]
and the rest. And if these severities will seem to be more
grievous than martyrdoms, yet once more he says: "Therefore I take pleasure in infirmities, in reproaches, in necessities, in persecutions, in distresses for Christ's sake."[4] He
also says, in verses occurring in a previous part of the
epistle: " Our condition is such, that we are troubled on
every side, yet not distressed; and are in need, but not in
utter want; since we are harassed by persecutions, but not
forsaken; it is such that we are cast down, but not destroyed;
always bearing about in our body the dying of Christ."[5]
"But though," says he, "our outward man perisheth"—the
flesh doubtless, by the violence of persecutions—"yet the
inward man is renewed day by day"—the soul, doubtless, by
hope in the promises. "For our light affliction, which is but
for a moment, worketh for us a far more exceeding and
eternal weight of glory ; while we look not at the things
which are seen, but at the things which are not seen. For
the things which are seen are temporal"—he is speaking of
troubles; " but the things which are not seen are eternal "
—he is promising rewards. But writing in bonds to the

[1] Rom. viii. 17.   [2] Rom. viii. 35.   [3] 2 Cor. xi. 23.
[4] 2 Cor. xii. 10.   [5] 2 Cor. iv. 8.

Thessalonians,[1] he certainly affirmed that they were blessed, since to them it had been given not only to believe on Christ, but also to suffer for His sake. "Having," says he, "the same conflict which ye both saw in me, and now hear to be in me."[2] "For though I am offered upon the sacrifice, I joy and rejoice with you all; in like manner do ye also joy and rejoice with me." You see what he decides the bliss of martyrdom to be, in honour of which he is providing a festival of mutual joy. When at length he had come to be very near the attainment of his desire, greatly rejoicing in what he saw before him, he writes in what terms to Timothy: "For I am already being offered, and the time of my departure is at hand. I have fought the good fight, I have finished my course, I have kept the faith; there is laid up for me the crown which the Lord will give me on that day"[3]—doubtless of his suffering. Admonition enough did he for his part also give in preceding passages: "It is a faithful saying: For if we are dead with Christ, we shall also live with Him; if we suffer, we shall also reign with Him; if we deny Him, He also will deny us; if we believe not, yet He is faithful: He cannot deny Himself."[4] "Be not thou, therefore, ashamed of the testimony of our Lord, nor of me His prisoner;"[5] for he had said before: "For God hath not given us the spirit of fear, but of power, and of love, and of a sound mind."[6] For we suffer with power from love toward God, and with a sound mind, when we suffer for our blamelessness. But further, if He anywhere enjoins endurance, for what more than for sufferings is He providing it? If anywhere He tears men away from idolatry, what more than martyrdoms takes the lead, in tearing them away to its injury?

14. No doubt the apostle admonishes the Romans[7] to be subject to all powers, because there is no power but of God, and because [the ruler] does not carry the sword without reason, and because he is the servant of God, nay also, says he, a revenger to execute wrath upon him that doeth

---

[1] Should be Philippians (Phil. i. 29, 30).   [2] Phil. ii. 17.   [3] 2 Tim. iv. 6.
[4] 2 Tim. ii. 11.   [5] 2 Tim. i. 8.   [6] 2 Tim. i. 7.   [7] Rom. xiii. 1.

evil. For he had also previously spoken thus: "For rulers are not a terror to a good work, but to an evil. Wilt thou then not be afraid of the power? Do that which is good, and thou shalt have praise of it. Therefore he is a minister of God to thee for good. But if thou do that which is evil, be afraid." Thus he bids you be subject to the powers, not on an opportunity occurring for his avoiding martyrdom, but when he is making an appeal in behalf of a good life, under the view also of their being as it were assistants bestowed upon righteousness, as it were handmaids of the divine court of justice, which even here pronounces sentence beforehand upon the guilty. Then he goes on also to show how he wishes you to be subject to the powers, bidding you pay "tribute to whom tribute is due, custom to whom custom,"[1] that is, the things which are Cæsar's to Cæsar, and the things which are God's to God;[2] but man is the property of God alone. Peter,[3] no doubt, had likewise said that the king indeed must be honoured, yet so that the king be honoured [only] when he keeps to his own sphere, when he is far from assuming divine honours; because both father and mother will be loved along with God, not put on an equality with Him. Besides, one will not be permitted to love even life more than God.

15. Now, then, the epistles of the apostles also are well known. And do *we*, [you say,] in all respects guileless souls and doves merely, love to go astray? I should think from eagerness to live. But let it be so, that meaning departs from their epistles. And yet, that the apostles endured such sufferings [as they enjoin], we know: the teaching is clear. This only I perceive in running through the Acts. I am not at all on the search. The prisons there, and the bonds, and the scourges, and the big stones, and the swords, and the onsets by the Jews, and the assemblies of the heathen, and the indictments by tribunes, and the hearing of causes by kings, and the judgment-seats of proconsuls, and the name of Cæsar, do not need an interpreter. That Peter is struck,[4]

---

[1] Rom. xiii. 6.   [2] Matt. xxii. 21.   [3] 1 Pet. ii. 13.
[4] It has been thought that the allusion is to the breaking of the legs

that Stephen is overwhelmed [by stones],[1] that James is slain[2] as is a victim at the altar, that Paul is beheaded, has been written in their own blood. And if a heretic wishes his confidence to rest upon a public record, the archives of the empire will speak, as would have the stones of Jerusalem. We read the lives of the Cæsars: At Rome Nero was the first who stained with blood the rising faith. Then is Peter girt by another,[3] when he is made fast to the cross. Then does Paul obtain a birth suited to Roman citizenship, when in Rome he springs to life again ennobled by martyrdom. Wherever I read of these occurrences, so soon as I do so, I learn to suffer; nor does it signify to me which I follow as teachers of martyrdom, whether the declarations or the deaths of the apostles, save that in their deaths I recall their declarations also. For they would not have suffered ought of a kind they had not previously known they had to suffer. When Agabus, making use of corresponding action too, had foretold that bonds awaited Paul, the disciples, weeping and entreating that he would not venture upon going to Jerusalem, entreated in vain.[4] For as for him, having a mind to illustrate what he had always taught, he says, "Why weep ye, and grieve my heart? But for my part, I could wish not only to suffer bonds, but also to die at Jerusalem, for the name of my Lord Jesus Christ." And so they yielded by saying, "Let the will of the Lord be done;" feeling sure, doubtless, that sufferings are included in the will of God. For they had tried to keep him back with the intention not of dissuading [from the kind of conduct contemplated], but to show love for him; as yearning for [the preservation of] the apostle, not as counselling against martyrdom. And if even then a Prodicus or Valentinus stood by, suggesting that one must not confess on the

---

of the crucified to hasten their death, not to the beating to which the apostles were subjected by the Jewish council (Acts v. 40).—Tr.

[1] Acts vii. 59.

[2] James the brother of our Lord, not the James mentioned Acts xii. 2.

[3] John xxi. 18.   [4] Acts xxi. 11.

earth before men, and must do so the less in truth, that God may not [seem to] thirst for blood, and Christ for a repayment of suffering, as though He besought it with the view of obtaining salvation by it for Himself also, he would have immediately heard from the servant of God what the devil had from the Lord: " Get thee behind me, Satan; thou art an offence unto me. It is written, Thou shalt worship the Lord thy God, and Him only shalt thou serve."[1] But even now it will be right that he hear it, seeing that, long after, he has poured forth these poisons, which not even thus are to injure readily any of the weak ones, if any one in faith will drink, before being hurt, or even immediately after, this draught of ours.

[1] Matt. xvi. 23 and iv. 10,—a mixing up of two passages of Scripture.

XVI.

AD NATIONES.[1]

CHAP. I.[2]—*The hatred felt by the heathen against the Christians is unjust, because based on culpable ignorance.*

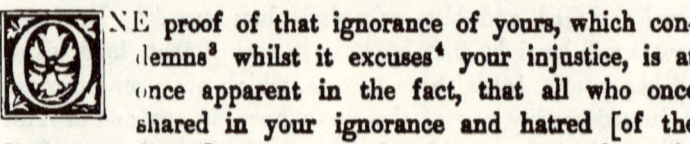NE proof of that ignorance of yours, which condemns[3] whilst it excuses[4] your injustice, is at once apparent in the fact, that all who once shared in your ignorance and hatred [of the Christian religion], as soon as they have come to know it, leave off their hatred when they cease to be ignorant; nay more, they actually themselves become what they had hated, and take to hating what they had once been. Day after day, indeed, you groan over the increasing number of the Christians. Your constant cry is, that the State is beset [by us]; that Christians are in your fields, in your camps, in your islands. You grieve over it as a calamity, that each sex, every age—in short, every rank—is passing over from you to us; yet you do not even after this set your minds upon reflecting whether there be not here some latent good. You do

---

[1] [This treatise resembles *The Apology* both in its general purport as a vindication of Christianity against heathen prejudice, and in many of its expressions and statements. So great is the resemblance, that this shorter work has been thought by some to have been a first draft of the longer and perfect one. Tertullian, however, here addresses his expostulations to the general public, whilst in *The Apology* it is the rulers and magistrates of the empire whom he seeks to influence.]

[2] [Comp. *The Apology*, c. i.]

[3] Revincit. ["Condemnat" is Tertullian's word in *The Apology*, i.]

[4] Defendit. ["Excusat" in *Apol.*]

not allow yourselves in suspicions which may prove too true,[1] nor do you like ventures which may be too near the mark.[2] This is the only instance in which human curiosity grows torpid. You love to be ignorant of what other men rejoice to have discovered; you would rather not know it, because you now cherish your hatred as if you were aware that, [with the knowledge,] your hatred would certainly come to an end. Still,[3] if there shall be no just ground for hatred, it will surely be found to be the best course to cease from the past injustice. Should, however, a cause have really existed, there will be no diminution of the hatred, which will indeed accumulate so much the more in the consciousness of its justice; unless it be, forsooth,[4] that you are ashamed to cast off your faults,[5] or sorry to free yourselves from blame.[6] I know very well with what answer you usually meet the argument from our rapid increase.[7] That indeed must not, you say, be hastily accounted a good thing which converts a great number of persons, and gains them over to its side. I am aware how the mind is apt to take to evil courses. How many there are which forsake virtuous living! How many seek refuge in the opposite! Many, no doubt;[8] nay, very many, as the last days approach.[9] But such a comparison as this fails in fairness of application; for all are agreed in thinking thus of the evil-doer, so that not even the guilty themselves, who take the wrong side, and turn away from the pursuit of good to perverse ways, are bold enough to defend evil as good.[10] Base things excite their fear, impious ones their shame. In short, they are eager for concealment, they shrink from publicity, they tremble when caught; when accused, they deny; even when tortured, they do not readily or invariably confess [their crime]; at all events,[11] they grieve when they are condemned. They reproach themselves for

---

[1] Non licet rectius suspicari.
[2] Non lubet propius experiri.
[3] At quin.
[4] Nisi si.
[5] Emendari pudet.
[6] Excusari piget.
[7] Redundantiæ nostræ.
[8] Bona fide.
[9] Pro extremitatibus temporum.
[10] [Or perhaps, " to maintain evil in preference to good."]
[11] Certe.

their past life; their change from innocence to an evil disposition they even attribute to fate. They cannot say that it is not a wrong thing, therefore they will not admit it to be their own act. As for the Christians, however, in what does their case resemble this? No one is ashamed, no one is sorry, except for his former [sins].[1] If he is pointed at [for his religion], he glories in it; if dragged to trial, he does not resist; if accused, he makes no defence. When questioned, he confesses; when condemned, he rejoices. What sort of evil is this, in which the nature of evil comes to a standstill?[2]

CHAP. II.[3]—*The heathen perverted judgment in the trial of Christians. They would be more consistent if they dispensed with all form of trial. Tertullian urges this with much indignation.*

In this case you actually[4] conduct trials contrary to the usual form of judicial process against criminals; for when culprits are brought up for trial, should they deny the charge, you press them for a confession by tortures. When Christians, however, confess without compulsion, you apply the torture to induce them to deny. What great perverseness is this, when you stand out against confession, [and] change the use of the torture, compelling the man who frankly acknowledges the charge[5] to evade it, him who is unwilling to deny it? You, who preside for the purpose of extorting truth, demand falsehood from us alone, that we may declare ourselves not to be what we are. I suppose you do not want us to be bad men, and therefore you earnestly wish to exclude us from that character. To be sure,[6] you put others on the rack and the gibbet, to get them to deny what they have the reputation of being. Now, when they deny [the charge against them], you do not believe them; but on our denial,

---

[1] Pristinorum. [In the corresponding passage (*Apol.* i.) the phrase is, "nisi plane retro non fuisse," *i.e.* "except that he was not [a Christian] long ago."]

[2] Cessat.   [3] [Comp. c. ii. of *The Apology.*]

[4] Ipsi.   [5] Gratis reum.   [6] Sane.

you instantly believe us. If you feel sure that we are the most injurious of men, why, even in processes against us, are we dealt with by you differently from other offenders? I do not mean that you make no account of [1] either an accusation or a denial (for your practice is not hastily to condemn men without an indictment and a defence); but, to take an instance in the trial of a murderer, the case is not at once ended, or the inquiry satisfied, on a man's confessing himself the murderer. However complete his confession,[2] you do not readily believe him; but over and above this, you inquire into accessory circumstances—how often had he committed murder, with what weapons, in what place, with what plunder, accomplices, [and] abettors after the fact[3] [was the crime perpetrated]—to the end that nothing whatever respecting the criminal might escape detection, and that every means should be at hand for arriving at a true verdict. In our case, on the contrary,[4] whom you believe to be guilty of more atrocious and numerous crimes, you frame your indictments[5] in briefer and lighter terms. I suppose you do not care to load with accusations men whom you earnestly wish to get rid of, or else you do not think it necessary to inquire into matters which are known to you already. It is, however, all the more perverse that you compel us to deny charges about which you have the clearest evidence. But, indeed,[6] how much more consistent were it with your hatred of us to dispense with all forms of judicial process, and to strive with all your might not to urge us to say "No," and so have to acquit the objects of your hatred, but to confess all and singular the crimes laid to our charge, that your resentments might be the better glutted with an accumulation of our punishments, when it becomes known how many of those feasts each one of us may have celebrated, how many incests have committed under cover of the night! What am I saying? Since your researches for rooting out our society must needs be made on a wide scale, you ought to extend your inquiry against our

---

[1] Neque spatium commodetis.
[2] Quanquam confessis.
[3] Receptoribus ["concealers" of the crime].
[4] Porro.   [5] Elogia.   [6] Immo.

friends and companions. Let our infanticides and the dressers [of our horrible repasts] be brought out,—ay, and the very dogs which minister to our [incestuous] nuptials;[1] then the business [of our trial] would be without a fault. Even to the crowds which throng the spectacles a zest would be given; for with how much greater eagerness would they resort to the theatre, when one had to fight in the lists who had devoured a hundred babies! For since such horrid and monstrous crimes are reported of us, they ought, of course, to be brought to light, lest they should seem to be incredible, and the public detestation of us should begin to cool. For most persons are slow to believe such things,[2] feeling a horrible disgust at supposing that our nature could have an appetite for the food of wild beasts, when it has precluded these from all concubinage with the race of man.

CHAP. III.[3]—*The great offence in the Christians lies in their very name. Tertullian rallies the persecutor for this absurdity, and pleasantly vindicates the name.*

Since, therefore, you who are in other cases most scrupulous and persevering in investigating charges of far less serious import, relinquish your care in cases like ours, which are so horrible, and of such surpassing sin that *impiety* is too mild a word for them, by declining to hear confession,

---

[1] [We have for once departed from Oehler's text, and preferred Rigault's: "Perducerentur *infantarii* et coci, ipsi canes pronubi, emendata esset res." The sense is evident from *The Apology*, c. vii.: "It is said that we are guilty of most horrible crimes; that in the celebration of our sacrament we put a child to death, which we afterwards devour, and at the end of our banquet revel in incest; that we employ dogs as ministers of our impure delights, to overthrow the candles, and thus to provide darkness, and remove all shame which might interfere with these impious lusts" (Chevallier's translation). These calumnies were very common, and are noticed by Justin Martyr, Minucius Felix, Eusebius, Athenagoras, and Origen, who attributes their origin to the Jews. Oehler reads *infantariæ*, after the Agobardine codex and *editio princeps*, and quotes Martial (*Epigr.* iv. 88), where the word occurs in the sense of an inordinate love of children.]

[2] Nam et plerique fidem talium temperant.

[3] [Comp. *The Apology*, cc. i. and ii.]

which should always be an important process for those who conduct judicial proceedings; and failing to make a full inquiry, which should always be gone into by such as sue for a condemnation, it becomes evident that the crime laid to our charge consists not of any sinful conduct, but lies wholly in our *name*. If, indeed,[1] any real crimes were clearly adducible against us, their very names would condemn us, if found applicable,[2] so that distinct sentences would be pronounced against us in this wise: Let that murderer, or that incestuous criminal, or whatever it be that we are charged with, be led to execution, be crucified, be thrown to the beasts. Your sentences, however,[3] import only that one has confessed himself a Christian. No name of a crime stands against us, but only the crime of a name. Now this in very deed is neither more nor less than[4] the entire odium which is felt against us. The name is the cause: some mysterious force intensified by your ignorance assails it, so that you do not wish to know for certain that which for certain you are sure you know nothing of; and therefore, further, you do not believe things which are not submitted to proof, and, lest they should be easily refuted,[5] you refuse to make inquiry, so that the odious name is punished under the presumption of [real] crimes. In order, therefore, that the issue may be withdrawn from the offensive name, we are compelled to deny it; then upon our denial we are acquitted, with an entire absolution[6] for the past: we are no longer murderers, no longer incestuous, because we have lost that name.[7] But since this point is dealt with in a place of its own,[8] do you tell us plainly why you are pursuing this name even to extirpation? What crime, what offence, what fault is there in a name? For you are barred by the rule[9] which puts it out of your power to allege crimes [of any man], which no legal action moots, no indictment specifies, no sentence

---

[1] Adeo si. [2] Si accommodarent. [3] Porro.
[4] Hæc ratio est. [5] Reprobentur. [6] Impunitate.
[7] [*i.e.* the name "Christians."]
[8] [By the "suo loco," Tertullian refers to *The Apology*.]
[9] Præscribitur vobis.

enumerates. In any case which is submitted to the judge,[1] inquired into against the defendant, responded to by him or denied, and cited from the bench, I acknowledge a legal charge. Concerning, then, the merit of a name, whatever offence names may be charged with, whatever impeachment words may be amenable to, I for my part[2] think, that not even a complaint is due to a word or a name, unless indeed it has a barbarous sound, or smacks of ill-luck, or is immodest, or is indecorous for the speaker, or unpleasant to the hearer. These crimes in [mere] words and names are just like barbarous words and phrases, which have their fault, and their solecism, and their absurdity of figure. The name *Christian*, however, so far as its meaning goes, bears the sense of anointing. Even when by a faulty pronunciation you call us "Chrestians" (for you are not certain about even the sound of this noted name), you in fact lisp out the sense of pleasantness and goodness.[3] You are therefore vilifying[4] in harmless men even the harmless name we bear, which is not inconvenient for the tongue, nor harsh to the ear, nor injurious to a single being, nor rude for our country, being a good Greek word, as many others also are, and pleasant in sound and sense. Surely, surely,[5] names are not things which deserve punishment by the sword, or the cross, or the beasts.

CHAP. IV.[6]—*The truth hated in the Christians; so in measure was it, of old, in Socrates. An eloquent eulogy on the virtues of the Christians.*

But the sect, you say, is punished in the name of its founder. Now in the first place, it is no doubt a fair and usual custom that a sect should be marked out by the name of its founder, since philosophers are called Pythagoreans and Platonists after their masters; in the same way physicians are called after Erasistratus, and grammarians after

---

[1] Præsidi.   [2] Ego.
[3] [Χρηστός means both "*pleasant*" and "*good;*" and the heathen confounded this word with the sacred name Χριστός.]
[4] Detinetis.   [5] Et utique.   [6] [See *The Apology*, c. iii.]

Aristarchus. If, therefore, a sect has a bad character because its founder was bad, it is punished[1] as the traditional bearer[2] of a bad name. But this would be indulging in a rash assumption. The first step was to find out what the founder was, that his sect might be understood, instead of hindering[3] inquiry into the founder's character from the sect. But in our case,[4] by being necessarily ignorant of the sect, through your ignorance of its founder, or else by not taking a fair survey of the founder, because you make no inquiry into his sect, you fasten merely on the name, just as if you vilified in it both sect and founder, whom you know nothing of whatever. And yet you openly allow your philosophers the right of attaching themselves to any school, and bearing its founder's name as their own also; and nobody stirs up any hatred against them, although both in public and in private they bark out[5] their bitterest eloquence against your customs, rites, ceremonies, and manner of life, with so much contempt for the laws, and so little respect for persons, that they even flaunt their licentious words[6] against the emperors themselves with impunity. And yet it is the truth, which is so troublesome to the world, that these philosophers affect, but which Christians possess: they therefore who have it in possession afford the greater displeasure, because he who affects a thing plays with it; he who possesses it maintains it. For example,[7] Socrates was condemned on that side [of his wisdom] in which he came nearest in his search to the truth, by destroying your gods. Although the name of Christian was not at that time in the world, yet truth was always suffering condemnation. Now you will not deny that he was a wise man, to whom your own Pythian [god] had borne witness. Socrates, he said, was the wisest of men. Truth overbore Apollo, and made him pronounce even against himself; since he acknowledged that he was no god, when he affirmed that that was the wisest man who was denying the gods. However,[8] on your principle he was the

[1] Plectitur. [2] Tradux. [3] Retinere. [4] At nunc.
[5] Elatrent. [6] Libertatem suam ["their liberty of speech"].
[7] Denique. [8] Porro.

less wise because he denied the gods, although in truth he was all the wiser by reason of this denial. It is just in the same way that you are in the habit of saying of us: Lucius Titius is a good man, only he is a Christian; while another says: I wonder that so worthy[1] a man as Caius Seius has become a Christian.[2] According to[3] the blindness of their folly, men praise what they know, [and] blame what they are ignorant of; and that which they know, they vitiate by that which they do not know. It occurs to none [to consider] whether a man is not good and wise because he is a Christian, or therefore a Christian because he is wise and good, although it is more usual in human conduct to determine obscurities by what is manifest, than to prejudice what is manifest by what is obscure. Some persons wonder that those whom they had known to be unsteady, worthless, [or] wicked before they bore this[4] name, have been suddenly converted to virtuous courses; and yet they better know how to wonder [at the change] than to attain to it; others are so obstinate in their strife as to do battle with their own best interests, which they have it in their power to secure by intercourse[5] with that hated name. I know more than one[6] husband, formerly anxious about their wives' conduct, and unable to bear even mice to creep into their bed-room without a groan of suspicion, who have, upon discovering the cause of their new assiduity, and their unwonted attention to the duties of home,[7] offered the entire loan of their wives to others,[8] disclaimed all jealousy, [and] preferred to be the husbands of she-wolves than of Christian women: they could commit themselves to a perverse abuse of nature, but they could not permit their wives to be reformed for the better! A father disinherited his son, with

---

[1] Gravem ["earnest"].
[2] [Comp. *The Apology*, c. iii.]
[3] Pro.   [4] [*i.e.* the Christian.]   [5] De commercio.
[6] Unum atque alium. [The sense being *plural*, we have so given it all through.]
[7] Captivitatis [as if theirs was a self-inflicted captivity at home].
[8] Omnem uxorem patientiam obtulisse [comp. *Apology*, middle of c. xxxix.].

whom he had ceased to find fault. A master sent his slave to bridewell,[1] whom he had even found to be indispensable to him. As soon as they discovered them to be Christians, they wished they were criminals again. For our discipline carries its own evidence in itself; nor are we betrayed by anything else than our own goodness, just as bad men also become conspicuous[2] by their own evil. Else how is it that we alone are, contrary to the lessons of nature, branded as very evil because of our good? For what mark do we exhibit except the prime wisdom,[3] which teaches us not to worship the frivolous works of the human hand; the temperance, by which we abstain from other men's goods; the chastity, which we pollute not even with a look; the compassion, which prompts us to help the needy; the truth itself, which makes us give offence; and liberty, for which we have even learned to die? Whoever wishes to understand who the Christians are, must needs employ these marks for their discovery.

CHAP. V.[4]—*The inconsistent life of any bad Christian no more condemns true disciples of Christ, than a passing cloud obscures a summer sky.*

As to your saying of us that we are a most shameful set, and utterly steeped in luxury, avarice, and depravity, we will not deny that this is true of some. It is, however, a sufficient testimonial for our name, that this cannot be said of all, not even of the greater part of us. It must happen even in the healthiest and purest body, that a mole should grow, or a wart arise on it, or freckles disfigure it. Not even the sky itself is clear with so perfect[5] a serenity as not to be flecked with some filmy cloud.[6] A slight spot on the face,

---

[1] In ergastulum.
[2] Radiant.
[3] [He means the religion of Christ, which he in b. ii. c. ii. contrasts with "*the mere wisdom*" of the philosophers.]
[4] [Compare *The Apology*, cc. ii. xliv. xlvi.]
[5] Colata ["filtered"].
[6] Ut non alicujus nubiculæ flocculo resignetur. [This picturesque language defies translation.]

because it is obvious in so conspicuous a part, only serves to show the purity of the entire complexion. The goodness of the larger portion is well attested by the slender flaw. But although you prove that some of our people are evil, you do not hereby prove that they are Christians. Search and see whether there is any sect to which [a partial shortcoming] is imputed as a general stain.[1] You are accustomed in conversation yourselves to say, in disparagement of us, Why is so-and-so deceitful, when the Christians are so self-denying? why merciless, when they are so merciful? You thus bear your testimony to the fact that this is not the character of Christians, when you ask, in the way of a retort,[2] how men who are reputed to be Christians can be of such and such a disposition. There is a good deal of difference between an imputation and a name,[3] between an opinion and the truth. For names were appointed for the express purpose of setting their proper limits between mere designation and actual condition.[4] How many indeed are said to be philosophers, who for all that do not fulfil the law of philosophy? All bear the name in respect of their profession; but they hold the designation without the excellence of the profession, and they disgrace the real thing under the shallow pretence of its name. Men are not straightway of such and such a character, because they are said to be so; but when they are not, it is vain to say so of them: they only deceive people who attach reality to a name, when it is its consistency with fact which decides the condition implied in the name.[5] And yet persons of this doubtful stamp do not assemble with us, neither do they belong to our communion: by their delinquency they become yours once more,[6] since we should be unwilling to mix even with them whom your violence and cruelty compelled to recant. Yet we should, of course, be more ready to have included amongst us those who have unwillingly forsaken our discipline than wilful apostates. However, you have no right to call them Christians, to whom the

---

[1] Malitiæ.
[2] Dum retorquetis.
[3] Inter crimen et nomen.
[4] Inter dici et esse.
[5] Status nominis.
[6] Denuo.

Christians themselves deny that name, and who have not learned to deny themselves.

CHAP. VI.[1]—*The innocence of the Christians not compromised or subverted by the iniquitous laws which were made against them.*

Whenever these statements and answers of ours, which truth suggests of its own accord, press and restrain your conscience, which is the witness of its own ignorance, you betake yourselves in hot haste to that poor altar of refuge,[2] the authority of the laws, because these, of course, would never punish the offensive[3] sect, if their deserts had not been fully considered by those who made the laws. Then what is it which has prevented a like consideration on the part of those who put the laws in force, when, in the case of all other crimes which are similarly forbidden and punished by the laws, the penalty is not inflicted[4] until it is sought by regular process?[5] Take,[6] for instance, the case of a murderer or an adulterer. An examination is ordered touching the particulars[7] of the crime, even though it is patent to all what its nature[8] is. Whatever wrong has been done by the Christian ought to be brought to light. No law forbids inquiry to be made; on the contrary, inquiry is made in the interest of the laws.[9] For how are you to keep the law by precautions against that which the law forbids, if you neutralize the carefulness of the precaution by your failing to perceive[10] what it is you have to keep? No law must keep to itself[11] the knowledge of its own righteousness,[12] but [it owes it] to those from whom it claims obedience. The law, however, becomes an object of suspicion when it declines to approve itself [thus]. Naturally enough,[13] then, are the laws against the Christians supposed to be just and deserving of respect

---

[1] [Compare *The Apology*, c. iv.]
[2] Ad arulam quandam.
[3] Istam. [4] Cessat ["loiters"]. [5] Requiratur.
[6] Lege. [7] Ordo. [8] Genus.
[9] [Literally, "holding the inquiry makes for the laws."]
[10] Per defectionem agnoscendi. [11] Sibi debet.
[12] Justitiæ suæ. [13] Merito.

and observance, just as long as men remain ignorant of their aim and purport; but when this is perceived, their extreme injustice is discovered, and they are deservedly rejected with abhorrence,[1] along with [their instruments of torture]—the swords, the crosses, and the lions. An unjust law secures no respect. In my opinion, however, there is a suspicion among you that some of these laws are unjust, since not a day passes without your modifying their severity and iniquity by fresh deliberations and decisions.

CHAP. VII.[2]—*The Christians defamed. A sarcastic description of* FAME; *its deception and atrocious slanders of the Christians lengthily described.*

Whence comes it to pass, you will say to us, that such a character could have been attributed to you, as to have justified the law-makers perhaps by its imputation? Let me ask on my side, what voucher they had then, or you now, for the truth of the imputation? [You answer,] Fame. Well, now, is not this [the thing which has been described as]—

"Fama malum, quo non aliud velocius ullum?"[3]
"Fame, than which never plague that runs
Its way more swiftly wins."[4]

Now, why "*a plague*," if it be always true? It never ceases from lying; nor even at the moment when it reports the truth is it so free from the wish to lie, as not to interweave the false with the true, by processes of addition, diminution, or confusion of various facts. Indeed,[5] such is its condition, that it can only continue to exist while it lies. For it lives only just so long as it fails to prove anything. As soon as it proves itself true, it falls; and, as if its office of reporting news were at an end, it quits its post: thenceforward the thing is held to be a fact, and it passes under that name. No one, then, says, to take an instance, "The report is that this happened at Rome," or, "The rumour goes that he has got a province;" but, "He has got a province," and, "This happened at Rome." Nobody mentions a rumour except at

[1] Despuuntur.   [2] [Comp. *The Apology*, cc. vii. viii.]
[3] [*Æneid*, iv. 174.]   [4] [Conington.]   [5] Quid? quod ["Yea more"].

an uncertainty, because nobody can be sure of a rumour, but only of certain knowledge; and none but a fool believes a rumour, because no wise man puts faith in an uncertainty. In however wide a circuit[1] a report has been circulated, it must needs have originated some time or other from one mouth; afterwards it creeps on somehow to ears and tongues which pass it on,[2] and so obscures the humble error in which it began, that no one considers whether the mouth which first set it a-going disseminated a falsehood,—a circumstance which often happens either from a temper of rivalry, or a suspicious turn, or even the pleasure of feigning news. It is, however, well that time reveals all things, as your own sayings and proverbs testify, yea, as nature herself attests, which has so ordered it that nothing lies hid, not even that which fame has not reported. See, now, what a witness[3] you have suborned against us: it has not been able up to this time to prove the report it set in motion, although it has had so long a time to recommend it to our acceptance. This name of ours took its rise in the reign of Augustus; under Tiberius it was taught with all clearness and publicity;[4] under Nero it was ruthlessly condemned,[5] and you may weigh its worth and character even from the person of its persecutor. If that prince was a pious man, then the Christians are impious; if he was just, if he was pure, then the Christians are unjust and impure; if he was not a public enemy, we are enemies of our country: what sort of men we are, our persecutor himself shows, since he of course punished what produced hostility to himself.[6] Now, although every other institution which existed under Nero has been destroyed, yet this of ours has firmly remained—righteous, it would seem, as being unlike the author [of its persecution]. Two hundred and fifty years, then, have not yet passed since our life began. During the interval there have been so many criminals; so many crosses have obtained immortality;[7] so

[1] Ambitione.
[2] Traduces.
[3] Prodigiam. [The word is "indicem" in *The Apology*.]
[4] Disciplina ejus illuxit.   [5] Damnatio invaluit.
[6] Æmula sibi.   [7] Divinitatem consecutæ.

many infants have been slain; so many loaves steeped in blood; so many extinctions of candles;[1] so many dissolute marriages. And up to the present time it is mere report which fights against the Christians. No doubt it has a strong support in the wickedness of the human mind, and utters its falsehoods with more success among cruel and savage men. For the more inclined you are to maliciousness, the more ready are you to believe evil; in short, men more easily believe the evil that is false, than the good which is true. Now, if injustice has left any place within you for the exercise of prudence in investigating the truth of reports, justice of course demanded that you should examine by whom the report could have been spread amongst the multitude, and thus circulated through the world. For it could not have been by the Christians themselves, I suppose, since by the very constitution and law of all mysteries the obligation of silence is imposed. How much more would this be the case in such [mysteries as are ascribed to us], which, if divulged, could not fail to bring down instant punishment from the prompt resentment of men! Since, therefore, the Christians are not their own betrayers, it follows that it must be strangers. Now I ask, how could strangers obtain knowledge of us, when even true and lawful mysteries exclude every stranger from witnessing them, unless illicit ones are less exclusive? Well, then, it is more in keeping with the character of strangers both to be ignorant [of the true state of a case], and to invent [a false account]. Our domestic servants [perhaps] listened, and peeped through crevices and holes, and stealthily got information of our ways. What, then, shall we say when our servants betray them to you?[2] It is better, [to be sure,][3] for us all not to be betrayed by any; but still, if our practices be so atrocious, how much more proper is it when a righteous indignation bursts asunder even all ties of domestic fidelity? How was it possible for it to endure what horrified the mind and affrighted the eye? This is also a wonderful thing, both

---

[1] See above, c. ii. note.
[2] [*i.e.* What is the value of *such* evidence?]
[3] [We have inserted this phrase as the sentence is strongly ironical.]

that he, who was so overcome with impatient excitement as to turn informer,[1] did not likewise desire to prove [what he reported], and that he who heard the informer's story did not care to see for himself, since no doubt the reward [2] is equal both for the informer who proves what he reports, and for the hearer who convinces himself of the credibility [3] of what he hears. But then you say that [this is precisely what has taken place]: first came the rumour, then the exhibition of the proof; first the hearsay, then the inspection; and after this, fame received its commission. Now this, I must say,[4] surpasses all admiration, that that was once for all detected and divulged which is being for ever repeated, unless, forsooth, we have by this time ceased from the reiteration of such things [5] [as are alleged of us]. But we are called still by the same [offensive] name, and we are supposed to be still engaged in the same practices, and we multiply from day to day; the more [6] we are, to the more become we objects of hatred. Hatred increases as the material for it increases. Now, seeing that the multitude of offenders is ever advancing, how is it that the crowd of informers does not keep equal pace therewith? To the best of my belief, even our manner of life [7] has become better known; you know the very days of our assemblies; therefore we are both besieged, and attacked, and kept prisoners actually in our secret congregations. Yet who ever came upon a half-consumed corpse [amongst us]? Who has detected the traces of a bite in our blood-steeped loaf? Who has discovered, by a sudden light invading our darkness, any marks of impurity, I will not say of incest, [in our feasts?] If we save ourselves by a bribe [8] from being dragged out before the public gaze with such a character, how is it that we are still oppressed? We have it indeed in our own power not to be thus apprehended at all.

[1] Deferre [an *infinitive* of purpose, of which construction of our author Oehler gives examples].
[2] Fructus.   [3] Si etiam sibi credat.   [4] Quidem.   [5] Talia factitare.
[6] [We read "quo," and not "quod," because.]   [7] Conversatio.
[8] [This refers to a calumny which the heathen frequently spread about the Christians.]

For who either sells or buys information about a crime, if the crime itself has no existence? But why need I disparagingly refer to [1] strange spies and informers, when you allege against us such charges as we certainly do not ourselves divulge with very much noise—either as soon as you hear of them, if we previously show them to you, or after you have yourselves discovered them, if they are for the time concealed from you? For no doubt,[2] when any desire initiation in the mysteries, their custom is first to go to the master or father of the sacred rites. Then he will say [to the applicant], You must bring an infant, as a guarantee for our rites, to be sacrificed, as well as some bread to be broken and dipped in his blood; you also want candles, and dogs tied together to upset them, and bits of meat to rouse the dogs. Moreover, a mother too, or a sister, is necessary for you. What, however, is to be said if you have neither? I suppose in that case you could not be a genuine Christian. Now, do let me ask you, Will such things, when reported by strangers, bear to be spread about [as charges against us]? It is impossible for such persons to understand proceedings in which they take no part.[3] The first step of the process is perpetrated with artifice; our feasts and our marriages are invented and detailed[4] by ignorant persons, who had never before heard about Christian mysteries. And though they afterwards cannot help acquiring some knowledge of them, it is even then as having to be administered by others whom they bring on the scene.[5] Besides, how absurd is it that the profane know mysteries which the priest knows not! They keep them all to themselves, then,[6] and take them for granted; and so these tragedies, [worse than those] of Thyestes or

---

[1] Detrectem [or simply "treat of," "refer to," like the simple verb "tractare"].

[2] [The irony of all this passage is evident.]   [3] Diversum opus.

[4] Subjiciuntur ["are stealthily narrated"].   [5] Inducunt.

[6] [It is difficult to see what this "tacent igitur" means without referring to the similar passage in *The Apology* (end of c. viii.), which supplies a link wanted in the context. "At all events," says he, "they know this afterwards, and yet submit to it, and allow it. *They fear to be punished*, while, if they proclaimed the truth, they would deserve

Œdipus, do not at all come forth to light, nor find their way [1] to the public. Even more voracious bites take nothing away from the credit [2] of such as are initiated, whether servants or masters. If, however, none of these allegations can be proved to be true, how incalculable must be esteemed the grandeur [of that religion], which is manifestly not overbalanced even by the burden of these vast atrocities! O ye heathen, who have and deserve our pity,[3] behold, we set before you the promise which our sacred system offers. It guarantees eternal life to such as follow and observe it; on the other hand, it threatens with the eternal punishment of an unending fire those who are profane and hostile; while to both classes alike is preached a resurrection from the dead. We are not now concerned [4] about the doctrine of these [verities], which are discussed in their proper place.[5] Meanwhile, however, believe them, even as we do ourselves. For I want to know whether you are ready to reach them, as we do, through such crimes. Come, whosoever you are, plunge your sword into an infant; or if that is another's office, then simply gaze at the [little] breathing creature [6] dying before it has lived; at any rate, catch its fresh [7] blood in which to steep your bread; then feed yourself without stint; and whilst this is going on, recline. Carefully distinguish the places where your mother or your sister may have made their bed; mark them well, in order that, when the shades of night have fallen upon them, putting of course to the test the care of every one of you, you may not make the awkward mistake of alighting on somebody else:[8] you would have to make an atonement, if you failed of the incest. When you have

universal approbation." Tertullian here states what the enemies of the Christians used to allege against them. After discovering the alleged atrocities of their secret assemblies, they kept their knowledge forsooth to themselves, being afraid of the consequences of a disclosure, etc.]

[1] [We have for convenience treated "protrahunt" (q.d. "nor do they report them") as a neuter verb.]
[2] [Even worse than Thyestean atrocities would be believed of them.]
[3] Miseræ atque miserandæ.
[4] Viderimus.
[5] [See below, in c. xix.]
[6] Animam.
[7] Rudem ["hardly formed"].
[8] Extraneam.

effected all this, eternal life will be in store for you. I want you to tell me whether you think eternal life worth such a price. No, indeed,[1] you do not believe it: even if you did believe it, I maintain that you would be unwilling to give [the fee]; or if willing, would be unable. But why should others be able if you are unable? Why should you be able if others are unable? What would you wish impunity [and] eternity to stand you in?[2] Do you suppose that these [blessings] can be bought by us at any price? Have Christians teeth of a different sort from others? Have they more ample jaws?[3] Are they of different nerve for incestuous lust? I trow not. It is enough for us to differ from you in condition[4] by truth alone.

CHAP. VIII.[5]—*The absurdity of the calumny against the Christians illustrated in the discovery of Psammetichus about the primeval nation; refutation of the story.*

We are indeed said to be the "third race" of men. What, a dog-faced race?[6] Or broad and clumsy footed?[7] Or some subterranean[8] Antipodes? If you attach any meaning to these names, pray tell us what are the first and the second race, that so we may know something of this "third." Psammetichus thought that he had hit upon the ingenious discovery of the primeval man. He is said to have removed certain new-born infants from all human intercourse, and to have entrusted them to a nurse, whom he had previously deprived of her tongue, in order that, being completely exiled from all

---

[1] Immo idcirco.   [2] Quanto constare.
[3] ["An alii ordines dentium Christianorum, et alii specus faucium?" (literally, "Have Christians other sets of teeth, and other caverns of jaws?") seems to refer to voracious animals like the shark, whose terrible teeth, lying in several rows, and greediness to swallow anything, however incongruous, that comes in its way, are well-known facts in natural history.]
[4] Positione.   [5] [Compare *The Apology*, c. viii.]
[6] Cynopæ. [This class would furnish the unnatural "*teeth*" and "*jaws*" just referred to.]
[7] Sciapodes [with broad feet *producing a large shade*; suited for the "incestuous lust" above mentioned].
[8] [Literally, "which come up from under ground."]

sound of the human voice, they might form their speech without hearing it; and thus, deriving it from themselves alone, might indicate what that first nation was whose speech was dictated by nature. Their first utterance was BEKKOS, a word which means "*bread*" in the language of Phrygia: the Phrygians, therefore, are supposed to be the first of the human race.[1] But it will not be out of place if we make one observation, with a view to show how your faith abandons itself more to vanities than to verities. Can it be, then, at all credible that the nurse retained her life, after the loss of so important a member, the very organ of the breath of life,[2] —cut out, too, from the very root, with her throat[3] mutilated, which cannot be wounded even on the outside without danger, and the putrid gore flowing back to the chest, and deprived for so long a time of her food? Come, even suppose that by the remedies of a Philomela she retained her life, in the way supposed by wisest persons, who account for the dumbness not by cutting out the tongue, but from the blush of shame; if on such a supposition she lived, she would still be able to blurt out some dull sound. And a shrill inarticulate noise from opening the mouth only, without any modulation of the lips, might be forced from the mere throat, though there were no tongue to help. This, it is probable, the infants readily imitated, and the more so because it was the only sound; only they did it a little more neatly, as they had tongues;[4] and then they attached to it a definite signification. Granted, then, that the Phrygians were the earliest race, it does not follow that the Christians are the third. For how many other nations come regularly after the Phrygians? Take care, however, lest those whom you call the third race should obtain the first rank, since there is no nation indeed which is not Christian. Whatever nation, therefore, was the first, is nevertheless Christian now.[5] It is ridiculous folly which makes you say we are the latest race, and then speci-

---

[1] [Tertullian got this story from Herodotus, ii. 2.]
[2] Ipsius animæ organo.   [3] Faucibus.   [4] Utpote linguatuli.
[5] [This is one of the passages which incidentally show how widely spread was Christianity.]

fically call us the third. But it is in respect of our religion,[1] not of our nation, that we are supposed to be the third; the series being the Romans, the Jews, and the Christians after them. Where, then, are the Greeks? or if they are reckoned amongst the Romans in regard to their superstition (since it was from Greece that Rome borrowed even her gods), where at least are the Egyptians, since these have, so far as I know, a mysterious religion peculiar to themselves? Now, if they who belong to the third race are so monstrous, what must they be supposed to be who preceded them in the first and the second place?

CHAP. IX.[2]—*The Christians are not the cause of public calamities; there were such troubles before Christianity.*

But why should I be astonished at your vain imputations? Under the same natural form, malice and folly have always been associated in one body and growth, and have ever opposed us under the one instigator of error.[3] Indeed, I feel no astonishment; and therefore, as it is necessary for my subject, I will enumerate some instances, that you may feel the astonishment by the enumeration of the folly into which you fall, when you insist on our being the causes of every public calamity or injury. If the Tiber has overflowed its banks, if the Nile has remained in its bed, if the sky has been still, or the earth been in commotion, if death[4] has made its devastations, or famine its afflictions, your cry immediately is, This is the fault[5] of the Christians! As if they who fear the true God could have to fear a light thing, or at least anything else [than an earthquake or famine, or such visitations].[6] I suppose it is as despisers of your gods that we call down on us these strokes of theirs. As we have

---

[1] De superstitione.   [2] [Comp. *The Apology*, cc. xl. xli.]

[3] [By the "manceps erroris" he means the devil.]

[4] Libitina.

[5] Christianorum meritum [which with "sit" may be also, "Let the Christians have their due." In *The Apology* the cry is, "Christianos ad leonem"].

[6] [We insert this after Oehler. Tertullian's words are, "Quasi modicum habeant aut aliud metuere qui Deum verum."]

remarked already,[1] three hundred years have not yet passed in our existence; but what vast scourges before that time fell on all the world, on its various cities and provinces! what terrible wars, both foreign and domestic! what pestilences, famines, conflagrations, yawnings, and quakings of the earth has history recorded![2] Where were the Christians, then, when the Roman state furnished so many chronicles of its disasters? Where were the Christians when the islands Hiera, Anaphe, and Delos, and Rhodes, and Cea were desolated with multitudes of men? or, again, when the land mentioned by Plato as larger than Asia or Africa was sunk in the Atlantic Sea? or when fire from heaven overwhelmed Volsinii, and flames from their own mountain consumed Pompeii? when the sea of Corinth was engulphed by an earthquake? when the whole world was destroyed by the deluge? Where *then* were (I will not say the Christians, who despise your gods, but) your gods themselves, who are proved to be of later origin than that great ruin by the very places and cities in which they were born, sojourned, and were buried, and even those which they founded? For else they would not have remained to the present day, unless they had been more recent than that catastrophe. If you do not care to peruse and reflect upon these testimonies of history, the record of which affects you differently from us,[3] in order especially that you may not have to tax your gods with extreme injustice, since they injure even their worshippers on account of their despisers, do you not then prove yourselves to be also in the wrong, when you hold them to be gods, who make no distinction between the deserts of yourselves and profane persons? If, however, as it is now and then very vainly said, you incur the chastisement of your gods because you are too slack in our extirpation, you then have settled the question[4] of their weakness and insignificance; for they would not be angry with you for loitering over our punishment, if they could do anything themselves,—although you admit the same thing indeed in another way, whenever by

[1] [See above, c. vii.]
[2] Sæculum digessit.
[3] Aliter vobis renuntiata.
[4] Absolutum est.

inflicting punishment on us you seem to be avenging them. If one interest is maintained by another party, that which defends is the greater of the two. What a shame, then, must it be for gods to be defended by a human being!

CHAP. X.[1]—*The Christians are not the only contemners of the gods: what greater contempt of them could be shown than was often displayed by heathen official persons? Homer made the gods contemptible.*

Pour out now all your venom; fling against this name of ours all your shafts of calumny: I shall stay no longer to refute them; but they shall by and by be blunted, when we come to explain our entire discipline.[2] I shall content myself now indeed with plucking these shafts out of our own body, and hurling them back on yourselves. The same wounds which you have inflicted on us by your charges I shall show to be imprinted on yourselves, that you may fall by your own swords and javelins.[3] Now, first, when you direct against us the general charge of divorcing ourselves from the institutions of our forefathers, consider again and again whether you are not yourselves open to that accusation in common with us. For when I look through your life and customs, lo, what do I discover but the old order of things corrupted, nay, destroyed by you? Of the laws I have already said, that you are daily supplanting them with novel decrees and statutes. As to everything else in your manner of life, how great are the changes you have made from your ancestors— in your style, your dress, your equipage, your very food, and even in your speech; for the old-fashioned you banish, as if it were offensive to you! Everywhere, in your public pursuits and private duties, antiquity is repealed; all the authority of your forefathers your own authority has superseded. To be sure,[4] you are for ever praising old customs; but this is only to your greater discredit, for you nevertheless per-

---

[1] [Comp. *The Apology*, cc. xii. xiii. xiv. xv.]

[2] [See *The Apology* (*passim*), especially cc. xvi.-xxiv. xxx.-xxxvi. and xxxix.]

[3] Admentationibus.   [4] Plane.

sistently reject them. How great must your perverseness have been, to have bestowed approbation on your ancestors' institutions, which were too inefficient to be lasting, all the while that you were rejecting the very objects of your approbation! But even that very heir-loom [1] of your forefathers, which you seem to guard and defend with the greatest fidelity, in which you actually [2] find your strongest grounds for impeaching us as violators of the law, and from which your hatred of the Christian name derives all its life — I mean the worship of the gods—I shall prove to be undergoing ruin and contempt from yourselves no less than [3] [from us], — unless it be that there is no reason for our being regarded as despisers of the gods like yourselves, on the ground that nobody despises what he knows has absolutely no existence. What certainly exists can be despised. That which *is* nothing, suffers nothing. From those, therefore, to whom it is an existing thing,[4] must necessarily proceed the suffering which affects it. All the heavier, then, is the accusation which burdens you who believe that there are gods and [at the same time] despise them, who worship and also reject them, who honour and also assail them. One may also gather the same conclusion from this consideration, above all : since you worship various gods, some one and some another, you of course despise those which you do not worship. A preference for the one is not possible without slighting the other, and no choice can be made without a rejection. He who selects some *one* out of many, has already slighted the other which he does not select. But it is impossible that so many and so great gods can be worshipped by all. Then you must have exercised your contempt [in this matter] even at the beginning, since indeed you were not then afraid of so ordering things, that all the gods could not become objects of worship to all. For those very wise and prudent ancestors of yours, whose institutions you know not how to repeal, especially in respect of your gods, are themselves found to have been impious. I am much mistaken, if they did not sometimes decree that no general should dedicate a temple, which he may

[1] Traditum. [2] Vel. [3] Perinde a vobis. [4] Quibus est.

have vowed in battle, before the senate gave its sanction; as in the case of Marcus Æmilius, who had made a vow to the god Alburnus. Now is it not confessedly the greatest impiety, nay, the greatest insult, to place the honour of the Deity at the will and pleasure of human judgment, so that there cannot be a god except the senate permit him? Many times have the censors destroyed[1] [a god] without consulting the people. Father Bacchus, with all his ritual, was certainly by the consuls, on the senate's authority, cast not only out of the city, but out of all Italy; whilst Varro informs us that Serapis also, and Isis, and Arpocrates, and Anubis, were excluded from the Capitol, and that their altars which the senate had thrown down were only restored by the popular violence. The Consul Gabinius, however, on the first day of the ensuing January, although he gave a tardy consent to some sacrifices, in deference to the crowd which assembled, because he had failed to decide about Serapis and Isis, yet held the judgment of the senate to be more potent than the clamour of the multitude, and forbade the altars to be built. Here, then, you have amongst your own forefathers, if not the name, at all events the procedure,[2] of the Christians, which despises the gods. If, however, you were even innocent of the charge of treason against them in the honour you pay them, I still find that you have made a consistent advance in superstition as well as impiety. For how much more irreligious are you found to be! There are your household gods, the Lares and the Penates, which you possess[3] by a family consecration:[4] you even tread them profanely under foot, you and your domestics, by hawking and pawning them for your wants or your whims. Such insolent sacrilege might be excusable, if it were not practised against your humbler deities; as it is, the case is only the more insolent. There is, however, some consolation for your private household gods under these affronts, that you treat your public deities with still greater indignity and insolence. First of all,

---

[1] Adsolaverunt ["thrown to the ground;" "floored"].
[2] Sectam. [3] Perhibetis.
[4] Domestica consecratione [*i.e.* "for family worship"].

you advertise them for auction, submit them to public sale, knock them down to the highest bidder, when you every five years bring them to the hammer among your revenues. For this purpose you frequent the temple of Serapis or the Capitol, hold your sales there,[1] conclude your contracts,[2] as if they were markets, with the well-known[3] voice of the crier, [and] the self-same levy[4] of the quæstor. Now lands become cheaper when burdened with tribute, and men by the capitation tax diminish in value (these are the well-known marks of slavery). But the gods, the more tribute they pay, become more holy; or rather,[5] the more holy they are, the more tribute do they pay. Their majesty is converted into an article of traffic; men drive a business with their religion; the sanctity of the gods is beggared with sales and contracts. You make merchandise of the ground of your temples, of the approach to your altars, of your offerings,[6] of your sacrifices.[7] You sell the whole divinity [of your gods]. You will not permit their gratuitous worship. The auctioneers necessitate more repairs[8] than the priests. It was not enough that you had insolently made a profit of your gods (if we would test the amount of your contempt); and you are not content to have withheld honour from them, you must also depreciate the little you do render to them by some indignity or other. What, indeed, do you do by way of honouring your gods, which you do not equally offer to your dead? You build temples for the gods, you erect temples also to the dead; you build altars for the gods, you build them also for the dead; you inscribe the same superscription over both; you sketch out the same lineaments for their statues—as best suits their genius, or profession, or age; you make an old man of Saturn, a beardless youth of Apollo; you form a virgin from Diana; in Mars you consecrate a soldier, a blacksmith in Vulcan. No wonder, therefore, if you slay the same victims and burn the same odours for your dead as you do for your gods. What excuse can be found for that insolence which classes the

---

[1] Addicitur.   [2] Conducitur.   [3] Eadem.
[4] Exactione ["as excise duty for the treasury"].   [5] Immo.
[6] ["In money," stipibus.]   [7] ["Victims."]   [8] Plus refigitur.

dead of whatever sort [1] as equal with the gods? Even to your princes there are assigned the services of priests and sacred ceremonies, and chariots,[2] and cars, and the honours of the *solisternia* and the *lectisternia*, holidays and games. Rightly enough,[3] since heaven is open to them; still it is none the less contumelious to the gods: in the first place, because it could not possibly be decent that other beings should be numbered with them, even if it has been given to them to become divine after their birth; in the second place, because the witness who beheld the man caught up into heaven [4] would not forswear himself so freely and palpably before the people, if it were not for the contempt felt about the objects sworn to both by himself and those [5] who allow the perjury. For these feel of themselves, that what is sworn to is nothing; and more than that, they go so far as to fee the witness, because he had the courage to publicly despise the avengers of perjury. Now, as to that, who among you is pure of the charge of perjury? By this time, indeed, there is an end to all danger in swearing by the gods, since the oath by Cæsar carries with it more influential scruples, which very circumstance indeed tends to the degradation of your gods; for those who perjure themselves when swearing by Cæsar are more readily punished than those who violate an oath to a Jupiter. But [of the two kindred feelings of contempt and derision] contempt is the more honourable, having a certain glory in its arrogance; for it sometimes proceeds from confidence, or the security of consciousness, or a natural loftiness of mind. Derision, however, is a more wanton feeling, and so far it points more directly [6] to a carping insolence. Now only consider what great deriders of your gods you show yourselves to be! I say nothing of your indulgence of this feeling during your sacrificial acts, how

---

[1] Utut mortuos.   [2] Tensæ.   [3] Plane.
[4] [Rigaltius has the name *Proculus* in his text; but Tertullian refers not merely to that case, but to a usual functionary, necessary in all cases of deification.]
[5] [Oehler reads "ei" (of course for "ii"); Rigalt. reads "ii."]
[6] Denotatior ad.

you offer for your victims the poorest and most emaciated creatures, or else of the sound and healthy animals only the portions which are useless for food, such as the heads and hoofs, or the plucked feathers and hair, and whatever at home you would have thrown away. I pass over whatever may seem to the taste[1] of the vulgar and profane to have constituted the religion[2] of your forefathers; but then the most learned and serious classes (for seriousness and wisdom to some extent[3] profess[4] to be derived from learning) are always, in fact, the most irreverent towards your gods; and if their learning ever halts, it is only to make up for the remissness by a more shameful invention of follies and falsehoods about their gods. I will begin with that enthusiastic fondness which you show for him from whom every depraved writer gets his dreams, to whom you ascribe as much honour as you derogate from your gods, by magnifying him who has made such sport of them. I mean Homer by this description. He it is, in my opinion, who has treated the majesty of the Divine Being on the low level of human condition, imbuing the gods with the falls[5] and the passions of men, who has pitted them against each other with varying success like pairs of gladiators: he wounds Venus with an arrow from a human hand; he keeps Mars a prisoner in chains for thirteen months, with the prospect of perishing;[6] he parades[7] Jupiter as suffering a like indignity from a crowd of celestial [rebels]; or he draws from him tears for Sarpedon; or he represents him wantoning with Juno in the most disgraceful way, advocating his incestuous passion for her by a description and enumeration of his various amours. Since then, which of the poets has not, on the authority of their great prince, calumniated the gods, by either betraying truth or

---

[1] Gulæ ["depraved taste"].
[2] Prope religionem convenire ["to have approximated to"].
[3] Quatenus.
[4] Credunt [one would expect "creduntur" ("are supposed"), which is actually read by Gothofredus].
[5] [Or, "circumstances" (casibus).] [6] Fortasse periturum.
[7] Traducit [perhaps "degrades"].

feigning falsehood? Have the dramatists also, whether in tragedy or comedy, refrained from making the gods the authors[1] of the calamities and retributions [of their plays]? I say nothing of your philosophers, whom a certain inspiration of truth itself elevates against the gods, and secures from all fear in their proud severity and stern discipline. Take, for example,[2] Socrates. In contempt of your gods, he swears by an oak, and a dog, and a goat. Now, although he was condemned to die for this very reason, the Athenians afterwards repented of that condemnation, and even put to death his accusers. By this conduct of theirs the testimony of Socrates is replaced at its full value, and I am enabled to meet you with this retort, that in his case you have approbation bestowed on that which is now-a-days reprobated in us. But besides this instance there is Diogenes, who, I know not to what extent, made sport of Hercules; whilst that Diogenes of the Roman cut,[3] Varro, introduces to our view some three hundred Joves, or, as they ought to be called, Jupiters,[4] [and all] without heads. Your other wanton wits[5] likewise minister to your pleasures by disgracing the gods. Examine carefully the sacrilegious[6] beauties of your Lentuli and Hostii; now, is it the players or your gods who become the objects of your mirth in their tricks and jokes? Then, again, with what pleasure do you take up the literature of the stage, which describes all the foul conduct of the gods! Their majesty is defiled in your presence in some unchaste body. The mask of some deity, at your will,[7] covers some infamous paltry head. The Sun mourns for the death of his son by a lightning-flash amid your rude rejoicing. Cybele sighs for a shepherd who disdains her, without raising a blush on your cheek; and you quietly endure songs which

---

[1] Ut dei præfarentur. [Oehler explains the verb "præfari" to mean, "auctorem esse et tanquam caput."]

[2] Denique.   [3] Stili.

[4] [Tertullian gives the absurd plural "*Juppiteres*."]   [5] Ingenia.

[6] [Because appropriating to themselves the admiration which was due to the gods.]

[7] Cujuslibet dei.

celebrate[1] the gallantries of Jove. You are, of course, possessed of a more religious spirit in the show of your gladiators, when your gods dance, with equal zest, over the spilling of human blood, [and] over those filthy penalties which are at once their proof and plot for executing your criminals, or else [when] your criminals are punished personating the gods themselves.[2] We have often witnessed in a mutilated criminal your god of Pessinum, Attis; a wretch burnt alive has personated Hercules. We have laughed at the sport of your mid-day game of the gods, when Father Pluto, Jove's own brother, drags away, hammer in hand, the remains of the gladiators; when Mercury, with his winged cap and heated wand, tests with his cautery whether the bodies were really lifeless, or only feigning death. Who now can investigate every particular of this sort, although so destructive of the honour of the Divine Being, and so humiliating to His majesty? They all, indeed, have their origin[3] in a contempt [of the gods], on the part both of those who practise[4] these personations, as well as of those[5] who are susceptible of being so represented. I hardly know, therefore, whether your gods have more reason to complain of yourselves or of us. After

[1] Sustinetis modulari.

[2] [It is best to add the original of this almost unintelligible passage: "Plane religiosiores estis in gladiatorum cavea, ubi super sanguinem humanum, super inquinamenta pœnarum proinde saltant dei vestri *argumenta et historias nocentibus erogandis, aut in ipsis deis nocentes puniuntur.*" Some little light may be derived from the parallel passage of the *Apology* (c. xv.), which is expressed somewhat less obscurely. Instead of the words in italics, Tertullian there substitutes these: "Argumenta et historias noxiis ministrantes, nisi quod et ipsos deos vestros sæpe noxii induunt "—" whilst furnishing the proofs and the plots for [executing] criminals, only that the said criminals often act the part of your gods themselves." Oehler refers, in illustration of the last clause, to the instance of the notorious robber Laureolus, who personated Prometheus; others, again, personated Laureolus himself: some criminals had to play the part of Orpheus; others of Mutius Scævola. It will be observed that these executions were with infamous perverseness set off with scenic show, wherein the criminal enacted some violent death in yielding up his own life. The indignant irony of the whole passage, led off by the "plane religiosiores estis," is evident.]

[3] Censentur.   [4] Factitant.   [5] [*i.e.* the gods themselves.]

despising them on the one hand, you flatter them on the other; if you fail in any duty towards them, you appease them with a fee;[1] in short, you allow yourselves to act towards them in any way you please. We, however, live in a consistent and entire aversion to them.

CHAP. XI.[2]—*The absurd cavil of "*THE ASS'S HEAD*" disposed of in some sentences of humorous irony.*

In this matter we are [said to be] guilty not merely of forsaking the religion of the community, but of introducing a monstrous superstition; for some among you have dreamed that our god is an ass's head,—an absurdity which Cornelius Tacitus first suggested. In the fourth book of his *Histories*,[3] where he is treating of the Jewish war, he begins his description with the origin of that nation, and gives his own views respecting both the origin and the name of their religion. He relates that the Jews, in their migration in the desert, when suffering for want of water, escaped by following for guides some wild asses, which they supposed to be going in quest of water after pasture, and that on this account the image of one of these animals was worshipped by the Jews. From this, I suppose, it was presumed that we, too, from our close connection with the Jewish religion, have ours consecrated under the same emblematic form. The same Cornelius Tacitus, however—who, to say the truth, is most loquacious in falsehood—forgetting his later statement, relates how Pompey the Great, after conquering the Jews and capturing Jerusalem, entered the temple, but found nothing in the shape of an image, though he examined the place carefully. Where, then, should their God have been found? Nowhere else, of course, than in so memorable a temple, which was carefully shut to all but the priests, and into which there could be no fear of a stranger entering. But what apology must I here offer for what I am going to say, when I have no other object at the moment than to

---

[1] Redimitis. [2] [Comp. *The Apology*, c. xvi.]
[3] [In *The Apology* (c. xvi.) the reference is to "the fifth book." This is correct. Book v. c. 3, is meant.]

make a passing remark or two in a general way which shall be equally applicable to yourselves?[1] Suppose that our God, then, be an asinine person, will you at all events deny that you possess the same characteristics with ourselves in that matter? [Not their heads only, but] entire asses, are, to be sure, objects of adoration to you, along with their tutelar Epona; and all herds, and cattle, and beasts you consecrate, and their stables into the bargain! This, perhaps, is your grievance against us, that, when surrounded by cattle-worshippers of every kind, we are simply devoted to asses!

CHAP. XII.[2]—*The charge of worshipping* A CROSS *met by a retort: the heathens themselves made much of crosses in sacred things; nay, their very idols were formed on a crucial frame.*

As for him who affirms that we are "the priesthood of a cross,"[3] we shall claim him[4] as our co-religionist.[5] A cross is, in its material, a sign of wood; amongst yourselves also the object of worship is a wooden figure. Only, whilst with you the figure is a human one, with us the wood is its own figure. Never mind[6] for the present what is the shape, provided the material is the same: the form, too, is of no importance,[7] if so be it be the actual body of a god. If, however, there arises a question of difference on this point, what, [let me ask,] is the difference between the Athenian Pallas, or the Pharian Ceres, and wood formed into a cross,[8] when each is represented by a rough stock, without form, and by the merest rudiment of a statue[9] of unformed wood? Every piece of timber[10] which is fixed in the ground in an erect position is a part of a cross, and indeed the greater portion of its mass. But an entire cross is attributed to us, with its transverse beam,[11] of course, and its projecting seat.

[1] In vobis [for "in vos"] ex pari transferendorum.
[2] [Comp. *The Apology*, c. xvi.] [3] Crucis antistites. [4] Erit.
[5] Consacraneus. [6] Viderint. [7] Viderit. [8] Stipite crucis.
[9] Solo staticulo. [The use of wood in the construction of an idol is mentioned afterwards.]
[10] Omne robur. [11] Antemna. [See our *Anti-Marcion*, p. 156.]

Now you have the less to excuse you, for you dedicate to religion only a mutilated imperfect piece of wood, while others consecrate to the sacred purpose a complete structure. The truth, however, after all is, that your religion is *all cross*, as I shall show. You are indeed unaware that your gods in their origin have proceeded from this hated cross.[1] Now, every image, whether carved out of wood or stone, or molten in metal, or produced out of any other richer material, must needs have had plastic hands engaged in its formation. Well, then, this modeller,[2] before he did anything else,[3] hit upon the form of a wooden cross, because even our own body assumes as its natural position the latent and concealed outline of a cross. Since the head rises upwards, and the back takes a straight direction, and the shoulders project laterally, if you simply place a man with his arms and hands outstretched, you will make the general outline of a cross. Starting, then, from this rudimental form and prop,[4] as it were, he applies a covering of clay, and so gradually completes the limbs, and forms the body, and covers the cross within with the shape which he meant to impress upon the clay; then from this design, with the help of compasses and leaden moulds, he has got all ready for his image which is to be brought out into marble, or clay, or metal, or whatever the material be of which he has determined to make his god. [This, then, is the process:] after the cross-shaped frame, the clay; after the clay, the god. In a well-understood routine, the cross passes into a god through the clayey medium. The cross then you consecrate, and from it the consecrated [deity] begins to derive his origin.[5] By way of example, let us take the case of a tree which grows up into a system of branches and foliage, and is a reproduction of its own kind, whether it springs from the kernel of an olive, or the stone of a peach, or a grain of pepper which has been duly tempered under ground. Now, if you transplant it, or take a cutting

---

[1] De isto patibulo.   [2] Plasta.   [3] In primo.   [4] Statumini.

[5] [Comp. *The Apology*, c. xii.: " Every image of a god has been first constructed on a cross and stake, and plastered with cement. The body of your god is first dedicated upon a gibbet."]

off its branches for another plant, to what will you attribute what is produced by the propagation? Will it not be to the grain, or the stone, or the kernel? Because, as the third stage is attributable to the second, and the second in like manner to the first, so the third will have to be referred to the first, through the second as the mean. We need not stay any longer in the discussion of this point, since by a natural law every kind of produce throughout nature refers back its growth to its original source; and just as the product is comprised in its primal cause, so does that cause agree in character with the thing produced. Since, then, in the production of your gods, you worship the cross which originates them, here will be the original kernel and grain, from which are propagated the wooden materials of your idolatrous images. Examples are not far to seek. Your victories you celebrate with religious ceremony[1] as deities; and they are the more august in proportion to the joy they bring you. The frames on which you hang up your trophies must be crosses: these are, as it were, the very core of your pageants.[2] Thus, in your victories, the religion of your camp makes even crosses objects of worship; your standards it adores, your standards are the sanction of its oaths; your standards it prefers before Jupiter himself. But all that parade [3] of images, and that display of pure gold, are [as so many] necklaces of the crosses. In like manner also, in the banners and ensigns, which your soldiers guard with no less sacred care, you have the streamers [and] vestments of your crosses. You are ashamed, I suppose, to worship unadorned and simple crosses.

CHAP. XIII.[4]—*The charge of worshipping* THE SUN *met by a retort. The heathen's respect for the great luminary.*

Others, with greater regard to good manners, it must be confessed, suppose that the sun is the god of the Christians,

---

[1] Veneramini.

[2] Tropæum [for "tropæorum." We have given the sense rather than the words of this awkward sentence].

[3] Suggestus. [4] [Comp. *The Apology*, c. xvi.]

because it is a well-known fact that we pray towards the east, or because we make Sunday a day of festivity. What then? Do you do less than this? Do not many among you, with an affectation of sometimes worshipping the heavenly bodies likewise, move your lips in the direction of the sunrise? It is you, at all events, who have even admitted the sun into the calendar of the week; and you have selected its day,[1] in preference to the preceding day,[2] as the most suitable in the week[3] for either an entire abstinence from the bath, or for its postponement until the evening, or for taking rest and for banqueting. By resorting to these customs, you deliberately deviate from your own religious rites to those of strangers. For the Jewish feasts are the Sabbath and "the Purification,"[4] and Jewish also are the ceremonies of the lamps,[5] and the fasts of unleavened bread, and the "littoral prayers,"[6] all which institutions and practices are of course foreign from your gods. Wherefore, that I may return from this digression, you who reproach us with the sun and Sunday should consider your proximity to us. We are not far off from your Saturn and your days of rest.

CHAP. XIV.[7]—*The vile calumny about "*ONOCOETES*" retorted on the heathen by Tertullian.*

Report has introduced a new calumny respecting our God. Not so long ago, a most abandoned wretch in that city of yours,[8] a man who had deserted indeed his own religion—a Jew, in fact, who had only lost his skin, flayed of course by wild beasts,[9] against which he enters the lists for hire day after day with a sound body, and so in a condition to lose

---

[1] [Sunday.]   [2] [Saturday.]   [3] Ex diebus.
[4] [On the "Coena pura," see our *Anti-Marcion*, p. 386, note 4.]
[5] [See Lev. xxiv. 2; also 2 Chron. xiii. 11. Witsius (*Ægyptiaca*, ii. 16, 17) compares the Jewish with the Egyptian "ritus lucernarum."]
[6] [Tertullian, in his tract *de Jejun.* xvi., speaks of the Jews praying (after the loss of their temple, and in their dispersion) in the open air, "per omne litus."]
[7] [Comp. *The Apology*, c. xvi.]   [8] In ista civitate [Rome].
[9] [This is explained in the passage of *The Apology* (xvi.): "He had for money exposed himself with criminals to fight with wild beasts."]

his skin[1]—carried about in public a caricature of us with this label: ONOCOETES.[2] This [figure] had ass's ears, and was dressed in a *toga* with a book, having a hoof on one of his feet. And the crowd believed this infamous Jew. For what other set of men is the seed-plot[3] of all the calumny against us? Throughout the city, therefore, Onocoetes is all the talk. As, however, it is less than "a nine days' wonder,"[4] and so destitute of all authority from time, and weak enough from the character of its author, I shall gratify myself by using it simply in the way of a retort. Let us then see whether you are not here also found in our company. Now it matters not what their form may be, when our concern is about deformed images. You have amongst you gods with a dog's head, and a lion's head, and with the horns of a cow, and a ram, and a goat, goat-shaped or serpent-shaped, and winged in foot, head, and back. Why therefore brand our one God so conspicuously? Many an *Onocoetes* is found amongst yourselves.

CHAP. XV.[5]—*The cruel charge of* INFANTICIDE, *made against the Christians by the heathen, retorted on the latter.*

Since we are on a par in respect of the gods, it follows that there is no difference between us on the point of sacrifice, or even of worship,[6] if I may be allowed to make good our comparison from another sort of evidence. We begin our religious service, or initiate our mysteries, with slaying an infant. As for you, since your own transactions in human blood and infanticide have faded from your memory, you shall be duly reminded of them in the proper place; we now postpone most of the instances, that we may not seem to be

---

[1] Decutiendus [from a jocular word, "decutire"].
[2] [This curious word is compounded of ὄνος, *an ass*, and κοιᾶσθαι, which Hesychius explains by ἱερᾶσθαι, *to act as a priest*. The word therefore means, "asinarius sacerdos," "an ass of a priest." Calumnious enough; but suited to the vile occasion, and illustrative of the ribald opposition which Christianity had to encounter.]
[3] [We take Rigaltius' reading, "seminarium."]
[4] Tanquam hesternum.   [5] [Comp. *The Apology*, c. ix.]
[6] Sacri.

everywhere[1] handling the selfsame topics. Meanwhile, as I have said, the comparison between us does not fail in another point of view. For if we are infanticides in one sense, you also can hardly be deemed such in any other sense; because, although you are forbidden by the laws to slay new-born infants, it so happens that no laws are evaded with more impunity or greater safety, with the deliberate knowledge of the public, and the suffrages[2] of this entire age.[3] Yet there is no great difference between us, only you do not kill [your infants] in the way of a sacred rite, nor [in the light of a service] to God. But then you make away with them in a more cruel manner, because you expose them to the cold and hunger, and to wild beasts, or else you get rid of them by the slower death of drowning. If, however, there does occur any dissimilarity between us in this matter,[4] you must not overlook the fact that it is your own dear children[5] whose life you quench; and this will supplement, nay, abundantly aggravate, on your side of the question, whatever is defective in us on other grounds. Well, but we are said to sup off our impious sacrifice! Whilst we postpone to a more suitable place[6] whatever resemblance even to this practice is discoverable amongst yourselves, we are not far removed from you in voracity. If in the one case there is unchastity, and in ours cruelty, we are still on the same footing (if I may so far admit our guilt[7]) in nature, where cruelty is always found in concord with unchastity. But, after all, what do you less than we; or rather, what do you not do in excess of us? I wonder whether it be a small matter to you[8] to pant for human entrails, because you devour full-grown men alive? Is it, forsooth, only a trifle to lick up human blood, when you draw out[9] the blood which was destined to live? Is it a

---

[1] [He refers in this passage to his *Apology*, especially c. ix.]
[2] Tabellis.
[3] Unius ætatis. [This Oehler explains by " per unam jam totam hanc ætatem."]
[4] Genere.
[5] Pignora [*scil.* amoris].
[6] [See *Apology*, c. ix.]
[7] Si forte.
[8] Parum scilicet?
[9] Elicitis.

light thing in your view to feed on an infant, when you consume one wholly before it is come to the birth?[1]

CHAP. XVI.[2]—*Other charges repelled by the same method of retort, especially that of* INCEST. *The story of the noble Roman youth and his parents.*

I am now come to the hour for extinguishing the lamps, and for using the dogs, and practising the deeds of darkness. And on this point I am afraid I must succumb to you; for what similar accusation shall I have to bring against you? But you should at once commend the cleverness with which we make our incest look modest, in that we have devised a spurious night,[3] to avoid polluting the real light and darkness—have even thought it right to dispense with earthly lights, and to play tricks also with our conscience. For whatever we do ourselves, we suspect in others when we choose [to be suspicious]. As for your incestuous deeds, on the contrary,[4] men enjoy them at full liberty, in the face of day, or in the natural night, or before high Heaven; and in proportion to their successful issue is your own ignorance of the result, since you publicly indulge in your incestuous intercourse in the full cognizance of broad day-light. [No ignorance, however, conceals our conduct from our eyes,] for in the very darkness we are able to recognise our own misdeeds. The Persians, you know very well,[5] according to Ctesias, live quite promiscuously with their mothers, in full knowledge of the fact, and without any horror; whilst of the Macedonians it is well known that they constantly do the same thing, and with perfect approbation: for once, when the blinded[6] Œdipus came upon their stage, they greeted him with laughter and derisive cheers. The actor, taking off his mask in great alarm, said, "Gentlemen, have I displeased you?" "Certainly not," replied the Macedonians, "you have played your part well enough; but either the author was very silly, if he invented [this mutilation as an

---

[1] Infantem totum præcocum.
[2] [Comp. *The Apology*, c. ix.]
[3] Adulteram noctem.
[4] Ceterum.
[5] Plane.
[6] Trucidatus oculos.

atonement for the incest], or else Œdipus was a great fool for his pains if he really so punished himself;" and then they shouted out one to the other, Ἤλαυνε εἰς τὴν μητέρα. But how insignificant, [say you,] is the stain which one or two nations can make on the whole world! As for us, we of course have infected the very sun, polluted the entire ocean! Quote, then, one nation which is free from the passions which allure the whole race of men to incest! If there is a single nation which knows nothing of concubinage through the necessity of age and sex—to say nothing of lust and licentiousness—that nation will be a stranger to incest. If any nature can be found so peculiarly removed from the human state as to be liable neither to ignorance, nor error, nor misfortune, that alone may be adduced with any consistency as an answer to the Christians. Reflect, therefore, on the licentiousness which floats about amongst men's passions[1] as if they were the winds, and consider whether there be any communities which the full and strong tides of passion fail to waft to the commission of this great sin. In the first place, when you expose your infants to the mercy of others, or leave them for adoption to better parents than yourselves, do you forget what an opportunity for incest is furnished, how wide a scope is opened for its accidental commission? Undoubtedly, such of you as are more serious from a principle of self-restraint and careful reflection, abstain from lusts which could produce results of such a kind, in whatever place you may happen to be, at home or abroad, so that no indiscriminate diffusion of seed, or licentious reception thereof, will produce children to you unawares, such as their very parents, or else other children, might encounter in inadvertent incest, for no restraint from age is regarded in [the importunities of] lust. All acts of adultery, all cases of fornication, all the licentiousness of public brothels, whether committed at home or perpetrated out of doors,[2] serve to produce confusions of blood and complications of natural relationship,[3] and thence to conduce to incest; from

[1] Errores.
[2] Sive statuto vel ambulatorio titulo.
[3] Compagines generis.

which consummation your players and buffoons draw the materials of their exhibitions. It was from such a source, too, that so flagrant a tragedy recently burst upon the public as that which the prefect Fuscianus had judicially to decide. A boy of noble birth, who, by the unintentional neglect of his attendants,[1] had strolled too far from home, was decoyed by some passers-by, and carried off. The paltry Greek[2] who had the care of him, or somebody else,[3] in true Greek fashion, had gone into the house and captured him. Having been taken away into Asia, he is brought, when arrived at full age, back to Rome, and exposed for sale. His own father buys him unawares, and treats him as a Greek.[4] Afterwards, as was his wont, the youth is sent by his master into the fields, chained as a slave.[5] Thither the tutor and the nurse had already been banished for punishment. The whole case is represented to them; they relate each other's misfortunes: they, on the one hand, how they had lost their ward when he was a boy; he, on the other hand, that he had been lost from his boyhood. But they agreed in the main, that he was a native of Rome of a noble family; perhaps he further gave some sure proofs of his identity. Accordingly, as God willed it for the purpose of fastening a stain upon that age, a presentiment about the time excites him, the periods exactly suit his age, even his eyes help to recall[6] his features, some peculiar marks on his body are enumerated. His master and mistress, who are now no other than his own father and mother, anxiously urge a protracted inquiry. The slave-dealer is examined, the unhappy truth is all discovered. When their wickedness becomes manifest, the parents find a remedy for their despair by hanging themselves; to their son, who survives the miserable calamity, their property is awarded by the prefect, not as an inheritance, but as the wages of infamy and incest. That one case was a sufficient example for public exposure[7] of the sins of

---

[1] Comitum.   [2] Græculus.   [3] ["Aliquis" is here understood.]
[4] Utitur Græco [*i.e.* cinædo, "for purposes of lust"].
[5] [Or, "is sent into the country, and put into prison."]
[6] Aliquid recordantur.   [7] Publicæ eruptionis.

this sort which are secretly perpetrated among you. Nothing happens among men in solitary isolation. But, as it seems to me, it is only in a solitary case that such a charge can be drawn out against us, even in the mysteries of our religion. You ply us evermore with this charge;[1] yet there are like delinquencies to be traced amongst you, even in your ordinary course of life.[2]

CHAP. XVII.[3]—*Other charges met; the Christian refusal to swear by "*THE GENIUS OF CÆSAR*;" flippancy and irreverence retorted on the heathen.*

As to your charges of obstinacy and presumption, whatever you allege against us, even in these respects there are not wanting points in which you will bear a comparison with us. Our first step in this contumacious conduct concerns that which is ranked by you immediately after[4] the worship due to God, that is, the worship due to the majesty of the Cæsars, in respect of which we are charged with being irreligious towards them, since we neither propitiate their images nor swear by their genius. We are called enemies of the people. Well, be it so; yet at the same time [it must not be forgotten, that] the emperors find enemies amongst you heathen, and are constantly getting surnames to signalize their triumphs —one becoming *Parthicus*,[5] and another *Medicus* and *Germanicus*.[6] On this head[7] the Roman people must see to it who they are amongst whom[8] there still remain nations which are unsubdued and foreign to their rule. But, at all events, you are of us,[9] and yet you conspire against us. [In reply to this, we need only state] a well-known fact,[10] that we acknowledge the fealty of Romans to the emperors. No conspiracy has ever broken out from our body: no Cæsar's

---

[1] Intentatis.
[2] Vestris non sacramentis [with a hyphen, "your non-mysteries"].
[3] [Comp. *The Apology*, c. xxxv.]   [4] Secunda.
[5] [Severus, in A.D. 198.]   [6] [These titles were borne by Caracalla.]
[7] [Or, "topic"—hoc loco.]
[8] [*i.e.* whether amongst the Christians or the heathen.]
[9] [A cavil of the heathen.]   [10] Sane.

blood has ever fixed a stain upon us, in the senate or even in the palace; no assumption of the purple has ever in any of the provinces been affected by us. The Syrias still exhale the odours of their corpses; still do the Gauls[1] fail to wash away [their blood] in the waters of their Rhone. Your allegations of our insanity[2] I omit, because they do not compromise the Roman name. But I will grapple with[3] the charge of sacrilegious vanity, and remind you of[4] the irreverence of your own lower classes, and the scandalous lampoons[5] of which the statues are so cognizant, and the sneers which are sometimes uttered at the public games,[6] and the curses with which the circus resounds. If not in arms, you are in tongue at all events always rebellious. But I suppose it is quite another affair to refuse to swear by the genius of Cæsar! For it is fairly open to doubt as to who are perjurers on this point, when you do not swear honestly[7] even by your gods. Well, we do not call the emperor God; for on this point "*sannam facimus,*"[8] as the saying is. But the truth is, that you who call Cæsar God both mock him, by calling him what he is not, and curse him, because he does not want to be what you call him. For he prefers living to being made a god.[9]

CHAP. XVIII.[10] — *The Christians charged with an obstinate "* CONTEMPT OF DEATH." *Tertullian shows how many instances of the same disposition are found amongst the heathen.*

The rest of your charge of obstinacy against us you sum up in this indictment, that we boldly refuse neither your swords, nor your crosses, nor your wild beasts, nor fire, nor tortures, such is our obduracy and contempt of death. But [you are inconsistent in your charges]; for in former times amongst your own ancestors all these terrors have come in

---

[1] Galliæ. [2] Vesaniæ. [3] Conveniam.
[4] Recognoscam. [5] Festivos libellos. [6] A concilio.
[7] Ex fide. [8] [Literally, " we make faces."]
[9] [Comp. *The Apology,* c. xxxiii., and Minucius Felix, *Octavius,* c. xxiii.]
[10] [Comp. *The Apology,* c. 50.]

men's intrepidity[1] not only to be despised, but even to be held in great praise. How many swords there were, and what brave men were willing to suffer by them, it were irksome to enumerate.[2] [If we take the torture] of the cross, of which so many instances have occurred, exquisite in cruelty, your own Regulus readily initiated the suffering which up to his day was without a precedent;[3] a queen of Egypt used wild beasts of her own [to accomplish her death];[4] the Carthaginian woman, who in the last extremity of her country was more courageous than her husband Asdrubal,[5] only followed the example set long before by Dido herself of going through fire to her death. Then, again, a woman of Athens defied the tyrant, exhausted his tortures, and at last, lest her person and sex might succumb through weakness, she bit off her tongue and spat out of her mouth the only possible instrument of a confession which was now out of her power.[6] But in your own instance you account such deeds glorious, in ours obstinate. Annihilate now the glory of your ancestors, in order that you may thereby annihilate us also. Be content from henceforth to repeal the praises of your forefathers, in order that you may not have to accord commendation to us for the same [sufferings]. Perhaps [you will say] the character of a more robust age may have rendered the spirits of antiquity more enduring. Now, however, [we enjoy] the blessing of quietness and peace; so that the minds and dispositions of men [should be] more tolerant even towards strangers. Well, you rejoin, be it so: *you* may compare *yourselves* with the ancients; *we* must needs pursue with hatred all that we find in you offensive to *ourselves*, because it does not obtain currency[7] among us. Answer me, then, on

[1] A virtute didicerunt.

[2] [With the "piget prosequi" to govern the preceding oblique clause, it is unnecessary to suppose (with Oehler) the omission here of some verb like "erogavit."]

[3] Novitatem ... dedicavit.

[4] [Tertullian refers to Cleopatra's death also in his tract *ad. Mart.* c. iv.]

[5] [This case is again referred to in this treatise (ii. 9), and in *ad Mart.* c. iv.]

[6] Eradicatæ confessionis.   [7] Non invenitur.

each particular case by itself. I am not seeking for examples on a uniform scale.¹ Since, forsooth, the sword through their contempt of death produced stories of heroism amongst your ancestors, it is not, of course,² from love of life that you go to the trainer's sword in hand and offer yourselves as gladiators,³ [nor] through fear of death do you enrol your names in the army.⁴ Since an ordinary ⁵ woman makes her death famous by wild beasts, it cannot but be of your own pure accord that you encounter wild beasts day after day in the midst of peaceful times. Although no longer any Regulus among you has raised a cross as the instrument of his own crucifixion, yet a contempt of the fire has even now displayed itself,⁶ since one of yourselves very lately has offered for a wager ⁷ to go to any place which may be fixed upon and put on the burning shirt.⁸ If a woman once defiantly danced beneath the scourge, the same feat has been very recently performed again by one of your own [circus-] hunters ⁹ as he traversed the appointed course, not to mention the famous sufferings of the Spartans.¹⁰

CHAP. XIX.¹¹—*If the Christians and the heathen are in these retorts shown to resemble each other, there is, after all, great difference in the grounds and nature of their apparently similar conduct.*

Here end, I suppose, your tremendous charges of obstinacy against the Christians. Now, since we are amenable to them in common with yourselves, it only remains that we compare

---

¹ Eadem voce.
² Utique. [The ironical tone of Tertullian's answer is evident.]
³ Gladio ad lanistas auctoratis.
⁴ [We follow Oehler in giving the clause this *negative* turn; he renders it: "Tretet nicht aus Furcht vor dem Tode ins Kriegsheer ein."]
⁵ Alicui.   ⁶ Jam evasit.   ⁷ Auctoravit.
⁸ Vestiendum incendiale tunica.
⁹ Inter venatorios ["venatores circi" (Oehler)].
¹⁰ ["Doubtless the stripes which the Spartans endured with such firmness, aggravated by the presence of their nearest relatives, who encouraged them, conferred honour upon their family."—*Apology*, c. 50.]
¹¹ [Compare *The Apology*, cc. xlvii. xlviii. xlix.]

the grounds which the respective parties have for being personally derided. All our obstinacy, however, is with you a foregone conclusion,[1] based on our strong convictions; for we take for granted[2] a resurrection of the dead. Hope in this resurrection amounts to[3] a contempt of death. Ridicule, therefore, as much as you like the excessive stupidity of such minds as die that they may live; but then, in order that you may be able to laugh more merrily, and deride us with greater boldness, you must take your sponge, or perhaps your tongue, and wipe away those records of yours every now and then cropping out,[4] which assert in not dissimilar terms that souls will return to bodies. But how much more worthy of acceptance is our belief which maintains that they will return to the same bodies! And how much more ridiculous is your inherited conceit,[5] that the human spirit is to reappear in a dog, or a mule, or a peacock! Again, we affirm that a judgment has been ordained by God according to the merits of every man. This you ascribe to Minos and Rhadamanthus, while at the same time *you* reject Aristides, who was a juster judge than either. By the award of the judgment, we say that the wicked will have to spend an eternity in endless fire, the pious and innocent in a region of bliss. In your view likewise an unalterable condition is ascribed to the respective destinations of Pyriphlegethon[6] and Elysium. Now they are not merely your composers of myth and poetry who write songs of this strain; but your philosophers also speak with all confidence of the return of souls to their former state,[7] and of the twofold award[8] of a final judgment.

CHAP. XX.—*In conclusion, Tertullian claims truth and reality for the Christians alone, and earnestly counsels the heathen to examine and embrace it.*

How long therefore, O most unjust heathen, will you refuse to acknowledge us, and (what is more) to execrate your own [worthies], since between us no distinction has

[1] Præstruitur.   [2] Præsumimus.   [3] Est.   [4] Interim.
[5] Traditum.   [6] [The heathen hell, *Tartarus* or *Orcus*.]
[7] Reciprocatione.   [8] Distributione.

place, because we are one and the same? Since you do not [of course] hate what you yourselves are, give us rather your right hands in fellowship, unite your salutations,[1] mingle your embraces, sanguinary with the sanguinary, incestuous with the incestuous, conspirators with conspirators, obstinate and vain with those of the selfsame qualities. In company with each other, we have been traitors to the majesty of the gods; and together do we provoke their indignation. You too have your "third race;"[2] not indeed third in the way of religious rite,[3] but a third race in sex, and, made up as it is of male and female in one, it is more fitted to men and women [for offices of lust].[2] Well, then, do we offend you by the very fact of our approximation and agreement? Being on a par is apt to furnish unconsciously the materials for rivalry. Thus "a potter envies a potter, and a smith a smith."[4] But we must now discontinue this imaginary confession.[5] Our conscience has returned to the truth, and to the consistency of truth. For all those points which you allege[6] [against us] will be really found in ourselves alone; and we alone can rebut them, against whom they are adduced, by getting you to listen[7] to the other side of the question, whence that full knowledge is learnt which both inspires counsel and directs the judgment. Now it is in fact your own maxim, that no one should determine a cause without hearing both sides of it; and it is only in our own case that you neglect [the equitable principle]. You indulge to the full[8] that fault of human nature, that those things which you do not disallow in yourselves you condemn in others, or you boldly charge[9] against others those things the guilt of which[10]

---

[1] Compingite oscula. [2] [Eunuchs (Rigalt.).]
[3] [As the Christians were held to be; coming after (1) the heathen, (2) the Jews. See above, c. viii., and *Scorpiace*, c. x.]
[4] [An oft-quoted proverb in ancient writers. It occurs in Hesiod (*Opp. et. Dies*) 25.]
[5] [Literally, "cease henceforth, O simulated confession."]
[6] Omnia ista.
[7] [This seems to be the force of the "agnitione," which Oehler renders "auditione."]
[8] Satisfacitis.   [9] Jactetis.   [10] Quorum reatum.

you retain a lasting consciousness of[1] in yourselves. The course of life in which you will choose to occupy yourselves is different from ours: whilst chaste in the eyes of others, you are unchaste towards your own selves; whilst vigorous against vice out of doors, you succumb to it at home. This is the injustice [which we have to suffer], that, knowing truth, we are condemned by those who know it not; free from guilt, we are judged by those who are implicated in it. Remove the mote, or rather the beam, out of your own eye, that you may be able to extract the mote from the eyes of others. Amend your own lives first, that you may be able to punish the Christians. Only so far as you shall have effected your own reformation, will you refuse to inflict punishment on them—nay, so far will you have become Christians yourselves; and as you shall have become Christians, so far will you have compassed your own amendment of life. Learn what that is which you accuse in us, and you will accuse no longer; search out what that is which you do not accuse in yourselves, and you will become self-accusers. From these very few and humble remarks, so far as we have been able to open out the subject to you, you will plainly get some insight into [your own] error, and some discovery of [our] truth. Condemn that truth if you have the heart,[2] but only after you have examined it; and approve the error still, if you are so minded,[3] only first explore it. But if your prescribed rule is to love error and hate truth, why, [let me ask,] do you not probe to a full discovery the objects both of your love and your hatred?

[1] Memineritis. [2] Si potestis. [3] Si putatis.

BOOK II.[1]

Chap. i.—*Tertullian, wishing to examine the heathen gods from heathen authorities, resorts to Varro, who had written a work on the subject. Varro's threefold classification stated, with general remarks on the changeable character of that which ought to be fixed and certain.*

Our defence requires that we should at this point discuss with you the character of your gods, O ye heathen, fit objects of our pity,[2] appealing even to your own conscience to determine whether they be truly gods, as you would have it supposed, or falsely, as you are unwilling to have proved.[3] Now this is the material part of human error, owing to the wiles of its author, that it is never free from the ignorance of error,[4] whence your guilt is all the greater. Your eyes are open, yet they see not; your ears are unstopped, yet they hear not; though your heart beats, it is yet dull, nor does your mind understand[5] that of which it is cognizant.[6] If indeed the enormous perverseness [of your worship] could[7] be broken up[8] by a single demurrer, we should have our objection ready to hand in the declaration[9] that, as we know all those gods of yours to have been instituted by men, all belief in the true Deity is by this very circumstance brought to nought;[10] because, of course, nothing which some time or other had a beginning can rightly seem to be divine. But the fact is,[11] there are many things by which tenderness of conscience is hardened into the callousness of wilful error. Truth is

---

[1] [In this part of his work the author reviews the heathen mythology, and exposes the absurdity of the polytheistic worship in the various classes of the gods, according to the distribution of Varro.]
[2] Miserandæ. [3] [Literally, "unwilling to know."]
[4] [i.e. it does not know that it is error.]   [5] Nescit.
[6] Agnoscit.   [7] Liceret.
[8] Discuti [or, in the logical sense, "be tested"].
[9] Nunciatio [legally, this is "an information lodged against a wrong"].
[10] Excidere ["falls through"].   [11] Sed enim.

beleaguered with the vast force [of the enemy], and yet how secure she is in her own inherent strength! And naturally enough,[1] when from her very adversaries she gains to her side whomsoever she will, as her friends and protectors, and prostrates the entire host of her assailants. It is therefore against these things that our contest lies—against the institutions of our ancestors, against the authority of tradition,[2] the laws of our governors, the reasonings of the wise; against antiquity, custom, submission;[3] against precedents, prodigies, miracles,—all which things have had their part in consolidating that spurious[4] system of your gods. Wishing, then, to follow step by step your own commentaries which you have drawn out of your theology of every sort (because the authority of learned men goes further with you in matters of this kind than the testimony of facts), I have taken and abridged the works of Varro;[5] for he in his treatise *Concerning Divine Things*, collected out of ancient digests, has shown himself a serviceable guide[6] for us. Now, if I inquire of him who were the subtle inventors[7] of the gods, he points to either the philosophers, or the peoples, or the poets. For he has made a threefold distinction in classifying the gods: one being the *physical* class, of which the philosophers treat; another the *mythic* class, which is the constant burden of[8] the poets; the third, the *gentile* class, which the nations have adopted each one for itself. When, therefore, the philosophers have ingeniously composed their physical [theology] out of their own conjectures, when the poets have drawn their mythical from fables, and the [several] nations have forged their gentile [polytheism] according to their own will, where in the world must truth be placed? In the conjectures? Well, but these are only a doubtful conception. In the

---

[1] Quidni?   [2] Receptorum.
[3] Necessitatem [answering to the "leges dominantium"].
[4] Adulterinam.
[5] [St. Augustine, in his *de Civit. Dei*, makes similar use of Varro's work on the heathen gods, *Liber Divinarum*.]
[6] Scopum [perhaps "mark"].   [7] Insinuatores.
[8] Volutetur.

fables? But they are at best an absurd story. In the popular accounts?[1] This sort of opinion,[2] however, is only promiscuous[3] and municipal. Now all things with the philosophers are uncertain, because of their variation; with the poets all is worthless, because immoral; with the nations all is irregular and confused, because dependent on their mere choice. The nature of God, however, if it be the true one with which you are concerned, is of so definite a character as not to be derived from uncertain speculations,[4] nor contaminated with worthless fables, nor determined by promiscuous conceits. It ought indeed to be regarded, as it really is, as certain, entire, universal, because it is in truth the property of all. Now, what god shall I believe? One that has been gauged by vague suspicion? One that history[5] has divulged? One that a community has invented? It would be a far worthier thing if I believed no god, than one which is open to doubt, or full of shame, or the object of arbitrary selection.[6]

CHAP. II.—*The philosophers had not succeeded in discovering God. The uncertainty and confusion of their speculations.*

But the authority of the physical philosophers is maintained [among you][7] as the special property[8] of wisdom. [You mean,] of course, that pure and simple wisdom of the philosophers which attests its own weakness mainly by that variety of opinion which proceeds from an ignorance of the truth. Now what wise man is so devoid of truth, as not to know that God is the Father and Lord of wisdom itself and truth? Besides, there is that divine oracle uttered by Solomon: "The fear of the Lord," says he, "is the beginning of wisdom."[9] But[10] fear has its origin in knowledge; for

---

[1] Adoptionibus.
[2] Adoptatio.
[3] Passiva ["a jumble"].
[4] Argumentationibus.
[5] Historia. [This word seems to refer to the class of *mythical* divinity above mentioned. It therefore means "fable" or "absurd story" (see above).]
[6] Adoptivum.
[7] Patrocinatur.
[8] Mancipium.
[9] [Prov. ix. 10; Ps. cxi. 10.]
[10] Porro.

how will a man fear that of which he knows nothing? Therefore he who shall have the fear of God, even if he be ignorant of all things else, if he has attained to the knowledge and truth of God,[1] will possess full and perfect wisdom. This, however, is what philosophy has not clearly realized. For although, in their inquisitive disposition to search into all kinds of learning, [the philosophers] may seem to have investigated the sacred Scriptures themselves, for their antiquity, and to have derived thence some of their opinions, yet because they have interpolated [these deductions], they prove that they have either despised them wholly, or have not fully believed them (for in other cases also the simplicity of truth is shaken[2] by the over-scrupulousness of an irregular belief[3]), and that they therefore changed them, as their desire of glory grew, into products of their own mind. The consequence of this is, that even that which they had discovered degenerated into uncertainty, and there arose from one or two drops of truth a perfect flood of argumentation. For after they had simply[4] found God, they did not expound Him as they found Him, but rather disputed about His quality, and His nature, and even about His abode. The Platonists, indeed, [held] Him to care about worldly things, both as the disposer and judge thereof. The Epicureans [regarded] Him as apathetic[5] and inert, and (so to say) a nonentity.[6] The Stoics believed Him to be outside of the world; the Platonists, within the world. The God whom they had so imperfectly admitted, they could neither know nor fear; and therefore they could not be wise, since they wandered away indeed from "the beginning of wisdom," that is, "the fear of God." Proofs are not wanting that among the philosophers there was not only an ignorance, but actual doubt, about the divinity. Diogenes, when asked what was taking place in heaven, answered by saying, "I have never been up there." Again, whether there were any

---

[1] Deum omnium notitiam et veritatem adsecutus [*i.e.* "following the God of all as knowledge and truth"].
[2] Nutat.   [3] Passivæ fidei.   [4] Solummodo.
[5] Otiosum.   [6] ["A nobody."]

gods, he replied, "I do not know; only there ought to be gods."[1] When Crœsus inquired of Thales of Miletus what he thought of the gods, the latter having taken some time[2] to consider, answered by the word "Nothing." Even Socrates denied with an air of certainty[3] those gods of yours.[4] Yet he with a like certainty requested that a cock should be sacrificed to Æsculapius. And therefore when philosophy, in its practice of defining about God, is detected in such uncertainty and inconsistency, what "fear" could it possibly have had of Him whom it was not competent[5] clearly to determine? We have been taught to believe of the world that it is god.[6] For such the physical class of theologizers conclude it to be, since they have handed down such views about the gods, that Dionysius the Stoic divides them into three kinds. The first, he supposes, includes those gods which are most obvious, as the Sun, Moon, [and] Stars; the next, those which are not apparent, as Neptune; the remaining one, those which are said to have passed from the human state to the divine, as Hercules [and] Amphiaraus. In like manner, Arcesilaus makes a threefold form of the divinity—the Olympian, the Astral, the Titanian—sprung from Cœlus and Terra; from which through Saturn and Ops came Neptune, Jupiter, and Orcus, and their entire progeny. Xenocrates, of the Academy, makes a twofold division—the Olympian and the Titanian, which descend from Cœlus and Terra. Most of the Egyptians believe that there are four gods—the Sun and the Moon, the Heaven and the Earth. Along with all the supernal fire Democritus conjectures that the gods arose. Zeno, too, will have it that their nature resembles it. Whence Varro also makes fire to be the soul of the world, that in the world fire governs all things, just as the soul does in ourselves. But all this is most absurd. For he says, Whilst it is in us, we have existence; but as soon as it has left us, we die. Therefore, when fire quits the world in lightning, the world comes to its end.

[1] Nisi ut sint expedire.   [2] Aliquot commeatus.   [3] Quasi certus.
[4] Istos deos.   [5] Non tenebat.
[6] De mundo deo didicimus.

CHAP. III.—*The physical philosophers maintained the divinity of the* ELEMENTS; *the absurdity of the tenet exposed.*

From these developments of opinion, we see that your[1] physical class [of philosophers] are driven to the necessity of contending that the elements are gods, since it alleges that other gods are sprung from them; for it is only from gods that gods could be born. Now, although we shall have to examine these other gods more fully in the proper place, in the mythic section of the poets, yet, inasmuch as we must meanwhile treat of them in their connection with the present class,[2] we shall probably even from their present class,[3] when once we turn to the gods themselves, succeed in showing that they can by no means appear to be gods who are said to be sprung from the elements; so that we have at once a presumption[4] that the elements are not gods, since they which are born of the elements are not gods. In like manner, whilst we show that the elements are not gods, we shall, according to the law of natural relationship,[5] get a presumptive argument that they cannot rightly be maintained to be gods whose parents (in this case the elements) are not gods. It is a settled point[6] that a god is born of a god, and that what lacks divinity[7] is born of what is not divine. Now, so far as[8] the world of which your philosophers treat[9] (for I apply this term to the *universe* in the most comprehensive sense[10]) contains the elements, ministering to them as its component parts (for whatever its own condition may be, the same of course will be that of its elements and constituent portions), it must needs have been formed either by some being, according to the enlightened view[11] of Plato, or else by none, according to the harsh opinion[12] of Epicurus; and since it was formed, by having a beginning, it must also have

---

[1] Istud.
[2] Ad præsentem speciem [the *physical* class].
[3] [Or, classification.]
[4] Ut jam hinc præjudicatum sit.
[5] Ad illam agnatorum speciem.
[6] Scitum.
[7] Non-deum.
[8] [" Quod," with a subj. mood.]
[9] Mundus iste.
[10] Summaliter.
[11] Humanitas.
[12] Duritia.

an end. That, therefore, which at one time before its beginning had no existence, and will by and by after its end cease to have an existence, cannot of course, by any possibility, seem to be a god, wanting as it does that essential character of divinity, eternity, which is reckoned to be [1] without beginning, and without end. If, however, it [2] is in no wise formed, and therefore ought to be accounted divine—since, as divine, it is subject neither to a beginning nor an end of itself—how is it that some assign generation to the elements, which they hold to be gods, when the Stoics deny that anything can be born of a god? Likewise, how is it that they wish those beings, whom they suppose to be born of the elements, to be regarded as gods, when they deny that a god can be born? Now, what must hold good of the universe [3] will have to be predicated of the elements, I mean of heaven, and of earth, and of the stars, and of fire, which Varro has vainly proposed that you should believe [4] to be gods, and the parents of gods, contrary to that generation and nativity which he had declared to be impossible in a god. Now this same Varro had shown that the earth and the stars were animated.[5] But if this be the case, they must needs be also mortal, according to the condition [6] of animated nature; for although the soul is evidently immortal, this attribute is limited to it alone: it is not extended to that with which it is associated, that is, the body. Nobody, however, will deny that the elements have body, since we both touch them and are touched by them, and we see certain bodies fall down from them. If, therefore, they are animated, laying aside the principle [7] of a soul, as befits their condition as bodies, they are mortal—of course not immortal. And yet whence is it that the elements appear to Varro to be animated? Because, forsooth, the elements have motion. And then, in

---

[1] Censetur.
[2] [*i.e.* "iste mundus."]
[3] Mundi [*i.e.* the universe; see above].
[4] [The best reading is "vobis credi;" this is one of Tertullian's "*final* infinitives."]
[5] [Compare Augustine, *de Civit. Dei*, vii. 6, 23, 24, 28.]
[6] Formam. [7] Ratione.

order to anticipate what may be objected on the other side, that many things else have motion—as wheels, as carriages, as several other machines—he volunteers the statement that he believes only such things to be animated as move of themselves, without any apparent mover or impeller from without, like the apparent mover of the wheel, or propeller of the carriage, or director of the machine. If, then, they are not animated, they have no motion of themselves. Now, when he thus alleges a power which is not apparent, he points to what it was his duty to seek after, even the creator and controller of the motion; for it does not at once follow that, because we do not see a thing, we believe that it does not exist. Rather, it is necessary the more profoundly to investigate what one does not see, in order the better to understand the character of that which is apparent. Besides, if [you admit] only the existence of those things which appear and are supposed to exist simply because they appear, how is it that you also admit them to be gods which do not appear? If, moreover, those things seem to have existence which have none, why may they not have existence also which do not seem to have it? Such, for instance, as the Mover[1] of the heavenly beings. Granted, then, that things are animated because they move of themselves, and that they move of themselves when they are not moved by another: still it does not follow that they must straightway be gods, because they are animated, nor even because they move of themselves; else what is to prevent all animals whatever being accounted gods, moving as they do of themselves? This, to be sure, is allowed to the Egyptians, but their [superstitious] vanity has another basis.[2]

CHAP. IV.—*Wrong derivation of the word Θεός, God. The name indicative of the real Deity. God without shape, and immaterial. Anecdote of Thales; its relevancy here.*

Some affirm that the gods [*i.e.* θεοί] were so called, because the verbs θέειν and σείεσθαι signify *to run* and *to be*

[1] Motatorem.   [2] Alia sane vanitate.

moved.¹ This term, then, is not indicative of any majesty, for it is derived from *running* and *motion*, not from any dominion² of godhead. But inasmuch as the Supreme God whom we worship is also designated Θεός, without however the appearance of any *course* or *motion* in Him, because He is not visible to any one, it is clear that that word must have had some other derivation, and that the property of divinity, innate in Himself, must have been discovered. Dismissing, then, that ingenious interpretation, it is more likely that the gods were not called θεοί from *running* and *motion*, but that the term was borrowed from the designation of the true God; so that you gave the name θεοί to the gods, whom you had in like manner forged for yourselves. Now, that this is the case, a plain proof is afforded in the fact that you actually give the common appellation θεοί to all those gods of yours, in whom there is no attribute of *course* or *motion* indicated. When, therefore, you call them both θεοί and *immoveable* with equal readiness, there is a deviation as well from the meaning of the word as from the idea³ of godhead, which is set aside⁴ if measured by the notion of *course* and *motion*. But if that [sacred] name be peculiarly significant of deity, and be simply true and not of a forced interpretation⁵ in the case of the [true] God, but transferred in a borrowed sense⁶ to those other objects which you choose to call gods, then you ought to show to us⁷ that there is also a community of character between them, so that their common designation may rightly depend on their union of essence. But the true God, on the sole ground that He is not an object of sense, is incapable of being compared with those false deities which are cognizable to sight and sense (to sense indeed is sufficient); for this amounts to a clear statement of the difference between an obscure proof and a manifest one. Now, since

¹ [This seems to mean: "because θέειν has also the sense of σείεσθαι (motion as well as progression)."]
² ["Dominatione" is Oehler's reading, but he approves of "denominatione" (Rigault's reading); this would signify "*designation* of godhead."]
³ Opinione.   ⁴ Rescinditur.   ⁵ Interpretatorium.
⁶ Reprehensum.   ⁷ Docete.

the elements are obvious to all, [and] since God, on the contrary, is visible to none, how will it be in your power from that part which you have not seen to pass to a decision on the objects which you see? Since, therefore, you have not to combine them in your perception or your reason, why do you combine them in name with the purpose of combining them also in power? For see how even Zeno separates the matter of the world from God: he says that the latter has percolated through the former, like honey through the comb. God, therefore, and Matter are two words [and] two things. Proportioned to the difference of the words is the diversity of the things; the condition also of matter follows its designation. Now if matter is not [God], because its very appellation teaches us so, how can those things which are inherent in matter—that is, the elements—be regarded as gods, since the component members cannot possibly be heterogeneous from the body? But what concern have I with physiological conceits? It were better for one's mind to ascend above the state of the world, not to stoop down to uncertain speculations. Plato's form for the world was round. Its square, angular shape, such as others had conceived it to be, he rounded off, I suppose, with compasses, from his labouring to have it believed to be simply without a beginning.[1] Epicurus, however, who had said, "What is above us is nothing to us," wished notwithstanding to have a peep at the sky, and found the sun to be a foot in diameter. Thus far you must confess[2] men were niggardly in even celestial objects. In process of time their ambitious conceptions advanced, and so the sun too enlarged its disk.[3] Accordingly, the Peripatetics marked it out as a larger world.[4] Now, pray tell me, what wisdom is there in this hankering after conjectural speculations? What proof is afforded to us, notwithstanding the strong confidence of its assertions, by the useless affectation of a scrupulous curiosity,[5] which is tricked out with an

---

[1] Sine capite.   [2] Scilicet.   [3] Aciem.
[4] Majorem orbem. [Another reading has "majorem orbe," q.d. "as larger than the world."]
[5] Morositatis.

artful show of language? It therefore served Thales of Miletus quite right, when, star-gazing as he walked with all the eyes he had, he had the mortification of falling[1] into a well, and was unmercifully twitted by an Egyptian, who said to him, "Is it because you found nothing on earth to look at, that you think you ought to confine your gaze to the sky?" His fall, therefore, is a figurative picture of the philosophers; of those, I mean,[2] who persist in applying[3] their studies to a vain purpose, since they indulge a stupid curiosity on natural objects, which they ought rather [intelligently to direct] to their Creator and Governor.

CHAP. V.—*The physical theory continued. Further reasons advanced against the divinity of the elements: they may be necessary, but their very necessity implies subordination and dependence.*

Why, then, do we not resort to that far more reasonable[4] opinion, which has clear proof of being derived from men's common sense and unsophisticated deduction?[5] Even Varro bears it in mind, when he says that the elements are supposed to be divine, because nothing whatever is capable, without their concurrence,[6] of being produced, nourished, or applied to the sustenance[7] of man's life and of the earth, since not even our bodies and souls could have sufficed in themselves without the modification[8] of the elements. By this it is that the world is made generally habitable,—a result which is harmoniously secured[9] by the distribution into zones,[10] except where human residence has been rendered impracticable by intensity of cold or heat. On this account, men have accounted as gods—the sun, because it imparts from itself the light of day, ripens the fruit with its warmth, [and] measures the year with its stated periods; the moon, which is at once the solace of the night and the controller of the months by its governance; the stars also, certain indications as they

---

[1] Cecidit turpiter.
[2] Scilicet.
[3] Habituros.
[4] Humaniorem.
[5] Conjectura.
[6] Suffragio.
[7] Sationem.
[8] Temperamento.
[9] Fœderata.
[10] Circulorum conditionibus.

are of those seasons which are to be observed in the tillage
of our fields; lastly, the very heaven also under which, and
the earth over which, as well as the intermediate space
within which, all things conspire together for the good of
man. Nor is it from their beneficent influences only that
a faith in their divinity has been deemed compatible with
the elements, but from their opposite qualities also, such as
usually happen from what one might call[1] their wrath and
anger—as thunder, and hail, and drought, and pestilential
winds, floods also, and openings of the ground, and earth-
quakes: these are all fairly enough[2] accounted gods, whether
their nature becomes the object of reverence as being favourable, or of fear because terrible—the sovereign dispenser,[3] in
fact,[4] both of help and of hurt. But in the practical conduct
of social life, this is the way in which men act and feel: they
do not show gratitude or find fault with the very things
from which the succour or the injury proceeds, so much as
with them by whose strength and power the operation of the
things is effected. For even in your amusements you do
not award the crown as a prize to the flute or the harp, but
to the musician who manages the said flute or harp by the
power of his delightful skill.[5] In like manner, when one is
in ill-health, you do not bestow your acknowledgments on
the flannel wraps,[6] or the medicines, or the poultices, but on
the doctors by whose care and prudence the remedies become
effectual. So, again, in untoward events, they who are
wounded with the sword do not charge the injury on the
sword or the spear, but on the enemy or the robber; whilst
those whom a falling house covers do not blame the tiles or
the stones, but the oldness of the building; as again shipwrecked sailors impute their calamity not to the rocks and
waves, but to the tempest. And rightly too; for it is certain
that everything which happens must be ascribed not to the
instrument with which, but to the agent by whom, it takes
place; inasmuch as he is the prime cause of the occurrence,[7]
who appoints both the event itself and that by whose instru-

[1] Tanquam. [2] Jure. [3] Domina. [4] Scilicet.
[5] Vi suavitatis. [6] Lanis. [7] Caput facti.

mentality it comes to pass (as there are in all things these three particular elements—the fact itself, its instrument, and its cause), because he himself who wills the occurrence of a thing comes into notice[1] prior to the thing which he wills, or the instrument by which it occurs. On all other occasions, therefore, your conduct is right enough, because you consider the author; but in physical phenomena your rule is opposed to that natural principle which prompts you to a wise judgment in all other cases, removing out of sight as you do the supreme position of the author, and considering rather the things that happen, than him by whom they happen. Thus it comes to pass that you suppose the power and the dominion to belong to the elements, which are but the slaves and functionaries. Now do we not, in thus tracing out an artificer and master within, expose the artful structure of their slavery[2] out of the appointed functions of those elements to which you ascribe [the attributes] of power?[3] But gods are not slaves; therefore whatever things are servile in character are not gods. Otherwise[4] they should prove to us that, according to the ordinary course of things, liberty is promoted by irregular licence,[5] despotism by liberty, and that by despotism divine power is meant. For if all the [heavenly bodies] overhead forget not[6] to fulfil their courses in certain orbits, in regular seasons, at proper distances, [and] at equal intervals—appointed in the way of a law for the revolutions of time, and for directing the guidance thereof—can it fail to result[7] from the very observance of their conditions and the fidelity of their operations, that you will be convinced both by the recurrence of their orbital courses and the accuracy of their mutations, when you bear in mind how ceaseless is

---

[1] Invenitur.
[2] Servitutis artem. ["Artem" Oehler explains by "artificiose institutum."]
[3] [We subjoin Oehler's text of this obscure sentence: "Non in ista investigatione alicujus artificis intus et domini servitutis artem ostendimus elementorum certis ex operis" (for "operibus," not unusual in Tertullian) " eorum quas facis potestatis?"]
[4] Aut.   [5] De licentia passivitatis libertas approbetur.
[6] Meminerunt.   [7] Num non.

their recurrence, that a governing power presides over them, to which the entire management of the world[1] is obedient, reaching even to the utility and injury of the human race? For you cannot pretend that these [phenomena] act and care for themselves alone, without contributing anything to the advantage of mankind, when you maintain that the elements are divine for no other reason than that you experience from them either benefit or injury to yourself. For if they benefit themselves only, you are under no obligation to them.

CHAP. VI.—*The changes of the heavenly bodies afford proof that they are not divine. Transition from the physical to the mythic class of gods.*

Come now, do you allow that the Divine Being not only has nothing servile in His course, but exists in unimpaired integrity, and ought not to be diminished, or suspended, or destroyed? Well, then, all His blessedness[2] would disappear, if He were ever subject to change. Look, however, at the stellar bodies; they both undergo change, and give clear evidence of the fact. The moon tells us how great has been its loss, as it recovers its full form;[3] its greater losses you are already accustomed to measure in a mirror of water;[4] so that I need not any longer believe in anywise what magians have asserted. The sun, too, is frequently put to the trial of an eclipse. Explain as best you may the modes of these celestial casualties, it is impossible[5] for God either to become less or to cease to exist. Vain, therefore, are[6] those supports of human learning, which, by their artful method of weaving conjectures, belie both wisdom and truth. Besides,[7] it so happens, indeed, according to your natural way of

---

[1] Universa negotiatio mundialis.   [2] Felicitas.

[3] [These are the moon's *monthly* changes.]

[4] [Tertullian refers to the Magian method of watching eclipses, the ἐνοπτρομαντεία.]

[5] [Instead of "non valet," there is the reading "non volet," "God would not consent," etc.]

[6] Viderint igitur ["Let them look to themselves," "never mind them"].

[7] Alias.

thinking, that he who has spoken the best is supposed to have spoken most truly, instead of him who has spoken the truth being held to have spoken the best. Now the man who shall carefully look into things, will surely allow it to be a greater probability that those elements which we have been discussing[1] are under some rule and direction, than that they have a motion of their own, and that being under government they cannot be gods. If, however, one is in error in this matter, it is better to err simply than speculatively, like your physical philosophers. But, at the same time,[2] if you consider the character of the *mythic* school, [and compare it with the *physical*,] the error which we have already seen frail men[3] making in the latter is really the more respectable one, since it ascribes a divine nature to those things which it supposes to be *superhuman* in their sensibility, whether in respect of their position, their power, their magnitude, or their divinity. For that which you suppose to be higher than man, you believe to be very near to God.

CHAP. VII.—*The gods of the* MYTHIC *class cursorily noticed. The poets, who are the authors thereof, are a very poor and whimsical authority in such matters. Homer and the mythic poets, why irreligious?*

But to pass to the *mythic* class of gods, which we attributed to the poets,[4] I hardly know whether I must only seek to put them on a par with our own [human] mediocrity, or whether they must be affirmed to be gods, with proofs of divinity, like the African Mopsus and the Bœotian Amphiaraus. I must now indeed but slightly touch on this class, of which a fuller view will be taken in the proper place.[5] Meanwhile, that these were only human beings, is clear from the fact that you do not consistently call them gods, but heroes. Why then discuss the point? Although divine honours had to be ascribed to dead men, it was not to them as such, of course. Look at your own practice, when with

[1] Ista. [2] Sedenim.
[3] Mortalitas. [4] [See above, c. i.]
[5] [See *The Apology*, especially cc. xxii. and xxiii.]

similar excess of presumption you sully heaven with the
sepulchres of your kings : is it not such as are illustrious for
justice, virtue, piety, and every excellence of this sort, that
you honour with the blessedness of deification, contented
even to incur contempt if you forswear yourselves[1] for such
characters? And, on the other hand, do you not deprive the
impious and disgraceful of even the old prizes of human
glory, tear up[2] their decrees and titles, pull down their statues,
and deface[3] their images on the current coin? Will He,
however, who beholds all things, who approves, nay, rewards
the good, prostitute before all men[4] the attribute of His own
inexhaustible grace and mercy? And shall men be allowed
an especial amount of care and righteousness, that they may
be wise[5] in selecting and multiplying[6] their deities? Shall
attendants on kings and princes be more pure than those
who wait on the Supreme God?[7] You turn your back in
horror, indeed, on outcasts and exiles, on the poor and weak,
on the obscurely born and the low-lived;[8] but yet you
honour, even by legal sanctions,[9] unchaste men, adulterers,
robbers, and parricides. Must we regard it as a subject of
ridicule or indignation, that such characters are believed to
be gods who are not fit to be men? Then, again, in this
mythic class of yours which the poets celebrate, how uncertain is your conduct as to purity of conscience and the maintenance thereof! For whenever we hold up to execration
the wretched, disgraceful, and atrocious [examples] of your
gods, you defend them as mere fables, on the pretence of
poetic licence; whenever we volunteer a silent contempt[10] of
this said[11] poetic [licence], then you are not only troubled

---

[1] Pejerantes.   [2] Lancinatis.   [3] Repercutitis.   [4] Vulgo.

[5] Sapere. [The infinitive of *purpose* is frequent in our author.]

[6] Distribuendis.

[7] [An allusion to Antinous, who is also referred to in *The Apology*, xiii.]

[8] Inhoneste institutos.

[9] [By the "legibus" Tertullian refers to the divine honours ordered to be paid, by decrees of the Senate, to deceased emperors. Comp. Suetonius, *Octav.* 88; and Pliny, *Paneg.* 11 (Oehler).]

[10] Ultro siletur.   [11] Ejusmodi.

with no horror of it, but you go so far as¹ to show it respect, and to hold it as one of the indispensable [fine] arts; nay,² you carry out the studies of your higher classes³ by its means, as the very foundation⁴ of your literature. Plato was of opinion that poets ought to be banished, as calumniators of the gods; [he would even have] Homer himself expelled from his republic, although, as you are aware,⁵ he was the crowned head of them all. But while you admit and retain them thus, why should you not believe them when they disclose such things respecting your gods? And if you do believe your poets, how is it that you worship such gods [as they describe]? If you worship them simply because you do not believe the poets, why do you bestow praise on such lying authors, without any fear of giving offence to those whose calumniators you honour? A regard for truth⁶ is not, of course, to be expected of poets. But when you say that they only make men into gods after their death, do you not admit that before death the said gods were merely human? Now what is there strange in the fact, that they who were once men are subject to the dishonour⁷ of human casualties, or crimes, or fables? Do you not, in fact, put faith in your poets, when it is in accordance with their rhapsodies⁸ that you have arranged in some instances your very rituals? How is it that the priestess of Ceres is ravished, if it is not because Ceres suffered a similar outrage? Why are the children of others sacrificed to Saturn,⁹ if it is not because he spared not his own? Why is a male mutilated in honour of the Idæan goddess [Cybele], unless it be that the [unhappy] youth who was too disdainful of her advances was castrated, owing to her vexation at his daring to cross her love?¹⁰ Why was not Hercules "a dainty dish" to the good ladies of Lanuvium, if it was not for the primeval offence which women gave to him? The poets, no doubt,

---

¹ Insuper.   ² Denique.   ³ Ingenuitatis.   ⁴ Initiatricem.
⁵ Sane.   ⁶ Fides.   ⁷ Polluuntur.   ⁸ Relationibus.
⁹ [Comp. *The Apology*, ix.]
¹⁰ [Comp. Minucius Felix, *Octav.* xxi.; Arnobius, *adv. Nat.* v. 6, 7; Augustine, *Civ. Dei*, vi. 7.]

are liars. Yet it is not because [of their telling us that][1] your gods did such things when they were human beings, nor because they predicated divine scandals[2] of a divine state, since it seemed to you more credible that gods should exist, though not of such a character, than that there should be such characters, although not gods.

CHAP. VIII.—*The gods of the different nations, Varro's* GENTILE *class; general remarks on them. Their inferiority. A good deal of this perverse theology taken from Scripture. Serapis is a perversion of Joseph.*

There remains the *gentile* class of gods amongst the several nations :[3] these were adopted out of mere caprice, not from the knowledge of the truth; and our information about them comes from the private notions [of different races]. God, I imagine, is everywhere known, everywhere present, powerful everywhere—an object whom all ought to worship, all ought to serve. Since, then, it happens that even they, whom all the world worships in common, fail in the evidence of their true divinity, how much more must this befall those whom their very votaries[4] have not succeeded in discovering! For what useful authority could possibly precede a theology of so defective a character as to be wholly unknown to fame? How many have either seen or heard of the Syrian Atargatis, the African Cœlestis, the Moorish Varsutina, the Arabian Obodas and Dusaris, [or] the Norican Belenus, or those whom Varro mentions—Deluentinus of Casinum, Visidianus of Narnia, Numiternus of Atina, [or] Ancharia of Asculum? And who have any clear notions[5] of Nortia of Vulsinii?[6] There is no difference in the worth of even their names, apart from the human sur-

[1] [This is the force of the *subjunctive* verb.]

[2] [By *divine scandals*, he means such as exceed in their atrocity even human scandals.]

[3] [See above, c. i.]

[4] Municipes. ["Their local worshippers or subjects."]

[5] Perceperint.

[6] [Literally, "Have men heard of any Nortia belonging to the Vulsinensians?"]

names which distinguish them. I laugh often enough at the little coteries of gods[1] in each municipality, which have their honours confined within their own city walls. To what lengths this licence of adopting gods has been pushed, the superstitious practices of the Egyptians show us; for they worship even their native[2] animals, [such as] cats, crocodiles, and their snake. It is therefore a small matter that they have also deified a man—him, I mean, whom not Egypt only, or Greece, but the whole world worships, and the Africans swear by; about whose state also all that helps our conjectures and imparts to our knowledge the semblance of truth is stated in our own [sacred] literature. For that Serapis of yours was originally one of our own saints called Joseph.[3] The youngest of his brethren, but superior to them in intellect, he was from envy sold into Egypt, and became a slave in the family of Pharaoh king of the country.[4] Importuned by the unchaste queen, when he refused to comply with her desire, she turned upon him and reported him to the king, by whom he is put into prison. There he displays the power of his divine inspiration, by interpreting aright the dreams of some [fellow-prisoners]. Meanwhile the king, too, has some terrible dreams. Joseph being brought before him, according to his summons, was able to expound them. Having narrated the proofs of true interpretation which he had given in the prison, he opens out his dream to the king: those seven fat-fleshed and well-favoured kine signified as many years of plenty; in like manner, the seven lean-fleshed animals predicted the scarcity of the seven following years. He accordingly recommends precautions to be taken against the future famine from the

---

[1] Deos decuriones [in allusion to the *small provincial senates* which in the later times spread over the Roman colonies and *municipia*].

[2] Privatas.

[3] [Compare Suidas, *s. v.* Σαράπις; Rufinus, *Hist. Eccl.* ii. 23. As Serapis was Joseph in disguise, so was Joseph a type of Christ, according to the ancient Christians, who were fond of subordinating heathen myths to Christian theology.]

[4] [Tertullian is not the only writer who has made mistakes in citing from memory Scripture narratives. Comp. Arnobius.]

previous plenty. The king believed him. The issue of all that happened showed how wise he was, how invariably holy, and now how necessary. So Pharaoh set him over all Egypt, that he might secure the provision of corn for it, and thenceforth administer its government. They called him Serapis, from the turban[1] which adorned his head. The peck-like[2] shape of this turban marks the memory of his corn-provisioning; whilst evidence is given that the care of the supplies was all on his head,[3] by the very ears of corn which embellish the border of the head-dress. For the same reason, also, they made the sacred figure of a dog,[4] which they regard [as a sentry] in Hades, and put it under his right hand, because the care of the Egyptians was concentrated[5] under his hand. And they put at his side Pharia,[6] whose name shows her to have been the king's daughter. For in addition to all the rest of his kind gifts and rewards, Pharaoh had given him his own daughter in marriage. Since, however, they had begun to worship both wild animals and human beings, they combined both figures under one form Anubis, in which there may rather be seen clear proofs of its own character and condition enshrined[7] by a nation at war with itself, refractory[8] to its kings, despised among foreigners, with even the appetite of a slave and the filthy nature of a dog.

CHAP. IX.—*The power of Rome in the world gave, in fact, a Romanized aspect to all the heathen mythology. Varro's threefold distribution of the Roman gods criticised. The chief of the Roman heroes, Æneas included, unfavourably reviewed.*

Such are the more obvious or more remarkable points which we had to mention in connection with Varro's threefold distribution of the gods, in order that a sufficient answer might seem to be given touching the physical, the poetic, and

---

[1] Suggestu.
[2] Modialis.
[3] Super caput esse [*i.e.* was entrusted to him].
[4] Canem dicaverunt.
[5] Compressa.
[6] [Isis; comp. *The Apology*, xvi.]
[7] Consecrasse.
[8] Recontrans.

the gentile classes. Since, however, it is no longer to the philosophers, nor the poets, nor the nations that we owe the substitution of all [heathen worship for the true religion], although they transmitted the superstition, but to the dominant Romans, who received the tradition and gave it its wide authority, another phase of the widespread error of man must now be encountered by us; nay, another forest must be felled [by our axe], which has obscured the childhood of the degenerate worship[1] with germs of superstitions gathered from all quarters. Well, but even the gods of the Romans have received from [the same] Varro a threefold classification into the *certain*, the *uncertain*, and the *select*. What absurdity! What need had they of uncertain gods, when they possessed certain ones? Unless, forsooth, they wished to commit themselves to[2] such folly as the Athenians did; for at Athens there was an altar with this inscription: "TO THE UNKNOWN GODS."[3] Does, then, a man worship that which he knows nothing of? Then, again, as they had certain gods, they ought to have been contented with them, without requiring select ones. In this want they are even found to be irreligious! For if gods are selected as onions are,[4] then such as are not chosen are declared to be worthless. Now we on our part allow that the Romans had two sets of gods, *common* and *proper;* in other words, those which they had in common with other nations, and those which they themselves devised. And were not these called the *public* and the *foreign*[5] gods? Their altars tell us so; there is [a specimen] of the foreign gods at the fane of Carna, of the public gods in the Palatium. Now, since their common gods are comprehended in both the physical and the mythic classes, we have already said enough concerning them. I should like to speak of their particular kinds of deity. We ought then to admire the Romans for

[1] Vitii pueritatem.
[2] Recipere [with a dative].
[3] IGNOTIS DEIS. [Comp. Acts xvii. 23.]
[4] Ut bulbi. [This is the passage which Augustine quotes (*de Civit. Dei*, vii. 1) as " too facetious."]
[5] Adventicii [" coming from abroad "].

that third set of *the gods of their enemies*,[1] because no other
nation ever discovered for itself so large a mass of superstition. Their other deities we arrange in two classes: those
which have become gods from human beings, and those
which have had their origin in some other way. Now, since
there is advanced the same colourable pretext for the deification of the dead, that their lives were meritorious, we are
compelled to urge the same reply against them, that no one
of them was worth so much pains. Their fond [2] father
Æneas, in whom they believed, was never glorious, and was
felled with a stone [3]—a vulgar weapon, to pelt a dog withal, inflicting a wound no less ignoble! But this Æneas turns out [4]
a traitor to his country; yes, quite as much as Antenor. And
if they will not believe this to be true of him, he at any rate
deserted his companions when his country was in flames, and
must be held inferior to that woman of Carthage,[5] who, when
her husband Hasdrubal supplicated the enemy with the mild
pusillanimity of our Æneas, refused to accompany him, but
hurrying her children along with her, disdained to take her
beautiful self and father's noble heart [6] into exile, but plunged
into the flames of the burning Carthage, as if rushing into the
embraces of her [dear but] ruined country. Is he " pious
Æneas " for [rescuing] his young only son and decrepid old
father, but deserting Priam and Astyanax? But the Romans
ought rather to detest him; for in defence of their princes
and their royal [7] house, they surrender [8] even children and
wives, and every dearest pledge.[9] They deify the son of
Venus, and this with the full knowledge and consent of [her
husband] Vulcan, and without opposition from even Juno.
Now, if sons have seats in heaven owing to their piety to

---

[1] [Touching these gods of the vanquished nations, compare *The Apology*, xxv.; below, c. xvii.; Minucius Felix, *Octav.* xxv.]
[2] Diligentem. [3] [See Homer, *Il.* v. 300.]
[4] Invenitur. [5] [Referred to also above, i. 18.]
[6] [The obscure " formam et patrem " is by Oehler rendered " pulchri-tudinem et generis nobilitatem."]
[7] [The word is " eorum " (possessive of " principum "), not " suæ."]
[8] Dejerant adversus.
[9] [What Tertullian himself thinks on this point, see his *de Corona*, xi.]

their parents, why are not those noble youths[1] of Argos rather accounted gods, because they, to save their mother from guilt in the performance of some sacred rites, with a devotion more than human, yoked themselves to her car and dragged her to the temple? Why not make a goddess, for her exceeding piety, of that daughter[2] who from her own breasts nourished her father who was famishing in prison? What other glorious achievement can be related of Æneas, but that he was nowhere seen in the fight on the field of Laurentum? Following his bent, perhaps he fled a second time as a fugitive from the battle.[3] In like manner, Romulus posthumously becomes a god. Was it because he founded the city? Then why not others also, who have built cities, counting even[4] women? To be sure, Romulus slew his brother in the bargain, and trickstily ravished some foreign virgins. Therefore of course he becomes a god, and therefore a Quirinus ["god of the spear"], because then their fathers had to use the spear[5] on his account. What did Sterculus do to merit deification? If he worked hard to enrich the fields *stercoribus*,[6] [with manure,] Augias had more dung than he to bestow on them. If Faunus, the son of Picus, used to do violence to law and right, because struck with madness, it was more fit that he should be doctored than deified.[7] If the daughter of Faunus so excelled in chastity, that she would hold no conversation with men, it was perhaps from rudeness, or a consciousness of deformity, or shame for her father's insanity. How much worthier of divine honour than this "good goddess"[8] was Penelope, who,

---

[1] [Cleobis and Biton; see Herodotus, i. 31.]
[2] [See Valerius Maximus, v. 4, 1.]
[3] [We need not stay to point out the unfairness of this statement, in contrast with the exploits of Æneas against Turnus, as detailed in the last books of the *Æneid*.] [4] Usque in.
[5] [We have thus rendered "quiritatem est," to preserve as far as one could the pun on the deified hero of the *Quirites*.]
[6] [We insert the Latin, to show the pun on *Sterculus*; see *The Apology*, c. xxv.]
[7] Curaria quam consecrari.
[8] Bona Dea [*i.e.* the daughter of Faunus just mentioned].

although dwelling among so many suitors of the vilest character, preserved with delicate tact the purity which they assailed! There is Sanctus, too,[1] who for his hospitality had a temple consecrated to him by king Plotius; and even Ulysses had it in his power to have bestowed one more god upon you in the person of the most refined Alcinous.

CHAP. X.—*It is a disgraceful feature of the Roman mythology, that it honours such infamous characters as* LARENTINA.

I hasten to even more abominable cases. Your writers have not been ashamed to publish that of Larentina. She was a hired prostitute, whether as the nurse of Romulus, and therefore called *Lupa*, because she was a prostitute, or as the mistress of Hercules, now deceased, that is to say, now deified. They [2] relate that his temple-warder [3] happened to be playing at dice in the temple alone; and in order to represent a partner for himself in the game, in the absence of an actual one, he began to play with one hand for Hercules and the other for himself. [The condition was,] that if he won the stakes from Hercules, he should with them procure a supper and a prostitute; if Hercules, however, proved the winner (I mean his other hand), then he should provide the same for Hercules. The hand of Hercules won. That achievement might well have been added to his twelve labours! The temple-warden buys a supper for the hero, and hires Larentina to play the whore. The fire which dissolved the body of even a Hercules [4] enjoyed the supper, and the altar consumed everything. Larentina sleeps alone in the temple; and [she], a woman from the brothel, boasts that in her dreams she had submitted herself to the pleasure of Hercules; [5] and she might possibly have experienced this, as it passed through her mind, in her sleep. In the morning, on going out of the temple very early, she is solicited by a

---

[1] [See Livy, viii. 20, xxxii. 1; Ovid, *Fasti*, vi. 213, etc. Compare also Augustine, *de Civ. Dei*, xviii. 19.]
[2] [Compare Augustine, *de Civ. Dei*, vi. 7.]   [3] Ædituum ejus.
[4] [That is, when he mounted the pyre.]
[5] Herculi functam. ["Fungi alicui" means to satisfy, or yield to.]

young man—"a third Hercules," so to speak.[1] He invites her home. She complies, remembering that Hercules had told her that it would be for her advantage. He then, to be sure, obtains permission that they should be united in lawful wedlock (for none was allowed to have intercourse with the concubine of a god without being punished for it); the husband makes her his heir. By and by, just before her death, she bequeathed to the Roman people the rather large estate which she had obtained through Hercules. After this she sought deification for her daughters too, whom indeed the divine Larentina ought to have appointed her heirs also. The gods of the Romans received an accession in her dignity. For she alone of all the wives of Hercules was dear to him, because she alone was rich; and she was even far more fortunate than Ceres, who contributed to the pleasure of the [king of the] dead.[2] After so many examples and [eminent] names among you, who might not have been declared divine? Who, in fact, ever raised a question as to his divinity against Antinous?[3] Was even Ganymede more grateful and dear than he to [the supreme god] who loved him? According to you, heaven is open to the dead. You prepare[4] a way from Hades to the stars. Prostitutes mount it in all directions, so that you must not suppose that you are conferring a great distinction upon your kings.

CHAP. XI.—*The Romans provided gods for every stage of possible human existence from the birth, nay, even before birth, to the death. Much indelicacy in this system.*

And you are not content to assert the divinity of such as were once known to you, whom you heard and handled, and whose portraits have been painted, and actions recounted, and memory retained amongst you; but men insist upon con-

---

[1] [The well-known Greek saying, "Άλλος οὗτος 'Ηρακλῆς.]
[2] [Pluto; Proserpine, the daughter of Ceres, is meant. Oehler once preferred to read, "Hebe, quæ mortuo placuit," *i.e.* "than Hebe, who gratified Hercules after death."]
[3] [Tertullian often refers indignantly to this atrocious case.]
[4] Subigitis.

secrating with a heavenly life[1] I know not what incorporeal, inanimate shadows, and the [mere] names of things—dividing man's entire existence amongst separate powers, even from his conception in the womb: so that there is a god Consevius,[2] to preside over concubital generation; and Fluviona,[3] to preserve the [growth of the] infant in the womb; after these come Vitumnus and Sentinus,[4] through whom the babe begins to have life and its earliest sensation; then Diespiter,[5] by whose office the child accomplishes its birth. But when women begin their parturition, Candelifera also [comes in aid], since childbearing requires the light of the candle; and other goddesses there are[6] who get their names from the parts they bear in the stages of travail. There were two Carmentas likewise, according to the general view: to one of them, called Postverta, belonged the function of assisting the birth of the introverted child; while the other, Prosa,[7] executed the like office for the rightly born. The god Farinus was so called from [his inspiring] the first utterance; while others believed in Locutius from his gift of speech. Cunina[8] is present as the protector of the child's deep slumber, and supplies to it refreshing rest. To lift them [when fallen][9] there is Levana, and along with her Rumina.[10] It is a wonderful oversight that no gods were appointed for cleaning up the filth of children. Then, to preside over their first pap and earliest drink, you have Potina

---

[1] Efflagitant cœlo et sanciunt [*i.e.* "they insist on deifying"].

[2] [Comp. Augustine, *de Civ. Dei*, vi. 9.]

[3] [A name of Juno, in reference to her office to mothers, "quia eam sanguinis fluorem in conceptu retinere putabant." Comp. August. *de Civ. Dei*, iii. 2.]

[4] [Comp. August. *de Civ. Dei*, vii. 2, 3.]

[5] [Comp. August. *de Civ. Dei*, iv. 11.]

[6] [Such as Lucina, Partula, Nona, Decima, Alemona.]

[7] [Or, Prorsa.]

[8] ["Quæ infantes *in cunis* (in their cradle) tuetur." Comp. August. *de Civ. Dei*, iv. 11.]

[9] Educatrix [Augustine says: "Ipse levet de terra et vocetur dea Levana" (*de Civ. Dei*, iv. 11)].

[10] [From the old word *ruma*, a teat.]

and Edula;[1] to teach the child to stand erect is the work of Statina,[2] whilst Adeona helps him to come [to dear Mamma], and Abeona to toddle off again; then there is Domiduca,[3] [to bring home the bride;] and the goddess Mens, to influence the mind to either good or evil.[4] They have likewise Volumnus and Voleta,[5] to control the will; Paventina, [the goddess] of fear; Venilia, of hope;[6] Volupia, of pleasure;[7] Præstitia, of beauty.[8] Then, again, they give his name to Peragenor,[9] from his teaching men to go through their work; to Consus, from his suggesting to them counsel. Juventa is their guide on assuming the manly gown, and "bearded Fortune" when they come to full manhood.[10] If I must touch on their nuptial duties, there is Afferenda, whose appointed function is to see to the offering of the dower; but, fie on you! you have your Mutunus,[11] and Tutunus, and Pertunda,[12] and Subigus, and the goddess Prema, and likewise Perfica.[13] O spare yourselves, ye impudent gods! No one is present at the secret struggles of married life. Those very persons who have a wish that way, go away and blush for very shame in the midst of their joy.

[1] [Comp. August. de Civ. Dei, iv. 9, 11, 36.]
[2] [See also Tertullian's de Anima, xxxix.; and Augustine's de Civ. Dei, iv. 21, where the god has the masculine name of Statilinus.]
[3] [See Augustine, de Civ. Dei, vi. 9 and vii. 3.]
[4] [Ibid. iv. 21, vii. 3.]
[5] [Ibid. iv. 21.]
[6] [Ibid. iv. 11, vii. 22.]
[7] [Ibid. iv. 11.]
[8] [Arnobius, adv. Nationes, iv. 8.]
[9] [Augustine, de Civ. Dei, mentions the goddess Agenoria.]
[10] [On Fortuna Barbata, see Augustine, de Civ. Dei, iv. 11, where he also names Consus and Juventa.]
[11] [Tertullian, in Apol. xxv., sarcastically says, "Sterculus, and Mutunus, and Larentina, have raised the empire to its present height."]
[12] [Arnobius, adv. Nationes, iv. 7, 11; August. de Civ. Dei, vi. 9.]
[13] [For these three gods, see Augustine, de Civ. Dei, vi. 9; and Arnobius, adv. Nationes, iv. 7.]

Chap. XII.[1]—*The original deities, Cœlus and Terra, were human in their character—with some very questionable characteristics.* Saturn *or* Time; *inconsistencies of opinion about him: he, too, was human.*

Now, how much further need I go in recounting your gods—because I want to descant on the character of such as you have adopted? It is quite uncertain whether I shall laugh at your absurdity, or upbraid you for your blindness. For how many, and indeed what, gods shall I bring forward? Shall it be the greater ones, or the lesser? The old ones, or the novel? The male, or the female? The unmarried, or such as are joined in wedlock? The clever, or the unskilful? The rustic or the town ones? The national or the foreign? For the truth is,[2] there are so many families, so many nations, which require a catalogue [3] [of gods], that they cannot possibly be examined, or distinguished, or described. But the more diffuse the subject is, the more restriction must we impose on it. As, therefore, in this review we keep before us but one object—that of proving that all these gods were once human beings (not, indeed, to instruct you in the fact,[4] for your conduct shows that you have forgotten it)— let us adopt our compendious summary from the most natural method [5] of conducting the examination, even by considering the origin of their race. For the origin characterizes all that comes after it. Now this origin of your gods dates,[6] I suppose, from Saturn. And when Varro mentions Jupiter, Juno, and Minerva, as the most ancient of the gods, it ought not to have escaped our notice, that every father is more ancient than his sons, and that Saturn therefore must precede Jupiter, even as Cœlus does Saturn, for Saturn was sprung from Cœlus and Terra. I pass by, however, the origin of Cœlus and Terra. They led in some unaccountable way [7] single lives, and had no children. Of course they required

---

[1] [Agrees with *The Apology*, c. x.] [2] Bona fide. [3] Censum.
[4] [There is here an omitted clause, supplied in *The Apology*, " but rather to recall it to your memory."]
[5] Ab ipsa ratione. [6] Signatur. [7] Undeunde.

a long time for vigorous growth to attain to such a stature.[1] By and by, as soon as the voice of Cœlus began to break,[2] and the breasts of Terra to become firm,[3] they contract marriage with one another. I suppose either Heaven[4] came down to his spouse, or Earth went up to meet her lord. Be that as it may, Earth conceived seed of Heaven, and when her year was fulfilled brought forth Saturn in a wonderful manner. Which of his parents did he resemble? Well, then, even after parentage began,[5] it is certain[6] that they had no child previous to Saturn, and only one daughter afterwards—Ops; thenceforth they ceased to procreate. The truth is, Saturn castrated Cœlus as he was sleeping. We read this name Cœlus as of the masculine gender. And for the matter of that, how could he be a father unless he were a male? But with what instrument was the castration effected? He had a scythe. What, so early as that? For Vulcan was not yet an artificer in iron. The widowed Terra, however, although still quite young, was in no hurry[7] to marry another. Indeed, there was no second Cœlus for her. What but Ocean offers her an embrace? But he savours of brackishness, and she has been accustomed to fresh water.[8] And so Saturn is the sole male child of Cœlus and Terra. When grown to puberty, he marries his own sister. No laws as yet prohibited incest, nor punished parricide. Then, when male children were born to him, he would devour them; better himself [should take them] than the wolves, [for to these would they become a prey] if he exposed them. He was, no doubt, afraid that one of them might learn the lesson of his father's scythe. When Jupiter was born in course of time, he was removed out of the way:[9] [the father] swallowed a stone instead of the son, as was pretended.

[1] Tantam proceritatem.
[2] Insolescere [*i.e.* at the commencement of puberty].
[3] Lapilliscere [*i.e.* to indicate maturity].
[4] [The nominative " cœlum " is used.]
[5] [It is not very clear what is the force of " sed et pepererit," as read by Oehler; we have given the clause an impersonal turn.]
[6] [" Certe " is sometimes " certo " in our author.]
[7] Distulit.   [8] [That is, to rain and cloud.]   [9] Abalienato.

This artifice secured his safety for a time; but at length the son, whom he had not devoured, and who had grown up in secret, fell upon him, and deprived him of his kingdom. Such, then, is the patriarch of the gods whom Heaven[1] and Earth produced for you, with the poets officiating as midwives. Now some persons with a refined[2] imagination are of opinion that, by this allegorical fable of Saturn, there is a physiological representation of *Time:* [they think] that it is because all things are destroyed by Time, that Cœlus and Terra were themselves parents without having any of their own, and that the [fatal] scythe was used, and that [Saturn] devoured his own offspring, because he,[3] in fact, absorbs within himself all things which have issued from him. They call in also the witness of his name; for they say that he is called Κρόνος in Greek, meaning the same thing as χρόνος.[4] His Latin name also they derive from *seed-sowing;*[5] for they suppose him to have been the actual procreator—that the seed, in fact, was dropt down from heaven to earth by his means. They unite him with *Ops,* because seeds produce the affluent treasure (*Opem*) of actual life, and because they develope with labour (*Opus*). Now I wish that you would explain this metaphorical[6] statement. It was either Saturn or Time. If it was Time, how could it be Saturn? If he, how could it be Time? For you cannot possibly reckon both these corporeal subjects[7] as co-existing in one person. What, however, was there to prevent your worshipping Time under its proper quality? Why not make a human person, or even a mythic man, an object of your adoration, but each in its proper nature, not in the character of Time? What is the meaning of that conceit of your mental ingenuity, if it be not to colour the foulest matters with the feigned appearance of reasonable proofs?[8] Neither, on the one hand, do

---

[1] [The word is "cœlum" here.]
[2] Eleganter.
[3] [*i.e.* as representing *Time.*]
[4] [So Augustine, *de Civ. Dei,* iv. 10; Arnobius, *adv. Nationes,* iii. 29; Cicero, *de Nat. Deor.* ii. 25.]
[5] [As if from "sero," *satum.*]
[6] Translatio.
[7] Utrumque corporale.
[8] Mentitis argumentationibus.

you mean Saturn to be Time, because you say he is a human
being; nor, on the other hand, whilst portraying him as Time,
do you on that account mean that he was ever human. No
doubt, in the accounts of remote antiquity your god Saturn
is plainly described as living on earth in human guise. Anything whatever may obviously be pictured as incorporeal
which never had an existence; there is simply no room for
such fiction, where there is reality. Since, therefore, there
is clear evidence that Saturn once existed, it is in vain that
you change his character. He whom you will not deny to
have once been man, is not at your disposal to be treated
anyhow, nor can it be maintained that he is either divine or
Time. In every page of your literature the origin [1] of Saturn
is conspicuous. We read of him in Cassius Severus and in
the Corneliuses, Nepos and Tacitus,[2] and, amongst the Greeks
also, in Diodorus, and all other compilers of ancient annals.[3]
No more faithful records of him are to be traced than in
Italy itself. For, after [traversing] many countries, and
[enjoying] the hospitality of Athens, he settled in Italy, or,
as it was then called, Œnotria, having met with a kind welcome from Janus, or Janes,[4] as the Salii call him. The
hill on which he settled had the name Saturnius, whilst the
city which he founded[5] still bears the name Saturnia; in
short, the whole of Italy once had the same designation.
Such is the testimony derived from that country which is
now the mistress of the world: whatever doubt prevails about
the origin of Saturn, his actions tell us plainly that he was a
human being. Since, therefore, Saturn was human, he came
undoubtedly from a human stock; and more, because he was
a man, he, of course, came not of Cœlus and Terra. Some
people, however, found it easy enough to call him, whose
parents were unknown, the son of those gods from whom all
may in a sense seem to be derived. For who is there that
does not speak under a feeling of reverence of the heaven
and the earth as his own father and mother? Or, in accord-

---

[1] Census.
[2] [See his *Histories*, v. 2, 4.]
[3] Antiquitatem canos ["hoary antiquity"].
[4] Jano sive Jane.
[5] Depalaverat ["marked out with stakes"].

ance with a custom amongst men, which induces them to say of any who are unknown or suddenly apparent, that "they came from the sky?" Hence it happened that, because a stranger appeared suddenly everywhere, it became the custom to call him a heaven-born man,[1]—just as we also commonly call earth-born all those whose descent is unknown. I say nothing of the fact that such was the state of antiquity, when men's eyes and minds were so habitually rude, that they were excited by the appearance of every newcomer as if it were that of a god: much more would this be the case with a king, and that the primeval one. I will linger some time longer over the case of Saturn, because by fully discussing his primordial history I shall beforehand furnish a compendious answer for all other cases; and I do not wish to omit the more convincing testimony of your sacred literature, the credit of which ought to be the greater in proportion to its antiquity. Now earlier than all literature was the Sibyl; that Sibyl, I mean, who was the true prophetess of truth, from whom you borrow their title for the priests of your demons. She in senarian verse expounds the descent of Saturn and his exploits in words to this effect: "In the tenth generation of men, after the flood had overwhelmed the former race, reigned Saturn, and Titan, and Japetus, the bravest of the sons of Terra and Cœlus." Whatever credit, therefore, is attached to your older writers and literature, and much more to those who were the simplest as belonging to that age,[2] it becomes sufficiently certain that Saturn and his family[3] were human beings. We have in our possession, then, a brief principle which amounts to a prescriptive rule about their origin serving for all other cases, to prevent our going wrong in individual instances. The particular character[4] of a posterity is shown by the original founders of the race—mortal beings [come] from mortals, earthly ones from earthly; step after step comes in due relation[5]—marriage, conception, birth—country, settlements,

---

[1] Cœlitem.　　[2] Magis proximis quoniam illius ætatis.
[3] Prosapia.　　[4] Qualitas.
[5] Comparantur.

kingdoms, all give the clearest proofs.¹ They, therefore, who cannot deny the birth of men, must also admit their death; they who allow their mortality must not suppose them to be gods.

CHAP. XIII.²—*As the gods were human at first, who had authority to make them divine?* JUPITER *not only human, but immoral.*

Manifest cases, indeed, like these have a force peculiarly their own. Men like Varro and his fellow-dreamers admit into the ranks of the divinity those whom they cannot assert to have been in their primitive condition anything but men; [and this they do] by affirming that they became gods after their death. Here, then, I take my stand. If your gods were elected³ to this dignity and deity,⁴ just as you recruit the ranks of your senate, you cannot help conceding, in your wisdom, that there must be some one supreme sovereign who has the power of selecting, and is a kind of Cæsar; and nobody is able to confer⁵ on others a thing over which he has not absolute control. Besides, if they were able to make gods of themselves after their death, pray tell me why they chose to be in an inferior condition at first? Or, again, if there is no one who made them gods, how can they be said to have been made such, if they could only have been made by some one else? There is therefore no ground afforded you for denying that there is a certain wholesale distributor⁶ of divinity. Let us accordingly examine the reasons for despatching mortal beings to heaven. I suppose you will produce a pair of them. Whoever, then, is the awarder [of the divine honours], exercises his function, either that he may have some supports, or defences, or it may be even ornaments to his own high dignity, or from the pressing claims of the meritorious, that he may reward all the deserving. No other cause is it permitted us to conjecture. Now there is no one who, when bestowing a gift on another, does

---

¹ Monumenta liquent.   ² [Comp. *The Apology*, c. xi.]   ³ Allecti.
⁴ [This is not so terse as Tertullian's "nomen et numen."]
⁵ Præstare.   ⁶ Mancipem.

not act with a view to his own interest or the other's. This conduct, however, cannot be worthy of the Divine Being, inasmuch as His power is so great that He can make gods outright; whilst His bringing man into such request, on the pretence that he requires the aid and support of certain, even dead, persons, is a strange conceit, since He was able from the very first to create for Himself immortal beings. He who has compared human things with divine will require no further arguments on these points. And yet the latter opinion ought to be discussed, that God conferred divine honours in consideration of meritorious claims. Well, then, if the award was made on such grounds, if heaven was opened to men of the primitive age because of their deserts, we must reflect that after that time no one was worthy of such honour; except it be, that there is now no longer such a place for any one to attain to. Let us grant that anciently men may have deserved heaven by reason of their great merits. Then let us consider whether there really was such merit. Let the man who alleges that it did exist declare his own view of merit. Since the actions of men done in the very infancy of time[1] are a valid claim for their deification, you consistently admitted to the honour the brother and sister who were stained with the sin of incest—Ops and Saturn. Your Jupiter too, stolen in his infancy, was unworthy of both the home and the nutriment accorded to human beings; and, as he deserved for so bad a child, he had to live in Crete.[2] Afterwards, when full-grown, he dethrones his own father, who, whatever his parental character may have been, was most prosperous in his reign, king as he was of the golden age. Under him, a stranger to toil and want, peace maintained its joyous and gentle sway; under him

"Nulli subigebant arva coloni"[3]—
"No swains would bring the fields beneath their sway;"[4]

and without the importunity of any one the earth would

[1] In cunabulis temporalitatis.
[2] [The ill-fame of the Cretans is noticed by St. Paul, Tit. i. 12.]
[3] [Virgil, *Georg.* i. 125.]   [4] [Sewell.]

bear all crops spontaneously.¹ But he hated a father who had been guilty of incest, and had once mutilated his² grandfather. And yet, behold, he himself marries his own sister; so that I should suppose the old adage was made for him: Τοῦ πατρὸς τὸ παιδίον—"Father's own child." There was "not a pin to choose" between the father's piety and the son's. If the laws had been just even at that early time,³ Jupiter ought to have been "sewed up in both sacks."⁴ After this corroboration of his lust with incestuous gratification, why should he hesitate to indulge himself lavishly in the lighter excesses of adultery and debauchery? Ever since⁵ poetry sported thus with his character in some such way as is usual when a runaway slave⁶ is posted up in public, we have been in the habit of gossiping without restraint⁷ of his tricks⁸ in our chat with passers-by;⁹ sometimes sketching him out in the form of the very money which was the fee of his debauchery —as when [he personated] a bull, or rather paid the money's worth of one,¹⁰ and showered [gold] into the maiden's chamber, or rather forced his way in with a bribe;¹¹ sometimes [figuring him] in the very likenesses of the parts which were acted¹²—as the eagle which ravished [the beautiful youth],¹³ and the swan which sang [the enchanting song].¹⁴ Well now, are not such fables as these made up of the most disgusting intrigues and the worst of scandals? or would not the morals and tempers of men be likely to become more wanton from such examples? In what manner demons, the offspring of evil angels who have been long engaged in their mission, have laboured to turn men¹⁵ aside from the faith to unbelief

---

¹ Ipsa.   ² [Jupiter's, of course.]
³ [The law which prescribed the penalty of the parricide, that he be *sewed up in a sack* with an ape, a serpent, and a cock, and be thrown into the sea.]
⁴ In duos culleos dividi.   ⁵ De quo.
⁶ De fugitivo.   ⁷ Abusui nundinare.
⁸ [The "operam ejus" = *ingenia et artificia* (Oehler).]
⁹ Percontationi alienæ.   ¹⁰ [In the case of Europa.]
¹¹ [In the case of Danäe.]   ¹² Similitudines actuum ipsas.
¹³ [In the case of Ganymede.]   ¹⁴ [In the case of Leda.]
¹⁵ Quos.

and to such fables, we must not in this place speak of to any extent. As indeed the general body [1] [of your gods], which took their cue [2] from their kings, and princes, and instructors, [3] was not of the self-same nature, it was in some other way [4] that similarity of character was exacted by their authority. But how much the worst of them was he who [ought to have been, but] was not, the best of them? By a title peculiar to him, you are indeed in the habit of calling Jupiter "the Best," [5] whilst in Virgil he is "Æquus Jupiter." [6] All therefore were *like* him—incestuous towards their own kith and kin, unchaste to strangers, impious, unjust! Now he whom mythic story left untainted with no conspicuous infamy, was not worthy to be made a god.

CHAP. XIV.—*Take the* FACTITIOUS *gods, those which were confessedly elevated to the divine condition, which they once did not possess, what pre-eminent right had they to such honour?* HERCULES *an inferior character.*

But since they will have it that those who have been admitted from the human state to the honours of deification should be kept separate from others, and that the distinction which Dionysius the Stoic drew should be made between the native and the factitious [7] gods, I will add a few words concerning this last class also. I will take Hercules himself for raising the gist of a reply [8] [to the question], whether he deserved heaven and divine honours? For, as men choose to have it, these honours are awarded to him for his merits. If it was for his valour in destroying wild beasts with intrepidity, what was there in that so very memorable? Do not criminals condemned to the games, though they are even consigned to the contest of the vile arena, despatch several of these animals at one time, and that with more earnest

---

[1] Plebs.   [2] Morata.   [3] Proseminatoribus.
[4] Alibi.   [5] Optimum.

[6] [There would seem to be a jest here; "æquus" is not only *just*, but *equal*, i.e. "on a par with" others—in *evil*, of course, as well as *good*.]

[7] Inter nativos et factos. [See above, c. ii.]

[8] Summa responsionis.

zeal? If it was for his world-wide travels, how often has the same thing been accomplished by the rich at their pleasant leisure, or by philosophers in their slave-like poverty?[1] Is it forgotten that the cynic Asclepiades on a single sorry cow,[2] riding on her back, and sometimes nourished at her udder, surveyed[3] the whole world with a personal inspection? Even if Hercules visited the infernal regions, who does not know that the way to Hades is open to all? If you have deified him on account of his much carnage and many battles, a much greater number of victories was gained by the illustrious Pompey, the conqueror of the pirates who had not spared Ostia itself in their ravages; and [as to carnage], how many thousands, let me ask, were cooped up in one corner of the citadel[4] of Carthage, and slain by Scipio? Wherefore Scipio has a better claim to be considered a fit candidate for deification[5] than Hercules. You must be still more careful to add to the claims of [our] Hercules his debaucheries with concubines [and] wives, and the swathes[6] of Omphale, and his base desertion of the Argonauts because he had lost his beautiful boy.[7] To this mark of baseness add for his glorification likewise his attacks of madness, adore the arrows which slew his sons and wife. This was the man who, after deeming himself worthy of a funeral pile in the anguish of his remorse for his parricides,[8] deserved rather to die the unhonoured death which awaited him, arrayed in the poisoned robe which his wife sent him on account of his lascivious attachment [to another]. You, however, raised him from the pyre to the sky, with the same facility with which [you have distinguished in like manner] another hero[9] also, who was destroyed by the violence of a fire from the gods. He having devised some few experiments, was said to have restored the dead to life by his cures. He was the son of Apollo, half human, although the grandson of Jupiter, and

[1] Famulatoria mendicitas. [2] Vaccula.
[3] Subegisse oculis ["reduced to his own eyesight"]. [4] Byrsæ.
[5] Magis obtinendus divinitati deputatur. [6] Fascias.
[7] [Hylas.] [8] [Here murders of children and other kindred.]
[9] [Æsculapius.]

great-grandson of Saturn (or rather of spurious origin, because his parentage was uncertain, as Socrates of Argos has related; he was exposed also, and found in a worse tutelage than even Jove's, suckled even at the dugs of a dog); nobody can deny that he deserved the end which befell him when he perished by a stroke of lightning. In this transaction, however, your most excellent Jupiter is once more found in the wrong—impious to his grandson, envious of his artistic skill. Pindar, indeed, has not concealed his true desert; according to him, he was punished for his avarice and love of gain, influenced by which he would bring the living to their death, rather than the dead to life, by the perverted use of his medical art which he put up for sale.[1] It is said that his mother was killed by the same stroke, and it was only right that she, who had bestowed so dangerous a beast on the world,[2] should escape to heaven by the same ladder. And yet the Athenians will not be at a loss how to sacrifice to gods of such a fashion, for they pay divine honours to Æsculapius and his mother amongst their dead [worthies]. As if, too, they had not ready to hand[3] their own Theseus to worship, so highly deserving a god's distinction! Well, why not? Did he not on a foreign shore abandon the preserver of his life,[4] with the same indifference, nay heartlessness,[5] with which he became the cause of his father's death?

---

[1] [Tertullian does not correctly quote Pindar (*Pyth.* iii. 54–59), who notices the skilful hero's love of reward, but certainly ascribes to him the merit of curing rather than killing: 'Αλλὰ κέρδει καὶ σοφία δέδεται· ἴατρεν καὶ κεῖνον ἀγάνορι μισθῷ χρυσὸς ἐν χερσὶν φανεὶς ἄνδρ' ἐκ θανάτου κομίσαι ἤδη ἀλωκότα· χερσὶ δ' ἄρα Κρονίων ῥίψαις δι' ἀμφοῖν ἀμπνοὰς στέρνων καθίλεν ὠκίως, αἴθων δὲ κεραυνὸς ἐνίσκιμψεν μόρον—" Even wisdom has been bound by love of gain, and gold shining in the hand by a magnificent reward induced even him to restore from death a man already seized by it; and then the son of Saturn, hurling with his hands a bolt through both, speedily took away the breath of their breasts, and the flashing bolt inflicted death" (Dawson Turner).]

[2] [Tertullian does not follow the legend which is usually received. He wishes to see no good in the object of his hatred, and so takes the worst view, and certainly *improves* upon it. The "bestia" is out of reason.]

[3] Quasi non et ipsi.   [4] [Ariadne.]   [5] Amentia.

CHAP. XV.—*The* CONSTELLATIONS *and the* GENII *very indifferent gods. The Roman monopoly of gods unsatisfactory; do not other nations require deities quite as much?*

It would be tedious to take a survey of all those, too, whom you have buried amongst the constellations, and audaciously minister to as gods.[1] I suppose your Castors, and Perseus, and Erigona,[2] have just the same claims for the honours of the sky as Jupiter's own big boy[3] had. But why should we wonder? You have transferred to heaven even dogs, and scorpions, and crabs. I postpone all remarks[4] concerning those whom you worship in your oracles. That this worship exists, is attested by him who pronounces the oracle.[5] Why; you will have your gods to be spectators even of sadness,[6] as is Viduus, who makes a *widow* of the soul, by parting it from the body, and whom you have condemned, by not permitting him to be enclosed within your city-walls; there is Cæculus also, to deprive the eyes of their perception; and Orbana, to bereave seed of its vital power; moreover, there is the goddess of death herself. To pass hastily by[7] all others, you account as gods the sites of places or of the city: such are Father Janus (there being, moreover, the archer-goddess[8] Jana[9]), and Septimontius of the seven hills.

Men sacrifice[10] to the same *Genii*, whilst they have altars or temples in the same places; but to others besides, when they dwell in a strange place, or live in rented houses.[11] I

---

[1] Deis ministratis.
[2] [The constellation Virgo.]
[3] Jovis exoletus [Ganymede, or *Aquarius*].
[4] [He makes a similar postponement above, in c. vii., to *The Apology*, cc. xxii. xxiii.]
[5] Divini.
[6] Et tristitiæ arbitros.
[7] Transvolem.
[8] Diva arquis.
[9] [Perhaps another form of Diana.]
[10] [Faciunt = ῥίζουσι.]
[11] [This seems to be the meaning of an almost unintelligible sentence, which we subjoin: "Geniis eisdem illi faciunt qui in isdem locis aras vel ædes habent; præterea aliis qui in alieno loco aut mercedibus habitant." Oehler, who makes this text, supposes that in each clause the name of some god has dropped out.]

say nothing about Ascensus, who gets his name for his
climbing propensity, and Clivicola, from her sloping [haunts];
I pass silently by the deities called Forculus from doors, and
Cardea from hinges, and Limentinus the god of thresholds,
and whatever others are worshipped by your neighbours as
tutelar deities of their front doors.[1] There is nothing strange
in this, since men have their respective gods in their brothels,
their kitchens, and even in their prison. Heaven, therefore,
is crowded with innumerable gods of its own, both these
and others belonging to the Romans, which have distributed
amongst them the functions of one's whole life, in such a
way that there is no want of the other[2] gods. Although, it
is true,[3] the gods which we have enumerated are reckoned as
Roman peculiarly, and as not easily recognised abroad, yet
how do all those functions and circumstances, over which
men have willed their gods to preside, come about,[4] in every
part of the human race, and in every nation, where their
guarantees[5] are not only without an official recognition, but
even any recognition at all?

CHAP. XVI.—*Inventors of useful arts are unworthy of deification; for they would themselves be the first to acknowledge a Creator of the things which they discovered. The arts, moreover, are changeable from time to time, and some become obsolete.*

Well, but[6] certain men have discovered fruits and sundry
necessaries of life, [and hence are worthy of deification].[7]
Now let me ask, when you call these persons "discoverers,"
do you not confess that what they discovered was already
in existence? Why then do you not prefer to honour the
Author, from whom the gifts really come, instead of converting the Author into [mere] discoverers? Previous to
his making the discovery, the inventor himself no doubt
expressed his gratitude to the Author; no doubt, too, he felt
that He was God, to whom really belonged the religious

[1] Numinum janitorum.   [2] Ceteris.   [3] Immo cum.
[4] Proveniunt.   [5] Praedes.   [6] Sedenim.
[7] [We insert this clause at Oehler's suggestion.]

service,[1] as the Creator [of the gift], by whom also both he who discovered and that which was discovered were alike created. The green fig of Africa nobody at Rome had heard of when Cato introduced it to the Senate, in order that he might show how near was that province of the enemy[2] whose subjugation he was constantly urging. The cherry was first made common in Italy by Cn. Pompey, who first imported it from Pontus. I might possibly have thought the earliest introducers of apples amongst the Romans deserving of the public honour[3] of deification. This, however, would be as foolish a ground for making gods as even the invention of the useful arts. And yet if the skilful men[4] of our own time be compared with these, how much more suitable would deification be to the later generation than to the former! For, tell me, have not all the extant inventions superseded antiquity,[5] whilst daily experience goes on adding to the new stock? Those, therefore, whom you regard as divine because of their arts, you are really injuring by your very arts, and challenging [their divinity] by means of rival attainments,[6] which cannot be surpassed.

CHAP. XVII.[7]—*Conclusion. The Romans owe not their imperial power to their gods. The great God alone dispenses kingdoms, by ordering the events which lead to their rise and fall. He is the God of the Christians.*

In conclusion, without denying all those whom antiquity willed [and] posterity has believed to be gods, to be the guardians of your religion, there yet remains for our consideration that very large assumption of the superstitions of Rome which we have to meet in opposition to you, O heathen, that the Romans have become the lords and masters

---

[1] Ministerium.
[2] [The incident, which was closely connected with the third Punic war, is described pleasantly by Pliny, *Hist. Nat.* xv. 20.]
[3] Præconium.   [4] Artifices.
[5] [" Antiquitas" is here opposed to " novitas," and therefore means "the arts of old times."]
[6] In æmulis. [" In," in our author, often marks the instrument.]
[7] [Compare *The Apology,* xxv. xxvi.]

of the whole world, because by their religious offices they have merited this dominion to such an extent that they are within a very little of excelling even their own gods in power. One cannot wonder that Sterculus, and Mutunus, and Larentina, have severally[1] advanced this empire to its height! The Roman people has been by its gods alone ordained to such dominion. For I could not imagine that any foreign [gods] would have preferred doing more for a strange nation than their own people, and so by such conduct become the deserters and neglecters, nay, the betrayers of the native land wherein they were born and bred, and ennobled and buried. Thus not even Jupiter could suffer his own Crete to be subdued by the Roman fasces, forgetting that cave of Ida, and the brazen cymbals of the Corybantes, and the most pleasant odour of [the goat] which nursed him on that [dear] spot. Would he not have made that tomb of his superior to the whole Capitol, so that that land should most widely rule which covered the ashes of Jupiter? Would Juno, [too,] be willing that the Punic city, for the love of which she even neglected Samos, should be destroyed, and that, too, by the fires of the sons of Æneas? Although I am well aware that

> "Hic illius arma,
> Hic currus fuit, hoc regnum dea gentibus esse,
> Si qua fata sinant, jam tunc tenditque fovetque."[2]

> "Here were her arms, her chariot here,
> Here, goddess-like, to fix one day
> The seat of universal sway,
> Might fate be wrung to yield assent,
> E'en then her schemes, her cares were bent."[3]

[Still] the unhappy [queen of gods] had no power against the fates! And yet the Romans did not accord as much honour to the fates, although they gave them Carthage, as they did to Larentina. But surely those gods of yours have not the power of conferring empire. For when Jupiter reigned in Crete, and Saturn in Italy, and Isis in Egypt, it was even as

---

[1] [The verb is in the *singular* number.]
[2] [*Æneid*, i. 16-20.]
[3] [Conington.]

men that they reigned, to whom also were assigned many to assist them.¹ Thus he who serves also makes masters, and the bond-slave² of Admetus³ aggrandizes with empire the citizens of Rome, although he destroyed his own liberal votary Crœsus by deceiving him with ambiguous oracles.⁴ Being a god, why was he afraid boldly to foretell to him the truth that he must lose his kingdom? Surely those who were aggrandized with the power of wielding empire might always have been able to keep an eye, as it were,⁵ on their own cities. If they were strong enough to confer empire on the Romans, why did not Minerva defend Athens from Xerxes? Or why did not Apollo rescue Delphi out of the hand of Pyrrhus? They who lost their own cities preserve the city of Rome, since [forsooth] the religiousness⁶ of Rome has merited the protection! But is it not rather the fact that this excessive devotion⁷ has been devised since the empire has attained its glory by the increase of its power? No doubt sacred rites were introduced by Numa, but then your proceedings were not marred by a religion of idols and temples. Piety was simple,⁸ and worship humble; altars were artlessly reared,⁹ and the vessels [thereof] plain, and the incense from them scant, and the god himself nowhere. Men therefore were not religious before they achieved greatness, [nor great] because they were religious. But how can the Romans possibly seem to have acquired their empire by an excessive religiousness and very profound respect for the gods, when that empire was rather increased after the gods had been slighted?¹⁰ Now, if I am not mistaken, every kingdom or empire is acquired and enlarged by wars, whilst they and their gods also are injured by conquerors. For the same ruin affects both city-walls and temples; similar is the carnage both of civilians and of priests; identical the plunder of profane things and of sacred. To the Romans belong as many sacrileges as trophies; and then as many triumphs over gods

¹ Operati plerique.
² Dediticius.
³ [Apollo; comp. *The Apology*, c. xiv.]
⁴ [See Herodot. i. 50.]
⁵ Veluti tueri.   ⁶ Religiositas.
⁷ Superstitio.
⁸ Frugi.   ⁹ Temeraria.
¹⁰ Læsia.

as over nations. Still remaining are their captive idols amongst them; and certainly, if they can only see their conquerors, they do not give them their love. Since, however, they have no perception, they are injured with impunity; and since they are injured with impunity, they are worshipped to no purpose. The nation, therefore, which has grown to its powerful height by victory after victory, cannot seem to have developed owing to the merits of its religion — whether they have injured the religion by augmenting their power, or augmented their power by injuring the religion. All nations have possessed empire, each in its proper time, as the Assyrians, the Medes, the Persians, the Egyptians; empire is even now also in the possession of some, and yet they that have lost their power used not to behave [1] without attention to religious services and the worship of the gods, even after these had become unpropitious to them,[2] until at last almost universal dominion has accrued to the Romans. It is the fortune of the times that has thus constantly shaken kingdoms with revolution.[3] Inquire who has ordained these changes in the times. It is the same [great Being] who dispenses kingdoms,[4] and has now put the supremacy of them into the hands of the Romans, very much as if [5] the tribute of many nations were after its exaction amassed in one [vast] coffer. What He has determined concerning it, they know who are the nearest to Him.[6]

[1] Morabantur. [We have taken this word as if from "mores" (character). Tertullian often uses the participle "moratus" in this sense.]

[2] Et depropitiorum.   [3] Volutavit.

[4] [Compare *The Apology*, c. xxvi.]

[5] [We have treated this "tanquam" and its clause as something more than a mere simile. It is, in fact, an integral element of the supremacy which the entire sentence describes as conferred on the Romans by the Almighty.]

[6] [That is, *the Christians*, who are well aware of God's purposes as declared in prophecy. St. Paul tells the Thessalonians what the order of the great events subsequent to the Roman power was to be: the destruction of that power was to be followed by the development and reign of Antichrist; and then the end of the world would come.]

Works Published by T. & T. Clark, Edinburgh.

LANGE'S
COMMENTARIES ON THE OLD TESTAMENT

AND ON

THE EPISTLES.

MESSRS. CLARK have now pleasure in intimating their arrangements, in conjunction with the well-known firm of SCRIBNER AND CO., of New York, and under the Editorship of Dr. PHILIP SCHAFF, for the Publication of Translations of the Commentaries of Dr. LANGE and his *Collaborateurs*, on the Old Testament and on the Epistles.

They have already published in the Foreign Theological Library the Commentaries on St. Matthew, St. Mark, St. Luke, and the Acts of the Apostles. They propose to issue in the same form the Commentary on St. John's Gospel, which will not, however, be ready for some time.

There are now ready, in *Imperial 8vo*, double columns—
  1st and 2d CORINTHIANS. One Volume.
  THESSALONIANS, TIMOTHY, TITUS, PHILEMON, and HEBREWS. One Volume.
  PETER, JOHN, JAMES, and JUDE. One Volume.

And they hope to publish in 1869 and 1870—
  ROMANS. One Volume.
  GALATIANS, EPHESIANS, PHILIPPIANS, and COLOSSIANS. One Volume.
  REVELATION. One Volume.

Of the OLD TESTAMENT they have already published the Commentary on
  THE BOOK OF GENESIS, *in Imperial 8vo, price* 21s.,
to which is prefixed a Theological and Homiletical Introduction to the Old Testament, and a Special Introduction to Genesis, with discussions on the most interesting and difficult questions in the interpretation of the book.

Messrs. CLARK will, as early as possible, announce further arrangements for the translation of the Commentaries on the Old Testament Books.

The price of each of the above Volumes will be TWENTY-ONE SHILLINGS.

Works Published by T. & T. Clark, Edinburgh.

In demy 8vo, price 10s. 6d.,

THE REVELATION OF LAW IN SCRIPTURE:

CONSIDERED WITH RESPECT BOTH TO ITS OWN NATURE, AND TO ITS RELATIVE PLACE IN SUCCESSIVE DISPENSATIONS.

The Third Series of the 'Cunningham Lectures.'

By PATRICK FAIRBAIRN, D.D.,

AUTHOR OF 'TYPOLOGY OF SCRIPTURE,' ETC.

'The theme is one of the grandest that can engage the attention of the most exalted intelligences, and few of our readers, we presume, will be satisfied without reading for themselves this masterly and eloquent contribution to our theological literature, which will not only sustain, but augment the reputation the author has acquired as an eminent theologian.'—*British and Foreign Evangelical Review.*

'It is impossible to give any idea, in a bare notice like the present, of the masterly manner in which, with the true instinct of the metaphysical divine, and the profound scholarship of the biblical interpreter, Dr. Fairbairn establishes his successive positions, and overthrows those of his various antagonists.'—*Evangelical Witness.*

In demy 8vo, price 10s. 6d.,

THE DOCTRINE OF JUSTIFICATION:

AN OUTLINE OF ITS HISTORY IN THE CHURCH, AND OF ITS EXPOSITION FROM SCRIPTURE, WITH SPECIAL REFERENCE TO RECENT ATTACKS ON THE THEOLOGY OF THE REFORMATION.

The Second Series of the 'Cunningham Lectures.'

By JAMES BUCHANAN, D.D.,

Professor of Divinity, New College, Edinburgh.

'This is a work of no ordinary ability and importance. Quite apart from the opinions of the author, it has a high value, as fairly exhibiting the history of the doctrine of justification at large, but especially in the early Church, the mediæval period, and the era of the Reformation. It gives us a most favourable opinion of the Scotch theological colleges, that works of such breadth of view, and exhibiting such solid learning, are produced by their professors, among whom Dr. Buchanan has long been distinguished.'—*Clerical Journal.*

'Our readers will find in them an able, clear, and comprehensive statement of the truth which forms the subject, clothed in language "suitable alike to an academic and to a popular audience." We only add, that the copious notes and references, after the manner of the Bampton and Hulsean Lectures, beside which it is worthy to stand, greatly enhance the value of the volume, and constitute it a capital handbook of the doctrine of justification.'—*Weekly Review.*

Works Published by T. & T. Clark, Edinburgh.

In Two Volumes 8vo, price 21s,

THE CHURCH OF CHRIST:

A TREATISE ON THE NATURE, POWERS, ORDINANCES, DISCIPLINE, AND GOVERNMENT OF THE CHRISTIAN CHURCH.

By the late JAMES BANNERMAN, D.D.,

Professor of Apologetics and Pastoral Theology, New College, Edinburgh.

Edited by his Son.

'Its intrinsic value makes it a rare accession to theological literature. . . . . We cannot but feel grateful that a posthumous work so complete and careful as this has appeared.'—*Daily Review.*

'Dr. Bannerman has argued his points with great clearness and force. . . . . The spirit with which he writes is beyond all praise, it is that of a scholar and Christian.'—*Church Review.*

'We commend these learned and masterly volumes to the careful study, not only of the scientific divine, but of all thoughtful men who would desire to understand some of the greatest and most vital questions of our time.'—*Presbyterian.*

'The book is very ably written; the various points involved in the extensive inquiry are handled with much care, acuteness, and power.'—*Evangelical Magazine.*

'This substantial and seasonable work is a fitting monument of the great abilities and wide research of its lamented author.'—*Watchman.*

PROF. EADIE'S NEW WORK.

Just published, in demy 8vo, price 10s. 6d.,

A Commentary on the Greek Text

OF THE

EPISTLE OF PAUL TO THE GALATIANS.

By JOHN EADIE, D.D., LL.D.,

Professor of Biblical Literature and Exegesis to the U.P. Church.

'Everything which lexical research and grammatical analysis can effect to bring out the most subtle and delicate shades of thought contained in St. Paul's writing, has been accomplished by the learned and painstaking Professor. The high tone of the book, too, is equal to its unquestionable scholarship.'—*Watchman.*

'This work will do more than preserve the well won reputation of Dr. Eadie. There is a considerable advance over his former expositions. There is a greater amount of resources at his disposal, and more freedom in his treatment of them.'—*Daily Review.*

Works Published by T. & T. Clark, Edinburgh.

In demy 8vo., price 10s. 6d.,

THE DOCTRINE OF THE ATONEMENT,

AS TAUGHT BY CHRIST HIMSELF;

OR,

THE SAYINGS OF JESUS ON THE ATONEMENT EXEGETICALLY EXPOUNDED AND CLASSIFIED.

By REV. GEORGE SMEATON,

PROFESSOR OF EXEGETICAL THEOLOGY, NEW COLLEGE, EDINBURGH.

'We recommend it as forming a most useful introduction to the study of a deep and mysterious doctrine, and likely to be profitable to the thoughtful and judicious reader. Its matter is carefully digested, and its argument is well thought and clearly reasoned.'—*Churchman.*

'We attach very great value to this seasonable and scholarly production. The idea of the work is most happy, and the execution of it worthy of the idea. On a scheme of truly Baconian exegetical induction, he presents us with a complete view of the various positions or propositions which a full and sound doctrine of the Atonement embraces.'—*British and Foreign Evangelical Review.*

In crown 8vo, price 3s. 6d.,

THE FOUR EVANGELISTS;

WITH THE DISTINCTIVE CHARACTERISTICS OF THEIR GOSPELS.

By EDWARD A. THOMSON,

Minister of Free St. Stephen's, Edinburgh.

'We have not seen for a long time a volume more fresh and scholarly, more suggestive and beautiful.'—*Freeman.*

Just published, in crown 8vo, price 3s. 6d.,

APOLOGETICAL LECTURES ON JOHN'S GOSPEL.

By J. J. VAN OOSTERZEE, D.D.,

Professor of Theology, University of Utrecht.

I. THE AUTHENTICITY OF ST. JOHN'S GOSPEL.
II. JOHN AND THE SYNOPTIC GOSPELS.
III. JOHN'S ACCOUNT OF CHRIST'S MIRACLES.
IV. THE JOHANNEAN CHRIST.
V. TABLE OF APOLOGETICAL LITERATURE ON JOHN'S GOSPEL.

TRANSLATED, WITH ADDITIONS, BY J. F. HURST, D.D.,
AUTHOR OF THE 'HISTORY OF RATIONALISM.'

'The small volume before us is the production of a strong and cultivated mind. . . . . Nothing could be more able, seasonable, and complete.'—*Watchman.*

Works Published by T. & T. Clark, Edinburgh.

COMMENTARIES ON THE OLD TESTAMENT
BY PROFESSORS KEIL AND DELITZSCH.

In Three Volumes, demy 8vo, price 31s. 6d.,
Biblical Commentary on the Pentateuch.
BY PROFESSOR KEIL.
TRANSLATED BY REV. JAMES MARTIN, B.A.

'There is a life in the criticisms, a happy realizing power in the words, which will make this work most acceptable. The Commentary, while it is verbal and critical, has also the faculty of gathering up and generalizing the lesson and the story, which will add immensely to its value. It aims to be an exegetical handbook, by which some fuller understanding of the Old Testament economy of salvation may be obtained from a study in the light of the New Testament teachings.'—*Eclectic Review.*

'We can safely recommend this work to the clergy and others who desire to study the Bible as the *Word of God.*'—*Scottish Guardian.*

BY THE SAME AUTHOR.

In 8vo, price 10s. 6d.,
Biblical Commentary on Joshua, Judges, and Ruth.

In 8vo, price 10s. 6d.,
Biblical Commentary on the Books of Samuel.

In Two Volumes, 8vo, price 21s.,
Biblical Commentary on the Book of Job.
BY PROFESSOR DELITZSCH.
TRANSLATED BY REV. FRANCIS BOLTON, B.A.

In Two Volumes, 8vo, price 21s.,
Biblical Commentary on the Prophecies of Isaiah.
BY PROFESSOR DELITZSCH.
TRANSLATED BY REV. JAMES MARTIN, B.A.

In Two Volumes, 8vo, price 21s.,
Biblical Commentary on the Minor Prophets.
BY PROFESSOR KEIL.
TRANSLATED BY REV. JAMES MARTIN, B.A.

In Two Volumes,
Biblical Commentary on the Epistle to the Hebrews.
BY PROFESSOR DELITZSCH.
TRANSLATED BY REV. T. L. KINGSBURY.
Volume I. is ready, price 10s. 6d.; Volume II. is in preparation.

In Preparation. In Three Volumes,
Biblical Commentary on the Book of Psalms.
BY PROFESSOR DELITZSCH.

Works Published by T. & T. Clark, Edinburgh.

DR LANGE'S COMMENTARIES.

⁎ For Dr LANGE'S LIFE OF THE LORD JESUS CHRIST, see *separate Prospectus*.

In Three Volumes, 8vo, £1, 11s. 6d.,
Theological and Homiletical Commentary
ON
THE GOSPELS OF ST MATTHEW AND MARK.
BY J. P. LANGE, D.D.,
PROFESSOR OF DIVINITY IN THE UNIVERSITY OF BONN.

In Two Volumes, 8vo, price 18s,
Theological and Homiletical
COMMENTARY ON THE GOSPEL OF ST LUKE.
BY DR J. VAN OOSTERZEE. EDITED BY J. P. LANGE, D.D.

In Two Volumes, 8vo, price 21s.,
Theological and Homiletical
COMMENTARY ON THE ACTS OF THE APOSTLES.
BY DRS LECHLER AND GEROK.
Edited by J. P. LANGE, D.D. Translated by Rev. P. J. GLOAG.

'The method which Professor Lange pursues in his Commentary, makes it exceedingly valuable both in an exegetical and practical point of view. Having portioned out the original narrative of the Evangelist into sections, according to the contents and connection of the passage, he subjects it to a threefold handling, in order to bring out the meaning and applications of the text. First of all we have a series of *critical notes*, intended to deal with the difficulties in the interpretation of the passage, and bringing all the aids which exegesis supplies to elucidate and exhibit its proper meaning. Next we have a series of *doctrinal reflections*, suggested by the passage interpreted, and intended to exhibit the substance of the scriptural truths which it contains. And lastly, we have a series of *homiletical hints*, founded on the passage elucidated.'—*Daily Review.*

In Four Volumes, crown 8vo, price 24s., *Cheap Edition*,
Biblical Commentary on the Gospels and Acts.
BY DR H. OLSHAUSEN.

'Olshausen is one of those persons whom the pious hearts of Germany will long remember with affection and veneration. . . . On the great and fundamental doctrines of Christianity, Olshausen is as fixed and as stable as the Rock on which the Church is built. The consciousness of sin is, as his translator well remarks, "the pivot in Olshausen's mind which moves all the rest;" deep inward experiences, and the pressing need of a Redeemer, make him ever feel and ever avow that we are not following cunningly devised fables, but real, substantial, and vital truths, which breathe and burn through every page of the blessed Gospels.'—*Christian Observer.*

In One thick Volume, 8vo, price 9s.,
Greek and English Lexicon of the New Testament.
BY EDWARD ROBINSON, D.D.,
LATE PROF. EXTRAORD. OF SAC. LIT. IN THE THEOL. SEM., ANDOVER.

A New and Improved Edition, Revised by ALEXANDER NEGRIS, Professor of Greek Literature, and by the Rev. JOHN DUNCAN, D.D., Professor of Oriental Languages in the New College, Edinburgh.

Works Published by T. & T. Clark, Edinburgh.

Just published, in Four Volumes 8vo, price 32s.,

THE

COMPARATIVE GEOGRAPHY OF PALESTINE

AND THE

SINAITIC PENINSULA.

BY PROFESSOR CARL RITTER, OF BERLIN.

Translated and Adapted for the Use of Biblical Students,

By WILLIAM L. GAGE.

'I have always looked on Ritter's *Comparative Geography of Palestine*, comprised in his famous "Erdkunde," *as the great classical work on the subject*; a clear and full résumé of all that was known of Bible Lands up to the time he wrote; and, as such, indispensable to the student of Bible Geography and History. This translation will open up a flood of knowledge to the English reader, especially as the editor is a man thoroughly imbued with the spirit of this noble-minded and truly Christian author.'—KEITH JOHNSTON, Esq., *Geographer in Ordinary to Her Majesty for Scotland.*

'One of the most valuable works on Palestine ever published.'—REV. H. B. TRISTRAM, *Author of 'The Land of Israel.'*

'By far the most important of Messrs. Clark's publications is this very handsome and complete edition of Ritter's *Palestine*. The great Berlin geographer *can never be out of date*; and though he did not live to complete his great work, by availing himself of the discoveries of recent explorers, yet the present editor has to a considerable extent supplied the deficiency; and we may say that, among the voluminous products of the well-known Edinburgh press, few exceed this publication in importance and completeness.'—*Christian Remembrancer, Jan.* 1867.

'To clergymen these volumes will prove not less interesting than instructive and useful. Theological students will find in them the most exhaustive storehouse of facts on the subjects existing in the language, while upon all the moot points of Palestinian and Sinaitic geography they will meet with a condensed summary of all the arguments of every writer of note, from the earliest ages down to the period of the author's death. In a word, these four volumes give the essence of the entire literature of the subject of every age and language. . . . . The readers of these volumes have every reason to be satisfied with the result. . . . . But it would be impossible to mention all the good things in these volumes. We must, however, say a few words upon Ritter's magnificent monograph on the situation of Ophir, which we regard as one of the gems of the work. . . . . Ritter's treatment of this apparently hopeless question is a masterpiece of mature scholarship and sound judgment. The whole monograph is a model of its kind. . . . . . What we are now saying of the monograph on the situation of Ophir, is, however, applicable to everything our author wrote.'—*Spectator.*

'Mr Gage has, with a perfect knowledge of the matter in hand, and by the use of a clear and lively style, produced a thoroughly readable book.'—*Daily Review.*

'By the publication of this geography of Palestine, Messrs. Clark have placed within the reach of a large number of students, clerical and lay, an exhaustive and comprehensive work on biblical geography, which will greatly facilitate the study of the sacred writings.'—*Churchman.*

'It is superfluous to commend a work of so peerless a character as this.'—*British Quarterly Review.*

'The translator has fulfilled his task admirably. . . . . . The book is pleasant to read, and will be found very interesting, not only by Biblical students, but by the public in general.'—*Evangelical Magazine.*

MACMILLAN AND CO.'S PUBLICATIONS.

DR. VAUGHAN'S WORKS.

TWELVE DISCOURSES ON SUBJECTS CONNECTED WITH THE LITURGY AND WORSHIP OF THE CHURCH OF ENGLAND. Fcap. 8vo, 6s.

LECTURES ON THE EPISTLE TO THE PHILIPPIANS. Second Edition. Crown 8vo, 7s. 6d.

LECTURES ON THE REVELATION OF ST. JOHN. Second Edition. Two vols. Crown 8vo, 15s.

MEMORIALS OF HARROW SUNDAYS. A Selection of Sermons preached in Harrow School Chapel. Fourth Edition. Crown 8vo, 10s. 6d.

THE BOOK AND THE LIFE, and other Sermons. Preached before the University of Cambridge. New Edition. Fcap. 8vo, 4s. 6d.

LESSONS OF LIFE AND GODLINESS. A Selection of Sermons preached in the Parish Church of Doncaster. Third Edition. Fcap. 8vo, 4s. 6d.

WORDS FROM THE GOSPELS. A Second Selection of Sermons preached in the Parish Church of Doncaster. Second Edition. Fcap. 8vo, 4s. 6d.

THE CHURCH OF THE FIRST DAYS. Series I.: The Church of Jerusalem. Series II.: The Church of the Gentiles. Series III.: The Church of the World. Second Edition. Fcap. 8vo, 4s. 6d. each.

LIFE'S WORK AND GOD'S DISCIPLINE. Three Sermons. Fcap. 8vo, 2s. 6d.

EPIPHANY, LENT, AND EASTER. Expository Sermons. Third Edition. Crown 8vo, 10s. 6d.

NOTES FOR LECTURES ON CONFIRMATION. With suitable Prayers. Sixth Edition. Fcap. 8vo, 1s. 6d.

THE WHOLESOME WORDS OF JESUS CHRIST. Sermons before the University of Cambridge. Second Edition. Fcap. 8vo, 3s. 6d.

FOES OF FAITH: Unreality, Indolence, Irreverence, and Inconsistency. Sermons before the University of Cambridge, November 1868. Fcap. 8vo, 3s. 6d.

CANON WESTCOTT'S WORKS.

A GENERAL VIEW OF THE HISTORY OF THE ENGLISH BIBLE. Crown 8vo, 10s. 6d.

'A brief, scholarly, and, to a great extent, an original contribution to theological literature.'—*Pall Mall Gazette.*

A GENERAL SURVEY OF THE HISTORY OF THE CANON OF THE NEW TESTAMENT DURING THE FIRST FOUR CENTURIES. Second Edition, revised. Crown 8vo, 10s. 6d.

INTRODUCTION TO THE STUDY OF THE FOUR GOSPELS. Third Edition. Crown 8vo, 10s. 6d.

'His "Introduction to the Study of the Gospels" and his "Canon of the New Testament" are two of the best works of the kind to be found in any literature, and exhibit the solidity of English judgment in combination with a fulness of learning which is often assumed to be a monopoly of the Germans.'—*Daily News.*

THE GOSPEL OF THE RESURRECTION. Thoughts on its Relation to Reason and History. New Edition. Fcap. 8vo, 4s. 6d.

THE BIBLE IN THE CHURCH. A Popular Account of the Collection and Reception of the Holy Scriptures in the Christian Churches. Second Edition. 18mo, 4s. 6d.

MACMILLAN AND CO., LONDON.

MACMILLAN AND CO.'S PUBLICATIONS.

PROFESSOR LIGHTFOOT'S WORKS.

ST. PAUL'S EPISTLE TO THE GALATIANS. A Revised Text, with Notes and Dissertations. Second Edition. 8vo, 12s.

ST. PAUL'S EPISTLE TO THE PHILIPPIANS. A Revised Text, with Introduction, Notes, and Dissertations. 8vo, 12s. Second Edition in the press.

'No commentary in the English language can be compared with it in regard to fulness of information, exact scholarship, and laboured attempts to settle everything about the Epistle on a solid foundation.—*Athenæum.*

THE ARCHBISHOP OF DUBLIN'S WORKS.

NOTES ON THE PARABLES OF OUR LORD. Tenth Edition. 8vo, 12s.

NOTES ON THE MIRACLES OF OUR LORD. Eight Edition. 8vo, 12s.

SYNONYMS OF THE NEW TESTAMENT. New Edition. One vol. 8vo, cloth, 10s. 6d.

COMMENTARY ON THE EPISTLES TO THE SEVEN CHURCHES IN ASIA. Third Edition, revised. 8vo, cloth, 8s. 6d.

ON THE AUTHORIZED VERSION OF THE NEW TESTAMENT. Second Edition. 8vo, cloth, 7s.

STUDIES IN THE GOSPELS. Second Edition. Demy 8vo, 10s. 6d.

SHIPWRECKS OF FAITH. Three Sermons preached before the University of Cambridge in May 1867. Fcap. 8vo, cloth, 2s. 6d.

SERMONS PREACHED IN WESTMINSTER ABBEY. Second Edition. 8vo, cloth, 10s. 6d.

THE FITNESS OF HOLY SCRIPTURE FOR UNFOLDING THE SPIRITUAL LIFE OF MAN. Hulsean Lectures. Fourth Edition. Fcap. 8vo, 5s.

SACRED LATIN POETRY, chiefly Lyrical, selected and arranged for Use. Second Edition, corrected and improved. Fcap. 8vo, cloth, 7s.

PROFESSOR KINGSLEY'S WORKS.

THE ROMAN AND THE TEUTON. A Series of Lectures delivered before the University of Cambridge. 8vo, cloth, 12s.

THE WATER OF LIFE, and other Sermons. Fcap. 8vo, cloth, 6s.

VILLAGE SERMONS. Seventh Edition. Fcap. 8vo, cloth, 2s. 6d.

THE GOSPEL OF THE PENTATEUCH. Second Edition. Fcap. 8vo, 4s. 6d.

GOOD NEWS OF GOD. Fourth Edition. Fcap. 8vo, cloth, 4s. 6d.

SERMONS FOR THE TIMES. Third Edition. Fcap. 8vo, 3s. 6d.

SERMONS ON NATIONAL SUBJECTS. First and Second Series. Second Edition. Fcap. 8vo, cloth, 5s. each.

DAVID. Four Sermons: David's Weakness—David's Strength—David's Anger—David's Deserts. Fcap. 8vo, cloth, 2s. 6d.

TOWN AND COUNTRY SERMONS. Second Edition. Fcap. 8vo, 6s.

DISCIPLINE, and other Sermons. Fcap. 8vo, 6s.

MACMILLAN AND CO., LONDON.

Works Published by T. & T. Clark, Edinburgh.

In Two Volumes, 8vo, price 21s.,
THE CHRISTIAN DOCTRINE OF SIN.

TRANSLATED FROM THE GERMAN OF DR. JULIUS MÜLLER,
Professor of Theology in the University of Berlin,

BY REV. WILLIAM URWICK, M.A.

'This is an *entirely new translation* of Müller's inestimable work, from the latest edition. No pains have been spared to make it a thoroughly good and reliable translation.

In 8vo, price 10s. 6d.,
CHRISTIAN DOGMATICS.
A COMPENDIUM OF THE DOCTRINES OF CHRISTIANITY.

BY H. MARTENSEN, D.D.,
Bishop of Seeland, Denmark.

TRANSLATED BY REV. WILLIAM URWICK, M.A.

I. Introduction. II. The Christian Idea of God. III. The Doctrine of the Father. IV. The Doctrine of the Son. V. The Doctrine of the Spirit.

'Every reader must rise from its perusal stronger, calmer, and more hopeful, not only for the fortunes of Christianity, but of dogmatical theology.'—*British Quarterly Review.*

'He enters into the various subjects with consummate ability; and we doubt whether there is in any language a clearer or more learned work than this on systematic theology.'—*Irish Ecclesiastical Gazette.*

'We have seldom seen any theological work, by a foreign author, which combines so profound a reverence for the Bible with such vigour and originality of independent thought.'—*London Review.*

In demy 8vo, price 10s. 6d.,
THE DIVINE REVELATION.
BY THE LATE CARL AUGUST AUBERLEN, PH.D., D.D.,
Professor at Basle.

The Pauline Epistles; The Gospels; The Old Testament; The great intellectual Conflict in the Christian World; The elder Protestantism and Rationalism; The Defeat of Rationalism.

BY THE SAME AUTHOR.

In crown 8vo, price 7s. 6d.,
The Prophecies of Daniel and the Revelation of St. John in their Mutual Relation.

'One of the latest contributions to the study of Apocalyptic prophecy. It is one of a very high order, and which must command attention. The author appears to us to possess, in no ordinary degree, those faculties of head and heart so absolutely necessary for the prosecution of this most difficult branch of sacred exegesis.'—*Ecclesiastic.*

Works Published by T. & T. Clark, Edinburgh.

In One volume 8vo, price 10s. 6d.,
ANALYTICAL COMMENTARY ON THE EPISTLE TO THE ROMANS,

TRACING THE TRAIN OF THOUGHT BY THE AID OF PARALLELISM; WITH NOTES AND DISSERTATIONS ON THE PRINCIPAL DIFFICULTIES CONNECTED WITH THE EXPOSITION OF THE EPISTLE.

By Rev. JOHN FORBES, LL.D.

'Altogether, it is one of the Commentaries on the Epistle to the Romans which ought to be found in the library of every Biblical student.'—*Weekly Review*.

'We are glad to give the very warmest commendation to a volume at once so original, so conservative, and so devout.'—*Churchman*.

'It is not a work to be judged of hastily, nor to be dismissed summarily, and we can aver from experience that a second perusal will well reward the thoughtful student. In every point of view it is a valuable addition to critical Biblical literature, and possesses many attractions even for the unlearned reader.'—*Contemporary Review*.

Now ready, in crown 8vo, price 6s., Second Edition, revised and enlarged,
THE TRIPARTITE NATURE OF MAN:
SPIRIT, SOUL, AND BODY.

Applied to Illustrate and Explain the Doctrines of Original Sin, the New Birth, the Disembodied State, and the Spiritual Body.

By the Rev. J. B. HEARD, M.A.

CHAP. I. The Case Stated. II. The Psychology of Natural and Revealed Religion contrasted. III. The Account of the Creation of Man. IV. The Relation of Body to Soul in Scripture. V. Of the Relation of Soul and Spirit in Scripture. VI. Psyche and Pneuma in the light of Christian Experience. VII. The Unity under Diversity of the Three Parts of Man's Nature. VIII. Analogies from the Doctrine of the Trinity to the Trichotomy in Man considered. IX. Of the Pneuma as the Faculty which distinguishes Man from the Brute. X. The state of the Pneuma in Man since the Fall. XI. The Question of Traducianism and Creationism solved by the distinction between Soul and Spirit. XII. Conversion to God explained as the quickening of the Pneuma. XIII. The Question of the Natural Immortality of Psyche considered. XIV. Application of the Doctrine of the Trichotomy to discover the Principle of Final Rewards and Punishments. XV. Intermediate State. XVI. The Resurrection and Spiritual Body. XVII. Summary.

'It will be seen that Mr. Heard's theme is a noble and important one, and he has treated it in a way to afford a high intellectual treat to the Christian philosopher and divine.'—*Clerical Journal*.

'We must congratulate our author on having, from a theological point of view, established satisfactorily, and with much thought, the theory he advocates, and with having treated a subject generally considered dry and unreadable, in an attractive style.' —*Reader*.

In Two Volumes crown 8vo, price 12s.,
BIBLICAL STUDIES ON ST. JOHN'S GOSPEL.
By Dr. BESSER.

'This book is full of warm and devout exposition. Luther's own rugged words start out, boulder-like, in almost every page.'—*News of the Churches*.

'We now call attention to the great merits of this volume. The character of this commentary is practical and devotional. There are often very exquisite devotional passages, and a vein of earnest piety runs through the whole work. We recommend the book most warmly to all.'—*Literary Churchman*.

'There is a quiet, simple, penetrating good sense in what Dr. Besser says, and withal a spirit of truly Christian devoutness, which the reader must feel to be in beautiful accordance with the inspired teachings which awaken it.'—*British Quarterly Review*.

JAMES NISBET & CO.'S PUBLICATIONS.

Post 8vo, each 7s. 6d. cloth,
A UNIFORM EDITION OF THE WORKS OF THE LATE JAMES HAMILTON, D.D., in Six Volumes.

Post 8vo, 7s. 6d. cloth,
A COMMENTARY ON ST. PAUL'S EPISTLE TO THE GALATIANS.
With Sermons on the Principal Topics contained in it.
By the Rev. EMILIUS BAYLEY, B.D.

Works by the Rev. J. A. ALEXANDER, D.D.

I. THE GOSPEL ACCORDING TO ST. MATTHEW EXPLAINED. Post 8vo, 5s. cloth.
II. THE GOSPEL ACCORDING TO ST. MARK EXPLAINED. Post 8vo, 5s. cloth.
III. THE ACTS OF THE APOSTLES EXPLAINED. Two Vols. post 8vo, 15s. cloth.

Works by the Rev. CHARLES HODGE, D.D.

I. A COMMENTARY ON ST PAUL'S EPISTLE TO THE EPHESIANS. Crown 8vo, 3s. 6d. cloth.
II. A COMMENTARY ON THE FIRST EPISTLE TO THE CORINTHIANS. Post 8vo, 5s. cloth.
III. A COMMENTARY ON THE SECOND EPISTLE TO THE CORINTHIANS. Post 8vo, 5s. cloth.

Works by the Rev. A. A. BONAR.

I. A COMMENTARY ON LEVITICUS, Expository and Practical. With Critical Notes. 8vo, 8s. 6d. cloth.
II. CHRIST AND HIS CHURCH IN THE BOOK OF PSALMS. Demy 8vo, 10s. 6d. cloth.

Complete in 6 vols. 4to, published at £4, 4s., now offered for £2, 10s.,
THE REV. THOMAS SCOTT'S COMMENTARY ON THE HOLY BIBLE,
comprising Marginal References, a copious Topical Index, Fifteen Maps, and Sixty-nine Engravings, illustrative of Scripture Incidents and Scenery.

Price £3, 3s. cloth,
MATTHEW HENRY'S COMMENTARY ON THE HOLY BIBLE,
comprising upwards of 7000 pages, well printed (the Notes as well as the Text in clear and distinct type), on good paper, forming Nine Imperial 8vo volumes, and handsomely bound in cloth.

London: JAMES NISBET & CO., 21, Berners Street, W.

JAMES NISBET & CO.'S PUBLICATIONS.

No. LXVIII., price 3s. 6d.,
THE BRITISH AND FOREIGN EVANGELICAL REVIEW
for APRIL contains:—
1. Christian Female Authorship.
2. Modern Judaism.
3. The Procession of the Holy Spirit from the Son.
4. The Antiquity of Man.
5. Romeward Tendencies of the Day.
6. Scottish Prelacy after the Restoration.
7. Hammerich's Ancient Church.
8. The Royal Supremacy and Religious Liberty.
9. General Literature.
10. Foreign Literature.
11. Critical Notices.

Works by the Rev. HORATIUS BONAR, D.D.
LIFE AND TRUTH—BIBLE THOUGHTS AND THEMES—THE GOSPELS. Crown 8vo, 5s. cloth.
LIGHT AND TRUTH—BIBLE THOUGHTS AND THEMES—OLD TESTAMENT. Crown 8vo, 5s. cloth.

Small crown 8vo, in Two Series, each 5s. cloth,
ILLUSTRATIVE GATHERINGS FOR PREACHERS AND TEACHERS:
A Manual of Anecdotes, Facts, Figures, Proverbs, Quotations, etc.
By the Rev. G. S. BOWES, M.A.

In Two Vols. post 8vo, 16s. cloth,
DEVOUT THOUGHTS BY DEEP THINKERS.
With a Preface by the Rev. J. C. RYLE, of Stradbroke, Suffolk.

Works by the Rev. ANDREW JUKES.
THE CHARACTERISTIC DIFFERENCES OF THE FOUR GOSPELS, considered as revealing various Relations of the Lord Jesus Christ. Small crown 8vo, 2s. 6d. cloth.
THE LAW OF THE OFFERINGS IN LEVITICUS, considered as the appointed Figure of the various Aspects of the Offering of the Body of Jesus Christ. Small crown 8vo, 3s. cloth.

Imperial 8vo, 12s. cloth,
THE BIBLE MANUAL:
An Expository and Practical Commentary on the Books of Scripture, arranged in Chronological Order; forming a Handbook of Biblical Elucidation for the use of Families, Schools, and Students of the Word of God. Translated from the German Work. Edited by the late Rev. Dr. C. G. BARTH, of Calw, Wurtemberg.

In Four Vols. crown 8vo, 16s. cloth,
OUR CHRISTIAN CLASSICS:
Readings from the best Divines. By JAMES HAMILTON, D.D.
Dedicated to the Lord Bishop of London.

London: JAMES NISBET & CO., 21, Berners Street, W.

Works Published by T. & T. Clark, Edinburgh.

In demy 8vo, price 10s. 6d.,

THE DOCTRINE OF THE ATONEMENT,
AS TAUGHT BY CHRIST HIMSELF;
Or, The Sayings of Jesus on the Atonement Exegetically Expounded and Classified.

BY REV. GEORGE SMEATON,
PROFESSOR OF EXEGETICAL THEOLOGY, NEW COLLEGE, EDINBURGH.

WORKS BY JAMES BUCHANAN, D.D.,
PROFESSOR OF DIVINITY, NEW COLLEGE, EDINBURGH.

In demy 8vo, price 10s. 6d.,

THE DOCTRINE OF JUSTIFICATION:
An Outline of its History in the Church, and of its Exposition from Scripture, with Special Reference to Recent Attacks on the Theology of the Reformation.

THE SECOND SERIES OF THE 'CUNNINGHAM LECTURES.'

'This is a work of no ordinary ability and importance. Quite apart from the opinions of the author, it has a high value, as fairly exhibiting the history of the doctrine of justification at large, but especially in the early church, and mediæval period, and the era of the Reformation. It gives us a most favourable opinion of the Scotch Theological Colleges, that works of such breadth of view, and exhibiting such solid learning, are produced by their professors, among whom Dr. Buchanan has long been distinguished.'—*Clerical Journal.*

'On two subjects this volume is highly valuable, and may be read with great advantage by the theological student, and by all who take an interest in questions of this kind. These subjects are, the history of the doctrine of justification, and of the true nature of justification itself. He has given the history of the doctrine as it is taught in the Old Testament; as it was held in the apostolic age; in the times of the fathers and scholastic divines; at the period of the Reformation; in the Romish Church after the Reformation; as a subject of controversy among Protestants; and as it is held in the Church of England.'—*Wesleyan Methodist Magazine.*

'After a careful perusal of the volume before us, we are bound to say that our expectations, high as they were, have not been disappointed. We have here the old doctrine about justification expounded with a fulness of learning, and a masterly grasp of all its principles and details, that would have gladdened the heart of a Turretine or a Davenant; while, at the same time, the exposition is suited in all respects to the wants and requirements, intellectual and spiritual, of the present nineteenth century. . . . . . . We would suggest, as eminently desirable, that some wealthy members of our churches would confer a lasting boon on their future ministry, by presenting a copy of it to all the students attending their theological halls.'—*Daily Review.*

Faith in God and Modern Atheism Compared, in their Essential Nature, Theoretical Grounds, and Practical Influence. Two Volumes 8vo, 12s.

Analogy, Considered as a Guide to Truth, and Applied as an Aid to Faith. 8vo, 10s. 6d.

On the Office and Work of the Holy Spirit. Crown 8vo, 6s.

On Comfort in Affliction: A Series of Meditations. Fcap. 8vo, 2s. 6d.

On Improvement of Affliction. Fcap. 8vo, 2s. 6d.

On the Essays and Reviews. 3s. 6d.

Works Published by T. & T. Clark, Edinburgh.

WORKS OF PATRICK FAIRBAIRN, D.D.,

PRINCIPAL AND PROFESSOR OF THEOLOGY IN THE FREE CHURCH COLLEGE, GLASGOW.

In Two Volumes, demy 8vo, price 21s., Fourth Edition,

THE TYPOLOGY OF SCRIPTURE,

VIEWED IN CONNECTION WITH THE WHOLE SERIES OF THE DIVINE DISPENSATIONS.

'One of the most sober, profound, and thorough treatises which we possess on a subject of great importance in its bearing on Christian doctrine.'—*Archdeacon Denison's Church and State Review.*

'As the product of the labours of an original thinker and of a sound theologian, who has at the same time scarcely left unexamined one previous writer on the subject, ancient or modern, this work will be a most valuable accession to the library of the theological student. As a whole, we believe it may, with the strictest truth, be pronounced the best work on the subject that has yet been published.'—*Record.*

'A work fresh and comprehensive, learned and sensible, and full of practical religious feeling.'—*British and Foreign Evangelical Review.*

In demy 8vo, price 10s. 6d., Third Edition,

EZEKIEL, AND THE BOOK OF HIS PROPHECY:

AN EXPOSITION; WITH A NEW TRANSLATION.

In demy 8vo, price 10s. 6d., Second Edition,

PROPHECY,

VIEWED IN ITS DISTINCTIVE NATURE, ITS SPECIAL FUNCTIONS, AND PROPER INTERPRETATION.

'We would express our conviction that if ever this state of things is to end, and the church is blest with the dawn of a purer and brighter day, it will be through the sober and well-considered efforts of such a man as Dr Fairbairn, and through the general acceptance of some such principles as are laid down for our guidance in this book.'—*Christian Advocate.*

In demy 8vo, price 10s. 6d.,

HERMENEUTICAL MANUAL;

OR, INTRODUCTION TO THE EXEGETICAL STUDY OF THE SCRIPTURES OF THE NEW TESTAMENT.

PART I. Discussion of Facts and Principles bearing on the Language and Interpretation of the New Testament.

PART II. Dissertations on particular subjects connected with the Exegesis of the New Testament.

PART III. On the Use made of Old Testament Scripture in the Writings of the New Testament.

'Dr Fairbairn has precisely the training which would enable him to give a fresh and suggestive book on Hermeneutics. Without going into any tedious detail, it presents the points that are important to a student. There is a breadth of view, a clearness and manliness of thought, and a ripeness of learning, which make the work one of peculiar freshness and interest. I consider it a very valuable addition to every student's library.'—*Rev. Dr. Moore, Author of the able Commentary on 'The Prophets of the Restoration.'*

NEW BOOKS.

HOMER'S ILIAD. In English Rhymed Verse. By Charles Merivale, B.D., D.C.L., Chaplain to the Speaker, etc. 2 vols. demy 8vo, 24s.

THE NEW TESTAMENT. A Revision of the Authorized Version. By Henry Alford, D.D., Dean of Canterbury. Crown 8vo, 6s.

THE MORAL USES OF DARK THINGS. By HORACE Bushnell, D.D., Author of 'The New Life,' etc. Crown 8vo. [*Nearly Ready.*

THE PRESENCE OF CHRIST. By the Rev. A. W. Thorold. Crown 8vo, 3s. 6d.

POEMS. (Including 'Lady Grace,' a Drama in Five Acts.) By Menella Bute Smedley. Crown 8vo, 5s.

'The time of this drama ("Lady Grace") is the present day, with its "girls of the period," its mildly fast young men, its selfish worldlings, and its Belgravian mothers. The scene is laid in the drawing-rooms, club-rooms, bachelor lodgings, and croquet-grounds of London life.... We should be more disposed to tell at length, but that we must not spoil the reader's enjoyment of a capital plot, which is as well carried out as it is conceived. The dialogue is wonderfully racy, and full of keen observation and satire.'—*Saturday Review.*

'"Lady Grace" is a drama scrupulously true and real, and is full of a delicate flavour of poetry. Instead of being just ideal enough to give a meretricious glitter to the conventional moralities of the hour, which is the case with the sentiment of most of our theatrical attempts at delineating modern life, there is a real poetical heart thrown into the meditation of the phenomena of modern society. It is a pity that while we see on the English stage plenty of plays as true as this to the conventional outside of our modern life, we cannot see any with the same delicate and ennobling spirit of poetry in them.'—*Spectator.*

PRIMEVAL MAN: Being an Examination of some Recent Speculations. By the Duke of Argyll. Crown 8vo, 4s. 6d.

'This volume is perhaps the most clear, graceful, pointed, and precise piece of ethical reasoning published for a quarter of a century. ... The book is worthy of a place in every library as skilfully popularizing science, and yet sacrificing nothing either of its dignity or of its usefulness.'—*Nonconformist.*

'This book shows great knowledge, unusual command of language, and a true sense of the value of arguments. ... It may be questioned and even confuted in some points without losing any of its claims as a candid, clear, and high-minded discussion.'—*Pall Mall Gazette.*

TWILIGHT HOURS: a Legacy of Verse. By SARAH Williams (Sadie). Crown 8vo, 5s.

'If we go on extracting all that seems to us the product of true genius, we should print nearly half of the volume. ... What a range of conception from the first fine piece, called "Baal," to the exquisite little children's poems, such as "Marjory's Wedding" and "Crutch the Judge," which show the divine light playing on children's nature with a spiritual truth, as it seems to us, infinitely superior to the higher touches in Mr Keble's beautiful "Lyra Innocentium."'—*Spectator.*

THE TRAGEDIES OF ÆSCHYLOS. A New Translation, with a Biographical Essay and an Appendix of Rhymed Choral Odes. By E. H. Plumptre, M.A. 2 vols. crown 8vo, 12s.

'Like his translations of Sophocles, Professor Plumptre's translation of Æschylos must, whoever comes after him, hold a very high place in our literature. In difficult passages he is never, to use the Italian proverb, a traditore. In the ordinary speeches he is faithful without being servile. And in the higher and more impassioned passages he shows himself to be a true poet. ... To English readers who wish to know something of one of the world's master poets, the present translation is indispensable.'—*Westminster Review.*

KRILOF AND HIS FABLES. By W. R. S. RALSTON. With Illustrations by Houghton and Zwecker. Crown 8vo, 5s.

'The translator has found a house full of "pearls and diamonds," and, with the help of the publisher and illustrator, has displayed his treasures in a fit and tasteful setting.'—*Saturday Review.*

'Krilof is the only Russian author who is read equally by young and old, rich and poor. He wrote the most idiomatic Russian that is known; and of this a certain aroma is presented in Mr. Ralston's flowing yet thoroughly faithful translation.'—*Pall Mall Gazette.*

CHILD-WORLD. By the Authors of, and uniform with, 'Poems Written for a Child.' With Illustrations. Square 32mo, 3s. 6d.

'Poems at once brilliant and playful, as full of glee and motion as those immortal wild daffodils on the shore of Wordsworth's lake. ... No one can read "The Fairies' Nest," "Mother Tabbyskins," or "Freddy's Kiss," and many others, without a real addition of happiness—not merely of enjoyment—so full of sunshine and sparkling air, of real imaginative gaiety and inventive humour, are each and all of them. Not that these are the only qualities. Besides the lightness of heart and humour, there are many lyrical touches which transmute the spiritual gaiety into true poetry.'—*Spectator.*

STRAHAN & CO., PUBLISHERS, 56, LUDGATE HILL.

On the 1st of May, price One Shilling, Part I. of

THE WORLD OF ANECDOTE:

AN ACCUMULATION OF

FACTS, INCIDENTS, AND ILLUSTRATIONS,

HISTORICAL AND BIOGRAPHICAL,

FROM BOOKS AND TIMES RECENT AND REMOTE.

BY

EDWIN PAXTON HOOD,

Author of 'Lamps, Pitchers, and Trumpets.'

To be completed in 9 monthly Parts.

The Volume will include among others Anecdotes referring to the following subjects:—

Ways and Means of doing Good—Romantic Transformations of Human Life—Oddities of Conversation—Table Talk—Dogs, Cats, and the Animal World—Prisons and Prisoners, Crimes and Criminals—Wasted Lives, Pleasure Seekers—Science and its Votaries—Foolish Wars—Benevolence—The Bible—Brands Plucked from the Burning—The Supernatural—Romance of the Peerage—Absence of Mind—Insanity, the Loosening of the Silver Cord—Industry and Perseverance—Singular Interpositions of Providence—Woman's Trials, Heroism in Woman—Wonders of Human Folly—Presence of Mind—Old Houses—Bench and Bar—The Pulpit, Eloquence—Self-Education—Death and Dying, the Breaking of the Golden Bowl.

Rev. Paxton Hood on Preachers and Preaching.

Second Thousand, price 10s. 6d., handsomely bound in cloth,

LAMPS, PITCHERS, & TRUMPETS.

LECTURES ON THE VOCATION OF THE PREACHER:

ILLUSTRATED BY ANECDOTES — BIOGRAPHICAL, HISTORICAL, AND ELUCIDATORY—OF EVERY ORDER OF PULPIT ELOQUENCE, FROM THE GREAT PREACHERS OF ALL AGES.

BY

EDWIN PAXTON HOOD.

'A book which we cordially recommend to all who take any interest in preaching. The book is a most valuable one, interesting as a romance, and quite unique in its kind. It is written in the most impartial Christianlike spirit—equally impartial in its views of some of the great mediæval saints, the lights of the Reformation, the enthusiasts of the Puritan Church, the great Anglican preachers, or the contemporary celebrities of sects differing from that of the author.'—*Dublin University Magazine.*

'Fresh, clever, sensible, and full of stimulus and thought for men aspiring to preach. The genius and power of the pulpit are vindicated, its character is pointed out, and the faults and merits of sermons are touched with a keen and racy criticism, and in the generous spirit of a man of large sympathies and culture.'—*Christian Work.*

Works Published by T. & T. Clark, Edinburgh.

WORKS BY THE LATE WILLIAM CUNNINGHAM, D.D.,
PRINCIPAL AND PROFESSOR OF CHURCH HISTORY, NEW COLLEGE, EDINBURGH.
COMPLETE IN FOUR VOLUMES 8VO, PRICE £2, 2s.

In Two Volumes, demy 8vo, price 21s., Second Edition,

HISTORICAL THEOLOGY:
A REVIEW OF THE PRINCIPAL DOCTRINAL DISCUSSIONS IN THE CHRISTIAN CHURCH SINCE THE APOSTOLIC AGE.

Chapter 1. The Church; 2. The Council of Jerusalem; 3. The Apostles' Creed; 4. The Apostolical Fathers; 5. Heresies of the Apostolical Age; 6. The Fathers of the Second and Third Centuries; 7. The Church of the Second and Third Centuries; 8. The Constitution of the Church; 9. The Doctrine of the Trinity; 10. The Person of Christ; 11. The Pelagian Controversy; 12. Worship of Saints and Images; 13. The Civil and Ecclesiastical Authorities; 14. The Scholastic Theology; 15. The Canon Law; 16. Witnesses for the Truth during Middle Ages; 17. The Church at the Reformation; 18. The Council of Trent; 19. The Doctrine of the Fall; 20. Doctrine of the Will; 21. Justification; 22. The Sacramental Principle; 23. The Socinian Controversy; 24. Doctrine of the Atonement; 25. The Arminian Controversy; 26. Church Government; 27. The Erastian Controversy.

In demy 8vo (624 pages), price 10s. 6d., Second Edition,

THE REFORMERS AND THE THEOLOGY OF THE REFORMATION.

Chapter 1. Leaders of the Reformation; 2. Luther; 3. The Reformers and the Doctrine of Assurance; 4. Melancthon and the Theology of the Church of England; 5. Zwingle and the Doctrine of the Sacraments; 6. John Calvin; 7. Calvin and Beza; 8. Calvinism and Arminianism; 9. Calvinism and the Doctrine of Philosophical Necessity; 10. Calvinism and its Practical Application; 11. The Reformers and the Lessons from their History.

'This volume is a most magnificent vindication of the Reformation, in both its men and its doctrines, suited to the present time and to the present state of the controversy.'
—*Witness.*

In One Volume, demy 8vo, price 10s. 6d.,

DISCUSSIONS ON CHURCH PRINCIPLES:
POPISH, ERASTIAN, AND PRESBYTERIAN.

Chapter 1. The Errors of Romanism; 2. Romanist Theory of Development; 3. The Temporal Sovereignty of the Pope; 4. The Temporal Supremacy of the Pope; 5. The Liberties of the Gallican Church; 6. Royal Supremacy in Church of England; 7. Relation between Church and State; 8. The Westminster Confession on Relation between Church and State; 9. Church Power; 10. Principles of the Free Church; 11. The Rights of the Christian People; 12. The Principle of Non-Intrusion; 13. Patronage and Popular Election.

In Two Volumes, demy 8vo, price 21s.,

INTRODUCTION TO THE PENTATEUCH:
AN INQUIRY, CRITICAL AND DOCTRINAL, INTO THE GENUINENESS, AUTHORITY, AND DESIGN OF THE MOSAIC WRITINGS.
BY REV. D. MACDONALD.

'The object of this work is very opportune at the present time. It contains a full review of the evidences, external and internal, for the genuineness, authenticity, and divine character of the Pentateuch. While it gives full space and weight to the purely critical and historical portions of the inquiry, its special attention is devoted to the certainly more profound and more conclusive considerations derived from the connection between the Pentateuch and the great scheme of revelation, of which it forms the basis; and this portion of the work is that upon which the author lays most stress. We entirely agree with him in his view of its importance. The work is singularly complete also in its view of the literature of the subject, as well as in the outline of its plan.'—*Guardian.*

WORKS BY REV. DR. KRUMMACHER.

In post 8vo, price 7s. 6d.,

David, the King of Israel;
A PORTRAIT DRAWN FROM BIBLE HISTORY AND THE BOOK OF PSALMS.

TRANSLATED UNDER THE EXPRESS SANCTION OF THE AUTHOR BY THE
REV. M. G. EASTON, M.A.

'From the author of "Elijah the Tishbite" we were entitled to expect no ordinary treat, when he proposed to lead us over a life fraught with such variegated interest as that of "David the King of Israel." In such a field Dr. Krummacher's well-known powers of description, his chaste fancy, his well-balanced judgment, and enlightened piety, were sure to find full scope; nor have our anticipations been disappointed. Time has not blunted the keen perception of the theologian; and though it may have sobered the exuberance, it has not withered the power, of the writer. In these pages, David passes before us, in the various phases of his character as shepherd, psalmist, warrior, and monarch. There is no attempt at originality of view, no prosy solution of difficulties, no controversial sparring; the narrative flows on like a well-told story; and the art of the writer lies in the apt selection of salient points, and in the naturalness of his reflections. A tone of spirituality is imparted to the narrative by linking it to the Book of Psalms.'—*British and Foreign Evangelical Review.*

'We have a lifelike picture of the prophet-king and of his times. The truths brought out are applied with marvellous skill and deep spiritual insight to the Christian state, so that every page is luminous with gospel lessons. The character of David is nobly drawn; and he stands before us as one of the greatest men and greatest saints of the Old Testament. We trust its venerable author will be rewarded by the abundant popularity of his picturesque and charming volume.'—*Evangelical Christendom.*

'Amongst the religious writers of modern Germany, few hold a higher place than Dr. Krummacher in the general estimation. The reputation his previous works—"The Suffering Saviour" and "Elijah the Tishbite"—have acquired for him in England, will at once attract attention to "David, the King of Israel." As the translator remarks, "Krummacher needs no introduction to English readers. His name is a household word in religious circles." The subject of the present volume is one that is especially adapted for skilful analysis and subtle comments. The character is excellently displayed in its many-sidedness and variety. It is almost unnecessary to remark that the treatment is marked by the acuteness of insight and the tenderness of sympathy that are characteristic of the author.'—*Imperial Review.*

'We would recommend this volume to the clergy as a storehouse of hints for pulpit use, and also as a valuable addition to our devotional literature.'—*Clerical Journal.*

'The volume is, on the whole, a very happy specimen of the style for which Dr. Krummacher is best known—at once vivid, imaginative, and experimental; and it exhibits more of the intellectual and robust than his earlier work. Should it direct the attention of ministers and students to the devout and practical study of the Old Testament narratives, as themes for pulpit exposition, it will confer a great boon on both preachers and hearers.'—*Freeman.*

BY THE SAME AUTHOR.

In crown 8vo, price 4s. 6d., Sixth Edition,

The Suffering Saviour;
OR, MEDITATIONS ON THE LAST DAYS OF THE SUFFERINGS OF CHRIST.

'We give it preference to everything hitherto produced by the gifted and devoted author. It is divinity of the most thoroughly evangelical description. Truth and tenderness have seldom been so successfully combined. A book of the heart, to *that* it appeals in every page, with a force which it will be difficult to resist.'—*Christian Witness.*

'The subject is a sublime and pathetic one, and is treated with much solemnity of feeling, together with great tenderness of sympathy.'—*Literary Churchman.*

WILLIAM HUNT & CO.'S PUBLICATIONS.

Dies Iræ: The Judgment of the Great Day, viewed in the light of Scripture and Conscience. By R. B. GIRDLESTONE, M.A., author of 'The Anatomy of Scepticism.' Crown 8vo, cloth extra, 6s.

CONTENTS.—Gravity and Difficulty of the Subject. The Divine Glory of Humanity. The True Nature of Sin. Men of all Ages and Dispensations reserved for Judgment. The Day of Judgment. Principles on which the Judgment will be conducted. The Position of the Saints on the Day of Judgment. The Nature of the Punishment of the Ungodly. The Duration of the Punishment of the Ungodly. The Meaning of the word 'Eternal' in the Old Testament. The Usage of the word 'Eternal' in the New Testament. Is Annihilation the Destiny of the Ungodly? Does Eternity of Punishment involve Eternity of Sin? Can there be any Proportion between the Sins of Time and the Punishment of Eternity? The Greatness of the Gulf between the Saved and the Lost. Is the Doctrine of Eternal Punishment Consistent with the Love of God? Will the Punishment of the Wicked be a Triumph of Evil over Good? The Principle of Retribution. The Glory of Christ and the Reconciliation of all Things. Satanic Temptation and Human Responsibility. Election and Reprobation. The Feeling of the Saved with regard to the Doom of the Lost. Repentance after Death. Summary and Conclusion.

How shall I Pray? Sermons for Children on the Lord's Prayer. By the Rev. CLAUDE BOSANQUET, M.A., Vicar of St. Nicholas, Rochester. Square 16mo, cloth, 1s. 6d.

Heaven's Whispers in the Storm. By the late Rev. FRANCIS J. JAMESON, M.A., Rector of Cotton, formerly Fellow and Assistant Tutor of St. Catharine's College, Cambridge. With a Biographical Sketch of the Author. Square 18mo, 2s.; with portrait, 3s.

CONTENTS.—Biographical Sketch of the Author.—I. Why am I thus?—II. Work for the Hands which hang down.—III. The Soul silent before God.—IV. Times of Visitation.—V. The Stability of Trust.—VI. God manifesting Himself in Sorrow.—VII. The disappointed Prayer.—VIII. God's fettered Workman.—XI. The Heart's Home. X. The coming Bridegroom.

Voices of the Church of England against Modern Sacerdotalism; Being a Manual of Authorities on the Nature of the Lord's Supper and the Christian Ministry. Selected and arranged, with Introduction, by the Rev. E. GARRETT, M.A., Vicar of Christ's Church, Surbiton, and Chaplain to the Right Hon. the Earl of Shaftesbury. Demy 8vo, 3s.

Preaching of the Cross. Sermons preached in St. Mary's Church, Bury St. Edmund's. By the Rev. JOHN RICHARDSON, M.A., Vicar. Post 8vo, 7s. 6d.

The Unseen Guide; or, Stories and Allegories to Illustrate the Fruits of the Spirit. Square 16mo. With Engravings by the Brothers Dalziel. By M. B. 3s. 6d.

The Religion of Redemption; or, The Doctrine of Man's Ruin and Christ's Salvation Defined and Defended. A Contribution to the Preliminaries of Christian Apology, by R. W. MONSELL, B.A., late Pastor of the Free Church of Neufchatel, Switzerland. 1 Vol. 8vo, 12s.

The Christian Life; Viewed under some of its more Practical Aspects. By EMILIUS BAYLEY, B.D., Incumbent of St. John's, Paddington, late Rector of St. George, Bloomsbury, and Rural Dean. Fcap. 8vo, extra cloth, 3s.; gilt edges, 3s. 6d.

The Word was Made Flesh. Short Family Readings on the Gospels for each Sunday of the Christian Year. 'In Cruce Victoria.' Crown 8vo, 6s.

Christian Experience; or, Words of Loving Counsel and Sympathy. Extracted from the unpublished Remains of the late Mrs. Mary WINSLOW. Edited by her son, the Rev. OCTAVIUS WINSLOW, D.D. 3s.

Living Jewels. Diversities of Christian Character, suggested by Precious Stones, with Biographical Examples. By A. L. O. E. With Illustrations. Small post 8vo, 2s. 6d.

The Ministry of Home; or, Brief Expository Lectures on Divine Truth. Designed especially for Family and Private Reading. By OCTAVIUS WINSLOW, D.D. Crown 8vo, 5s.; extra binding, gilt edges, 6s. This volume forms the first of a Series of Short Expository Readings on Scripture Doctrines, History, and Biography.

The Intermediate State of the Blessed Dead; in a Series of Meditational Expositions. By the Rev. JOSEPH BAYLEE, D.B., late Principal of St. Aidan's, Birkenhead. Second Edition, enlarged. Extra cloth, bevelled boards, 3s. 6d.

William Hunt and Co.'s Publications—*continued.*

Day by Day; or, Counsels to Christians on the Details of Every-day Life. By the Rev. GEORGE EVERARD, M.A., Incumbent of St. Mark's, Wolverhampton. With Introduction by the Rev. T. VORES, M.A., Incumbent of St. Mary's, Hastings. Fourth Edition, fcap. 8vo, cloth extra, 3s.; gilt edges, 3s. 6d.

BY THE SAME AUTHOR.

Home Sundays; or, Help and Consolation from the Sanctuary. Uniform with 'Day by Day.' Cloth extra, 3s.; gilt edges, 3s. 6d.

Expository Thoughts on the Gospels. Designed especially for Family and Private Reading. By the Rev. J. C. RYLE, B.A.

ST. MATTHEW. Complete in one Vol. 6s. cloth.
ST. MARK. Uniform with the above. 5s.
ST. LUKE. Vol. I. 5s. 6d.
ST. LUKE. Vol. II. 7s.
ST. JOHN. Vol. I. 6s. 6d.
ST. JOHN. Vol. II. In course of Publication.

This work is also kept in half morocco, at an excess of 2s. 6d. per volume. In extra half morocco binding, at 4s. 6d.; or whole Turkey morocco, 6s. per volume.

BY THE SAME AUTHOR.

Hymns for the Church on Earth. Being Three Hundred Hymns, for the most part of Modern Date. Selected and Arranged by the Rev. J. C. RYLE, B.A. Eighth Edition. In small 8vo, black cloth, red edges, 4s.; Black antique, 4s. 6d.; Violet and extra cloth antique, gilt edges, 5s.; Turkey morocco, 10s.

Bishops and Clergy of other Days. With an Introduction on the Real Merits of Reformers and Puritans. Crown 8vo, extra cloth, 4s.

Home Truths. Being the Miscellaneous Writings of the Rev. J. C. RYLE. Revised. Fcap. 8vo, extra cloth, lettered. Seven Series, each complete with Frontispiece and Vignette Title. 3s. 6d. each volume. This work is also kept in morocco binding.

Coming Events and Present Duties. Being Miscellaneous Sermons and Addresses on Prophetical Subjects. Arranged, Revised, and Corrected by the Rev. J. C. RYLE, B.A., Vicar of Stradbroke, Suffolk. Crown 8vo, 3s. 6d.

The Two Bears, and other Sermons for Children. Illustrations by Dalziel. This day. Cloth extra, 1s. 6d.

The Rich Man and Lazarus. A Practical Exposition. By BROWNLOW NORTH, B.A. Uniform with 'Ourselves.' Cloth boards, 1s. 6d.; antique, 2s.

Ourselves. A Picture, sketched from the History of the Children of Israel. Uniform with 'Yes! or No!' Fourth Edition. Cloth boards, 2s. 6d.; extra binding and toned paper, 3s.

Yes! or No! Or, God's Offer of Salvation. Uniform with 'Ourselves.' Third Edition. Cloth boards, 2s. 6d.; extra binding, and toned paper, 3s.

Earnest Words. New and Old. A Series of Addresses, with Prayers and Hints for Christians. Uniform with 'Gathered Leaves.' Limp cloth, 6d.

Gathered Leaves. Uniform with 'Earnest Words.' Large type, limp cloth, 6d.

Think! Earnest Words for the Thoughtless. Large type, limp cloth, 6d.

Words for the Anxious. Uniform with 'Earnest Words.' Large type, limp cloth, 6d.

The Rock, and other Short Lectures on Passages of Holy Scripture. By Miss HASELL, Dalemain, Author of 'Saturday Afternoons,' and of 'Sunday Evenings.' Dedicated to Sir George Musgrave of Edenhall, Bart. Fcap. 8vo, cloth boards, 2s.; extra binding, 2s. 6d.

Nature and Art; or, Reminiscences of the International Exhibition, opened in London on May 1st, 1862. A Poem. With Occasional Verses and Elegiac Stanzas. By RICHARD TONSON EVANSON, M.D., F.R.C.P., etc. Post 8vo, cloth extra, gilt edges, 9s.

The Golden Chain of Praise. Hymns by THOMAS H. GILL, Author of 'The Papal Drama,' etc. Crown 8vo, cloth extra, gilt edges, 6s.

Signs of the Times; showing that the Coming of the Lord draweth near. By SAMUEL GARRATT, M.A., Vicar of St. Margaret's, Ipswich, Author of 'A Commentary on the Revelation of St. John,' etc. Fcap. 8vo, cloth limp, 1s. 6d.

Words of Eternal Life; or, the First Principles of the Doctrine of Christ, set forth in Eighteen Sermons. By the Hon. the Right Rev. SAMUEL WALDEGRAVE, D.D., Lord Bishop of Carlisle. Crown 8vo, 7s., cloth.

BY THE SAME AUTHOR.

New Testament Millenarianism; or, the Kingdom and Coming of Christ, as taught by Himself and his Apostles. 10s. extra cloth.

The Way of Peace; or, the Teaching of Scripture concerning Justification, Sanctification, and Assurance: in Sermons before the University of Oxford. Crown 8vo. Fourth Edition. Cloth, 4s. 6d.

LONDON: WILLIAM HUNT AND COMPANY, 23, HOLLES STREET, W.

Works Published by T. & T. Clark, Edinburgh.

Third Edition, One volume, crown 8vo, price 5s.,
GOTTHOLD'S EMBLEMS;
OR, INVISIBLE THINGS UNDERSTOOD BY THINGS THAT ARE MADE.
By CHRISTIAN SCRIVER,
MINISTER OF MAGDEBURG IN 1671.

Translated from the Twenty-eighth German Edition.

'Finds tongues in trees, books in the running brooks,
Sermons in stones, and GOD in everything.'

Among other emblems (there is one for every day in the year) are—'The Dial-Plate; Snow; The Child learning to Walk; The Paper Mill; The Wolf; The Diamond; Angry Alms; The Hot Coals; The Trees in Winter; The Magnet; The Watchmaker; Conscience; The Milky Way; The Rainbow; The Lark; The Violet; Feeding the Hens; The Best Chamber; The Young Lamb; The Sleepy Child; The Richest Prince; The Clout; The Evening Shadow; The Stork; The Caterpillar; Wormwood; Sharp Air; The Silkworm; The Folded Hands; The Rye in Flower; The Wearisome Rain; The Midge; The Wasp; The Weed; The Orphans; The Dismantled House; The Ropemaker; A Strange Sea; Washing the Hands; Tears; The Faggot Beam; The Strange Bargain; The Smoky Chimneys; Grey Hairs; The Howling Dog; Blind Man's Buff; The Pillow; The New-Born Babe; The Death of the Christian.'

'For simple poetical fancy, deep sentiment, religious wisdom, and quaint suggestiveness, we know no devotional book that is its equal.'—*Nonconformist.*

'It is a book for all men, from the beggar on his pallet of straw to the prince upon his throne. With a strangely childish eye and charming lip, Scriver leads us forth into nature, as into a vault of mirrors, from which the image of God everywhere shines forth.'—*Clerical Journal.*

'A peculiarly fascinating volume. It is rich in happy and beautiful thoughts, which grow on the root of genuine piety.'—*Witness.*

In crown 8vo, price 3s.,
MANUAL OF HERMENEUTICS
FOR THE WRITINGS OF THE NEW TESTAMENT.
By J. J. DOEDES, D.D.,
PROFESSOR OF THEOLOGY, UNIVERSITY OF UTRECHT.

'This little volume is a very valuable summary of the history and principles of sound exegesis of the New Testament.'—*British Quarterly Review.*

'We have here an elaborate and painstaking system of what might be called cautions to be observed in the unfolding of the New Testament Text. . . . Its ample and continuous references to the literature of the subject add to its value as a handbook.'—*Literary Churchman.*

In crown 8vo, price 5s.,
THE FATHERHOOD OF GOD,
AND ITS RELATION TO THE PERSON AND WORK OF CHRIST, AND THE OPERATIONS OF THE HOLY SPIRIT.

By C. H. H. WRIGHT, M.A., T.C.D., British Chaplain at Dresden.

'The evangelical view is that maintained by our author, who is a linguist and a man of many accomplishments, besides being, what is much better, "a workman that needeth not to be ashamed, rightly dividing the word of truth." . . . . . His volume is almost a body of divinity, so wide is the scope of doctrines discussed in it in connection with his principal theme; and it is well worthy the attention of ministers and young divines, for the establishment and confirmation of the truth as it is in Jesus.'—*Irish Ecclesiastical Gazette.*

'It exhibits large argumentative powers, combined with considerable learning and research.'—*Bell's Weekly Messenger.*

'The various subjects are treated clearly, calmly, and judiciously.'—*British Quarterly Review.*

'Mr. Wright has given a very useful manual on the entire subject discussed; and the manly, free, generous spirit in which he has accomplished his task, deserves all recognition.'—*English Independent.*

www.ingramcontent.com/pod-product-compliance
Lightning Source LLC
Chambersburg PA
CBHW031945290426
44108CB00011B/678